# WOMEN PASTORS?

**The Ordination of Women in Biblical Lutheran Perspective**

A COLLECTION OF ESSAYS
THIRD EDITION

Edited by Matthew C. Harrison
and John T. Pless

CONCORDIA PUBLISHING HOUSE · SAINT LOUIS

This edition published 2012 Concordia Publishing House

3558 S. Jefferson Ave.
St. Louis, MO 63118-3968
1-800-325-3040 • cph.org

First edition published 2008 Concordia Publishing House
Second edition published 2009 Concordia Publishing House

Manufactured in the United States of America

---

Library of Congress Cataloging-in-Publication Data

　　Women pastors : the ordination of women in biblical Lutheran perspective : a collection of essays / edited by Matthew C. Harrison and John T. Pless.

　　　　p. cm.

　　ISBN-978-0-7586-3142-8

　　1. Ordination of women—Lutheran Church. 2. Ordination of women—Biblical teaching. 3. Pastoral theology—Lutheran Church. 4. Lutheran Church—Clergy. I. Harrison, Matthew C. II. Pless, John T., 1953–

　　BX8071.2.W66　　　　2008

　　262'.1441082—dc22　　　　　　　　　　　　　　　　　　　　　　　2007039704

---

7 8 9 10 11 12 13 14 15 16　　　　30 29 28 27 26 25 24 23 22 21

# CONTENTS

# PUBLISHER'S PREFACE

When I first set eyes on the list of articles for *Women Pastors? The Ordination of Women in Biblical Lutheran Perspective*, I quickly concluded that this would be a timely and helpful volume. However, in discussing the project with colleagues, I learned that the manuscript was being delayed in the publication process because of various permission issues and the fact that some of the anticipated essays were not ready for publication. In fact, the project had been shelved. To start it moving again, I made a number of pragmatic decisions: cutting articles that still required permission, dropping incomplete essays, and directing the remaining manuscript back into our publishing plans. This allowed the team to move the project forward. The first press run sold out, and, once again, we made pragmatic decisions that enabled us to release a second edition quickly.

As I saw the second edition likewise selling out, I proposed a third edition of *Women Pastors?* that would allow us to incorporate something we had lost in the pragmatic choices for the earlier editions: essays from Lutheran women who served in leadership positions of the church. Thanks be to God, this third edition fills this important gap, which was wholly my responsibility as a get-it-done editor.

I trust that readers will find this third edition more thorough, fulfilling the original intentions for the book. I would like to thank, first, the editors of the volume for their patience with my pragmatic choices and, second, the church for embracing *Women Pastors? The Ordination of Women in Biblical Lutheran Perspective*.

In Christ,
Rev. Edward A. Engelbrecht, STM
Concordia Publishing House
Senior Editor for Professional and Academic Books & Bible Resources

# Preface to Third Edition

It is with great thankfulness that we are now into the third edition of *Women Pastors?* The book has been a substantial contribution to the debate on the ordination of women as churches, theologians, and thoughtful men and women all over the world wrestle with this question.

John Pless and I continue to be delighted with the response the book has received. We are, however, especially pleased with this new edition prepared by our able compatriots at Concordia Publishing House for the cause of biblical orthodoxy.

This new edition contains three additional essays written by articulate and learned female theologians. You will quickly recognize their value for anyone struggling to understand this challenging issue. John Pless has also given us another essay demonstrating the truth that women's ordination and the acceptance of homosexuality are intimately connected. As a woman ordained to the ministry in the ELCA told me twenty years ago, while she was already then strongly advocating for a hermeneutic favorable to homosexuality, "You can't have one without the other."

As the assault on creedal, biblical Christianity only intensifies in these gray and latter days, we shall hold fast, "as in all the churches" that bow before the Sacred Scriptures, humbly, kindly, to be sure . . . but unwaveringly.

Matthew C. Harrison
Epiphany 2012

# Preface to First and Second Editions

The question of the ordination of women to the pastoral office is not likely to go away. Given our culture's preferential option for inclusiveness and egalitarianism that is unwilling to make any distinctions based on gender, the pressure to ordain women to the pastoral office will only increase. Large ecumenical organizations such as the Lutheran World Federation assume that the ordination of women is the norm, and they will bring their weighty wealth to pressure member churches to forsake a male-only pastorate as a relic of a patriarchal era that is best forgotten. Lutheran churches that have opted to ordain women have become increasingly intolerant of those who reject the practice. Church bodies such as the Church of Sweden that for a time allowed a "conscience clause" for pastors who could not support the ordination of women, now refuse to ordain men who will not acknowledge the legitimacy of women's ordination. Thus a brave African bishop, Walter Obare of the Evangelical Lutheran Church in Kenya, had no choice but to journey to Sweden in the winter of 2005 to officiate at the consecration of a bishop for the Mission Province, an ecclesial organization of Swedish Lutherans who are determined to remain faithful.

The essays in this volume will strengthen Lutheran pastors and laity worldwide in their confession of the truth of the Holy Scriptures as it speaks to this issue. It has been thirty-five years since the first woman was ordained in a Lutheran Church in the United States. With more than 3,000 women (roughly 25 percent) on the clergy roster of the Evangelical Lutheran Church in America, it is no longer rare to see a woman functioning as a pastor. As the ordination of women has become commonplace in North American and European Protestant communions, it is becoming increasingly important for faithful Lutherans to be able to articulate why authentic, genuine, historical Lutheranism, because of the teachings of Holy Scripture, does not ordain women to serve as pastors.

This book provides a witness of encouragement to struggling brothers and sisters in Christ in Lutheran churches around the world. From our contacts with Lutherans overseas, we know of ridicule that faithful pastors and people endure in Sweden for their refusal to compromise biblical truth. We have observed the coercive tactics of the Lutheran World Federation in Africa and Eastern Europe as attempts are made to push women's ordination on churches by threatening the withdrawal of financial support. We have witnessed the bold leadership of Archbishop Janis Vanags, who brought an end to the ordination of women in the Lutheran Church of Latvia, though he was severely criticized by church leaders in North America and Europe. Several of the essays in this volume come from pastors and theologians in the Lutheran Church of Australia as it is at the present time deeply divided on this issue. We want to support and assist Lutherans both in our sister churches and in the global Lutheran community to maintain a God-pleasing confession and practice.

A variety of issues emerge surrounding women's ordination. While not every conceivable dimension of the problem of women's ordination is covered in the essays assembled herein, the wide variety of authors do address many of them. Biblical mandates (1 Cor. 14:33b–38 and 1 Tim. 2:11–14) certainly prohibit women from serving in the pastoral office. Ordaining women to serve in the pastoral office is a denial of biblical authority. It should come as no surprise that a leading and early proponent was Krister Stendahl,[1] one of the most notorious advocates of the higher critical approach to the Holy Scripture in the twentieth century. The method of interpreting the Bible that was used forty years ago to bring women into the pastoral office is now being employed to bring homosexuals into the ministry. In both the case of women's ordination and the endorsement of homosexuality there is a "flight from creation."[2] There are other problems as well. Such as how does the admission of a woman to the pastoral office transform the dominically established office? What is the relation of the practice of women's ordination to ancient and contemporary forms of Gnosticism? Is the doctrine of the Trinity distorted by the ordination of women? What does the catholicity of the church have to do with women's ordination? These and other questions are engaged by our essayists.

While we contend that all the essays in this collection fall within the pale of opinion governed by the Sacred Scriptures and the Lutheran Confessions, we grant that not all of the arguments offered by individual authors are equally weighty or ultimately acceptable. Some of the essays are by nature more probing and exploratory as the author seeks to uncover the biblical foundation upon which the apostolic prohibition of placing women in the pastoral office rests. We are firmly convinced that the Gospel is ultimately at stake and that is no small matter. When the Church of Sweden made the decision to ordain women, the renowned theologian and bishop Anders Nygren spoke prophetically: "As this current decision not only means a determination of the specific issue concerning female pastors, but, I am convinced, also means that our church has now shifted onto a previously unknown track heading in the direction of Gnosticism and the *Schwaermerei* . . . I must declare my deep sorrow regarding the decision and give notice of my reservation of the same."[3] How far this direction of Gnosticism and Enthusiasm has progressed is now quite apparent in the Swedish church's blessing of same-sex unions and the ordination of practicing homosexuals.

---

1   See Krister Stendahl, *The Bible and the Role of Women* (Philadelphia: Fortress, 1966).

2   For an examination of how a hermeneutic that denies the orders of creation leads from the ordination of women to endorsement of homosexuality, see John T. Pless, "Using and Misusing Luther on Homosexuality," *Lutheran Forum* (Summer 2005).

3   *Kyrkomoetets protokoll*, nr. 4, 158, p. 154. Our thanks to Pastor Eric R. Andrae for his translation from the Swedish into English.

The editors wish to thank all those who allowed their essays to be included in *Women Pastors? The Ordination of Women in Biblical Lutheran Perspective.* Although he did not live to see this book come to fruition, we gratefully acknowledge the encouragement given us in this undertaking from the sainted Rev. Dr. Louis Smith, a clergyman of the ELCA who himself came to a change of mind in regard to women's ordination. His essay "How I Changed My Mind" is included here with the kind permission of the editor of *Lutheran Forum* where it first appeared. We also acknowledge with appreciation the assistance of seminarian Jason Lane of Concordia Theological Seminary, Fort Wayne, Indiana, in preparing this volume. We offer it now with the prayer that Christ Jesus would have good use of it to strengthen His people in the confession of His name, edify His Church, and extend His kingdom to all nations.

The Editors
Matthew C. Harrison
John T. Pless
Pentecost 2005

# SECTION I

# EXEGETICAL STUDIES

The prophetic and apostolic Scriptures, given by the Spirit's inspiration, are the inerrant judge and norm for all that is said and done within the Church of our Lord Jesus Christ. The Church does not stand over the Scriptures but under them in order to receive all that the Lord would give her for her life and blessing. Confessional Lutherans do not seek God's will apart from the Scriptures, or behind them in supposed oral traditions or precanonical documents, but in the text itself. The essays included in this section take up the two Pauline texts that prohibit women from being placed in the pastoral office: 1 Corinthians 14:33b–38 and 1 Timothy 2:11–14.

Henry P. Hamann, long-time principal of Luther Seminary, Adelaide, Australia, looks at the issue of women's ordination in light of the totality of the New Testament. Bertil Gärtner, formerly a professor of New Testament at Princeton and later bishop of the Diocese of Gothenburg in the Church of Sweden, takes up the biblical definition of teacher, *didaskalos*, demonstrating that this office requires qualified men according to the will of Him who is Teacher of us all.

Dr. Cynthia Lumley, associate director of deaconess studies at Concordia Theological Seminary, Fort Wayne, Indiana, takes up the case of Phoebe, who is mentioned briefly in Rom. 16:1–2. Lumley demonstrates how this Christian woman served not as a minister of the Word but in a way that reflected the sacrificial character of Jesus Christ in her support of the work of apostolic ministry.

Disciples are made through Baptism and teaching (Matt. 28:18–20), but not all disciples are teachers. Dr. John W. Kleinig, recently retired after a distinguished teaching career as pastor and seminary professor in the Lutheran Church of Australia, examines 1 Cor. 14:33b–38 and 1 Tim. 2:11–15, demonstrating that women are and must be disciples of Jesus Christ but are not to teach in the liturgical assembly.

1

Australian pastors Peter Kriewaldt and David W. Bryce also provide exegetical studies of the 1 Corinthians and 1 Timothy passages. And Charles A. Gieschen of Concordia Theological Seminary, Fort Wayne, Indiana, examines the 1 Timothy text, asking whether the Lord wills women to be quiet learners or ordained proclaimers.

Women in positions of cultic leadership were not unknown in the ancient world. Louis A. Brighton of Concordia Seminary, St. Louis, Missouri, suggests that the ordination of women into the pastoral office is a modern form of the ancient heresy of Gnosticism.

John Kleinig returns with a study of order and subordination in the New Testament in an essay entitled "Ordered Community," which contrasts the biblical understanding of subordination in the context of the primacy of communal existence with the individualism that dominates modern thought. God's ordering of human life reflects the order of self-giving love within the Holy Trinity.

Another Australian Lutheran scholar, Dr. Gregory J. Lockwood, who has served on the faculty at Concordia Theological Seminary in Fort Wayne, Indiana, and more recently at the Australian Lutheran College in Adelaide, provides a biblical overview of the case for a male-only pastorate, addressing modern challenges to the apostolic practice that arise not from the scriptural narrative but from the presuppositions of modernity.

# THE NEW TESTAMENT AND THE ORDINATION OF WOMEN

## HENRY P. HAMANN

The Lutheran Church of Australia has taken a very definite position on the matter of the ordination of women to the Holy Ministry. The Theses of Agreement, which forms part of the Document of Union, states very briefly and very categorically:

> Though women prophets were used by the Spirit of God in the Old as well as in the New Testament, 1 Cor. 14:34–35 and 1 Tim. 2:11–14 prohibit a woman from being called into the office of the public ministry for the proclamation of the Word and the administration of the Sacrament. This apostolic rule is binding on all Christendom; hereby her rights as a member of the spiritual priesthood are in no wise impaired.

These words were formulated early in the 1950s, when the agitation about and for female ordination had hardly begun, which explains the brevity of the Theses on this matter. This present essay is concerned only with the position and teaching of the New Testament, not with other important aspects of the issue, like its ecumenical implications, the question of historical continuity, and others which are all involved in any ecclesiastical decision. However, the New Testament position is the most important aspect of the whole problem and that which is finally decisive. For, it is taken for granted and as beyond all debate, here, as in all articles of this Journal, that the Sacred Scripture is source and judge of all teachers and teachings. It is also taken for granted, but perhaps it needs restatement, that the authority enunciated does not mean merely showing that the NT in such-and-such a place takes such a position on the ordination of women, but also that such a position is in line with, harmonious with the Gospel of Jesus Christ.

It is clear from a position like the one enunciated that arguments drawn from reason, experience, or a humanistic philosophy can have no authority when measured against the statements of the Word of God. These arguments dare not be ignored; on the contrary, they must be taken seriously, examined, refuted. They may lead us to a closer examination even of the Scriptural texts themselves; they may lead us to make sure that what may be a traditional exegesis is not merely traditional, without being in fact true and accurate. But these arguments of human reason enjoy no final authority, they are not a final source of truth beyond which we cannot go.

It is not very likely that the reader will find something new in these lines. Too much has been written on this subject from various points of view for anything not to have been said that is really of value. All that can reasonably be expected are a new emphasis and a new ordering of material that is on the whole well-known.

I

The first assertion or thesis to be put forward in this paper is: *The New Testament gives no support at all for the ordination of women.* Ordination I define as authorization and commissioning to do the work of a pastor or minister of the church, a task involving control and pastoral care of a congregation, the public, independent teaching of the Gospel and the administration of the sacraments of Baptism and the Lord's Supper, and the public carrying out of the task of announcing the absolution or, on occasion, the retention of sins. Offices exactly corresponding to this definition cannot be shown to have existed in the New Testament, but something approximating it, closely enough for our present purposes, is presupposed in a direction like that of Paul to the elders of Ephesus: "Take heed to yourselves and to all the flock, in which the Holy Spirit has made you guardians, to feed the church of the Lord which he obtained with his own blood" (Acts 20:28 RSV).

The plain fact is that there is no example in the NT of any woman occupying such an office. Christ chose only men to be His close disciples, the Twelve. Only men were in the 70 (72) sent out to go before Him and assist Him in His mission. Only men took part in the last Passover, where Jesus instituted the Lord's Supper, in spite of the fact that the Passover was celebrated in families. There are no female counterparts to Timothy, Titus, Aristarchus, Mark, Jesus Justus, and Epaphras. Only men appear among the larger group of apostles. A number of editors accent *Iounian* in Rom. 16:7 so as to get the name "Junia"; however, there seems little likelihood that they can be right, and the masculine "Junias" of the RSV is the right translation, also in view of all the masculine forms in the verse mentioned.

Women are entrusted with all sorts of important functions in the life of the church, but always in a subordinate or supporting or private role. Women look after Jesus and His disciples, Luke 8:1–3. Paul also is supported by a number of women. Lydia provided him with a base of operations. Priscilla (or

Prisca) instructed the gifted Apollos besides being a help to the apostle Paul in other ways. Since she is always mentioned before her husband Aquila, she seems indeed to have been the more prominent of the two. Phoebe, the deaconess of the church in Cenchreae, was entrusted with the important letter to the Romans. Of especial interest are Euodia and Syntyche, of whom it is said that "they labored side by side with me in the gospel together with Clement and the rest of my fellow workers" (Phil. 4:3 RSV). In spite of this high praise and association with a number of mostly-nameless male workers, these women are not described as having an independent charge. No woman appears in the NT as carrying out an independent pastoral charge, as defined above. There may conceivably be an explanation for this state of affairs. However, it is clear that the fact itself is not at all favorable for those pressing for the ordination of women. It is, rather, something to be explained away, if possible.

The only text supplying anything like support for female ordination is Gal. 3:28: "There is neither Jew nor Greek, there is neither slave nor free, there is neither male nor female; for you are all one in Christ Jesus." In fact, the text has been hailed as a "breakthrough" in this whole question. Far from being a breakthrough, it does not even dent the NT wall against the ordination of women. The previous verse, v. 27, in the Galatians paragraph runs: "For as many of you as were baptized into Christ have put on Christ." The declaration of the next verse, then, has to do with the oneness of all those who are in Christ, infants included. Paul could quite easily have gone on: "there is neither young nor old" . . . "for you are all one in Christ Jesus." The oneness of man and woman in Christ, as baptized members of the body of Christ, as co-sharers of the eschatological Kingdom—this is what is asserted here. The fact of baptism and oneness in Christ's body allows no argument as to the proper ordering of the church. Nor does it annul the facts of life in this aeon into which we are all born. It does not suddenly eliminate the fact of sex. Believing and baptized women do not suddenly cease to be women. Schlier has made the very appropriate comment in his work on Galatians:

> Once this limitation (i.e. that of v. 27) of the assertion in v. 28 is recognized, then one will refrain from drawing from it direct conclusions for the ordering of the ministerial office or of society. For the ministry does not rest directly on baptism, but on the call into it, and society is never identical with the body of Christ.

However important Gal. 3–28 is for the relation of men and women in the church, and for the proper respect and dignity they are to accord one another, it does not speak of female ordination directly or indirectly.

The most that could be supported by Gal. 3:28 would, so it seems to me, be pastoral activity of women in cases of real emergency. If somewhere, sometime, because of extraordinary circumstances, there just were no men capable of carrying out the pastoral office, and there happened to be a woman or women available capable of fulfilling the office, there would be nothing to prevent such an abnormal functioning of a woman as a pastor. The welfare of the church there would be the supreme law, and the oneness of man and woman in Christ might well then be involved as a reason for such a non-normal action. It would be the understood thing in that situation that the abnormal activity of the emergency woman "pastor" would cease as soon as the normal order of ministry could be restored. Acceptance by the church of the validity of the ministrations of women in emergency situations would be a confession of the wide principle of Gal. 3:28, and also obedience to the apostolic direction for the normal ordering of the church in this matter. To this apostolic direction we now turn.

2

The second thesis or assertion to be put forward in this paper is that *there is specific NT prohibition of the ordination of women.*

This prohibition is contained in the well-known texts of 1 Cor. 14:34–35 and 1 Tim. 2:11–14. There is a close connection between these two short paragraphs and the whole teaching contained in them may best be unfolded by a parallel display of the corresponding phrases in both.

| *1 Corinthians 14* (RSV) | | *1 Timothy 2* (RSV) | |
|---|---|---|---|
| v. 34 | "they are not permitted to speak" | v. 12 | "I permit no woman to teach or to have authority over *men*" (! *andros*, singular in Greek) |
| | "but should be subordinate" | | "she is to keep silent" |
| v. 35 | "If there is anything they desire *to know*" [*mathein*] | v. 11 | "Let a woman learn (*manthanetō*)" |
| | "let them ask their husbands at home" | | "in silence with all submissiveness" |
| v. 34 | "as even the law says" | vv. 14–15 | Adam and Eve in creation and sin. |

There are two ways of judging a comparison like this. The critical and suspicious scholar judges 1 Timothy as non-Pauline, in spite of the evidence which quite definitely supports the Pauline authorship. (The epistle would still be rightly regarded as Pauline if we adopt the attractive suggestion that Paul made use of an amanuensis who worked with some freedom.) The critical scholar often goes on to draw the conclusion that the similar material of 1 Corinthians has been modeled on that of 1 Timothy and has been interpolated into the text of 1 Cor. 14, without leaving a trace in the manuscripts of the text which did not contain the interpolation. If, on the other hand, you are simple, uncritical, and unsuspicious, then the correspondence between 1 Corinthians and 1 Timothy shows a consistent attitude of St. Paul extending over a number of years, and if anything, increasing in firmness. Without pursuing the matter further and without any more demonstration, I shall assume that the latter position is the surer one historically and operate from that base.

If we have the same writer in both letters writing on the same matter, we have the right to allow one text to explain the other, and especially to let the clearer or more definite throw light on the less precise. So 1 Tim. 2 is the key for the understanding of 1 Cor. 14. One of the difficulties of the passage in 1 Cor. 14 is the statement of v.34. This seems to prohibit all speaking of women in congregational assemblies, and this in turn is a fruitful source of many problems. The immediate difficulty, if 1 Cor. 14:34 is understood as a blanket prohibition of all speaking by women in congregational assemblies, is that we have apparently an irremovable contradiction between 1 Cor. 11:2–16 and 14:34. The former permits a speaking (*lalein*) by the prophetess, the second forbids all speaking (*lalein*) on the part of women.

Some of the ways of getting around the difficulty within Corinthians are less than convincing: that prophetesses represented an exceptional situation (1 Cor. 14 has only prophets in mind, since only the masculine is used there), and that they had to be given permission to speak because "the Spirit was not to be quenched, nor prophesying despised," 1 Thess. 5:19–20—so that the whole direction represented an unwilling concession on the part of the apostle; that St. Paul has only a home situation in mind in 1 Cor. 11; that Paul unawares to himself wrote inconsistently. Among the unsuccessful ways of getting around the difficulty is that which argues that *lalein* in 1 Cor. 14:34 is related to the idea of congregational order, which is Paul's big concern in the context in which the prohibition concerning speaking is found. *Lalein* is then understood as referring to undisciplined interjections or foolish chatter. But would Paul have permitted men to take part in undisciplined interjections or foolish chatter? Wouldn't their *lalein*, if that is the meaning of the word, have upset congregational order as much as the same activity by women? Or is the suggestion that women only are given to this sort of *lalein*? I hardly think that Else Kähler, where I first saw this suggestion, would have *that* in mind (*Die Frau in den paulinischen Briefen*. Zürich/Frankfurst am Main: Gotthelf Verlag, 1960). There is a second and more important reason why the suggested solution of the problem is unsatisfactory. *Lalein* is not really contrasted with the idea of order. The contrast in the Greek sentence marked by the *ou gar* . . . *alla* sets in opposition *lalein* and *hypotassesthōsan*, speaking and being subordinate. A speaking is involved which is the opposite of being subordinate, a speaking with authority, teaching, preaching with the implicit demand for obedience. The parallel in 1 Tim. supports this understanding of *lalein* to the hilt. In 1 Tim. Paul does not use *lalein* but *didaskein, authentein andros*, teaching and having authority over men. So, understanding 1 Cor. 14 in the light of 1 Tim. 2, we see that *lalein* is a sign of a ruling position, the behavior of a dominant person, and it is not to be taken literally as meaning any sort of speaking in church.

The understanding of *lalein* suggested by the parallel in 1 Tim. 2 is supported by a further argument. We are still concerned in part with the apparent contradiction between 1 Cor. 11 and 1 Cor. 14. Now, the contradiction is eliminated if we fix on the apostle's real concern in both chapters. In 1 Cor. 11 he is evidently not concerned about the speaking of prophetesses at all, but about their head-covering; in 1 Cor. 14 he is concerned with speaking only in so far as it is a sign of authority. In both passages he is concerned about the same thing really, the subordinate relation of women to men as part of the creation. It is only by accident that a contradiction has come about or seems to have come about. Margaret E. Thrall (*The Ordination of Women to the Priesthood*) points out the true relation as follows:

> Both the matter and the style of the verses (1 Cor. 14:34–35) are Pauline. The demand that women should be in subjection fits in with what the apostle has previously said about the man as the head of woman, and here, as in Chapter 11, reference is made to the Genesis narrative for support. There is contradiction only if we suppose that *lalein* refers specifically to prophetic utterance, which it need not do, apart from the context.

There *is*, of course, a problem of context here. The verses of 1 Cor. 14 with which we have been dealing do not very well fit the context in which they are found. The context, both that which precedes and that which follows, has to do with congregational order. And we have seen that the attempt to make vv. 34–35 fit into the scheme of order is a failure. Some textual witnesses, the Greek manuscripts D and G, some manuscripts of the Old Latin or Itala, and certain Church Fathers, have these verses right at the end of the chapter, after v. 40, where they stand as a kind of appendix or postscript. They actually don't fit much better there than they do in their present position, but one sees the reason for the change of position. Either of two explanations can account for the awkwardness of vv. 34–35 in their present context. It is possible that Paul inserted the material in its present place at a later stage of composition of the letter. There are examples of this having occurred in other letters of the apostle. Romans 9–11 interrupts the smooth course of the argument proceeding from chapter 8 to chapter 12; if we had never seen chapters 9–11 in our copies of Romans we would never have noticed their absence! Gal. 4:21–31 looks very much like an afterthought, as does Phil. 3:2–4:1. The repeated use of *lalein, sigato* in previous verses, and of *hypotassetai* in v. 32 would suggest the present place for the insertion of this new, but heterogeneous material. Or, again, Paul could have from the very beginning included vv. 34–35 where they are because of the association of the words just mentioned. The value that Paul saw in the material itself would have been more important to him than its lack of aptness for the context. I think the second of the two suggestions more likely. And, in any case, no one expects perfect logical arrangement in a letter, and we are never upset by even jumbles of ideas in a letter when we know where it comes from.

The upshot of this investigation into these two key passages, 1 Cor. 14:34–35 and 1 Tim. 2:11–14, is that they both teach the same thing, that a ruling, authoritative role in the church is not for women, is unbecoming to them, in fact (*aischron*, 14:35). The pastoral office, the highest office in the church, where the pastor represents Christ Himself, would be the obvious case in our modern church-life which would be affected by the apostolic injunction. If it did not apply to the pastoral office it could not be applied to any. We shall touch on this point again at a later stage of this essay.

For the moment, we must address ourselves to an important and common objection to the use of these texts in the ordination-of-women question. It is asserted by many writers with considerable confidence that the Pauline restriction on the activity of women in the church was meant only as a direction for that time and that place, being determined by social customs of the day, and that it is a mistake to see in Paul's prohibition a directive for the church of today. Frequently, Paul's prohibition of unveiled women in church is seen as a parallel case. We disregard the latter prohibition—why insist on the former?

It is not easy to assess the evidence about women's status in the society of Paul's day. Are we to think of Jewish, Greek, or Roman society? Were there local variations of importance? On the whole, we should not be far wrong in supposing that Paul had Jewish Jerusalem society in mind. The role of Jewish women in worship both in the Old Testament and in New Testament times was restricted. Israel never had priestesses, although women took part in various folk festivals, in sacrificial meals, and in the Passover. Women were not allowed beyond the court of the women when they attended the temple services. They attended the services of the synagogue, but their place was behind a screen, and they were only listeners. On the other hand, women were quite prominent in heathen cults, not only in the family cult, but also in the public cults. From the point of view of the heathen, Paul's limitation on the activity of women in worship might well have appeared abnormal, as contrary to the customs of the day! Even from the Jewish point of view, some of Paul's rules for worship might have seemed opposed to prevailing custom, as, for example, his observation that men should worship with their heads uncovered, 1 Cor. 11:4. Peter Brunner, accordingly, makes the statements:

Quite often his (Paul's) instructions seem directly opposed to that which was the custom in the synagogue or in the Hellenistic world. When seen in relationship to their day, the New Testament injunctions against women taking an active role in the congregation represent exactly a rejection of those practices that were current in the social surroundings. Thus it is not at all certain that Paul in this passage (1 Cor. 11:2–12) has taken as his standard one of the then prevailing value judgments as to what is decent and proper for a woman. It seems much more likely to me that the reason behind Paul's considering this kind of conduct as shameful is because it violates the express will of God. (See *The Ministry and the Ministry of Women*, [St. Louis: Concordia, 1971], p. 23.)

That Paul is concerned about the will of God and not about prevailing custom both in 1 Cor. 14 and 1 Tim. 2 seems evident from the fact that he appeals to the Old Testament as the solid basis for his directions. In the former passage he writes: "For they are not permitted to speak, but should be subordinate, as even the law says." In the latter passage, he refers first to the creation of Eve as subsequent to that of Adam, and then to the role of Eve in the Fall; she was tempted, deceived, not Adam. The point of Paul in these two references of 1 Tim. 2 to Adam and Eve is the subordinate position of Eve: she was created second, i.e., to help and serve Adam—the mere succession of time is surely not the point—and she is mentally (morally?) inferior. The specifics of Paul's argument are certainly not very happy or convincing, but the appeal to the Old Testament and to the beginning of things surely is important. It shows, at the least, that he is not arguing on the basis of custom. He sees God's will behind his decision. The same appeal to the will of God comes out, of course, in his reference to the law in 1 Cor. 14:34. It is doubtful which passage or passages of the Old Testament Paul has in mind, whether Gen. 3:16 or 18:12, or perhaps, better still, passages like Lev. 12; 27:1–5; Num. 30. It may even be that he has only the general tenor of the Old Testament in mind.

Then, too, we must not forget 1 Cor. 14:37: "If anyone thinks that he is a prophet, or spiritual, he should acknowledge that what I am writing to you is *a command of the Lord.* " It seems necessary to relate this assertion to the whole of the preceding exposition of the chapter, including the statements of vv. 34–35.

We should note also that Paul argues differently on the matter of proper womanly conduct in church in the two chapters of 1 Corinthians, i.e. 11 and 14. In the case of the demand for silence and the non-assumption of authority in ch. 14 he appeals, as has been just shown, to the will of God and the command of the Lord. He does not do this in the case of head-covering. He makes important statements in connection with it, statements to which we shall turn in the third section of this essay, but he does not finally say: "You must wear veils, you women, because that is the will of God." When he has come to the end of his involved, and even tortuous, argumentation calling for the acceptance of veils by the Corinthian women, he finally does, almost in desperation, leave the matter with an appeal to *custom*: "However, if you insist on arguing, let me tell you, there is no such custom among us, or in any of the congregations of God's people" (1 Cor. 11:16 NEB). Paul, then, does not see his demand that women keep silence in the church as a demand limited by time, place, custom! The prohibition of Paul stands, as far he is concerned, on the law and will of God.

## 3

One might get the impression that the prohibition of female leadership in the church is something of an arbitrary opinion of the apostle, one unrelated to his theology or to the Gospel generally—that is, if one judges solely from the sudden and unprepared way in which his statements appear in 1 Corinthians and 1 Timothy. However, such an impression would be a wrong one, for Paul's views on this matter are embedded in his theology of creation, the fall of man, and the redemption through Jesus Christ. This whole web of thought, which we might call the theology of female ordination, has been specially carefully worked out by Peter Brunner in the work mentioned earlier, and what follows now is a mere resume of his thoughts in the chapter headed "Place of Woman in Creation."

Brunner's chief passages are 1 Cor. 11:2–16, Genesis 2, and Eph. 5:22–33. From the passage in 1 Corinthians he derives his term "*kephale*-structure."

The man is the head of the woman; Christ is the head of the man; God is the head of Christ. The "head" is that which is prior, that which determines, that which leads. . . . It involves the kind of relationship for which one can never substitute a polar *schema*. (p. 25)

The actual relationship of woman according to this fundamental order is that she is "from" man and "for the sake of man." And these positions cannot be interchanged.

Only where the woman in her concrete practical relationships lives what she is by *virtue* of the creaturely existence given her in the creation is she a woman as God meant her to be (p. 27).

This *kephale*-structure is visible also in the event of the Fall. Eve heard through Adam, of the command of God concerning the tree that was not to be eaten of, Gen. 2:16–18. Eve was less capable of preserving these original words of God since she did not hear the word of God directly, but by way of Adam. And her fall into sin did not become the fall of man (*homo!*) till it also became the sin of Adam.

The first Adam proved himself also to be the "head," in that sin and death entered into the world through him. The statement in 1 Tim. 2:14 must be amplified by Rom. 5:12, and this must be said: To be sure, Adam was led astray through Eve, but through Adam the fall was "fulfilled." (p. 28)

And, finally, the *kephale*-structure is seen also in the redemption, but an eschatological quality has been given to it. In Eph. 5:22–33 the relationship between man and woman is compared to the relationship between Christ and His church.

Three events join in a mysterious way to determine the relationship of man and woman to each other: the creation in the beginning, the original fall into sin with the resulting judgment on it, and the saving act of Christ with its fruits. (p. 29)

The event of Christ does not eliminate the relationship between man and woman that was given at the creation. The *kephale*-structure still remains, but through the new Christ-church reality, and in it, that relation begins to be transformed.

Despite the individual differences of the various forms of subordination, the subordination of the woman to the man is mysteriously bound up with the subordination of the church to Christ and Christ to the Father. . . . The Christian woman could not mistake or belie the dignity that is hers in a more basic manner than by attempting to step out of the *kephale*-struc- ture that governs her relationship with the man and by trying to usurpand assume the place accorded to him either in the church or in marriage. (p. 30)

In contrast with this reading of the new reality in Christ, a reading which sees the new as transforming the orders of creation from within without trying to remove them, is another view which would like to see the new eliminate the old where it can be done, now, in this life. This comes out very clearly in a major article by John Reumann, "What in Scripture Speaks to the Ordination of Women," *Concordia Theological Monthly* XLIV, 1 (January 1973), He writes:

At several points it has been suggested that the meaning of key texts depends on the eschatological stance involved. If the new age has come, then the old order is changed, and "in Christ" the new obtains. If, on the other hand, we are still in the old order or not fully in Christ in the new, then the orders of creation still hold, at least in some respects (p. 29).

The statements of Paul in 1 Cor. 11 and 14 are understood by Reumann as showing Paul between new and old, concerned about the introduction of the new (1 Cor. 11—which allows women prophetesses to speak) and at the same time "invoking the order of the original creation as a restraint on going too far too fast (1 Cor. 14). And the conclusion Reumann draws is as follows:

It follows that in our vastly changed day and generation the ordination of women is often culturally more easy and obvious than in Paul's, and that Biblically there is a case for allowing it. Church leaders must ask whether the movement toward it is a prompting of the Spirit or whether one should continue to cling to the old and to the traditions long established. If they conclude for the work of the Spirit in drawing women into the ministry, these leaders still have the duty of regulating it, for the edification of the church and its mission, for the sake of good order, and to show that, while the new has dawned for believers, all is not yet the fullness of the kingdom (p. 30).

It is hardly a sound eschatology that lies behind the words of Reumann just quoted. We are not to see the new order in Christ as gradually transforming the old orders of creation, until the new order of things has completely dispossessed the old. A true understanding of the New Testament rather sees the old order of creation, in fact, the old order of creation as ruined by sin, continuing till the end when Christ returns, while the new order of things in Christ ("the old has passed away, behold, the new has come," 2 Cor. 5:17) runs parallel with the old—there is an overlapping of the two aeons—till that same return of Christ. But the new is there in faith, not sight. Nothing of the new is visible, demonstrable: not Christ, not the Spirit, not the *Una Sancta*, not the new birth in Baptism, not the body and blood of the Sacrament, not the forgiveness of sins—nothing. All these are realities, and faith is sure of them, because of the Word of God, but they are all hidden in this world, where what is visible is exactly what has been there from the beginning. There is a realism about this proper view of eschatology which stands in marked contrast to the wishful thinking and enthusiasm of all eschatologies which look for a change of the present world's basic structure. The same realism should be applied to the whole question of women's liberation.

4

The final section of this essay is really an appendix, or rather, two appendixes. The first takes up for brief comment two common objections to the teaching of St. Paul as presented and defended in this essay.

The first objection is that the church is inconsistent in prohibiting the ordination of women while allowing women a whole host of other activities which are just as contrary to the apostolic directive as the pastorate. Reumann, for instance, in the essay mentioned earlier, says in respect of the 1 Timothy 2 passage:

If 2:11–12 forbids their ordination, it also precludes their praying, prophesying, perhaps even singing or speaking liturgical response and teaching males. At the least one must grant that the Jewish synogogal attitude toward women of the early Christian period, here imported into a "church order," has scarcely been universally observed in worship, church schools, and so forth (p. 21).

If the exegesis proposed above is right, viz., that the kind of speaking and teaching involved is that which is of an independent kind, characteristic of authority, then the objection seems to lose much of its force. Onè would be right in making the observation that the pastoral office is the most obvious example of that independent, authoritative activity which the apostle declares is not for women. Here we must start in the application of Paul's prohibition. However much else of our customary churchly activity is involved, would have to be examined, each function for itself; but most of the items mentioned by Reumann and others, I should say, would not fall under Paul's rule. The second appendix below suggests a quite considerable scope for women's gifts in the church.

Another objection to the view defended in this essay is very much like the first. It, too, has to deal with inconsistency. It is held that, if the church rejects the ordination of women on the basis of the arguments derived from St. Paul, then it should protest against women taking up positions of authority in non-ecclesiastical spheres, in society and in politics. The answer here is in part that, if anywhere, then at least in the church Christians should insist on the role of women which fits the created order. Not every development in the world can be changed or even challenged by the church, but a witness to the proper state of affairs can be given by what goes on in the church. And the complaint of the prophet may not be so far off the mark: "My people—children are their oppressors and women rule over them" (Is. 3:12).

The second appendix is merely an enumeration of possible roles for women in the church taken from the work by Peter Brunner referred to in this essay a number of times already. He writes:

> With no dogmatic difficulties, the following functions can be separated from the pastoral office and can be organized into an official assisting ministry into which a woman with theological training can be installed through prayer and the laying on of hands:
>
> 1. the Christian instruction of the catechumens, also confirmation instruction, above all the training of groups of members, also the introduction to the interpretation of the Scriptures that takes the form of a Bible study;
>
> 2. baptizing those who have been approved by the pastor of the congregation, and the dispensing of the cup at the Lord's Supper;

3. home visitations and visits to the sick with the care and counseling that is involved, in fact, individual counseling, particularly with women, and also in hospitals and prisons;

4. devotions in houses such as retreat centers, hospitals, prisons, and charitable institutions;

5. assisting in the training of other official orders such as catechists, congregational helpers, deacons, and deaconesses;

6. cooperating in the maintenance of correct doctrine through theological research (pp. 36–37).

We end with the observation with which we began. The Christian's guide in this matter, as in all others, is the Sacred Scripture and not any human philosophy nor the popular clamor of the day. Christian women, like Christian men, will be led by "the command of the Lord". They will be submissive to the better knowledge and understanding of Him who at the beginning created them male and female. Insistence on rights in any case, except in certain exceptional circumstances like Paul's appeal to his Roman citizenship in the face of unjust treatment, Acts 16:37, is not a Christian virtue, Matt. 5:38–42. Christ our Lord did not come to be served but to serve, and the whole of the Christian life, every Christian's life, is to be seen as an *imitatio Christi*. "You know that the rulers of the Gentiles lord it over them, and their great men exercise authority over them. It shall not be so among you; but whoever would be great among you must be your servant, and whoever would be first among you must be your slave" (Matt. 20:25–27). No life of faith, lived in this spirit of service and submission to the will of God, can be without the blessing of God.

# DIDASKALOS

## THE OFFICE, MAN AND WOMAN IN THE NEW TESTAMENT

## BERTIL GÄRTNER

### THE LARGER DOCTRINAL CONTEXT

Does the New Testament contain any direct teaching about the relationship between man and woman and the office of the ministry? The answer to this question is an unequivocal yes. In fact it is easy to see that the office and the division of the office in relation to man and woman is set in a larger context from which these questions cannot be separated without making the office something other than what it is in the New Testament. If we think that what the apostle says (e.g., in 1 Cor. 14:34 and 1 Tim. 2:12) is only a casual directive intended to correct some irregularities then current in the external order, then the New Testament does not present any teaching concerning the office and woman. However, the above view does not correspond to the material Paul presents. From the way the apostle argues, it is clear that he is not seeking to solve any casual conflict, but that he is giving a normative teaching about the problem and that he himself considers it a question of doctrine.

Consider the construction of 1 Corinthians. The apostle deals with a number of questions which have been put to him by the congregation. They deal with marriage, immorality, meat offered to idols, loveless relationships at the common meal, certain basic principles in worship, etc. None of these questions is dealt with by the apostle as an unimportant detail; rather he sets them in their larger context: the relation to creation, the relation to the Christian life in the world, the connection between the problem and the absoluteness of living *en kyrio* ("in the Lord"). To illustrate how important it is to see all of these questions in their proper context, consider chapter 8. It seems to be a trivial matter: can the Christians in Corinth eat meat which is sold in the marketplace without asking where the meat comes from? The apostle does not simply refer them to "evangelical freedom," nor does he say that it is obvious that a Christian can do as he likes in the matter, but he places the question in the larger context. Fear of being contaminated by meat offered to idols is considered in relation to the doctrine of God as the only God, which excludes the possibility of other gods (v. 4). In his teaching freedom is motivated from the center of the Christian doctrine. But the problem is still not answered. It has another side that is equally important. The "weak" of conscience can be harmed by the other's freedom. This would be a sin against the fellow Christian for whom Christ died. But if the fellow Christian suffers (the perspective deepens again), it is not only a sin against him, it is also a sin which harms the body of Christ: "In thus sinning against your brothers and wounding their consciences, you sin against Christ" (v. 12). True love for Christ places demands upon the one who has a "strong" conscience; this perspective is so important that the apostle concludes this section with this summation: "And therefore, if food be the downfall of my brother, I will never eat meat any more, for I will not be the cause of my brother's downfall" (v. 13).

In this manner the problem which has arisen in Corinth is solved. Placed in the context of Christian doctrine, it receives its proper clarification and gains a solution which the apostle considers absolutely normative.

In the problem of woman and the office, a problem which really exists in the New Testament and which is dealt with, it is important to discover how the problem is resolved, what arguments are used, the context in which the question is placed. Individual texts should not be taken by themselves and an opinion built on them; rather the problem must be considered more deeply and the total concept of what is involved developed so that we may see the context in which the individual texts are set.

## Jesus and Woman: The Choosing of the Apostles

The portrayal of Jesus' relation to women in the Gospels can be said to be revolutionary, in comparison to both the Jewish and Greek environment. He opposes putting limits on her in regard to faith and the religious life. He gives her the same rights as men have and places the same demands on her as on men. Equality is underscored. Jesus frees woman from being a minor. In His proclamation of the kingdom, He draws no limits on who may belong. The only limit to His activity is the concentration on the proclamation to the people of Israel. But He breaks down this boundary when Israel does not receive the Gospel, and thereby the kingdom is opened to all alike, irrespective of sex, nation, or race. This point of view runs through the whole New Testament. The manner in which Jesus associates freely with women goes beyond the Jewish rules. Often the stories show that Jesus did not share the viewpoint of His contemporaries that woman was a lower being, nor did He share the rules of propriety created by this viewpoint. Jesus arrives at His stand because of a new and shocking message. The disciples are surprised by the natural relation He has with the Samaritan woman in John 4:27, but none of the disciples says anything about it because, as the Messiah, He breaks human rules and in a sovereign manner creates anew. The sinful woman in the house of Simon is received by Jesus and is placed by Him, even before the Pharisees, as an example for them to follow (Luke 7:36–50).

It is important to consider Jesus' choice of apostles. He chooses men for this service. The purpose of choosing apostles is not only to have messengers in a particular situation needing messengers (as for example, when He sent out disciples according to Matt. 10 or Luke 10); there it was natural to send men and not women. Instead it happens that Jesus sets the apostles as leaders of the new people of God (church), which is to be comprised of all the nations. The extraordinary importance of the role of the office of the apostle develops *inter alia* from Jesus' words about the church and the apostolate in Matthew 16:18. The same thing happens in the Missionary Command where the task does not concern work limited in time and space, but to a worldwide task: to make all people disciples. The task of the apostle can be fully understood first when Christ completed His work of salvation and "was ascended." By instituting the apostolate Jesus must have intended to create an office that by necessity would belong to the phenomenon of the church in the world. (That Jesus really expected a period of time between His death and the *parousia* has become clearer in recent research: the institution of the office, of Baptism and the Eucharist, and the giving of the Missionary Command indicate this). We shall see that Jesus had a purpose in limiting this office to men from the role that this office played in some important contexts, as this office was developed and divided into different functions during the period of the church of the New Testament times.

For example, although the most esteemed women (such as Jesus' mother), who were part of the closest circle of disciples, were present in Jerusalem during the Passover festival, it was only the apostles themselves who were invited to be present at the Last Supper. It was the Passover meal that was eaten that last evening. By immemorial custom both women and children shared in this dinner fellowship. Yet, this is the time that Jesus breaks that tradition and gathers only the twelve around Him. We know from the Gospel tradition of no other such limitation of participants at meals during Jesus' lifetime. This limitation at the Last Supper must have a very special importance: namely, that the apostles shall handle the mystery of the Eucharist and receive the charge to celebrate it anew in the congregation after His death. Just as the apostles were made bearers of Christ's teaching and the teaching about Christ and received the charge to proclaim it, so the resurrected Christ delivers to them three further commissions: Eucharist, Baptism, and the power of the Keys. It is important to note that doctrine, Eucharist, Baptism, and the power of the Keys are placed in relationship to the apostles, to the leaders of the people of God. In the texts that deal with the time between Easter and the ascension these things are also central in the Resurrected One's teaching to the apostles: the commission to preach (Matt. 28:16ff.); Baptism (Matt. 28:16ff., cf. Mark 16:15ff.); Eucharist (John 21:12ff., cf. Mark 16:14, Luke 24:30); the power of the Keys (John 20:21ff.); doctrine (Luke 24:44ff.).

It is clear that in the early church there was a distinct tradition that Jesus had both instituted the office and given instructions concerning it. We shall cite the following passage from I Clement (ca. A.D. 90):

> Our apostles knew through our Lord Jesus Christ that there would be strife over the name of the bishops' office. For this cause, therefore, having received complete foreknowledge, they appointed the aforesaid persons, and afterwards they provided a continuance, that if these should fall asleep, other approved men should succeed to their ministration (44:1ff.).

According to Clement, the apostles had received in advance the basic principles of the office. It would be difficult to imagine that this office had been dreamed up in its entirety.

## Jesus' Conception of Marriage and Creation

Already in Jesus one meets a principle which has a direct bearing on the relationship between man, woman, and the office. In Matthew 19:3ff. Jesus discusses the subject of marriage with the Pharisees, and in this discussion it is important to note how Jesus works with three periods of time. First He tells how it was "in the beginning," in creation as it was formed by God. "In the beginning God created them man and woman. . . ." Through the fall into sin, however, God's creation was disturbed and the Law given by Moses presupposes this disturbance: "For the sake of your hardness of heart" easy divorce was permitted, but "it was not so from the beginning." To these two periods is now added a third, the time of the kingdom of heaven, which already begins to manifest itself around Jesus. For the one who enters the kingdom of heaven and lives there, what the Messiah reveals is now relevant, when He points back to the order and meaning of creation ("But I say to you . . ."). The superficial view of marriage is not in accordance with the unity in marriage that was intended at the creation, says Jesus. But in the kingdom of God there is the possibility and the power to achieve God's intention at creation in this matter. This principle, that for the first time since the fall into sin the order of creation is able to be realized, also lies beneath the apostle Paul's teaching of the relation of the church to creation in 1 Corinthians.

# The Christian Is a New Creation

That the church received, in Christ, a revelation about male and female in the order of creation may be concluded from the texts in which the apostle Paul describes the manner in which the church should function. The basic principle is this: the Christian, at the same time as he lives in the fallen world in a completely determined milieu, in a certain concept of society, is also a "new creation," living his life according to the rules governing the life in Christ, in the church where the revealed meaning of creation shall be realized. He who is "in Christ" is a new creation (2 Cor. 5:17; Gal. 6:15). By carefully showing what it means to be a member of Christ, the apostle points out the necessity for the individual Christian to stand in solidarity with the order that governs the life situation "in Christ." This solidarity and order stretches out towards God, who has established it, and to the individual Christian who will be helped by it to actualize the Christian life. The life of the church functions this way. Something entirely new enters in here so that the Christian is placed in the world as something more than merely belonging to the fallen world. In the new context, in the life of the church, the true relationship between male and female can take place. The new order which exists in Christ is not, however, something spiritual, having nothing to do with physical reality. It is directly anchored in concrete existence and this can be seen as it restores existence to its state at the creation. The church and the life "in Christ" fulfill the basic intention of the creation, according to the New Testament. This cannot be understood unless one receives it by the revelation which comes through Christ and His apostles. Before dealing with the various Pauline texts concerning man and woman it is necessary to explain the church's relationship to creation.

# The Church and Creation: Heresy in Corinth

One of the very important concepts of Pauline teaching on the church is that the concept of the church is directly related to the concept of creation. In 1 Corinthians this may be seen clearly. Within the young congregation at Corinth the apostle found a strange distortion of the doctrine of the Sacraments, and of the place of the Spirit in the congregation. Probably under the influence of the contemporary mystery cults and other pneumatic circles, people thought that they lived a perfect Christian life. Through Baptism and the Spirit they shared in the heavenly life and, when the Spirit worked in them, they were completely freed from all rules and regulations. Because of this the kerygma and dogma were blurred, and there was a strong influence from the surrounding wisdom cults that dealt in knowledge, the complete knowledge of the mysteries and the philosophical *gnosis*. People were above the office and authority of the apostle. According to the Corinthian heresy, the one who had the gifts of the Spirit received a direct revelation; thus the apostle was no longer needed as the bearer of the teaching concerning Christ and the fixed norms of doctrine. Through tongues and revelations they could speak directly with the angels and God. They set themselves above the commandments on marriage and discipline. Everything was spiritualized, and the individual was self-sufficient in his own faith and concepts and his relationship with God. He could, therefore, set aside the fundamental command of fellowship and love to the neighbor.

The apostle gives several instances of where this leads. When the Corinthians thought that life in the church was the complete realization of the eternal life on earth and that the grace of the Spirit broke down all regulations that belonged to creation, the basic idea of the early Christian church was torn to shreds. According to it, only the beginning of eternal life has taken place at present in the church. The powers of the heavenly world are active, but they work in things which are part of creation. According to the apostolic concept, the church is not only a spiritual quality; but it is so arranged that the Spirit, in the church, through created things, shares the gifts of salvation which Christ gave and gives. When, in Corinth, the distinction between man and woman in the office was disregarded there was a misconception as to the nature of the church. As a result of this misconception the division of functions in the office between man and woman was removed and disorder took control. At the Lord's Supper things went awry; disorder came into the worship; women took over the functions of the office, etc. Therefore the apostle became involved in restoring the right concept of the church in this congregation. He does not give rules which are of limited duration and are designed to create order; but he motivates his teaching, as in chapter 8, from the basic dogmatic propositions and points to the final authority, Christ Himself, to show that disorder does not in the final analysis proceed from questions of order, but, far more importantly, from completely wrong concepts of creation, the church, and the office. The negative opinion of the congregation in Corinth on order and organization is easily explained by their Hellenistic training with its low opinion of the creation and material reality. Paul instructs them that, in the teaching of Jesus, salvation rests upon creation. According to the whole New Testament, both creation and the new creation (salvation) proceed from God and belong together. In the Letter to the Corinthians Paul points out this radical disparity between the Biblical world view and that of the Hellenists. The apostolic, Biblical concept is seen as being in conflict with the cultural spirit of that time and society.

The early Christian concept, here presented by Paul, considers the act of Christ as having revolutionary importance for the world. In Christ, full salvation has been realized. But this salvation is related to the church, which appears within the created world and follows the orders of this world and its divisions of roles as they have been revealed in Christ. The Sacraments are not only spiritual. They impart the gifts of the Spirit under the forms of water and bread and wine. It is not surprising that Paul must correct their concepts of Baptism and Eucharist inasmuch as the pneumatic aspect has been grossly exaggerated. To the phenomenon of the church in the world belongs also the office, and that is borne by certain people. As a visible thing, the office is related to the order of creation; and according to the order of creation, the human race is divided into man and woman. This division is given in creation and is not caused by the fall into sin. Therefore it is not changed by the redemptive work of Christ; it only receives its rightful evaluation. This proceeds from the aforementioned view of Jesus about marriage. In another connection Jesus says that the time will come when the created orders of this world will be done away with, but this will happen at the resurrection "when the world is born anew." Then the distinction between man and woman which was established at creation will be done away with. Then the faithful will be "like angels" (Luke 20:36); then the relations between men and women will be completely changed. But as long as the church functions in the world, it functions in accordance with the revealed order of God in creation. The office which is one part of the phenomenon of the church in the world reflects the church's relation to creation. In worship, in the liturgy, the separation of men and women is expressed in different ways as customs and concepts differ. In the early Christian church it was the custom for women to have "veils" on their heads, but not men ("there is no such custom among us, or in any of the congregations of God's people" [1 Cor. 11:16]). But it is interesting to note that the apostle does not describe these details as being other than customs. At the same time the meaning of these customs is to make visible the order of creation, the distinction between men and women.

The apostle presumes that not all the details of the office are everywhere the same, but the basic concept of man's and woman's relation to the office he considers as fixed. Here it is not a question of custom or human order, but it concerns a basic relationship with creation, which the apostle states is a command of the Lord.

This does not mean that woman has no function in the congregation. Such a view is not in accord with other instructions of Paul. The woman has her functions and her gifts of grace. In the first place, the order of creation is realised when men and women have their given functions in the congregation. But the apostolic teaching on this matter is disobeyed both when the distinction between man and woman is obliterated and when the woman is denied the task that she has in the congregation. What women's duties are in the congregation is not described in detail. Those that are mentioned in the New Testament have a variety of functions, the concrete shape of which we do not know. Euodia and Syntyche had "shared my struggles in the cause of the Gospel" (Phil. 4:3). Some women are mentioned in Romans 16 who "toil in the Lord's service." Priscilla and her husband took charge of Apollos; in their home they gave him a more basic instruction in Christian doctrine (Acts 18:26). The status of "widows" clearly entailed a care for souls and loving work in the service of the congregation (1 Tim. 5:9ff). Man and woman in the early church worked side by side "in the Gospel," completing each other; but their roles were not mixed.

## THE BASIC CONCEPT OF SAINT PAUL IN FIRST CORINTHIANS

In order to gain a better understanding of this division of functions it is helpful to analyze in detail some of the more important texts.

*First Corinthians 12*: The basic thought of the apostle is that there is a distribution, a division (*diairesis*) of services and gifts of grace in the congregation. But this distribution does not entail division but unity. The Spirit is the same, but the one Spirit works through a distribution of differing tasks, responsibilities, and gifts. This distribution is a divine ordinance and it is God who works through the different gifts and tasks, the apostle says. The purpose of these services is not that each one should be important for himself; but that each shall be *pros to sympheron*, "for some useful purpose," so that the whole, the church, the congregation, functions best. To illustrate this important concept the church is depicted as a body which has many parts. Thus it is underscored that in services and assignments and functions in the congregation we are dealing with a living fellowship. Everything should serve to help the congregation live the life which Christ has intended for it. The purpose of the various members of the body is to make the body function together in the correct way. It is never a question of one part considering itself the finest, or sufficient unto itself. Only in the common function the part has its special task. "For Christ is like a single body," writes the apostle (v. 12). The church is a body and every baptized person is a member in that body. In that respect there is no difference between Jew or Greek, slave or free (v. 13). But this similarity between Baptism and salvation does not mean that all the baptized have the same function or that all have a right to the same service or position. This is made clear in the following verses.

Having shown that there is an allotment of functions by explaining the relationship between the members in the body, the apostle comes to the point of his simile about the body and its members: showing that the division of function relates to the office and services in the church. "Within our community God has appointed, in the first place apostles, in the second place prophets, thirdly teachers; then miracle workers, then those who have the gifts of healing, or ability to help others or power to guide them, or the gift of ecstatic utterances of various kinds. Are all apostles? all prophets? all teachers? . . ." (vv. 28ff.).

It could be thought that the gifts of the Spirit which the apostle describes in this section of the text are all equal in the sense that anyone in the congregation can be an apostle or a prophet or a teacher or be active in the work of the church. But in chapter 13 there is a limitation. In this text the apostle Paul separates the pneumatic functions. Speaking with tongues, prophecy and knowledge, and the works of love are special spiritual gifts. But because they are spiritual, the danger is present, as may be seen in the congregation in Corinth, that they who own them and use them may be puffed up by a sense of their own importance and spirituality. The pneumatics have a direct contact with God and are above the office which has been given by God in the congregation, the apostolic authority. Therefore these pneumatic gifts must always be placed in connection with love, which is the specific Christian relationship to our neighbor. This is their right context, that they, in humility and with the help of the Spirit, are an essential part in the building up of the congregations and of individuals. Naturally it is also a pneumatic function to be an apostle and "teacher," and the holder of the office has received a special charismatic gift. And naturally, these "ordinary" offices must also be characterized by love and unselfish service to the whole, the congregation. But there is a difference between these offices and the above mentioned pneumatic gifts; for the latter can come to any member of the congregation as a gift of grace, directly from God, whereas the "ordinary" offices are given to those who are called and consecrated in the proper order. The apostle points here to the orders given by God.

This is also the meaning of Galatians 3:26ff. In Baptism all have "put on" Christ and become a unity: "There is no such thing as Jew or Greek, slave or freeman, male and female; for you are all one person in Christ Jesus." (N.B.: the NEB translation does not make the distinction that Paul does and has "and" throughout the sentence.) The apostle underscores that the wall of separation between Israel and the heathen, between the slave and the free, and between man and woman has been broken down in Christ. A holy fellowship having no boundaries or valuations has been created. But in this connection the apostle does not say anything about how this unity functions. When he wants to portray the functions in this unity, he draws on the comparison between the body and the members, where the point is that all are baptized into Christ's body, but that all do not have the same functions, for unity is not the same as uniformity. Consider the parallel passage (1 Cor. 12:13), where the words about Jew and Greek, slave and free are placed within the explanation of the body as having many members. Unfortunately, this is not the place to deal with the interesting circumstance, namely, that the apostle deals with the relationship between man and woman in Christ in a different way from other relationships (slave *or* free; man *and* woman).

*First Corinthians 11*: This section is introduced by the apostle with an exposition of how the congregation has received the apostolic tradition, the *paradosis*, namely through Paul. In relation to this doctrinal tradition he takes up the question of man and woman and places it in relation to creation. He thinks that the division into man and woman at the creation has relevance for worship. Again he follows his principle of deciding a question on the basis of the larger doctrinal interconnection. It is in this way that he finds a basic principle for the regulation of the life of the congregation. Because the Corinthian spiritualists misunderstood man's and woman's position in creation and in the "new life," the consequence is that disorder has arisen in the congregation. To the apostle, this is contrary to the will of God and leads to individualism.

To explain the doctrinal question that lies at the base of his teaching, the apostle points to the relationship between Christ, man and woman, and God ("Christ is the man's head, etc."). The details of his understanding of "head" are not clear, but the idea is important for the apostle. In verse 7 we see again the same relationship between man and woman, where it is said, however, that man is God's image and *doxa*, while woman is man's *doxa*. The decisive factor for the teaching of man and woman in 1 Corinthians can be stated in the following manner: according to Genesis 2 the creation narrative which is especially concerned with man, God created mankind, that is, a man (v. 15). But the man did not really "function"; the original text says that "he could not get the help which corresponded to his need." Man needed a *completion*. Thus, when woman was created, created from the man who already existed, the human was "whole." This is underlined by the repeated word that the man and woman are one flesh (vv. 23ff.). It is this passage that the apostle refers to, as did Jesus also when He taught about marriage. ("For man did not originally spring from woman, but woman was made out of man; and man was not created for woman's sake, but woman for the sake of man," writes the apostle in 1 Cor. 11:8ff.). There is a relationship of dependency according to this view, between man and woman. ("And yet, in Christ's fellowship woman is as essential to man as man to woman," the apostle writes in v. 11.) The apostle follows the mainstream of Jesus' interpretation, when he lets the new situation, the new life "in Christ," refer back to creation, and thinks that first in the kingdom of God, "in Christ," the order and meaning of creation comes to its complete revelation and reality. "In the Lord" man and woman are two different sides of mankind, differing in natures and functions, but together making up a "wholeness," the full interplay between masculine and feminine. "If woman was made out of man, it is through woman that man now comes to be; and God is the source of all" (v. 12). This fullness and interplay between man and woman should be reflected in the liturgy. The "veil" on the head and woman's long hair were ways that the early church expressed this relationship (v. 16).

*First Corinthians 14*: The chapter is introduced by repeating what was said in chapter 12, viz., anyone can speak in tongues and prophesy if these gifts of the Spirit have been given him, but because these are the gifts of the Spirit it must be pointed out that these gifts cannot be an end in themselves or a means for calling attention to the spiritual gift as such, but that they should have as their purpose the building up of the congregation; for it was as a member of the congregation that the individual received his gift of grace—to serve the congregation. The whole body shall profit from the gift to the individual. It is this very part of worship (where the uncontrolled pneumatic gifts are given expression) that bears the risk of losing the very meaning of the worship, the building up of the congregation. Thus the apostle deals with these matters in great detail; and so some people have been led by this fact to believe that the early Christian worship was almost completely dominated by the working of the free, pneumatic gifts of grace. But there were also other aspects to the liturgy in which the office of teacher (those who had this gift through call and consecration) carried on instruction, proclamation, and administered the Sacraments. At this point it was not easy to change the order of worship, even if we can see that ignorance about the order of creation at times could have this consequence (1 Cor. 14:34ff.; 1 Tim. 2:12).

The order of creation, in this case the right relationship between man and woman, had been set aside in Corinth; but the apostle calls the congregation back to the order of the Christian teaching ("not a God of disorder, but of peace" [1 Cor. 14:33]). Apart from what had gone wrong with charismatic gifts mentioned in earlier chapters (which in principle are for the use of all), there is also disorder concerning the office so that women, in accordance with this wrong view of the order of creation and with the appearance of the new life in the church, "in Christ," had taken upon themselves these functions. (The warning to women "to be silent" is the same as that directed against those who speak in tongues when there is no interpreter; it is not a crass command to forbid women from taking part in the service.) "They have no license to speak (*lalein*), but should keep their place (*hypotassesthai*) as the Law (*nomos*) directs" (v. 34). At this point we will discuss these three words: speak, subordinate, and law.

*Nomos*: Here the apostle Paul is referring to the Pentateuch, the Torah. What passages in this large collection of writings are being referred to is not made clear, but the reference is probably to the account of creation and the conception of man and woman therein which the apostle had developed earlier. His method of debate is important to observe: he gives the command from the church's *paradosis*, but also finds support in the Law. The direction from the Torah is a subordinate argument; note the formulation, "as also the Law says."

*Lalein*: It would be absurd to say that the apostle meant to speak about women who sat and whispered, disturbing the service, and so are admonished to keep silence. Such an interpretation cannot be drawn from either text or context. Nor can these words of Paul be meant to forbid women from speaking in the service *in toto*; the apostle in 11:5 clearly says the women both pray and prophesy through gifts of the Spirit, just as he says "all" in regard to prophecy, speaking in tongues, and the other spiritual gifts mentioned in chapter 14. *Lalein* must, therefore, refer to the teaching which went on in public worship. (Trans. note: see the translation in the NEB.) Where *lalein* is used in connection with the service in the New Testament it always means "to preach" (proclamation, exposition, teaching). It is a *nomen technicum* for "to preach"; the following references are a few examples from the New Testament: Matthew 9:18; 12:46; Mark 2:2; Luke 9:11; John 8:12; Acts 4:1; 8:25; 13:43; 1 Corinthians 2:7; 2 Corinthians 12:19; Ephesians 6:20; Philippians 1:14, etc. That in 1 Corinthians 14 the word means to speak as the *didaskalos* may be seen from the parallel text in 1 Timothy 2:11ff. (where the word *didaskein*, "to instruct," "to teach," is used). But one ought to observe the different ways the apostle expresses himself when he uses *lalein* ("to preach"), or *lalein glossais* ("to speak in tongues") or *glosse*, or *propheteuein* ("to speak a prophetic word").

*Hypotassesthai*: This verb, "to subordinate oneself," is often understood as involving the slavish submission to a tyrant. But if one examines the usage of the New Testament, one will find a different meaning. (See also the section on subordination below.) For this reason we must compare 14:34 with other texts in which this word is used. In 1 Corinthians 16:16 the apostle admonishes the congregation to submit itself to Stephanas. Here we see another aspect of subordination. It is evident that Stephanas, together with Fortunatus and Achaicus, has held the office in the congregation. ("You know that the Stephanas family were the first converts in Achaia, and have laid themselves out to serve God's people. I wish you to give their due position [*hypotassesthai*] to such persons, and indeed to everyone who labours hard at our common task"). The subordination of woman, spoken of in 14:34, should be compared with the subordination to one installed in the office by the apostle. To take upon oneself the function of the *didaskalos*, "teacher in the congregation," is to disobey God's order and His peace. Note that the apostle differentiates between the public worship (*en ekklesia*) and conversation about doctrine at home (*en oiko*). A detailed knowledge of what lies behind the words, "If there is something [a doctrine] they want to know, they can ask their own husbands at home," is not clear. That both verbs (*manthanein* and *eperotan*) have to do with doctrinal teaching is obvious, but we know little as to the exact content and form of this side of the congregation's activity.

First Timothy 2:11ff. is an important parallel text where the same terminology appears (*manthanein* and *hypotage*). Here "subordination" is also placed in relation to the command that women shall not hold the office of teacher. The verb used here is not *lalein*, but *didaskein*. The two verbs are parallel in the two passages. In 1 Timothy 2 creation is also mentioned as being basic to the doctrine. From these two texts it can be seen that the conviction that woman had spiritual equality with man led to a mistake about the division of man and woman that was laid down in the creation. This was true at Corinth and other Hellenistic congregations. This mistake is corrected by the apostle with a well-defined teaching which is given the highest divine authority.

In order to underline further the meaning of this basic teaching, Paul points out that the norm for the congregation is the "Word of God." The tendency in the Corinthian congregation to provincialism and self-made rules is repeated: "Did the Word of God originate with you? Or are you the only people to whom it came?" (v. 36). The apostle is not to present his own thoughts or counsel, but he is to be in agreement with the teaching of Christ. ("It is the command of the Lord" [v. 37].) The pneumatics of Corinth in their spiritual enlightenment ought to understand this basic fact. "If anyone claims to be inspired or to be a prophet, let him recognize that what I write has the Lord's authority" (v. 37). How important it is to be obedient in this matter is pointed out by the apostle in these words: "If he does not acknowledge this, God does not acknowledge him" (v. 38).

As to the meaning of "it is the law of the Lord" (*entole kyriou*), it should be pointed out that the apostle is careful to note whether he is citing something said by the Lord, or giving his own advice. In 1 Corinthians 7:10 we read in the advice about marriage: "I give this ruling, which is not mine but the Lord's." The apostle recalls what Jesus Himself has taught, and this tradition is written down in the Gospels for the same advice. Further, in the same passage, on the other hand he writes: "To the rest I say this, as my own word, not as the Lord's" (v. 12). In the same chapter, verse 25, he writes, "On the question of celibacy I have no instruction from the Lord." Instead he says that he gives his own advice (*gnome*). The same term appears in 2 Corinthians 8:10 about advice which the apostle gives to the congregation. In 1 Corinthians 9:14 the apostle points to a command from the Lord that is also contained in the Gospels. Concerning the words of Jesus in the account of the Lord's Supper, we are told expressly that they are from the Lord (11:23). The question of the "veil" on the head and hair styles is answered only with a reference to what is the custom (*synetheia*). But the apostle says that his views on woman and the teaching office are a "law of the Lord."

The word, *entole* ("law"), in the New Testament means, in general, a Law of God, the Decalogue, or the Law of God received in Christ. In this connection notice that the same word is used in the Missionary Command (Matt. 28:20). In this word of Jesus the apostles are given authority to make disciples of all nations. ("Baptize men . . . and teach them to observe [*terein*] all that I have commanded [*entellesthai, entole*] you.") Paul is following faithfully the ordinance which is contained in the words of the Lord as being unreservedly authoritative norms for the life of the church.

One more thing should be observed in the construction of the above-mentioned passage from 1 Corinthians, and that is, when the apostle *begins* his teaching about the order of creation and the functions in worship and congregation (chaps. 11–14), he proceeds from the premise that that which follows is part of the universal Christian doctrine, the apostolic tradition (11:2). The apostle refers to the tradition that he has received and now passes on. At the end of this section on the teaching in chapter 14, when the apostle goes on to correct a false belief about another part of the content of the faith, the resurrection, (chap. 15) he does this in the same manner. He introduces his teaching by pointing to the early Christian tradition about the resurrection of Christ, as it has been formed in a short "creed." Again the apostle shows that his teaching is the same as the doctrine of the early church, which he has received and passes on in his work as an apostle. (The words used here are *paradidonai*, "to pass on as tradition," and *paralambanein*, "to receive as tradition" [15:3].)

## THE SUBORDINATION OF WOMEN

When considering the relationship of man and woman, and especially the relationship of woman and the office, it is of basic importance that the principle of "subordination" be considered. According to the usual interpretation of the need for "subordination," it has been seen as an outcropping of an antique, patriarchal viewpoint and as a sign that the apostle Paul had fallen into "rabbinical thinking." But by this simplification of the problem, one loses the specifically Christian content in the idea of marriage and in the view of the office as the New Testament presents it.

First, it should be said that the apostle Paul is by no means alone in his advocacy of the basic-ness of "subordination." The same teaching is clearly seen in the apostle Peter's instruction in 1 Peter. In the nature of the case, it is possible to offer strong proof that this is a universal, basic idea in early Christian thinking.

The doctrine of "subordination" cannot be explained as merely an example of the patriarchalism of that time. Instead the Christian idea of man and woman signifies something completely new, that is not at all the same as that found in the Jewish conception of woman and marriage. Neither can it be compared with the Greek-Hellenistic conception. On this point the Christian doctrine is unique. It is thoroughly permeated by faith in Christ, and has an organic connection with the new life "in Christ." The New Testament makes new evaluations about man and woman, marriage, and the office. For the sake of clarification this can be pointed out in the letter of Clement; in those sections which deal with the body and its members, the letter is completely in accord with the teaching of the apostle in 1 Corinthians 12. This letter was written to the same congregation in Corinth some decades after St. Paul wrote his letters and shows that the concept of function was still a stumbling-block.

> There is a certain mixture in all things and therein lies utility. Let us take our body as an example. The head without the feet is nothing, so likewise the feet without the head are nothing, even the smallest limbs of our body are necessary and useful for the whole body: but all the members conspire and unite in subjection (*hypotage*), that the whole body may be saved. (Note: "conspire" [*sympnei*] means "to breathe together," "work together.") So in our case let the whole body be saved in Christ Jesus and let each man be subject (*hypotassesthai*) unto his neighbor, according as also he was appointed with special grace.

That the differing members have differing tasks so that the whole body may function in its entirety has been mentioned. above in connection with 1 Corinthians 12. But it should be noted that subordination is natural for being "in Christ" (i.e., it is a basic natural principle for the one who lives in the new life, "in Christ"); there must be dependency upon each other. The apostle Paul expresses the same thing in Ephesians 5:20: "Be subject [*hypotassesthai*] to one another out of reverence for Christ." Subordination occurs in relation to the grace one has received, to the place in the whole which one has.

That the special content of subordination comes from the life "in Christ" follows from Colossians 3. There the women are warned to "be subject to your husbands; that is your Christian duty," which is part of life "in Christ" (v. 18). The same admonishment is also given to children who are to subject themselves to their parents in everything "for that is pleasing to God and is the Christian way" (v. 28). (Cf. Eph. 6:1 where the same expression occurs.) It is important to note in Colossians 3 that the subordination of slaves to their masters is not motivated from the point of "in the Lord." The relationship of slavery is not comparable to a child's subordination to its parents or a woman's "subordination" to her husband. Servants shall, of course, be subject to their master (they shall subject themselves but this is not "in the Lord"

[1 Pet. 2:18]). But in the pastoral teaching about subordination of servants the motivation is different. In their service they are ultimately serving Christ (Eph. 6:5; Col. 3:22ff.), but this does not mean that slavery as such should be maintained as proper "in the Lord."

When it is said that woman shall "subordinate herself" to her husband, this admonishment is not merely to be understood as subordination "in the Lord," "in Christ," for the very special thought which is involved comes to clearest expression in Ephesians 5. There man and woman are placed in a "type relation" that gives Christian marriage its specific character. Christ is the head of the church. In every way Christ serves His church in love and humility. The church subordinates itself to Christ, but Christ in His love gives Himself for the church, offers His life for her. Man is the head of woman and therefore she shall be subject to him. In no way is he to be a tyrant over his wife; this has no prototype in Christ who came "not to be served but to serve." That man should reflect Christ's glory (as in 1 Cor. 11:7) means, *inter alia*, (above all, self-giving love belongs to His glory) that he should be the servant of his wife, in the same way that Christ was the servant of His church. The man should realize a love towards his wife after the prototype of Christ. When a man is said to be "placed over" his wife it does not mean that he should appear as her lord. Any attempt from the side of man to rule would harm the wholeness, marriage. Any attempt from the woman's side to "domineer over man" (1 Timothy 2:12) would harm the wholeness, marriage. Thus it is mutual service and love which creates wholeness between man and woman. This relationship between man and woman, that is mirrored in the relationship of Christ and the church, is a great mystery whose depth one can only understand through the revelation of the Spirit.

So, when it is said only of woman that she should "subject herself," while the man receives the admonishment to "love his wife," the difference in ter-minology is based on the analogy of Christ and the church. Thus, when this prototype of Christian marriage is kept in mind, then the New Testament doctrine on this point can be understood. Through this analogy the central principle is expressed that man and woman in marriage, through the differ-ence in their beings, can realize wholeness. Both verbs, "to subject oneself" and "to love," express a "serving relationship." The apostle thinks that this is a revelation of the meaning of creation, when God created man to be man and woman and said that they should be one flesh. By pointing to the teach-ing about the church as the body of Christ and the Christians as members in the body (v. 30) the apostle has pointed out in what context the principle of subordination must of necessity be understood. (That the apostle has not forgotten the unwed or single woman is seen, e.g., in 1 Cor. 7. Through her freedom from the "trouble of a family" and such things she has a special call to serve the Lord in an undivided manner, "The unmarried or celibate woman cares for the Lord's business; her aim is to be dedicated to Him in body as in spirit" [v. 34]. She can also make clear in all of her dealings an immediate relationship with Christ.)

Finally, it should be stressed that in this context one of the most important ideas about the office is to be understood. Despite his high office, the apostle is not "lord" or tyrant over the congregations, but a servant who serves the congregations with God's gifts. Despite the dizzyingly high authority Jesus gave His disciples, He taught them about the specific nature of their office: "In the world kings lord it over their subjects, and those in authority are called their country's 'Benefactors.' Not so with you; on the contrary, the highest among you must bear himself like the youngest, the chief of you like a servant. For who is greater—the one who sits at table or the servant who waits on him? Surely the one who sits at table. Yet here am I among you like a servant" (Luke 22:25ff.). At the same time, the apostles had to give diligent care to their tasks and teaching, and personally had to be only "humble servants." And with this, all patriarchalism is turned upside down.

# PHOEBE

## A ROLE MODEL FOR DEACONESSES TODAY

## CYNTHIA LUMLEY

## THE OFFICE OF THE HOLY MINISTRY—FOUNDED IN THE GOSPEL

Lutheran doctrine is biblical teaching—holding firmly to the principle of *sola scriptura*. What, then, does Scripture teach regarding the ordination of women, an issue on which we are constantly challenged today? In a "What About" pamphlet,[1] sainted LCMS president A. L. Barry states that "the Lord teaches us through His Word that women are not given the responsibility of serving the church as pastors," and then he cites the well-known passages from 1 Corinthians (13:33–34, 37) and 1 Timothy (2:11–12; 3:1–2), where Paul provides "commands" concerning the role of women in the Church. Countless word studies have been conducted and numerous books have been written on these few verses, with both the proponents and the opponents of women's ordination claiming to prove their case. Barry concludes that "the church which wishes to remain faithful to the Word of God cannot permit the ordination of women to the pastoral office." This view is entirely consistent with Scripture, but this, together with almost all publications on this issue, starts and ends with the Law. As Luther stated, "without the Gospel the Law is ugly and terrible."[2] Perhaps one reason for the controversy over the issue of women's ordination is the difficulty people have accepting the Law-based argument made by those who oppose women's ordination. We live in the freedom of the Gospel, and it is important therefore to understand from a

---

1   A. L. Barry, *What about the Ordination of Women to the Pastoral Office* (St. Louis: LCMS Office of the President, 1997).

2   Quoted in Ewald M. Plass, comp., *What Luther Says, An Anthology* (St. Louis: Concordia, 1959), 739.

Gospel perspective God's establishment of the Office of the Holy Ministry as an office to be filled by males.

The Gospel is God's free gift of salvation, won for us not by any merit or worthiness on our part, but through Christ's suffering, death, and resurrection. Even before He created human beings, God knew that His creation would fall (Ps. 139:15–16). His order for salvation was therefore in place before He breathed life into Adam (Eph. 1:4–10; Matt. 25:34; Heb. 4:3; Rev. 13:8). And that salvation order was that His own Son, Jesus Christ, would be incarnate as a male human, the second (1 Cor. 15:21–22, 44–49) and perfect Adam (Rom. 5:14), and would give His life for His Bride, the Church (Matt. 9:15; John 3:29; Eph. 5:23–32; Rev. 9:7–9; 21:2). What a wonderful, loving God and heavenly Father we have! He created us, even knowing we would fall to the temptation of the devil and knowing that He would give His only Son as a ransom for us (Matt. 20:28; Mark 10:45).

God's creation order was therefore based on what would transpire when the Word Himself would become flesh (John 1:14). Creation order did not determine salvation order; rather, it is the other way around. At creation, God gave headship and authority to the man, Adam (Gen. 1:26), in light of the fact that Christ, the Head (Bridegroom) of His Church, would be incarnate as a male human. As William Weinrich points out, all the Old and New Testament figures who serve as "types of the redemptive purposes of God in Christ are male figures": Adam, Abraham, Moses, David, the first-born son, the sacrificial Passover lamb, the scapegoat. Also, "Christ Himself, to whom all these masculine types point, assumed His human nature in the masculine mode of human being."[3] Jesus "continues his own ministry in and through those he commissions,"[4] as affirmed in John 20:22ff. Through the holy office established by Christ, we receive the gifts of hearing Christ Himself speak (Luke 10:16), receiving absolution from Christ Himself (Matt. 16:19–20; John 20:21–23), being taught and baptized by Christ Himself (Matt. 28:16–20; cf. Mark 16:15–16), and receiving the Lord's Supper from Christ Himself (1 Cor. 11:23–25).[5] God the Father revealed Himself to us through His incarnate (male) Son (John 14:9–11). "That Jesus' maleness is basic to his role as our incarnate Saviour is a matter of Biblical revelation."[6] What a wonderful gift that the office which belongs to Christ and through which He delivers His gifts is filled by males!

---

3   William Weinrich, "It Is Not Given to Women to Teach," 478 in this volume.

4   William Weinrich, "Called and Ordained: Reflections on the New Testament View of the Office of the Ministry," *Logia* 2, no. 1 (January 1993): 24–25.

5   Thomas M. Winger, "The Office of the Holy Ministry According to the New Testament Mandate of Christ," *Logia* 7, no. 2 (1998): 40.

6   J. I. Packer, "Let's Stop Making Women Presbyters," *Christianity Today* (February 11, 1991): 20.

If the Office of the Holy Ministry is reserved for males, what, then, are the opportunities for women to serve in the Church? St. Paul, who is so often quoted in support of reserving the office for males, "himself shows us that he is perfectly convinced of the blessing which godly women wrought in the Apostolic Church."[7] According to Roger Gryson, "there is no doubt that Paul often benefited from the cooperation of women in his apostolic labours and that the women did not prove themselves less fervent than the men in spreading the Good News."[8] For example, Paul includes several women among those whom he calls his "fellow workers" (τοὺς συνεργούς μου) in Romans 16, who have "worked hard in the Lord."

One way in which women can enter consecrated service in The Lutheran Church—Missouri Synod (LCMS) is through the office of deaconess, which has been established by the church to strengthen and support the Office of the Holy Ministry and to assist the faithful in their God-given vocations. The Lutheran deaconess is called and commissioned by the church to provide care through various vocations and tasks, with special emphasis on

- demonstrating the compassion of Christ through acts of mercy;
- providing spiritual care for the shut-in, infirm, and all in need; and
- teaching the faith, especially to women, youth, and children.

Through these activities the deaconess witnesses to the Christian faith and guides others to the Word and Sacraments provided by the Office of the Holy Ministry.

Many writers have linked the roots of the office of deaconess to Phoebe, referred to by Paul in Rom. 16:1–2, because one of the words Paul uses to describe her is διάκονον, which, in some English translations is transliterated as "deacon." Whether or not Phoebe filled an office of deaconess or assisted in a nonofficial capacity, her support for the apostle Paul and the church at Cenchreae can be studied as a model for a diaconal identity and the ways in which a deaconess today provides support for the Office of the Holy Ministry and for Christ's Body, the Church.

## PHOEBE: SISTER, HELPER, AND PATRON

Who was Phoebe? The only information we have is that which is provided in Rom. 16:1–2. Paul tells us that she lived in Cenchreae, the eastern seaport of Corinth. Corinth followed Roman cultural parameters, and this suggests that Phoebe may have had more possibility of achieving a high status in society

---

7    C. Golder, *History of the Deaconess Movement in the Christian Church* (Cincinnati: Jennings & Pye, 1903), 19.

8    Roger Gryson, *The Ministry of Women in the Early Church* (Collegeville, MN: Liturgical Press, 1976), 5.

than women elsewhere in Greece.[9] Most commentators highlight three particular words used by Paul that describe her status. First, she is described as "our sister" (τὴν ἀδελφὴν ἡμῶν). This is generally taken to mean a sister "in Christ" rather than a blood relative. This view is supported by her pagan name, which indicates that she was probably a Gentile who became a Christian.[10] According to Joan Campbell, "Paul identifies Phoebe as 'our sister' (Rom 16:1) to underscore that she shares an intimate bond with every member of the Jesus' group regardless of where they are located. As a disciple of Jesus, she is one of them, their sister. Because of this, she deserves the love and care that biological siblings owe one another."[11]

There is considerable controversy regarding the meaning of the next descriptor, διάκονον. In some English translations, this word is transliterated as "deacon." There is some debate as to whether or not this is a reference to the office of deacon as defined in Phil. 1:1. Some commentators suggest that the use of the phrase οὖσαν [καὶ] διάκονον τῆς ἐκκλησίας τῆς ἐν Κεγχρεαῖς ("being also of the assembly in Cenchrea"[12]), suggests that in Rom. 16:1 "deacon" is a recognized leadership role, status, or office of service "of the church at Cenchrea."[13] Others suggest that it refers either to the role that Phoebe had in representing Paul to the Romans[14] or to the help she provided in her role as προστάτις,[15] the third descriptor. Regardless, it is apparent that Phoebe played an important role in helping the church and supporting Paul's ministry.

The word προστάτις does not occur anywhere else in the New Testament, thus there is some debate as to its precise meaning. However, forms of the verb that corresponds to the noun προστάτις do occur in the New Testament

---

9 Antti Marjanen, "Phoebe, a Letter Courier," in *Lux Humana, Lux Aeterna: Essays on Biblical and Related Themes in Honour of Lars Aejmelaeus*, ed. Antti Mustakallio, et al. (Göttingen: Vandenhoeck & Ruprecht, 2005), 500.

10 Jonathan F. Grothe, *The Justification of the Ungodly: An Interpretation of Romans* (Canada, 2005), 2:806; Robert H. Mounce, *Romans*, New American Commentary 27 (Nashville: Broadman & Holman, 1995); Sojung Yoon, "Phoebe, a Minister in the Early Christian Church," in *Distant Voices Drawing Near: Essays in Honor of Antoinette Clark Wire*, ed. Holly E. Hearon (Collegeville, MN: Liturgical Press, 2004), 26.

11 Joan Cecelia Campbell, *Phoebe: Patron and Emissary* (Collegeville, MN: Liturgical Press, 2009), 32.

12 Kurt Aland, et al., *The Greek New Testament*, 4th rev ed. (Stuttgart: Deutsche Bibelgesellschaft, 1993), S. Ro 16:1.

13 Marjanen, "Phoebe," 503; Grothe, *Justification of the Ungodly*, 2:806; Yoon, "Phoebe," 26.

14 John N. Collins, *Deacons and the Church: Making Connections between Old and New* (Harrisburg, PA: Morehouse, 2002), 73–75.

15 Aimé Georges Martimort, *Deaconesses: An Historical Study* (San Francisco: Ignatius Press, 1986), 19–20. Cf. C. K. Barrett, *The Epistle to the Romans*, 2nd ed. (London: A&C Black, 1991), 258; Paul J. Achtemeier, *Harper's Bible Dictionary* (San Francisco: Harper & Row, 1985), 791.

and mean "to exercise a position of leadership,"[16] suggesting that προστάτις could be a term that was used to identify someone in authority.[17] It could also have been used to denote a patron or benefactor.[18] Thus the use of this term suggests that Phoebe had prestige (she was probably higher in social ranking than Paul[19]) and probably possessed the financial means to support private individuals or institutions. Paul's commendation confirms this, and he includes himself among those whom Phoebe helped (Rom. 16:2). Theodoret of Cyrus, writing in the early fifth century, defines Phoebe's patronage as "hospitality and protection," indicating his understanding of "the function of patronage as care exercised from a more powerful social position than the recipient's."[20] Several authors draw a parallel between Phoebe's role as a benefactor and that of one of her contemporaries, Junia Theodora of first-century Corinth. Junia's work is described by a cognate of the word προστάτις, which was applied to Phoebe.[21] The patronage of Junia, as recorded in first-century documents, included the provision of hospitality in her own home for Lycians traveling through Corinth and also the cultivation of Roman authorities on their behalf.[22] The inscriptions relating to Junia indicate that women of wealth could and did hold influential positions in the society of Paul's lifetime. In light of this, and of the description of Phoebe as προστάτις, it is reasonable to assume that Phoebe was a benefactor and patron of the Christian believers in Cenchreae and of Paul himself.[23]

Although these two brief verses are the only descriptions we have of Phoebe, it is possible to learn much from them about the identity of a deaconess.

---

16  Campbell, *Phoebe*, 80.

17  Matushka E. Gvosdev, *The Female Diaconate: An Historical Perspective* (Minneapolis: Light & Life, 1991), 7.

18  προστάτις: a woman in a supportive role, patron, benefactor (the relationship suggested by this term should not be confused with the Roman patron-client system, which was of a different order and alien to Greek tradition). See Frederick W. Danker, Walter Bauer, and William Arndt, *A Greek-English Lexicon of the New Testament and Other Early Christian Literature* (Chicago: University of Chicago Press, 2000), 885 (hereafter BDAG 2000).

19  Kevin Madigan and Carolyn Osiek, *Ordained Women in the Early Church: A Documentary History* (Baltimore, MD: Johns Hopkins University Press, 2005), 13.

20  Madigan and Osiek, *Ordained Women in the Early Church*, 16.

21  R. A. Kearsley, "Women in Public Life in the Roman East: Iunia Theodora, Claudia Metrodora and Phoebe, Benefactress of Paul," *Tyndale Bulletin* 50, no. 2 (1999): 189–211.

22  Kearsley, "Women in Public Life in the Roman East," 194; Campbell, *Phoebe*, 91; Madigan and Osiek, *Ordained Women in the Early Church*, 13.

23  Kearsley, "Women in Public Life in the Roman East," 202.

Consider first the term "sister." In biblical society, two people would be considered siblings only if they shared the same father (their biological mother would not determine a sibling relationship).[24] Because it is highly unlikely that Phoebe was a blood relative to Paul, her relation as sister is the result of her Baptism, through which she received a new identity as a member of Christ's Body, the Church, and adoption as a child of God. Members of the early church were to "relate to each other with the affection of biological brothers and sisters . . . under the care of one father, God."[25] "Thus, the early Christians seemed to think of the church not as a substance, a thing, or an institution but as a person or relation, living within the communication that exists between the Father, the Son, and the Spirit. This relation, this communication, this eternal sharing of life that exists eternally in the triune God is experienced [today] by the church in her liturgical, sacramental life. This is *leitourgia*."[26]

Just as Phoebe was a sister to Paul and the members of the church at Cenchreae, deaconesses are sisters to all members of God's family. As such, they share an intimate bond with all whom they serve, exercising the same love for them that they would extend to a biological sibling. Because of this bond of love, a deaconess is concerned with the cares of those members of God's family whom she serves, recognizing need and organizing acts of mercy to address those needs. Mercy begins and ends with God. We learn the true meaning of mercy in His free gift of salvation, won for us not by any merit or worthiness on our part, but through Christ's suffering, death, and resurrection. By first referring to Phoebe as "our sister," Paul firmly grounds her actions in the sacramental life of the Church, where she receives God's gifts of Word and Sacrament through the hands of her pastor and to whom she points others to receive those gifts.

The second term, διάκονον, can be translated in a general sense as "servant." In the Greek society in which Phoebe lived, service was considered to be undignified; men were born to rule, not to serve.[27] Jesus, however, reversed this, coming not to be served but to commit the ultimate service of laying down His life for all (Matt. 20:28). Christ's Body, the Church, is called to extend His loving service to others, and Phoebe epitomized this life of service, of *diakonia*. "*Diakonia* is the church personally opening herself up to the world. The Father's communication of His own being to the Son, and

---

24 Campbell, *Phoebe*, 25.

25 Campbell, *Phoebe*, 32.

26 James Bushur, "*Leitourgia* and *Diakonia*" (lecture, Concordia Theological Seminary, Fort Wayne, Indiana, October 3, 2010).

27 Gerhard Kittel, Gerhard Friedrich, Geoffrey William Bromiley, *Theological Dictionary of the New Testament* (Grand Rapids: Eerdmans, 1995), 152.

through the Son to the church, is now communicated to the world through the church's *diakonia* or service. . . . *Leitourgia*—our participation in God's own trinitarian life—calls the church to a life of sacrifice for the world."[28] For the deaconess, service is not something she does; it is her identity. This is emphasized by Paul's reference to Phoebe not as someone who performs a service, but as a διάκονον. Thus he emphasizes that it is her identity, rather than a task or duty she performs. "*Diakonia* is not simply an act of will or an external function that is performed; rather, *diakonia* is an identity, a relation to the world that completes the economy of the Gospel. . . . Being a deaconess is defined by the relations that are established, to the church, to the pastor, to those in her care."[29]

*Diakonia* is equally as critical to the life of the Church as is *leitourgia*. James Bushur points out three consequences for *leitourgia* if it is separated from *diakonia*:[30]

1. *The Gospel remains abstract and has no concrete reality.* The love and righteousness received by the Church from God is never lived out before the world or communicated to our neighbor. Golder suggests that this was happening in the church of his day, pointing out that the church "subordinated such temporal affairs as the physical welfare of the poor, the sick, the widows and orphans, prisoners, etc., altogether too much to her spiritual interests, and Church organizations have too often forgotten that the Judge of the world will say on that great day: 'I was an hungered, and ye gave me meat: I was thirsty, and ye gave me drink: I was a stranger, and ye took me in; naked, and ye clothed me: I was sick and ye visited me: I was in prison, and ye came to me,' or the reverse. (Matt. xxv, 35, 36)."[31]

2. *The Church's life is reduced to consumerism, leading to an individualism that we see all around us today.* Yet this is not confined to our age; even Jesus' disciples were concerned with themselves and their own status, requesting high positions in Christ's kingdom (Mark 10:35–37) and arguing among themselves more than once as to which of them was the greatest (e.g., Luke 9:46; 22:24). It is significant that "Jesus responds to their dispute by speaking of greatness in the kingdom of God in terms of service—*table* service: 'For who is greater, the one who reclines [at table] or the one who serves?' (Lk 22:27; τίς γὰρ μείζων, ὁ ἀνακείμενος ἢ ὁ διακονῶν . . . )."[32]

---

28  Bushur, "*Leitourgia* and *Diakonia*."

29  Bushur, "*Leitourgia* and *Diakonia*."

30  Bushur, "*Leitourgia* and *Diakonia*."

31  Golder, *History of the Deaconess Movement in the Christian Church*, 15.

32  Arthur A. Just Jr., *Luke 9:51–24:53* (St. Louis: Concordia, 1998), 845.

3. *The Church loses her connection to the world, the horizontal dimension of her fellowship.* The deaconess does not wait for the people to step into the Church; rather, she goes out from the door of the church to extend Christ's hands of mercy to those in need. For example, she may be involved in providing meals; visiting the sick, the lonely, and the suffering; assisting the poor to find the resources they need; organizing a care and compassion committee; teaching women and children; or simply being present and offering a listening ear. A deaconess is trained to recognize need. Serving alongside the pastor, she uses her skills and theological training to embody Christ's incarnational care, pointing to the light of Christ through her presence, devotions, and prayers and thereby pointing to the church, where the pastor administers Christ's mercy through the gifts of Word and Sacraments.[33]

The third term Paul uses to describe Phoebe is προστάτις. As pointed out earlier, this difficult term carries the connotation of patron, benefactor, or helper. We can infer from this that Phoebe was continuing the tradition of the women who supported Jesus and His disciples by providing for them out of their own means. Of course, most deaconesses today are not in a position to provide this type of help. However, a deaconess can follow the example of Phoebe by not eschewing humble service to others. There is no task too menial, whatever the social standing of the deaconess. Furthermore, a deaconess by example and through teaching can lead the church in showing Christ's incarnational mercy to others. Phoebe was certainly an example of humble service, for which she is commended by Paul.

## Phoebe's Role as a Letter Carrier

Paul's recommendation of Phoebe indicates that she might be the carrier of his letter to the Romans, a possibility that the remainder of this article will explore.[34] The Epistle to the Romans has been described as St. Paul's greatest piece of sustained theological writing.[35] Martin Luther called Romans a light that illuminates the entire Scripture, and Philip Melanchthon described it as a compendium of Christian doctrine.[36]

---

33  See Sara M. Bielby and Arthur A. Just Jr., "Serving Christ by Serving Our Neighbor: Theological and Historical Perspectives on Lutheran Deaconesses," *Issues in Christian Education* 39, no. 1 (2005).

34  Marjanen, "Phoebe," 495; Grothe, *Justification of the Ungodly*, 2:806; Mounce, *Romans*.

35  Barrett, *Romans*, 1.

36  Bo Reicke, David P. Moessner, and Ingalisa Reicke, *Re-examining Paul's Letters: The History of the Pauline Correspondence* (Harrisburg, PA: Trinity Press International, 2001), 68.

It is likely that Paul wrote his letter to the Romans to introduce himself prior to his intended visit, which was to be preliminary to his planned missionary trip to Spain. The Roman Christians had developed independently of Paul and did not always see eye to eye with him.[37] Thus the Epistle to the Romans is Paul's exposition of his theological position in advance of his visit.[38] Furthermore, it has been suggested Paul's letter is directed specifically to those Christians in Rome who opposed Paul's Gospel because they were reluctant to accept that Jews and Gentiles should come together in a "Law-free, faith alone life in Christ."[39]

## THE ROLE OF THE LETTER CARRIER

It is apparent that Romans is a critical letter, and, as with all of Paul's letters, he would have wanted to ensure its safe delivery. At the time Paul was writing, no organized postal system for personal correspondence existed, though there was such a system for official state correspondence. Private citizens had to look for other ways to deliver letters. The wealthy could send their slaves or use independent couriers. Anyone undertaking a journey could be given letters—family members, friends, merchants, passing travelers, soldiers.[40] That there actually was a culture of letter writing depends not least on the fact that "each traveler was also (at least potentially) a postman at the same time."[41] The more important the message, the more trustworthy the letter carrier had to be.

Many scholars have suggested that often the letter carrier had a more important role than merely delivering the letter.[42] He or she may have been expected to read the letter aloud. This was important for three reasons.

---

37   Barrett, *Romans*, 6; Grothe, *Justification of the Ungodly*, 1:8.

38   Barrett, *Romans*, 7.

39   Grothe, *Justification of the Ungodly*, 1:8.

40   Eldon Jay Epp, "New Testament Papyrus Manuscripts and Letter Carrying in Greco-Roman Time," in *The Future of Early Christianity: Essays in Honor of Helmut Koester*, ed. Helmut Koester, Birger A. Pearson, A. Thomas Kraabel, George W. E. Nickelsburg, and Norman R. Petersen (Minneapolis: Fortress, 1991), 43.

41   Hans-Josef Klauck and Daniel P. Bailey, *Ancient Letters and the New Testament: A Guide to Context and Exegesis* (Waco, TX: Baylor University Press, 2006), 62; S. R. Llewelyn, "The Conveyance of Letters," in *New Documents Illustrating Early Christianity* 7 (Macquarie University, NSW: Ancient History Documentary Research Centre, 1994), 26.

42   M. Luther Stirewalt, *Paul, the Letter Writer* (Grand Rapids: Eerdmans, 2003), 3–5; R. McL. Wilson, *A Critical and Exegetical Commentary on Colossians and Philemon*, International Critical Commentary on the Holy Scriptures of the Old and New Testaments (London: T&T Clark, 2005), 296; J. Ross Wagner, *Heralds of the Good News: Isaiah and Paul "in Concert" in the Letter to the Romans*, Supplements to Novum Testamentum 101 (Leiden: Brill, 2002), 38; Klauck and Bailey, *Ancient Letters and the New Testament*, 65.

First, only about 5 percent of the population could read,[43] so there was a general distrust of the written word. The oral message may have been important corroboration of the letter. Second, as the text at the time would have been written without spaces, to be able to read it required familiarity with the content. Third, reading the letter conveyed a sense of the writer's personal presence. In addition to reading the letter, the carrier may also have been expected to answer questions about the content or to help interpret the material, and, in some cases, to convey additional messages that had not been committed in writing. J. Ross Wagner quotes several examples of this from nonbiblical ancient letters,[44] and Paul's letters to the Colossians (4:7–9) and to the Ephesians (6:21–22) refer to additional information to be provided by the carrier.

Ward gives even more weight to the potential role of Paul's letter carriers, referring specifically to one of his letters to Corinth:

> When Paul's emissary stood before the Corinthians to speak the letter, he would have internalized the contents of the letter and would be prepared to interpret the whole of Paul's logos to the Corinthians. . . . In any case, Paul must have carefully considered the ability of his reciter to render his text in accordance with the standards of excellence of the time. Titus, or some other emissary, through the skilful rendering of Paul's letter, intended to guide the audience through an *experience* of the situation from Paul's perspective. . . . Given the conventions of performing letters in antiquity, we can imagine the reciter giving Paul's letter fullness, not simply by rendering the written word but by adding oral commentary in the spirit and attitude of Paul himself.[45]

Recently, Peter Head reported on his detailed examination of the Oxyrhynchus Papyri, which were discovered in 1897, specifically in relation to the role of Paul's letter carriers. He concludes overall that, "in general, the evidence from the documentary papyri of Oxyrhynchus consistently underscores the idea that the named letter-carrier often has an important role in extending the communication initiated by the letter. . . . On occasions the named letter-carrier did function in some way or another to 'represent' the sender, to expand on details within the letter, and even to expound and reinforce the primary message of the letter in oral communication. The clearest examples of such a role or function focus on reinforcing the main message of the letter, and not on the exposition of obscure details."[46] Eldon Jay Epp,

---

43  Campbell, *Phoebe*, 4.

44  Wagner, *Heralds of the Good News*, 38.

45  Ward 1995: quoted by Wagner, *Heralds of the Good News*, 38.

46  Peter Head, "Named Letter-Carriers among the Oxyrhynchus Papyri," *Journal for the Study of the New Testament* 31, no. 3 (2009): 296–97.

who has also studied a number of papyri, found at least one case in which a letter carrier was recommended to the addressees as qualified to expand on the situation treated in the letter.[47]

## The Case of Phoebe

Turning to Romans, the letter itself gives no direct indication as to how it was sent. However, in Rom. 16:1–2 Paul commends Phoebe and asks that she be received and helped. As found by Head[48] and Llewelyn,[49] the letter carrier was often recommended, particularly if not known to the addressee(s), and letters of recommendation in antiquity were neither restricted to men nor written primarily for women.[50] These facts lend weight to the supposition that Phoebe was the bearer of the letter.[51] As the bearer of the letter, it would be quite natural for Paul to have commended Phoebe and to have made special mention of her to the recipients of the letter (Συνίστημι δὲ ὑμῖν).[52]

If Phoebe was indeed the letter carrier, this raises the question of whether it was usual at that time for a woman to undertake such a long journey. We know that travel could be hazardous, not least from Paul's list of the dangers he had been exposed to in his missionary career, which includes many associated with traveling (2 Cor. 11:25–27). There are few known examples of traveling women in antiquity—from Scripture we know that Priscilla and Junia traveled, Priscilla with her husband (Acts 18:2) and Junia possibly with her husband (Rom. 16:7). There are also two fourth-century papyri that specifically mention Christian women as letter carriers, one of whom traveled with a man[53] and one that names only the woman.[54] Thus it seems unusual, but not unique, for Phoebe to undertake a journey such as the one to Rome.

As to why Phoebe was selected as the letter carrier, most commentators believe the primary purpose of Phoebe's journey to Rome was personal business.[55] The use of the word πράγματι suggests to some commentators that it

---

47  Epp, "New Testament Papyrus Manuscripts and Letter Carrying in Greco-Roman Time," 46.

48  Head, "Named Letter-Carriers among the Oxyrhynchus Papyri," 285–86.

49  Llewlyn, "Conveyance of Letters," 51.

50  Elisabeth Schüssler Fiorenza, "Missionaries, Apostles, Coworkers: Romans 16 and the Reconstruction of Women's Early Church History," *Word and World* 6 (4) (1986): 424.

51  Marjanen, "Phoebe," 495; Grothe, *Justification of the Ungodly*, 2:806; Mounce, *Romans*.

52  Mounce, *Romans*.

53  Stanley Kent Stowers, *Letter Writing in Greco-Roman Antiquity*, Library of Early Christianity 5 (Philadelphia: Westminster Press, 1986), 157–58.

54  Llewelyn, "Conveyance of Letters," 169–70.

55  Marjanen, "Phoebe," 501; Grothe, *Justification of the Ungodly*, 2:808; Barrett, *Romans*, 258.

may have been legal business,[56] as this term is used in the papyri and in 1 Cor. 6:1 in the sense of "lawsuit."[57] It is possible, then, that Paul took advantage of the fact that Phoebe was traveling to Rome and sent his letter with her. However, this would not have been purely opportunistic. He would have had to be certain that Phoebe could accomplish the task. Perhaps more important, he would also need to have known that it was not a "theological risk" to have a woman present his letter to the leadership of the Roman church.[58] Some authors suggest that this was not the only time Phoebe would have been entrusted to act as an emissary on behalf of the church at Cenchreae; "[Phoebe] was probably a woman of means who had been sent to Rome to use her influence, perhaps her wealth, in matters affecting her community."[59]

## Phoebe's Role as the Letter Carrier

This brings us back to two points: the importance of Paul's letter to the Romans and the role of the letter carrier. In writing to Rome, Paul may have had several motives: he was initiating a dialog with those living in the empire's capital city; he was seeking support for his forthcoming mission to Spain; he was expounding "his" Gospel to a Gentile church that he had not founded; and he was introducing himself to people who did not know him, in preparation for his visit to Rome.[60] Each of these on its own is important; taken together they emphasize the importance of the letter and particularly the need for it to be well-received in Rome.

To carry his letters, Paul used people who supported him and shared his ministry. Some letter carriers, such as Titus, appear to have served him regularly; all seem to have been capable and trustworthy—traits essential in those chosen for such an important task.[61] The key question is whether the letter carrier had a role in extending the communication process. Head's examination of the Oxyrhynchus papyri shows that this was common in letters of antiquity, and he supports the idea that "in the Pauline tradition the accredited letter-carriers functioned not only as personal private postmen, but as personal mediators of Paul's authoritative instruction to his churches, and as the earliest interpreters of the individual letters."[62]

---

56  Marjanen, "Phoebe," 502; H. D. M. Spence-Jones, ed., *The Pulpit Commentary: Romans* (Bellingham, WA: Logos Research Systems, 2004), 454.

57  BDAG (2000) lists four definitions for this term; Rom. 16:2 is associated with "thing, matter, affair" and 1 Cor. 6:1 with "dispute, lawsuit."

58  Marjanen, "Phoebe," 506.

59  John N. Collins, *Diakonia: Re-interpreting the Ancient Sources* (Oxford: Oxford University Press, 1990), 225.

60  Barrett, *Romans*, 6.

61  Stirewalt, *Paul, the Letter Writer*, 13.

62  Head, "Named Letter-Carriers among the Oxyrhynchus Papyri," 298.

Therefore the notion that Phoebe was the carrier of the letter to the Romans could have wider implications than the fact that she was a trusted colleague of Paul. If it could be demonstrated clearly and conclusively that Phoebe was the carrier, it would suggest that she also had a role in representing Paul to the Romans and in explaining and expounding his theology as presented in the letter. Would Paul, who in 1 Cor. 14:34 instructed that "the women should keep silent in the churches" and who did not "permit a woman to teach or to exercise authority over a men" (1 Tim. 2:12), have trusted a woman to be the first person to speak "his" Gospel to the Romans, even one as senior in the church as Phoebe?[63]

In this context it is helpful to remember that Jesus chose women to announce His resurrection to the apostles. "The women who were with Jesus in Galilee, supported him with their own resources (Luke 8:3), and viewed the crucifixion (Luke 23:49) are the first witnesses of the resurrection. Luke repeats that these women are the first evangelists to announce to the apostles the resurrection facts."[64] However, Jesus did not choose women to be His apostles. Thus there is an important distinction between the deaconess, who can fulfill the role of an "emissary,"[65] and the pastor, who stands "in the stead and by the command of Christ." The possibility that Paul chose Phoebe to deliver this important letter would be significant. He would have trusted her to deliver his message on his behalf, with no question of her aspiring to his office. Here the cultural values of families during the first century are important to bear in mind. "Those who love the family do what the family values. Moreover, they defer to parental authority and will not disobey their parents in public because doing so would shame the entire family."[66] There would be no question of Phoebe disobeying or dishonoring her Father's authority, vested in His apostle Paul. Despite her wealth, culture, abilities, and high social standing, she assumed the role of a servant not just to the church in Cenchreae but also to Paul. And perhaps this is the most important lesson we can learn from our reflections on what little we know about their relationship. The Office of the Holy Ministry was established by Christ Himself and, in the same way that Jesus' maleness is basic to His role as our incarnate Savior, the pastor's maleness is essential to his office. Women who are called to the office of deaconess in the confessional Lutheran Church continue in Phoebe's footsteps in loving service to others and by upholding and supporting the Office of the Holy Ministry.

---

63  Given that many regard Paul's Epistles as sermons, this point is worthy of further study.

64  Just, *Luke 9:51–24:53*, 970.

65  Collins, *Diakonia*, 225.

66  Campbell, *Phoebe*, 20.

# BIBLIOGRAPHY

Achtemeier, Paul J. *Harper's Bible Dictionary*. San Francisco: Harper & Row, 1985.

Aland, Kurt, Matthew Black, Carlo M. Martini, Bruce M. Metzger, Maurice Robinson, and Allen Wikgren. *The Greek New Testament*. 4th revised edition. Stuttgart: Deutsche Bibelgesellschaft, 1993.

Barrett, C. K. *The Epistle to the Romans*. 2nd edition. London: A&C Black, 1991.

Bielby, Sara M., and Arthur A. Just Jr. "Serving Christ by Serving Our Neighbor: Theological and Historical Perspectives on Lutheran Deaconesses." *Issues in Christian Education* 39, no. 1 (2005): 7–13.

Bushur, James. "*Leitourgia* and *Diakonia*." Lecture, Concordia Theological Seminary, Fort Wayne, IN. October 3, 2010.

Campbell, Joan Cecelia. *Phoebe: Patron and Emissary*. Collegeville, MN: Liturgical Press, 2009.

Collins, John N. *Deacons and the Church: Making Connections between Old and New*. Harrisburg, PA: Morehouse, 2002.

———. *Diakonia: Re-interpreting the Ancient Sources*. Oxford: Oxford University Press, 1990.

Cranfield, C. E. B. *Romans 1–8*. International Critical Commentary. London: T&T Clark, 2001.

Elwell, Walter A., and Philip Wesley Comfort. *Tyndale Bible Dictionary*. Wheaton, IL: Tyndale House, 2001.

Epp, Eldon Jay. "New Testament Papyrus Manuscripts and Letter Carrying in Greco-Roman Times." Pages 35–36 in *The Future of Early Christianity: Essays in Honor of Helmut Koester*. Edited by Helmut Koester, Birger A. Pearson, A. Thomas Kraabel, George W. E. Nickelsburg, and Norman R. Petersen. Minneapolis: Fortress, 1991.

Fiorenza, Elisabeth Schüssler. "Missionaries, Apostles, Coworkers: Romans 16 and the Reconstruction of Women's Early Church History." *Word and World* 6 (4) (1986): 42–433.

Golder, C. *History of the Deaconess Movement in the Christian Church*. Cincinnati: Jennings & Pye, 1903.

Grothe, Jonathan F. *The Justification of the Ungodly: An Interpretation of Romans*. 2 volumes. Canada, 2005.

Gryson, Roger. *The Ministry of Women in the Early Church*. Collegeville, MN: Liturgical Press, 1976.

Gvosdev, Matushka E. *The Female Diaconate: An Historical Perspective*. Minneapolis: Light & Life, 1991.

Head, Peter M. "Named Letter-Carriers among the Oxyrhynchus Papyri." *Journal for the Study of the New Testament* 31, no. 3 (2009): 279–99.

Kearsley, R. A. "Women in Public Life in the Roman East: Iunia Theodora, Claudia Metrodora and Phoebe, Benefactress of Paul." *Tyndale Bulletin* 50, no. 2 (1999): 189–211.

Klauck, Hans-Josef, and Daniel P. Bailey. *Ancient Letters and the New Testament: A Guide to Context and Exegesis.* Waco, TX: Baylor University Press, 2006.

Llewelyn, S. R. "The Conveyance of Letters." Pages 1–57 in vol. 7 of *New Documents Illustrating Early Christianity.* Macquarie University: Ancient History Documentary Research Centre, 1994.

Madigan, Kevin, and Carolyn Osiek. *Ordained Women in the Early Church: A Documentary History.* Baltimore, MD: Johns Hopkins University Press, 2005.

Marjanen, Antti. "Phoebe, a Letter Courier." Pages 495–508 in *Lux Humana, Lux Aeterna: Essays on Biblical and Related Themes in Honour of Lars Aejmelaeus.* Edited by Antti Mustakallio, et al. Göttingen: Vandenhoeck & Ruprecht, 2005.

Martimort, Aimé Georges. *Deaconesses: An Historical Study.* San Francisco: Ignatius Press, 1986.

Mounce, Robert H. *Romans.* New American Commentary 27. Nashville: Broadman & Holman, 1995.

Petersen, Norman R. "On the Ending(s) to Paul's Letter to Rome." Pages 337–47 in *The Future of Early Christianity: Essays in Honor of Helmut Koester.* Edited by Helmut Koester, Birger A. Pearson, A. Thomas Kraabel, George W. E. Nickelsburg, and Norman R. Petersen. Minneapolis: Fortress, 1991.

Reicke, Bo, David P. Moessner, and Ingalisa Reicke. *Re-examining Paul's Letters: The History of the Pauline Correspondence.* Harrisburg, PA: Trinity Press International, 2001.

Spence-Jones, H. D. M., ed. *The Pulpit Commentary: Romans.* Bellingham, WA: Logos Research Systems, 2004.

Stirewalt, M. Luther. *Paul, the Letter Writer.* Grand Rapids: Eerdmans, 2003.

Stowers, Stanley Kent. *Letter Writing in Greco-Roman Antiquity.* Library of Early Christianity 5. Philadelphia: Westminster Press, 1986.

Wagner, J. Ross. *Heralds of the Good News: Isaiah and Paul "in Concert" in the Letter to the Romans.* Supplements to Novum Testamentum 101. Leiden: Brill, 2002.

Whelan, Caroline. "Amici Pauli: The Role of Phoebe in the Early Church." *Journal of New Testament Studies* 49 (1993): 67–85.

Wilson, R. McL. *A Critical and Exegetical Commentary on Colossians and Philemon.* International Critical Commentary on the Holy Scriptures of the Old and New Testaments. London: T&T Clark, 2005.

Yoon, Sojung. "Phoebe, a Minister in the Early Christian Church." In *Distant Voices Drawing Near: Essays in Honor of Antoinette Clark.* Edited by Holly E. Hearon. Collegeville, MN: Liturgical Press, 2004.

# Disciples But Not Teachers

## 1 Corinthians 14:33b–38 and 1 Timothy 2:11–15

## John W. Kleinig

In 1976 The Pontifical Biblical Commission decided that by itself the New Testament does not permit exegetes to settle the problem of the accession of women to the presbyterate. This uncertainty may explain why, in 1994, Pope John Paul II did not refer to 1 Corinthians 14:33b–35 and 1 Timothy 2:11–12 in *Ordinatio Sacerdotalis*, his *Apostolic Letter on Reserving Priestly Ordination to Men Alone*, but based his case on the precedent of Christ in choosing male apostles.

The church has not in the past shared this diffidence, since right from the beginning it justified the reservation of the apostolic ministry for men by recalling these two texts. Nor need it share this diffidence now, for they explain why the ministry of the gospel should still be reserved for men. I would therefore like to examine them closely to show how they forbid the ordination of women in the church.

## I. 1 Corinthians 14:33b–38

### Translation and Structure

While commentators have often found it hard to make sense of this passage, rhetorical analysis has shown the unity of vv 33b–38 as a coherent argument.[1] Its argument may be set out as follows:

> As in all the churches of the saints,
> let the women remain silent in the churches,
> > for it is not permitted for them to speak,
> > but let them be subordinate, as the law says.
> If they wish to learn something,

---

1 Dautzenberg: 253–73, 291–98; Hauke: 364–96

> let them interrogate their husbands at home,
>> for it is shameful for a woman to speak in church.
>> What, did the word of God go out from you,
>> or has it reached you alone?
> If anyone considers that he is a prophet or a spiritual person,
> let him recognise that what I write is a command of the Lord.
> If, on the other hand, anybody does not acknowledge (this), he is not
> acknowledged (by God).

Rhetorically speaking, the passage falls into two main parts. It begins with an unqualified directive for silence from women in all churches, followed by a subordinate clause explaining why they are not to speak. This reverses the previous pattern in 27, 28 and 29–33a of reference to 'speaking' before mentioning some restriction of it with 'silence'. Paul then treats three problems associated with this directive in three conditional sentences.

In keeping with the pattern established in vv 26–33a, the flow of the argument is determined by two third person jussives for silence and subordination in v 34, followed by two conditional jussives about the questioning of husbands and the acknowledgment of Christ's authority in vv 35–37. This culminates in the conditional threat in v 38 against those who reject this teaching.

Thus this passage is a coherent piece of Pauline rhetoric. It is presented in the form of regulations for the operation of the church as a liturgical community.[2]

## The Place of the Passage in 1 Corinthians 14:26–40

Paul's directives on the silence of women are part of his larger discussion in 1 Corinthians chapters 12–14 about the use of spiritual gifts in church that culminates in a discussion on the place of tongues and prophecy in public worship. More immediately, it comes as the climax of Paul's liturgical regulations in 1 Corinthians 14:26–40. In this last section Paul deals with three problems: the demand by some tongues' speakers for the right to 'speak' in tongues in the church; the demand by some prophets for the right to 'speak' their words of prophecy; and the demand by some female prophets for recognition as 'speakers in church'. Paul counters these demands for the right to speak with the demand for appropriate silence in vv 28, 30, and 34.

In keeping with this theme, the structure of 1 Corinthians 14:26–40 is as follows:

a.  Introduction (26)

> General problem: the use of spiritual gifts in public worship
>
> General directive: the edification of the congregation

---

2    Hauke: 267, 370–71.

b. Speaking in tongues (27–28)

Permissible *speaking*, if there is an interpreter

**Silence**, with private speaking to God, if there is no interpreter

c. Speaking of prophecy (29–33a)

Permissible *speaking* with assessment of prophecies

**Silence**, if another prophet receives a revelation

d. Speaking of women (33b–38)

**Silence** of women in the church

Prohibition of *speaking* except for questioning at home

e. Conclusion (39–40)

Encouragement of prophecy without prohibition of tongues

Need for order in worship.

There is growing recognition among scholars that the link between 14:27–33a and 14:33b–38 is provided by Paul's requirement in 14:29 that all prophecies must be duly weighed and assessed to discover their significance and proper application.[3] Paul does not state exactly how this is to be done. He does, however, indicate that the whole congregation ('the others') should somehow be involved in this. It probably involved a general discussion that resulted in an authoritative judgment on its sense and its application by the teachers of the congregation in the light of Christ's teaching (Matt 7:15–27; Rev 19:10), the confession of Jesus as Lord (1 Cor 12:3), and the analogy of faith (Rom 12:6).

As Johansson[4] has shown from Acts 20:7–12, this kind of discussion was not restricted to the weighing of prophecies; it seems also to have been associated with the homilies given by teachers in the early church. While all members could share their insights into the meaning and application of a text from the Old Testament, they could not challenge the final teaching given by the leaders of the congregation, as some women seem to have done in Corinth (1 Cor 14:35).

Paul's argument runs as follows. Speaking in tongues is allowed in worship provided that it is properly interpreted. It thereby becomes a prophecy for the congregation. Prophecies may also be given in the church provided that they are limited in number and weighed in the light of the apostolic teaching, since all prophecy is to be understood and evaluated in the light of the apostolic tradition. The reason for this is that God's Spirit does not contradict

---

3    Clark: 186; Hurley: 188–92; Grudem: 250–251; Bacchiocchi: 167; Hauke: 376; Carson: 151; Witherington, 102; Thiselton, 1158.

4    57–71.

himself. So, those who hand on the apostolic tradition are finally responsible for assessing prophecy. They are the speakers in the church, those who have been appointed to teach the word of God and to ensure that it is heeded in the liturgical assembly.

## The Nature of the Demand for Silence from Women

Paul's demand for the silence of women is explained in two ways. They are not permitted by God to be 'speakers' in the liturgical assembly. While the verb *lalein* is used in many different ways in the New Testament, it is never used in the sense of chattering.[5] Here, as is often the case, it is a synonym for the teaching of God's word (e.g. Acts 4:1; 18:25; 1 Cor 2:6–7; 2 Cor 2:17; Heb 13:7). In addition, the silence of the women involves subordination. Remarkably, Paul does not mention the object of their subordination. He does not refer to the general subordination of all women to all men, or the subordination of wives to husbands. Context indicates that they are to be subordinate to the male teachers of God's word and so to the word itself. Women are therefore not allowed to be speakers in the liturgical assembly, but, like all the other members of the congregation, they must be subordinate to those who have been appointed to fulfill that task. By their subordination they fit into the liturgical order that is established by the ministry of God's word in the church.

Paul quite clearly insists on relative rather than absolute silence, since he allows women to speak in tongues (1 Cor 14:5, 23), prophesy (1 Cor 11:5; 14:5, 23, 31), and engage in liturgical prayer (1 Cor 11:5; 1 Tim 2:1–10). The kind of speaking that Paul prohibits is defined in three ways. First, a woman may not 'be a speaker in a liturgical assembly' (14:35). The unusual absolute form for 'speaking' indicates that Paul uses it as a technical term for someone authorized to speak in an official capacity.[6] Since this prohibition does not apply at home it has nothing to do with the subordination of a wife to her husband.

Secondly, the forbidden speaking is associated with God's word which has come to Corinth via its apostolic emissaries from Jerusalem (14:36; see Acts 1:8; 1 Thess 2:13). We may therefore conclude that its content was the transmission and application of the apostolic teaching that had been entrusted to the leaders of the congregation, as described by Paul in 2 Timothy 2:2.

Thirdly, while this kind of 'speaking' is related to prophecy and the disputation that is connected with the weighing of prophecy in the congregation, it is nevertheless distinguished from prophecy and is more authoritative than prophecy, since it transmits the commands of Christ and requires the

---

5    Barrett, 332.

6    Johansson: 53f.

acquiescence of prophets (14:37–38). So when Paul forbids women to act as speakers in a liturgical assembly of the church, he excludes them from the ministry of the apostolic word.

## The Basis and Authority for the Prohibition

Paul bases his case on four sets of authority that he marshals in ascending order of importance.

First, he appeals to ecumenical practice (14:33b). Some scholars claim that, since Paul uses a similar ecumenical formula in 1 Cor 4:17; 7:17 and 11:16 to conclude a section of argument, this phrase must belong to v 33a. Yet that is most unlikely, since it is not used as a conclusion in 7:17 and it functions elsewhere to assert the catholicity of Paul's teaching.[7] Paul claims that his ruling does not just apply to the church in Corinth, but to all churches everywhere.

Secondly, he appeals to the law in the Old Testament. The absence of the far more common citation formula, 'it is written' makes it unlikely that he refers only to Genesis 3:16 or any other specific verse. Rather the use here of the summary formula: 'as the law says' (see 1 Cor 9:8), shows that Paul has in mind the whole of Genesis 2 and 3. It is best understood in the light of Paul's teaching in 1 Timothy 2:12 on the primacy of Adam, his headship as the husband of Eve, and God's commission to him in Genesis 2:15–17.

Thirdly, he appeals to his hearers' sense of shame in 14:35. For Paul, shame did not just arise from failure to meet the social expectations of peers according to customary norms, as in 1 Corinthians 11:6, but also from loss of face with God (Phil 1:20; 2 Tim 1:12), and at the failure to meet his expectations (Rom 6:21; 2 Cor 4:2; Eph 5:4, 12; Col 3:8; Phil 3:19). In fact, in Eph 5:12, the only other place apart from 1 Cor 11:6 where Paul uses the formula, 'it is shameful', that formula covers what is unacceptable to God rather than what is merely socially unacceptable. In 14:35–36 the appeal to shame is closely allied with Paul's challenge to the presumptuousness of certain women prophets in questioning their teachers and in regarding themselves as either the generators or exclusive recipients of God's word.

Lastly and most significantly, Paul appeals to a specific command of the Lord in 14:37 which he has received together with other sayings of Jesus. It, like 1 Thessalonians 4:15, is not recorded in any of the gospels.[8] As last in the list, this most weighty authority is meant to clinch the argument. When Paul speaks about the Lord's command, he most likely refers to the prohibition in v 34. Its passive formulation denotes that it comes from God himself. Only its divine origin provides an adequate basis for his unequivocal pronouncement in 14:38 that those who reject Paul's ruling on the silence of women in

---

7    Witherington: 96; Carson: 140–41; Thiselton: 1155.

8    See Johansson: 90–98; Hauke: 385–90; Lockwood, 511–14.

the church will not be recognized by God as prophets or Spirit-filled people. Since they do not base their ministry on Christ and his word, their work will not survive the fire of God's judgment on the last day (1 Cor 3:11–14).[9] That grave threat makes sense only in the light of Christ's prohibition of women as speakers in the church.

The appeal of Paul to such a full range of authorities discloses the gravity of the matter under discussion. If he were dealing with culturally inappropriate behavior or disruptive chatter by women, he would have had no need to employ all these authorities. Indeed, its force would be totally disproportionate to the alleged offence, much like the use of a steamroller to squash a bull ant. A simple appeal to their better senses would suffice.

To conclude: Paul's appeal to such a wide range of authorities, his mention of Christ's command, his reference to the apostolic tradition and his responsibility for it, and his threat of divine disapproval for those who reject his teaching, makes sense only if he is engaged in the defense of the divinely instituted ministry of the word.

## 2. 1 TIMOTHY 2:11–15

It is generally agreed that this passage, more clearly than 1 Corinthians 14:33b–38, excludes women from the apostolic ministry of the word. Whereas that text deals with a specific situation in Corinth, Paul here gives far more general instructions to his pastoral protégé Timothy about the reorganization of the church in Ephesus.

### TRANSLATION AND STRUCTURE

1 Timothy 2:11–15 forms a single literary unit with 2:8–10. The following translation of that unit indicates its basic structure:

> I therefore require
> > that in every place men should pray,
> > > lifting holy hands without anger and quarrelling,
> > and that women too (should pray), dressing themselves with
> > modesty and chastity by means of respectable deportment,
> > > not by means of gold-braided hair or pearls or expensive
> > > dress,
> > > but through good works, as is suitable for women who
> > > profess reverence for God.
> Let a woman learn in quietness with entire subordination.
> Yet I do not permit a woman to teach
> or to have authority over a man.
> But she must remain in quietness;

---

9   See Hauke: 383–85; Lockwood, 514.

for Adam was formed first, then Eve;
and Adam was not deceived, but the woman, being deceived,
came into transgression.
Nevertheless a woman will be saved through child bearing,
provided that she remains with chastity in faith and love and
sanctification.

Two things are worth noting in this. First, the repetition of 'chastity' in
vv 9 and 15 acts as a bracket that introduces and closes the teaching on the
participation of women in public worship. Secondly, the repetition of 'quietness' in vv 11 and 12 creates a chiastic construction which is highlighted by
the contrast between woman and man in v 12a. This is how it is structured:

a. Let a woman learn in **quietness** with entire subordination.

b. Teaching, on the other hand, for a <u>woman</u> I do not permit,

b' nor having authority over a <u>man</u>,

    a' but being in **quietness** (I permit).

It follows from this that Paul's main concern here is with learning as a
disciple rather than with teaching, and that 'teaching' and 'having authority'
are to be regarded as complementary activities.

## THE PLACE OF 1 TIMOTHY 2:11–15 IN ITS CONTEXT

This passage is part of Paul's written pastoral 'charge' to Timothy about
his work in the church at Ephesus and the need to combat the teachers of
false doctrine there (1 Tim 1:3, 18; 4:11; 5:7; 6:17). The heart of this charge
is the congregational code in 2:1–3:16. This code gives instruction on how
the household of God, the church of the living God, is to operate liturgically
(1 Tim 3:14, 15).

The congregational code covers the following matters:

a. The nature and basis of congregational prayer (2:1–7)

b. The involvement of both sexes in congregational prayer

c. Praying by men without anger and quarrelling (2:8)

d. Praying by women without ostentatious dress (2:9, 10)

e. The involvement of women in learning rather than in teaching
(2:11–15)

f. Qualifications for leaders in public worship

g. Bishops as teachers in God's household (3:1–7)

h. Deacons as their assistants (3:8–13)

i. The purpose of Paul's charge (3:14–16)

## THE AUTHORITY OF PAUL IN 1 TIMOTHY 2:11–15

Even though Paul uses 'I' in addressing Timothy in 1 Timothy 2:1, 7, 8, 12, he does not give his personal opinions on congregational worship. Rather, in 2:7 he emphasizes that he has been appointed by God both as an 'apostle' (see 1:1) and as a 'teacher of the faith and its truth to the gentiles'. He therefore writes about what 'must' (*dei*) be done not just in Ephesus, but in the whole church which is God's household (1 Tim 3:14, 15).[10] His teaching therefore transcends the particular local problems of the church in Ephesus.

## THE MEANING OF 'TEACHING' IN THE PASTORAL LETTERS

Since 'teaching' is the key term in this text, its exact sense needs to be established before we can examine Paul's argument. Paul uses the terms for 'teaching' in a much narrower, technical sense than we do in modern English (e.g. 1 Cor 12:28; Eph 4:11). It usually refers to the teaching and application of God's word by Jesus and his apostles. A teacher hands on the apostolic tradition and uses it to build up the church as a liturgical community.

As the teacher of the gentiles (1 Tim 2:7), the apostle Paul is also a teacher of the gospel (2 Tim 1:11) which God has entrusted to him (1 Tim 1:11). He has been Timothy's teacher (1 Tim 1:2; 2 Tim 2:2) and has passed on to him what he himself has received from Christ (2 Tim 1:13, 14). Paul therefore urges Timothy to teach what he has received from him (1 Tim 4:11; 6:2) and to live a life consistent with that teaching (1 Tim 4:16). Timothy is to use the Old Testament (2 Tim 3:16) and the words of Jesus (1 Tim 4:6; 6:3) in his teaching which is usually associated with the public reading of the Scriptures (1 Tim 4:13) and the preaching of the word to the congregation (2 Tim 4:2). By teaching he convinces and encourages his hearers (2 Tim 4:2); he rebukes and corrects those who teach what is contrary to the apostolic tradition (1 Tim 1:3). So Timothy is required to hand on to other faithful men what he has been taught by Paul, and to appoint them as teachers in the church (2 Tim 2:2).

Paul uses a number of terms to describe the role of the teachers in the church. As 'bishops' they supervise the worship and life of the congregation (1 Tim 3:2). As 'elders' they arrange the worship of the congregation and manage its operation (1 Tim 5:17). As 'servants' of the risen Lord they represent him in their teaching and work with him (2 Tim 2:24). Their basic qualification is that they are teachable and skilled in teaching (1 Tim 3:2; 2 Tim 2:24). They teach God's word in the church (1 Tim 5:17); they use the healing doctrine of Christ to encourage the faithful and to refute those who contradict it (Tit 1:9).

---

10 See Hurley: 196; Bacchiocchi: 145–48, 151–52.

So then, for Paul a teacher is a minister of God's word, a pastor who has been authorized to teach what the apostles taught.

## THE ARGUMENT OF 1 TIMOTHY 2:11–15

Paul makes it quite clear that, unlike Jewish women who did not join in the public prayers of the synagogue and were not allowed to be students of the rabbis, Christian women were expected to join in the intercession of the church for the world and to 'learn' God's word as disciples of Jesus Christ. In fact, he commands them to be disciples, students who learn God's word. The unusual absolute form of this verb suggests that this command has to do with being disciples rather than with learning a particular lesson. Like all the men, they too are recipients of the apostolic tradition (2 Tim 3:14). As disciples they are to pray and do good works. These activities, rather than teaching, are the marks of their discipleship.

Their proper disposition as disciples is characterized by two terms. First, they are to learn in quietness. This describes their attitude to God's word, their state of being as disciples. Such quietness involves stillness and harmony, receptivity and teachability, respectful listening and readiness to receive direction (see Acts 11:18; 21:14; 22:2; 1 Thess 4:11; 2 Thess 3:12; 1 Tim 2:2). It is the mark of a wise learner, a sage who never ceases to be student. Secondly, women are to be in a state of entire subordination. As in 1 Corinthians 14:34, Paul does not mention the object of their subordination. Since it is linked with being a disciple, it refers to Christ's word and to those who teach that word rather than to men in general.[11]

Even though women must be disciples, they are not permitted to teach in the liturgical assembly. The use of *de* introduces a contrast between learning which is commanded and teaching which is forbidden.[12] In other words, 2:12 explains the concept of subordination in negative terms. The responsibility for teaching in public worship is associated with the 'exercise of authority' over a man. The sense of 'a man' is not immediately clear. While it could be men in general or a husband, it most obviously refers to the male teacher(s) of the congregation. The relationship between teaching and exercising authority can be taken in three ways. Paul could be prohibiting two separate activities or two identical activities or, most likely, from the syntax, two similar activities.[13] Whatever the case, it is clear that Paul does not allow women to be teachers in the church.

Paul bases the subordination of women to their male teachers on God's will as revealed in the priority of Adam's creation. God appointed him as the

---

11  Moo: 183.

12  Bacchiocchi: 149; Moo: 184.

13  Köstenberger.

teacher of his wife and his family by giving him his original command and promise (Gen 2:16, 17). The priority of Adam established his God-given responsibility to be the head of the human family; it also established firstborn males as the heads of every Israelite family. As such they were the teachers of their families. In worship they represented their families before God. This role of Adam as the liturgical head of the human family was fulfilled by Christ (see Col 1:15–23); it is now exercised by him through the male teachers in the church.

While Paul's mention of Adam's priority over Eve establishes the position of male teachers in the congregation, his subsequent reference to Eve's deception is a warning against the refusal of some women in Ephesus to remain students of God's word. The point of comparison is between Eve as an insubordinate student of God's word and all Christian women as receptive disciples. Thus Paul does not assert that women should be excluded from the ministry of the word because they are more responsible for the fall than Adam, or because they are somehow more susceptible to deception by Satan than men. That is obviously not so. Rather, he warns that Christian women should not become teachers like Eve, but remain disciples of Christ, subordinate to him and his word and to those who teach that word.

So, while Paul teaches the full involvement of all women in the public worship of the church as intercessors and disciples, he does not allow them to be teachers in the church.

## 3. Conclusion

The exalted Lord Jesus has appointed ministers of the gospel to convey his gifts to the faithful in the church. He has chosen to do so by calling male apostles and male teachers of his word. But he has not authorized any women to perform this ministry. Paul, in fact, claims that Christ has forbidden women to be teachers in the assembly of the saints. Christ has not given them the task of giving his word and his sacraments to the people of God. So, since he has not been given it to them, they cannot exercise this ministry without usurping that office in violation of Christ's command.

### References

Aalen, S. "A Rabbinical Formula in 1 Corinthians 14:34," in F L Cross, *Studia Evangelica* 11/1, Akademie-verlag, Berlin, 513–25, 1964.

Bacchiocchi, Samuele. *Women in the Church. A Biblical Study on the Role of Women in the Church*, Biblical Perspectives 7, Berrien Springs, 1987.

Barrett, C K. *A Commentary on the First Epistle to the Corinthians*, Black: London, 2d ed, 1971.

Brunner, Peter. *The Ministry and the Ministry of Women*, Concordia: St. Louis, 1971.

Carson, D A. "'Silent in the Churches': On the Role of Women in 1 Corinthians 14:33b–36," in J. Piper and W. Grudem, *Recovering Biblical Manhood and Womanhood*, Crossway Books: Wheaton, 140–53, 1991.

Clark, Stephen. *Man and Woman in Christ*, Servant Publications: Ann Arbor, 1980.

Dautzenberg, Gerhard. *Urchristliche Prophetie. Ihre Forschung, ihre Voraussetzungen im Judentum und ihre Struktur im ersten Korintherbrief*, BWANT 104, Kohlhammer: Stuttgart, 1975.

Fee, Gordon. *The First Epistle to the Corinthians*, Eerdmans: Grand Rapids, 1987.

Grudem, Wayne. *The Gift of Prophecy in 1 Corinthians*, University Press of America: Washington DC, 1982.

Hauke, Manfred. *Women in the Priesthood. A Systematic Analysis in the Light of the Order of Creation and Redemption*, Ignatius Press: San Francisco, 1988.

Hurley, James B. *Man and Woman in Biblical Perspective. A Study in Role Relationships and Authority*, Intervarsity Press: Leicester, 1981.

Johansson, Nils. *Women and the Church's Ministry: An Exegetical Study of 1 Corinthians 11–14*, St Barnabas: Ottawa, 1972.

Käsemann, E. "Sentences of Holy Law in the NT," in *NT Questions of Today*, Eng. Trans., SCM: London, 66–81.

Kleinig, John W. "Scripture, and the Exclusion of Women from the Pastorate (I)," *Lutheran Theological Journal* 29/2 (1995): 74–81, and "Scripture, and the Exclusion of Women from the Pastorate (II)," *Lutheran Theological Journal* 29/3 (1995): 123–29.

Knight, George. "*Authentein* in reference to women in 1 Timothy 2:12," *New Testament Studies* 30 (1984): 143–157.

Köstenberger, Andreas J. "Syntactical Background Studies to 1 Timothy 2:12 in the New Testament and Extrabiblical Greek Literature," in Stanley E. Porter and D. A. Carson, *Discourse Analysis and Other Topics in Biblical Greek*, Sheffield Academic Press: Sheffield, 156–179, 1995.

Lockwood, Gregory J. *1 Corinthians*. Concordia Commentary Series. Concordia: St. Louis, 2000.

Moo, Douglas. "What Does It Mean Not To Teach or Have Authority Over Men?, 1 Timothy 2:11–15," in J. Piper and W. Grudem, *Recovering Biblical Manhood and Womanhood*, Crossway Books: Wheaton, 179–93, 1991.

Panning. Armin J. "*Authentein*—A Word Study," *Wisconsin Lutheran Quarterly* 78 (1981): 185–191.

Pope John Paul II. *Ordinatio Sacerdotalis. Apostolic Letter on Reserving Priestly Ordination to Men Alone*, at: http://www.cin.org/users/james/files/w-ordination.htm, 1994-May-22.

Thiselton, Anthony C. *The First Epistle to the Corinthians*. The New International Greek Testament Commentary. Eerdmans: Grand Rapids, and Paternoster Press: Carlisle, 2000.

Towner, Philip H. *The Goal of Our Instruction: The Structure of Theology and Ethics in the Pastoral Epistles*, JSOT Supplement 34, JSOT Press: Sheffield, 1989.

Witherington, Ben. *Women in the Earliest Churches*, Cambridge University Press: Cambridge, 1988.

# 1 Corinthians 14:33b–38, 1 Timothy 2:11–14, and the Ordination of Women

## Peter Kriewaldt

It goes without saying that Jesus elevated the status of women. He regarded them as equal members of the community and encouraged them to study the Scriptures. Jesus broke with Judaism, which did not allow women to learn God's Word.

Therefore it is highly significant that Jesus entrusted the oversight of the Church to men only, and that the apostles appointed only males leaders in the Church. Indeed, Paul says that women are to be silent in the churches, not speak, be in submission, and not teach or have authority over the male leaders. Clement of Rome, writing in the first century, records that Jesus gave precise instructions to His apostles that only proven men should continue the Office of the Ministry after the apostles died (1 Clement 42:1–4).

## 1 Corinthians 14:33b–38

It is not always easy to define the culture of any given place. But we do know that Corinth had a number of cults that included priestesses, for example, the cults of Artemis, Demeter and Kore, Dionysos, Isis, and Aphrodite. So Paul's command for women to be silent runs counter to pagan culture in Corinth. He is not culturally conditioned. Therefore if it really was Jesus' will for women to become priests, Paul would have had a good opportunity for introducing them in this church. It is our contention that Paul explicitly prohibited women from becoming teachers in the Corinthian church.

First Corinthians 14 does not deal with the office of priest but rather imparts a ban on teaching by women. It is aimed at official and public activity as teacher, whereas teaching outside of this office seems thoroughly appropriate for women in the Pauline community. For this reason the passage has always been seen as a clear prohibition against women entering the priest-hood. For sixty generations, catholic Christian orthodoxy has interpreted 1 Corinthians 14 in this way. There are no biblical grounds for challenging or neutralizing this understanding.

The integrity of this passage is certain. There is no manuscript evidence for the omission of these verses from chapter 14, though some manuscripts place them after v. 40. A structural analysis shows that the section fits well into the context. The interpolation theory owes more to perceived difficulties of harmonization than to actual textual problems.

Paul's setting has to do with the worship life of the Church. Paul sets out to regulate speaking in tongues, the speaking of prophecy, and the speaking of women. In each case he says, "Yes, but." Tongues—yes, but only two or three in one session, and none if no interpreter is present. Prophecy—yes, but only two or three in one session and the prophecy must be weighed by the congregation or, more likely, the male leaders. Speaking by women—yes, they may prophesy, but when the prophecy is discussed and debated, they are to be silent, at least until they get home!

Paul says that his commands are followed in all the churches. Therefore the church at Corinth should follow suit. Even if v. 33b is to be read with v. 33a, nothing is lost, for "in the churches" also appears in v. 34. Paul's injunctions are therefore meant for all the churches, regardless of their cultural background—Paul transcends culture.

> 33b–34: "As in all the congregations of the saints, women should remain silent in the churches. They are not allowed to speak, but must be in sub-mission, as the Law says."

Who is being addressed here? Married and unmarried women. Although Paul talks of wives in v. 35, it would be ludicrous to limit his commands to wives. If wives are to be silent, so also those who are single—an *a fortiori* argument.

Women can prophesy. Prophecy is not preaching; it is speech directly inspired by God; the message is received through revelation (cf. 14:30). Although instruction and learning are connected with prophecy, it is not an institution that is constantly ready for action; rather, it is dependent on the activity of the Spirit that is not at our disposal. It is quite different from preaching and official teaching of the apostolic word. Prophecy, then, is open also for women. Scripture refers to a number of women prophets. Indeed, at Pentecost, Peter said that the prophecy of Joel was now being fulfilled in that sons and daughters, men and women, will prophesy.

When were women to be silent? When the prophecy was being weighed and evaluated. Why did prophecy need to be evaluated? Because it didn't have the same authoritative status as that of the Old Testament. Indeed, that is the reason why Paul elevates teaching above prophecy (cf. 14:26 and the context of this passage, which submits prophecy to testing by the teaching). The evaluation of prophecy probably involved a general discussion (1 Thess. 5:19–22), which resulted in an authoritative judgment on its sense and application by the leaders of the congregation in the light of the apostolic tradition (Rev. 19:10; cf. Matt. 7:15–27) and the analogy of faith (Rom. 12:6). Through questioning, women began to take possession of the service of teacher.

Acts 20:7–12 shows that this kind of discussion was not restricted to the weighing of prophecies but also was associated with homilies given by teachers in the Early Church.

Thus women are to be silent. They are not allowed to speak in assessing prophecy, since this involves the teaching of Scripture according to the apostolic tradition.

"Speak" confirms that authoritative teaching is what is meant. "Speak," or *lalein*, is a synonym for authoritative teaching (Matt. 9:18; Acts 18:25; 2 Cor. 2:17). *Lalein* also means the giving of a sermon.

It is thus authoritative teaching that women were not to give. It certainly doesn't mean chattering or strident speaking. *Lalein* never means "to chatter, to interrupt." Moreover it would be odd for Paul to appeal to church custom, the law, shame before God, and a command of Jesus to quieten chattering of *all* the women, for apparently they must have all been at it. It should be noted that this passage does not prevent women from teaching other women or children.

Paul says women "are not allowed to speak." Or, "It is not permitted." The use of the passive indicates that it is God Himself who does not permit women to speak or teach.

There are four reasons why women are to be silent and are not to speak. First, it is the ecumenical practice of all the churches. We have referred to that. Second, women "must be in submission as the Law says." The Law probably has to do with the whole Pentateuch, but especially Gen. 2:18–25 (cf. 1 Tim. 2:11–12). The derivation of woman from man indicates that the woman is to submit to him. Submission is based on the order of creation and is not a result of the fall. It applies to both the family and the liturgical setting. It does not apply to government and business. Paul's point is that the order of creation, in which women are to submit, is not preserved if women become teachers in the public worship of the Church.

Submission is a somewhat dirty word today. Yet it shouldn't be. For Paul says that Christ will be made subject (*upotagesatai*) or submissive to the Father at the end of time (1 Cor. 15:28). So submission has nothing to do with inequality. Woman is equal to man but is to be submissive.

But, some may say, what of Eph. 5:21? Doesn't it talk of mutual submission? "Submit to one another out of reverence for Christ." This could be a general command of Paul directed to all members of the church to show reverence and to defer to one another. Having said that, in v. 22 it is wives who are to submit to husbands; it is never husbands who are to submit to wives.

At the same time one could argue that v. 21 does not teach mutual submission at all, but only teaches that we should all be subject to those whom God has put in authority over us—such as husbands, parents, or employers. Talk of reciprocal submission in Ephesians 5 is saying too much. Are parents to submit to children? It is much better to understand Eph. 5:21 according to this paraphrase: "Be subject to one another, that is, to some others, in the fear of Christ."

The Greek verb for subjecting oneself, *upotassesthai*, always implies a relationship of submission to an authority. For example, Jesus submits to his parents (Lk. 2:52); demons are subject to the disciples (Lk. 10:17); citizens are subject to government authorities (Rom. 13:1); Christ is to be subject to the Father (1 Cor. 15:28). None of these relationships is ever reversed. That is, husbands are never told to be subject to wives, the government to citizens, masters to servants, disciples to demons etc. The word is never mutual in its force. It is always one directional in its reference to submission to an authority. So also in Eph. 5:21. The submission Paul has in mind is submission to a higher authority, not mutual submission.

What then does it mean to "submit to one another"? It means to submit to some others, not everyone to everyone. There are many passage where "to one another" means "some others" (Rev. 6:4; Gal. 6:2; 1 Cor. 11:33; Lk. 2:15; 21:1; 24:32). For example, Rev. 6:4 says the rider of the red horse was given power "to make men slay each other." This means that some would kill others. It could hardly be reciprocal! As if to say that those people being killed would mutually kill those who were killing them!

Ephesians 5:21 is thus saying, "those who are under authority (wives, children, slaves) should be subject to others among you (husbands, parents, masters) who have authority over them."

35: "If they want to inquire about something, they should ask their own husbands at home; for it is disgraceful for a woman to speak in the church."

Wives should be silent, not speak, but be in submission. Hence they should leave their questions for later—outside of the liturgical assembly.

Why? We come now to the third reason Paul gives for women to be silent and not speak: "It is disgraceful." In the LXX (Greek OT) and the NT, shame has primarily a theological rather than a social meaning (in Eph. 5:12, shame is what is unacceptable to God and society). So, then, Paul is saying it is shameful to God for a woman to assume a teaching role in the church. For women to speak in the church is unacceptable to God.

36: "Did the word of God originate with you? Or are you the only people it has reached?'

Paul tells the church that it is not free to create God's Word and apply it as it sees fit. The word originated with Jesus and was passed on to His apostles. It was this word that Paul was communicating to them. They dare not refuse it or disobey it. The word of God Paul now gives them included the command for women to be silent and not speak the authoritative teaching in the assembly.

37: "If anybody thinks he is a prophet or spiritually gifted, let him acknowledge that what I am writing to you is the Lord's command."

Fourthly, women are to be silent and not speak because anyone filled with the Spirit would have to admit that what Paul is saying is really a command of the Lord! Paul had access to Christ's commands outside of Scripture (see, e.g., Acts 20:35; 1 Thess. 4:5; cf. John 20:30; 21:25). One of these commands prohibited women from teaching in the churches.

This interpretation of the text, as already mentioned, has been consistently applied for sixty generations by the Church. It is presumptuous for us living in the twentieth century to change or disobey the command of Christ. According to many of the Church Fathers, it is heretical and sectarian to do so.

38: "If he ignores this, he himself will be ignored."

Paul warns the church against ignoring what he has written. If they disobey this word, they will be ignored or not recognized. This could mean that they won't be recognized by God as prophets and Spirit-filled people. Or it could even mean that God will ignore them on the Day of Judgment. It is a serious thing to disobey God's Word.

There is some debate as to which word Paul is referring to here. Paul would hardly threaten the congregation with eternal punishment in hell for violation of his directives concerning those who speak in tongues: "only two or at most three, and each in turn." Or his word concerning prophets: "If a revelation is made to another sitting by, let the first be silent." Surely what Paul is defending is not merely such disciplinary norms but rather the command of the Lord as it relates to the ban on women speaking the apostolic word in the liturgical setting.

# 1 Timothy 2:11–15

This letter was sent to Timothy in Ephesus, the economic, political, and religious center of Asia Minor. In that region the social position of women was well developed. There were numerous female doctors there. In politics, women were thoroughly involved in leadership. Female philosophers were known to teach, probably appearing publicly in the same way as did Paul, who chose a lecture hall in Ephesus as a place of work.

In Paul's day the Greek and Roman world was awash with priestesses. In Crete, men, not women, were banned from the priesthood. In Ephesus, the Phrygian cult of Cybele, in which the mother goddess played the central role, was well established, along with its priestesses and priests. There were also the priestesses of Demeter and of the mystery cult of Isis, which had made equal rights for women its platform. Leading positions were held by women in the cult of Dionysus, in whose worship ceremonies all members had equal rights. Most characteristic of Ephesus, however, was the cult of Artemis. In it, priestesses had a higher position than priests.

Thus the social environment was anything but hostile to women priests; indeed, this question was very much in the air. That Paul took a strong stand against the culture of the day is most significant. He did not tailor his message or his commands to fit with the milieu, though this step may have brought easier passage for the Gospel.

Paul was not even guided by the Jewish influence in Ephesus. Clear differences from Judaism are evident in 1 Timothy. Judaism banned women from learning; Paul made learning a duty for women. Paul also encouraged women to teach—other women and children; men could also be taught outside the worship setting (Acts 18:26; 2 Tim. 4:19). Many other fields of service were given to women (1 Tim. 5:10; Titus 2:3–5). Paul's only "no" had to do with official teaching in the liturgical assembly.

The setting for 1 Timothy 2 is public worship. It has to do with instructions for worship; "how people ought to conduct themselves in God's household, which is the church of the living God" (1 Tim. 3:15). Paul uses the word *dei*, "must." What he writes is a matter of necessity, divine obligation, meant for all the churches. Paul does not give his personal opinion. In 1 Timothy 2:7 he emphasizes that he has been appointed as an apostle by God to be a "teacher" of the Christian faith to the Gentiles. He therefore speaks with apostolic authority in his instruction and prohibition in 2:11–12.

False teaching had invaded the church at Ephesus (1 Tim. 1:3; 6:20). It had sowed dissension. One of its features led women to discard traditional roles. Those misled believed that marriage and male/female distinctions were no longer relevant to them. They were to disregard their appropriate roles, especially vis-à-vis their husbands (1 Tim. 2:9–15; 5:13–14; Titus 2:3–5).

Paul addresses some of this false teaching in chapter 2, including how women are to relate to men in public worship. Paul seeks to right the balance by reasserting the importance of the created order and the ongoing significance of those role distinctions between men and women that he saw rooted in creation.

This passage strongly reemphasizes the message of 1 Corinthians 14:33b–38 that women are not to take a lead role in the worship service. It reads like a commentary of 1 Corinthians 14. Paul directs women to learn in the worship assembly with a quiet and submissive attitude rather than to teach or have authority over a man in that context. He gives two reasons for this directive. First, the pattern of male headship was established in creation, and Paul wanted to see this principle affirmed in the Church. Second, the principle of male headship was violated through the reversal of authority roles in the fall with devastating consequences, and Paul wanted the believers to avoid such a role reversal in the Church.

In this pericope, *gyne* must mean woman, not wife. *Gynaikas* (v. 9) and *gynaiksin* (v. 10) refer to female worshipers. *Gyne* (v. 11) must also mean "woman," not "wife." Furthermore, it is clear that Paul has Genesis 2–3 in mind in these verses (the creation and fall accounts). Following the Septuagint, when Paul means "wife" he uses *gyne* with a personal pronoun, and when he means "woman" he uses *gyne* without a pronoun. *Gyne* appears in this passage without a personal pronoun, so Paul must be speaking of women generally rather than wives specifically.

Unlike Jewish women, Christian women are to join in the public prayer of the church and to "learn" God's Word as disciples of Christ. Their learning is to be characterized by two states of mind.

First, "in quietness." This has to do with receptivity, peacefulness, harmony, and respectful listening rather than total silence. Paul was concerned that women were not learning "in quietness." They were endeavoring to teach the apostolic word. The false teaching that blurred role distinctions had led them where they were not permitted to go. There is no evidence that they were teaching falsely and, for this reason, Paul ordered them to be quiet—as if to say that if they taught truly Paul would have no problems with that. Paul orders them to listen respectfully to the word.

Second, women are to learn in "full submission." That is, they are to submit to Christ's Word and those who teach it. Paul is not saying that women are to be submissive to all males. Submission does not deal with the question of equality or esteem or worth or any possible lack of it. It has to do with an ordering or arranging of oneself—equal though the two subjects may be in essence, glory, worth, esteem—beneath (*hypo*) the other. The term describes relationships between two parties—perfect relationships. It has to do with the willing assumption of a relationship, under the motivation of Christ's Gospel, which does not insist that one has a right, power, or authority over the other.

In public worship some are called to teach; some are called to learn. Verse 11 suggests that Christian women will, under the Gospel, willingly place themselves in the latter category—just as the majority of men have to as well.

12: "I do not permit a woman to teach or to have authority over a man; she must be silent."

The Greek word order of the first part of the sentence is: "To teach to a woman I do not permit." Paul's sense is this: Let the women learn with full submission; but (*de*) full submission means also that I do not permit a woman to teach or to exercise authority over a man. She must be silent.

Some think that when Paul says "I do not permit" this only has to do with his personal opinion rather than with a permanent command of the Lord. Therefore it is only a temporary instruction that applies to Ephesus. This is wishful thinking. Paul's letter bristles with apostolic authority (1:1, 3,18; 2:1, 7, 8, 11, 14; 4:6, 11, 16; 6:2c, 13). This suggests that apostolic authority underlies and pervades this whole section in such a way as to make it unthinkable to propose that the use of "I do not permit" implies something less than a firm apostolic command.

What are women not permitted to do? They are not permitted to teach the apostolic doctrine or engage in the apostolic ministry of the Word in the worship assembly. Women are certainly allowed to teach as we already mentioned, but not in the worship service of the Church.

Nor are women permitted to exercise authority over a male teacher in the Church. They are to be silent. The Greek of verse 12 makes it clear that it should be translated in this fashion: "I do not allow a woman to teach; and I do not allow a woman to exercise authority over a man." *Authentein* ("exercise authority") is used only here in the NT. But in other Greek literature it almost invariably has to do with the concept of "authority." Such authority is a positive concept and is in no way regarded as having any overtone of misuse of position or power, i.e., to "domineer."

Some have understood this verse to mean that women can teach if it is not done in a domineering way. The verse doesn't say that. Paul simply says, "I do not allow a woman to teach; and I do not allow a woman to exercise authority over a man."

Paul appeals to the Scriptures in two ways to support his assertion that male teachers are the liturgical leaders of God's family and that women are to be submissive to such leaders.

13: "For Adam was formed first, then Eve."

"For" (*gar*) provides the initial reason as to why women are to learn in full submission, not teach, not exercise authority over the male leaders, and be silent. This reason is found in God's will as revealed through the priority of Adam's creation (Gen. 2:18). Adam was created first. "First" is not merely first in time, but carries with it a position of leadership, authority, and responsibility (1 Cor. 12:28; 15:3; 1 Tim. 1:15–16; 2:1). The priority of Adam established the divinely instituted role of Adam as the priestly head of the human family and of firstborn Israelite males as the heads of their families. As such they were teachers of their families. In worship they represented their families before God and represented Him to their families. This role of Adam as the liturgical head of the human family was fulfilled by Christ (see Col. 1:15–23) and is now exercised by Him through the male teachers in God's family, the Church.

Some commentators reject Paul's argument. They say that if priority means authority, then animals are our masters! That is really scraping the barrel!

In rooting these prohibitions in the circumstances of creation rather than in the circumstances of the fall, Paul shows that he does not consider these restrictions to be the product of the curse and presumably, therefore, to be phased out by redemption. And by citing creation rather than cultural circumstances as his basis for the prohibitions, Paul makes it clear that cultural issues do not provide the reason for his advice. His reason for the prohibitions of verse 12 is the created role relationship of man and woman, and we may justly conclude that these prohibitions are applicable until the return of Christ.

14: "And Adam was not the one deceived; it was the woman who was deceived and became a sinner."

Paul's second appeal to Scripture concerns the fall. Paul does not assert that women alone are responsible for the fall or that they are more susceptible to deception by Satan than men. But the woman ceased to be a disciple and became insubordinate by assuming authority in making the wrong decision and then pressing her decision onto the man. The man, who was meant to be leader and head, fell down on the job with eyes wide open. He deliberately and knowingly chose to listen to the woman and thereby sinned by following her teaching.

If women at the church in Ephesus proclaim their independence from the male leaders, refusing to learn "in quietness and full submission," seeking roles that have been given to men in the church, they will make the same mistake Eve made.

So today, Christian worship is to reflect the order established by God in creation, not followed in Eden, in which males have the responsibility for teaching God's Word.

# The Authority of These Texts for Today

Are these texts still in force today? Let's have a look at the evidence.

(1) These texts give us commands of Jesus (1 Cor. 14:37). There is no hint that Jesus' commands are to be restricted to the Early Church. Certainly the Church for sixty generations has believed them to be in force. Who gives us the right to tamper with Christ's commands? No one!

It is sometimes argued that the Holy Spirit and the apostles issued an edict concerning the requirements for Gentile believers (Acts 15:28–29), some of which requirements were not enforced for any length of time. The problem was that there was no clear word from Jesus to direct the Church. So a different procedure to handle the question was used. Obviously the requirements concerning food, blood, and meat had a limited application. Paul even says already in Romans 14 that all food is clean. But the requirement to abstain from sexual immorality was surely meant to be observed in the Church of all ages! One can hardly use this passage to say that Paul's argument concerning the silence of women is time-bound. There is no passage in Scripture that gives us the right to relax that command, as there is with some of the requirements in Acts 15.

(2) Paul commands that his instructions be kept until Christ's coming (1 Tim. 6:14).

(3) To reject these commands is to prove oneself unspiritual (1 Cor. 14:37).

(4) Paul says that he delivers trustworthy sayings worthy of full acceptance (1 Tim. 1:15; 3:1; 4:9). We have no right reject these sayings of Paul.

(5) Paul's injunctions are not just for the church at Corinth, but for all the churches (1 Cor. 14:33; 1:2). They are also for the LCA.

(6) If Jesus had wanted women for this office, He would not have permitted Paul to speak so strongly against them assuming spiritual leadership in the Church.

(7) The original order of creation with man as the head is continued throughout the whole OT and reiterated in the NT. What right have we to change God's order of creation? (Slavery is not a rejoinder, as slavery was never part of God's original creation order for human relationships.)

(8) If Jesus wanted women to be priests, then:

a. the apostles failed to divine His intentions, or

b. they deliberately disobeyed Jesus to the extent that they twisted the words of Jesus, or

c. Christ erred in not declaring clearly to His apostles that this was His intention, for the apostles wrote against it.

(9) The Montanist sect believed that the Holy Spirit had led them to ordain women. The Church said, "No, this is not from the Holy Spirit or

Jesus or the apostles." Similarly, to ordain women today is not of the Holy Spirit or Jesus or the apostles.

(10) Paul's commands fly in the face of the culture of his day with its priestesses. So Paul is not bound to culture.

(11) Galatians 3:28 does not negate these passages. This text has to do with the baptismal identity of all believers as God's children in Christ Jesus. That is, Galatians 3:28 says that the basis for becoming a child of Abraham has nothing to do with race, gender, or station in life but with faith in Christ alone. It is not talking of roles or service in the Church—or ministry.

(12) The Gospel does not abolish these prohibitions. The Gospel does not establish doctrine. It does not tell us that the bread is the body of Christ or that Christ will return on the Last Day to judge the living and the dead. These teachings must be drawn from the relevant Scripture passages that talk about these subjects. So, too, whether women may become priests or not is not derived from the Gospel. We contend that Scripture clearly rules out the ordination of women. Men and women are one in Christ, but God has given them different roles in the Church.

(13) The Holy Spirit does not contradict Himself. He has spoken to the Church with one voice for almost 2,000 years and said that women are not to teach in the worship assembly. We have no right to reinterpret Scripture in such a way that we contradict the Church's clear teaching of Scripture for all these years.

(14) The Church for sixty generations has said that these passages prohibit women from the ordained ministry. I believe that our *Theses of Agreement* have got it right:

> Though women prophets were used by the Spirit of God in the Old as well as in the New Testament, 1 Cor. 14:34, 35 and 1 Tim. 2:11–14 prohibit a woman from being called into the office of the public ministry for the proclamation of the Word and the administration of the Sacraments. This apostolic rule is binding on all Christendom; hereby her rights as a member of the spiritual priesthood are in no wise impaired." (*TA* VI, 11).

## Bibliography

Strelan, Rick. *Paul, Artemis, and the Jews in Ephesus*. Berlin: de Gruyter, 1996.

Theissen, Gerd. *The Social Setting of Pauline Christianity*. Philadelphia: Fortress, 1982.

# "As in All the Churches of the Saints"

## A Text-Critical Study of 1 Corinthians 14:34,35

## David W. Bryce

### I. Introduction

Peter Lockwood asks, 'Does 1 Corinthians 14:34,35 exclude women from the pastoral office?' (*LTJ* 30/1 May, 1996). He answers in the negative and claims that

> the most compelling way of accounting for the problems raised by 1 Corinthians 14:34,35 is that the regulation [for women being silent in the church] does not come from Paul's hand at all . . . Rather the 'mulier taceat' was a marginal note that was incorporated into the text by a copyist who agreed with its ruling. (33)

Although there are no extant New Testament manuscripts which omit 14:34,35 from 1 Corinthians, a number of Western manuscripts place it after 14:40 (Lockwood: 34). Since the appearance of Hans Conzelmann's commentary on 1 Corinthians, the text critical evidence has largely been ignored when examining 14:34,35. Those who hold that these verses are an interpolation cite the variant placement as evidence. As a result they have shifted their focus from text criticism in favour of literary criticism (Hauke: 366).

This paper will examine 1 Corinthians 14:34,35 text-critically. In particular we will examine the variant texts which place 14:34,35 after 14:40. We will also discuss what may have led to the variant, and its possible origins.

The interpolation theory, as it attempts to explain away the import of 14:34,35, rests on shaky foundations (Hauke: 366). Text-critically, the evidence that 14:34,35 is original and should be placed in its traditional location, and not after 14:40, is substantial (Carson: 124).

# Excursus i

The Alexandrian-type text which gives broad support to the traditional placement of 1 Corinthians 14:34,35 is usually considered to be the best text and the most faithful in preserving the original. Evidence from the Bodmer Papyri, in particular **p66** and **p75**, takes the Alexandrian type of text back to an archetype that must be dated early in the second century (Metzger: xviii). The traditional placement is confirmed by the significant fourth century parchments Codex Vaticanus and Codex Sinaiticus. Furthermore, the proto-Alexandrian Chester Beatty 2 papyri **p46** (about AD 200) and the later Alexandrian type uncials Codex Alexandrinus and Codex Athous Laurae, together with the minuscules **33 81 104 326** and **1739**, also corroborate this placement. The Coptic Sahidic and Bohairic versions frequently contain typically Alexandrian readings.

The textual evidence for the traditional placement follows:

*Papyri*: one (**p46**) ca AD 200.

*Uncials*: three from the 4th and 5th century; two from the 8th and 9th century; one from the 10th century.

Sinaiticus ca IV.

**A** Alexandrinus. Ca V.

**B** Vaticanus. Ca IV.

**K** Moscow. Ca IX.

**Ψ** Athos. Ca VIII/IX.

**0234** ca X.

*Minuscules*: one from the 9th century; one from the 10th century; six from the 11th century; five from the 12th century; two from the 13th century; five from the 14th century; one from the 14/15th century; one from the 16th century.

*Ancient Versions*:

(a) Old Latin (witnesses either in whole or in part) one codex from the 8th century; one codex from the 9th century; one codex from the 13th century.

(b) Vulgate of the 4/5th century.

(c) Syriac: Peshitta of the 5th century; Harclean of the 7th century; Palestinian of the 5th century.

(d) Coptic: Sahidic dialect of the 3rd century; Bohairic dialect of the 4th century; Fayyumic dialect of the 4th century.

(e) Armenian: Zohrab of the 5th century.

The majority of the Byzantine manuscripts.

The reading of the majority of Lectionaries in the Synaxarion and in the Menologion when these agree.

The variant placement of 14:34,35 after 14:40 is witnessed by the **Western** type text. The chief characteristic of Western readings is their fondness for paraphrase. Words, clauses, and even whole sentences are freely changed, omitted, or inserted. Motives for these may be to bring harmony, or to enrich the narrative by including traditional or apocryphal material. A most important Greek manuscript that presents a Western-type of text in the Pauline epistles is Codex Claromontanus **D**. The Old Latin versions are noteworthy witnesses to a Western type text. It was used by Tatian, Irenaeus, Tertullian, Cyprian and Marcion (Metzger: xviii).

The variant texts which place 14:34,35 after 14:40 follow.

*Papyri*: None

*Uncials*: one from the 6th century; two from the 9th century; one from the 9/10th century.

**D** Claromontanus. Ca VI.

**F** Cambridge. Ca IX.

**G** Boererianus. Ca IX.

*Minuscules*: one from the 12th century.

*Old Latin Version*: one codex from the 5/6th century; three from the 9th century.

*Church Fathers*: Ambrosiaster from the 4th century;

Sedulus-Scotus from the 9th century.

## II. Examination of the Texts

Antoinette Wire examines those manuscripts which place 1 Corinthians 14:34,35 after 14:40, and reveals (149) that the texts are all either Greek-Latin bilinguals or Latin texts. The exception is the minuscule **88\*** from the twelfth century. We will examine this manuscript later.

The manuscripts can be traced with some certainty:

(a) The manuscripts **D, E, F, G** are all bilingual (Greek and Latin) forms of 1 Corinthians.

(b) The text **E** Sangermanensis is a direct copy of **D** Claromontanus and bears no direct evidence (Clabeaux: x; Wire: 149).

(c) The two manuscripts, **F** and **G** are so close to each other that textual critics such as Scrivener and Frede, either consider that the writer of **F** copied **G**, or that both writers copied the same Greek text.

(d) The parallel omissions of major units of material in the Greek and Latin of **F** and **G** also confirm their common source.

(e) Critics have named this source manuscript X (Wire: 149, 284).

We can say accurately that the variant is present, therefore, in two Greek witnesses among the bilinguals, that is, **D** and **G** (or **X**). These two texts agree in diverging from the Alexandrian text type six times in our two verses in the Nestle-Aland 26th edition. As a result, the theory of a single common archetype of these two Greek texts, called **Z**, is well established (Wire: 149).

We also find that the Latin texts **d e f g** of the Pauline epistles also place 14:34,35 after 14:40.

The following points are of note:

(a) It would appear that the Old Latin text tradition arose when the gospel spread away from the groups who spoke Greek well and into other provinces and ethnic groups.

(b) The Old Latin texts come to us from an already complex tradition which existed by the time the first of the bilinguals is made about the fourth century (Clabeaux: 6ff).

(c) Scholars have classified the Old Latin tradition according to three different text types. There is the so-called African or North African type which had a fixed form by the third century. Two European type texts originate soon after and become mixed in different ways. Clabeaux (9) assigns **d f g** to a southern Italian tradition.

(d) Text **E** Sangermanensis has no independent value for our discussion since it is a copy of **D** Claromontanus (Clabeaux: 9n).

(e) It is generally regarded that **it dem** and **it x** are not Old Latin but Vulgate with some Old Latin readings. The codex **it z** is Old Latin only in Hebrews 10:13 (Wire: 284). These codices witness the traditional placement of 14:34,35.

(f) All extant Old Latin manuscripts of 1 Corinthians, regardless of their type, agree with the bilingual texts in placing 14:34,35 at the end of the chapter. The Latin texts which have survived show the broadest possible early Latin evidence for locating 14:34,35 after verse 40 (Wire: 150).

(g) These texts do not provide us with a wide range of independent witnesses which corroborate a broad tradition. Rather they indicate a shared, common origin (Wire: 150).

When the Old Latin tradition is compared with the most reliable Greek texts, such as Chester Beatty 2 **p46**, Vaticanus **B**, and Goltz Manuscript **1739**, the Old Latin disagrees so frequently with the Greek that the Latin texts are taken together as signs that they have been derived from the same primary sources (Wire: 150; Hauke: 366). These primary sources can be narrowed down even further:

(a) Scholars regularly trace back the African and both European text types to a single original Greek text.

(b) When the second of these European text types was later copied opposite a Greek text, the single archetype of the Greek bilinguals **Z** closely resembles the Greek text behind the Latin.

The manuscripts which place 1 Corinthians 14:34,35 at the end of chapter 14 belong to the Western tradition. The text-critical evidence leads to a reasonable conclusion that all most likely derive from a single textual source which is no longer extant (Wire: 150).

The twelfth-century minuscule **88\*** in the original hand places 14:34,35 at the end of chapter 14 also. However, it departs from the pattern set by the other texts with this variant placement:

(a) When the twelfth-century scribe found verses 34,35 at the end of the chapter being copied, he recognised that it had been omitted after verse 33 and misplaced there.

(b) The scribe made two short slashes on the line of writing to indicate the reversal of order before he wrote these two verses.

(c) As part of the correction, the scribe put similar marks some lines earlier to show where they belonged.

Scholars argue (Wire: 151) that the scribal slashes and marginal marks in the manuscript **88\*** represent the final demise of the Western tradition with its placement of 14:34,35 at the end of chapter 14.

In the sixth century Victor of Capua corrected the Vulgate manuscript Codex Fuldensis using what is thought to be a text very close to the Vulgate manuscript Codex Vaticanus Reginensis. Reginensis contains the variant placement.

(a) Victor inserted 14:36–40 in the margin **before** 14:34,35 to match the sequence of Reginensis.

(b) He did not, however, eliminate 14:36–40, which already followed 14:34,35 in Fuldensis according to the usual Vulgate order (Wire: 285; Metzger: 565).

(c) This deuterograph has been wrongly seen as evidence that Paul glossed his own letter in this way (Wire: 285).

Codex **Fuldensis** and **88\*** give us important evidence of scribal attempts to place 14:34,35 appropriately within 14:33–40 (Metzger: 565). The evidence also supports the theory that those who originally excised 14:34.35 from 1 Corinthians 14 were not necessarily the same people who placed the verses at the end of chapter 14. The variant placement of 14:34,35 in differ-ent manuscripts could very well be the result of an original scribal attempt to replace 14:34,35 in a manuscript where it was absent.

## EXCURSUS 2

A comparison of 1 Corinthians 14:34,35 with 1 Timothy 2:12 provides further evidence against an interpolation theory. There are no variant readings within 1 Timothy 2:11–15. There is no evidence to suggest that 1 Timothy 2:12 is an interpolation. The Corinthian and Timothy texts bear clear similarities. In the Pauline corpus, outside of the two mentioned texts, the verb *epitrepein*, to permit, only occurs in 1 Corinthians 16:7 with *Kyrios* as its subject and in Hebrew 6:3 with *Theos* as its subject.

If the interpolation theory were correct it would be reasonable for an editor to use the thrust and vocabulary of the Timothy passage to construct his interpolation. If that were the case, the Timothy passage would predate the Corinthian insertion. But when we compare the two texts we see the same thrust of argument but a significant difference in vocabulary. It is unrea-sonable to suggest that an interpolator constructed his exclusion of women 'speaking authoritatively' by changing the technical verb *didaskein*, 'to teach', in Timothy for the more general verb *lalein*, 'to speak', in Corinthians.

It is more reasonable to see that the resemblance between 1 Corinthians 14:34,35 and 1 Timothy 2:14 is because the Corinthian text predates the Timothy texts and they both come from the same person or school or tradi-tion writing to different environments (Kleinig 1995a: 123).

## III. WHO MIGHT BE THE AUTHOR
## OF THE VARIANT PLACEMENT?

The apostle Paul appeals to five authorities in his ruling on the silence of women in 14:33–40:

(a) ecumenical practice (33b)

(b) the law (34)

(c) a command of the Lord (37b)

(d) evangelical decorum (40)

When 14:34,35 is removed from its traditional placement, his appeals to ecumenical practice and a command of the Lord is also removed.

Those who support the ordination of women often discount 14:34,35 as a later Judaic, proto-Catholic or misogynist interpolation. Those who orig-inally removed 14:34,35 from its traditional placement may have regarded 14:34,35 as a similar interpolation.

With this in mind, we will attempt to construct a profile of the person or persons who may have been responsible for removing 14:34,35 from its original, traditional placement.

(a) Since the apostle Paul wrote 1 Corinthians in AD 55 or AD 56 near the end of his stay in Ephesus (Pfitzner: 18), and the earliest record of the variant placement is Ambrosiaster around AD 375, the exciser probably lived between AD 56 and AD 375.

(b) Because of the Greek-Latin bilingual and Latin textual evidence, he may have influenced the Old Latin textual tradition.

(c) Similarly, he probably lived and worked within Rome or Western Europe.

(d) He was interested in the recording and editing of the Pauline epistles.

(e) He opposed the exclusion of women from the ordained ministry and sought to reverse the traditional ecclesiastical practice of his day.

(f) He may well have judged that tradition and practice as apostate.

(g) He rejected the law of Moses in the Old Testament.

(h) He may well have dissociated the message and ministry of Jesus and his apostle Paul from the Old Testament entirely.

# IV. A Culprit?

In the early church one man exerted enormous influence on the emerging texts of the New Testament. The formal recognition of a fixed list, or canon, of New Testament writings can be dated about the middle of the second century. The first person to draft one, so far as surviving evidence shows, was Marcion.

Marcion was a native of Sinope in Pontus who came to Rome shortly before AD 140. He was a member of an orthodox community until his excommunication from the Catholic Church in Rome in AD 144 (Blackman: 2,3). As Marcion was unable to convert the Catholic Church to his philosophy, he began his own church (Blackman: 2). Although none of his writings has survived, we are able to reconstruct large portions of his *Antithesis* from the extensive quotations in Tertullian's *Against Marcion*, as well as from other church fathers such as Ireneaus.

Marcion did not avail himself of the allegorical method of exegesis current in the church of his day. Subsequently he found the Old Testament impossible to reconcile with the gospel of Christ. From this impasse Marcion held that there must be two Gods, a lower Demiurge who created the universe (ie, the God of Judaism) and the supreme God made known for the first time in Christ (Kelly: 57). This dualism led Marcion to reject the Old Testament. Furthermore, Marcion canonised an alternative set of Scripture for use in his church. He regarded all Christian writings which seemed in the slightest way infected with a Jewish outlook as suspect (Kelly: 57; Dunbar: 331).

The apostle Paul, the champion of the gospel against the law, was Marcion's hero. Marcion believed that all the original apostles had fallen away from the truth revealed in Jesus. Only Paul represented Jesus' teaching in its pure form (Dunbar: 331).

Marcion set about restoring the true text of the New Testament. The letter to the Galatians became Marcion's hermeneutical principle for understanding Paul (Hauke: 392; cf Habel and Wurst: 130). He was convinced that in the Pauline epistles there were interpolations and alterations by Judaising interests anxious to make the apostle say that the Old Testament contained divine revelation (Chadwick: 40). Tertullian (Stevenson: 181) described Marcion's approach to text criticism by saying, '[he] used the knife, not the pen'. Ireneaus writes of Marcion:

> He mutilates the Gospel which is according to Luke . . . He dismembered the epistles of Paul removing . . . also those passages from the prophetic writings which the apostle quotes in order to teach us that they announced beforehand the coming of the Lord. (Steveson: 97)

Scholars agree that Marcion used the Western type text, influencing it and the Old Latin tradition along the way. The degree of Marcion's influence on these texts, however, remains a subject of dispute. The Marcionite canon consisted of the ten letters of the *Apostles* (ie, the Pauline corpus minus the Pastoral Epistles) and the *Gospel*, an edited version of Luke.

Marcion's theology has been described as a combination of Christianity and Syrian gnosis (Dunbar: 331). Since Marcion rejected the inferior God of Creation, he rejected the created orders also. Marcion rejected marriage and taught a strict asceticism. For Marcion, the lesser God devised the humiliating method of sexual reproduction, the discomfort of pregnancy, and the pains of childbirth, the mere contemplation of which filled Marcion with nausea (Chadwick: 39). A Marcionite innovation was the permission given to women to hold office in the church, to teach and to baptise (Blackman: 5; Stevenson: 154, 182, 184). Marcion claimed that the Holy Spirit bestows his various gifts on each one, without taking notice of pre-existing differences (Hauke: 391, cf Habel and Wurst: 132). For Marcion this included the gifting of the Holy Spirit as the only qualification for the public ministry.

For Marcion, the message of 1 Corinthians 14:33–40 would have contained all the hallmarks of interpolation and alteration by the Judaising elements:

(a) women were portrayed as in subjection to their husbands;

(b) they were made to be silent in the church in keeping with the Catholic ('apostate') practice of his day;

(c) the text that sanctioned this made its appeal through the law and a command of the Lord.

Clearly, Marcion had motive, opportunity and an established *modus operandi* to excise this offensive passage and reclaim, what was for him, the pure text of St Paul.

## V. CONCLUSION

The textual evidence does not support the theory that the apostle's prohibition on women speaking in the church was a marginal note that was incorporated into the text by a copyist who agreed with its ruling (*contra* Lockwood: 33).

The textual evidence supports a conclusion that Paul's prohibition was excised from its original placement by a person(s) who disagreed with his ruling. In addition:

(a) The textual evidence strongly supports that the Western-type text tradition which places 14:34,35 after 14:40 is dependent on one, no longer extant, variant text.

(b) The textual evidence gives little support either to its original placement after 14:40 or to its interpolation into the text by a later scribe under the influence of 1 Timothy 2:12.

(c) 1 Corinthians was part of Marcion's canon. The Pastoral epistles, which includes 1 Timothy, were not. 1 Timothy 2:12, which supports the apostle's teaching in 14:34,35, is free from any textual variants.

(d) It is reasonable to suggest that the original editor who excised from 1 Corinthians the apostle's prohibition of women speaking in the chuch was Marcion or Marcionite.

(e) Likewise, it is reasonable to see the variant placement of 14:34,35 as evidence of an attempt to again include Paul's teaching concerning women into an appropriate position within the context of 14:33–40 (Metzger: 565).

The Lutheran Church of Australia publicly teaches that the rule of the apostle excludes the possibility of women acting as pastors and shepherds of congregations (*DSTO* F2.) There is extensive textual evidence that requires the LCA to continue to apply 1 Corinthians 14:34,35 in any discussion on the ordination of women. The text is part of Paul's apostolic teaching for the church: *as in all the congregations of the saints* (1 Cor 14:33b [NIV]).

REFERENCES

Blackmann, E.C.
1948    *Marcion and his Influence*, SPCK, London.

Carson, D.A.
1988    *Showing the Spirit*, Lancer, Homebush West.

Chadwick, Henry
1967    *The Early Church*, Penguin Books, Harmondsworth.

Clabeaux, John J.
1989    'A Lost Edition of the Letters of Paul: A Reassessment of the Text of the Pauline Corpus Attested by Marcion', *The Catholic Biblical Quarterly* Monograph Series 21, The Catholic Biblical Association of America, Washington.

Conzelmann, Hans
1975    *1 Corinthians*, Fortress, Philadelphia.

Dunbar, David G.
1986    'The Biblical Canon', in *Hermeneutics, Authority and Canon*, ed. D.A. Carson and John D. Woodbridge, InterVarsity, Leicester, 295–360.

Habel, Norman and Shirley Wurst
1994    'The Gospel and Women in Ministry', *Lutheran Theological Journal* 28/3, 129–134.

Hauke, Manfred
1988    *Women in the Priesthood. A Systematic Analysis in the Light of the Order of Creation and Redemption*, Ignatius Press, San Francisco.

Kelly, J.N.D.
1958    *Early Christian Doctrine*, A & C Black, London.

Kleinig, John W.
1995a   'Scripture and the Exclusion of Women from the Pastorate (I)', *Lutheran Theological Journal*, 29/2 74–81.

1995b   'Scripture and the Exclusion of Women from the Pastorate (II)', *Lutheran Theological Journal*, 29/3 123–129.

Lockwood, Peter F.
1996    'Does 1 Corinthians 14:34,35 Exclude Women from the Pastoral Office?' *Lutheran Theological Journal*, 30/1, 30–38.

Metzger, Bruce
1971    *A Textual Commentary on the Greek New Testament*, UBS, Stuttgart.

Pfitzner, Victor C.
1982    *First Corinthians*, Lutheran Publishing House, Adelaide.

Stevenson, J. (ed)
1957    *A New Eusebius*, SPCK, London

Wire, Antoinette Clark
1990    *The Corinthian Women Prophets*, Fortress, Minneapolis

# Ordained Proclaimers or Quiet Learners?

## Women in Worship in Light of 1 Timothy 2

### Charles A. Gieschen

Few biblical texts present more poignant guidance to those concerned about women's roles in the worship life of the Christian Church than the second chapter of 1 Timothy.[1] This chapter has become one of the key "battle-grounds" in the Church when decisions concerning women have been considered—whether it is granting women suffrage in the congregation voters' assembly, having women serve as lectors in public worship, or ordaining women into the pastoral office. This chapter contains, among other things, the stark apostolic command: "I do not permit a woman to teach or to exercise authority over a man, but [I want her] to keep quiet" (2:12).[2] Many Christians of the twenty-first century see this command as insensitive—at the least—and even discriminatory, including more than a few pastors.[3]

There are a least three reasons why this biblical command was overrun in the course of the past century by Christians who espoused women's ordination. First, biblical authority has eroded within many parts of the Church to

---

1   This is widely recognized; see especially the essays in *Women in the Church: A Fresh Analysis of 1 Timothy 2:9–15*, ed. A. J. Köstenberger, T. R. Schreiner, and H. S. Baldwin (Grand Rapids: Baker, 1995). This volume is a very helpful resource in studying current evangelical scholarship on 1 Timothy 2. See also the essays in *Recovering Biblical Manhood and Womanhood: A Response to Evangelical Feminism*, ed. J. Piper and W. Grudem (Wheaton: Crossway, 1991). I was asked to address this text and topic for the 1999 Annual Theological Convocation of the Pacific Southwest District of The Lutheran Church—Missouri Synod. This article is a slightly revised form of that paper.

2   All translations of biblical texts are my own. The other biblical text that issues a similar command is 1 Cor. 14:33b–40, as discussed below.

3   The prevalence of this attitude toward 1 Timothy 2 is apparent from the fact that many Christian denominations began ordaining women in the twentieth century, despite this biblical mandate.

the point where the demands of biblical texts are simply not heeded. This erosion of biblical authority within the Church has been aided by the historical-critical work of biblical scholars that has called historical claims and authorship into question. More specifically, many New Testament scholars have concluded that the Pastoral Epistles were not written by Paul and even are at odds with some Pauline teaching; therefore, 1 Timothy is sometimes dismissed as nonapostolic and marginalized as less authoritative for the life of the Church.[4] This situation has led some Christians to view commands such as this one as an expression of human authority and nonbinding. Second, some who respect the authority of this Epistle as part of the Christian canon, or even accept Pauline authorship of the Pastoral Epistles, still view this command as "culturally conditioned" or a "contingent" command.[5] This means that they understand this command to be reflecting a first-century bias toward women or a command limited to this particular situation that is not applicable to the Church of every locale and era. Third, and closely related, feminism had a profound impact on the Western world, including much of the Christian Church, in the nineteenth and twentieth centuries.[6] It is clear that the Church has often conformed to feminist perspectives on gender and family within Western culture rather than transforming them. A feminist approach to texts such as 1 Timothy 2 recognizes their claims and then judges these claims to be patriarchal and wrong, with the result that the texts are deconstructed and their teaching is replaced by the "enlightened" feminist perspective on the issues addressed by the texts.[7]

This study will re-examine the significance of 1 Timothy 2 for understanding women's roles in Christian worship. It will demonstrate that 1 Tim. 2:8–15 provides legitimate and applicable guidance for women's roles in the Church's worship, including the prohibition of women's ordination, which is congruent with the wider revelation of God in the Holy Scriptures.

---

4  For example, Robin Scroggs, "Paul and the Eschatological Women," *Journal of the American Academy of Religion* 40 (1972): 283–303. A similar thing is sometimes done with 1 Corinthians by pitting 11:2–16 (women engaged in prophecy) against 14:34–35 (women are to be quiet) and dismissing the latter text as a later non-Pauline gloss; see the critique by Gregory J. Lockwood, *1 Corinthians*, Concordia Commentary (St. Louis: Concordia, 2000), 527–34.

5  For example, David Scholer, "1 Timothy 2:9–15 and the Place of Women in the Church's Ministry," in *Women, Authority and the Bible*, ed. Alvera Mickelsen (Downers Grove: InterVarsity, 1986), 193–219.

6  There is certainly a genealogical relationship between feminism in wider Western culture at the start of the twentieth century and the push for women's ordination in the Church; see Mary A. Kassian, *The Feminist Gospel: The Movement to Unite Feminism with the Church* (Wheaton: Crossway, 1992).

7  For example, Elizabeth Schüssler Fiorenza, *In Memory of Her: A Feminist Theological Reconstruction of Christian Origins* (New York: Crossroad, 1983).

# I. INTERPRETATIVE FOUNDATIONS

Before commencing an exegesis of 1 Tim. 2:8–15, it is important to state the basic convictions about 1 Timothy and the hermeneutical task that undergird this study, since these convictions have a profound impact on the process of interpreting the text. First, I am convinced that the author of this chapter, as the Epistle itself claims, is the apostle Paul.[8] This means that I consider this letter to have the same apostolic authority as Paul's other letters and that it should be interpreted in light of them. Therefore, unlike some critical scholars, the content of this Epistle will not be discounted or dismissed as being post-apostolic or at odds with "true" Pauline theology.[9] This is especially visible in attempts to trump the so-called "pseudo-Pauline" stress on the order of creation in 1 Tim. 2:13 with the so-called "authentic Pauline" emphasis on the order of redemption in Gal. 3:28: "there is neither male nor female, for you are all one in Christ Jesus."[10] Equality before God does not erase created gender distinctions between male and female.

Second, and in line with this understanding of apostolic authorship and authority, I regard this Epistle to be the Word of God; therefore it is a revelation of God's will that is normative for the Church's doctrine and practice. As such, I do not regard 1 Timothy 2 as some isolated one-of-a-kind "proof text" that reflects the flawed ideology and bias of some late first-century Christians or as a text that is addressed to such a specific situation and is so culturally conditioned that it has little to say to the wider Church of the first century or the Church today. I regard 1 Timothy 2 as a text that reveals truth in continuity with the broader truth of God's revelatory and salvific deeds and words throughout history, especially the revelation of God in our Lord Jesus Christ. Thus, though 1 Timothy is addressed to Timothy and the Church in a particular historical context, its content is also sufficiently general that it can be understood and applied in other contexts. Note what Paul himself says in 1 Tim. 3:14–15: "I hope to come to you soon, but I am writing these instructions to you so that, if I am delayed, you may know how one ought to behave in the household of God, which is the church of the living God, the pillar and bulwark of truth."

This understanding of the authority of the Scriptures is not shared by all who respect the Bible as the Word of God. For example, David Scholer, an

---

8   See the defense of Pauline authorship in Donald Guthrie, *New Testament Introduction*, rev. ed. (Downers Grove: InterVarsity, 1990), 607–49.

9   See esp. Scoggs, "Paul and the Eschatological Women," 283–303. For a more moderate example, see Jouette M. Bassler, *1 Timothy 2 Timothy Titus*, Abingdon NT Commentaries (Nashville: Abingdon, 1996).

10  See Arland J. Hultgren, *I–II Timothy, Titus*, Augsburg Commentary on the NT (Minneapolis: Augsburg, 1984), 67–68.

evangelical scholar who expresses a high regard for the Scriptures, emphasizes that 1 Timothy is "an occasional ad hoc letter directed specifically towards enabling Timothy and the church to avoid and combat the false teachers and teaching at Ephesus."[11] Although there is an inherent danger in labeling any apostolic letter as "ad hoc," I certainly agree that this letter is addressed to specific situations in the Church. He goes on to state that what is said about women in the worship service is not normative for the wider Church because these instructions are conditioned by the "cultural settings of the first century A.D., which assumed male dominance and a belief in women's subordination and inferiority."[12] Scholer concludes that these "ad hoc instructions" were directed solely against women who "are abusing the normal opportunities women had within the church to teach and exercise authority."[13] If this was the case, one would think that the apostle Paul would have made this explicit in the text in order that such commands would not be misunderstood by the various congregations whom the apostle knew would come to read them.[14] The point is simply this: Although this chapter is addressed to a specific historical context, as the Word of God it reveals unchanging and significant truth for the life of the Church (1 Thess. 2:13). To use terms coined by J. Christiann Beker, Paul's message has "coherence" as it is proclaimed in "contingent" circumstances.[15] Some scholars overemphasize that Paul's commands are contingent to particular circumstances; I am aware of these contingent circumstances but will argue that these commands also cohere with his theology and, most important, with the theology of the rest of the Scriptures.

My third introductory point is this: I am convinced that a vital part of the interpretative process is to identify the "implied reader" of this document and then seek to understand the text as this implied reader.[16] James Voelz describes the importance of this relationship between the "implied reader" and the interpreter in this manner:

---

11  Scholer, "1 Timothy 2:9–15 and the Place of Women," 200.

12  Scholer, "1 Timothy 2:9–15 and the Place of Women," 202. The accuracy of this rather typical characterization of first-century Greco-Roman society as supporting "male dominance and a belief in women's subordination and inferiority" is questionable; see esp. S. M. Baugh, "A Foreign World: Ephesus in the First Century," in *Women in the Church: A Fresh Analysis of 1 Timothy 2:9–15*, ed. A. J. Köstenberger, T. R. Schreiner, and H. S. Baldwin (Grand Rapids: Baker, 1995), 13–52.

13  Scholer, "1 Timothy 2:9–15 and the Place of Women," 203.

14  Although addressing a particular historical context, Paul himself states in 1 Tim. 2:9 that there is a wider context for his instructions: "I desire that *in every place . . .*"

15  *Paul the Apostle* (Philadelphia: Fortress, 1980), 11–19.

16  See James W. Voelz, *What Does This Mean? Principles of Biblical Interpretation in the Postmodern World*, 2nd ed. (St. Louis: Concordia, 1997), 218–29.

This implied reader is a person, a receptor, with that knowledge, those abilities, that competency, which enables him to "actualize" the text. He is a conception of the author—it is for him which the author writes (though he in no actual fact corresponds to any actual reader of the text). Who, then, is a valid interpreter of the text? It is he who conforms to the expectations of the author. It is he who conforms himself to the given text's assumptions. It is he who becomes the implied reader—and only such a one—of a given text. Which means that an "objective" reading of a text is not only impossible; it is not to be desired.[17]

Although 1 Timothy is addressed to Timothy (1 Tim. 1:2), it was also intended to be shared with the Church, including congregations other than those in Ephesus (1 Tim. 4:6; cf. 3:14–15). Therefore, the "implied reader" is not simply Timothy, but Timothy and the first-century members of Christian congregations with whom he was working, primarily in Asia Minor.[18] It must be our endeavor as interpreters to share—as much as is possible—the beliefs, knowledge, experiences, and attitudes of this "implied reader" as we seek to interpret this text.

The modern study of hermeneutics has become increasingly aware of the huge role that the reader plays in the communication process.[19] The reader becomes, in effect, a "second text" of beliefs, knowledge, experiences, attitudes, and the like that is used to understand the text to be read.[20] Some hermeneutical approaches, however, have little concern for the "implied reader"; rather, they emphasize that the modern reader should, indeed must, give meaning to the text that may be quite different from the meaning intended by the author for the implied reader. For example, it was already noted above that a feminist approach to 1 Timothy 2 will usually admit that the text does say something about the limits of women's roles in the Church to its implied reader, but such assertions are judged to be patriarchal and wrong by the modern reader.[21]

---

17  Voelz, *What Does This Mean?* 219.

18  Recent scholarship has often focused too narrowly on the Christians at Ephesus as those whom Paul is addressing with the content of 1–2 Timothy. They then attempt to reconstruct the historical situation that this Epistle is addressing from both the content of this Epistle and the historical/archaeological evidence of this city. See esp. Baugh, "A Foreign World," 13–52.

19  See esp. the work of Anthony C. Thiselton, *The Two Horizons: New Testament Hermeneutics and Philosophical Description* (Grand Rapids: Eerdmans, 1980); *New Horizons in Hermeneutics: The Theory and Practice of Transforming Biblical Reading* (Grand Rapids: Zondervan, 1992); and *Interpreting God and the Post-Modern Self: On Meaning, Manipulation and Promise* (Grand Rapids: Eerdmans, 1995).

20  Voelz, *What Does This Mean?* 209.

21  For a survey of feminist hermeneutical approaches and relevant bibliography, see Thiselton, *New Horizons*, esp. 430–62. Thiselton emphasizes the relationship between liberation and feminist hermeneutics.

Much more subtle are those approaches that claim a high respect for the text but are driven by ideological concerns that cause them to read the text and any other evidence in a manner that supports their concerns.[22] In both examples, the modern reader reigns supreme in the hermeneutical process.

These introductory remarks have focused on the basic communication process: the author, the text, and the implied reader. First Timothy 2, like the rest of the Holy Scriptures, does not have an ever-changing "meaning" in different generations, as it seems to be the case if one examines the multifarious secondary literature produced on this text. The text has a consistent meaning; it is the applications of the text that are multiple and open to change.[23] For example, I could take the consistent meaning of this chapter and apply it one way to a denomination considering women's ordination, but I could take that same meaning and apply it in a much different manner during a congregational study of biblical roles in Christian marriage. Therefore, Parts II–VII of this study will present the consistent meaning of this chapter, and Part VIII will apply this meaning to the life of the· Church, especially to the issue of women's ordination.

## II. THE CONTEXT, TEXT, AND CENTRAL QUESTIONS

The broader context of 1 Timothy 2 contains warnings of false teaching (chapter 1) and the qualifications for those who hold particular offices in the congregation (chapter 3). After a brief greeting, Paul does not write a thanksgiving as is typical in many of his letters but moves directly to the subject of false teaching. Although elaborate and very specific historical reconstructions have been offered by scholars for the situation that Paul is addressing, the general nature of much of the content of this letter renders many of these reconstructions problematic.[24] After addressing false teaching and before discussing congregational offices, Paul turns his attention to matters of public worship. This immediate context for all of 1 Timothy 2 is signaled with the opening sentence his exhortations: "First of all I urge that supplications, prayers, intercessions and thanksgivings be made for all men, for kings and all who are in high positions, that we may lead a quiet and peaceable life" (1 Tim. 2:1). This is liturgical language directed to the life of the Church in public

---

22  For example, see Gretchen Hull, *Equal to Serve: Women and Men in the Church and Home* (Old Tappen, NJ: Revell, 1987).

23  See the discussion of application in Voelz, *What Does This Mean?* 322–41.

24  See analysis and relevant research in Thomas R. Schreiner, "An Interpretation of 1 Timothy 2:9–15: A Dialogue with Scholarship," in *Women in the Church: A Fresh Analysis of 1 Timothy 2:9–15*, ed. A. J. Köstenberger, T. R. Schreiner, and H. S. Baldwin (Grand Rapids: Baker, 1995), 107–14.

worship. Therefore, the rest of chapter two should be understood as directed toward matters of public worship.

The exegesis of this chapter is based upon the Greek text provided below that is followed by a translation.[25] Because women are not mentioned until verse 9, this study will focus primarily on 2:8–15:

[8] Βούλομαι οὖν προσεύχεσθαι τοὺς ἄνδρὰς ἐν παντὶ τόπῳ ἐπαίροντας ὁσίους χεῖρας χωρὶς ὀργῆς καὶ διαλογισμοῦ. [9] Ὡσαύτως [καὶ] γυναῖκας ἐν καταστολῇ κοσμίῳ μετὰ αἰδοῦς καὶ σωφροσύνης κοσμεῖν ἑαυτάς μὴ ἐν πλέγμασιν καῖ χρυσίῳ ἢ μαργαρίταις ἢ ἱματισμῷ πολυτελεῖ, [10] ἀλλ' ὃ πρέπει γυναιξὶν ἐπαγγελλομέναις θεοσέβειαν, δι' ἔργων ἀγαθῶν. [11] Γυνὴ ἐν ἡσυχίᾳ μανθανέτω ἐν πάσῃ ὑποταγῇ· [12] διδάσκειν δὲ γυναικὶ οὐκ ἐπιτρέπω οὐδὲ αὐθεντεῖν ἀνδρός, ἀλλ' εἶναι ἐν ἡσυχίᾳ. [13] Ἀδὰμ γὰρ πρῶτος ἐπλάσθη, εἶτα Εὔα. [14] καὶ Ἀδὰμ οὐκ ἠπατήθη, ἡ δὲ γυνὴ ἐξαπατηθεῖσα ἐν παραβάσει γέγονεν· [15] σωθήσεται δὲ διὰ τῆς τεκνογονίας, ἐὰν μείνωσιν ἐν πίστει καὶ ἀγάπῃ καὶ ἁγιασμῷ μετὰ σωφροσύνης·

[8] Therefore, I want the men in every place to pray, lifting holy hands without anger or strife; [9] likewise [in every place, I want] women to dress themselves in appropriate attire with modesty and good judgment, not with braided hair or gold or pearls or costly clothes, [10] but with what is fitting for women who profess worship of God: with good deeds. [11] Let a woman learn in quietness with all submissiveness. [12] I [also] neither permit a woman to teach, nor [do I permit a woman] to exercise authority over a man, but [I want her] to keep quiet. [13] For Adam was formed first, then Eve; [14] and Adam was not deceived [first], but the woman was deceived [first] and became a transgressor [before Adam]. [15] Yet she [woman] will be "saved" through the [God-ordained role of] childbearing, if they [women] remain in faith and love, and holiness, with modesty.

Five primary questions arise from this text that must be addressed in the exegesis below. First, what is the significance of Paul's discussion of women's attire? Second, how are we to understand Paul's command that a woman "learn in quietness"? Third, what is the meaning of the command that "a woman is not to teach, nor to exercise authority over a man"? Fourth, why is the order of creation the basis of this command that women are not to teach or exercise authority over men? And fifth, what is the relationship between childbearing and salvation?

---

25  The Greek text is from Nestle-Aland, *Novum Testamentum Graece*, 27th ed. (Stuttgart: Deutsche Bibelgesellschaft, 1993).

## III. The Focus on Women in Worship

Our first question concerns the significance of Paul's discussion of women's attire. Paul placed his instructions about women's attire in 1 Tim. 2:9–10 in a parallel construction with his instruction about men praying in 2:8.[26] He had already urged that supplications, prayers, intercessions, and thanksgivings be made for all men in 1 Tim. 2:1. In light of this dictum for public worship (see οὖν in v. 8), he now adds these parallel exhortations using two infinitives: "I want *men* (ἄνδρας) in every place *to pray* (προσεύχεσθαι), lifting holy hands without anger or quarreling; likewise [in every place, I want] *women* (γυναῖκας) *to dress* (κοσμεῖν) themselves in appropriate attire with modesty and good judgment, not with braided hair or gold or pearls or costly clothes." The "in every place" (ἐν παντὶ τόπῳ) is significant for understanding the wide context and broad application of this apostolic guidance. This is probably a reference to the various meeting places of public worship, namely house churches.[27] It communicates the sense that these convictions about worship are not restricted to one worshiping congregation or even a few congregations but have a broader application to the worship services of the wider Church. Paul's statement of his desire with specific details indicates that the situation was probably not always as he wanted it to be in the congregations who were to hear this letter, as well as in wider Christendom: some men had been quarreling and angry with one another in worship, while some women were coming to worship with braided hair, gold, pearls, and costly clothing.[28] Both of these situations probably caused disruptions and distractions in worship services. The attire of women that is outlined here suggests that 1 Tim. 2:9–10 form a polemic against an ostentatious or seductive appearance in worship.[29]

---

26 Paul is surely speaking broadly of men and women here with the use of the terms ἄνδρας and γυναῖκας, not only husbands and wives in the context of their homes as argued by Gordon P. Hugenberger, "Women in Church Office: Hermeneutics or Exegesis? A Survey of Approaches to 1 Tim 2:8–15," *JETS* 35 (1992): 341–60. For example, Paul's concern about adornment would not be limited to *married* women; see also the critique by Schreiner, "An Interpretation of 1 Timothy 2:9–15," 115–16.

27 George W. Knight III, *The Pastoral Epistles*, NIGTC (Grand Rapids: Eerdmans, 1992), 128. J. M. Holmes oddly argues that these commands are not focused on women in worship but that the author seeks to regulate everyday behavior of women; see *Text in a Whirlwind: A Critique of Four Exegetical Devices at 1 Timothy 2.9–15*, JSNTSup 196 (Sheffield: Sheffield Academic Press, 2000).

28 The problems Paul is facing are often reflected in the content of his Epistles. The process of reading the historical situation that the Epistles are addressing out of the text is sometimes referred to as "mirror reading"; see esp. John M. G. Barclay, "Mirror-Reading a Polemical Letter: Galatians as a Test Case," *Journal for the Study of the New Testament* 31 (1987): 73–93. The accuracy of such readings, however, is largely dependent on the specificity of the Epistle in reflecting the position of the opponents that Paul is combating.

29 Schreiner, "An Interpretation of 1 Timothy 2:9–15," 119.

The concern for attire voiced here is not unique to Paul but is found in other early Christian writings, as well as the literature of the wider Greco-Roman world.[30] First Peter 3:3–5 is especially noteworthy:

> [3] Let not the outward adorning with braiding of hair, decoration of gold, and wearing of fine clothing characterize you, [4] but let it be the hidden person of the heart with the imperishable jewel of a gentle and quiet spirit, that is very precious in God's sight. [5] In like manner the holy women who hoped in God used to adorn themselves and were submissive to their husbands.

Paul desires a different scene for the worship of the Church: Men at peace with one another being active in prayers of the worship service and women whose primary noteworthiness is not visible in attire that calls attention to itself but in good deeds. These verses should not be understood as prohibiting women from participating in worship by praying since 1 Tim. 2:8 speaks only of men praying. First Corinthians 11:5 makes it clear that Paul encouraged women at Corinth to participate in prayer as long as they were not rejecting the basic authority structure of creation. Such liturgical participation in worship was probably done in unison with other worshipers; it was probably not seen as the "teaching" that Paul prohibits in 1 Tim. 2:12.

Therefore, is Paul setting forth a command concerning women's attire that stands for all time and contexts, or is this command contingent on particular "culturally conditioned" circumstances? One could answer "yes" to both of these questions, but not a simple "yes." In a manner similar to the head coverings discussed in 1 Corinthians 11, it is the basic principle behind the command that is enduring, though some of the details of this command still speak pointedly to our time and culture.[31] Ostentatious or seductive

---

30 See the textual evidence, not the conclusions, in David Scholer, "Women's Adornment: Some Historical and Hermeneutical Observations on the New Testament Passages," *Daughters of Sarah* 6, no. 1 (January/February 1980): 3–6; see also the critique of Schreiner, "An Interpretation of 1 Timothy 2:9–15," 118–21. For the relationship between this text and contemporary Roman women, see Bruce W. Winter, "The 'New' Roman Wife and 1 Timothy 2:9–15: The Search for a *Sitz Im Leben*," *Tyndale Bulletin* 51 (2000): 285–94.

31 The issue of head coverings for women primarily grows out of a problem with the rejection of the authority of the husband that certain hairstyles exhibited; see James B. Hurley, "Did Paul Require Veils or the Silence of Women? A Consideration of I Cor. 11:2–16 and I Cor. 14:33B–36," *Westminster Theological Journal* 35 (1973): 190–220. Although the mandate for head coverings is not operative in much of the church today, the principle behind head coverings—namely, authority/headship—should remain operative in the Christian Church and family today. For a discussion of the distinction between assertions that address conduct that is a "manifestation" of the human condition and those that address conduct that is essentially "symptomatic" of the human condition, see Voelz, *What Does This Mean?* 326–28. For a further exegesis of this text, see Lockwood, *1 Corinthians*, 359–68.

appearance is discouraged in worship with this command. This command continues to stand "in principle," though braiding of hair or wearing of some gold or pearls may not be ostentatious or seductive in many modern contexts. This command still speaks to situations where outward appearance is reflecting rejection of divinely instituted authority, whether it be that of God, husband, or parent. Furthermore, Paul's encouragement to be dressed with "good deeds" (1 Tim. 2:10) also has obvious ongoing significance for the Church.

## IV. The Posture of Women in Christian Worship

The second question being addressed by this study concerns how we are to understand Paul's imperative that "a woman learn in quietness with all submissiveness." Before examining the prepositional phrases that nuance this command, it is important to notice that this imperative affirms the role of women as learners in the worship service. This text is not trying to keep women spiritually shackled because of the lack of education or participation in worship. Paul makes it clear that women are engaged in learning (μανθανέτω). He is not attempting to eliminate this learning.

The real purpose of this exhortation is to qualify the manner or mode of learning in public worship for women.[32] Paul does this with the prepositional phrases that specify the circumstances of the learning: ἐν ἡσυχίᾳ ("in quietness") and ἐν πάσῃ ὑποταγῇ ("in all submission"). One should not understand ἐν ἡσυχίᾳ as advocating that women be completely "silent" and say nothing in worship, much less in other congregational contexts.[33] With this in mind, ἐν ἡσυχίᾳ has been translated more understandably as "in quietness." The context of the command, however, is learning in worship. The phrase ἀλλ᾽ εἶναι ἐν ἡσυχίᾳ ("but to be quiet") in 1 Tim. 2:12 makes it clear that women are not to be in a verbal *teaching* mode during the service, but rather they are to be in a "quiet" *learning* mode. This command suggests that Paul had experienced some problems with women setting aside the authority structure within the Church during the learning process and even assuming the teaching role in worship on occasion.[34] The suggestion of some interpreters that this imperative as well as the command "I permit no woman to teach"

32  Schreiner, "An Interpretation of 1 Timothy 2:9–15," 122.

33  Schreiner, "An Interpretation of 1 Timothy 2:9–15," 123–24; see also Lockwood, *1 Corinthians*, 527–34.

34  See relevant bibliography in Schreiner, "An Interpretation of 1 Timothy 2:9–15," 127 n. 97. Paul's concern for the authority structure of the Christian family and Church is visible elsewhere, including 1 Corinthians 11.

is directed exclusively toward women who are uneducated is another example of constructing a context that is not apparent from the text.[35]

The prepositional phrase "in all submission" (ἐν πάσῃ ὑποταγῇ) is more difficult to understand. The referent question is important: Submission *to what* or *to whom?* The context helps a great deal in determining the referent. Thomas Schreiner has made the following perceptive observations:

> Verses 11 and 12 constitute an inclusio; verse 11 begins with "in silence" and verse 12 concludes "in silence." The permission for women to "learn" is contrasted with the proscription for them "to teach," while "all submissiveness" is paired with "not exercising authority over a man." The submission in view, then, is likely to be men, since verse 12 bans women from exercising authority over men. Yet the context of verse 12 suggests that the submission of all women to all men is not in view, for not all men taught and had authority when the church was gathered. Thus, we should not separate submission from what is taught from submission to those who taught it. Women were to learn with entire submissiveness from the men who had authority in the church and manifested that authority through their teaching.[36]

Although this command reinforces the fact that women are and should be actively learning in public worship, it *primarily* emphasizes that the manner of such learning is to be one of quiet listening in submission to the men who are the authoritative teachers of the congregation.

Moreover, this command and its application to the wider Church is congruent with Paul's teaching in 1 Corinthians. Gregory Lockwood argues persuasively that 1 Cor. 11:2–16 reflects Paul's gentle "pastoral" approach toward the problematic situation of women prophesying and speaking in tongues during worship. Then 1 Cor. 14:33b–38 makes explicit the command that women are not to be engaged in authoritative speaking (speaking in tongues, prophesying, or preaching/teaching) in a worship service.[37] Paul's instruction in 1 Cor. 14:33b–36, which he calls "the Lord's command" (14:37), is very close to 1 Tim. 2:11–12:

> [33b] As in all the churches of the saints, [34] let the women stay silent in the churches [αἱ γυναῖκες ἐν ταῖς ἐκκλησίαις σιγάτωσαν]. For it is not permitted for them to speak, but they should be subordinate, as the Law also says. [35] If they wish to learn something, let them ask their own husbands at home. [36] For it is shameful for a woman to speak in church.

---

35 For example, Bilezikian, *Beyond Sex Roles*, 179. See the critique by Schreiner, "An Interpretation of 1 Timothy 2:9–15," 121–23.

36 Schreiner, "An Interpretation of 1 Timothy 2:9–15," 124.

37 See discussion of the interrelationship between 1 Cor. 11:2–16 and 14:33b–38 in Lockwood, *1 Corinthians*, 527–34.

Finally, it should be noted that this submissive posture in worship that is commanded is theologically related to the posture of a Christian wife toward her husband who is to be her head, even as Christ is head of the Church.[38] The possession of authority in the Church is, for Paul, directly related to Christian marriage since marriage is to be a reflection of the Church's union with Christ.

## V. THE COMMAND NOT TO TEACH OR EXERCISE AUTHORITY OVER MEN

Our third question focuses on the meaning of the command that a woman is not to teach or exercise authority over a man. Paul sets forth this blunt command in 1 Tim. 2:12: "I do not permit a woman to teach or to exercise authority over a man, but to be quiet" (διδάσκειν δὲ γυναικὶ οὐκ ἐπιτρέπω οὐδὲ αὐθεντεῖν ἀνδρός, ἀλλ᾿ εἶναι ἐν ἡσυχίᾳ). Questions concerning the infinitives διδάσκειν and αὐθεντεῖν need to be answered before discussing the wider scope of this verse.

Let us begin with διδάσκειν ("to teach"). What is the content of this teaching and who is the object of this teaching? It is clear from the content of the Pastoral Epistles as well as the worship context of this pericope that the "teaching" here is "the authoritative and public transmission of tradition about Christ and the Scriptures."[39] The object of the teaching is men since both infinitives have ἀνδρός ("a man") as their object. Teaching by women of women and children is certainly not prohibited here, but such teaching also would be seen as being done under the authority of the bishops and elders of the congregation. The first part of this phrase, therefore, is expressing this meaning: "I do not permit a woman to engage in the authoritative and public transmission of tradition about Christ and the Scriptures to men." This command clearly prohibits woman from holding the pastoral office since authoritative and public teaching about Christ is central to this office.[40]

There have also been problems with understanding both the verb αὐθεντέω in its infinitive form as well as the syntax of the phrase οὐδὲ [ἐπιτρέπω] αὐθεντεῖν ἀνδρός. The conclusion of scholars who have done extensive study of αὐθεντέω, which only appears here in the New Testament, is that its usage in ancient literature centers around the concept of authority, especially the

---

38  Submission is also characteristic of this relationship; see Eph. 5:21–23 and 1 Peter 3:1–6 (cf. 1 Cor. 11:3).

39  See Schreiner, "An Interpretation of 1 Timothy 2:9–15," 127; cf. 1 Cor. 12:28–29; Eph. 4:11; 1 Tim. 2:7; 2 Tim. 3:16; James 3:1. Concerning the synecdoche ("part for the whole") in this text, see Voelz, *What Does This Mean?* 172.

40  See Augsburg Confession V. Ephesians 4:11 presents the actions of shepherd and teacher as one office: pastors and teachers.

active use of authority.[41] It can be considered part of the semantic domain of
ἐξουσία ("authority"), but with the added nuance of *exercising* authority rather
than *inherently possessing* authority. Therefore, "to exercise authority" in the
sense of ruling, controlling, or dominating without inherently possessing the
authority to do so appears to be what Paul is signifying with his use of this
term. Again the object of the infinitive is ἀνδρός ("a man"). The οὐκ οὐδὲ
("neither, nor") syntax sets these phrases in parallel construction with the
main verb: "I permit a women *neither* to teach, *nor* to exercise authority [she
does not inherently possess], over a man." The final clause, ἀλλ᾿ εἶναι ἐν ἡσυχίᾳ
("but to be quiet"), both reinforces the quiet learning mode emphasized in
2:11 and reaffirms the context for this command is the public proclamation
and teaching of the Church, namely, public worship and related settings of
biblical teaching.

There are three primary ways that interpreters have sought to avoid the
apparent wide scope of this command, namely, that women are not to teach in
the public worship of the Church. Some have argued that it is not an imperative since Paul's use of the present indicative form of ἐπιτρέπω ("I permit")
implies he is giving a temporary instruction or prohibition for the Church.[42]
It must be stated that commands can be rendered without using the imperative mood. One need only to look at Paul's use of βούλομαι ("I want") in
1 Tim. 2:8 (see also 1 Tim. 5:14; Titus 3:8) and his frequent use of παρακαλέω
("I exhort") elsewhere (Rom. 12:1; 1 Cor. 1:10; Eph. 4:1; Phil. 4:2; 2 Tim. 1:6)
to see that a present indicative verb can function as a command. Furthermore,
the use of ἐπιτρέπω ("I permit") elsewhere in the New Testament does not
imply any temporary sense to Paul's command here.[43]

A second approach that is often used to set aside this command is to
emphasize that this command is conditioned by the Greco-Roman and Jewish
social and cultural milieu of the author since, as the argument goes, women
in this milieu simply did not have such roles.[44] Certainly one can selectively
present evidence to support such a position. A more inclusive examination of
the evidence, however, does not indicate the Church was merely conforming

---

41   See esp. H. Scott Baldwin, "A Difficult Word: αὐθεντέω in 1 Timothy 2:12," in *Women in
     the Church: A Fresh Analysis of 1 Timothy 2:9–15*, ed. A. J. Köstenberger, T. R. Schreiner,
     and H. S. Baldwin (Grand Rapids: Baker, 1995), 65–80.

42   For relevant bibliography, see Schreiner, "An Interpretation of 1 Timothy 2:9–15," 125
     n. 91.

43   See 1 Cor. 14:34; 16:7; Heb. 6:3. See also Schreiner, "An Interpretation of 1 Timothy
     2:9–15," 125–26.

44   See James G. Sigountos and Mygren Shank, "Public Roles for Women in the Pauline
     Church: A Reappraisal of the Evidence," *Journal of the Evangelical Theological Society* 26
     (1983): 283–95.

to cultural or societal norms with such a command. William Weinrich offers this balanced assessment:

> Nor, it must be said, did the Church's obedience to the apostolic command reflect an unevangelical accommodation to social and cultural circumstances. In fact, the social and cultural context of early Christianity at times very much favored the introduction of women into teaching, priestly or sacramental offices. In 1st and 2nd century Asia Minor, for example, the social position of women was well developed. There were female physicians, and Ephesus had its female philosophers among the Stoics, Epicureans, and Pythagoreans, who were known to teach, perhaps also publically. Female leadership and priesthood were well-known in the local religious cults of Cybele, Isis, Demeter, and Artemis. In the Greek cults of Demeter and Artemis the holiest places were open only to female priestesses. Generally in the mystery cults women shared "equal rights" with men and women were initiated into all the mysteries. Often women performed the ceremonies and delivered the instructions, even to the male participants. This is, for example, documented in the cult of Dionysius in which all distinctions between men and women, adults and children, freemen and slaves, were broken down.[45]

A third way to set aside this command is to argue that it must be interpreted in light of all the evidence in early Christian texts that demonstrate women were engaged in authoritative teaching in worship. David Scholer, for example, states: "Careful examination of Acts and Paul's letters demonstrates that women engaged in the gospel ministry in Paul's churches *just as men did*."[46] Women were certainly active in the Christian Church; this is visible already in the ministry of Jesus and clearly continues in the life of the Early Church.[47] To assert that the evidence demonstrates that they were the authoritative teachers of the Church or holders of the "pastoral office," however, is very difficult to defend.[48] This teaching, "the authoritative and public transmission of tradition about Christ and the Scriptures" mentioned above, is not to be done

---

45   William Weinrich, " 'It Is Not Given to Women to Teach': A Lex in Search of a Ratio," in *Church and Ministry Today: Three Confessional Lutheran Essays*, ed. John A. Maxfield (St. Louis: Luther Academy, 2001), 174–75. See also Baugh, "A Foreign World," 13–52.

46   Scholer, "1 Timothy 2:9–15 and the Place of Women," 205 (*emphasis added*).

47   See the discussion in "Women in the Church: Scriptural Principles and Ecclesial Practice," a Report of the Commission on Theology and Church Relations of The Lutheran Church—Missouri Synod (September 1985): 5–17.

48   Here one should not only consider the testimony of Holy Scripture but also the overwhelming witness of the Church to this understanding of Scripture; see Weinrich, "It Is Not Given to Women to Teach," 175–182, and esp. William Weinrich, "Women in the Church: Learned and Holy, But Not Pastors," in *Recovering Biblical Manhood and Womanhood: A Response to Evangelical Feminism*, ed. J. Piper and W. Grudem (Wheaton: Crossway, 1991), 263–79.

by women according to 1 Tim. 2:12; rather, such "teaching" is integral to the offices of bishops and elders, as Paul states elsewhere in 1 Timothy (3:2; 5:17). There also appears to be some clear distinctions between such public teaching and prophesying.[49]

The importance of *not* placing this command in the same basket as commands that do have some cultural conditioning, such as women's attire or veils, is expressed very pointedly by Weinrich:

> What therefore seems to be indicated by Paul in these passages is that a woman ought not to take the position of the one who preaches or teaches in an authoritative way, that is, a woman ought not to speak the message of the Church for the Church and unto the Church. Now, the Church relates to such speaking in a vastly more significant way than the Church relates to the wearing of veils. The Church organically relates to such preaching and teaching as that which is created by and through such speaking. In short, the Church is constituted in the hearing of faith which arises out of such authoritative speaking. And this fact, I would like to argue, possesses a substantive and organic relation to the relational order of man and woman given in creation.[50]

# VI. The Order of Creation
## as the Basis for Paul's Command

This analysis by Weinrich is also relevant for addressing the fifth question that concerns the order of creation as the basis of this command. Some have argued that the basis for these commands concerning learning, teaching, and exercising authority was the situation that women at Ephesus were teaching heresy or were simply uneducated.[51] Therefore, the reasoning goes, if we remove these problems in the modern Church by making sure that women are educated and orthodox, then they obviously can teach. Paul, however, does not base his prohibition on such criteria; he simply refers to Genesis 2 as the basis for the prohibition of women's public teaching of men in the the Church: "For Adam was formed first and then Eve; and Adam was not deceived, but the woman was deceived and became a transgressor" (1 Tim. 2:13–14).

It must be emphasized that Paul saw his commands as grounded in the created order; it is not simply as an authority structure set in place after (and because of) the fall into sin or an ad hoc structure that mirrored the

---

49  See analysis and bibliography in Schreiner, "An Interpretation of 1 Timothy 2:9–15," 129.

50  Weinrich, "It Is Not Given to Women to Teach," 190.

51  See discussion in Schreiner, "An Interpretation of 1 Timothy 2:9–15," 128.

contemporary culture in which he lived.[52] Paul grounds his commands in the creation of man and woman: "Adam was formed first, then Eve" (2:13). The Church does not set aside the order of creation; the Church, along with the Christian family, should be one of the (few) places where the order of God's creation is still respected, honored, and upheld. The basis for the setting aside of this created order by some in the Church is almost always the "neither male nor female" of Gal. 3:28, wherein the "order of redemption" is understood to trump and transform the "order of creation" so that the latter ceases to function within the Church.[53] For example, Gilbert Bilekizian of Wheaton College states: "The concept of sex roles is one of those bondages from which the gospel can set us free."[54]

The redemption accomplished by Christ restores the fallen creation, including the gender distinctiveness of male and female; it does not change the basic nature of creation. Weinrich has also reflected on this issue and states:

> From the very beginning of the Bible, therefore, it is evident that male-ness and femaleness are constitutive aspects of the human being. There is no humanity, there is no personhood apart from male humanity, male personhood and female humanity, female personhood. Masculinity and femininity are . . . constitutively connected to the person; they are modes of human being, ways of being human. . . . The gift of the Holy Spirit which we receive when we are united into Christ does not, as it were, impart some sort of spiritual nature to our natural selves, so that, apart from our human selves as man and woman, there is a new, undifferentiated spiritual nature, common to both man and woman, which manifests itself by producing or allowing only the selfsame, undifferentiated activities for both man and woman.[55]

Differences in genders and roles do not imply that women are inferior to men or less important to God than men. Galatians 3:28 makes this clear. These created differences, however, remain within the kingdom of God. Weinrich further explains: "The Bible does speak of a mutuality and reciproc-ity between the sexes, which mutuality and reciprocity however entails no interchangeability or confusion between the distinctions but rather a mutual-ity and reciprocity that has its own intrinsic order."[56]

---

52  This understanding within The Lutheran Church—Missouri Synod is expressed in "Women in the Church: Scriptural Principles and Ecclesial Practice," 21.

53  Weinrich, "It Is Not Given to Women to Teach," 192; see also Lockwood, *1 Corinthians*, 525–27.

54  *Beyond Sex Roles*, 208.

55  Weinrich, "It Is Not Given to Women to Teach," 191–92.

56  "It Is Not Given to Women to Teach," 186. One can see this, by way of analogy, in the nature of the Holy Trinity. There is distinction, mutuality, and reciprocity without

The 1985 Lutheran Church—Missouri Synod Commission on Theology and Church Relations document on "Women in the Church" argues that the order of redemption has not "nullified" the order of creation.[57] I do not disagree with this logic, but it does not go far enough in expressing the inherent relationship between creation and redemption. They are not two orders functioning in different realms that do not cancel one another out; redemption is nothing less than the redemption *of creation*. Weinrich emphasizes this organic relationship between creation and redemption:

> Perhaps one can express the point like this: the redemptive work of God brings the creative work of God, presently under the alien dominion of sin and death, to its intended purpose and goal. If this is the case, then the "Order of creation" is not transformed in the "order of redemption": but is rather illuminated in the "order of redemption". We perceive the "order of creation" most clearly in the "order of redemption." That Christ, the Head of the new humanity, was male was not due, therefore, to some requirement to maintain the "order of creation". It is not that Christ was a male human person because in the "order of creation" God has given headship and authority to man, Adam. Rather, God who created humankind in order that he might have communion with it in and through his word gave the headship of humanity to the man, Adam, *in view of* the eschatological goal of humanity which is Christ and His Church. Because in the final purpose and *telos* of God for the world the man Jesus Christ was to be the Head of his Body, the Church, God in the beginning gave Adam to be head to Eve.[58]

One can see that 1 Timothy 2 is *not* merely an isolated proof text for the order of creation; rather, it is an expression of the much broader contours of biblical theology. One can also conclude that the conviction concerning the holders of the pastoral office being male does not grow out of first-century Jewish social convention. The fact that Eve was deceived first is also mentioned by Paul as an additional affirmation of the created order of male headship in the midst of the fallen creation.[59]

---

interchangeability or inequality. The Son is distinct from the Father and submitted to the Father, yet He is equal with the Father and one with the Father.

57  "Women in the Church: Scriptural Principles and Ecclesial Practice," 27.

58  Weinrich, "It Is Not Given to Women to Teach," 200–201.

59  This support for Paul's command is secondary and supplementary. It should be noted that though Paul stresses Eve's openness to deception here as a reason for women not to be engaged in authoritative teaching in public worship, he elsewhere stresses *Adam's* role in bringing sin to all creation; see Rom. 5:12–21.

# VII. "Saved through Child-Bearing"

We now arrive at the final question: What is the connection between child-bearing and salvation? Paul states: "Yet she/he will be 'saved' through child-bearing, if they remain in faith and love, and holiness, with modesty" (1 Tim. 2:15). Once again, a challenge for interpreting this text is the referent: Who is the third person singular subject of σωθήσεται ("will be saved") and the third plural subject of μείνωσιν ("they remain")? The most natural answer is "woman" in general as the referent of both, rather than a specific person (e.g., Eve, Mary, etc.). It is very tempting to argue, as many faithful interpreters have, that τῆς τεκνογονίας ("childbearing") has as its referent the birth of the Messiah, Jesus Christ.[60] If this was the intended meaning of Paul, however, it is much more likely that he would have expressed it explicitly rather than allusively.

The historical context points to the probability that Paul is affirming childbearing as an important role of women through these words. It appears that some Christians were forbidding or belittling the importance of marriage and procreation in the congregations that Paul is addressing (1 Tim. 4:3). They saw these natural aspects of creation as part of the old fallen order caused by sin. Thus, in light of the overwhelming testimony of Paul elsewhere, one should not understand διὰ τῆς τεκνογονίας ("through childbearing") as the means of salvation but as an important God-ordained role of women established in creation that is not set aside through redemption. The understanding that salvation is not through childbearing but through faith is also clear from the mention of πίστει καὶ ἀγάπη ("faith and love"). Therefore, Paul emphasizes that women who bear children are not part of the fallen and lost order of creation as some false teachers appear to have claimed, as long as these women remain in faith that shows itself in love (1 Tim. 2:15b).

# VIII. The Application of 1 Timothy 2
## in the Twenty-first-century Church

It is important to begin this section on application by explicitly stating something that is merely implicit in the exegesis above: It is absolutely vital that we interpret these (Law) commands in their *Gospel* context. Paul states in 1 Tim. 2:3–7:

> [3] This is good, and it is acceptable in the sight of God our Savior, [4] who desires all men to be saved and to come to the knowledge of the truth. [5] For there is one God and there is one mediator between God and men, the man Christ Jesus, [6] who gave Himself as a ransom for all,

---

60 Schreiner, "An Interpretation of 1 Timothy 2:9–15," 146–53.

the testimony to which was borne at the proper time. [7] For this I was appointed a preacher and apostle (I am telling the truth, I am not lying), a teacher of the Gentiles in faith and truth.

Paul is not giving his commands in the latter part of 1 Timothy 2 in a theological vacuum. He is addressing people who were called, gathered, and enlightened by the Gospel of our Lord Jesus Christ which is the "power of God unto salvation" (Rom. 1:17). Everything that Paul says to the Church about women is done with the understanding that through Holy Baptism we have been buried with Christ and have been raised with Him; through our union with Him we have died to sin and have been raised to newness of life (Rom. 6:1–14). This means we should also preach, teach, and discuss these commands in a *Gospel* context in the Church. This does not mean, however, that the Gospel leads us to set aside or marginalize the imperatives of this text.[61] Within a Gospel context several applications of this text can be made.[62] The focus here will be on the application of Paul's words to the modern-day issue of women's roles in worship, especially women's ordination.

As demonstrated from the context and content of 1 Timothy 2, this text clearly addresses women's roles in public worship. The posture of women in worship is introduced by Paul's discussion of women's appearance. He then emphasizes that women should not teach in worship but should learn in quietness with all submissiveness. A woman is not to teach men or exercise authority over them in the context of the Church. Both the appearance and the actions of women in worship are to reflect respect for and submission to God and those whom He has placed in authority in the Christian Church and home. This does not mean, however, that women should say nothing during the worship service or other church activities nor does this command support an unloving and hierarchical attitude toward women. They, too, are to participate in worship and to serve as a vital part of the Body of Christ. They, too, are to function as part of the priesthood of all believers in their individual vocation and family.[63]

---

61  This problematic approach is discussed by Lockwood, *1 Corinthians*, 522–25.

62  See the applications mentioned in "Women in the Church: Scriptural Principles and Ecclesial Practice," 39–47. There is a clear shift in application in "The Service of Women in Congregational and Synodical Offices," a Report of the Commission on Theology and Church Relations (September 1994). This document was not brought to a convention of The Lutheran Church—Missouri Synod and approved until 2004, largely because of disagreement within the commission and Synod over its content. The "order of creation" is not the scriptural principle guiding the practice suggested in this document.

63  Furthermore, this text can also be applied to matters of women's teaching outside the worship service (e.g., teaching children or other women, but not teaching a Sunday morning Bible Class where men and women attend) and their exercising of authority over men outside of worship (e.g., though the equivalent of a congregational voters'

In the face of increasing pressure on the Church to abandon its teaching about men and women, Gregory Lockwood sets forth the value of this teaching for the Church in our postmodern and religiously pluralistic world:

> Thus Paul's command that the women be silent in the churches (1 Cor 14:34) must be understood, in part, as countercultural and antisyncretistic. It is a command that distinguishes and separates the Christian church from other religions. Inspired by the Spirit of God, its roots are deep in the biblical revelation, which always runs counter to the spirit and wisdom of this world ([1 Cor] 2:12).[64]

In light of the teaching of 1 Timothy 2 concerning women in worship, it can and should be used in support of the doctrine that women are not to function in or hold the pastoral office. The significance of women taking on pastoral functions should not be ignored. We should consider what kind of message we send to our congregations if we say that a woman should not be ordained, but then vest her in an alb and have her read the Scriptures or assist with the distribution of the Sacrament in a worship service. Practice influences change in doctrine; the two should be in harmony.[65] Furthermore, it is amazing that a significant portion of the modern Church, for whom scriptural texts like this one are to be authoritative, has ignored the clear implications of this text for prohibiting the ordination of women into the pastoral office. This was clearly understood, confessed, and practiced by Christendom until the twentieth century.[66] Too much of the Church has capitulated to the claim that restricting the pastoral office to selected male members of the Church is a discriminatory and outmoded practice.

Our exegesis of 1 Timothy 2, especially with Paul's appeal to the order of creation, has also shown that the office of the public ministry as a male office should not be understood solely from the basis of a few isolated proof texts, as important as they are, but also in light of wider biblical theology, even the nature of God Himself, especially Jesus Christ. Weinrich writes: "Just as in the person of the incarnate Son who in his male humanity communicates to us the Father's grace, so also it is proper and right—and this in terms of the whole salvific economy of God from the beginning—that the human instrument of the Father's grace in Christ, in the concreteness of male humanity, be an

---

assembly is not mentioned in Holy Scripture, there may be issues that arise in this setting related to the pastoral office or worship that women should not address, either verbally or by vote).

64  Lockwood, *1 Corinthians*, 518.

65  See David P. Scaer, "Doctrine and Practice: Setting the Boundaries," *Concordia Theological Quarterly* 66 (2002): 307–14.

66  See Daniel Doriani, "A History of the Interpretation of 1 Timothy 2," in *Women in the Church: A Fresh Analysis of 1 Timothy 2:9–15*, ed. A. J. Köstenberger, T. R. Schreiner, and H. S. Baldwin (Grand Rapids: Baker, 1995), 213–67.

image of the incarnate Image of the eternal Father."[67] Adam was created first in the image of the Son; those who represent the incarnate Son and second Adam, therefore, are also to be males who were created in the image of the Son like the first Adam.

We have also demonstrated that this text maintains the importance of gender roles that result from creation. Distinctions in gender and roles that have been established by God in creation are not set aside by Christ and the redemption He has accomplished. These distinctions do not, in any manner, support unbiblical attitudes and behavior by men in the Church. These distinctions, rather, help us to see how God has created us to function as His people. Furthermore, bearing children is held up in this text as a significant role of women. Unfortunately, our culture has assaulted and decimated this important role like few others. Childbearing is not an antiquated societal or cultural imperative for women from past generations; it is part of the created order established when the Creator formed Eve and brought her to Adam. This does not mean that women must be married and have children to please God, but it does mean that the role of wife and mother are God-pleasing, important, and valuable roles for Christian women—indeed for all women and for the future of the Church and world. The Church must trumpet this message to the world as it degrades this basic and blessed gender role.

In our approach to this text and the issues it addresses within the Church, we do well to heed the advice that the apostle Paul gave to Timothy and the Church at the close of this Epistle: "Guard what has been entrusted to you. Avoid the godless chatter and contradictions of what is falsely called knowledge, for by professing it some have missed the mark as regards the faith" (1 Tim. 6:20–21).

---

67  Weinrich, "It Is Not Given to Women to Teach," 210; see also Nathan Jastram, "Man as Male and Female: Created in the Image of God," *Concordia Theological Quarterly* 68 (2004): 5–96.

# The Ordination of Women

## A Twentieth-Century Gnostic Heresy?

## Louis A. Brighton

### Introduction

What does the modern practice of ordaining women to the public ministry of Word and Sacraments in the church reveal about her theology? Is there a relationship between one's theology of God and the practice of the ordination of women into the clergy of the church? Why did the early church refute and reject such a practice? Did the fathers of the early church reject the ordination of women because they saw in it a denial of the apostolic catholic faith? These questions are asked because I believe that the modern practice of the ordination of women has not been adequately thought out with regard to the Christian doctrine of God. This paper poses the question: How did the role of women in Gnosticism relate to Gnostic theology, specifically the article of God? Secondly, this paper notes the opposition of the early church to both the Gnostic practice of ordaining women and the Gnostic doctrine of God. This paper is offered then in the hope that it can be a contribution to the whole subject of the ordination of women, particularly in the province of the church's doctrine of God and the practice of the ordination of women.

It is quite clear that the early church saw an important and intimate connection between the practice of women serving as priests before the Christian altar and the doctrine and teaching about God. This is revealed to us particularly in the writings of those fathers who addressed themselves against the heretical teachings of Gnosticism. For example, Irenaeus tells us that women were especially attracted to Gnosticism because of its references to God as Wisdom and female.[1] Certain Gnostic teachers encouraged women to preach and to prophesy, to celebrate the Eucharist, to consecrate the cup before

---

1    Irenaeus *Against Heresies* I.13.3–5.

the altar, which practices were strictly forbidden by the orthodox catholic church according to Irenaeus and Hippolytus.[2] Tertullian, speaking against women participating in the public act of worship, says, "It is not permitted for a woman to speak in the church, nor is it permitted for her to teach, nor to baptize, nor to offer the eucharist, nor to claim for herself a share in any masculine function—not to mention any priestly office."[3] Tertullian expresses outrage against such women being used in public worship by the Gnostics. "These heretical women—how audacious they are! They have no modesty; they are bold enough to teach, to engage in argument, to enact exorcisms, to undertake cures, and, it may be, even to baptize!"[4] He speaks also against those who had scandalized the orthodox church by appointing women on an equal basis with men as priests and bishops.[5] Why did the early church reject the practice of ordaining women to her public ministry? Was it because such a practice was not socially accepted by society? Or was there a theological reason for such a rejection?

## THE EARLY CHURCH AND SOCIETY

It is fashionable today to espouse the thesis that in the early church, even in the canonical Scriptures, there was a correlation between religious theory and social practice. That is, the orthodox catholic church kept its theology and practice in line with what was socially acceptable.[6] This thesis, however, is not so easy to demonstrate. In fact the evidence appears to give a mixed picture. Throughout the Graeco-Roman world of both the New Testament and the early church, there seems to have been no set social practice with regard to the status and rights of women. In some parts of the Roman Empire women were, for example, involved in business, social life, theater, music, sports, traveling, with or without their husbands and as equals with men. They took part in a wide range of activities that society has often in more modern times denied

---

2  Ibid. I.13.1–4; Hippolytus *Ref.* 6.25; cf. Elaine Pagels, *The Gnostic Gospels* (New York: Random House, 1979), pp. 59–60.

3  Tertullian *De Virginibus Velandis* 9.

4  Tertullian *De Praeser* 41.

5  Ibid.; cf. Pagels, *Gnostic Gospels*, pp. 60, 65; Irenaeus *Against Heresies* I.25.6; and *Apostolic Church Order-Apostolic Tradition* 18.3.

6  Pagels, *Gnostic Gospels*, p. 60ff. Pagels suggests that the evidence indicates such a correlation. She maintains that the orthodox church kept its theology and practice in line with what was socially accepted, while some Gnostics did not. Among the Valentinians women were considered equal to men as prophets, teachers, priests, and possibly also as bishops. Pagels contends that the orthodox church held to its view on rejecting such use of women in the ministry of the church because it was not socially accepted, while the Gnostics, at least some of them, were not so influenced by society.

to women, such as athletics and the bearing of arms in war.[7] Of course, much of society, if not even most of it, in the Roman Empire did not accept such a role for women, at least not in public life. But in some strata of society it was accepted and may have been even encouraged. It is difficult, however, to be dogmatic, and certainly it is not possible to make a blanket statement about what was or was not socially acceptable.[8]

The religious movements of the first century, the influence of which increased during the second and third centuries, attaining their greatest influence in the fourth, also encouraged women to act independently of and/or equally with men in public life, especially in religious practices.[9] At best all that can be said is that in the Graeco-Roman world of the early church position of women was as varied and difficult to assess as it is in the twentieth century. Certainly we cannot say without serious qualifications, even if we should say it at all, that the orthodox church tempered its theology according to the accepted customs of society. What can be demonstrated is that there was a wide cleavage between the attitude of the orthodox church and that of heretical sects towards the role of women in the church, and that this attitude was not based on what was or was not socially acceptable, but rather on strongly held theological positions. Such a sect was the Gnostics.[10]

---

7  L. Swidler, "Greco-Roman Feminism and the Reception of the Gospel," in *Traditio-Krisis-Renovation*, ed. B. Jaspert (Marburg, 1976):41–55. Swidler says that under the Roman Empire "women were everywhere involved in business, social life, such as theaters, sports events, concerts, parties, traveling—with or without their husbands. They took part in a whole range of athletics, even bore arms and went to battle." Cited by Pagels, *Gnostic Gospels*, p. 62.

8  L. Friedlander, *Roman Life and Manners Under the Early Empire*, 7th ed., trans. Leonard A. Magnus (London: George Routledge & Sons, n.d.), pp. 228–267. According to the author, wives were equal economic partners with their husbands. As early as Augustus wives were almost unrestricted socially in sharing with their husbands' social station. Wives were given consular rank; they were independent in society, even as early as the Republican days; they could marry whom they chose, elope, and divorce. Such independence made women seek to throw off the restrictions of society and nature and custom and follow male pursuits in public, civic, and political activities.

9  Ibid., pp. 255ff. These facts refer only to women of upper classes and even among them there were great variations. Cf. Pagels, *Gnostic Gospels*, p. 62, "At the beginning of the Christian era, the archaic, patriarchal forms of Roman marriage were increasingly giving way to a new legal form in which the man and woman bound themselves to each other with voluntary and mutual vows. . . . Upper-class women often insisted upon living their own life'." See also J. Carcopino, *Daily Life in Ancient Rome*, trans. E. O. Lorimer (New York: Yale University Press, 1940), pp. 95–100.

10  For further reading compare Carcopino, *Daily Life in Ancient Rome*, pp. 76–100. For example, Carcopino says, "Contrary to general opinion . . . it is certain that the Roman woman of the epoch we are studying enjoyed a dignity and an independence at least equal if not superior to those claimed by contemporary feminists. More than one ancient champion of feminism under the Flavians, Musonius Rufus for one, had claimed for women this dignity and independence on the ground of moral and intellectual equality of the two sexes" (p. 85). Again, "If the Roman women showed reluctance to perform

## GNOSTIC SOURCES

Gnosticism flourished during the second century of the Christian era, though its roots and origins are much earlier. Justin and Irenaeus and later Tertullian, Hippolytus, and Epiphanius wrote refutations of Gnostic doctrines. Other fathers such as Origen and Clement of Alexandria have references concerning Gnosticism and its influence. The earliest detailed discussion of the systems of Gnosticism is that of Irenaeus in his famous work *Against Heresies*, written around 180. Irenaeus relied in part on an earlier work of Justin, written around 150 but now lost. He also used oral and written testimony from the Gnostics themselves, including a work called *The Apocryphon of John*.

Until the nineteenth century the only sources of our knowledge of Gnosticism were the early church fathers, although such sources as the sacred books of the Mandaeans and the writings of the Manichaeans had been used and compared.[11] But this began to change in 1945 when a library of Gnostic texts was discovered at Nag Hammadi in Upper Egypt.[12] Thirteen leather-bound codices were found containing fifty-two texts or tractates, most

---

their maternal functions, they devoted themselves on the other hand, with a zeal that smacked of defiance, to all sorts of pursuits which in the days of the republic men had jealously reserved for themselves. In his sixth satire Juvenal sketches for the amusement of his readers a series of portraits, not entirely caricatures, which show women quitting their embroidery, their reading, their song, and their lyre, to put their enthusiasm into an attempt to rival men, if not to outclass them, in every sphere" (p. 91). Carcopino further says, "To live your own life was a formula which women had already brought into fashion in the second century" (p. 93).

11 Hans Jonas, *The Gnostic Religion*, 2nd ed. (Boston: Beacon Press, 1967), pp. 39, 126ff. Jonas gives a detailed description of the teachings and cultic practices of the Mandaeans. For further reading on Gnosticism in general, in addition to Jonas, cf. G. Van Groningen, *First Century Gnosticism, Its Origins and Motifs* (Leiden: E. J. Brill, 1967), and Werner Foerster, ed. *Gnosis: A Selection of Gnostic Texts*, 2 vols., trans. R. McL. Wilson et al. (Oxford: University Press, 1972), Vol. 1, *Patristic Evidence*; Vol. 2, *Coptic and Mandaean Sources*.

12 For a brief description of this archaeological discovery Pagels, *Gnostic Gospels*, pp. xiii–xxxvi; and James M. Robinson, gen. ed., *The Nag Hammadi Library* (San Francisco: Harper & Row, 1977), pp. 1–25. A *Facsimile Edition of the Nag Hammadi Codices* published under the auspices of the Dept. of Antiquities of the government of Egypt by E. J. Brill, is nearing completion; ten volumes thus far have appeared. A second series of volumes is to appear, *The Coptic Gnostic Library*, a set of eleven volumes when completed, published by E. J. Brill in the Nag Hammadi Studies series. This second series of volumes will provide Coptic transcriptions, English translations of the texts, commentaries, introductions, notes, and indices for all the texts of the Nag Hammadi Library. Thus far two volumes have been published, volumes 4 and 11. The Nag Hammadi Studies series under the editorship of M. Krause and others, and published by E. J. Brill, in addition to containing the critical texts of the *Coptic Gnostic Library*, will also contain essays and studies on various aspects of the Nag Hammadi Library. Thus far fourteen volumes have been published, including the above two volumes of 4 and 11. A third work of interest is the volume mentioned above, Robinson, *The Nag Hammadi Library*. This volume gives all of the texts of the Nag Hammadi Library in English. It

of which exhibit Gnostic teachings and practices. Among the texts are *The Gospel of Thomas*, *The Gospel of Philip*, *The Gospel of Truth*, and *The Gospel of the Egyptians*. Another group of texts consists of sayings attributed to Jesus' disciples and followers, such as *The Secret Book of James*, *The Apocalypse of Paul*, *The Letter of Peter to Philip*, and *The Apocalypse of Peter*. In addition to the texts of Christian Gnostics there are texts that seem to exhibit Jewish Gnostic thought such as *The Testimony of Truth* and *The Apocalypse of Adam*. All the texts are in the Coptic language and are translations of originals which were composed in Greek. The dating of the texts is still uncertain, although dates ranging from the beginning to the end of the fourth century have been proposed. The Nag Hammadi library was hidden in a jar possibly for the same reason that the Dead Sea Scrolls (though at a later date) were hidden in jars, to preserve them from destruction because of the approach of Roman authorities. The discovery of this Gnostic library probably will be as important to the study of Gnosticism as the Dead Sea Scrolls are proving to be to the study of the Old Testament and related disciplines.

## GNOSTICISM AND THE ROLE OF WOMEN

In some of the Gnostic texts women appear equal to men in being authorities for the establishment of doctrine. In the tractate *The Dialogue of the Savior* sayings of Jesus are given which are comparable to those in *The Gospel of Thomas*. Jesus gives these sayings to His disciples, three of whom are selected for receiving them, Matthew, Judas, and Mariam (Mary Magdalene). This Mariam is an authoritative receiver of these sayings together with Matthew and Judas.[13] She was chosen by Jesus to receive these sayings so that she could be a "revealer" to others, and in this capacity is described as a woman who knows all things.[14] Elaine Pagels in a recent study correctly states, "*The Dialogue of the Savior* not only includes Mary Magdalene as one of three disciples chosen to receive special teaching but also praises her above the other two."[15] So highly does Gnosticism regard Mary Magdalene as an authoritative "revealer" of the thoughts and sayings of Jesus, that they have a gospel named after her. In *The Gospel of Mary*, the first of four tractates found in the Berlin Gnostic Codex, Mary is described in the role of "comforter" and "revealer." At the departure of the resurrected Lord she comforts the disciples and then at the request of

---

is the only source to date which contains all of the texts of the Nag Hammadi Library, although only the English translations.

13  *The Dialogue of the Savior*, pp. 229–238 in *The Nag Hammadi Library* (*TNHL*). Cf. "Then he (Jesus) took Judas and Matthew and Mariam . . . at the end, the whole of heaven and earth. And when he set his hand upon them . . ." 134.24–135.4; p. 234 in *TNHL*.

14  *The Dialogue of the Savior* 139.10–13; 140.15–20; pp. 235–236 in *TNHL*.

15  Pagels, *Gnostic Gospels*, p. 64.

Peter tells them some sayings of the Savior which she alone knew. Mary then relates a vision in which Jesus told her these sayings.[16] Throughout this tractate the role of Mary as an authority on the sayings of Jesus, equal to that of Peter and the twelve, is upheld and enhanced.

The role of women in Gnosticism is in striking contrast to the role that women held in orthodox Christianity. While Gnostics developed the principle of equality between men and women in the social and political structures of their religious communities, so that at times women were looked upon even as the source of authoritative teachings as well as serving as priests and bishops, orthodox Christianity reserved the role of authority, including that of bishop and priest, exclusively for men.[17] These two different patterns of attitudes between Gnosticism and orthodox Christianity are correlated to their respective understandings and descriptions of God. Both Gnosticism and orthodox Christianity derived and supported their attitudes concerning the role of women from their theologies of God and their teachings of God's relationship to the human race.[18]

## FEMINISM AND THE GNOSTIC THEOLOGY OF GOD

The role of women in Gnosticism ought not to surprise us when seen against and compared to its theology of God. Deeply embedded in its thought and teachings of God is the feminine idea. Throughout the Gnostic texts sexual symbolism is used to describe both masculine and feminine elements in God. This is in marked contrast to both the canonical Scriptures and the orthodox church's belief, in which the feminine element is absent in both thought and symbolism of God.[19] The Gnostic texts of Nag Hammadi, while exhibiting a diversity in their descriptions of God in both masculine and feminine thought

---

16  *The Gospel of Mary*, 10.1ff.; p. 472 in *TNHL*.

17  Cf. Pagels, *Gnostic Gospels*, p. 66. Not all Gnostics were unanimous in affirming the equality of women with men in the teaching office of the community and in the public functions of the worship life of the community. Some Gnostic texts reflect an inferior status for women as can be seen in *The Gospel of Thomas* (37.20–35; 43.25–35; 51.23–26; pp. 121, 124–125, and 130 in *TNHL*) and even in *The Gospel of Mary* (9.20; p. 472 in *TNHL*). And conversely not all orthodox fathers rejected such equality, i.e., Clement of Alexandria (*Paidagogos* 1.4; 1.6; 1.19; cited by Pagels, *Gnostic Gospels*, pp. 67–69).

18  Pagels believes that both Gnosticism and orthodox Christianity based their respective theologies on the canonical Scriptures, but arrived at different and opposing patterns because of a difference in interpretation (*Gnostic Gospels*, pp. 65–67). However, she arrives at this conclusion because of a selective choosing of canonical texts. She does not, for example, refer to the whole text of Eph. 5:22–33 but only to verse 24, and she does not refer to a passage like 1 Cor. 11:3 at all.

19  "Indeed, the absence of feminine symbolism for God marks Judaism, Christianity, and Islam in striking contrast to the world's other religious traditions, whether in Egypt, Babylonia, Greece, and Rome, or in Africa, India, and North America, which abound in feminine symbolism" (Pagels, *Gnostic Gospels*, p. 48).

and symbolism, share the common idea and notion that God is both masculine and feminine, and that the feminine element is as essential in the idea of God as is the masculine.

The church fathers were aware of this notion and, of course, refuted it.[20] Irenaeus in particular was well acquainted with this Gnostic notion of the feminine element in God. In *Against Heresies* he relates how several Gnostic groups such as the Valentinians thought of God as a dyad, one who is both "Primal Father" and the "Womb" or "Mother of All." The followers of Valentinus prayed to this "Mother of All," whom they also called "Silence" and "Grace," so that they might receive knowledge. Valentinus attributed the origin of all created things to "Wisdom," whom he called Eve, "the Mother of all living." To manage her creation, "Wisdom" brought forth the demiurge, the creator-God of Israel, as her agent. At times the Valentinians refer to the feminine element of God, as "Truth," because she, the "Mother of All," was the source and dispenser of knowledge.[21] Irenaeus relates an instance of how a certain Valentinian by the name of Marcus, when celebrating the Mass, called upon "God the Mother," whom he also addressed as "Grace," to drop her own blood into the chalice so that those who drink of the cup might receive the flowing in of "Grace."[22] According to Irenaeus the Gnostics differed in their understanding of God as a dyad. Some insisted that God be thought of as the "great male-female power," that is, an hermaphrodite. Others suggested that God was neither male nor female nor hermaphroditic but neuter, and that the descriptive terms male and female were only metaphors. Still others assigned a spouse to God in order to explain the male-female nature of God.[23]

That Irenaeus was not distorting or exaggerating in his citations and references to Gnostic sources can be seen from a perusal of the texts of the library from Nag Hammadi. Throughout the texts God is referred to, pictured, and thought of as both male and female in various ways. The idea that God had a spouse, Wisdom (*Sophia*), is present, along with the idea that the Holy Spirit is this female person or element of God. In *The Apocryphon of John*[24] the author describes a vision in which God as a light appeared to him in a likeness of

---

20  Clement of Alexandria attests that Wisdom, "Mother of all the living," was thought of by several Gnostics as being the "first universal creator" who created all creatures, enlightens human beings, and makes them wise (*Excerpta* 47.1). Origen quotes or refers to the Gospel according to the Hebrews where Jesus calls the Holy Spirit His Mother (*Commentary on John* 2.12; *Commentary on Matthew* 15.14; *Hom. on Jeremiah* 15.4). Cf. Eusebius *Ecclesiastical History* I.11.14–15.

21  Irenaeus *Against Heresies* I.1.1; I.2.2–3; I.4.1–5.4; I.11.1; I.13.2. Cf. Pagels, *Gnostic Gospels*, pp. 50, 54.

22  Irenaeus *Against Heresies* I.13.1–2, cited by Pagels, *Gnostic Gospels*, p. 50.

23  Irenaeus *Against Heresies* I.11.5, cited by Pagels, *Gnostic Gospels* p. 51.

24  *The Apocryphon of John* 5.5–15; p. 101 in *TNHL*. Cf. Gilles Quispel, "Jewish Gnosis and Mandaean Gnosticism: Some Reflections on the Writing Bronté," *Les Textes De Nag*

multiple forms, specifically in three forms: the Father; the Mother; and the Son.[25] Again in the same work the author quotes God as saying, "I am the one who is with you forever. I [am the Father], I am the Mother, I am the Son."[26] In *The Gospel of Philip* the author denies that Mary conceived Jesus by the Holy Spirit. Because the Holy Spirit is feminine, a woman, she could not have been the cause of Mary's conception.[27] In the same work it is said that "Adam came into being from two virgins, from the Spirit and from the virgin earth."[28] In *The Gospel of Thomas* Jesus contrasts His earthly parents, Mary and Joseph, with His divine Father, the Father of Truth, and His divine Mother, the Holy Spirit.[29] In the tractate *Trimorphic Protennoia* ("The Three-Formed First Thought") we are told that Protennoia first appeared as Father (or Voice); second, as Mother (or Sound); and third, as Son (or *Logos*). "Now the Voice that originated from my thought exists as three permanences: the Father, the Mother, the Son."[30] And again in the same tractate, "I am androgynous. [I am both Mother and] Father since [I copulate] with myself."[31] In the tractate *The Thunder, Perfect Mind* a female revealer in a discourse says, "I am the first and the last. I am the honored one and the scorned one. I am the whore and the holy one. I am the wife and virgin. I am the mother and the daughter."[32] In *The Gospel of the Egyptians* (known also as *The Holy Book of the Great Invisible Spirit*) we are told that "three powers came forth from him (the great invisible

*Hammadi*, Jacques-E. Menard, ed., *Nag Hammadi Studies*, vol. 7. ed, Martin Krause, James M. Robinson, and Frederik Wisse (Leiden: E. J. Brill, 1975), pp. 94ff.

25   *The Apocryphon of John* I.31–2.14; 5.5–14; pp. 99, 101 in *TNHL*.

26   Ibid., 1.2; p. 99 in *TNHL*.

27   *The Gospel of Philip* 55.24–30; p. 134 in *TNHL*. Cf. 59.10–60.1; p. 136 in *TNHL*.

28   Ibid, 71.15–20; p. 143 in *TNHL*.

29   *The Gospel of Thomas* 49.32–50.1; pp. 128–129 in *TNHL*; G. Quispel et al. *The Gospel of Thomas* (New York: Harper and Brothers, 1959), pp. 50–51. As can be seen when compared to n. 17 above, *The Gospel of Thomas* is ambivalent in its attitude toward the idea of the female sex. While attributing a female characteristic or person to God, it also exhibits a condescending attitude toward women. For example, it ends with the words, "Simon Peter said to them, 'Let Mary leave us, for women are not worthy of Life.' Jesus said, 'I myself shall lead her in order to make her male, so that she too may become a living spirit resembling you males. For every woman who will make herself male will enter the Kingdom of Heaven,'" 50.19–25; p. 129 in *TNHL*; Quispel, *The Gospel of Thomas*, p. 15. *The Gospel of Mary* shows a similar ambivalence, cf. n. 17 above. Cf. also *The First Apocalypse of James* 41.15–20 where it is stated, "The perishable has gone up to the imperishable and the female element has attained to this male element"; p. 248 in *TNHL*.

30   *Trimorphic Protennoia* 37.10–15; p. 463 in *TNHL*. Cf. 38.10–15; 35.30–38.15; and 42.1–2; pp. 462–463 and 465–466 in *TNHL*.

31   Ibid., 45.1–10; p. 467 in *TNHL*.

32   *The Thunder, Perfect Mind* 13.16–21; pp. 271–272 in *TNHL*.

Spirit); they are the Father, the Mother, and the Son."[33] And again in the same tractate, ". . . giving glory with one voice, with one accord, with a mouth which does not rest, to the Father, and the Mother, and the Son, and their whole pleroma."[34] Clearly we have here an example of another version and expression of the Trinity, one in which one person of God is female.

## WHENCE THE FEMININE NOTION OF GOD IN GNOSTICISM?

What were the sources for the Gnostic notion of female element or person in God? One source was the wisdom literature of the Old Testament. In the book of Proverbs wisdom is feminine, and throughout book wisdom speaks with a feminine voice (cf. Prov. 1:20ff.; 8:1ff.; 9:1ff.). At times wisdom is personified as the agent of God's creation (3:19); as the one that is to be exalted (4:8); who existed with Yahweh before creation (8:22–31); and is Yahweh's delight (8:30). This tradition, in which wisdom is personified, voiced in Proverbs and found elsewhere in Jewish literature (Siracides 24:1–22; Wis. of Sol. 4–10; Bar. 3:9–4:4; and 1 Enoch 84:3), helped to give birth to the feminine figure or person of "Wisdom" (*Sophia*) found in both Jewish and Christian Gnosticism.[35] Both Jewish and Christian Gnostics pondered the meaning of "wisdom" in Proverbs and elsewhere, wondering whether it (she) was the feminine power or person of God. In *The Apocalypse of Adam* and in the tractate *Trimorphic Protennoia* the feminine power or person of God is connected with "wisdom" and has creative ability.[36] According to Clement of Alexandria several Gnostics thought that "Wisdom" was the "first universal creator" who created all creatures and gave to human beings enlightenment and wisdom.[37] In the first book of *Against Heresies* Irenaeus gives a lengthy and detailed description of this "Wisdom figure" under the name of Sophia and of the role she played in Gnosticism, particularly in Valentinianism. Sophia was one of the thirty aeons making up the pleroma (the totality or whole

---

33 *The Gospel of the Egyptians* 41.9; p. 196 in *THNL*; pp. 54–55 in *Nag Hammadi Codices III, 2 and IV, 2—The Gospel of the Egyptians*, ed. and trans. A. Böhlig and F. Wisse in cooperation with P. Labib, vol. 4 in the Nag Hammadi Studies, ed. M. Krause, J. M. Robinson, and F. Wisse (Leiden: E. J. Brill, 1975). Cf. also 41.15–42.20; p. 196 in *TNHL*; pp 55–56 in A. Böhlig, *The Gospel of the Egyptians*.

34 *The Gospel of the Egyptians* 55.4–11, p. 200 in *TNHL*; Böhlig, *The Gospel of the Egyptians*, p. 112.

35 For a discussion of the Sophia figure see George W. MacRae, "The Jewish Background of the Gnostic Sophia Myth," *Novum Testamentum*, 12 (1970):86–101; and G. C. Stead, "The Valentinian Myth of Sophia," *Journal of Theological Studies*, 20 (1969):75–104.

36 *The Apocalypse of Adam* 64.10–20 and 81.2–9; pp. 257, 262 in *TNHL*; *Trimorphic Protennoia* 35.1–15; pp. 461–462 in *TNHL*. Cf. Pagels, *Gnostic Gospels*, pp. 53–56.

37 Clement of Alexandria *Excerpta* 47.1.

of the divine sphere, the invisible spiritual world in contrast to the visible material world—in Valentinianism the aeons were created divine entities or emanations, among whom were Christ and the Holy Spirit). At times Sophia was named and identified with the Holy Spirit (I.4.1). At other times she was called "Mother" (I.4.5). She formed the "Demiurge," and together they created the visible world, that is, everything outside of the pleroma (I.5.1,3). She was instrumental with her spouse, the savior, in leading into the pleroma those human beings who were spiritual and who called and worshiped her as "Mother" (I.7.1–3 and I.13.1–6). According to Irenaeus this "Wisdom" figure was known by both her Greek name of "Sophia" and also by her Hebrew name of "Achamoth," evidently from the Hebrew word for wisdom (I:4:1). In *The First Apocalypse of James* this Sophia figure was in the Father and was the mother of the human race through Achamoth. In this tractate from Nag Hammadi, Sophia at times is a separate female entity from Achamoth, for it is said that Sophia produced Achamoth, who in turn produced the human race. At other times they seem to be the same female figure bearing two names. Sophia (and Achamoth) is imperishable and is the one through whom man will be redeemed.[38] In *The Apocryphon of John* Sophia is referred to as the spouse of God and as being invoked in creation.[39] In the tractate *On the Origin of the World* Sophia is described as an agent of God's creation.[40]

From the descriptions of Sophia in Irenaeus and now also further confirmed and elaborated in the Gnostic texts from Nag Hammadi, it is quite clear that the female element or notion attached to God in Gnosticism by way of the figure of Sophia is a fanciful creation of a mind working with an unrestrained imagination rather than with reason or experience. While one can postulate as the basis for this female figure the idea of "wisdom" in wisdom literature, the creation of the Sophia myth is due to an illusion of the mind rather than to an exegesis of the concept of "wisdom." An example of such an illusionary imagination at work can be seen in *The Apocryphon of John*, where

---

38  *The First Apocalypse of James* 34.1–36.15; pp. 246–247 in *TNHL*. Throughout the Gnostic texts there is a confusion of ideas and concepts, and oftentimes an ambivalence (cf. n. 29 above). With regard to the redemption of man there is not only a confusion and indecisiveness as to what it really is and consists of, there is also a confusion as to whom it is to be attributed. Even in the same tractate this confusion appears. In *The Second Apocalypse of James* redemption is attributed to James himself (55.15–25); to God the Father (62.15–25); and to the Holy Spirit (63.25–30), pp. 252, 255 in *TNHL*. According to Irenaeus the tradition of the Gnostics "respecting redemption is invisible and incomprehensible. . . . It is fluctuating. . . . There are as many schemes of 'redemption' as there are teachers" (*Against Heresies* I.21.1). Cf. also *Against Heresies* I.21.5, where Irenaeus refers to Sophia and redemption.

39  *The Apocryphon of John* 5.5–15; 9.26ff.; pp. 101, 103–104 in *TNHL*.

40  *On the Origin of the World* 98.10–20; 99.24–100.15ff., pp. 162–163 in *TNHL*. In this tractate, which is an apologetic essay explaining the world view of Gnosticism, Sophia evolves or flows out of Pistis, and they then are both involved in creation.

a reference to Sophia describes her as creating a likeness from herself.[41] What she brought forth out of herself changed into the form of a lion-faced serpent, because she did this act of creation without the consent of the Spirit. Because of this independent act of creation, evil in addition to good now becomes associated with Sophia. In turn she becomes the genesis and the *agent provocateur* by which the origin of evil is attached to God.

In some of the texts from Nag Hammadi the figure of Sophia is identified with the Holy Spirit, and by way of such an identification the notion of the female element is no longer merely related to God as an aeon of the pleroma, or as a consort or spouse, but now as a part of God Himself. Many of the church fathers reveal an awareness of this identification.[42] Epiphanius, for example, says that Simon the Magician identified Helena-Sophia with the Holy Spirit. Simon and his followers also came to the paradoxical conclusion that because Sophia, the female deity, was the author of evil and thus an harlot, the Holy Spirit was prostitute.[43] The Gnostics could claim justification for this identification because of the Hebrew word for "spirit." While the Greek word for spirit is neuter and thus would require that the Holy Spirit be asexual, the Hebrew word is feminine, as are both the Greek and Hebrew words for "wisdom."[44] Thus throughout the text of *The Apocryphon of John* the Holy Spirit is this feminine person of God.[45]

The concept of "wisdom" in Jewish wisdom literature was not the only source for the Gnostic notion of the feminine element and person of God. There is evidence that both Jewish and Christian Gnostics also resorted to the mythological cults of the ancient peoples of Canaan and Egypt—vestiges of which were still present in the Hellenistic world—and to Greek philosophy for the creation and development of their feminine notion of God. Once the idea was conceived that the figure of Sophia was the source of both good and evil and that in the relationship between Sophia and the Holy Spirit the source of evil was attached to God, Gnosticism developed the idea of the "sacredness of evil" in connection with their feminine figure of God. From the ancient cultic rituals of the Near Eastern world Gnosticism took the idea of the "sacred prostitute" and attached it to their Sophia figure.[46] They welded together the love goddesses of Near Eastern, West Semitic, and Greek cultic

---

41 *The Apocryphon of John* 9.26ff.; pp. 103–104 in *TNHL*.

42 See notes 20 and 21 above. Cf. Quispel, "Jewish Gnosis and Mandaean Gnosticism," p. 100.

43 *Panarion* 21.2, 4; cited by Quispel, "Jewish Gnosis and Mandaean Gnosticism," p. 100.

44 Cf. Pagels, *Gnostic Gospels*, pp. 51–53.

45 *The Apocryphon of John* 2.10–25; 4.34–5.20; 6.1–35; pp. 99–102 in *TNHL*.

46 Cf. Quispel, "Jewish Gnosis and Mandaean Gnosticism," pp. 89ff., 94–100, and 100–103.

rituals (Ishtar, Astarte, and Aphrodite) as well as the Egyptian goddess Isis together with the "wisdom figure" to create the notion of their "feminine figure" of God, Sophia. Both the idea that this feminine figure of Sophia was the spouse and consort of God and that this divine spouse at the same time was the cause and symbol of all fornication resulted from such a syncretism.[47] Even the Holy Spirit among some of the Christian Gnostics could paradoxically be conceived of as a sacred prostitute because the female figure or deity of Sophia as a harlot was associated and at times identified with the Holy Spirit.[48]

The feminine figure of God in the Gnostic texts appears under various names and guises. In addition to that of Sophia, she appears as the Mother, the Sound, the Thought of the Father, the Image of the Invisible Spirit, Barbelo, the Invisible One, the Perfect Mind, the First and the Last, Bronte (the Thunder), the Whore, the Holy One, the Mother of All, the Mother, the Virginal Barbelon, the Uninterpretable Power, the Ineffable Mother who presides over heaven.[49] These are but a sampling from the Gnostic texts of Nag Hammadi. From the writings of the Mandaean Gnostic sect a further listing could be added with descriptive titles or names such as Mother, Divine Mother, Wellspring of Life, Mother of Life, Spouse of the great Principle of Divine Enlightenment.[50] From Simonian Gnostic sources we meet the title of "the First Idea," which is certainly "a Stoical and highly philosophical terminology."[51] The Nag Hammadi text, *The Apocryphon of John*, while not using the title "the First Idea," attributes to the divine feminine figure similar philosophical qualities. For example, she is spoken of as "the first thought" in the same context where she is described as "the womb of everything, the eternal aeon, the first to come forth, the invisible virginal Spirit, that is, Barbelo."[52] What Quispel concludes concerning Jewish and Mandaean Gnosticism can be said of Christian Gnosticism as well:

---

47  Ibid., pp. 94ff., 99. For example, see *The Apocryphon of John* 5.5–15; p. 101 in *TNHL*.

48  *Panarion* 21.2, 4; cited by Quispel, "Jewish Gnosis and Mandaean Gnosticism," p. 100.

49  *Trimorphic Protennoia* 37.20–38.20, p. 463 in *TNHL*; *The Thunder, Perfect Mind* 13.16–21, pp. 271–272 in *TNHL*; *The Dialogue of the Savior* 144.8–15, p. 237 in *TNHL*; *The Gospel of the Egyptians* 42.10–15, pp. 60–61 in *TNHL*.

50  Quispel, "Jewish Gnosis and Mandaean Gnosticism," p. 101. The Mandaeans are a Gnostic sect which originated as a small community east of the Jordan River in the first and second centuries. They were supposedly to have had association with John the Baptist, but this today is held in doubt. They still survive today as a small community south of Baghdad. Their chief writing, *Ginza* (Treasure), setting forth their teachings and cultic rituals, is dated from the seventh/eighth centuries. For further information see Hans Jonas, *The Gnostic Religion*, esp. pp. 39ff. and 125–140.

51  Quispel, "Jewish Gnosis and Mandaean Gnosticism," p. 103.

52  *The Apocryphon of John* 5.1–15; p. 101 in *TNHL*.

It is only in the perspective of Jewish wisdom speculations that this ambivalence can be understood. Ruah (Spirit] is called at the same time the Holy Spirit and the prostitute, just as Sophia in Bronte [as found in the Nag Hammadi texts of *The Thunder, Perfect Mind* and *On the Origin of the World*] is the saint and the whore, just as in Simonian Gnosis Sophia is called the Holy Spirit and the harlot. It would even seem that her dialectical nature goes back further than Bronte or Simon the Magician or the *Apocryphon of John*, to the syncretism of Israel before, during and after the prophets. In any case we have in Mandaeanism a parallel development as in later Cabbalism, where the Shechina is the divine Mother and yet shows demonic features.[53]

To the Christian mind molded by the canonical Scriptures of the Old and New Testaments, this ambivalence of good and evil in the character of the Gnostic divine feminine figure is certainly disturbing. It is not the only disturbing factor in this whole discussion of the feminine element and figure of God in Gnosticism. Mention could be made of the polytheism that is met in Gnosticism, a polytheism that is a part of the Gnostic doctrine of God because of the additional feminine figure and its teaching concerning the pleroma, a polytheism that is a denial of monotheism even in the Platonic sense—not to mention in the sense of the Old and New Testaments.[54] And certainly mention could be made of the Gnostic notion of salvation in connection with their divine feminine figure, a notion of salvation which is contradictory to that found in the Old and New Testaments.[55] However, here only a few thoughts of the Gnostic notion of good and evil with regard to the feminine figure and with regard to their theology of God can be given.

Not only do we see God as the source of evil, as well as good, through the divine feminine figure in Gnosticism, we also observe the idea that evil can be holy. At times in the Gnostic texts, when man's creation is attributed to Sophia, she is referred to as the whore.[56] When she is spoken of as the Mother or the Great Mother, negative (as well as positive) aspects and characteristics are attributed to her almost as if she were the female counterpart

53  Quispel, "Jewish Gnosis and Mandaean Gnosticism," p. 102. The brackets and enclosures have been added for clarity.

54  Cf. *The Apocryphon of John* 13.10ff.; 15.1–17; 19.1–5; pp. 106–109 in *TNHL*.

55  See n. 38 above. Cf. also *The Scond Treatise of the Great Seth* 55.25–56.20; p. 332 in *TNHL*; and *The Apocalypse of Peter* 81.15–25; p. 355 in *TNHL* for further examples. Not only is the Gnostic view of the death of Jesus Christ Docetic in character, but it also makes the teaching of salvation by the cross of Jesus Christ something to be laughed at and ridiculed. Similarly, the resurrection of Jesus Christ is ridiculed and denied in the Gnostic texts. For examples see *The Gospel of Mary* 7.10; p. 472 in *TNHL*; and *The Gospel of Philip* 2.73; p. 144 in *TNHL*. Cf. Pagels, *Gnostic Gospels*, pp. 10–16 for discussion and comment.

56  Cf. *The Second Treatise of the Great Seth* 50.25–30; p. 330 in *TNHL* for an example.

of the devil.[57] On occasion when she is referred to as the Holy Spirit, she is also called the prostitute or whore or harlot. Gnosticism thus pictured this feminine divine figure as dialectical in nature, as good and evil, as saint and whore, as divine Mother and yet as one that shows demonic features.[58] This dialectical view of the divine feminine figure was one way that Gnosticism attempted to come to terms with the mystery of the origin of evil. However, far from solving the problem, it only intensified it. For this divine feminine figure not only caused such paradoxical conclusions and aberrations as that of the Holy Spirit being a prostitute—an extreme conclusion not held by all Gnostics—it was also responsible for much of Gnostic aestheticism as well as libertinism and antinomianism.

## CONCLUSION

It is the contention of this study that the early church rejected the ordination of women on theological grounds, specifically its theology of God. This paper presents a review of the theology of God in Gnosticism as seen through its notion of the divine feminine figure of God in order to suggest a correlation between it and the Gnostic practice of the ordination of women. In view of this theology of God in Gnosticism, this paper concludes that orthodox Christianity of the early church, with its theology of the Triune God, could not but reject the practice of the ordination of women into the public ministry.

---

57  Cf. Quispel, "Jewish Gnosis and Mandaean Gnosticism," p. 102; and the Gnostic tractate *The Hypostasis of the Archons*, where the serpent in paradise is called the "Female Spiritual Principle" (89.30–35; p. 155 in *TNHL*).

58  Cf. Quispel, "Jewish Gnosis and Mandaean Gnosticism," pp. 102–103; and *The Thunder, Perfect Mind* 13.15–35; pp. 271–272 in *TNHL* for an example.

# ORDERED COMMUNITY

## ORDER AND SUBORDINATION IN THE NEW TESTAMENT

## JOHN W. KLEINIG

Years ago when I was working as a chaplain at Saint Peters Lutheran College, I had a conversation with three Aboriginal girls about their difficulties in fitting into the boarding school and feeling at home in it. In the course of the conversation one of them remarked that as soon as they set foot on the campus, they had to switch from "we" to "I", from thinking of themselves as part of a community to regarding themselves as individuals apart from their community.

We, I hold, must do the reverse, if we are to make sense of the New Testament teaching on subordination. Subordination presupposes the primacy of community over individuality, the need for communal solidarity for the wellbeing of each person. Unlike many modern western thinkers, the writers of the New Testament assume that we can only truly be ourselves as persons, and find lasting personal fulfilment, in community. None of us is ever independent and autonomous; we are all interdependent, like the leaves and branches in a tree, in our family, our workplace, our society, our nation, and our church. We are, as the New Testament reminds us, members of a body. This applies for our life in the human family as well as for life in God's family. Our prosperity comes from receiving and giving in community. We suffer if we separate ourselves from our given social matrix. We damage our community if we go our own way and refuse to cooperate with each other under the supervision of our leaders. We threaten the health of the church if we, like a cancerous organ, disorder its ecology by taking what we want from it for ourselves, without giving what is required of us for its wellbeing. Community depends on subordination. Without subordination there is no true community.

The term subordination, like the Christian teaching about it,[1] has, I concede, fallen into disrepute. Most people equate subordination with destructive subservience to authoritarian leaders, enforced servitude to power-mongers, and a disabling sense of inferiority in a hierarchy of domination. It bespeaks all that we abhor most. Yet, if I may put my case most provocatively, the proper practice of subordination, as taught in the New Testament, contributes much more to our experience of love, joy, contentment and peace than we realise. It has to do with a good conscience that comes from living a God-pleasing life in our station and vocation (Rom 13:5; Col 3:19; 1 Pet 3:18–21; 1 Clem 41:1). Subordination supplies the context for self-giving love to flourish in our families and our church, without the abuse of power. In fact, I maintain that the practice of subordination is a bulwark against authoritarianism, with its abuse of power and authority in the church.

The apostolic teaching on subordination should not be identified, as is commonly done, with inferiority, or subservience. It is possible to be subordinate and yet equal. So, for example, I am subordinate as a lecturer to the principal of the Australian Lutheran College, just as I am subordinate to my national president as a pastor and to my pastor as congregational member. But that does not make me inferior to any of them, a lesser person, or lesser Christian, or lesser pastor than they. Even though I respect and obey them, I am not subservient to them, nor do they run roughshod over me as if I were their underling. None of them has ever dominated or exploited me, just because I am subordinate to them.

Subordination involves our willing acceptance of our given communal leaders and our whole-hearted cooperation with them because they are our leaders. We are subordinate to those who are our heads,[2] because they occupy an office[3] over us, a divinely instituted position of leadership in our community. We are subordinate to them in their office.

Since headship exists in community and works for its common good, it depends on that community for its existence and its legitimacy. Like the head of a body, leaders who exercise headship must be responsive and responsible,

---

1     Richard Foster asserts: "Of all the Spiritual Disciplines none has been more abused than the Discipline of submission. Somehow the human species has an extraordinary knack for taking the best teaching and turning it to the worst ends. Nothing can put people into bondage like religion, and nothing in religion has done more to manipulate and destroy people than a deficient teaching on submission" (96).

2     See 1 Cor 11:3; Eph 1:22; 4:15; 5:23; Col 1:18; 2:10. The sense of the Greek word κεπηαλε in the New Testament has been the subject of some debate. While some have followed the lead of Kroeger in arguing for the use of this term in the sense of a 'source' rather than 'a person in authority', this has been challenged lexically by the work of Grudem (1994).

3     This is Luther's favoured term. It is still by far the best term for this reality, because it puts the accent on the position of leadership rather than on the person of the leader.

accessible and accountable, to the people that make up their community, for they cannot lead effectively unless they gain and retain their acquiescence and cooperation, their willing subordination.

My basic premise is that God has instituted certain basic orders for community, such as the family, government, and the church, with offices for leadership within them, for the delivery and distribution of his blessings to the people who live and work in them. By their subordination to these offices people receive and share God's blessings. That is the purpose of subordination.

In this paper which is a tribute to my teacher and dear colleague Vic Pfitzner, I would like to explore the startling teaching on subordination in the New Testament.[4] It is offered to him as a token of appreciation for showing me that it is possible to engage in theological controversy in a peaceful godly way. Even though we have stood on opposite sides in the debate on the ordination of women, his generosity of spirit, his brotherly love, has kept us from falling out with each other but has, in fact, drawn us closer to each other in Christ. And so I thank him most warmly for reflecting God's loving kindness and patience in his interaction with me.

This is, in many ways, an exercise in the rehabilitation of a teaching that has fallen out of favour among us. There are three reasons for this exercise. First, subordination is one of the key terms in the two texts that have been used to restrict the ordained ministry to men, which is presently under discussion among us. Second, the apostolic teaching on subordination provides some very helpful orientation in the rather contentious areas of debate about marriage, family, and ministry in our society and the church. Third, the concept of certain divinely instituted communal orders that is implied by this term, could, in the future, prove to be useful in evangelising some of the young people in our society, who are so fed up with disordered freedom that they long for a given social ecology, a cosmic order that provides a measure of harmony and stability for them.

## 1. CLARIFICATION OF TERMINOLOGY

The New Testament uses a whole body of words in its teaching on subordination. As they all interact with each other semantically, they help to define what is meant by this term.

The idea of order is basic to all talk about subordination.[5] The Greek word for this is *taxis*. This is basically a military term (1 Clem 37:1–4; Thiselton, 1168). It was used, most commonly, in the Hellenistic world for the order of a military unit, a century, under its officer, a centurion. It does not usually refer

---

4   This essay is a revision of a paper that was given in June 9, 2004, to the Pastors' Conference of the Queensland District of the Lutheran Church of Australia.

5   See Delling, 42; Yoder, 172; and Eliott, 486f.

to the ranking of soldiers in a military hierarchy, but to the organisation of a unit in battle order, around its commander and under its standard. He usually led from the centre of front line for battle, with his soldiers around him. This is how that word is used in a few places in the LXX (Num 1:52; 2 Macc 8:22; 13:21).[6] At the time of Christ Jewish writers had also begun to use *taxis* for the liturgical order of the synagogue. It described the set pattern of leadership in prayer with communal responses, and in reading from the Scriptures and the exposition of them with communal silence, as well as the custom of sitting to teach and standing to pray.[7] Similarly, the noun *taxis* is used as a liturgical term in the New Testament. Thus, while Luke 1:8 tells us that Zechariah was officiating as a priest on duty in the "order" of his division, Hebrews contrasts the priestly "order" of Melchizedek (5:6, 10; 6:20; 7:11, 17, 21) with the priestly "order" of Aaron (7:11). Paul instructs the Corinthian congregation that in their worship everything must be done according to the right pattern and in "order" (1 Cor 14:40;[8] see also 1 Clem 40:1). This instruction does not just insist that their worship should be orderly, which would mean that any order was acceptable. It implies that the service should be done according to an established order, God's order, the right pattern for speaking and hearing

---

6    It was also used in the LXX for God's heavenly army (Judg 5:20; Job 38:12; Hab 3:11).

7    The best compilation and analysis of the data on this comes from Dautzenberg, 278–84.

8    1 Clement 40–42 shows how this concept of a liturgical order was understood in the Early Church by reference to the service at the temple: "Now that we have looked into the depths of divine knowledge, we ought to do all those things in **order** (*taxis*) that the Master of the House has commanded to be performed at **ordered** (*tetagmenous*) times. He did not command that the liturgical offerings should be performed arbitrarily or **disorderly** (*'ataktôs*), but at appointed times and hours. By his supreme will he himself has appointed where and through whom he wished them to be performed, so that they may all be done devoutly with his approval and be most acceptable to his will. Therefore those who make their offerings at the **ordered** (*prostetagmenois*) times are most acceptable and blessed, for, since they follow the regulations of the Master of the House, they do not go wrong. For to the high priest has been given his own liturgical tasks, and their own place has been **ordered** (*prostetaktai*) for the priests, and their own ministries have been assigned to the Levites, while the layperson has been bound by lay **orders** (*prostagmasin*). Let each of us, brothers, be well-pleasing to God in our own **order** (*tagma*), with a good conscience, without transgressing the appointed rule (*kanōn*) of our liturgical service, and with reverence. . . . The apostles received the gospel for us from the Lord Jesus Christ; Jesus the Christ was sent from the Father. So Christ is from God, and the apostles are from Christ. Both came to be in a **well-ordered** way (*'eutaktôs*) by the will of God. After they had received their instructions and been fully assured through the resurrection of our Lord Jesus Christ and convinced by the word of God, they went out with the full assurance of the Holy Spirit and preached the good news that the kingdom of God was about to come. So, as they preached from region to region and from town to town, they appointed their first fruits, after testing them by the Spirit, as bishops and deacons."

God's word and for giving and receiving Christ's body and blood. Paul also tells the Colossians that he rejoices in their "order" as a congregation (Col 2:5).[9]

The opposite of *taxis* is *'akatastasia*, disorder, whether it be political (Luke 21:9; 2 Cor 6:5), social (2 Cor 12:20; see James 3:8), liturgical (1 Cor 14:33), or spiritual (James 3:16; see 1:8) in character. Those who refuse to work for a living act *disorderly* (*'ataktôs*) in their community (2 Thess 3:6, 11), while those who disrupt its worship are *disorderly* (*'ataktous*) people (1 Thess 5:14; see 1 Clem 40:2).

The noun *taxis* is connected with verb *tassô*, which means to put or arrange a person or thing in a set place (BAGD, 1). It can also mean to establish an office (eg. Rom 13:11) or to appoint a person to a position, like the centurion in Luke 7:8, or for a particular task (Acts 15:2; 22:10).

From *tassô* comes the compound verb *hypotassô*, which means to put someone or something in a position *under* someone or something.[10] In its active voice it is used only of God in the New Testament (1 Cor 15:27, 28; Phil 3:21; Heb 2:5, 8; see Herm Man 12:42; Diog 10:2).[11] Likewise its passive voice is used only for God's placement of angels (1 Pet 3:22) and the whole universe (1 Cor 15:27, 28; Heb 2:8) under himself and Christ. The verb *hypotassô*, however, is most commonly used in the middle voice for self-subordination, the voluntary placement (Delling, 42) of oneself under God or his appointed agents (Rom 8:7; 10:3; 13:1; 1 Cor 14:34; 15:28; 16:16; Eph 5:21, 24; Col 3:18; Tit 2:5, 9; 3:1; Heb 12:9; James 4:7; 1 Pet 2:13, 18; 3:1, 5; 5:3). The noun from this verb is *hypotagê*, *subordination* (2 Cor 9:13; Gal 2:5; 1 Tim 2:11; 3:4; see 1 Clem 37:5; Ign Eph 2:2). With respect to Christ, no human being is *anhypotaktos*, exempted from his headship and *independent* from him (Heb 2:8). So those who refuse to accept God and the positions of leadership established by him are also regarded as *anhypotaktos*, *insubordinate* (1 Tim 1:9; Tit 1:6, 10).

From this overview of the terminology we may conclude that subordination has to do with order. God subordinates people to himself and his agents

---

9  The connection in Col 2:5 of 'order' with 'firmness of faith in Christ' does not make sense unless we take the order as the firm foundation for the stability of their faith in him.

10  While Thiselton quite rightly recognises that the notion of divine 'order' is implied by the use of this verb, he ignores the force of the prefix ηψπο and so argues that in 1 Cor 14:34 *hypotassesthōsan* should be translated: 'let them keep their ordered place' (1153–55). He therefore disconnects Paul's term from any implied link with the reality of headship as authority. Yet the regular use of this verb with the dative for the person as its indirect object shows that it always describes the acceptance of two things: the order of a community and the leadership of those who are responsible for its maintenance. Subordination is therefore always associated with an ordered community and its legitimate leadership.

11  All these passages allude to the Messianic Psalm 8:6, an indication of the importance of this text in the development of the teaching on subordination in the Early Church and its connection with christology.

in the orders that he has ordained for human life on earth. Subordination is a voluntary act by which people cooperate with God by fitting into his arrangement for them in the world and in the church.[12]

## 2. THE PATTERN OF SUBORDINATION
## IN THE NEW TESTAMENT

The references to subordination in the New Testament show that there are three basic temporal orders which have been ordained by God, two that belong to the realm of creation, the world, and one that belongs to the realm of redemption, the church.[13] St Peter maintains that each of these is *anthrôpinê ktisei*;[14] they are not human inventions but divinely established positions of leadership, offices created by God for humanity (1 Pet 2:13).[15] This means that there is no single general order of creation.[16] Each order differs from the

---

12　The question remains whether the words 'subordinate' and 'subordination' are the best English translations for *hypotassô* and its cognates. Translators have used terms such as 'be subject/subjection', or 'submit/be submissive/submission', or 'be obedient/obedience'. Yet as Yoder has shown (172), none of these translations is entirely satisfactory. Subjection conveys the notion of forceful debasement and domination by a person in power. Submission suggests passive subservience to the will of another person. Obedience touches only on one aspect of subordination in some contexts, for even if people carry out the commands of another, they can still be inwardly insubordinate and refuse to accept their situation. The advantage that the term subordination has over all these, despite its possible modern connotations of inequality and inferiority, is that, as Elliott notes (487), it carries with it the notion of adjustment to an order, rather than subservience to a person.

13　In contrast to the medieval teaching on the holy order of the monasticism, Luther maintains that there are three divinely instituted 'holy orders', the order of the ministry, the order of marriage, and the order of civil government. These holy orders are instituted by God's most holy word, the same word that sanctifies them and the believers who faithfully do the work of God in them. They and their work are sanctified by God's word and faith in it. Luther's teaching on these three holy orders is summarised most succinctly in his 'Confession Concerning Christ's Supper' of 1528 (LW 37, 364f). This teaching has confessional status by virtue of its inclusion in part nine of the Small Catechism in 'The Table of Duties'. Kolb and Wengert translate Luther's heading accurately by stating that these passages are God's word for the 'holy orders' that God has established. See Bayer and Wannenwetsch for two perceptive analyses of Luther's teaching on these three holy orders.

14　While Peter's call for Christians to be subordinate 'to every divinely instituted authority' clearly refers to the Roman emporer and the governors under him, his use of 'every' shows that it also introduces his call for the subordination of slaves to their masters (2:18), wives to their husbands (3:11), and church members to their presbyters (5:5).

15　The German text of Article 16 of the Augsburg Confession echoes this by asserting that the government and the family are 'true orders of God' (wahrhaftige Gottesordnung) in which each person, according to his own calling, is required to 'manifest Christian love and genuine good works in his station of life' (Tappert, 38).

16　Elliott quite rightly observes that '(t)he societies of the Greco-Roman period were greatly concerned with the establishment and maintenance of "order" (*taxis*) in all areas

other. What applies to one does not necessarily apply to the other. Likewise there is no general concept of subordination. It means something different in each different context.

First, we have **the order of the household**, the family. In keeping with the definition of the household by the tenth commandment in Exodus 20:17, it includes three different sets of relationships: wives and husbands (Eph 5:24; Col 3:18: Tit 2:5; 1 Pet 3:1, 5); children and parents (Luke 2:51; Tit 2:9; 1 Pet 2:18); servants and masters (Tit 2:9; 1 Pet 2:18). The husband, whose head is Christ (1 Cor 11:3), is the head of the wife (1 Cor 11:3; Eph 5:23). Surprisingly, the call for subordination of a Christian wife to her husband does not focus on her obedience to him, but on her respect for him as her head (Eph 5:22, 33; 1 Pet 3:2). Its purpose is for her to receive his love (Eph 5:24–27), and, if she is married to an unbeliever, to gain his conversion (1 Pet 3:1–2). While the father is the head of the family, both parents are the heads of their children. Like Jesus with his parents (Luke 2:51), the subordination of children to their parents involves reverence (1 Tim 3:4) and obedience (Eph 6:1; Col 3:20). Its purpose is the reception of prosperity and enjoyment of longevity in the family (Eph 6:1–3). Since slaves are considered part of the family,[17] their status is similar to the children. Their subordination to their masters also involves obedience (Eph 6:1; Col 3:20) and reverence (1 Tim 3:4), as well as acceptable behaviour and utter reliability (Tit 2:9,10). Its purpose is the reception of Christ's approval and his reward (Eph 6:8; Col 3:24; 1 Pet 2:22). In all these cases the attitude of subordination results in the kind of behaviour that is appropriate to the relationship.

Second, we have **the order of government** (Rom 13:1, 5; Tit 3:1; 1 Pet 2:13). The subordination of Christian citizens to their rulers involves obedience with four kinds of good works (Tit 3:2): the payment of taxes, the payment of custom's duties, respect for them, and honouring them (Rom 13:7). In this they do exactly what all good pagan citizens do. They, however, differ from them by their acceptance of their rulers as God's agents, his ministers (Rom 13:4) and assistants (Rom 13:6). The purpose of their subordination

---

of public and private life as a replication of an ordered universe (*kosmos*)' (486). He therefore assumes that this world view was adopted uncritically by the Early Church. Yet that does not quite fit the evidence. The apostles Peter and Paul and the apostolic authors, such as Clement and Ignatius, did not urge Christians to harmonise themselves and their behaviour to the natural order of the world or even its created order, but called on them to align themselves with the risen Lord Jesus as the head of the church and the cosmos by subordinating themselves to those whom God had set over them as their heads in the family, government and the church. They therefore did not promote the principle of order but the word of God that ordered the foundational communities for human life in the world and conveyed his blessings to those who lived in them.

17  See Exod 20:17.

is the reception of benefits from God through their rulers and the possession of a good conscience before God (Rom 13:3–5; 1 Pet 2:14).

Third, we have **the order of the church** (1 Cor 14:40). Here the risen Christ is the head (Eph 5:24; cf. Eph 4:15; Col 1:18; 2:19) with God the Father as his head (1 Cor 11:3). Within that order everybody is subordinate to some others (Eph 5:21).[18] The congregation is subordinate to God the Father for the reception of life from him (Heb 12:9; James 4:7) and to Christ for the reception of its salvation (Eph 5:24; see 4:15–16). Its subordination involves adherence to God's word (Rom 8:7) and the gospel as it is confessed in the creedal statements of the church (2 Cor 9:13).[19] The members of the congregation are subordinate to its leaders who teach God's word (1 Cor 16:15,16[20]; 1 Pet 5:5[21]; see Ign Eph 2:2; Ign Mag 2; 13:2; Ign Tr 2: 1, 2; 13:2; Ign Pol 6:1; 1 Clem. 1:3; 57:1, 2; Pol. Phil. 5:3).[22] This includes the silent subordination of women (and men!) to the men who teach God's word in their congregation (1 Cor 14:34; 1 Tim 2:11). The purpose of subordination is the reception of all that Christ gives to the church through his word.

---

18  The participial clause in Eph 5:21 can be construed in two ways grammatically, either as the fifth consequential participial after the imperative, 'be filled with the Spirit' in 5:18, or as a new participial imperative that serves as a summary introduction to the instructions in 5:22–6:11 (Barth, 608f, and Clark, 365). I take it to function both ways. Over the last fifty years this verse has been understood as a call for mutual, reciprocal subordination either for husbands and wives to each other in marriage, or else for all members to each other in a family. This interpretation, however, is questionable, as has been shown by Doriani and Grudem (2002b). It is contradicted by the specific call for the subordination of wives to husbands in 5:22,24, without any corresponding call for reciprocation from their husbands. It has, traditionally, been taken to mean that all Christians are to be subordinate to those others who are their leaders. This remains a viable interpretation, since the pronoun *'allêlois* is not only used reciprocally to refer to 'each other' and 'all others'. It can, in some cases, also be used distributively to refer 'each to another/each to some others' (see Matt 24:10; Luke 2:15; 12:1; 24:32; 1 Cor 11:33; Gal 6:2; Rev 6:4). 1 Clem 2:1 seems to paraphrase Paul's admonition: 'You were all humble-minded and not at all arrogant, subordinating yourselves rather than subordinating others, giving more gladly than taking.' See also its elaboration in 1 Clem 38:1–2.

19  See Pfitzner, 135.

20  1 Clem 42:4 tells us that the elders in the church at Corinth came from the 'first converts' there, who, according to Paul in 1 Cor 16:15, were from the household of Stephanas. So, when Paul urges the Corinthians to be subject to the household of Stephanas, he, most likely, refers to the elders in Corinth (Grudem, 2002b, 226, foonote 10).

21  The contrast between 'elders' as pastor-teachers in 1 Pet 5:1–4 and 'younger men' in 5:5 is rather puzzling. As Elliott has shown (838–41), the comparative adjective *neôteros* could refer to those who were later converts. It is used in Luke 22:26 for those who are led, in contrast to the 'great', those who lead. This pair of terms reflects the common Hebrew idiom, 'small and great' (Gen 19:11; 1 Sam 30:2,19; 1 Kgs 22:31; 2 Kgs 23:2; 25:26; 1 Chr 25:8; 26:13; 2 Chr 15:13; Job 3:19). As in Polycarp's Letter to the Philippians 5:3, Peter most likely uses it to refer to the lay members of the congregation.

22  For an analysis of the teaching of Ignatius on subordination to the leaders of the church, see Hensley.

Three things are worth noting from this data. First, the New Testament does not teach that there is a general universal order of creation. Second, it does not speak of the general subordination of all women to all men but only their subordination in particular relationships, according to their station, such as wives to husbands. There is therefore no theological reason why women cannot be leaders in government. Third, subordination means different things in different contexts and different relationships. While a woman may not speak as teacher in the liturgical assembly, she may question her husband at home (1 Cor 14:33–35) and teach younger women to be good wives and mothers (Tit 2:3–5).

Besides the earthly orders of family, government, and the church, there are three heavenly orders, **the order of the church triumphant**, **the angelic order** and **the order of the Holy Trinity**. In the order of the church triumphant God the Father has made Jesus the royal head of the universe for the benefit of the church and its mission to the world (1 Cor 15:25–27; Phil 3:21; Heb 2:5–8; 1 Pet 3:22). In the angelic order all the angels and the all things in the cosmos are now subordinate to Christ (1 Pet 3:22; 1 Cor 15:27; Eph 1:22; see Phil 2:9–11).

## THE SEMANTIC FIELD OF SUBORDINATION IN THE NEW TESTAMENT

| Relationship of Subordination | Order | Nature of Subordination | Benefits of Subordination |
|---|---|---|---|
| Wives to husbands | Family | Respect | Husband's love Husband's conversion |
| Children to parents | Family | Reverence Obedience | Prosperity Longevity |
| Slaves to masters | Family | Reverence Obedience Winsomeness Fidelity | Christ's approval Christ's reward |
| Christian citizens to rulers | State | Tax payment Duties payment Respect Honour | God's gifts Good conscience |
| Christians to God and his word | Church | Obedience (?) | Life from God |
| Christians to Christ | Church | Love (?) | Salvation |
| All Christians to the men who teach them | Church | Silent listening | Learning as disciples |
| Universe to Christ | Church triumphant | | |
| Angels to Christ | Angelic order | | |

## 3. Subordination and the Great Reversal

In the New Testament most of the teaching on subordination is found in the so-called *Haustafeln*, the house tables, the tables of domestic duty (Eph 5:21–6:9; Col 3:18–4:1; Tit 2:1–3:7; 1 Pet 2:11–3:22; 5:1–5).[23] They seem to reflect the tradition of catechesis in the Early Church. While they do reflect some common aspects of ethical teaching in the Ancient World, they themselves are quite unique in their form and content.[24]

First, they are not primarily addressed to those free individuals who enjoy the independence and power that come from an assured income and a high position in society, and allow them to exercise benevolent patronage with their dependants and clients. Instead, they first address those who are dependent on others for their livelihood, wives, children, and slaves. They treat these "subordinate" people as moral agents, people who are responsible for social cohesion and communal solidarity. Only then do they speak to the people who are the leaders, their husbands, parents, and masters. Thus we have matching sets of instructions that presuppose reciprocity and focus on the importance of the rank and file members of the family for its prosperity.

- Wives    → Husbands    (Eph 5:22–33; Col 3:18–19; 1 Pet 3:1–7)
- Children → Parents     (Eph 6:1–4; Col 3:20–21)
- Slaves   → Masters     (Eph 6:5–9; Col 3:22–4:1[25])

Second, the moral philosophers in antiquity did not call on wives, children, and slaves to be subordinate, because they had no choice but to submit to their superiors. In contrast, the call for subordination by Paul and Peter arises from their equality before God (Yoder, 175).[26] Through baptism and union with Christ each Christian has gained the same royal status and worth. All the saints share the same status as Christ the Son because they are all

---

23  See Elliott, 503–11, for a recent summary of the debate about the origin, nature and function of the so-called house tables as well as a bibliography on them and subordination in them.

24  Delling makes this claim about the teaching on subordination in the New Testament: 'This word which belonged originally to the sphere of worldly order is now filled with new content as a term of order' (45). In what follows I am much indebted to the work of Yoder on the revolutionary teaching on subordination in the New Testament.

25  Note that in 1 Pet 2:18–25 and Tit 2:9–14 the mention of slaves is not followed by the mention of their masters.

26  It is worth noting that there is very little explicit teaching about equality in the New Testament. Jesus never mentions it. The apostles teach about five aspects of it: the equality in divinity of the Son with the Father (Phil 2:16; see John 5:18), the equal bestowal of the Holy Spirit on Jews and Gentiles (Acts 11:7), the equal possession of faith by all Christians (2 Pet 1:1), the equal provision for the needs in the church through the offering for the poor in Jerusalem (2 Cor 8:13), and the equal treatment of slaves by their Christian masters (Col 4:1).

"sons" of the heavenly king and coheirs with him Gal 3:26–4:7). They then have even greater freedom and dignity than the aristocracy in their society. This makes them people that matter, holy people who make a difference, God's coworkers.

Third, while the teaching of moral philosophy in antiquity tried to prevent a social-political revolution upwards in which the ruled displaced their former rulers, the apostolic teaching on subordination presupposes a spiritual revolution downwards that was accomplished by the incarnation, death, and resurrection of God's Son. Through him the original order of the human family has been redeemed and transformed so that it now provides the framework for the life of God's heavenly family here on earth. In this new order the abuse of power is arrested and undone by self-sacrificial love.

In their epistles St Paul and St Peter promote a kind of revolutionary subordination that involves a complete reversal of social values.[27] In the ancient world the ideal person was an independent man, with economic resources and political clout, a self-sufficient autonomous person. Yet in the church this is reversed. There the ideal human being is a dependent person, someone who is subordinate and reliant on others, such as a wife or a child or a servant. Thus the church is the bride of Christ; all Christians are children of God and servants of Christ. The ideal state for the Christian is now no longer to be a master, with legally assured status, wealth and power, but to be a servant, free from enslavement to social status, wealth and power (1 Pet 2:16). Subordination has therefore become the normal condition in the church. All Christians are subordinate to Christ (Eph 5:21, 23), to God the Father (Heb 12:9; James 4:7), and to the orders that God has established (1 Pet 2:13). So, every Christian is in subordination to someone else. All are under headship and authority. None are self-sufficient and autonomous

Fourth, the revolutionary character of the apostolic teaching on subordination is most evident in the content of the house tables. Even though the apostles accepted the given structure of the family and their societies, they called for a change in the attitude of those who lived in these communities. There are two surprises! On the one hand, by their subordination to their heads, wives, children, slaves and citizens are expected to do nothing more than what was normally required of them. In one very significant case the usual demands have been lightened. Thus, in a society where wives were often expected to serve their husbands sexually and to use their sexual assets to gain what they wanted, the apostles merely urge wives to "respect" their husbands (Eph 5:33) and to be fearless in doing what is good, without using

---

27 See Yoder, 185-87, and Foster, 101–05.

their sexuality to manipulate their husbands (1 Pet 3:1–7).[28] On the other hand, the apostles required much more of husbands, fathers, and masters than what was demanded by custom and law. They were, in fact, to act as if they stood in the shoes of their subordinates. Instead of requiring their wives to demonstrate their love for them, husbands were to love their wives demonstrably and self-sacrificially, like Christ with the church (Eph 5:25–28; Col 3:19); instead of expecting their wives to meet their needs and honour them, they were to honour their wives and consider their needs (1 Pet 3:7). Paul does not demand that children should avoid provoking and angering their fathers; instead, fathers should not provoke and anger their children (Eph 6:4; Col 3:21). Most radically, masters were not just urged to treat their slaves fairly as if they were equals[29] (Col 4:1), but to do God's will by wholeheartedly "serving" them (Eph 6:9).[30]

Fifth, even though the apostles teach that God has created the order of the family and government (Rom 13:2; 1 Pet 2:13), they do not base their teaching on how and why Christians are to be subordinate to their leaders on God's creation of these orders or on a universal cosmic order. Instead, they find both the reason for subordination and the model of right subordination in Christ and his self-sacrificial service (Eph 5:21–27; Tit 2:9–10; 3:1–7; 1 Pet 2:13, 21–25). Since they are in Christ and have him as their Lord (Eph 6:1; Col 3:18), they are to be subordinate to others out of reverence for him (Eph 5:22). Subordination is the apt thing to do for those who are in Christ (Col 3:18). Since willing subordination reflects Christ's attitude and character, it sends out the right message to the world and so promotes the mission of the church (Tit 2:4–5, 9–14; 1 Pet 2:13–15; 3:1–2).

If Christ is the basis and the model for subordination, then only those who are in Christ can be truly subordinate, for they alone have been transformed by him and conformed to him by the Holy Spirit (Tit 3:1–7). Thus in Ephesians 5:18–21 Paul associates subordination with the communal performance of thanksgiving to God the Father through Jesus, and regards both as products of the Holy Spirit.[31] As we are filled with the Holy Spirit we receive the ability and desire to practice full subordination.

## 4. CONCLUSION

When the apostles Peter and Paul teach subordination, they do not thereby sanction the social, political, economic status quo, but, in fact, acknowledge

---

28  In fact, in 1 Cor 7:3–4 Paul teaches that Christian husbands and wives should, by common consent, provide mutual sexual access to each other.

29  While the term *'isotês* can mean 'fairness' and 'equity', it may also mean 'equality'.

30  The phrase *ta panta poieîte* refers back to *met' 'eunoias douleuontes* in 6:7.

31  See footnote 18.

how riddled it is with sin and the abuse of power. They do not propose a social or political agenda for the reformation and transformation of a society by the behaviour of its lower classes. Nor do they reinforce cultural roles or stereotypical patterns of behaviour in marriage, family life, and society at large. Instead, they show how Christians can already now, by faith, live with God as citizens of heaven within the earthly orders of a fallen world, because Christ has transformed the whole human life cycle from the womb to the tomb by his incarnation and his exaltation. Christ does not abolish the old divinely instituted orders of family and government to free his disciples from life in community, but he redeems these orders so that they can accomplish their proper purpose. In practical terms, the apostles do not assimilate the church to the patriarchal family, which is modelled on the state with its coercive structures of power. On the contrary, Christ rules as the head of all principalities and powers in all governments and all families for the sake of the church (Eph 1:20–23). The family and government are meant to serve Christ and his church. By fulfilling its vocation of serving others in self-giving love, the church provides the model for life in community as it reflects the order of self-giving in the Holy Trinity.

In sum: the apostolic teaching on subordination does not establish a chain of command for the exercise of power by those who sit at the top; it promotes a chain of transmission from the triune God for the delivery of blessings through his appointed agents in the church and in the world.

No one has summed this whole teaching up more vividly and aptly than Clement in his First Letter to the Corinthians. He writes these glowing words to that congregation which had been riddled with insubordination (37–38):[32]

> Brothers, let us therefore campaign most strenuously under the Son's blameless **orders** (*prostagmata*). Let us consider those who campaign with our leaders, with what **good order** (*eutaktôs*), with what willingness, and with what **subordination** (*hypotetagmenôs*) they fulfil their **orders** (*diatassomena*). They are not all generals or colonels or captains or lieutenants, or so forth; but each one in his own **order** (*tagma*) fulfils the **orders** (*epitassomena*) given by the emperor and the leaders. The great cannot exist without the small, nor the small without the great. There is a kind of mixture that is beneficial to all.
>
> Take our body! The head without the feet is nothing; likewise, the feet without the head are nothing. Even the smallest parts of the body are necessary and useful to the whole body. But all breathe together and act in single **subordination** (*hypotagê*), so that the whole body may be saved.
>
> So let our whole body be saved in Christ Jesus, and let each person be **subordinate** (*hypotassomai*) to his neighbour, as appointed with his **gift**

---

32   This translation is a slightly modified version of the text in Goodspeed, 67f.

(*charisma*). Do not let the strong neglect the weak, and let the weak respect the strong. Let the rich provide for the poor, and the poor give thanks to God, because he has given them someone to fill up what they lack. Let the wise show their wisdom in good deeds rather than in words. Do not let the humble-minded speak about themselves, but let others speak about them. Do not let those who are sexually chaste boast, knowing that it is someone else who grants them this self-control.

So brothers, let us consider how we were begotten, how we entered the world, how God has shaped and created us from a dark grave and brought us into his world, where he had prepared his benefits for us before we were even born. Since therefore we have received all these things from him, we ought to give thanks to him for everything, to whom be the glory forever and ever. Amen.

## BIBLIOGRAPHY

Barth, Markus
1974    *Ephesians, Translation and Commentary on Chapters 4–6*, Anchor Bible Commentary, Doubleday, New York.

Bayer, Oswald
1998    'Nature and Institution: Luther's Doctrine of the Three Orders,' *Lutheran Quarterly* 12, 125–59.

Clark, Andrew T
1990    *Ephesians*, Word Bible Commentary, Word Books, Dallas.

Dautzenberg, Gerhard
1975    'Das Einhalten der schönen Ordnung beim Gottesdienst', *Urchristliche Prophetie. Ihre Forschung, ihre Voraussetzungen im Judentum und ihre Struktur im ersten Korintherbrief*, BWANT 104. Kohlhammer, Stuttgart, 278–84.

Delling, Gerhard
1972    'hypotassô', *Theological Dictionary of New Testament* 8, Gerhard Kittel and Gerhard Friedrich (eds), Geoffrey W Bromiley (tr), Eerdmans, Grand Rapids, 39–46.

Doriani, Daniel
2002    'The Historical Novelty of Egalitarian Interpretations of Ephesians 5:21–22', in Wayne Grudem ed, *Biblical Foundations for Manhood and Womanhood*, Crossway Books, Wheaton, 203–31.

Eliott, John H
2000    *1 Peter. A New Translation with Introduction and Commentary*, Anchor Bible Commentary, Doubleday, New York.

Foster, Richard
1978    *Celebration of Discipline*, Hodder & Stoughton, London.

Goodspeed, Edgar J
1950    *The Apostolic Fathers. An American Translation*, The Independent Press,
        London.

Grudem, Wayne
1991    'The Meaning of *kephale*: A Response to Recent Studies', *Recovering
        Biblical Manhood and Womanhood*, John Piper and Wayne Grudem eds,
        Crossway Books, Wheaton, 425–68.

2002a   'The Meaning of *kephale* ("Head"): An Evaluation of New Evidence,
        Real and Alleged', in *Biblical Foundations for Manhood and Womanhood*,
        Wayne Grudem ed, Crossways Books, Wheaton, 145–202.

2002b   'The Myth of Mutual Submission as an Interpretation of Ephesians
        5:21', in *Biblical Foundations for Manhood and Womanhood*, Wayne
        Grudem ed, Crossway Books, Wheaton, 221–31.

Hensley, Adam
2001    'Submission to Bishop, Presbytery and deacons in the Letters of St
        Ignatius of Antioch', *Lutheran Theological Journal* 35/2, 75–86.

Pfitzner, Victor C
1991    *Strength in Weakness. A Commentary on 2 Corinthians*, Lutheran
        Publishing House, Adelaide.

Kolb, Robert, and Timothy J. Wengert
2000    *The Book of Concord: The Confessions of the Evangelical Lutheran Church*,
        Fortress Press, Minneapolis.

Kroeger, Catherine
1991    'Head', *Dictionary of Paul and His Letters*, Gerald F. Hawthorne, Ralph
        P. Martin, and Daniel G. Reid eds, InterVarsity, Downers Grove and
        Leicester, 375–77.

Luther, Martin
1961    'Confession Concerning Christ's Supper' (1528), in Robert H. Fischer
        ed, *Luther's Works* 37, Fortress, 151–59.

Tappert, Theodore G
1959    *The Book of Concord: The Confessions of the Evangelical Lutheran Church*,
        Fortress, Minneapolis.

Thiselton, Anthony C
2000    *The First Epistle to the Corinthians*, The New International Greek
        Testament Commentary, Eerdmans, Grand Rapids and Paternoster,
        Carlisle.

Yoder, John Howard
1994    'Revolutionary Subordination,' *The Politics of Jesus. Behold the Man! Our
        Victorious Lamb*, Second Edition, Eerdmans, Grand Rapids, 162–92.

Wannenwetsch, Bernd
2001    'Luther's Moral Theology', *The Cambridge Companion to Martin Luther*,
        Donald K McKim ed, Cambridge University Press, Cambridge, 120–35.

# The Ordination of Women[1]

## Gregory J. Lockwood

Wherever the Gospel has free course, it has a liberating effect on women (as indeed the Gospel liberates all people, Jn 8:31–36). In the South Pacific nation of Papua New Guinea, for example, where women were traditionally treated as chattels,[2] the advent of Christianity has often brought them a new dignity and respect. Indeed there are countless societies where many women, once regarded merely as garden beds for raising children[3]—to be discarded if they proved unfruitful—have found their Christian husbands treating them with courtesy and affection.

This Christian regard for women is, of course, inspired by "the meekness and gentleness of Christ" (2 Cor 10:1). Jesus himself set the pattern for his church by his own respect for women, beginning with his childhood submission to his mother (Lk 2:51). To women he extended his healing hand; with women he was happy to converse, to the amazement of his disciples (Jn 4:27); to women and men alike he taught the Word of God. Luke records how on one occasion the Lord took time to teach a class consisting of one woman, Mary, who received his praise because she "chose the best part, which will not be taken away from her" (Lk 10:38–42). Paul commands husbands to love their wives "as Christ loved the church and gave himself up for her" (Eph 5:25). Peter counsels husbands to "live considerately . . . with [their] wives, bestowing honor [on the women] as joint heirs of the grace of life" (1 Pet 3:7). Thus biblical Christianity elevates women, honors them as equal members of the Christian community, and encourages them to study the Scriptures. The

---

1   A fuller discussion of some of the topics in this essay can be found in G. Lockwood, *The Women's Ordination Debate in the Lutheran Church of Australia* (privately printed, second ed. 1999; reprinted Concordia Theological Seminary Press, Fort Wayne, IN, 2000).

2   See *Pigs, Pearlshells, and Women: Marriage in the New Guinea Highlands*, ed. R. M. Glasse and M. J. Meggitt (Englewood Cliffs, NJ: Prentice-Hall, 1969).

3   W. Trobisch describes the "garden concept of marriage" common to pagan cultures in *I Married You* (Leicester: Inter-Varsity, 1972) 29–32.

same is true of the Lutheran church in particular. The Lutheran Confessions sharply criticize misogyny: "Daniel says that it is characteristic of Antichrist's kingdom to despise women."[4]

Whereas the OT honors women as equal members of the worshiping community (Ex 19:6–8; Deut 29:10–12), rabbinic Judaism during the days of Jesus and Paul was developing in a direction which relegated women to an inferior status. Women could worship only in the forecourt of the Herodian temple (the court of the women) or in the gallery or outer chamber of the synagogue. The Tosefta includes this second-century A.D. rabbinic teaching:

> R. Judah says, "A man must recite three benedictions every day: (1) 'Praised [be Thou, O Lord, our God, King of the universe,] who did not make me a gentile'; (2) 'Praised [be Thou, O Lord . . .] who did not make me a boor'; (3) 'Praised [be Thou, O Lord . . .] who did not make me a woman.' . . .
>
> "[Praised be Thou, O Lord . . . who did not make me] a woman—for women are not obligated [to perform all] the commandments."[5]

Most rabbis did not see themselves under obligation to teach women the Torah; indeed, some discouraged the practice.[6]

At the opposite extreme from rabbinic Judaism, the Greco-Roman culture of Paul's day frequently allowed women a leading role in religious rites. Whereas the Jewish Torah restricted the priesthood to men, there were no explicit prohibitions of priestesses in other religions.[7] Thus women priests may be found at any time and in any place in the Hellenistic world. On the basis of inscriptional evidence, Gill states categorically: "Woman priests were present in [imperial] Corinth."[8] Gooch adduces evidence from the large sanctuary of Demeter and Kore in Roman Corinth, where women are known to

---

4    Ap XXIII 25, citing Daniel 11:37.

5    *Berakhot*, 6.18, *The Tosefta*, first division, ed. J. Neusner and R. Sarason (Hoboken, NJ: KTAV, 1986) 40. This rabbinic saying is quoted in the Jerusalem Talmud, *Berakhot*, 9.1 (see *The Talmud of the Land of Israel*, vol. 1, trans. T. Zahavy [Chicago: Univ. of Chicago Press, 1989] 318). Cf. M. Hauke, *Women in the Priesthood?* 327.

6    Thus Rabbi Eliezer wrote (around A.D. 90): "If any man gives his daughter a knowledge of the Law it is as though he taught her lechery" (Mishnah, *Sotah*, 3.4; ed. H. Danby, 296).

7    M. Hauke, *Women in the Priesthood?* 191–92. Hauke adds: "In Egypt and Greece, for instance, women stood *pari cum pari* ['equals with equals'] with their professional colleagues of the opposite sex in the service of male deities. Naturally, priestesses play a special role in the service of female deities, and particularly of mother goddesses."

8    "The Importance of Roman Portraiture for Head-Coverings in 1 Corinthians 11:2–16," 252. Gill points to a marble block discovered in imperial Corinth bearing the following inscription:

> To Polyaena, daughter of Marcus, priestess of Victory. The high priest [Publius] Licinius Priscus Juventianus, [while still living, (set up this monument)] with the official sanction of the city council to (this) excellent woman. (Citing J. H.

have played a prominent role in the fertility rites. Each October/November the festival known as Thesmophoria was held in honor of Demeter and Kore. Gooch describes the rites:

> On the first night of the festival women gathered to drink and participate in rites of foul, abusive language and sexual joking (*aischrologia* [αἰσχρολογία, the activity Paul condemns in Col 3:8; cf. αἰσχρόν, "shameful," in 1 Cor 11:6; 14:35]). . . . There is evidence for feasts held on the last day of the festival, *presided over by women elected to office in the cultus*. Finally, associated with the festival are sacrificial cakes made into the shape of phalli. . . . Sexual organs made from pastry were set out on the tables.[9]

Whether all cults in which women figured as priestesses were as gross as the Demeter cult is not the issue here. The point is simply that a number of ancient cults, including those represented in Corinth, featured female priests.[10]

In the light of the contrasts with its religious environment, the apostolic teaching on the role of women in worship is *countercultural*. Whereas the male chauvinism characteristic of some[11] cultures (in Paul's day and ours) regards women as mere chattels, and rabbinic Judaism tended to treat them as second-class members of the community, the apostles counsel husbands to cherish and honor their wives.[12] On the other hand, in contrast to the permissiveness of pagan religions, which often allowed women to serve as priestesses and instructors in the cult, the biblical revelation does not permit them to serve as priests (Ex 28:1) or pastors (1 Tim 3:2; Titus 1:6). Thus Paul's command that the women be silent in the churches (1 Cor 14:34) must be understood,

---

Kent, *Corinth: The Inscriptions 1926–1950* [Princeton, NJ: American School of Classical Studies at Athens, 1966] p. 89, no. 199, plate 17)

9   *Dangerous Food*, 11; emphasis added.

10   Further evidence is found in Pausanias, the second century A.D. travel-writer, who describes a festival of the goddess Artemis at Patras in the northern Peloponnese (a little to the south of Corinth): "The festival opens with a most gorgeous procession in honour of Artemis, the rear being brought up by the virgin priestess" (D. Gill, "Behind the Classical Façade," 77).

    The above evidence relates directly to Corinth and its environs. From other parts of the empire sporadic references are found to priestesses functioning in the pagan cults. In Ephesus, for example, a priestess had become the cult's chief official by A.D. 104 (P. Trebilco, "Asia," *The Book of Acts in Its Graeco-Roman Setting*, ed. D. Gill and C. Gempf, 324). According to Strabo (ca. A.D. 20), when the Artemis cult expanded into Phocaea, a Greek colony in western Anatolia, the Phocaeans paid the woman Aristarcha the honor of appointing her priestess (P. Trebilco, "Asia," 334, citing Strabo, *Geography*, 4.1.4.). The role of the Vestal Virgins in Roman rites is also well known.

11   The choice of the word "some" is deliberate; women at times achieved high status in some non-Christian cultures (cf. Acts 17:12).

12   See the commentary on 1 Cor 10:25–30 for further examples of how Paul's teaching was emphatically countercultural in relation to rabbinic Judaism.

in part, as countercultural and antisyncretistic. It is a command that distinguishes and separates the Christian church from other religions. Inspired by the Spirit of God, its roots are deep in the biblical revelation, which always runs counter to the spirit and the wisdom of this world (2:12).

## THE SCRIPTURES ARE THE BASIS FOR DECIDING THE ISSUE

There is a broad consensus among those who desire to remain faithful to historic Christianity that the issue of whether or not to ordain women must be decided on the basis of the biblical evidence. Only the most radical postmodernist would disagree with Reumann: "Any decision about women functioning in the ordained Ministry of the church must rest . . . on careful examination of the scriptural data."[13]

There is also consensus that the results of this biblical study will depend on the principles of interpretation (the hermeneutics) employed. Reumann continues: "The whole question is basically one of hermeneutics: how do you interpret and apply the Scripture?"[14] Beyond this point of consensus, however, the ways divide. While there is general agreement that different hermeneutical approaches are at the root of the differing conclusions, some maintain that these variations in approach and result should not trouble the church; after all, the divergence is *merely* a matter of hermeneutics and should not be considered church divisive.

Others object that much more is at stake in one's choice of a hermeneutical approach. Not every way of interpreting the Bible is equally true to the Bible's self-understanding and therefore equally faithful to God and helpful in building up the church. No matter what assurances may be given regarding a common commitment to the Bible, it is by no means insignificant that higher-critical methodologies foster a critical stance toward the authority, truthfulness, and clarity of parts of the Bible. Again the church faces this old question: Is the Bible the Word of God, as a whole and in all its parts (1 Thess 2:13), or does it merely contain the Word of God? And—a corollary to that primary question—is the Bible clear, harmonious, and self-consistent, or does it contain (as critical scholars suggest) divergent theological strands which

---

13  *Ministries Examined*, 78. The postmodernist school of thought has difficulty accepting any authority-claims or truth-claims, including the claims of the Bible. For the postmodernist, the chief authority is his or her own self, his or her personal life experience, perception, and judgment. Cf. G. Veith: "Postmodernists tend on principle to rebel against authority. . . . All authority is assumed to be intrinsically oppressive" (*Postmodern Times: A Christian Guide to Contemporary Thought and Culture* [Wheaton, IL: Crossway, 1994] 108).

14  *Ministries Examined*, 98.

make it "possible to draw different, even diametrically opposed, conclusions on the subject [of women's ordination] from different parts of Scripture"?[15] Thus the issue of women's ordination is no isolated phenomenon.[16] Rather, the church's stance on the issue will be symptomatic of its attitude to more fundamental questions of hermeneutics and the doctrine of Scripture.

The question, then, is whether to adopt (1) an understanding of the entire Bible as the Word of God, together with a hermeneutic which allows Scripture (rather than culture) to interpret Scripture ("the hermeneutics of appreciation"),[17] or (2) whether to follow a critical approach to the Scriptures, which to a greater or lesser extent questions the authority, clarity,[18] and relevance of foundational texts (a hermeneutic which in its crasser forms has been called "the hermeneutics of suspicion").

Despite assurances that the differences among Christians on the issue are merely a matter of hermeneutics, the advocates of women's ordination themselves do not accept all hermeneutical approaches as equally salutary. Reumann, for example, describes two different ways of interpreting Scripture.

---

15  R. T. France, *Women in the Church's Ministry: A Test-Case for Biblical Interpretation* (Grand Rapids: Eerdmans, 1995) 27.

16  In addition to its relationship to the doctrine of Scripture and the doctrine of the public ministry, the issue of women's ordination regularly brings in its train such questions as these: "(1) Is God male or female, and what difference does it make? (2) Can a male Savior save women? (3) Is a woman included in the traditional category formerly known as 'man'?" (G. Grindal, "Luther's Theology as a Resource for Feminists," *Dialog* 24.1 [Winter 1985] 32). In other words, it raises gender questions with regard to the nature of the Trinity and biblical anthropology. Arguments for the ordination of women are often coupled with extensive critique of patriarchal tendencies in the Scriptures. For a fine presentation of the Bible's portrait of God as a loving, caring Father, in contrast to pagan depictions of divinities as males (or females), see W. Weinrich, "*It Is Not Given to Women to Teach*": *A Lex in Search of a Ratio* (Fort Wayne, IN: Concordia Theological Seminary Press, 1993) 24–27. Weinrich observes: "The Christian Church does not worship a male god, nor does it worship a female goddess. This does not mean, however, that the Christian does not worship God the **Father** and God the **Son**" (p. 25).

17  Cf. Ps 119:72: "The Torah [teaching instruction] from your mouth is more precious to me than thousands of gold and silver pieces."

18  The essential clarity of the Scriptures is a vital point in the church's doctrine of Scripture. Against Erasmus, Luther argued for the perspicuity of Scripture: "The notion that in Scripture some things are recondite [obscure] and all is not plain was spread by the godless Sophists. . . . And Satan has used these unsubstantial spectres to scare men off reading the sacred text, and to destroy all sense of its value" (*The Bondage of the Will*, trans. J. I. Packer and O. R. Johnston [London: James Clarke, 1957] 71; cf. LW 33:25).

Luther adds: "Those who deny the perfect clarity and plainness of the Scriptures leave us nothing but darkness" (*The Bondage of the Will*, 128; cf. LW 33:94). In support of his position Luther cites Pss 19:8; 119:105; Is 8:20; Mal 2:7; 2 Pet 1:19.

The clarity of the key NT texts which teach that women are not given the pastoral office can hardly be disputed (see 1 Cor 14:33b–38; 1 Tim 2:11–14; 3:1–7; Titus 1:5–9).

One approach, he writes, "argues by proof texts," the other supposedly is Gospel-centered. Thus we face this question: "Does a central gospel or do individual texts . . . prevail in reaching a decision?"[19] Already the dice are loaded: one approach professes to be Gospel-centered, and therefore good; the other, by implication, is not Gospel-centered, and therefore is legalistic and bad. This latter approach, it is claimed, sets too much store by "proof texts" and "individual texts."

Those expressions have been used, without proper definition, to disparage any appeal to the key foundational texts which have served as the church's basis in determining its teaching and practice. If employing "proof texts" means that a person appeals to biblical texts without regard to their context, then all would agree that this is bad. But what Reumann (among others) attacks specifically is making too much of texts that speak directly to the issue: "To begin with the Old Testament, with 1 Corinthians 14, or 1 Timothy 2, can lead only to the exclusion of women from ordained Ministry."[20] But that is not the method Reumann advocates.

Again one must ask, What is wrong with appealing to key foundational texts? Jesus himself, immersed in the Scriptures as he was,[21] constantly appealed to individual texts from the OT as the foundation for his teaching and practice (see the thrice-repeated "it is written" in Mt 4:1–13, for example). A reading of the Small Catechism will show that Luther also quotes the Bible over and over as the foundation of the teaching he expounds. He uses texts that speak to the specific issue. In elucidating the doctrine of Baptism, for example, he does not appeal in general terms to "the Gospel." Rather, he adduces individual texts (the *sedes doctrinae*) that deal specifically with Baptism (Mt 28:19; Titus 3:5–8; Rom 6:4).[22]

---

19  J. Reumann, *Ministries Examined*, 99.

20  J. Reumann, *Ministries Examined*, 117.

21  Indeed, Jesus is the Word incarnate (Jn 1:1–14), and the Spirit of Christ inspired the OT prophets (1 Pet 1:11).

22  SC IV 4, 10, 14. This *sedes doctrinae* approach also characterizes Luther's attitude to women's ordination (LW 41:154–55):

> It is . . . true that the Holy Spirit has excepted women, children, and incompetent people from this function, but chooses (except in emergencies) only competent males to fill this office, as one reads here and there in the epistles of St. Paul that a bishop must be pious, able to teach, and the husband of one wife—and in I Corinthians 14 [:34] he says, "The women should keep silence in the churches." In summary, it must be a competent and chosen man. Children, women, and other persons are not qualified for this office, even though they are able to hear God's word, to receive baptism, the sacrament, absolution, and are also true, holy Christians, as St. Peter says [I Pet. 3:7].

# APPLYING THE SCRIPTURES TODAY: BRIDGING THE "GAP" BETWEEN THE BIBLE AND THE MODERN WORLD

Advocates of women's ordination see enormous significance in the cultural, linguistic, and historical gaps that divide the first century from the twenty-first. They assert that what the biblical text meant then may be different from what it means today.[23] Biblical texts are said to be "time conditioned" and "culture bound." In view of this gulf between the biblical and the modern "horizons," it should not be surprising (it is alleged) that whereas in Paul's day to have ordained women would have been harmful to the church's mission, in our day it would be helpful to her mission.

We must, indeed, deal discriminatingly with the Scriptures. Not all is on the same level, not all is as equally and directly applicable to the church today. For example, much of the OT law has been fulfilled and thus superseded: the ceremonial law has been fulfilled in Christ, our great high priest; the civil law applied specifically to the nation of Israel,[24] and no longer applies to us. The Ten Commandments, on the other hand, still do apply; Jesus and the apostles constantly confirmed them (e.g., Lk 18:18–20; Rom 13:8–10). And the NT is the authoritative interpreter of the OT. Consequently we need to be careful before concluding that any NT teaching no longer applies. To be sure, we no longer wash one another's feet (John 13). But that custom is not prescribed in the NT, anyway; Jesus simply refers to it as an "example" or "pattern" (Jn 13:15) of how we are to serve one another in Christian love. What is commanded, *mandated*, is that we love one another,[25] however that love may be expressed in our modern culture. Similarly, in 1 Cor 11:2–16, Paul urges the women to conform in feminine modesty to the custom of their day by wearing a head-covering at public worship. *Customs* of dress may change, but the *principle* of male headship and female subordination (1 Cor 11:3) remains in effect. We have no authority to abrogate a command, a mandate of the Lord. To do so involves disobedience to the Lord of the church.

Certainly the first-century world differed from ours in a host of ways (the practices of foot-washing and head-coverings are but two examples). But the significance of these differences should not be exaggerated. Cultures vary from one another in their surface configurations—thus the fascination of studying other cultures and languages. But the longer one is immersed in another

---

23  Cf. R. T. France, *Women in the Church's Ministry*, 24–25: "The question is not now what the text *meant*, but what it *means* to me in my situation and to you in yours."

24  Luther said: "Moses is the *Sachsenspiegel* [Saxon code of law] for the Jews" (LW 35:167).

25  See Jn 13:34: "A new commandment [Vulgate: *mandatum novum*] I give you, that you love one another." The word "commandment" in Greek is ἐντολή, the very word Paul uses in 1 Cor 14:37 in undergirding his injunction (in 14:34) that the women be silent in the churches: "it is the Lord's command [ἐντολή]" (14:37).

culture, whether ancient or contemporary, the more one realizes that under the surface all human beings have the same desires, weaknesses, aspirations, and so forth. It is a myth that modern men and women are thoroughly different from the people of biblical times. Deep down, all share a common humanity which is far more important than anything that appears on the surface.

And the same Word of God is addressed to all. From one point of view, indeed, there are two horizons; we need to dig into the biblical world and its history and languages if we are to grasp it accurately. But the more we enter that world sympathetically, the more we hear the same Word that was addressed to people of biblical times addressing us today. For, from the divine perspective, there is really only one horizon. The OT prophets were taken up into God's council (his סוֹד, Jer 23:22) and enabled to see past, present, and future from God's vista. Similarly, the apostles and evangelists of the NT are given the Word of the One who sees and foresees all human history. As H. Wheeler Robinson observed, God's people across the generations have a "corporate personality."[26] Thus Moses can speak to the Israelites some forty years after the exodus and revelation at Mt. Sinai: "The Lord our God made a covenant with us at Horeb. *It was not with our fathers* that the Lord made this covenant, *but with us*, with all of us who are alive here today" (Deut 5:2–3). What God said to our forefathers and mothers he still says to us "today" (Ps 95:7)—unless there are clear indications to the contrary in Scripture. The God in whom there is "no change or shadow of turning" (James 1:17), the Lord who is "the same yesterday, today, and forever" (Heb 13:8) has given the same clear Word to all generations of his church.

## THE GOSPEL

Some have argued that the only link between the first and twenty-first centuries that remains unchanged is the Gospel: "The gospel principle is a long-standing Lutheran principle governing both how we 'do theology' and how we interpret the Scriptures."[27] Indeed, if there is one thing on which both the advocates and opponents of women's ordination are agreed, it is the importance of the Gospel as the *cantus firmus*, the great central theme of the Scriptures. In 1 Corinthians, Paul's argument concerning the role of women in the church is embedded in his magnificent presentation of the Gospel. This Gospel is first articulated in his announcement of the epistle's theme—the word of the cross (1:18)—then reiterated throughout the epistle in keeping

---

26 *Corporate Personality in Ancient Israel* (Philadelphia: Fortress, 1964). The expression "corporate personality" may not be the most felicitous. It may be better to speak of the community, the solidarity of all human beings in Adam, and of all believers in Christ.

27 N. Habel and S. Wurst, "The Gospel and Women in the Ministry," *Lutheran Theological Journal* 28.3 (December 1994) 129.

with his desire to know only "Jesus Christ and him crucified" (2:2). Finally it is taken up again immediately after Paul's discussion of the role of women as he reminds the Corinthians of their basic lessons in the Gospel: "I delivered to you as of first importance what I also received: that Christ died for our sins . . ." (15:3). On the importance and permanence of this golden theme we are all agreed.

Disagreement begins to arise, however, when we consider the relationship of this fundamental article of the Christian faith to other articles. While we agree that every other article will—if correctly stated—be in harmony with the Gospel,[28] this appreciation of the way the various articles of the faith form one perfect tapestry does not provide a warrant to drain individual articles of their color. Thus our adherence to the Gospel principle—the centrality of the Gospel—and our appreciation of the new creation in Christ does not warrant reduction and homogenization of other doctrines (most importantly in this context, the ongoing significance of the original order of creation,[29] the fall into sin, the Law, and the doctrine of the ministry) so that these collapse and cease to have significance.

Paul defines and spells out the Gospel of justification in very specific ways and continually highlights it as his great central theme. But he addresses other topics as well and deserves an attentive hearing on each issue. These other topics are relevant for the faith and life of the church, and ultimately they are connected in an organic way to the Gospel, even if they may appear otherwise. Thus in this epistle we hear him speaking to a great variety of topics, and even making "rules, regulations, and conditions,"[30] as when he commands the Corinthians to "remove the wicked person from among yourselves" (5:13) or solemnly warns them that wicked people will not inherit the kingdom (6:9). Likewise, this thoroughly Gospel-centered apostle does not see any inconsistency with the Gospel in laying down rules and regulations for the proper conduct of divine worship, using a string of imperatives to demand silence from the tongues-speaker who has no interpreter, from the prophet who finds that another has just received a revelation, and, finally, from the women (14:28–34).

---

28  Cf. N. Habel and S. Wurst, "The Gospel and Women in the Ministry," 129–30: "Maintaining a gospel focus involves asking a series of questions. Do our discoveries clarify and highlight the gospel? Are they consistent with the gospel as central to our faith? Are they consistent with the Lutheran understanding of the gospel's essence: justification by grace alone through faith in Christ alone?"

29  See further below.

30  N. Habel and S. Wurst, "The Gospel and Women in the Ministry," 130, state that "whenever the gospel is bounded by rules, regulations, and conditions, it is diminished and changed."

Thus the advocates of women's ordination must concede that Paul does from time to time use his apostolic authority to lay down "rules, regulations, and conditions." This is not a naked use of authority for its own sake; it always expresses a fatherly concern (4:14–16) for the eternal welfare of the saints. At the same time, opponents of women's ordination must concede, indeed, must wholeheartedly agree that the same Gospel which makes saints is the Gospel which makes ministers. The same "grace" (χάρις) of God, richly poured out on all "called saints" in Corinth (1:2–5) had bestowed on Paul and his fellow apostles and pastors the gracious gift and calling which was the basis of their ministry (4:1; 9:1–2). By grace alone a person became a saint; by that same grace some were called to the public ministry. Thus Paul praises God: "To me as the very least of all saints was given this grace, to preach to the Gentiles the unfathomable riches of Christ" (Eph 3:8). And in the following chapter of Ephesians he prefaces his discussion of the ministry of apostles, prophets, pastors and teachers with these words: "To each one of us was given grace according to the measure of the gift of Christ" (Eph 4:7).

Thus it is freely granted that there can be no proper discussion of the pastoral ministry which does not have its foundation in the doctrine of God's grace, his grace in calling all Christians to be saints, and in calling some to be pastors.[31] As for the saints, their call to be Christians was not through their own willing or running, but through God's mercy alone (Rom 9:16). As for pastors, what the author of Hebrews says of the Jewish high priest applies: "No one takes the honor upon himself, but he is called by God" (Heb 5:4; cf. 1 Cor 15:10).

But just as not all are apostles, not all are prophets, so not all are pastors and teachers (1 Cor 12:29; Eph 4:11). And not only women are excluded from the pastoral office, but also most men. For most men have not been called to the office, nor have they been given sufficient aptitude in teaching. The ministry can be difficult enough, in these turbulent times, even for men who are "apt to teach" (1 Tim 3:2). This catechetical aptitude is the one qualification on Paul's lists of qualifications for pastors (1 Tim 3:2–7; Titus 1:6–9)

---

31  Cf. A. L. Barry, "What about . . . the Ordination of Women to the Pastoral Office," 1: "We receive what God gives, in the way He has given it, and in the form He has given it. We do not tell God that His gift is not good enough for us, or that we don't like the form in which He has given the gift" (St. Louis: The Office of the President, The Lutheran Church—Missouri Synod, 1997). The public ministry is not an office one should campaign for. Even though C. R. Klein is a supporter of the ordination of women, she sounds a concern about

a Pelagian bias in the contemporary women's movement. We fall into the trap set by our culture when we measure our worth primarily by what the world deems accomplishment. . . . Have we not pinned women's ultimate worth to their "works," so that, like the Pelagians of the fifth century, we equate human effort with God's salvation? ("Women's Concerns in Theological Education," *Dialog* 24.1 [Winter 1985] 26)

which is not required of every Christian man. Since God has called the church into existence through the Gospel, he has every right to select those whom he chooses to be pastors, and to establish such qualifications as he desires pastors to have. Just as in Israel the eleven other tribes had no right to cry foul because God selected only the Levites to serve at his sanctuary, and only the sons of Aaron to be his priests, so Christians have no right to criticize God for limiting the pastoral office to those who meet his qualifications, including that of gender. It is not inconsistent for the God of the Gospel also to establish such an order in his church: "God is not [a God] of disorder" (1 Cor 14:33).

## CREATION AND THE NEW CREATION

The relationship between the order of creation and the order of redemption is another key topic where hermeneutical assumptions will lead to certain conclusions relevant to the ordination of women.[32] For example, the paragraphs by Habel and Wurst under the heading "Women and the New Creation" totally dissolve the tension between the overlapping old and new aeons and accord no ongoing significance to the order of creation.[33] Reumann asserts:

> The early church, with its eschatological consciousness of the Spirit's presence as a token of the New Age, did not opt just for retaining such [headship] structures, but at times—in spite of its historical circumstances, in a culture where the role of women in society was often severely limited—allowed women in ministry roles, as foretaste of the new creation "in Christ" or fulfillment of God's original will for male and female in Genesis, Chapter 1.[34]

But nowhere in his book does Reumann give serious consideration to Genesis 2–3. Furthermore, there is no hard evidence that women served as apostles, bishops, or pastors in the early church.[35]

Responding to Reumann, Hamann argues persuasively:

> We are not to see the new order in Christ as gradually transforming the old orders of creation, until the new order of things has completely dispossessed the old. A true understanding of the New Testament rather sees the old order of creation . . . continuing till the end when Christ returns, while the new order of things in Christ ("the old has passed away, behold, the new has come," 2 Cor. 5:17) runs parallel with the old—there is an overlapping of the two aeons—till that same return of Christ. But the new is there

---

32  See further the commentary on 11:7–10 regarding the order of creation and on 11:11–12 regarding the order of redemption.

33  "The Gospel and Women in the Ministry," 132–33.

34  *Ministries Examined*, 97.

35  See further below.

in faith, not sight. Nothing of the new is visible, demonstrable: not Christ, not the Spirit, not the *Una Sancta*, not the new birth in Baptism, not the body and blood of the Sacrament, not the forgiveness of sins—nothing. All these are realities, and faith is sure of them, because of the Word of God, but they are all hidden in this world, where what is visible is exactly what has been there from the beginning. There is a realism about this proper view of eschatology which stands in marked contrast to the wishful thinking and enthusiasm of all eschatologies which look for a change in the present world's basic structure.[36]

The order of creation is not merely a construct of theologians but has deep roots in the Scriptures. When Jesus and Paul provide guidance for the proper ordering of marriage and relations between the sexes, they go back to the order of creation set forth in the first three chapters of Genesis. Thus Jesus, in speaking against lax attitudes toward divorce, says, "In the beginning it was not so" (Mt 19:8), and quotes Gen 1:27 and Gen 2:24 in Mt 19:3–9 and Mk 10:2–12. And Paul, in arguing that the woman is not to function as head and teacher of the church family at worship, grounds his injunction "I do not permit a woman to teach . . ." (1 Tim 2:12) in the order of creation and fall established in Genesis 2 and 3: "For Adam was formed first, then Eve. And Adam was not deceived, but the woman was deceived and fell into transgression" (1 Tim 2:13–14). In other words, Adam reneged on his spiritual responsibilities. He failed to exercise his headship by following his wife instead of correcting her after she had given a false lead. Finally, when Paul appeals to "the Law" as the basis for his ruling in 1 Cor 14:34 ("it is not permitted for [the women] to speak . . . as the Law also says"), he almost certainly has in mind the same passages of Genesis 2–3 which he cites in his epistle to Timothy (1 Tim 2:13–14).

In 1 Corinthians, when discussing worship practices and the conduct of women Paul invokes the order of the original creation in 11:7–10. God's activity in creation is in harmony with his activity in redemption (11:11–12). These two activities of God are not in conflict with each other or contradictory; the goodness of God the orderly Creator is manifested also in the *ordo salutis*, the order of redemption.

The fifth argument of the case "for the ordination of men only," outlined in *The Ordination of Women: Initial Report of the Commission on Theology and Interchurch Relations of the Lutheran Church of Australia*, is entitled "the representation of Christ's headship." The argument aptly expresses the significance of the order of creation in the debate:

36  "The New Testament and the Ordination of Women," 107; cf. also F. Zerbst, *The Office of Woman in the Church*, 118–19.

The ordination of women contradicts the reality of male headship in the church and family which was established by God in the creation of Adam and fulfilled by the incarnation of God's Son as a male person (1 Cor 11:3, 8, 9; Eph 5:22–24; 1 Tim 2:13). It therefore involves disobedience to Christ, the head of the church, and disrespect for his gift of order in the church (1 Cor 14:34; 1 Tim 2:11).[37]

That apostles and pastors are representatives and ambassadors of Christ is the clear teaching of the NT (Lk 10:16; 2 Cor 5:20). The Apology of the Augsburg Confession states: Pastors "do not represent their own persons but the person of Christ, because of the church's call, as Christ testifies (Luke 10:16), 'He who hears you hears me.' When they offer the Word of Christ or the sacraments, they do so in Christ's place and stead" (Ap VII and VIII 28). However, that does not, in itself, necessarily imply that a pastor must be a man. The NT never develops an argument that because the first person of the triune God is the Father and the second person, the Son of God, was incarnate as the man Jesus, therefore only a man can serve *in persona patris* ("as a personal representative of the Father") and *in persona Christi* ("as a personal representative of Christ"). Whereas the catholic wing of the Church of England and the Roman Catholic and Orthodox churches ground their opposition to women's ordination partly "on the belief that it is 'ontologically' impossible for a woman to be a priest since Christ was a man, and the priest represents Christ at the altar,"[38] the Scriptures themselves go back to the order of creation (1 Cor 14:34; 1 Tim 2:12–14; cf. 1 Cor 11:3). Christ's incarnation as a man is ultimately rooted in this divinely willed order. A man (Adam) was head of the old humanity; so, in the divine economy, a man (the second Adam) is head of the new humanity (Rom 5:12–19). And because Christ chose to follow (and fulfill) the old order of creation rather than overturn it, he chose only men to serve as apostles and pastors and thus provide the leadership for his church.

---

37  *The Ordination of Women* (1998) 6.

38  R. T. France, *Women in the Church's Ministry*, 10. Eastern Orthodoxy regards the priest as an "icon" of Christ: "In offering the unbloody sacrifice . . . the bishop (or the priest . . .) becomes . . . the icon of the Word incarnate. It is this iconic character of the figure of the priest in Orthodox worship that, it seems to me, embodies the strongest argument against the admission of women to the . . . sacramental priesthood" (E. Behr-Sigel, "The Participation of Women in the Life of the Church," *Martyria/Mission: The Witness of the Orthodox Churches Today*, ed. I. Bria [Geneva, 1980] 59, cited by M. Hauke, *Women in the Priesthood?* 50). Roman Catholic theology understands the role of the priest as the "representation of Jesus Christ" in a similar manner to Orthodoxy. See M. Hauke, *Women in the Priesthood?* 330–32. In each case, there is a heavy emphasis on the priest's sacramental role. The NT, on the other hand, places primary emphasis on the pastor's role as teacher (1 Tim 2:12; 3:2; Titus 1:9).

## The Relationship between 11:2–16 and 14:33b–38

One of the main questions which must be addressed is the relationship between 1 Cor 11:2–16 (especially 11:5), where Paul seems to accept that women may pray or prophesy in worship, and 14:33b–38 (especially 14:34), where he seems to forbid any speaking by women. Advocates of women's ordination often assert one or more of the following: (1) The two passages simply contradict one another.[39] (2) Since they conflict, the apparently more lenient passage (11:2–16) is to be preferred. (3) By means of a text-critical argument 14:34–35 is deleted as inauthentic.[40] (4) The import of 14:34–35 is reduced to a mere ban on women asking disruptive questions.[41]

The following may be said in response. First, the apparent discrepancy between 11:5 and 14:34 should not be exaggerated. After all, the "heading"— the thematic verse that sets the tone for 11:2–16 (especially 11:3–10)—is the introductory statement on headship (11:3). And unless the meaning of κεφαλή ("head [of]") in 11:3 is reduced to "source [of]," this headship/subordination theme in 11:2–16 plays in perfect harmony with 14:34. Second, the larger passage which speaks directly to the issue of women speaking in worship (the *sedes doctrinae*, 14:33b–38) should be given more weight than 11:5.[42] And third, a number of solutions are at hand which do not assume a contradiction between 11:5 and 14:34.

The following five harmonizations have been proposed by various scholars. They are presented in order from least likely to more probable. This commentary's view is that the fifth explanation is the best. The fourth has much to recommend it, but the second and third are less plausible, and the first is not supported by sound evidence.

---

39 Notably G. Fee, *The First Epistle to the Corinthians*, 702: "These verses [14:34–35] stand in obvious contradiction to 11:2–16." Cf. W. Linss: "This [14:33b–36] contradicts what we just heard in ch[apter] 11 about women praying or prophesying in church" ("St. Paul and Women," *Dialog* 24.1 [Winter 1985] 39).

40 Fee dismisses 14:34–35 as "not authentic" and "certainly not binding for Christians" (*The First Epistle to the Corinthians*, 708). Regarding the textual authenticity of 14:34–35, see further below and see also the textual note and commentary on it.

41 An optional solution for Linss, who also considers option 3 above to be a possible solution, is that Paul is merely admonishing the women not to ask disruptive questions ("St. Paul and Women," 39).

42 By the same token, the more extensive, explicit treatments of women's roles in 1 Cor 14:33b–38 and 1 Tim 2:11–14 should carry more weight than brief references to the roles played by some women in the early church, including Priscilla (Acts 18:26), Phoebe (Rom 16:1–2), or the women who labored with Paul "in the Gospel" (Phil 4:3). Besides, Priscilla taught Apollos *privately*; Phoebe is described as a "deacon" and "patron," not a "pastor" (ποιμήν) nor "bishop, overseer" (ἐπίσκοπος) nor "elder" (πρεσβύτερος). And women have always labored alongside pastors in the Gospel in various non-ordained capacities.

Post-Enlightenment exegesis tends to presuppose that contradictions will be found in many parts of the Scriptures. Apparent difficulties and discrepancies are often blown out of proportion, while attempts to supply harmonizing solutions are disparaged. The alternative approach adopted in this commentary is based on the belief that the Scriptures are a unity, the Word of one primary, divine author—the Holy Spirit—speaking through prophets, apostles, and evangelists as secondary authors, and that consequently the Scriptures are all true and consistent.[43] This assumption that the Scriptures possess the integrity, consistency, truthfulness, and authority of God himself legitimizes the attempt to demonstrate their unity and harmony in particular cases. For this purpose it is sufficient to show that one or more plausible explanations exist, even if the state of our knowledge does not permit us to state definitively that one explanation is right and all others are wrong.

1. Many advocates of women's ordination "solve" the "problem" by arguing that the offensive verses in which Paul prohibits women from speaking in church, 14:34–35, are inauthentic.[44] Having eliminated these verses from the picture, it is readily concluded on the basis of 11:5 that Paul is content to allow women to pray and prophesy in church, and generally to take a leading speaking role in worship. One of the great popularizers of this view in recent times has been the influential commentary by Fee.[45] A number of commentators make a similar case with regard to the authenticity of 1 Timothy by classifying it and the other pastoral epistles (2 Timothy and Titus) as "pseudepigraphical" (i.e., forgeries) and thus unworthy of the same regard as the "authentically Pauline" epistles.[46] Thus at a stroke two of the most significant texts (1 Cor 14:34–35 and 1 Tim 2:11–12) are eliminated from consideration, undercutting the ecumenical doctrine and practice of the Christian church over the last two millennia of not ordaining women.

The problem with this explanation is that the actual manuscript data support the authenticity of 1 Cor 14:34–35.[47] In the overwhelming majority of manuscripts these two verses are found in their normal location between 14:33 and 14:36. In a few manuscripts, however, they are placed after 14:40.[48]

---

43 See FC Ep, Rule and Norm 1; FC SD, Rule and Norm 1–3.

44 P. Brunner, *The Ministry and the Ministry of Women*, 22, notes that "this thesis [that 11:33b–36 is a later interpolation] was first proposed by Semler (d. 1791)."

45 *First Corinthians*, 699–708.

46 For example, Reumann thinks that "14:33b–36 is a later gloss which we place in the trajectory at the same points where 1 Tim. 2:11–12 arises" (*Ministries Examined*, 112).

47 See the textual note on 14:34–35.

48 Again, see the textual note on 14:34–35, and also see the critical apparatus of NA27 and UBS4.

Hauke set himself the detective task of trying to track down who may have been responsible for moving 14:34–35 in some manuscripts.[49] While the case against the suspected culprit falls short of final proof, Hauke uses an array of circumstantial evidence to argue that it was Marcion who took offense at the references to creation and Law in these verses and excised them from the text, thus leaving an enduring mark on the "Western" textual tradition. He believed that the creator God of the OT was an inferior being different from the God of the NT. Marcion, of course, also removed the pastoral epistles from his canon. Should Marcion be the culprit, we would face the intriguing question of whether there could be a parallel between him and those modern scholars who show a similarly cavalier attitude—a parallel not only in excising canonical texts, but also in the basis for their excisions: the distaste for anything in Paul that smacks of Law and the OT.[50]

Hauke's speculations, however, probably outrun the evidence. Niccum's approach is more restrained. His detailed study refutes the case for the inauthenticity of 14:34–35 and points to "northern Italy and neighbouring Alpine regions" as the source of the scribal transposition. He concludes: "The motivation for displacing the text may never be discovered."[51]

2. A second suggestion is that when Paul insists a woman wear a head-covering (11:2–16) he has in mind private devotions in the home. Thus there is no conflict between his apparent tolerance for a woman praying and prophesying in that private setting, and his later insistence that she should not speak "in the churches" (14:33). But this solution to the difficulty does not seem tenable. Among the arguments Carson advances against it, most noteworthy is his reference to Paul's statement in 11:16: "We have no such custom, nor do the churches of God."[52] Paul's concern from 11:2 to 14:40 is what happens *in the churches*. Thus the Jerusalem Bible sees a major section of the epistle as beginning at 11:2 and places a major heading over that verse: "C. Decorum in Public Worship."

3. Carson offers a more plausible reconciliation between chapters 11 and 14 in his book *Showing the Spirit*.[53] He proposes that Paul expects the women to be silent in church only when it comes to "weighing" prophecies, that is, giving an authoritative interpretation of what the prophecy means for the church's faith and life (cf. 14:29). By no means is the apostle banning

---

49 *Women in the Priesthood?* 390–94. Cf. D. Bryce, "'As in All the Churches of the Saints': A Text-Critical Study of 1 Corinthians 14:34, 35," *Lutheran Theological Journal* 31 (May 1997) 31–39.

50 Paul's affirmation of the created order impacts his view of human sexuality. Cf. also the excursus "Homosexuality."

51 "The Voice of the Manuscripts on the Silence of Women"; quotes on pp. 252 and 254.

52 *Showing the Spirit*, 123.

53 *Showing the Spirit*, 129–31.

the women from any kind of speaking in the assembly. They may, as can be assumed from 11:5, pray and prophesy; they may also speak in tongues. Only the evaluation of prophecies is prohibited. Carson then explains that the parallel in 1 Tim 2:11–12 shows that the apostolic injunction in 1 Cor 14:34–35 applies to authoritative speaking, that is, to teaching the Word of God to the assembled congregation ("I do not permit a woman to teach," 1 Tim 2:12). The interpretation of prophecies is a kind of authoritative teaching, according to Carson.

Carson certainly is correct that the parallel injunction in 1 Tim 2:11–12 shows that in 1 Cor 14:34–35 Paul is prohibiting women from teaching authoritatively (as a pastor does) in the church's worship. Carson is also certainly correct in saying that 14:34–35 should not be interpreted so broadly as to prohibit women from joining in the church's prayers, hymns, liturgical responses, and confessions of faith in the worship services.

However, Carson's view suffers from a weakness. If interpreting prophecies (a form of authoritative teaching) were the only restriction Paul had in mind in 14:34–35, it is surprising he did not spell it out: "Let the women be silent in the churches by not weighing prophecies, but let them speak in tongues and prophesy." If this was what the apostle meant, the best that can be said is that he did not express himself—or God's will—unambiguously. Throughout the chapter Paul has used λαλέω ("to speak") in connection both with speaking in tongues[a] and with prophecy.[b] Tongues-speakers may speak (λαλέω) if there is an interpreter; two or three prophets may speak (λαλέω) if they take their turn (14:26–32). But then Paul declares—and there is no way of getting around the abruptness—that the women are *not* permitted "to speak " (λαλέω). There is no exception clause.

As attractive, then, as Carson's proposal may be in allowing women some latitude to speak in the assembly (hymns, prayers, and so on), and in harmonizing 11:5 and 14:34, it does not fit the flow of Paul's argument in chapter 14. Nevertheless, it is one of the most plausible of the solutions that have been offered.

4. A fourth interpretation is that in 14:34–35 Paul is prohibiting women from speaking authoritatively in church.[54] As in 1 Tim 2:11–12, in 1 Cor 14:34–35 Paul prohibits women from preaching and authoritative (pastoral) teaching of the church in worship. Thus there is no conflict with 11:5, where Paul apparently accepts that women with head-coverings may pray and prophesy in church. Teaching is an activity distinctly different from praying

---

54 This is the interpretation advocated in *Women in the Church*, a report of the Commission on Theology and Church Relations of The Lutheran Church—Missouri Synod (pp. 32–38). It is also the interpretation of N. Johansson, *Women and the Church's Ministry: An Exegetical Study of 1 Corinthians 11–14*, trans. C. J. de Catanzaro (Ottawa, 1972) 51–89, and B. Gärtner, *Das Amt, der Mann und die Frau im Neuen Testament*, 19.

and prophesying.[55] In 14:34–35 Paul, then, is permitting the women to prophesy and speak in tongues, but he is not permitting them to preach and teach.
This would coincide with 1 Tim 2:12, where he states: "I do not permit a
woman to teach."

This view is expressed well in the CTCR document *Women in the Church*:

First, that [in 1 Cor 14:34–35] Paul is not commanding *absolute*,[56] unqualified silence is evident from the fact that he permits praying and prophesying in 1 Corinthians 11. The silence mandated for women in 1 Corinthians
14 does not preclude their praying and prophesying.[57] Accordingly, the
apostle is not intimating that women may not participate in the public
singing of the congregation or in the spoken prayers. It should be noted in
this connection that Paul uses the Greek word *laleo* [λαλέω] for "speak" in
1 Cor. 14:34, which frequently means to "preach" in the New Testament
(see Mark 2:2; Luke 9:11; Acts 4:1; 8:25; 1 Cor. 2:7; 2 Cor. 12:19; Phil.
1:14; *et al.*), and not *lego* [λέγω], which is the more general term. . . . When
*laleo* has a meaning other than religious speech and preaching in the New
Testament, this is usually made clear by an object or an adverb (e.g., to
speak like a child, 1 Cor. 13:11; to speak like a fool, 2 Cor. 11:23). Secondly,
it must be underscored that Paul's prohibition that women remain silent
and not speak is uttered with reference to the worship service of the
congregation (1 Cor. 14:26–33). . . . Thus, Paul is not here demanding
that women should be silent at all times or that they cannot express their
sentiments and opinions at church assemblies. The command that women

---

55 See διδάσκω, "to teach," διδάσκαλο, "teacher," and διδασκαλία, "teaching, doctrine" in,
for example, Rom 12:6–7; 1 Cor 12:28–29; Eph 4:11; 1 Tim 2:7, 12; 4:6, 11; 6:2–3.

56 To support this, *Women in the Church* cites NT verses that have forms of the Greek
word ἡσυχία, "silence"; these words are not in 1 Cor 14:34–35, but in the similar
passage 1 Tim 2:11–12 Paul uses the word ἡσυχία, "silence," and in 1 Tim 2:2 he uses
the related adjective ἡσύχιος, "quiet." The noun ἡσυχία, "silence," also occurs in Acts
22:2 and the related verb ἡσυχάζω, "be quiet, remain silent," in Acts 11:18 and 21:14.
In Acts 11:18; 21:14; and 22:2 "total silence is not implied" (*Women in the Church*, 33,
n. 47).

57 A footnote at this point (*Women in the Church*, 33, n. 48) references George Stoeckhardt's
discussion (originally published in 1897) in "Von dem Beruf der Lehrerinnen an christ-
lichen Gemeindeschulen," *Concordia Theological Monthly* 5 (October 1934) 764–73, and
quotes Stoeckhardt, who writes (p. 769):

No, the apostle's words will hardly allow another interpretation than that he
finds nothing objectionable in the public praying and prophesying in itself, if
only it occurs with a covered head. But thereby he has not in the least limited
or weakened what he writes in 1 Cor. 14 regarding the silence of women.
Neither the praying or the prophesying belongs to that speaking which he
forbids for women directly in 1 Cor. 14:33–36. The women are not to teach in
the assembly of the congregation. They are not to appear as teaching women,
nor to instruct the men, nor to dispute publicly before and with men. This
is, as we have recognized, the understanding of St. Paul in the latter passage
quoted. Neither the praying nor the prophesying belongs in this category.
Obviously the praying is not teaching or disputing.

keep silent is a command that they not take charge of the public worship service, specifically the teaching-learning aspects of the service.[58]

According to this view, women may teach as long as they are not occupying the pastoral office, that is, if their teaching is done under the supervising authority of the pastor,[59] or in a private setting. For example, Paul tells Titus to "speak" (λαλέω, Titus 2:1; the same activity women are prohibited from carrying out in 1 Cor 14:34; NIV translates it as "teach" in Titus 2:1) to the older women so that those women may be "good teachers [καλοδιδασκάλους]" who can "advise [σωφρονίζωσιν] the younger women to be lovers of their husbands and lovers of their children" (Titus 2:3–4). Older women were to teach younger women, and women were expected to teach children. A woman like Priscilla could also give private instruction in the faith to a man like Apollos (Acts 18:26). Nor should it be understood as an absolute ban prohibiting women from joining in the hymns and prayers, creeds and responses.

A difficulty with this view is Paul's use of λαλέω earlier in 1 Corinthians 14 in connection with tongues and prophecy (e.g., 14:2–6, 27–29). One might naturally assume that λαλέω in 14:34 refers to the same kind of speaking: to speak in a tongue or to speak a prophecy. In that case, Paul would be telling the women that they cannot speak in a tongue or prophesy in church, in a worship service (that is the next explanation, number 5, below).

However, against that objection, and so in favor of this explanation (number 4), is a different approach to the understanding of the verb λαλέω. The verb itself can refer to a variety of kinds of speaking (see BAGD). The *kind* of speaking must be determined by the context, the words and phrases used with the verb. In 14:2, "the person who speaks in a tongue [λαλῶν γλώσσῃ]" obviously refers to tongues-speaking, while in the next verse, in the phrase "the person who prophesies speaks to people [προφητεύων ἀνθρώποις λαλεῖ]," the same verb is in the context of prophesying. Speaking in tongues and prophesying are distinctly different activities, even though the same verb, λαλέω, can be used for either. It entails tongues-speaking in 14:2, 4–6a, 9, 11, 13, 18, 21, 23, 27–28, 39, but prophesying in 14:3, 6b, 29.

In 14:34–35, λαλέω is used absolutely; there are no modifying or qualifying words such as "in a tongue" or "a prophecy." The only qualifying phrases are "in the churches" in 14:34 and "in church" in 14:35. This absolute kind of speaking may then be interpreted in light of the similar passage in 1 Tim 2:11–12, which leaves no doubt that the kind of speaking prohibited

---

58  *Women in the Church*, 33.

59  One NT term for a pastor is ἐπίσκοπος, "an overseer, supervisor, bishop," found, for example, in Acts 20:28 (with ποιμαίνω, "to shepherd, to pastor"); Phil 1:1; 1 Tim 3:2; Titus 1:7. In 1 Pet 2:25 Christ himself is "the shepherd/pastor [ποιμήν] and overseer [ἐπίσκοπος] of your souls."

for women is the authoritative teaching of men. Therefore 1 Cor 14:34–35 prohibits women from assuming the role of authoritative (pastoral) speaking (preaching and teaching) of the church in worship.

5. A fifth explanation is preferred by this commentary. This explanation assumes that because λαλέω, "to speak," earlier in chapter 14 referred to speaking in tongues and prophesying (see number 4 above), that same verb (λαλέω) must entail those same kinds of speaking in 14:34–35. This reading of 14:33b–38 is that here Paul prohibits the women from speaking in tongues, prophesying, and, a fortiori, authoritative (pastoral) preaching and teaching in the worship service.[60] Nevertheless, this should not be understood as a blanket ban on women prophesying or speaking in tongues in *any* context. Philip's daughters, presumably, would still be permitted to prophesy in private (Acts 21:8–9), and Priscilla could still give private instruction (Acts 18:26).

If this interpretation is correct, the question arises why Paul did not make his position clearer back in 1 Corinthians 11, where he seems to allow properly covered women to speak in tongues and prophesy (11:5). Here it may be helpful to consider his pastoral approach in other parts of the letter. A close parallel may be found in his discussion of food offered to idols (chapters 8–10). In chapter 8 he lays the theological foundation for approaching the issue and gently suggests that reclining in an idol temple could be an offense to the weaker brother. Then by way of a lengthy excursus (chapter 9) he points to his own example as the free Christian apostle who has voluntarily given up some of his rights for the sake of the church, including the weak brother. Then he firmly forbids any participation in cultic meals (10:14–22). His position in both chapters 8 and 10 is that the Christian should not partake of meals in pagan temples, but his appeal in chapter 8 is based on Christian love, and he saves his explicit command until chapter 10. A similar dynamic may explain the relationship between chapters 11 and 14. In chapter 11 Paul appeals to the Corinthians on the basis of Christ's headship and their natural sense of propriety and decorum. He calls his description a "custom" (συνήθεια, 11:16), not a "command" (ἐντολή, the word in 14:37 that refers to 14:34–35).

---

60  F. Bruner thinks Paul places a prohibition particularly "on the glosso-*lalic* participation of women in the congregational meetings" (*A Theology of the Holy Spirit*, 300–301).

Cf. P. Brunner, *The Ministry and the Ministry of Women*, 21–22: "When we consider this passage only in the context of chapter 14 of 1 Corinthians, it raises no exegetical difficulties worth mentioning. . . . When [Paul] commands [the women] to be silent, . . . he is at the same time denying them the right to prophesy, the regulation of which plays an important part in this chapter." The exegetical problem, Brunner continues, is the relationship of 14:33–38 to 11:2–16. Brunner notes that "the most common interpretation . . . is that Paul [in chapter 14] forbids women the right to preach but not the right to prophesy." Since, however, the "spirits of prophets are subject to prophets" (14:32), "one can with good reason conclude that the apostle also sought to bid the spirits of the prophetesses to keep silence in the congregation."

Then in chapter 12 he lays the theological foundation regarding spiritual gifts and follows it up with an excursus on Christian love (chapter 13). Paul then concludes the more detailed discussion of tongues and prophecy in chapter 14 with a number of directives regarding the proper role of tongues, prophecy, and the appropriateness of women holding the teaching office.[61]

Paul's approach, then, is a fine example of wise pastoral care. Not everything can be addressed at once. A foundation must first be laid before the more difficult things that must be said can be said. Thus Paul in 11:2–16 is not yet ready to issue "the Lord's command" (14:37) regarding the women. He restricts himself primarily to the issue of their head-coverings and prayer. Although he briefly mentions prophesying (11:5), he leaves his direct orders regarding the more sensitive issue of their speaking during worship (including prophesying and speaking in tongues) to the end of chapter 14.[62]

## Objections to "the Lord's Command"

As is well known, the apostle's injunction in 14:34–35 is encountering more opposition today than at any time since the Gnostic, Marcionite, and Montanist movements of the second century A.D.[63] The objections are legion; to respond to them all with any measure of adequacy would require another book.[64] Six of

---

61  Fee notes with regard to chapters 8–10: "The answer lies with Paul's understanding of the relationship between the indicative and the imperative (see on 5:6–8). Paul seldom begins with an imperative. As in 6:12–20; 1:10–4:21; 12:1–14:40, he begins by correcting serious theological misunderstandings and then gives the imperative" (*The First Epistle to the Corinthians*, 363, n. 23). J. Smit analyzes the relationship between chapters 8 and 10 along similar lines: "In 1 Cor 8:9 Paul takes a very reserved and disapproving stand on the presumed 'power' of the Corinthians to take part in sacrificial meals," preparing the way for the "prohibition" which "he frankly states in 10:1–22" ("The Rhetorical Disposition of First Corinthians 8:7–9:27," *CBQ* 59.3 [July 1997] 490).

62  Thus the verb λαλέω, "to speak," in 14:34–35, occurs a total of twenty-four times in chapter 14 but is completely absent from chapter 11. Also absent from chapter 11 are the tongues (γλῶσσα), which do not appear in 1 Corinthians until 12:10.

63  On these second-century movements as "a prelude to the modern controversy," see M. Hauke, *Women in the Priesthood?* 404–11. L. Brighton has documented how certain second-century Gnostic teachers "encouraged women to preach and to prophesy, to celebrate the Eucharist, to consecrate the cup before the altar" ("The Ordination of Women: A Twentieth-Century Gnostic Heresy?" *Concordia Journal* 8.1 [January 1982] 12–18; quote on p. 12). Gnostics also promoted feminine conceptions of God (pp. 14–18).

64  None of the arguments for the ordination of women carries much weight in itself. By comparison with the significant *sedes doctrinae* (1 Cor 14:33b–38; 1 Tim 2:11–14; 3:1–7; Titus 1:5–9) which have supported the church's traditional stand on the issue for two millennia, each individual argument for women's ordination is easily rebutted. How, then, has the movement for women's ordination been so successful in Protestant churches? An analogy used by E. Linnemann to explain the dominance of historical-critical methodology in biblical scholarship may also explain the success of the exegetical case that has been advanced for women's ordination. Linnemann draws an analogy

the most significant may be singled out for discussion: the crucial NT passage Gal 3:28; the appeal to justice and human rights; the appeal to "inclusivity"; the appeal to women's giftedness; the argument that the case against women's ordination rests on the "subordinationist heresy"; and the appeal to the role of prophetesses in both testaments.[65]

## GALATIANS 3:28

Gal 3:28 is the text most frequently cited by the women's ordination movement. Reumann hails Gal 3:28 as "the breakthrough," "the crucial New Testament [text] . . . cited for ordaining women." Reumann draws out what he believes to be the implications of the text: just as "women, like men, have experienced the gospel of grace" through "the 'Christ event,' " so "women too are to witness to the gospel of grace and minister in its name."[66]

While the argument from Gal 3:28 may seem persuasive, if one examines its context even cursorily, it is obvious that Paul is not speaking to the issue of ordination—of women or of men—at all! The topic is the baptismal identity of all believers as God's "sons" and "heirs" of the Abrahamic promise of eternal life in Christ Jesus.[67] The verse must be read in context: "You are all

---

from the use of corrugated cardboard in the packing industry: while a flat piece of cardboard is easily torn to bits, corrugated pieces, when piled on top of one another, eventually possess great strength. So a new idea, though based on a series of flimsy premises, can often gain enormous weight (*Historical Criticism of the Bible: Methodology or Ideology?* trans. R. Yarbrough [Grand Rapids: Baker, 1990] 136).

65 Other arguments include these: the alleged ambiguous nature and irrelevance of the key texts (1 Cor 14:33b–38; 1 Tim 2:11–14; 3:1–7; Titus 1:5–9); the so-called mission imperative (whereas first-century Jews would have found women pastors offensive, potential converts today would find a male-only pastorate offensive); the various roles played by women in the early church; an emphasis on Christ's assumption of a generic human nature (rather than his nature as a male) which makes it possible for a woman to represent him in the public ministry (this argument responds to those who argue for a male-only pastorate chiefly on the basis of Christ's maleness, rather than understanding the Pauline instructions as rooted above all in the order of creation); alleged difficulties in accepting the authority of Paul, coupled with charges that the apostle has a different spirit from the spirit of Christ; claims that arguments against the ordination of women are irrelevant, since there is no divinely instituted or divinely mandated office of the ministry at all; assertions that the changing culture opens up new possibilities for the life of the church which would not have been culturally acceptable in earlier ages; and the desire to join other church bodies which condone the practice. Additional arguments could be added.

66 *Ministries Examined*, 86.

67 As long as "priestly vocation" refers to the priesthood of all believers in their vocations (roles in life) but does not refer to the pastoral office, one can affirm "the indisputable equality [with regard to men and women] of priestly vocation, grounded in baptism, according to the order of creation and the multiplicity of gifts in the fellowship of the Body of Christ" (R. Slenczka, "Is a Criticism of Women's Ordination a Church Divisive Heresy?" trans. H. Oberscheidt [*Forum News* 2.4 (December 1997)] 6; this article is translated from R. Slenczka, "Ist die Kritik an der Frauenordination

sons of God through faith in Christ Jesus, for as many of you as were baptized into Christ have been clothed with Christ. There is neither Jew nor Greek, there is neither slave nor free, *there is neither male nor female*; for you are all one in Christ Jesus. If you are of Christ, therefore you are Abraham's seed and heirs according to the promise" (Gal 3:26–29). Ordination is another topic, which Paul addresses elsewhere.[68] If Gal 3:28 is taken as the standard for determining who may be ordained, what prevents the church from ordaining incompetent Christians, children, or for that matter, homosexuals?[69] To such questions, proponents of women's ordination often respond that one must then look elsewhere, for example to 1 Tim 3:2, which says a pastor should be "apt to teach." But that is precisely the point: we must look to other passages, not to Gal 3:28, to find the qualifications for ordination. These are set out in 1 Tim 3:1–7 and Titus 1:5–9, where "husband of one wife" (1 Tim 3:2 and Titus 1:6), together with the masculine Greek nouns and adjectives, limits the office to qualified men. That conclusion is corroborated by 1 Cor 14:33b–38 and 1 Tim 2:11–14.

## JUSTICE AND HUMAN RIGHTS

For some, the case for women's ordination is straightforward: it is a matter of simple justice. The movement toward justice and equal rights for women in the workplace or political arena is taken as a normative signal to the church that Christian women should be eligible to be ordained. Although this argument can appeal in general terms to the biblical theme of "justice," its real impetus is in the secular culture. The church should not be shaped by the world, but by the Word.

Advocates of the ordination of women sometimes draw a parallel between the way the church was slow to recognize the evils of slavery but eventually was led by the Gospel to denounce slavery, and the way the church was slow to recognize the evils of "patriarchy" but is now being led by the Gospel to protest "patriarchy" and the withholding of the pastoral office from women. But the two cases are vastly different. Slavery was a powerfully entrenched

---

eine kirchentrennende Irrlehre? Dogmatische Erwägungen zu einer Erklärung des Rates der EKD vom 20 Juli 1992," *Kirche in der Schule Luthers: Festschrift für D. Joachim Heubach* [Erlangen: Martin Luther Verlag, 1995] 185–98).

68  1 Cor 14:33b–38; 1 Tim 2:11–14; 3:1–7; Titus 1:5–9.

69  Gal 3:28 has been used in some churches as an argument for the ordination of gays. Indeed, the pattern of argumentation for the ordination of homosexuals follows the same hermeneutical lines as the argument for the ordination of women: (a) The appeal to Gal 3:28. (b) The notion that the biblical writers were conditioned by their culture and time, so that the scriptural condemnations against homosexuality had only temporary significance; "what it meant" then is not necessarily "what it means" for us today. (c) Appeals to inclusivity and other modern cultural trends and values are given weight than the sacred Scriptures.

system of the Roman state, imposed on Christian and non-Christian alike by Roman society. Yet Paul could say, "But if indeed you are able to become free, by all means make use of [the opportunity]" (1 Cor 7:21b). The headship of the man, on the other hand, applied only to the Christian home and the Christian church, where Christians were free to order their relationships in keeping with the Word of God. Paul never said to the women: "If you can assume the leading teaching office in the congregation, by all means avail yourself of the opportunity." Rather, he insisted that "the Lord's command" (14:37) ruled it out (14:34–38).

## INCLUSIVITY

More recently, "inclusivity" often replaces "justice" as one of the movement's buzz words. In keeping with Gal 3:28, the church should abolish all social barriers between Jew and Greek, slave and free, male and female. The ordination of women serves as an important sign of greater openness and inclusivity.

The "inclusivity" slogan confuses the issue. On the one hand, to be sure, the Gospel is inclusive: "God wants *all people* to be saved" (1 Tim 2:4; ἀνθρώπου there is inclusive: "people," not just "men"). Through Baptism into Christ *all* Christians share a oneness in Christ Jesus (Gal 3:28). This does not mean, however, that all are called to the public ministry. It is God who calls certain individuals into the pastoral ministry in accordance with his Word; the church has no right to add unbiblical requirements or to abolish biblical prerequisites.

The "inclusivity" argument unfairly brands those who do not accept women's ordination as "exclusive" and narrow minded, in contrast to those who are "inclusive," "open minded," and so on. It is also infinitely elastic and raises these questions: "Whom would you debar from the public ministry? Why not ordain practicing homosexuals, or children, or the intellectually disabled? Where do you draw the line? And on what basis?" All Christians will agree that not *everyone* is fit for the ministry. The question then becomes whether the criteria will be determined by human reasoning or by the Word of God.

## THE GIFTEDNESS OF WOMEN

The claim is often advanced that women should be ordained because they too have been endowed with the Spirit's gifts and should therefore be given an opportunity to exercise them in the public ministry.[70] While it is true that the

---

70  Johansson criticizes the view of A. von Harnack that the apostles, prophets, and teachers all performed their function on the basis of their spiritual gifts (*Women and the Church's Ministry*, 71–77). According to von Harnack, "they are all charismatics, i.e., their calling rests on a gift of the Spirit, which is a permanent possession for them" (*The Constitution and Law of the Church in the First Two Centuries*, trans. F. Pogson [London:

modern emphasis on the giftedness of all Christians has sometimes led to aberrations such as the construction of "inventories" of gifts in terms of people's personal qualities and abilities, the NT does indeed teach that God's multifaceted grace has endowed every Christian with a "gift of grace" (χάρισμα), either for speaking or for service (1 Pet 4:10–11; see the commentary on 1 Cor 12:8). Christian women also have a station and vocation in life, as do Christian men—in family, church, community, and workplace. As with all Christians, this gives women ample opportunity to speak "the words of God" to others, and to serve "out of the strength which God supplies, so that in everything God may be glorified through Jesus Christ" (1 Pet 4:11). But the gift of the public ministry has not been given to them (nor to most men).

## THE "SUBORDINATIONIST HERESY"

In an article in *Dialog* entitled "The Trinity, Ordination of Women, and the LCMS," C. Volz charged that some theologians of The Lutheran Church—Missouri Synod, as part of their defense of that church body's practice of not ordaining women, were developing a "new exegesis of 1 Cor 15:28 . . . identical with that of the Arians in 357 A.D."[71] The debate between Volz and these theologians takes us into areas of patristic theology which lie outside the scope of this excursus. But on the basis of our common grounding in the NT and the Athanasian Creed the following comments can be made.

The Greek verb ὑποτάσσω occurs nine times in 1 Corinthians, each time indisputably carrying the active meaning "to subordinate or subject" or the middle or passive meaning "to be subordinate or be subject to someone."[72] In chapter 14 it refers to the subjection of the spirits of prophets to prophets (14:32), and the subordination of women in the churches (14:34). In chapter 15 it refers first to the Father subjecting everything, including death, to the

Williams and Norgate, 1910] 24). It is true that apostles, prophets, and teachers are all the triune God's gift to the church (1 Cor 12:28; Eph 4:11). Johansson is correct, however, in stating: "We can rest assured that as little as the apostles . . . received their office by virtue of any special endowment of the spirit, no more was this true of the teachers in the Church. Paul states that God appointed them" (*Women and the Church's Ministry*, 77). Johansson rejects "the supposition that, as long as he had the needed charismata ['gifts of grace,' as in 1 Cor 12:4, 9, 28, 30, 31], anyone in the church had the right to act as a teacher" (p. 79). Luther emphasizes that the prophetesses of the Old and New Testaments did not prophesy without being called; they did not proceed "as a result of their own reflections nor on the basis of their own pietistic impulses" (P. Brunner, *The Ministry and the Ministry of Women*, 9, citing WA 30 III, 524, 10 ff. [LW 40:390]). Luther's view is supported by passages such as Judg 4:4–10, which portrays the prophetess Deborah as a reluctant leader who would have preferred Barak (a man) to be the sole leader in battle, and by 2 Pet 1:20–21.

71  *Dialog* 35.3 (Summer 1996) 164.

72  1 Cor 14:32, 34; 15:27 (three times); 15:28 (three times); 16:16. See the textual note on ὑποτασσέσθωσαν in 14:34.

Son, and then the Son's subjecting himself to the Father (15:27–28). Finally, in 16:16 it refers to the need for the Corinthian Christians to subject themselves to Stephanas and the other church servants like him.

Significant in the context in 1 Corinthians are two nouns from the same word-family, τάξις (14:40) and τάγμα (15:23). Both words have to do with the proper "order" of things. Everything in the church's worship must be done "properly and in order" (14:40). And the resurrection will take place "each in its proper order": Christ is raised first as the firstfruits, then those who belong to him, and then comes the end (15:23–24). Thus whether Paul is speaking of "order" or "subordination," he has in mind "a divinely willed order."[73]

In Eph 5:21, 24 Paul uses the verb ὑποτάσσω in close conjunction with the concept of headship (Eph 5:23). This supports the assumption that his statement about headship in 1 Cor 11:3 ("the head of every man is Christ, the head of the woman is the man, and the head of Christ is God") implies the subordination or subjection of the woman to the man, the man to Christ, and Christ to God the Father.

Given this headship structure, then, it is proper to view the apostolic word on women's subordination in the light of what Paul says in the context (11:3; 15:28) regarding Christ's subordination to the Father. Moreover, this broader context leads inescapably to the conclusion that it is no more demeaning for the woman to be subject to the man than it is for the man to be subject to Christ, and Christ to the Father. Conversely, the man's headship (properly exercised according to the divine order) over the woman is no more oppressive than Christ's headship over the man and the Father's headship over Christ.

Paul never calls on the Christian men to make the women submit.[74] There is nothing in Pauline theology providing a warrant for men to be oppressive, dictatorial, or misogynistic. The pattern Paul holds before men is the self-sacrificing love of Christ for his bride, the church (Eph 5:25–33). When he speaks of the submission of women, he always appeals to the women themselves to submit voluntarily (1 Cor 14:34; Eph 5:22–24).

As A. Pfeiffer has commented, this Christian "submission is a gift. Submission cannot be demanded or forced, it can only be given. As submission is a gift, so love is a gift, the right use of authority is a gift, obedience is a gift, honor is a gift and so on. Christians live in their society, family and work place this way by exercising their Christian freedom to give and serve, not to revolutionize and overthrow."[75] Some may take offense that it is Paul, a

---

73  G. Delling, "ὑποτάσσω," *TDNT* 8:43.

74  The fallen creation was unwillingly subjected to futility (Rom 8:20)! But Paul is not speaking there about the relationship between men and women, and nowhere does he say something similar about that relationship.

75  "A Comparative Study of Ephesians, Colossians, and First Peter, Drawing Implications for the Evangelism of Adults," unpublished manuscript presented to a Doctor of

man, who demands this submission. However, Paul is not speaking in a private capacity, but as the "apostle of Christ Jesus" (1 Cor 1:1). The Gospel provides the motivation for men and women joyfully to take their appointed places in God's order, especially in the church. It is possible to resist and reject the Gospel, as Paul himself once did, but such rejection is "to kick against the goads" (Acts 26:14). On the other hand, the person of faith—the new creation in Christ—delights in God's order (cf. Pss 1:2; 112:1; 119:16, 24, 35).

## PROPHETESSES IN THE OLD AND NEW TESTAMENTS

The occasional references to prophetesses in both testaments have been taken as a warrant for ordaining women.[76] But as has been argued in the excursus "Spiritual Gifts in 1 Corinthians," we cannot draw a straight line from the office of the prophet to that of a pastor. Unlike pastors, prophets speak on the basis of special revelations.[77] When the Montanists allowed women to make public speeches in church, referring for support to the prophetesses Miriam (Ex 15:20), Deborah (Judg 4:4), and Huldah (2 Ki 22:14; 2 Chr 34:22) in the OT, and to Philip's daughters (Acts 21:9) and Anna (Lk 2:36) in the NT, Hauke notes that

> Origen counters that all these women would never have spoken in public in the presence of men. Acts mentions nothing about prophesying by the daughters of Philip in the congregation, nor is that reported of Anna. Miriam only directed the singing of a group of women. In contrast to Jeremiah and Isaiah, we hear of no address to the people by Deborah. Huldah, likewise, did not address the people; rather, it was necessary to go to her home to hear her.[78]

Among the slighter arguments are the appeal to supposed NT precedents in the case of Priscilla, who assisted her husband Aquila in giving private instruction to Apollos (Acts 18:26), or Phoebe, the deaconess at Cenchrea (Rom 16:1), or Junia, whom some take to be a female apostle (Rom 16:7).[79] But Origen's comments apply here too; none of these women preached, led, or taught the church in worship or administered the Sacraments. It may be added that, in contrast to the few women who were OT prophets, all the priests were men.

---

Missiology seminar at Concordia Theological Seminary, Fort Wayne, IN, Winter 1996–97, p. 16.

76  J. Jarick, "The Seven (?) Prophetesses of the Old Testament," *Lutheran Theological Journal* 28.3 (December 1994) 116–21. Luther anticipated this argument and responded to it (LW 40:390–91).

77  G. Friedrich, "προφήτης κτλ.," *TDNT* 6:854.

78  *Women in the Priesthood?* 410, citing a commentary on 1 Cor 14:34–35 by Origen that has been preserved in a catena (for the text, see C. Jenkins, "Origen on 1 Corinthians," *Journal of Theological Studies* 10 [1909] 41–42).

79  See the response in M. Hauke, *Women in the Priesthood?* 358–59.

And it may be argued that the priests' responsibilities in teaching the Torah and administering the sacrifices bear the closest relationship to those of the NT ministers of Word and Sacrament.

## Conclusion

The above will have to suffice in response to the array of arguments advanced by the advocates of women's ordination. None of those arguments stands up to serious exegetical scrutiny. Nor is that surprising, for the movement to ordain women does not really have its starting point in the Scriptures, but in the sociology and spirit of the modern age (cf. 1 Cor 2:12). It is a novelty, an aberration from the Scriptures and from the universal doctrine and practice of the church for almost two millennia.

Nonetheless, Christians are subjected to emotive arguments like these: "We must go forward in faith, not hold back in fear."[80] Naturally no one wants to be charged with fear and cowardice and hesitancy to go forward in faith. But how are commands to go forward in faith and not be afraid used in the Bible? One passage that comes to mind is the Lord's word to Moses as the Egyptians pursued the Israelites to the shore of the Red Sea: "Tell the Israelites to go forward!" (Ex 14:15). Here indeed was a situation where the people were called to go forward in faith and not hold back in fear. But they were to go forward *at the command of God—a clear word from the Lord*. And as they obeyed that divine word, God blessed and delivered them through the waters of the Red Sea.[81]

It is a perilous situation, however, when Christians are told to go forward in defiance of the Lord's command. In such a situation, we should take notice rather of texts like Is 66:2: "This is the person for whom I [the Lord] will have regard: for the one who is humble and contrite in spirit, and trembles at my word."

Thus the apostolic command that women be silent in the churches (1 Cor 14:34), as it is "*the Lord's command*" (14:37), binds the church's conscience to "the obedience of Christ" (2 Cor 10:5).[82] Christians who submit their thinking

---

80  This psychological approach played a prominent role in the Church of England's debate on women's ordination in 1992. In the final two sentences of the final speech before the vote was taken, the Bishop of Guildford said: "So I ask the Synod to take a step forward into the future, God's future, confident that he will lead us into this truth. I ask the Synod to vote firmly, clearly and confidently for this legislation" (*The Ordination of Women to the Priesthood: The Synod Debate* [London: Church House, 1993] 76).

81  See similar divine commands to be courageous, not fearful, and to carry out God's explicit instructions in, for example, Deut 11:8; 31:6–7; Josh 1:6–9; 10:25; 23:6.

82  Johansson observes: "Had he [Paul] not so strongly stressed the necessity for obeying the commands of God and of Christ as he does in 1 Corinthians 11–14, it [Christianity]

and living to this obedience will not be deterred by ostracism and anathemas, even as Luther ignored the papal bull and took his stand on the Word of God. This has been ably expressed by Slenczka in response to the Evangelical Church in Germany's 1992 anathematizing of even the criticism of women's ordination by its pastors:

> Whether we like it or not, the literal meaning of the text here concerns itself . . . with a matter that affects our salvation. This means that Women's Ordination is not just a question of ecclesiastical order, or historical custom. Here the Apostle is concerned with the fellowship of the churches and their obedience to the Word of the Lord. . . . A church is not to place itself above the Word of God and a clear command of the Lord and at the same time sever its fellowship with other churches in other places and times. Such a decision is aimed against the church itself. The church disintegrates when it no longer clings to the Word of its Lord; and it sinks as it subjects itself to the throw of a dice (Eph. 4:14) of human opinion and social currents. . . . You can neither alter the Word of God in the literal rendering of the Holy Scriptures nor abolish its effect on consciences.[83]

## APPENDIX

On November 11, 1992, at about 4:30 p.m., the Church of England approved the ordination of women to the priesthood. The vote was carried by majorities of over two-thirds in each of the synod's three houses (bishops, clergy, and laity). The earlier part of the day was devoted to speeches for and against the legislation. Of those who spoke against the legislation, one of the most eloquent was Mrs. Sara Low. Her speech may be described as a cry from the heart, or in C. S. Lewis' terms, the bleating of a sheep trying to catch the ear of her shepherds.[84] I believe she is an able spokesperson for all Christians who desire to remain faithful to their Lord.

> When I was converted to Jesus Christ in my early twenties and came into the Church of England, I was told by my first parish priest, now a bishop on these benches, that the Church of England based itself on Holy

---

would have become an antinomian and libertinistic gnostic sect which would scarcely have survived the classical world" (*Women and the Church's Ministry*, 57). Brunner also notes that in Paul's instructions in 14:34–38, "as in 1 Cor. 11:16, the apostolic character of the Corinthian church is at stake, and its reaction to this problem will ultimately determine whether it remains within the folds of the apostolic church or becomes a syncretistic sect" (*The Ministry and the Ministry of Women*, 24).

83   "Is a Criticism of Women's Ordination a Church Divisive Heresy?" 5, quoting from his earlier paper "The Ordination of Women to the Office of the Church: Lecture to the State Synod of Schaumburg-Lippe, Bückeburg [October 5, 1991]."

84   See *Fern-Seed and Elephants and Other Essays on Christianity*, ed. W. Hooper (Glasgow: Collins/Fountain, 1975) 105.

Scripture, holy tradition and human reason. This legislation gives me the gravest possible concern on all three counts.

One of the things that I have learned in my time as a Christian is that where we are faithful to the revealed truth, there the promises of the New Testament are fulfilled. The Churches that believe this and do it are, in my experience, those that are blessed.

Like many of those here, I have listened for nearly twenty years to this debate. I listened very carefully to the early arguments about Jesus' cultural conditioning and the claim that Jesus did not have the freedom to appoint women. If cultural conditioning was determinative for Jesus, then all his teaching and all his actions are thus heavily influenced. We are no longer talking about the eternal Son of God. Jesus Christ is different today from what he was yesterday, and he will be different again tomorrow. I have listened to the arguments that the early Church was equally unable to make this change, yet, on the contrary, what could have made a bigger bridgehead with the pagan world than the introduction of women priests, with which they were already familiar? I have listened to arguments on St Paul where one classic quotation [Gal 3:28] has been wrenched out of context, given a meaning that no previous generation of believers has given it, and seen it used to deny the clear teaching on headship in the rest of St Paul's letters. I have listened to the doctrine of creation being divided into greater and lesser truths, so that the complementarity of male and female has been debased to a banal interchangeability. I have listened patiently to talk of prayerful, thoughtful majorities when surely our problem is that the minority is also prayerful and thoughtful.

These are not comfortable things to say, but they must be said because if the Synod overturns scriptural authority today it will be no good coming back next time and hoping to impose it on other issues. For the Church, the authority of the Scriptures and the example of Jesus has always been determinative; I do not believe that this House has the authority to overturn them.

My second concern is the legislation itself. What of those who dissent? It seems strange, does it not, to call those who faithfully believe what the Church has always believed "dissenters"? Bishops and archbishops may give verbal assurances that there will be no persecution against such priests and laypeople, but it is with great sadness that I have to tell the bishops that I have not met one opponent of the measure who believes them. The reasons are simple. First, no verbal assurance can undo the fact that you are legislating for two classes of Christian; any good intentions that may exist will wither before the law and practice, as in other provinces. Second, in many dioceses the spirit of this legislation has been in operation for some years. Orthodox clergy are excluded from appointments and orthodox laity are made to feel excluded from that warm glow of official approval, as if they are suffering from some embarrassing handicap. I have experienced that myself often enough in these corridors.

However, if the human injustice of this legislation, which eases old men into retirement and condemns others to serve forever under authorities whose primary qualification is compromise, is disgraceful, it is as nothing besides its theological arrogance and blasphemy. The legislation clearly instructs the Lord God Almighty whom he may raise up to lead the Church. The Holy Spirit will be told, "You may choose anyone you want so long as it is one of us." A Church that denies the sovereignty of God is no longer a Church. The fruits of this debate are not the fruits of the Holy Spirit.

What of tomorrow? If you wake in the morning having voted yes, you'll know that you have voted for a Church irreconcilably divided, for whom the revealed truth of God is no longer authoritative. If you vote no, you will wake to tears and a healing ministry, but above all to the possibility of a renewed New Testament Church, for all of us could then be united in encouraging, training and funding the ministry of priest, deacon, teacher, prophet, healer, administrator, spiritual director—all promised by the Holy Spirit.

I urge Synod to vote for the authority of the Word of God, for the unity of Christ's Church and against this ruinous legislation.[85]

---

85   *The Ordination of Women to the Priesthood: The Synod Debate*, 42–43.

# SECTION II

# HISTORICAL STUDIES

The practice of ordaining women to the pastoral office is a novelty in the history of the Church. In the United States, the first woman to be ordained was Antoinette L. Brown in 1853 at a small Congregationalist congregation in upstate New York. The twentieth century would witness a widespread embrace of women's ordination both in the United States and Europe. Fueled by theological movements that set the charismatic distribution of the Spirit in opposition to an established office, the emerging egalitarianism of the feminist movement, historical criticism's distrust of the biblical text, and in some cases a pragmatism that saw the ordination of women as a way to alleviate the clergy shortage brought on by World War II, many Protestant denominations took steps to ordain women.

The essays in this section seek to set the practice of the ordination of women in historical context. William Weinrich, professor of historical theology and academic dean at Concordia Theological Seminary, Fort Wayne, Indiana, gives an overview of the many ways that faithful women have been active in the life of the Church—noting that these women were holy and learned but never pastors.

In a short piece on "The Use of Tractate 26 to Promote the Ordination of Women," John W. Kleinig argues that Philip Melanchthon's confession that the ministry of the New Testament is not bound to persons, as was the Levitical priesthood of the Old Testament, does not open the way for the ordination of women. On the contrary, Melanchthon grounds the authority of the office on the institution of Christ in contrast with the purely human authority of the papacy. The ordination of women is an act of human authority; it cannot be demonstrated as being instituted by Christ.

Some Lutherans have argued that the supposed silence of the Lutheran Confessions on the question of the gender of the office bearer makes the ordination of women an open question. Roland Ziegler, assistant professor of systematic theology at Concordia Theological Seminary, Fort Wayne, Indiana, gives a reading of the leading ladies in feminist theology. A pastor from the Church of Sweden, Fredrik Sidenvall, reflects on the negative effects of the ordination of women in his homeland over the past forty years.

John T. Pless, assistant professor of pastoral ministry and missions at Concordia Theological Seminary, Fort Wayne, Indiana, examines the coherence and parallelism of theological arguments now being offered for the ordination of practicing homosexuals with those arguments that were and are made for the ordination of women in "The Ordination of Women and Ecclesiastical Endorsement of Homosexuality: Are They Related?"

The advocates of women's ordination are right about at least one thing. Ordination of women is a monumental turn in the history of the Church. Yet the practice is not a progressive step forward; it is a veering away from the received tradition of the Church. It puts those church bodies that practice it on dangerous ground, for it indicates that they are out of step not only with two thousand years of Christian history but also with the will of the Lord of the Church.

# WOMEN IN THE HISTORY OF THE CHURCH

## LEARNED AND HOLY, BUT NOT PASTORS

## WILLIAM WEINRICH

If it was once true that women were a neglected factor in church history, that imbalance is quickly being rectified. There is a spate of recent books on the history of women in the church that chronicle their institutions, their influence, and their contributions. As typical examples one may mention the three-volume collection of scholarly essays, *Women & Religion in America*, edited by Rosemary Ruether and Rosemary Keller, and the monograph *Holy Women in Twelfth-Century England*, by Sharon K. Elkins.[1] There is little doubt that such scholarship is making a significant contribution to our understanding of the church's past and, specifically, of the place and importance of women in it.

From within evangelical circles, the most important contribution to the history of women in the church is *Daughters of the Church*, by Ruth A. Tucker and Walter Liefeld.[2] This book offers historical vignettes about women who have in one way or another exercised active, public leadership roles in the centuries of the church's past. While striving to be objective, Tucker and Liefeld nevertheless exhibit a predilection for feminist interpretations of the evidence. Yet, that aside, they have amassed a considerable amount of mate-

---

1  Rosemary Radford Ruether and Rosemary Skinner Keller, eds., *Women & Religion in America*, three vols. (San Francisco: Harper & Row, 1982–1986); Sharon K. Elkins, *Holy Women of Twelfth-Century England* (Chapel Hill, NC: The University of North Carolina Press, 1988). The importance of women in the history of the church was never a totally neglected theme. Before it was fashionable to do so, Roland H. Bainton wrote his three-volume *Women of the Reformation* (Minneapolis: Augsburg, 1971–1977). See also Edith Deen, *Great Women of the Christian Faith* (New York: Harper & Brothers, 1959), and her bibliography, pp. 411–415.

2  Ruth A. Tucker and Walter Liefeld, *Daughters of the Church: Women and Ministry from New Testament Times to the Present* (Grand Rapids, MI: Zondervan, 1987).

171

rial so that their book can nicely serve as a kind of women's "Who's Who in Church History."[3]

In a short article, we cannot encompass the full breadth of women's contributions to the church's life and faith through the centuries. We do wish, however, briefly to indicate some of the ways women have contributed to the church as well as the unbroken teaching and practice of the church that the recognized teaching and sacramental ministry of the church is to be reserved for men.

# I. "DAUGHTERS OF THE CHURCH" IN WORD AND DEED

## A. SERVICE OF PRAYER AND CHARITY

It is, I suppose, impossible to escape the trap of describing the contributions of women, or of men, to the church primarily in terms of leadership and influence. After all, historical sources tend to focus on persons who did something or said something of extraordinary importance and therefore have been remembered and recorded. Yet we ought not be oblivious to one-sided activistic assumptions. The life of faith can be "active" in prayer, contemplation, and charity, and there have been myriad women, and men, who have excelled in these "silent works."

In fact, the early church had a distinct group of women called "widows" who were dedicated to prayer and intercession.[4] The *Apostolic Tradition* of Hippolytus (c. 210 A.D.) speaks of widows as "appointed for prayer" (chap. 11), and the *Didaskalia Apostolorum* (Syria, c. 230 A.D.) similarly speaks of the widows as having prayer as their primary duty: "for a widow should have no other care save to be praying for those who give and for the whole Church."[5] Other early Christian writers make clear that widows as a group held a place of considerable honor and dignity. Often they are listed along with the bishop, elders, and deacons (e.g., Origen, *Hom. in Luc.* 17), and Tertullian calls them an "order" and says that widows were assigned a place of honor within the assembled congregation (*On Modesty* 13.4).[6] Although prayer and intercession

---

3   More recently Ruth A. Tucker has produced a similar but more focused book on women in modern missions: *Guardians of the Great Commission: The Story of Women in Modern Missions* (Grand Rapids, MI: Zondervan, 1988).

4   See 1 Timothy 5:3–10. Ignatius of Antioch speaks of "virgins called widows" (*Smyrna* 13:1), a phrase that indicates that *widow* designated a specific group of women within the church. Polycarp of Smyrna calls the widow an "altar of God" (Philippians 4:3), probably because widows were recipients of Christian charity.

5   R. Hugh Connolly, *Didaskalia Apostolorum* (Oxford: The Clarendon Press, 1929), p. 132.

6   See also Tertullian, *Exhortation to Chastity* 13:4; *On Modesty* 13:7; *To His Wife* 1.7.4. This does not imply that widows were "ordained" or considered part of the clergy. Indeed, the *Apostolic Tradition* of Hippolytus expressly forbids the laying of hands on the widow.

were the primary tasks of the widow, the *Didaskalia* indicates that by the third century the widows in some churches were engaged in charitable work. Such charity would consist in hospitality, working at wool to assist those in distress, and visiting and laying hands on the sick.[7] The *Apostolic Church Order* (Egypt, fourth century) evinces a similar two-fold division of prayer and service. Three widows are to be appointed: "Two of them are to dedicate themselves to prayer for all those in trial and to be ready for revelations. . . . The one is to be ready to serve, attending upon those women who are ill" (chap. 21).[8]

Especially in eastern Christianity (Syria, Chaldea, Persia), social mores that severely limited social access to women required the creation of a distinctly female diaconal ministry for the evangelization and care of women. The order of deaconess first takes concrete form in the *Didaskalia*.[9] The first duty of the deaconess was to assist the bishop in the baptism of women by anointing their bodies and ensuring that their nudity was not seen. Beyond this duty, the *Didaskalia* says that the deaconess had the responsibility of teaching and instructing the newly baptized women, apparently serving as a spiritual mother exhorting them to chastity. In addition, the deaconess was to visit Christian women in the homes of the heathen, to visit women who were ill, to bathe those women who were recovering from illness, and to minister to women in need.[10]

Subsequent ecclesiastical legislation in eastern Christianity reiterates these functions of the deaconess, but they add other responsibilities. The *Apostolic Constitutions* (Syria, fourth century) indicate that the deaconess supervised the seating and behavior of the female part of the worshiping community. She was

---

She is to be appointed "by the word alone" and is distinct from the clergy (*Apost. Trad.* 11).

7  Connolly, pp. 136, 138, 140.

8  The *Apostolic Constitutions* (Syria, fourth century), the *Canons of Hippolytus* (Egypt, fourth century), and the *Testament of our Lord Jesus Christ* (Syria, fifth century) continue to depict the widow as given to prayer and charity. The *Testament* gives the widow a place of considerable prominence and even appears to place her among the clergy. One should note that the ministry of the widow was exclusively toward other women. For general discussion of the widow, see Mary McKenna, *Women of the Church: Role and Renewal* (New York: P. J. Kennedy & Sons, 1967), pp. 35–63; Bonnie Bowman Thurston, *The Widows: A Women's Ministry in the Early Church* (Minneapolis: Fortress Press, 1989); Roger Gryson, *The Ministry of Women in the Early Church* (Collegeville, MD: The Liturgical Press, 1976, 1980) *passim*.

9  That social conditions demanded an order of deaconess is evident from the *Didaskalia* itself: "for there are houses to which you (the bishop) cannot send a (male) deacon to the women, on account of the heathen, but you may send a deaconess" (Connolly, p. 146). The best study on the deaconess is Aimé Georges Martimort, *Deaconesses: An Historical Study* (San Francisco: Ignatius Press, 1986); see also Gryson, *Ministry of Women*.

10  Connolly, pp. 146–148.

a keeper of the doors to prevent men from mingling in the women's section of the church, and she served as intermediary between the male clergy and the women of the congregation (*Apost. Const.* 2.57ff.; 2.26; 3.15ff., 19).[11] The *Testament of Our Lord Jesus Christ* (Syria, fifth century), which gives to the widow what other legislation gives to the deaconess, does give the deaconess one duty, to bring communion to pregnant women unable to attend Easter mass (*Test.* II 20.7).

Such legislation reveals a feminine ministry of considerable significance and responsibility. Indeed, the importance of the deaconess is indicated by the fact that she was an ordained member of the clergy.[12] In other regions, where the separation of the sexes was not so strict, such a female diaconate was not required, but the title of deaconess was introduced as a degree of honor to enhance the dignity of a woman religious called upon to oversee a convent. Such a deaconess-abbess not only would administer the life of the convent and oversee its charitable activities, but also could perform certain liturgical services in the absence of a priest.[13]

Typical of this kind of deaconess was Olympias. Born into wealth in fourth-century Constantinople, she used her wealth to found a convent that included a hostel for priests as well as a number of hospitals. Her fame was enhanced by her friendship with John Chrysostom, with whom she corresponded while he was in exile.[14] According to Palladius, Olympias "catechized many women."[15] Perhaps another such deaconess-abbess was a certain Mary who is known only from her tombstone (found in Cappadocia): "according to the text of the apostle, raised children, practiced hospitality, washed the feet of the saints and distributed her bread to those in need."[16] In the East where convents frequently were located in isolated places and priests might not be present, a deaconess-abbess could perform certain liturgical services:

---

11 See also the fifth- through seventh-century legislation from Chaldea and Persia adduced by Martimort, *Deaconesses*, pp. 52–58.

12 For discussion see Gryson, *Ministry of Women*, pp. 62–64; Kyriaki Fitzgerald, "The Characteristics and Nature of the Order of the Deaconess," *Women and the Priesthood*, ed. Thomas Hopko (Crestwood, NY: St. Vladimir's Seminary Press, 1983), pp. 84–89. *Apost. Const.* 8.20 gives an ordination prayer for the deaconess. It is necessary to make clear that ordination placed one into a *specific* service. It did not mean that one could perform any and all churchly acts. The deaconess performed by ordination the functions of deaconess. Her ordination did not authorize her to perform the tasks of elder or bishop. No office was simply interchangeable with another office.

13 For discussion of the deaconess-abbess, see Martimort, *Deaconesses*, pp. 134–143, 205–206; Gryson, *Ministry of Women*, p. 90.

14 See Martimort, *Deaconesses*, pp. 136–137.

15 Palladius, *Lausiac History*, 56.

16 Martimort, *Deaconesses*, pp. 125–126. Most likely "the text of the apostle" is 1 Timothy 5:10.

distribute communion to the nuns, read the Gospels and the holy books in a worship assembly, etc.[17]

Although the West never had a developed female diaconate[18] and the deaconess disappeared also in the East by the twelfth century, the deaconess ideal of charity and teaching for the sick and poor experienced a significant renewal in the nineteenth century. Indeed, Kathleen Bliss would write that in terms of its subsequent influence, the revival of deaconess in Germany in the early nineteenth century was "the greatest event in the life of women in the Church since the Reformation."[19] In Germany the deaconess trained primarily as a nurse and only secondarily as a teacher. The model for this nurse-deaconess was the deaconess home at Kaiserwerth begun in the 1830s by a Lutheran pastor, Theodore Fliedner. Its focus was the care of the sick poor, the orphan, discharged women prisoners, and the mentally ill.[20] Other deaconess training schools on the Kaiserwerth model began all over Germany, such as that in Neuendettelsau in 1854, but the success of Fliedner's enterprise was measured in international terms. By the mid-nineteenth century, Kaiserwerth nurses and teachers were staffing hospitals and schools in America, Constantinople, Smyrna, Alexandria, Jerusalem, Bucharest, and Florence.[21]

A different type was the Anglican deaconess, whose training was mostly theological and pastoral. The inspiration for this female diaconate came from Elizabeth Ferard, who—with six other women—founded the London Deaconess Institution in 1862. Unlike the German deaconess, who worked largely independently of the church, the Anglican deaconess was responsible to the bishop of the diocese in which she worked. Well-trained theologically, the Anglican deaconess worked in the parish or taught in school.[22]

In her 1952 report on the function and status of women in the member churches of the World Council of Churches, Kathleen Bliss listed in addition to the deaconess these types of women parish workers: (1) the trained lay parish worker whose duties might include Sunday school and youth work, Bible study, home visitation, hospital visiting, preparation for confirmation,

---

17  See especially Martimort, *Deaconesses*, pp. 138–143.

18  Martimort, *Deaconesses*, pp. 187–216.

19  Kathleen Bliss, *The Service and Status of Women in the Church* (London: SCM Press, 1952), pp. 80–81.

20  Perhaps the most famous of Kaiserwerth's nurses was Florence Nightingale, who went there after she could find no similar training in England.

21  For a brief account of the history and influence of the German type of deaconess, see Bliss, *Service and Status of Women*, pp. 80–89.

22  For the Anglican deaconess, see *ibid.*, pp. 89–91. Bliss noted a third type of deaconess as well, one common to Presbyterian, Baptist and Methodist churches. Their work ranged "from parish work to institutional work in orphanages, homes for the aged, and other church-supported institutions" (pp. 92–94).

and social case work; (2) parish helpers; (3) directors of religious education; (4) trained youth leaders; (5) church social workers; (6) Sunday school organizers.[23] Throughout the history of the church thousands of dedicated women have carried on the tradition of prayer, Christian charity, and care begun in the early church by the widow and deaconess. Happily, the stories of some of these women are being told. An example of this is a recent book by Barbara Misner, who chronicles the history and work of eight different groups of Catholic women religious in America between 1790 and 1850.[24] Among their "charitable exercises" she mentions especially the care of the sick, work during cholera epidemics, and care of orphans.

## B. SERVICE OF MIND AND PEN

Although the opportunity to exercise their literary and intellectual abilities could vary considerably given historical circumstances, Christian women nonetheless have bequeathed to the church a respectable literary and intellectual legacy. From the beginning, Christian women have been interested in the study of the Scripture and Christian theology. Already in the second century we hear of a young woman named Charito who was martyred with Justin Martyr, most probably because she was associated with Justin's school in Rome (*Martyrdom of Justin* 4). We know also that the lectures of Origen were well attended by women, the most famous being Mammaea, the mother of Emperor Alexander Severus, who had a military escort bring Origen to Antioch so she could test his understanding of the divine things (Eusebius, *Hist. eccl.* 6.21.3ff.). Yet, it was the great Roman matrons of the fourth century whose combination of the ascetic life and the study of the Scriptures and the Church Fathers became, through the influence of Jerome, the ideal image of women dedicated to the religious life. Two of these highborn ladies, Marcella and Paula, founded circles of ascetic women in their homes whose central purpose was the intensive study of the Bible. Jerome became their mentor and introduced them to the study of the Old Testament in Hebrew. Paula learned Hebrew so well that she could chant the Psalms without a trace of Latin accent. Marcella is called by Jerome his "task-mistress" because she incessantly demanded of him complete explanations of Hebrew words and

---

23  *Ibid.*, pp. 94–103. This informative report, now almost forty years old, deserves an update, if it has not already received one.

24  Barbara Misner, *"Highly Respectable and Accomplished Ladies": Catholic Women Religious in America 1790–1850* (New York/London: Garland, 1988). The eight groups Misner discusses are the Carmelites, Visitation Sisters, Sisters of Charity-Emmitsburg, Sisters of Loretto, Sisters of Charity of Nazareth, Dominican Sisters of St. Catherine Kentucky, Oblate Sisters of Providence, and Sisters of Our Lady of Mercy.

phrases.[25] "With her probing mind Marcella wished to have all the obscurities, especially the linguistic ones, of the text cleared up; and although their meetings were frequent, she often insisted on his setting down his solutions on paper."[26] Paula and Jerome eventually established monastic communities for women and for men in Bethlehem.

Another Roman ascetic matron who conjoined learning and monastic life was Melania the Elder. She, along with Rufinus of Aquileia, formed monasteries in Jerusalem. Palladius speaks of Melania's deep learning:

> Being very learned and loving literature, she turned night into day perusing every writing of the ancient commentators, including the three million (lines) of Origen and the two hundred and fifty thousand of Gregory, Stephen, Pierius, Basil and other standard writers. Nor did she read them once only and casually, but she laboriously went through each book seven or eight times. (*Lausiac History* 55)

A similar circle of studious women gathered in Constantinople around Theodosia, the sister of Amphilocius of Iconium. Olympias, deaconess and friend of John Chrysostom, was educated in this circle.

In this context we should mention also Macrina, whose strength as a woman ascetic and a theological mind is glorified by her brother, Gregory of Nyssa, in his *Life of Macrina*. Gregory's *On the Soul and the Resurrection* is presented as a Socratic dialogue between Gregory and Macrina in which Macrina is depicted as the protagonist and teacher.

The tradition of learned monastic women continued into the medieval period. Lioba (eighth century), sister of St. Boniface, "had been trained from infancy in the rudiments of grammar and the study of the other liberal arts." "So great was her zeal for reading that she discontinued it only for prayer or for the refreshment of her body with food or sleep: the Scriptures were never out of her hands." "She read with attention all the books of the Old and New Testaments and learned by heart all the commandments of God. To these she added by way of completion the writings of the Church Fathers, the decrees of the Councils and the whole of ecclesiastical law."[27] Princes and bishops, we are told, "often discussed spiritual matters and ecclesiastical discipline with her" because of her knowledge of the Scripture and her prudent

---

25  Jeome, *Letters* 28; 29. These two letters answer Marcella's questions about "ephod" (1 Samuel 2:18) and "teraphim" (Judges 17:5).

26  J. N. D. Kelly, *Jerome: His Life, Writings, and Controversies* (New York: Harper & Row, 1975) p. 94. Jerome says that some, including priests, inquired of Marcella concerning "doubtful and obscure points" (*Letter* 127).

27  For these quotes, see the *Life of St. Lioba*, in *The Anglo-Saxon Missionaries in Germany*, ed. C. H. Talbot (London: Sheed and Ward, 1954, 1981), p. 215.

counsel.[28] The Venerable Bede (eighth century) reports that Abbess Hilda of Whitby required those under her direction "to make a thorough study of the Scriptures" and that she did this to such good effect "that many were found fitted for Holy Orders and the service of God's altar."[29] Indeed, five bishops trained at Whitby under Hilda's direction.

The love of reading the Scriptures and the Church Fathers led convents also to the copying of manuscripts. In c. 735, St. Boniface wrote to Abbess Eadburga requesting that she have a copy of the epistles of Peter made in letters of gold. "For many times by your useful gifts of books and vestments you have consoled and relieved me in my distress."[30] Among other things, these words of Boniface reveal how logistically important and supportive English convents were to the Anglo-Saxon missionaries on the Continent.

Although the volume of theological and spiritual literature composed by Christian women is less than that written by Christian men, throughout the history of the church there have been capable women who have been productive with the pen. We have mentioned already women like Marcella and Olympias, who engaged in correspondence with Jerome and John Chrysostom. Their letters, unfortunately, no longer exist. However, a not inconsiderable body of writing by Christian women is extant.

Perhaps the earliest writing we have from a Christian woman is the account of Vibia Perpetua of her sufferings and visions as a Christian martyr. Martyred under Septimius Severus (c. 202 A.D.), Perpetua's personal account was included by an unknown redactor in the *Martyrdom of Perpetua and Felicitas*, which became a model for later Acts of the martyrs, especially in North Africa.[31] One of the most fascinating documents of the early church is the travel diary of Egeria (late fourth century). Egeria, a noble woman from southern France, spent several years as a pilgrim in the East, traveling to Egypt, Palestine, Syria, and Asia Minor. Taking notes along the way, she later wrote them up as her *Travels*. It is clear from her narrative that Egeria was steeped in the classics of the church, and "her language often echoes that

---

28  *Life of St. Lioba*, p. 223.

29  Bede, *History of the English Church and People*, 4.23. Whitby was a double monastery of both women and men. In Celtic and Anglo-Saxon monasticism, such monasteries were usually under the direction of an abbess.

30  Boniface's letter may be found in *Christianity and Paganism, 350–750: The Conversion of Western Europe*, ed. J. N. Hillgarth (Philadelphia: University of Pennsylvania Press, 1986), p. 175.

31  In the present form of the *Martyrdom of Perpetua*, chapters 3–10 constitute the prison diary of Perpetua. The *Martyrdom of Montanus and Lucius* and the *Martyrdom of Marian and James* (both c. 250 A.D.) are patterned after the *Martyrdom of Perpetua*.

of the Bible or of formal prayer."[32] Her account contains some of the most helpful and informative detail we possess of early monasticism and liturgy.

A rather unique contribution to Christian literature is the Virgilian cento by Proba. Born a pagan in fourth-century Rome, Proba was educated in the classical writers of Latin literature, especially in Virgil, whom she especially loved. In the fourth century it was fashionable to write cento poetry. A cento is a poem produced by piecing together lines from the works of another poet, resulting in a new poem with a new theme. After becoming a Christian, Proba wrote a cento, borrowing from the works of Virgil, in which she intended to present the whole of the Biblical history.[33] About one-half of the 694 lines relates the beginning of the Old Testament (creation, fall, flood, the exodus), but then Proba moves to the gospel story of Jesus. Although Jerome harshly criticized it, and the Gelasian Decretal "On Books to be Received and not to be Received" (496 A.D.) placed it among the apocryphal writings, Proba's *Cento* became a popular school text in the Middle Ages.[34] Its frequent use is attested by the number of manuscripts containing it and the catalogues of monastic libraries.

Eudoxia is another Christian woman who produced a respectable literary output. The daughter of a pagan philosopher, Eudoxia was instructed "in every kind of learning" (Socrates, *Hist. eccl.* 7.21). She was later baptized a Christian and became the wife of Emperor Theodosius II (408–450). The greater part of her writing has been lost.[35] However, much of a cento drawn from the works of Homer is extant, as is the so-called *Martyrdom of St. Cyprian*. The *Martyrdom* tells of a certain Antiochian magician named Cyprian who fails in his effort to tempt a young Christian virgin and is rather himself led to

---

32  John Wilkinson, ed., *Egeria's Travels* (London: SPCK, 1971), p. 5.

33  Virgilian cento poetry existed already at the time of Tertullian. In her *Cento*, Proba used especially Virgil's *Aeneid*, *Eclogues*, and *Georgics*.

34  For Jerome's criticism, see *Letter* 53.7, where he calls Christian cento literature "puerile" (also *Letter* 130). The most easily accessible English translation of Proba's *Cento* is in Patricia Wilson-Kastner, G. Ronald Kastner, et al., *A Lost Tradition: Women Writers of the Early Church* (Washington, D.C.: University Press of America, 1981), pp. 45–68. The *Cento* was not Proba's only writing. The beginning lines indicate that while still a pagan she had written of civil war, probably referring to the uprising of Magnus Magnentius against the Emperor Constantius (351–353 A.D.).

35  Socrates (*Hist. eccl.* 7.21) speaks of a "poem in heroic verse" that Eudoxia composed on the occasion of Theodosius' victory over the Persians (422 A.D.). Evagrius Scholasticus (*Hist. eccl.* 1.20) has preserved one verse of a poetic address to the people of Antioch. Photius, ninth-century Patriarch of Constantinople, mentions a poetic paraphrase of the first eight books of the Bible (*Bibliotheca* 183) and also a poetic paraphrase of the prophetic books of Daniel and Zechariah.

become a Christian. The story ends with the martyr death of Cyprian and of the young maiden under the Emperor Diocletian.[36]

The tradition of literary Christian women continued into the Middle Ages. Abbess Hildegarde of Bingen (1098–1179) was an extremely influential visionary and prophetess whose correspondence included "four popes, two emperors, several kings and queens, dukes, counts, abbesses, the masters of the University of Paris, and prelates including Saint Bernard and Thomas à Becket."[37] Commanded by a heavenly voice to write down her visions, Hildegarde wrote two major works, *Know the Ways of the Lord* (*Scivias*) and *Book of Divine Works*. Both works belong to the medieval genre that "combined science, theology, and philosophy in a description of the universe, internal (the human body) and external (the earth and the heavens)."[38] Her works evince a familiarity with Augustine and Boethius as well as with contemporary scientific writers. Portions of her *Scivias* were read by Pope Eugenius III and St. Bernard and elicited from the pope a letter of praise and approval.[39] In addition to her two major works and her extensive correspondence, Hildegarde wrote lives of St. Disibod and St. Rupert, hymns, books on medicine and natural history, fifty allegorical homilies, and a morality play.

In Spain, the Catholic Reformation had a major female voice in St. Teresa of Avila (1515–1582). As a young woman she entered the Carmelite convent at Avila. There, later in life, she began to experience visions and ecstasies, and these in turn led her to propose a reform of the Carmelite order according to its original, more austere rule. Although there was powerful opposition to Teresa, support from Pope Paul IV and from King Philip II enabled her to establish many convents for her "discalced" (barefoot) Carmelite nuns. Of her most important writings, two are autobiographical. The *Life* describes her visions and discusses the centrality of prayer, and *Foundations* describe the establishment of her convents. Teresa wrote her most important mystical writings for her nuns. The *Way of Perfection* teaches the virtues of the religious (monastic) life and uses the Lord's Prayer as the vehicle for teaching prayer. The *Interior Castle* presents mature Teresian thought on the spiritual life. Growth in prayer enables a person to enter into deeper intimacy with God, who dwells in the soul or "interior castle" of the person. Some thirty-one poems and 458 letters of Teresa are extant.

---

36  For an English translation of Eudoxia's Martyrdom of Cyprian, see Wilson-Kastner, et al., *Lost Tradition*, pp. 149–171.

37  Frances and Joseph Gies, *Women in the Middle Ages* (New York: Harper & Row, 1978), p. 84.

38  *Ibid.*, p. 78.

39  *Ibid.*, p. 81. Other nuns of the twelfth century who followed Hildegarde as intellectual mystics and writers were Herrad of Landesberg, Elizabeth of Schönau, Mechtild of Magdeburg, Mechtild of Hackeborn, and Gertrude the Great (*ibid.*, pp. 85–86).

Not all significant writing by women, however, issued from the religious orders. Marguerite Porete (c. 1300) was an important leader in the Beguine movement. The Beguines were pious laywomen who practiced poverty, chastity, and charity but belonged to no monastic order and took no vows. Their independence from church authority sometimes brought them into suspicion of heresy, and this was the fate of Marguerite as well. Nevertheless, her book, *The Mirror of Simple Souls*, enjoyed considerable popularity in France, Italy, and England.[40] Another such woman was Mme. Jeanne Guyon, who—with Fenelon—was a spiritual leader in the Quietist movement in late seventeenth-century France. Her literary production amounted to some forty books, including a multi-volume commentary on the Bible.

In the nineteenth century, hymn writing by women came into its own.[41] Anna Laetitia Barbauld (1743–1825) wrote *Hymns in Prose for Children*, which was popular for many years and was translated into French, Spanish, and Italian. "Praise to God, Immortal Praise" is one of her best-known hymns. Charlotte Elliot (1789–1871) wrote around 150 hymns, including "Just As I Am." Sarah Adams (1805–1848) wrote "Nearer, My God, to Thee." But in addition to her hymns Adams wrote also *Vivia Perpetua*, a dramatic poem about the conflict between paganism and Christianity, and *The Flock at the Fountain*, a catechism and hymnbook for children. Cecil Frances Alexander (1823–1895) wrote around four hundred hymns, mostly for children. Among her most beloved hymns are "There Is a Green Hill Far Away," "Once in Royal David's City," and "Jesus Calls Us O'er the Tumult." Frances R. Havergal (1836–1879), well trained in the classics and mistress of several foreign languages, composed over fifty hymns. These include "Take My Life and Let It Be," "I Am Trusting You, Lord Jesus," and "Now the Light Has Gone Away." From the twentieth century we may mention Dorothy F. Gurney (1858–1932), who wrote "O Perfect Love," and Julia C. Cory (1882–1963), who wrote "We Praise You, O God." And it is hard to imagine how anyone can top Fanny J. Crosby (1820–1915), author of over three thousand hymns, including the well-known "Pass Me Not, O Gentle Savior," "Rescue the Perishing," and "Sweet Hour of Prayer."

Two women have been significant as translators of hymns. The foremost translator of German hymnody has been Catherine Winkworth (1829–1878),

---

40  See Robert E. Lerner, *The Heresy of the Free Spirit in the Later Middle Ages* (Berkeley: University of California Press, 1972), pp. 68–78. For a theological description of *The Mirror of Simple Souls*, see Lerner, pp. 200–208.

41  Examples of pre-nineteenth-century female hymn writers are Emilie Juliane (1637–1706), to whom some six hundred hymns are attributed, and Henriette Luise von Hayn (1724–1782), who wrote over four hundred hymns, the most famous of which is perhaps "I Am Jesus' Little Lamb." For this topic, cf. Tucker and Liefield, *Daughters*, pp. 256–257.

whose renderings are the most widely used of any from the German language. Her translations are contained chiefly in her *Lyra Germanica: Hymns for the Sundays and Chief Festivals of the Church Year* and *Christian Singers of Germany*. Winkworth was sympathetic with any practical efforts for the benefit of women, and from that interest wrote the *Life of Pastor Fliedner*, about the chief architect of the German deaconess movement. Second only to Winkworth as a translator of German hymns is Jane Borthwick (1813–1897). Her *Hymns from the Land of Luther* contains "Be Still, My Soul" (itself composed by a woman, Catharina von Schlegel, b. 1697).

The literary contribution of women to the faith and life of the church has continued into our own century. Of great influence was Evelyn Underhill (1875–1941). Born into an agnostic home, she converted to Roman Catholicism through a religious experience that led her to investigate spiritual experience. Underhill became an internationally recognized authority in mystical theology, and her book *Mysticism* (1911) became a standard text in that discipline. In *Worship* (1936), Underhill studied the nature and forms of Christian worship. Eventually Underhill was led into the Anglican communion by Baron Friedrich von Hegel, with whom she shared a long and fruitful spiritual relationship. Underhill herself served as a spiritual director for many, and she conducted many retreats in spirituality. Underhill's distinction is indicated by the fact that she was the first woman invited to give a series of theological lectures at Oxford University (1921). She became a Fellow of King's College, Cambridge, and received a Doctor of Divinity degree from Aberdeen.

Dorothy L. Sayers (1893–1957) is another example of an influential woman thinker and writer. The daughter of an Anglican minister, Sayers studied medieval literature at Oxford. While her initial success was as a writer of detective novels, her renown comes from her work as an expositor of orthodox Christian faith through translations, plays, and books. Her play *The Man Born to Be King* (written for BBC) was a dignified presentation of the life of Christ. Her background in medieval literature bore fruit in her translation of Dante's *Divine Comedy*, which is perhaps the most-used English translation of that classic. Sayers was a lay theologian of some merit. Her treatment of God and the creative process, *The Mind of the Maker* (1942), argues that the creative process is analogous to the government of the world by the Trinity wherein both the sovereignty of God and the freedom of man are preserved. Sayers was a prolific writer, whose works, both popular and scholarly, require their own book to catalogue.[42]

---

42  See Colleen B. Gilbert, *A Bibliography of the Works of Dorothy L. Sayers* (Hamden, CN: Archon Books, 1978).

Women also have written popular and devotional literature. As a representative of this writing we mention Corrie ten Boom, whose popular books— *The Hiding Place*, *Tramp for the Lord*, *In My Father's House*—detail her courageous love to Jew and Christian during and after World War II.

## C. SERVICE OF SPIRITUAL POWER AND ADMINISTRATION

Christian women have exercised spiritual power in many ways. The early church praised the steadfastness of its female martyrs and saw in them examples of Christ's victory over Satan and death. Some of these female martyrs were clearly instrumental in eliciting faithfulness also from others. Blandina (d. 177 A.D.), apparently a slave girl, was hung on a post and seemed to hang in the form of a cross. Her earnest prayer "aroused great desire in those who were suffering," for with their eyes they saw in the person of Blandina "Him who was crucified for them" (Eusebius, *Hist. eccl.* 5.1.41). Similarly, Potamiaena (d.c. 210 A.D.), a pupil of Origen in Alexandria, is said to have influenced the soldier who led her to her death to become a Christian martyr himself, and "it is related that many others of those at Alexandria came over all at once to the word of Christ . . . because Potamiaena appeared to them in dreams and invited them" (Eusebius, *Hist. eccl.* 6.5.7). Writing around a century later, Eusebius says that Potamiaena "is to this day still loudly sung by her fellow-countrymen" (*Hist. eccl.* 6.5.1).[43]

Female prophetic figures have on occasion exercised considerable spiritual direction and influence in the church. In the second century there were a number of female prophetesses in the churches of Asia Minor. We hear of the daughters of Philip the evangelist, who were active at Hierapolis (Eusebius, *Hist. eccl.* 3.31.4; cf. Acts 21:8ff.), and of a certain Ammia who prophesied at Philadelphia (*Hist. eccl.* 5.17.2–5). *The Acts of Paul* mention Theonoe, a prophetess at Corinth.

Yet, it is especially in the Middle Ages that one finds powerful, prophetic women. We have already mentioned Hildegarde of Bingen, who wrote her visions down and whose advice and counsel were sought by popes and princes

---

43 The story of Potamiaena is told also in Palladius, *Lausiac History* 3. Other female martyrs may be briefly mentioned: along with Blandina were martyred her mistress and a certain Biblis (Eusebius, *Hist. eccl.* 5.1.18, 25f); along with Potamiaena were martyred her mother, Marcella, and a certain Herais (Eusebius, *Hist. eccl.* 6.5.1). We have already mentioned Perpetua, who wrote of her visions. A certain Felicitas was martyred with her. Eusebius quotes a letter of Bishop Dionysius of Alexandria to Bishop Fabian of Antioch in which five women, martyred under Decius (c. 250 A.D.) are mentioned by name: Quinta, Appollonia, Mecuria, Dionysia, Ammonarion (*Hist. eccl.* 6.41). Finally, we mention Agape, Irene, and Chione, who were martyrs under Diocletian in Thessalonica (304 A.D.). The *Martyrdom* of these three women mentions another four women who were arrested but not killed (Agatha, Cassia, Philippa, Eutychia). The deaths of Agape, Irene, and Chione were adapted by the tenth-century nun, Hroswitha of Gandersheim, in her Latin play, *Dulcitius*.

so that her influence was perhaps not excelled in the Middle Ages. Of similar influence was Catherine of Siena (1347–1380) who was instrumental in the return of Pope Gregory XI to Rome from the Papal "Babylonian Captivity" in Avignon. Indeed, Walter Nigg can write that "no man has yet dared to speak to a wearer of the tiara as radically and openly as she spoke to Pope Gregory XI in Avignon."[44] Another prophetess contemporary to Catherine was Bridget of Sweden (1302–1373). Her visions and revelations led her also to work for the reform of ecclesiastical abuse and for the return of the papacy to Rome.[45] Finally, we may mention Caterina Fieschi Adorno, known as Catherine of Genoa (1447–1510). Following an ecstatic conversion, she committed herself to personal austerity and to the care of the poor and diseased at the Genoese hospital. She was also a mystical writer of merit.

Especially in the religious orders the spiritual power of Christian women could be ordered, officially recognized, and institutionalized. Nowhere was this more strikingly the case than with the medieval abbesses, whose powers could approach those of a bishop. The double monasteries in the seventh- and eighth-century Merovingian and Anglo-Saxon kingdoms were normally governed by abbesses. These women were ordinarily from royal or noble lineage, and the monasteries that they administered were extensions of royal power and were means for maintaining the wealth of the family.[46] "They were masterful and formidable ladies and they did not forget that they belonged to a ruling caste."[47] As such, these noble abbesses ruled their monasteries, nuns and monks alike. They were builders of churches and monasteries and demonstrated administrative wisdom.[48] They attended royal councils and ecclesiastical synods. One may mention Abbess Hilda at the Council of Whitby (664 A.D.) and Abbess Aelffled at the Synod of Nidd (706 A.D.).[49]

---

44  Walter Nigg and H. N. Loose, *Katharina von Siena* (Freiberg: Herder, 1980), p. 8.

45  Bridget founded the Bridgettine Sisters (1370), who were dedicated to humility and simplicity. The original monastery in Vadstena, Sweden, established one of the first printing presses in Sweden.

46  See Jane Tibbets Schulenberg in *Women & Power in the Middle Ages*, ed. Mary Erler & Maryanne Kowaleski (Athens, GA, and London, England: The University of Georgia Press, 1988), pp. 105–109. Many of these noble women who exerted power as abbesses achieved sainthood (Schulenberg, pp. 105ff.).

47  R. W. Southern, *Western Society and the Church in the Middle Ages* (Baltimore: Penguin Books, 1970), pp. 309–310.

48  See Gregory of Tours, *History of the Franks* 2.17; Bede, *History of the English Church and People* 4.6, 19; also the discussion of Schulenberg, pp. 110–112.

49  *The Life of St. Wilfrid* 60 calls Aelffled "always the comforter and best counselor of the whole province" and makes clear that Aelffled's speech was the determining factor at Nidd.

Yet, it is doubtful whether one can speak meaningfully of the "egalitarianism of the double monasteries," as do Tucker and Liefeld.[50] Although nuns and monks shared common functions in the scriptoria, the schools, and perhaps the divine services, the early double monasteries were, as noted, extensions of a ruling family's power and as such governed by a member of the ruling family, the abbess, who "ruled the whole organization in the spirit of one accustomed to command."[51] Moreover, nuns and monks lived separately, and their work was divided, the nuns doing the less strenuous work and the monks the rougher work. Finally, the abbesses had no episcopal power and no power to excommunicate or to administer the sacraments (note the case of the abbess of Quedlinburg, below, p. [186]).

The institution of the double monastery and female monasticism in general declined during the ninth and tenth centuries. However, in the eleventh and twelfth centuries there was a revival of the double monastery, nurtured by the piety of the *vita apostolica* (which emphasized poverty and personal holiness) and utopian enthusiasm. This renewal culminated in the founding of the Premonstratensian Order by Norbert of Xanten and of the Order of Fontevrault by Robert of Arbrissel. In these foundations, nuns lived with monks, with an abbess usually at the head. In the case of Fontevrault, this rule of the abbess may have reflected the view that men should be obedient to women as St. John was to the Virgin Mary.[52] Similar were the Gilbertines founded by Gilbert of Sempringham. The Gilbertines were founded on a millennial vision of the kingdom of God encompassing all, men and women.[53]

Although there were variations, the abbesses of such foundations could have considerable authority. They administered community property, awarded benefices and spiritual offices, held their own chapter meetings, gave the benediction to their own nuns, and received ofttimes an oath of obedience from all those in the community, both men and women. And this power was not only tolerated but defended by the church, even against offending clergy.

---

50  Tucker and Liefeld, *Daughters*, p. 137.

51  Southern, *Western Society*, p. 310.

52  See Jacqueline Smith, "Robert of Arbrissel: Procurator Mulierum," in *Medieval Women*, ed. Derek Baker (Oxford: Basil Blackwell, 1978), p. 180 n. 34. Smith points out that at Fontevrault the building that housed the virgins, widows, and matrons was dedicated to the Virgin Mary, while the men stayed in a building dedicated to St. John. For a general discussion of Prémontré, Fontevrault, and similar foundations for women, see Brenda Bolton, "Mulieres Sanctae," in *Women in Medieval Society*, ed. Susan Mosher Stuard (University Park, PA: University of Pennsylvania Press, 1976), pp. 141–158.

53  See Elkins, *Holy Women*, pp. 130–134. The utopian/millennial vision could go to heretical extremes. The Guglielmites believed that a certain Guglielma of Milan was the incarnation of the Holy Spirit and wished to establish a church with a female pope and female cardinals. Stephen E. Wessley, "The Guglielmites: Salvation Through Women," in *Medieval Women*, ed. Baker, pp. 289–303.

For example, in 1222 Pope Honorius III upheld the authority of the abbess of Quedlinburg, who had suspended from office and benefice a number of canonesses and clergy because of disobedience and certain other offenses. The Pope wrote to the abbot of Michelstein that he was to force the offenders, by ecclesiastical censure if necessary, to obey and defer to proper authority.[54]

However, in these institutions where the equal status of women in the communal life of the monastery was unquestioned and even held high, ultimate spiritual jurisdiction was not accorded to the abbess. Even the Gilbertines had a male master general who was "the judge to whom all controversial or difficult decisions were referred" and who heard "any confessions that the prioresses had reserved for his special attention, especially first confessions and those considered grave."[55] Also, in the case involving Pope Honorius III it is clear that the abbess had no power to excommunicate. It is for that reason that the abbot of Michelstein was called in. He could censure with excommunication.[56] The abbess was not merely the equivalent of the abbot or bishop.

The tradition of spiritual influence by women in religious orders continued after the Reformation. We have mentioned already Teresa of Avila, who gained the support of Pope Paul IV and King Philip II for her reform of the Carmelite Order. Closer to our own time is Elizabeth Bayley Seton (d. 1821). Born into a distinguished colonial, Episcopalian family, Seton early evinced great concern for the sick and poor, earning the name of the Protestant Sister of Charity. When she converted to Roman Catholicism, she went to Baltimore and eventually to Emmitsburg, Maryland, where she founded the American Sisters of Charity. Under her leadership, orphanages were opened in Philadelphia and New York, and in 1818 Seton started the first free parochial school in America. For such schools she trained teachers and prepared textbooks. After her death, the Sisters of Charity opened the first Catholic hospital in the United States (St. Louis, 1828).

In the same tradition was Frances Xavier Cabrini (d. 1917), the first American citizen to be canonized (1946). Born and raised in Italy, she was sent to America to work among the thousands of Italian immigrants. In that work she founded orphanages, schools, and hospitals, not only in the United States but also in South America and Europe.

Nor was it always the activist and organizer who exerted spiritual influence. Not until after her death did Therese of Lisieux (d. 1897) become known through her autobiography. But then her simplicity and humility elicited such

---

54   Ida Raming, *The Exclusion of Women From the Priesthood: Divine Law or Sex Discrimination?* (Metuchen, NJ: The Scarecrow Press, 1976), pp. 73–74.

55   Elkins, *Holy Women*, pp. 135–136.

56   Raming, *Exclusion*, p. 74.

worldwide reaction that Rome hastened the process of canonization. Therese was sainted in 1925.

Within Protestantism too the influence of women of faith has been significant. Wibrandis Rosenblatt (d. 1564) was married successively to three major reformers (John Oecolampadius, Wolfgang Capito, Martin Bucer) and gave gracious, intelligent hospitality to their guests. Calvin was supported by two prominent noblewomen: Marguerite of Navarre (d. 1549), the sister of King Francis I, and Renee of Ferrara (d. 1575). Especially supportive of the Protestant cause in France was Jeanne d'Albret (d. 1572), the daughter of Marguerite and the mother of King Henry IV.[57]

However, given the Reformation emphasis on proclamation, not surprisingly Protestant women too were interested in preaching and outreach. A central figure in the evangelical revival of eighteenth-century England was Selina Hastings, Countess of Huntingdon (d. 1791). Through her status and wealth she was the benefactress of John Wesley, George Whitefield, and other itinerant Methodist preachers. She founded colleges for the training of evangelical, even dissident, preachers and built chapels for them to preach in. Selina was interested in Whitefield's mission to Georgia and organized the sending of preachers to the Indians there. In that she was "a forerunner of those Wesleyan women in the nineteenth century who would find their first public identity in the development of missionary societies and social reform organizations."[58]

Indeed, the influence and participation of women in mission work has been considerable. Tucker and Liefeld document some of the primary figures and contributions in this area.[59] Here we may refer to those numerous women who have supported missions through various mission societies such as the Baptist Missionary Union, the Woman's Foreign Missionary Society of the Methodist Church, and the Lutheran Women's Missionary League.

As individual examples of women in missions we may mention Clara Swain (d. 1910), who was the first female medical missionary to a non-Christian land (India), and Mary Slessor (d. 1915), who served for thirty-eight years as missionary in Calabar (modern Nigeria). There she built churches and schools, preached, taught, and even served as a magistrate on behalf of the government.

---

57 For these women and others who played a role in the Reformation, see Bainton, *Women of the Reformation*. For Reneé of Ferrara, see F. Whitfield Barton, *Calvin and the Duchess* (Louisville, KY: Westminster/John Knox Press, 1989).

58 Martha Tomhave Blauvelt and Rosemary Skinner Keller, "Women and Revivalism: The Puritan and Wesleyan Traditions," in Ruether and Keller, *Women & Religion in America*, vol. 2, p. 325.

59 Tucker and Liefeld, *Daughters*, pp. 291–327.

## II. "It Is Not Given to Women to Teach": The Central Tradition

By selected example we have illustrated the broad and respected contributions that Christian women have made to the church throughout its history. These contributions have been intellectual, diaconal, and evangelical, and have carried with them spiritual power and recognized authority. Many women have achieved sainthood, and some have received titles of highest honor. Within Eastern Orthodoxy a number of women—Mary Magdalene, Thekla, Helena, and Nina, missionary to the Georgians—are regarded as "equal to the apostles," and Catherine of Siena and Teresa of Avila were named "doctors of the church" by Pope Paul VI.

In fact, women have done almost everything men have, and have done it just as well. The significant exception to that generalization is that, until the very recent past, the "office" of teaching and of the sacramental ministry, with the jurisdictional powers this implies, has been reserved for men. Of course, there have been historical anomalies, and there have been sects and peripheral groups that accepted women preachers who may also have offered the eucharist.[60] Yet, in its broad central tradition and practice, the church—East and West and in a multiplicity of cultural and social settings—has consistently maintained that to men alone is it given to be pastors and sacramental ministers.

Tertullian (second century) may be taken as a representative voice of this viewpoint: "It is not permitted to a woman to speak in church. Neither may she teach, baptize, offer, nor claim for herself any function proper to a man, least of all the sacerdotal office" (*On the Veiling of Virgins* 9.1). Photius, ninth-century Patriarch of Constantinople, echoes the same sentiment for Eastern Christendom: "A woman does not become a priestess" (*Nomocanon* 1.37). This general prohibition did not rest on some idea of a natural inferiority of women to men in intellect or spiritual stature. John Chrysostom writes that "in virtue women are often enough the instructors of men; while the latter wander about like jackdaws in dust and smoke, the former soar like eagles into higher spheres" (*Epistle to Ephesians*, Hom. 13.4). Commenting on Priscilla's teaching of Apollos in view of 1 Timothy 2:12, Chrysostom says that "Paul does not exclude a woman's superiority, even when it involves teaching," when

---

60 For the anomalies, see Joan Morris, *The Lady Was a Bishop: The Hidden History of Women with Clerical Ordination and the Jurisdiction of Bishops* (New York: Macmillan, 1973), who vastly overrates the significance of her evidence; for the sects, see Friedrich Weichert, "Der Dienst der Frau ausserhalb der Grosskirche," *Eine Heilige Kirche* 21 (1939): 129–139; Gottfried Koch, *Frauenfrage und Ketzertum im Mittelalter* (Berlin: Akademie-Verlag, 1962).

the man is an unbeliever and in error (*Greet Priscilla and Aquila* 3).[61] We have already noted Christian women whose counsel, advice, and intellectual gifts were valued by men. To those may be added the three "ammas" or "mothers" (Theodora, Sarah, Synkletika) whose sayings are included in the Eastern church's *Geronikon* ("Sayings of the Desert Fathers").[62]

Nor does the evidence suggest that the church's exclusion of women from the preaching and teaching "office" was an unevangelical accommodation to social and cultural pressures. In fact, the social and cultural context of Christianity at times favored the church's admitting women to the teaching "office." In first- and second-century Asia Minor, for example, the social position of women was well developed. There were female physicians, and Ephesus had its female philosophers among the Stoics, Epicureans, and Pythagoreans, who were known to teach, perhaps publicly. Likewise, female leadership and priesthood were well known in the local religious cults (Cybele, Isis, Demeter, Artemis).[63]

The first clear patristic opposition to female teachers and ministers is in reaction to Gnostic groups that often regarded women as the special bearers of revelation.[64] In their denial of the creation, the Gnostics refused to take seriously any fleshly, creaturely differences, so that Tertullian complains that among them no distinctions are made between catechumens and believers, women and men, neophyte and experienced faithful, layman and priest. In his rejection of such Gnostic egalitarianism, Tertullian writes of their women: "how wanton they are! For they are bold enough to teach, to dispute, to enact exorcisms, to undertake cures, it may be even to baptize" (*Prescription Against Heretics* 41.5). It is evident that Tertullian believes the Gnostics are engaging in a practice contrary to the standing practice of the church. Otherwise his point that in creed and practice the Gnostics are contrary to the church would lose all force. It is equally evident that a distinction of functions between man and woman in the church relates in some way to actual distinctions in creation.

---

61   Illustrations of this attitude can easily be multiplied. *The Acts of Peter* (second century) tell of Candida, who taught her pagan husband the gospel and converted him (chapter 1). In Syria, a widow could answer pagan inquirers in refuting polytheism and demonstrating the unity of God (*Didaskalia*, Connolly, 132; *Apostolic Constitutions* 3.5). Widows could not teach about the "mystical points" of Christ's incarnation and passion. For this the unbeliever should be sent to the elders.

62   The monk Isaias (c. 1200 A.D.) compiled a Meterikon ("Sayings of the Mothers") parallel to the *Paterikon* ("Sayings of the Fathers").

63   Manfred Hauke, *Women in the Priesthood? A Systemic Analysis in the Light of the Order of Creation and Redemption* (San Francisco: Ignatius Press, 1988), pp. 401–402.

64   The Simonians had Helen (Irenaeus, *Adv. Haer.* 1.23.2); the Naassenes had Marianne (Hippolytus, *Adv. Haer* 10:5); Mary Magdalene is revealer of secret knowledge in *Pistis Sophia, Gospel of Mary*, and *The Dialogue of the Savior*. In the *Egyptian Gospel*, Salome is vehicle of secret tradition.

Against the Gnostic, to maintain a distinction of male and female function was to confess a creation theology that respected the concrete, fleshly differences between man and woman.[65]

Montanism was also important in early patristic prohibitions of women teaching and baptizing in the church. Montanism was an outburst of Christian apocalypticism that taught that a new outpouring of the prophetic Spirit had begun the last days. With Montanus and two prophetesses, Prisca and Maximilla, as its leaders, Montanism held to a spiritual egalitarianism based on the common outpouring of the end-time, prophetic Spirit. Montanism appears then to have granted women a more extensive participation in the worship services. Yet, even Montanism seems generally to have respected functional distinctions in the church. The general prohibition by Tertullian, "it is not permitted to a woman to speak in Church" (*Veiling of Virgins* 9.1), was written within his Montanist period. The account of a Montanist woman who had visions "amidst the sacred rites of the Lord's day in the church" and who "after the people are dismissed at the conclusion of the sacred services" reports her visions to the church's leaders illustrates how Montanist prophecy and Tertullian's prohibition coexisted (Tertullian, *On the Soul* 9).

The basic question raised by Montanism was whether the church understood itself to be essentially apostolic or essentially prophetic. The apostle, witness to the resurrection and confined to the first generation of the church, represented the finality of the revelation of the Word that happened once in history. The prophet, who rises again and again, does not and cannot represent Christ as final truth. When the prophet asserts his independence and autonomy, the finality of the revelation in Christ is threatened. The prophetic must be subordinated to the apostolic. Not surprisingly, therefore, the Fathers appeal to Pauline (apostolic) statements against women speaking in church as well as to the practice of Christ and the completed canonical histories of the Old and New Testaments.

Commenting on 1 Corinthians 14:34–35, Origen (third century) criticizes the Montanist prophetesses. Apparently the Montanists justified their prophetesses by an appeal to the four prophet daughters of Philip and to Old Testament prophetesses. To this Origen replies: "If the daughters of Philip prophesied, at least they did not speak in the assemblies; for we do not find this fact in the Acts of the Apostles." Deborah, Miriam, and Huldah were prophetesses. Yet, "there is no evidence that Deborah delivered speeches to the people, as did Jeremias and Isaias." Miriam and Huldah also did not speak to the people. Similarly, in the Gospel the prophetess Anna "did not speak

---

65  Tertullian, *Prescription Against the Heretics* 41.1: "I must not omit an account also of the heretics—how frivolous it is, how worldly, how merely human, without authority, without discipline, as suits their *creed*" (italics mine).

publicly." The apostolic statements in 1 Corinthians 14:34 and 1 Timothy 2:12 correspond to the Biblical history.[66]

Epiphanius provides similar argumentation against two fourth-century "feminine" movements. The "Quintillians," an aberrant Montanist group, appealed to Eve, who had eaten of the tree of knowledge, as prototype for a female clergy. Epiphanius explicitly says that they had women bishops and women presbyters and that they justified this on the basis of Galatians 3:28. To counter the appeal to Eve, Epiphanius quotes Genesis 3:16 and 1 Timothy 2:14 ("Adam was not deceived, but Eve was first to be deceived") along with 1 Timothy 2:12 and 1 Corinthians 11:8 (*Against the Heresies* 49.1–3). The Collyridians venerated Mary as a virtual goddess, and women in the group served as priests in offering up a sacrifice of bread rolls in her name. Epiphanius attacks the women's claim to exercise the sacerdotal ministry: "Never from the beginning of the world has a woman served God as priest." In litany fashion Epiphanius runs through the Old and New Testaments pointing out that God's priests were always men but never a woman. Mary herself, the mother of the all-ruling Son of God, was not entrusted to baptize, that being given to John (*Against the Heresies* 78–79). Similar appeals to the Biblical history and to the example of Christ are made by the *Didaskalia* (Connolly, 133, 142), the *Apostolic Constitutions* (3.6, 9), and the *Apostolic Church Order* (24–28).

Fourth-century Latin opposition to women teaching in the church was probably occasioned by a Montanist-like revival named "Priscillianism." The sect was popular with women, and to give them an official function it seems to have imported from the East the title of "deaconess," which until then was not known in the West. In their commentaries on Paul, "Ambrosiaster" and Pelagius both express the view that it is contrary to the order of nature and against apostolic injunction for women to speak in an assembly of men. Ambrosiaster is especially harsh in his attitude.[67] In view of Priscillianism church councils also condemned the public teaching by women and reiterated the apostolic prohibition against women speaking in the church. The Council of Saragossa (380 A.D.) warned Catholic women not to attend Priscillian meetings where women might give readings and teach. The Council of Nimes (396 A.D.), reacting to reports that certain ones were admitting women to the "Levitical ministry," rejects such a practice as an innovation "contrary to apostolic discipline" and not permitted by the ecclesiastical rule.[68]

---

66  *Fragments on I Corinthians* 74. For the full Origen quotation, see Gryson, *Ministry of Women*, pp. 28–29.

67  See especially Ambrosiaster, *Comm. on I Corinthians*, 14:34–35, and Pelagius, *Comm. on I Corinthians*, 14:34–35. For Ambrosiaster and Pelagius, see Gryson, *Ministry of Women*, pp. 92–99; Martimort, *Deaconesses*, pp. 191–192; Hauke, *Women*, pp. 421–423.

68  For the Councils of Saragossa and Nimes, see Gryson, *Ministry of Women*, pp. 100–102.

There were occasional instances into the early Middle Ages when women did serve at the altar. Invariably this practice received stiff ecclesiastical censure. To bishops in southern Italy and Sicily, Pope Gelasius I "with vexation" speaks of reports of women who "serve at holy altars": "everything that is entrusted exclusively to the service of men is performed by the sex that has no right to do so" (*Letter* 11.26). In the early sixth century, two priests in Brittany allowed women to assist them in the celebration and distribution of the Lord's Supper. This elicited a letter from three Gallic bishops. The distribution of the blood of Christ to the people by women was "a novelty, and unheard-of superstition."[69] In the early ninth century, several bishops wrote to Louis the Pious that "contrary to divine law and canonical directive, women enter the sanctuary, handle the consecrated vessels without fear, pass clerical vestments to the priests, and . . . distribute the Body and Blood of the Lord to the people." They had tried to take measures to prevent such liberties. "It is most astonishing that this practice, which is forbidden in the Christian religion, could have crept in from somewhere; . . . undoubtedly it took hold through the carelessness and negligence of some bishops."[70] While the details of what was prohibited and allowed to women might vary, "there was complete constancy regarding the bans on ministering and especially . . . on 'female ministers of Communion.' "[71]

It is perhaps necessary to mention the fifth- and sixth-century Gallic councils, for they have been cited recently as proof that there was a gradual suppression of ordained female ministry in the early Middle Ages. The Council of Orange (441 A.D.) ruled: "Deaconesses are absolutely not to be ordained; and if there are still any of them, let them bow their head under the benediction which is given to the congregation." The subsequent councils of Epaon (517 A.D.) and Orleans (533 A.D.) finally prohibited the consecration of women to the diaconate. Suzanne Wemple claims these councils were "a battle against female ministers." Of the Council of Orange she writes: "We do know that, by 441, the Gallican church had ordained deaconesses who regarded themselves as equals to the male clergy. . . . The bishops assembled at Orange were apparently determined to abolish the feminine diaconate, to humiliate the women who had already been ordained, and to assert the exclusivity of male authority in the church."[72] Tucker and Liefeld give a similar judgment. Quoting the "commonly used" ordination prayer for the deaconess in the *Apostolic Constitutions* (8.20), they comment: "By the sixth century, such

---

69   See Gryson, *Ministry of Women*, p. 106; Martimort, *Deaconesses*, p. 195.

70   For the text, see Hauke, *Women*, pp. 423–424.

71   Hauke, *Women*, p. 424.

72   Suzanne Fonay Wemple, *Women in Frankish Society: Marriage and Cloister 500–900* (Philadelphia: University of Pennsylvania Press, 1981), pp. 138–140.

consecrations were becoming less and less common in the Western church. . . . church councils during the sixth century gradually lowered the status of these women until the position of deaconess was virtually nonexistent."[73]

The fact is that "such consecrations" were never common, indeed never existed in the West. Also, to my knowledge the "commonly used" prayer of the *Apostolic Constitutions* was used nowhere else than in the provenance of the *Constitutions* themselves, that is, in eastern Syria. The mixing of eastern and western evidence by Tucker and Liefeld produces quite a false historical reconstruction. Detailed study of the deaconess has amply shown that there is no evidence that such deaconesses like those in the *Apostolic Constitutions* with social and limited liturgical duties ever existed in the West.[74] Ambrosiaster and Pelagius reveal no knowledge of deaconesses in the West. The language of the councils itself indicates that the practices they opposed were unfamiliar and uncommon. The Council of Nimes acts on a report and does not even know the location where the abuse is taking place ("one knows not where"). The Council of Orange wonders "if there are still any" of the ordained deaconesses. They also speak of innovation and novelty. The claim of Wemple that between 395 and 441 the ordination of deaconesses had become "common practice in the churches of Gaul" is wholly overdone.[75] The title *deaconess* appears to have been an import from the East. The reality behind the title in the West was the widow who wished to be consecrated to the ascetic life.[76]

In sum, there never was recognized ordained female ministry in the West (or East) that involved teaching in the assembly and ministering at the altar.

The canonical regulations that govern church life and circumscribe what is permissible are consistent throughout the Middle Ages in prohibiting women from teaching in the assembly and performing priestly and episcopal functions. The *Statuta Ecclesiae antiqua* of Gennadius of Marseilles (c. 480 A.D.), which adapts eastern practice for western life, allows the nuns and widows to teach women who are to be baptized ("to teach clearly and with exactitude unlearned women from the country"), but it also repeats the general prohibitions: "a woman, however learned and holy, may not presume to teach men in the assembly" (*in conventu*); and, "a woman may not presume to baptize." Again and again this text is cited in bans on teaching. Likewise, the ban of Pope Innocent III (thirteenth century) on the preaching and hearing of confession by powerful abbesses is a commonplace in canon law: "No matter whether the most blessed Virgin Mary stands higher, and is also more illustrious, than all the apostles together, it was still not to her, but to them, that

---

73   Tucker and Liefeld, *Daughters*, pp. 132–133.

74   Gryson, *Ministry of Women*, p. 102.

75   Wemple, *Women in Frankish Society*, p. 138.

76   Gryson, *Ministry of Women*, pp. 102–108; Martimort, *Deaconesses*, pp. 193–200.

the Lord entrusted the keys to the Kingdom of heaven."[77] The *Corpus Iuris Canonici*, the present-day book of canon law in the Roman Catholic Church, is the final recipient of the long tradition that has its origin in Paul: "Only a baptized man validly receives sacred ordination" (canon 1024).

Sometimes it is asserted that the canonical prohibitions were motivated by misogyny and false evaluations of women's intellectual and moral capacities. Misogynous remarks and opinions of inferiority do exist. Yet, Manfred Hauke correctly notes that the language of Gennadius' *Statuta*—"however learned and holy"—and of Innocent III—whether Mary "stands higher than all the apostles"—indicates that ultimately and officially considerations of intellect and sanctity were not determinative. Determinative were the Biblical history, the example of Jesus, and the apostolic injunctions.[78]

Within Protestantism, the major Reformation and post-Reformation leaders assumed without question the practice of reserving the office of pastor and sacramental minister to men. Their strong "Scripture alone" principle led them, however, to rely almost exclusively on actual apostolic prohibition. Appeal to the Biblical history and to the example of Jesus is correspondingly less frequent.

Against Rome's use of 1 Corinthians 14:34 to argue the existence of a special priesthood not common to all Christians, Martin Luther (d. 1546) consistently maintained a priesthood of all believers (especially on the basis of 1 Peter 2:9). This common priesthood possesses the right and power to exercise all "priestly offices" (teach, preach, baptize, administer the Eucharist, bind and loose sin, pray for others, sacrifice, judge doctrine and spirits).[79] Yet, Luther habitually combines 1 Corinthians 14:34 with Genesis 3:16 to assert that women are excluded from the public exercise of the common priesthood. In view of the "ordinance and creation of God" that women are subject to their husbands, Paul forbade women to preach in the congregation where men are present who are skilled in speaking, so that respect and discipline may be maintained.[80] However, if no man is present to preach, then "it would be necessary for the women to preach."[81] For Luther, the apostolic prohibition of 1 Corinthians 14:34 was determinative.

John Calvin (d. 1564) also understood Paul's prohibitions as excluding women from speaking in an "ordinary service or where there is a Church in

---

77  Quoted in Hauke, *Women*, p. 447.

78  Hauke, *Women*, pp. 446–447.

79  *Luther's Works*, American Edition (St. Louis: Concordia Publishing House; Philadelphia: Fortress Press, 1955ff.), 40.21–34; 36.150, 152; 39.234–235.

80  *Luther's Works*, 36.152; 41.154–155; 30.55; 28.276–277.

81  *Luther's Works*, 36.152; 30.55. For discussion of Luther's position, see Wilhelm Brunotte, *Das geistliche Amt bei Luther* (Berlin: Lutherisches Verlagshaus, 1959), pp. 193–199.

a regularly constituted state." The office of teaching is "a superiority in the Church," and therefore it is inconsistent that a woman, who is under subjection, should preside over the entire body.[82] Commenting on 1 Corinthians 14:34, Calvin writes: "It is therefore an argument from things inconsistent—If the woman is under subjection, she is, consequently, prohibited from authority to teach in public."[83] In his commentary on 1 Timothy, Calvin writes similarly: Paul "excludes [women] from the office of teaching, which God has committed to men only."[84] Although Calvin recognizes that some women in the Old Testament were supernaturally called by the Spirit to govern the people, "extraordinary acts done by God do not overturn the ordinary rules of government, by which he intended that we should be bound."[85]

The only significant group that denied the continuing applicability of Paul's prohibitions was the Society of Friends (Quakers). Their strong emphasis on the interiority of the Spirit militated against any distinctions in church life. George Fox (d. 1671), founder of the Quakers, and especially Margaret Fell (d. 1702) argued that the authority of the indwelling Spirit gave women equal right and obligation to speak, even in public assemblies.

John Wesley (d. 1791) repeatedly attempted to distinguish Quaker views and practices from those of Methodism, in which women also at times spoke in public. Wesley's own view was conservative. The ordinary rule of discipline, based on 1 Corinthians 14:34, was that women should be in subjection "to the man whose proper office it is to lead and to instruct the congregation."[86] Nonetheless, Wesley claimed that "an extraordinary impulse of the Spirit" suspends the apostolic regulation and allows a woman to speak in public.[87] Yet, the Methodists are not like the Quakers, who "flatly deny the rule, although it stands clearly in the Bible." The Methodists, however, "allow the rule; only we believe it admits of some exceptions." Indeed, Wesley regarded Methodism itself to be "an extraordinary dispensation" of divine providence, so that he did not wonder "if several things occur therein which do not fall under the ordinary rules of discipline."[88]

---

82  John Calvin, *Commentary on the Epistles of Paul the Apostle to the Corinthians*, trans. John Pringle (Grand Rapids, MI: Eerdmans, 1948), vol. 1, pp. 467–468.

83  Calvin, *Corinthians*, vol. 1, p. 468.

84  Calvin, *Commentary on the Epistles to Timothy, Titus, and Philemon*, trans. William Pringle (Grand Rapids, MI: Eerdmans, 1948), p. 67.

85  Calvin, *Timothy*, p. 67.

86  John Wesley, *Explanatory Notes upon the New Testament* (1754; Naperville, IL: Alec R. Allenson, rpt. 1966), p. 632 (on I Corinthians 14:34).

87  Wesley, *Explanatory Notes*, p. 632.

88  For Wesley's view and practice, see especially Earl Kent Brown, "Women of the Word: Selected Leadership Roles of Women in Mr. Wesley's Methodism," in *Women in New*

Other Reformation and post-Reformation groups largely concurred with the views of Luther, Calvin, and Wesley. The Anabaptists, the Anglicans, the Puritans, and the Separatists all prohibited women from the public ministry of preaching and teaching. While groups that emphasized religious experience and interior calling did allow women to assume (more or less restricted) public preaching, not until the nineteenth century did women begin to make significant strides toward a ready acceptance of any public ministry. It has been only in the last half of the twentieth century that the major Protestant church bodies have begun to accept women as regular preachers and pastors.

## III. CONCLUSION

We have emphasized the practice and argument of the patristic and medieval periods of the church's history. It was during these centuries that patterns of conduct and ecclesial behavior were developed and solidified. The evidence shows that the Pauline statements against women speaking in the church were consistently upheld. Contrary practices were regarded as innovative and opposed to the truth and were, by ecclesiastical discipline and censure, excluded from the church. The practice of the early and medieval church was followed without question by the churches of the Reformation, both Reformed and Lutheran, and by virtually all other communions until the most recent past. Although they are favorable to the full participation of women in all functions of the church, Tucker and Liefeld note that even women who did seek a position of prominence rarely evinced "feminist impulse" but rather were "very hesitant to challenge the 'rightful' leadership of men."[89] That observation as much as anything testifies to the pervasive and universal faithfulness of the church to the Biblical and apostolic word throughout its history. The utter paucity of instances adduced where women were given or took the function of public preaching and teaching confirms it.

---

*Worlds*, ed. Hilah F. Thomas and Rosemary Skinner Keller (Nashville: Abingdon, 1981), pp. 69–81. For the above, pp. 74–76.

89  Tucker and Liefeld, *Daughters*, p. 16.

# The Use of Tractate 26 to Promote the Ordination of Women

## John W. Kleinig

1. In par 26 of the Treatise on the Power and Primacy of the Pope Melanchthon says:

   'Besides, the ministry of the New Testament is not bound to places and persons, as the Levitical priesthood is, but is spread abroad through the whole world and exists wherever God gives his gifts; apostles, prophets, pastors, teachers. Nor is this ministry valid because of any individual's authority but because of the word given by Christ'.

2. This passage has been misused by those who advocate the ordination of women to the public ministry of the gospel.

   a. They assume that, when Melanchthon speaks about 'the word given by Christ', he refers to the gospel which is preached by the minister. The validity of the ministry is therefore held to depend on the proclamation of the gospel rather than the person who proclaims the gospel. The authority of the person is derived from that proclamation.

   b. They back up this functional interpretation of these words by the German addition to par 26:

      'The person adds nothing to this Word and office [*Amt*] commanded by Christ. No matter who it is who preaches and teaches (the Word), if there are hearts that hear and adhere to it, something will happen to them according [*sic*] as they hear and believe because Christ commanded such preaching and demanded that his promises be believed'.

197

c. Since it does not matter who the person is that preaches, as long as the word is preached and received in faith, they conclude that a person of either sex can be a minister of the gospel. What's more, those who exclude women from the ministry err in basing the authority and power of the ministry on the sexual nature and masculine qualities of the pastor as a male person.

3. This interpretation cannot be sustained for two reasons.

a. It misunderstands what is meant by 'the word given in Christ', in par 26. There Melanchthon argues that Christ instituted the office of the ministry. Neither the person nor the pope through the bishops in fellowship with him create this office and give it its authority. The authority of the ministry rests on 'the word of Christ' (par 10). Its mandate is from Christ (par 31). Hence when Christ promised to Peter that he would build his church 'on this rock' in Matthew 16:18, he did not refer to Peter as a private person, nor to his personal confession of faith, but to Peter as 'a public person' (Latin *persona communis*) who represented all the apostles (par 23, 24), and as a 'minister' whose 'ministry' it was to preach, teach and confess that Jesus was the Christ, the Son of God (par 25). This passage does not then distinguish between the person of the pastor and the ministerial function performed by that pastor, but distinguishes between the divinely instituted office of the ministry and those who occupy that office and perform its tasks. No human person, whether he be an apostle or the pope, gives that office its authority and power. The office lends its authority to the person in it. Thus, when the German text maintains that it does not matter 'who preaches and teaches', it does not open the office of the ministry to all comers. It does not promote a purely functional understanding of the ministry which could be performed by anybody, but rather champions the authority of divinely instituted office of the ministry which Christ has instituted and empowered for the proclamation of the gospel and for the creation of faith in its hearers. The validity of the office does not depend on the minister nor on the ministry done by that person, but on Christ's institution (which has traditionally been taken to include 1 Cor 14:34–37) and the faithfulness of the church to his mandate.

b. The use of Tr 26 to argue for the ordination of women from a functional understanding of the public ministry ignores the context and purpose of this passage. It is part of a larger argument against the power of the pope. It not only attacks the pretensions of the papacy but also defends the right of the evangelical churches to ordain pastors without episcopal and papal involvement. The purpose of the treatise is to argue that, whereas the office of the papacy had not been instituted by Christ, the ministry of the gospel had been instituted as an office by Christ. He had conferred this office equally on all the twelve apostles and confers it equally on all pastors through the church. Neither the church nor the apostles nor Peter as the first pope created this office. Nor did they determine its function. Rather 'the office of the ministry derives from the common call of the apostles' (par 10, German). Unlike the ministry of the gospel, the papacy had no divine mandate, for the words of Christ to Peter in Matthew 16:18, 19 and John 21:17 apply to the public ministry of the word which is given to all the apostles and to all properly called and ordained pastors. If Melanchthon were truly arguing for the functional view of the ministry ascribed to him by some advocates for the ordination of women, he could easily have jettisoned these arguments about the nature and purpose of the divinely instituted office. Instead, he could have argued that the authority of the evangelical pastors did not rest on their office and its institution by Christ but on their zeal in preaching the gospel and their faithfulness in administering the sacraments.

4. *The Treatise on the Power and Primacy of the Pope* cannot therefore legitimately be used to promote the ordination of women. In fact, if its line of argument is correct, it could even be used to maintain that, like the papacy, the ordination of women has no mandate from Christ but is based on dubious theological inferences from passages in the Scriptures which have little or nothing to do with it. Like the papacy, it is not valid because it rests on human authority rather than on divine commission.

John W. Kleinig
Luther Seminary
15 October 1997

# Liberation Theology in the Leading Ladies of Feminist Theology

## Roland Ziegler

## Introduction

### Definition of Terms:
### Liberation Theology, Feminist Theology

Feminist liberation theology—this is a rather unusual combination of words. More often, only feminist theology or liberation theology is used. The title suggests that feminist theology is a subcategory of liberation theology— which is an accurate description of the relationship of the two. Liberation theology is a child of the 1960s.[1] The civil rights movement and the resurgence of Marxism have influenced theology deeply. The question was asked of the relevance (or irrelevance) of theology and Christianity in the struggle for the liberation of the oppressed and marginalized in society. The tradition of Christianity to sanction the societal status quo, and thereby be part of the oppressive system rather than supportive of the poor, was questioned in the light of early Christian tradition and the experience of those struggling for freedom and justice. Soon, different strands of liberation theology emerged, reflecting different groups of people seeking freedom from repression. A black liberation theology came into existence in the United States.[2] The struggle in Latin America was reflected by the Theology of Liberation, probably the

---

1    Cf. Stanley J. Grenz; Roger E. Olson, *20th-Century Theology: God and the World in a Transitional Age* (Downers Grove, IL: InterVarsity Press, 1992), 200–224.

2    E. g., James H. Cone, *Liberation: A Black Theology of Liberation* (Philadelphia & New York: J. B. Lippincott Company, 1970).

most influential and productive group.[3] In South Korea, Minjung theology reflected the struggle for democratic and economic rights. The common features of different forms of liberation theology can be summarized as follows.[4] First, it is *contextual*, i.e., it stresses the importance of the context of the theologian for doing theology and rejects the idea of an eternal, non-contextual method of theology. The Gospel addresses people in their concrete situation. The situation of the oppressed is at least the necessary hermeneutical key to understand the Gospel; sometimes it is source and norm for doing theology. Second, it is *practical*. Theology aims at the action, at a change of the situation of the oppressed. Third, it sees God as the *liberator* and the Gospel as the message of *liberation* from all forms of oppression and alienation. Finally, sin and salvation are seen communally, not in an individualistic way. "Sin to us is eminently a political, a social term."[5] That means that salvation is not primarily in an afterlife, but the creation of a new just society, the reign of *shalom* on earth.

Feminist theology is theology done in the context of women's experience today. It is part of liberation theology because women are an oppressed group in society and church. As liberation theology fights a denigrating and exploitative capitalist and hierarchical system, so feminist theology fights patriarchy, the system of male intellectual, religious, and social domination over women to restore true personhood to women—and men. As in Marxist analysis of society, which holds that not only the proletarian but also the bourgeois are alienated from true humanity, so also feminist theology teaches that patriarchy deforms women *and* men. Feminist theology is practiced mostly by women, but this is not necessarily so. Men who join the effort to combat patriarchy can do feminist theology as well.

## HISTORY OF FEMINIST THEOLOGY, MAIN PROPONENTS, AND MAIN BRANCHES (LIBERAL, RADICAL, EVANGELICAL)

Feminist theology as a form of liberation theology became visible in the 1970s. There are precursors of such an approach to theology in representatives of the women's rights movement in the nineteenth century, when the equality of women also in church was asserted. This involved a critique of the Christian tradition, including Holy Scripture, as we can see, e.g., in the project of the Women's Bible.[6] Nevertheless, as a widespread movement,

---

3   Gustavo Guitiérrez, *A Theology of Liberation*, first published in 1971.

4   Cf. Letty M. Russell, *Human Liberation in a Feminist Perspective: A Theology* (Philadelphia: Westminster Press, 1974), 50–71.

5   Dorothee Sölle, "The Gospel and Liberation," *Commonweal* (Dec. 22, 1972): 273.

6   Elizabeth Stanton Cady, *The Woman's Bible* (New York, Arno Press, 1972 [original c. 1895–98]).

feminist theology is relatively new. Feminist theology is a movement that transcends denominational borders, for there are women struggling for equal rights in all churches. As a movement, it has certain common features, but also a great variation in statements concerning dogmatic *loci* (topics). After all, it is *not* something like a creedal church. Statements like "feminist theology asserts . . ." therefore have to be made and received cautiously.

If one tries to categorize feminist theology, one may distinguish using the terms mainstream, radical, and evangelical.[7] *Mainstream feminist theology* is feminist theology in a liberal Christian setting. By "liberal Christian" I mean a concept of theology that on the one hand appreciates and wants to continue the Christian tradition, while on the other hand sees contemporary religious consciousness as a critical norm for Christian tradition, maybe even as a source of new tradition. Major representatives of this expression of feminist theology in the United States are Rosemary Radford Ruether, Letty M. Russell, and Elisabeth Schüssler-Fiorenza.

*Radical feminist theology* is a post-Christian theology. Christianity is rejected as an inherently patriarchal, misogynist tradition. A new religion emerges from the experience of the divine in women today. Often a connection with pre-Christian religions is sought, as for example in the revival of Wicca as a religion that supposedly predates patriarchy and Christianity, or in the revival of shamanistic practices. A prominent representative here is Mary Daly, a former Roman Catholic theologian.[8]

*Evangelical feminist theology* is feminist theology done in the context of modern Evangelicalism. It shares the basic points of Evangelicalism,[9] e.g., a high view of Scripture and the centrality of redemption through Christ, while with feminism it shares a concern for the equal rights of women in society and church. It sees patriarchalism as not inherent in Scripture but rather as a later addition to Christianity, and tries to show that Scripture has an egalitarian view of the sexes. Representatives of this strand include Letha Scanzoni and Nancy Hardesty, Catherine Clark Kroeger, and Gretchen Gaebelein Hull.[10]

---

7  David L. Smith, *A Handbook of Contemporary Theology* (Grand Rapids: Baker Books, 1998), 248.

8  Cp. also Daphne Hampson, *Theology and Feminism* (Oxford, UK and Cambridge, MA: Basil Blackwell, 1990).

9  Evangelicals have been described as "Protestant Christians who stress belief in personal conversion and salvation by faith in the atoning death of Christ, and in the Bible as the sole authority in matters of faith: stress is also laid on evangelism." *Oxford Dictionary of World Religions*, ed. John Bowker (Oxford and New York: Oxford University Press, 1997), 326.

10 Cp. a critique of evangelical feminist theology, *Recovering Biblical Manhood and Womanhood: A Response to Evangelical Feminism*, ed. John Piper and Wayne Grudem (Wheaton, IL.: Crossway Books, 1990).

In this paper I will concentrate on mainstream feminist theology. I will first deal with the method of feminist theology, then show its implications in several central points of the Christian faith: Scripture, God, Christ, and redemption.

## THE METHOD OF FEMINIST THEOLOGY

Methodology seems to be a dry subject, if you think of methods as techniques that have no inner connection to the subject matter to which they are applied. At least in theology, there is no such thing as a neutral method. Methods are part of the content, or, to say it differently, the way you approach theology says a lot about the content of your theology, or even shapes the content of your theology. If you ask certain kinds of questions, you get certain kinds of answers.

Feminist theology wants to ask *new* questions from the perspectives of women doing theology. Rosemary Radford Ruether distinguishes three stages of the development of feminist theology: "The first moment of feminist theology is the critique of the masculine bias of theology."[11] Traditional theology was done and is done by men in a patriarchal society. It is shaped by specific male traits, and the perspective of women is excluded. Women do not talk in this theology; they are talked about. The male is taken as the normative human subject, and females are subordinate and auxiliary. Everything in theology, every single concept, starting from God and ending with the view of the final things (eschatology), is shaped—or one should rather say, *misshaped*—by males. The first step is to realize this bias and to evaluate everything in Christian tradition (and that includes Holy Scripture) with this suspicion: a domineering male has formed this in his image, which is not simple "human being." By doing this, women free themselves from the intellectual and spiritual domination of men over them. They are rejecting the male power to define who God is, who they are, what Christianity is. The first step, therefore, is to denounce androcentrism (male-centeredness) and misogyny in Christian tradition.

"The second moment in feminist theology is one which seeks alternative traditions which support the autonomous personhood of women."[12] Although the Christian tradition as we have it today is shaped by men, nevertheless it is not purely a patriarchal culture. Women and their view were present, even when their accounts and deeds were later distorted or completely suppressed, and there are traditions in Christianity that have the power to help women in their struggle for liberation today. This second moment in feminist theology

---

11  Rosemary Radford Ruether, "The Future of Feminist Theology in the Academy," *Journal of the American Academy of Religion* 53 (1985): 706.

12  Ibid., 707.

therefore looks in Scripture for non-patriarchal, non-androcentric traditions. It unearths the contribution of women in church history, their fight against patriarchy, and it cherishes small groups in which countercultural Christianity was lived in an egalitarian way.

"The third moment of feminist theology then takes the form of tentative efforts to restate the norms and methods of theology itself in the light of this critique and alternative tradition."[13] After distortions have been eliminated— the ground is so to say *cleared*—and stones have been retrieved, it is now time to build a new building. After all, theology is not simply an academic discipline. Feminist theology shares with liberation theology the emphasis on theology as praxis, as changing things. Feminist theology therefore tries to serve the building of a community of faith "which seeks to live its faith as repentance of sexism, exodus from patriarchy, and entrance into a new humanity."[14]

As a summary, one might say that feminist theology criticizes an androcentric, oppressive patriarchal Christian tradition. It seeks the suppressed voice of women in it, in order to build a non-sexist (i.e. non-discriminatory and egalitarian) liberated community. Everything that follows is simply an application of these steps to dogmatic topics.

## EXPERIENCE AND TRADITION: THE BASIS OF FEMINIST THEOLOGY

### THE CHARACTER OF HOLY SCRIPTURE: COLLECTION OF EXPERIENCES—THE NATURE OF SCRIPTURE—A NEO-LIBERAL CONCEPT, EXPRESSION OF RELIGIOUS CONSCIOUSNESS

Foundational for any Christian theology is Holy Scripture, simply because it is the oldest and most influential document in Christianity. The question is whether it is the only foundation. Against a Protestant *sola scriptura* stands the Roman Catholic view of tradition as supplementary foundation (a widening of the basis) and a neo-Protestant approach to Scripture that distinguishes in the Bible normative from non-normative parts.

Feminist theology can neither accept Scripture plus tradition nor Scripture alone, because Scripture and tradition are products of men, with all the implications that this fact has. Scripture is not seen as God's Word; rather, it is the written account of encounters with the divine. Feminist theology can talk of revelation. But revelation is not in any way propositional. It is not a god speaking to man. It is, rather, the appearance of meaning in life: "By *revelatory* we mean breakthrough experiences beyond ordinary fragmented

---

13 Ibid., 709.
14 Ibid., 709–10.

consciousness that provide interpretive symbols illuminating the means of the *whole* of life."[15]

This encounter with ultimate reality is essentially non-verbal, so that any account of it in words implies the reflection of the authors on this encounter. An author is always limited in his accounts by his cultural and personal frame. Up till now feminist theology is essentially following the classical liberal concept of Scripture that sees Holy Writ as an expression of the religious consciousness of the authors. It is also not foreign to liberal theology to assert that the authors were limited in their outlook. This gives the present generation, which no longer shares these limitations, the right to ignore the cultural accidentals, and go to the center—the experience—and rephrase in words and concepts of today's culture. Feminist theology goes a step further by stating that one of these cultural limitations was patriarchy. It is therefore the task of feminist theology to find authentic experiences of the divine in Scripture and reject patriarchal distortions. Feminist theologians approach Holy Scripture with a hermeneutic of suspicion: androcentric and misogynist traditions have to be identified and eliminated. Any statement that does not comply with the critical principle of feminist theology—"the promotion of the full humanity of women"[16]—has to be rejected as non-redemptive, not divine. Any talk about subordination of women—like that of Paul does in Ephesians 5 (cf. 1 Pt 3:1), statements that exclude women from full participation in offices in the church (1 Cor 14:34; 1 Tm 2:12), notions that see women as the "weaker sex" (1 Pt 3:7), or women as secondary (1 Cor 11:9)—must be excised as patriarchal. Feminist theology thus establishes a "new canon."[17] Also the sole use of male metaphors for God has to be rejected as caused by the fact that men wrote the biblical books.

The second step is the rediscovery of women-friendly traditions in the Bible, e.g., the egalitarian and non-sexist attitude of Jesus and the first Christian communities, before they conformed to the hierarchical setting of surrounding society. Or the important role women played in the early Christian church: Mary Magdalene as the first apostle. Also, traditions in

---

15   Rosemary Radford Ruether, *Sexism and God-Talk* (Boston: Beacon, 1983), 13.

16   Ibid., 18.

17   Elisabeth Schüssler-Fiorenza, "Toward a Feminist Biblical Hermeneutics: Biblical Interpretation and Liberation Theology," in *The Challenge of Liberation Theology*, ed. Brian Mahan and L. Dale Richesin (Maryknoll, NY: Orbis Books, 1981), 108: "A feminist theological interpretation of the Bible that has as its canon the liberation of women from oppressive sexist structures, institutions, and internalized values, must, therefore, maintain, that only the nonsexist and non-androcentric traditions of the Bible and the nonoppressive traditions of biblical interpretation have the theological authority of revelation if the Bible is not to continue as a tool for the oppression of women. The 'advocacy stance' demands that oppressive and destructive biblical traditions cannot be accorded any truth and authority claim today."

Scripture that use female imagery for God have to be emphasized, so that the image of God as an old *man* is corrected.

The third step goes beyond Scripture as a source and norm for theology. It includes the present experience of women as basis and source of theology.[18] A new beginning has to be made, a third covenant.[19] In Ruether's words: "This means that feminist theology cannot just rely on exegesis of past tradition, however ingeniously redefined to appear inclusive. It is engaged in a primal re-encounter with divine reality and, in this re-encounter, new stories will grow and be told as new foundations of our identity."[20] Ruether gives an example for that: "One woman in the class [on violence against women] recounted her experience of being raped in a woods. During the rape she became convinced that she would be killed and resigned herself to her impending death. When the rapist finally fled and she found herself still alive, she experienced a vision of Christ as a crucified woman. This vision filled her with relief and healing, because she knew, that 'I would not have to explain to a male God that I had been raped. God knew what it was like to be a woman who had been raped.' "[21] Feminist theology goes beyond Scripture, because the liberated women will "generate new stories, new primal data of religious experience which will become the symbols of a new tradition. This may not [!] be experienced as total discontinuity with the past . . ."

## THE DOCTRINE OF GOD IN FEMINIST THEOLOGY

The traditional doctrine of God has to be critiqued insofar as it is oppressive to women and must be reconstructed in a non-sexist way, including thereby the experience of women.

### WHO IS GOD?

When talking about God, other terms are used and sometimes preferred. Not only "Goddess" or "God/ess" but also terms like "the divine," "the ground of being," "the matrix." God is here not a person, but rather beyond personality—though in a different way than C. S. Lewis used this term to explain the Trinity. The personhood of God is seen as a way of human beings perceiving God rather than as He is. Ruether, though she uses "God/ess," still prefers to use the term "matrix" for the reality of the divine. The divine is not

---

18  Letty Russell, "Authority and the Challenge of Feminist Interpretation," in *Feminist Interpretation of the Bible*, ed. Letty M. Russell (Philadelphia: Westminster Press, 1986), 146: "The shift in interpretive framework means that we no longer need to divide feminist experience and biblical witness."

19  Ruether, "Future of Feminist Theology," 711.

20  Ibid., 710.

21  Ibid., 710–711.

transcendent in the traditional sense; rather it is the foundation of everything, and everything by existing participates in the divine. Some statements strongly suggest an almost pantheistic identification of world and God: "The God/ess who is the foundation (at one and the same time) of our being and our new being embraces both the roots of the material substratum of our existence (matter) and also the endlessly new creative potential (spirit)."[22] God as male is emphatically rejected, and this concept of God is seen as a root of the secondary status of women in patriarchal society. But a view of God as male *and* female, as androgynous, is not viewed as the solution of a sexist idea of God, since it presupposes that there are essentially male and female characteristics. Feminist theologians who reject this anthropology in favor of a view that sees male and female as essentially the same (claiming that anything beyond the purely biologically is generated by society) reject an androgynous view of God as a continuation of gender stereotypes on a metaphysical level. Therefore also the terminology of "Goddess" is not universally approved, because it may lead to a reversed sexism. Ruether tries to solve the dilemma by introducing the term "God/ess," which cannot be pronounced, as a code for the non-sexist God. Phyllis Trible tries to keep up the distinction between *God* as a being in himself (itself/herself) and the images we have of him, reversing Gn 1:27. We have to use images of male and female, but God is the transcendent creator who is neither male nor female nor a combination of both.[23] Sally McFague wants to overcome a patriarchal view of God by favoring the terms God as *Mother, Lover,* and *Friend*.[24]

## THE NATURE OF BIBLICAL LANGUAGE ABOUT GOD: METAPHORICAL

The way God is described in Scripture is not a self-revelation of God, and therefore we have human efforts to describe God that must not be taken literally. All names of God say something about God, but are inadequate to describe God. "Classical Christian theology teaches that all names for God are analogies. The tradition of negative or *apophatic* theology emphasizes the unlikeness between God and human words for God." "God is both male and female and neither male nor female. One needs in inclusive language for God that draws on the images and experiences of both genders."[25]

---

22  Ruether, *Sexism and God-Talk*, 70–71.

23  Phyllis Trible, *God and the Rhetoric of Sexuality* (Philadelphia: Fortress Press, 1978), 200–201.

24  Sally McFague, *Models of God: Theology for an Ecological, Nuclear Age* (Philadelphia: Fortress Press, 1987), 91–180.

25  Ruether, *Sexism and God-Talk*, 67.

## GOD IS BIBLICALLY DEPICTED
## IN MALE AND FEMALE METAPHORS[26]

Although God is referenced in Holy Scripture overwhelmingly in male terms, there are also female terms for God. God is described like a mother (Is 49:14–15) or a woman in travail (Is 42:14). The word for God's mercy is *rechem*, "womb"; God's presence is seen in His wisdom (*Hokmah*); God's spirit is *ruach*, a feminine word. God is compared to a women seeking the lost coin (Luke 15). The rather infrequent findings reflect, of course, the patriarchal redaction of Holy Scripture, but are sufficient to claim that female references are part of the Christian tradition and not simply an innovation. This strain of female imagery for God is then continued in marginal groups in the history of Christianity: Gnostics, Montanists, certain mystics, the Shakers. We can see here also the rejection of the traditional distinction between "orthodox" and "heretical." Feminist theology freely draws on sources outside mainstream Christianity to recover women's experience.

Ruether has another, more indirect, approach. She traces the history of the image of the God who is not the guarantor of the status quo—like the patriarchal gods of surrounding peoples—but rather on the side of the oppressed, of those who oppose hierarchy—the image of the God who liberates. Even naming God Father can be liberating, since this does not serve the sacralization of the authority of the fathers on earth, but rather serves to free human beings from the authority of earthly fathers.[27] This in itself is non-patriarchal speech about God, even if the oppression of women is not specifically mentioned in the Old Testament. Christ's use of "Abba" for God inaugurates a new non-hierarchical relationship.

### A NEW LITURGICAL LANGUAGE

The consequence of this view of God leads to a reconstruction also of liturgical language. Since an exclusively male language for God is idolatrous and leads to the sacralization of men and denigration of women, female imagery has to be incorporated also into liturgical language about God. It starts with avoiding male pronouns when referring to God (repeating instead "God") and titles like "Lord" that can be misunderstood in a patriarchal way. But the recovery of forgotten biblical tradition and inclusion of women's experience leads to a new language, finally bringing wholeness to our image of God. A prayer for the second Sunday of Easter:

> Heartbeat of this Earth, / in the ebb and flow / of your steadfast love / You bring us into being / and make us one flesh with You. / Throb within the

---

26  Cp. Trible, *God and the Rhetoric of Sexuality*.

27  Ruether, *Sexism and God-Talk*, 65.

breasts of all believers: that your church become the pulse / of your body
the universe, and share in the process / of the redemption of all creation;
Lover, beloved and Love itself. Amen.[28]

# CHRIST

## REJECTION OF TRADITIONAL CHRISTOLOGY

"Traditional Christology" is the Christology formulated in the dogmatic
struggles of the early church and confessionally stated especially in the Nicene
and Athanasian creeds. It confesses that Christ is true man and God, being of
one substance of the Father, consubstantial with the Father according to His
divinity and consubstantial to human beings according to His humanity. This
is rejected by feminist theology. The development that led to Chalcedon is
not in harmony with the witness of the New Testament but "represents a
rejection of key elements of Jewish messianic hope and their replacement by
ideas that Judaism continues to reject as idolatrous."[29] Instead of accepting a
"mythology" of the divine Logos or the Messiah, Christology rather has to
start with the historical Jesus.[30]

## THE IMPORTANCE OF CHRIST: EXAMPLE OF NEW RELATIONSHIPS, RENEWER OF PROPHETIC TRADITION

If Christ's importance is not that He is God in the flesh, why is He important? And can He, as a male, be of ultimate importance for women? He can,
but only if His maleness is accidental to His continuing function.[31] The term
"function" indicates a concept of Christ where He is primarily an example
that encourages and serves as a model. Any traditional concept of Jesus as
Savior, as the one who atones for us, appeases God's wrath, or overcomes for
us the power of sin and death, has no place in feminist theology. Feminist
theology has a different concept of sin and redemption, which makes traditional soteriology unnecessary. Also, the entire concept of our relationship of
God as an ethical relationship in which we failed, that is, that we are guilty
and in need of forgiveness, is virtually non-existent. Judgment Day is just a

---

28  Mary Kathleen Speegle Schmitt, *Seasons of the Feminine Divine: Christian Feminist
    Prayers for the Liturgical Cycle* (New York: Crossroad, 1993), 88–89.

29  Ruether, *Sexism and God-Talk*, 116.

30  Ibid., 135.

31  Patricia Wilson-Kastner, *Faith, Feminism & the Christ* (Philadelphia: Fortress Press,
    1983), 115: "No one can deny that Jesus the Christ was a male person, but the sig-
    nificance of the incarnation has to do with his humanity, not his maleness." Also see
    Russell, *Human Liberation*, 138–39: "To think of Christ first in terms of his male sex or
    his racial origin is to revert again to *biological* determinism, which affirms that the most
    important thing about a person is her or his sex or color."

mythological figure. So, if we do not need Christ to save us from damnation and to bring us into eternal life (which also are mythological concepts), why then do we need Him? Again, He is an example. He can be the paradigm of true humanity, living in harmony with the divine, free from all patriarchal distortions, as Letty Russell sees Him.[32] In Ruether's view, Jesus is important as the prophet of the coming kingdom of God. Jesus expects the reign of God as the vindication of the poor and the oppressed. This coming reign is not other-worldly; it happens here on earth. So Jesus gives us a vision of a society that is egalitarian and non-exploitive.[33]

In turning against the authorities of His time, Jesus "frees religious experience from the fossilization of the past traditions,"[34] thereby setting an example for the ongoing possibility of new religious experience and the rejection of one normative pattern.

## CHRIST AND WOMEN

Christ is not the first feminist: that would be an anachronistic view.[35] But Christ in His critique of religious and social hierarchy is compatible and parallel to feminist criticism. In His preaching He renews the view of God that we find in the prophetic protest in the Old Testament, where God is not seen as the one who guarantees the existing society of lords and servants. Jesus revises the language for God in using the name *Abba*, thereby correcting a patriarchal understanding. In the new community of disciples around Jesus, women play an important role and the difference between male and female does not structure this new society. "Male" and "female" are not in any way categories of the Gospel; therefore, no metaphysics of the sexes has any foundation in the gospels. Jesus knows only human beings.

## CHRIST AS SPIRIT: TRANSCENDING MALENESS, HIS MALENESS IS THEOLOGICALLY INSIGNIFICANT (REJECTION OF ARGUMENTATION FROM CHRIST'S MALENESS TO FORBIDDING WOMEN'S ORDINATION)

All this relates to Jesus as an historical person. The next step is the question of Jesus as the Christ or, to put it differently, Christ not as a past person but as present reality. Ruether sees as a viable paradigm a Spirit-Christology. In the time of the New Testament a Christology emerged which saw Christ living on in the prophetic Spirit which the early church experienced in its

---

32  Russell, *Human Liberation*, 139.

33  Ruether, *Sexism and God-Talk*, 120.

34  Ibid., 121.

35  But Russell does call Jesus a "feminist"—though in quotation marks. *Human Liberation*, 138.

midst and which was the source also for the New Testament. This was later suppressed in favor of a church that was ruled by officials (not charismatics) according to the book (the Bible) instead of present experience. Christ today means: living like Jesus, continuing in the community that comes from Him:

> Christ, as redemptive person and Word of God, is not to be encapsulated "once-for-all" in the historical Jesus. The Christian community contin- ues Christ's identity. As vine and branches Christic personhood continues in our sisters and brothers. In the language of early Christian prophe- tism, we can encounter Christ *in the form of our sister*. Christ, the liberated humanity, is not confined to a static perfection of one person two thousand years ago. Rather, redemptive humanity goes ahead of us, calling us to yet uncompleted dimensions of human liberation.[36]

## CHRIST—FINAL OR PRELIMINARY?

Jesus is not the final and "once-for-all" revelation of God. To see Him as such would indeed be a repudiation of that for what Christ stood, and those Christians who claim such a position for Christ repeat the error of the Pharisees and scribes.[37] He is a viable and liberating symbol for the divine and the struggle of humans for a society with liberty and justice for all, but in other cultures there can be other symbols. Feminist theology therefore tends to be non-exclusive, or universalistic.

# IMAGES OF SALVATION

I have already touched on the question of salvation in discussing Christology. Feminist theology differs from traditional theology also in these concepts.

## RE-DEFINITION OF SIN FOLLOWING LIBERATION THEOLOGY

Sin is not a transgression of a divine rule of God. It is the distortion of the self-other relationship through the superior-inferior dualism. Sin therefore is first and foremost an inter-human category. This distortion of the relation between human beings leads to alienation between humans, alienation from oneself, and alienation from nature and God. Sin then is so to say objecti- fied by structures in society that enforce and reproduce this superior-inferior dualism. But evil is something human beings created, something which in turn, in the shape of these structures, forms human beings. But there is no super-human evil that is out of the reach of mankind.

---

36  Ruether, *Sexism and God-Talk*, 138.

37  Ibid., 122.

## RE-DEFINITION OF SALVATION: SHALOM, THE NEW SOCIETY

Salvation is thus the restoration of relationships between persons from a hierarchical to an egalitarian society, from a mindset that does not think in relational terms to a mindset that recognizes and honors the interdependence of all things. This renewal of relationship has to start on an individual level, but also includes the fight against the systemtic evil that rules society at large. The concept of the reign of God gives hope and a certain utopia in this struggle.

## INNER-WORLDLY SALVATION AND ESCHATOLOGY, REJECTION OF PERSONAL IMMORTALITY

Redemption happens in this world in the building of new relations, in the building of a new society. Feminist theologians do not regard the question of immortality as central or even important to the Christian faith. As Ruether put it: agnosticism is the appropriate attitude.

## CONCLUSION: CONFESSIONAL LUTHERANISM AND FEMINIST THEOLOGY[38]

Feminist theology is by now firmly a part of mainstream theology. It is academically established, and since it has the backing of a general social trend—the emancipation of women and a rather egalitarian concept of the relationship of women and men—it will not go away early. A legitimate question might be to ask if feminist theology is in itself stable, or whether it is not itself so fraught with tensions that it will eventually develop into an openly post-Christian spirituality.

In my estimation, mainstream feminist theology is, viewed from its basic approaches, old-fashioned liberalism turned feminist.[39] Basically liberal is the

---

38  For a critique of feminist theology see Susanne Heine, *Matriarch, Goddesses, and Images of God: A Critique of a Feminist Theology* (Minneapolis: Augsburg, 1989) (moderate mainstream Protestantism, useful to evaluate post-Christian feminists); also Donald G. Bloesch, *The Battle for the Trinity: The Debate over Inclusive God-Language* (Ann Arbor: Servant Publications, 1985) (conservative Evangelical); William Oddie, *What Will Happen to God? Feminism and the Reconstruction of Christian Belief* (San Francisco: Ignatius Press, 1988) (Anglican); Vern S. Poythress and Wayne Grudem, *The Gender-Neutral Bible Controversy: Muting the Masculinity of God's Words* (Nashville: Broadman and Holman, 2000) (Reformed). See also two papers written by pastors of the LCMS, available at www.scholia.net: Michael L. McCoy, "Male and Female He Created Them: An Exegetical Paper in Response to a Book Entitled Different Voices/Shared Visions" and Tim Pauls, "Feminism and the Church. A Seminar for Youth, Parents, and Anyone Else Who's Interested."

39  Dorothee Sölle, *Gott denken. Einführung in die Theologie* (Stuttgart: Kreuz Verlag, 1990), 17–34, distinguishes three paradigms of doing theology: orthodox, liberal, radical. She distinguishes radical from liberal theology in terms of the former's rejection of the

view that Holy Scripture is a residue of religious experiences—that whatever is authoritative in it is not the text itself but some layer behind the words, some basic premises which have to be excavated. In that process, modern consciousness of what is right and acceptable cannot be ignored but is (more or less) normative.[40] Liberal theology was always open to religious experiences outside of Christianity, although there were often viewed as "inferior."

Feminist theology shares the liberal view of Holy Scripture. Its distinct feature is the feminist critique of Christian tradition. With the Social Gospel, another offspring of theological liberalism, it shares the concern for the social existence of human beings. As a movement in a pluralistic society that has given up belief in the superiority of Western civilization, it will not rate other religious experiences but rather regards their truth as an open question, with a strong tendency to accept them as different forms of encounter.

Confessional Lutheranism therefore has to reject the basic premises of feminist theology. Holy Scripture is God's Word to man, God is speaking not in a metaphorical way—He actually communicates through human language to mankind, making propositional assertions. The statements of Holy Scripture are accurate statements by and about God. Even though they are given in the language and culture of a certain time, this context in no way distorts them. That includes also all charges of patriarchalism. If there is patriarchalism in Holy Scripture, then this is in no way accidental, but is part of God's revelation. That includes also the language about God. God revealing His name is not solely the *I am who I am* of Ex 3:14, for the names of God in Holy Scripture are not projections and metaphors given by men but are part of God's self-revelation. Therefore, the unique and dominant position of "Father" cannot be given up or developed into a language which includes feminine images in order to express also the experiences of women.[41]

---

liberal separation of church and state and the resulting privatization of religion, as well as the rejection of the individualistic understanding of religion in favor of a communal concept of theology (p. 29).

40   Elizabeth A. Johnson rejects an understanding of revelation as "rational, linguistic statements communicated by God without error that give information about divine mystery and dealing with the world." Instead she favors an understanding that reinterprets these texts. "The context for reinterpretation is a common life in faith, with the communities that produced the texts and the communities reading them today living in response to the covenanting God. In this perspective, when the interpreting community today is women themselves, or women and men together in the struggle for emancipation from sexism, then what ensues is interpretation guided by a liberating impulse." Idem, *She Who Is. The Mystery of God in Feminist Theological Discourse* (New York: Crossroads, 1995), 77. The same understanding of revelation is voiced in Schüssler-Fiorenza, "Toward a Feminist Biblical Hermeneutics," 96–97.

41   To this question compare *Speaking the Christian God. The Holy Trinity and the Challenge of Feminism*, ed. Alvin F. Kimel, Jr. (Grand Rapids, MI: William B. Eerdmans Publishing Company and Leominster, UK: Gracewing, 1992).

"Father" is not arbitrary metaphor but is an integral part of God's revelation. The concept that scriptural language about God is strictly metaphorical truly means that human beings are creating God in their own image. On the contrary, "Father" is first and foremost the name of God due to the inner-trinitarian relationship between Father and Son, and definitely not a projection of human experiences on God.[42]

Regarding the inclusion of human experience as a source and norm of theology, nothing better can be said than Luther's statements in the Smalcald Articles:

> In these matters, which concern the external, spoken Word, we must hold firmly to the conviction that God gives no one his spirit or grace except through or with the external Word which comes before. Thus we shall be protected from the enthusiasts—that is, from the spiritualists who boast that they possess the Spirit without and before the Word and who therefore judge, interpret, and twist the Scriptures or spoken Word according to their pleasure. . . . Accordingly, we should and must constantly maintain that God will not deal with us except through his external Word and sacrament. Whatever is attributed to the Spirit apart from such Word and sacrament is of the devil.[43]

Feminism as a philosophy has to be rejected by Christianity, and feminist theology is another form of apostasy in Christianity, leading us to the worship of another god. A post-Christian theologian, Daphne Hampson, has recognized this fact: "It is conservative Christians who, together with more radical feminists, perceive that feminism represents not just one crisis among many. For the feminist challenge strikes at the heart of Christianity."[44]

Feminism points to many instances where Christianity derogates women. This accusation has to be taken seriously. Here, as in other respects, the history of Christianity is far from spotless and Christians have not lived up to the message of the New Testament. To accept this critique means also a renewed study of the witness of Holy Scripture and its teaching of the relation of women and men. Such a study cannot aim at a reconciliation of the present emancipatory mindset and the Bible. It has to be open to accept the fact that Holy Writ is far from egalitarian, without being simply patriarchal. Man and woman are not interchangeable, and they are ordered to each other in a certain relationship, without making women in any way inferior or less human than men. This will also be a challenge to men, if they are willing to fulfill their God-given role. It will be a challenge to an economic system that

---

42   Patrick Henry Reardon, "Father, Glorify Thy Name," *Pro Ecclesia* VII/No. 2 (1998): 138–51.

43   SA III.viii.3, 10. Tappert, 312–13.

44   Hampson, *Theology and Feminism*, 1.

basically views men and women as interchangeable resources for the labor market and has a tendency to ignore the fact that families, not isolated men and women, are the basic units of society.

Feminist theology in the form presented here might be seen as an extreme view, being of not much relevance to the conservative milieu of the Missouri Synod. And certainly there are safeguards against its inroads into the LCMS in its high view of the Scripture and the knowledge of Christian doctrine that enables people to sense the alien spirit in feminism. Nevertheless, it would be negligence to underestimate the overall pressure of a feminist mindset that permeates the air we breathe. Views of the Bible as patriarchal and therefore in that respect no longer authoritative are common beyond the circles of Ruether and Schüssler-Fiorenza.[45] Therefore also the topic *Feminism and the Church* will not go away, as long as our culture remains the way it is now. The debate on women's ordination, for example, will become more heated in the future. An awareness and critique of theological trends in the religious scene, and a renewed study of the language about God and of the relation of man and women in the light of Holy Scripture, is the best contribution we can make so that the LCMS will not, like so many other churches, succumb to the spirit of this age.

---

45  Cp. the collection of essays by Marie Meyer et al., *Different Voices/Shared Visions: Male and Female in the Trinitarian Community* (Delhi, NY: ALPB Books, 1992), advocating a feminist viewpoint in the LCMS and the network for the introduction of women's ordination in the LCMS, www.voicesvision.org, situated not far from here in Oak Park. Its mission statement says: "We work to bring about a theologically correct understanding, by both clergy and laity, of the value of the ministry of women, one that affirms women in all roles in the church and in the world, and we seek to support all women in the work and ministry of their choosing. We are committed to, and actively seek, a change in the present understanding of the role of women in the ministries of the Lutheran Church—Missouri Synod, that no longer will a woman be restricted by her gender in serving the Body of Christ in any role to which the Lord has called her."

# Forty Years of Female Pastors in Scandinavia

## Fredrik Sidenvall

When I focus this paper on the experiences in Sweden it is not an expression of old imperial Swedish ambitions of domination of Scandinavia. Rather, it is partly an expression of my limited knowledge of the history of female pastors in the Lutheran churches of Denmark, Norway, and Finland, and also an expression of the common insight that the battle over the question of ministry has nowhere been more difficult or had a deeper impact on the church than in the Church of Sweden. Surely many sincere Christians could accuse a congress with a theme such as this to be out of touch with time. Should we not, after terrifying experiences of violent evil in the world, try to focus on the essentials, on those tenets that could unite and strengthen Christendom? My answer to such a remark would be that the theological motivation and the political introduction of female pastors has proved this issue to be a secret weapon of a spiritual terrorism that has devastated the life of our church. Mark ye well, I do not call the female pastors spiritual terrorists—many of them work faithfully and honestly to build up the church. But the theological way of thinking that has motivated the order to ordain women and—I must tell you—some of the theology that tried to stop this order has, unconsciously, prepared the way for the worst of all monsters: the *monstrum incertitudinis*, the leading terrorist in the field of the Spirit, which attacks the assurance of souls.

In *De captivitate Babylonica ecclesiae* Luther defends the church against a reductionistic way of reading St. Paul. Here the issue is what could be called a periphery matter, the question of the chalice offered to laymen. A papist theologian had said that what St. Paul writes in 1 Cor 11:25–26 is only valid for that current parish and time. Luther writes:

> If the church universal receives, reads and follows this epistle as written for itself in all other respects, why should it not do the same with this portion also? If we admit that any epistle, or any part of any epistle of Paul, does

not apply to the church universal, then the whole authority of Paul falls to the ground. Then the Corinthians will say that what he teaches about faith in the Epistle of Romans does not apply to them. What greater blasphemy and madness can be imagined than this? God forbid that there should be one jot or tittle in all of Paul which the whole church universal is not bound to follow and keep![1]

The arguments of Luther have proved themselves to be true. After more than forty years with female pastors and fifty years with the theology that motivates this order, it is impossible to proclaim any truth based on Scripture in our church. The liberals try to maintain trust in a psychological way, based on promises they do not believe are true. They try to give people ethical guidelines from commandments they do not believe are divine or eternal. Having abandoned the formal principle, the Bible alone, the leaders of our church in the course of time abandoned the material principle, faith alone. The aim of this paper is to try to help you protect yourselves against this form of spiritual terrorism that our church has suffered from for such a long time. It will try to do so by pointing out the complexity in the discussion that led to the decision to ordain women into the office of the ministry, the effects of this decision, and mistakes made by the opposition to this decision.

On Palm Sunday 1960 the first three female pastors were ordained in the Cathedral of Uppsala by Archbishop G. Hultgren. This historical fact raises some questions. Why did this happen? Why did it not happen earlier? What impact has the ongoing ordination of women had on the life and doctrine of our church? How did the opposition react? Finally, what are their hopes for the future?

## WHY DID THE ORDINATION OF WOMEN NOT TAKE PLACE EARLIER?

Already in 1923 there was a motion in the Parliament proposing that women should have the right to hold positions as pastors in the Church of Sweden. The background was, among other things, that in 1918 women were granted the right to vote in common elections. Sweden had also elected its first social-ist government. The Minister of Ecclesial Matters, Arthur Engberg, had already in 1912, at the congress of the Social Democratic Party, gathered a majority for a proposal to change the program of the Party so it would not demand a separation of state and church. This should not be done until the Church of Sweden was so changed from the inside that there would be no space for any black frocks, and the Church of Sweden would teach only a

---

1   Timothy F. Lull, ed., *Martin Luther's Basic Theological Writings* (Minneapolis: Fortress Press, 1989), 281.

common religious atheism. The Church of Sweden was not only attacked by radical political groups but also from various free church revivalist groups that questioned the biblical basis for the church as institution, her sacraments, and her ministry. Liberal theology dominated the universities.

Among the bishops there were still some who stood in the tradition of Lutheran orthodoxy. The status of the ministry in society was low at this time. In defense of the church and her practice of baptizing children, orthodox and liberal theologians formed an alliance against biblicistic critics. They argued that an evangelical church is not bound to a special church order revealed in the New Testament. Christ is not the giver of a new law. The liberals did not believe in the authority of the Scriptures at all and the orthodox of course had confessional arguments based on the Scripture as whole.

After decades of decay a new movement started within the Church of Sweden. In Swedish its name became "ungkyrkorörelsen," the neo-church movement. In the same atmosphere that gathered cadres of young people in communist or fascist groups in Europe, this movement gathered thousands of youth and students. Under slogans such as "church of our fathers in the land of Swedes, dearest among churches on earth," they filled old, tired pastors with new hope. There came a new, fearless spirit among the faithful people of the church. This movement, which in a romantic way celebrated the histori-cal and national heritage of the church, had a charismatic leader in Nathan Söderblom, later archbishop. He was in many senses liberal in doctrine but catholic in ecclesiology. This was the answer to the challenge from free-church groups and also to political attempts to control the Church of Sweden.

This movement later on went in two directions. One searched deeper for the content of the church and became a confessional and liturgical movement of great blessing to the Church of Sweden. Bo Giertz became the personal icon of this direction. The other direction was so focused on the unity of the destiny of the church and people that in the end it became a tragic captive of political groups that strived to assimilate the church with the culture. In the late 1920s and early 1930s, a new school of exegesis was formed at the University of Uppsala under the leadership of the Norwegian professor Anton Fridrichsen. In a radical reaction against liberal theology, the exegetes of this school tried to rediscover the message of the NT as it was intended from the beginning. Instead of answering the free-church critics only with confes-sional arguments, they could prove that the idea of the church, the ministry instituted by Christ Himself, and the sacraments are all essential parts of the NT message.

This exegetical program, together with an eagerness to enrich the sacra-mental and liturgical life of the church as well as confessional reflection, made the two decades from around 1938 until 1958 very fruitful and rich years for the church. In the 1920s very few wanted to accept vocations to holy ministry, but by the end of the 1930s it was hard to get a position as pastor. So the status of pastors had increased while the religious motivation of ministry was strengthened, as was the whole inner life of the church.

This of course made it more interesting for those working for the equality of women to renew the efforts to open the ministry of the church to women. When there came a new initiative in the 1964 Parliament to investigate the matter of the ordination of women, the government appointed an exegete[2] who, though far from having any position in the faculties, had the qualifications to produce the answers the politicians wanted. In 1950 this disentanglement was published. Here the way of thinking that will be crucial in the following debate in the Church of Sweden is first manifested. Dr. Sjöberg writes,

> As fundamental questions have been raised against the admittance of women to the ministry in the debate during later years, this is connected to a pronounced tendency to stress more strongly the normative significance of the Bible for the church. . . . If you presuppose that the church is bounded to the Bible in such a way that every biblical statement—or at least every saying in the NT—binds the church in duty, then the question is solved by the direct prohibitions in 1 Cor 14 and 1 Tim 2. Such a mere mechanical authority is not, however, in accordance with the Evangelical-Lutheran view on Scripture. . . . Obviously one here works with a theory of an infallibility of the Apostle, when he speaks in his ministry, strikingly similar to the Roman-Catholic doctrine on the infallibility of the Pope, when he speaks *ex cathedra*.[3]

In response, all the leading exegetes in Sweden published in 1951 an official declaration. Professors A. Fridrichsen and H. Odeberg, together with assisting professors B. Reicke and H. Riesenfeld, declared "that the introduction of so called female pastors in the church would be incompatible with the views of the New Testament and would mean a desertion from the faithfulness to the Holy Scripture. Both Jesus' choice of apostles and Paul's words about the position of the women in the congregation are fundamental and independent of circumstances and views of the period."[4] The scholarly authority of these exegetes, and the years of experience of what "blessings" this way of ransacking the Scriptures have had for the church, made the resistance in the Church of Sweden very strong. This is the historical answer to the question put above.

---

2   Teol.dr. Erik Sjöberg. See Dag Sandahl, *Kyrklig splittring* (Stockholm: Verbum, 1993), 16.

3   Ibid., 16; *Statens offentliga utredningar* [The Official Disentanglements of the State] (Stockholm: Riksdagens förlag, 1950), 48.

4   *Svensk Kyrkotidning* (1951): 678 (my translation); Sandahl, *Kyrklig splittring*, 18.

The essential answer is of course the power of the Word and Spirit of God and the royal government of Christ.

## Why Were Female Pastors Introduced after All, Forty Years Ago?

The political pressure on the church was massive. A church meeting, the General Synod of the Church of Sweden, was convened in 1957. A majority of bishops, pastors, and laymen refused the proposition to allow women to become pastors. This showed the great influence of the renewal movement. The General Synod was not usually convened more often than every sixth year. But after this defeat for the secular powers, the government convened a new General Synod already the following year, in 1958. When the lay representatives were elected the chief whips from the political parties were very busy. But even so, had it not been for the bishops and pastors, the proposal would have been rejected. Now the votes were 69 for and 29 against. When the result was announced the Bishop of Lund, world-famous theologian Anders Nygren, rose from his bench and uttered prophetic words:

> As the decision that now has been made not only resolves the limited question of female pastors but also, according to my conviction, includes that our church switch to the track that points towards gnosticism and enthusiasts (svärmares), that until now has been alien for her, . . . I have to convey my deepest regrets concerning the decision that has been made and announce my reservation.[5]

In a national church such as the Church of Sweden, which at the time had almost 100% of the population as members and had a democratic structure, it is not at all surprising that the ideals of the times have a deep impact on the church. What could be more applicable for churches with a different structure would be to study how those who had taken an oath at their ordination to keep the confession according to the Book of Concord fought for this new order, that is, how they argued. Already in the arguments of E. Sjöberg (quoted above) there were some hints of the line of reasoning. Sjöberg and other exegetes, such as Krister Stendahl (who recently took part in a controversial ordination of a bishop in the ELCA), could really accept the exegetical conclusions of those scholars who had signed the declaration mentioned above. But for them the authority of the Bible was limited. They raised the questions of hermeneutics and confessional principles. In many ways, theological thinking among us has been dominated by the trauma from the *fin de siecle* when the Church of Sweden lost its hegemony over the soul of Sweden and was questioned by Baptists and others coming back from the USA with

---

5    Dag Sandahl, *Kyrkomötesprotokoll* 4 (1958): 154.

a new religion. When the exegetes suggested that a question concerning the church order should be resolved by studying the situation of the NT, it was easy to make parallels with the biblicist critics against the ministry, liturgy, and sacraments of the church.

The systematic theologians in Lund, Dr Gustaf Wingren[6] and Bishop Martin Lindström, tried to maintain that they fought for a confessional standpoint against the Uppsala school of exegetical theology, with its "mechanical" understanding of biblical authority. They carefully avoided mentioning and arguing with the professor of Systematic Theology in Uppsala, Hjalmar Lindroth, who really represented a confessional standpoint. What had happened in the theological debate during the 1950s was a polarization in the theology of ministry. The disciples of Anton Fridrichsen, Bertil Gärtner[7] and Harald Riesenfeld[8] went further in their quest for motivation for church and ministry. Riesenfeld followed the lines of evolution in the early church and Gärtner argued for the practice of the laying on of hands at ordination and for the significance of apostolic succession. Wingren and other neo-protestant scholars, e.g., Ruben Josefsson and Ragnar Askmark, stressed that the ministry is only functional and is a delegation from the priesthood of all believers. How the ministry is organized in different times and cultures is an adiaphoron. Wingren could write, "The nourishment that Christ has prepared for humanity is now contained within the Scripture. It lies, so to say, in the pot on the table: no waiting at the table in the world can give nutrition to this food but it has nutrition in itself. The whole matter of the ecclesiastical ministry is a question of waiting at the table and not about preparing, cooking, or creating."[9] The position and influence of the exegetes were weakened by these kinds of pseudo-confessional and hermeneutic arguments.[10] But the influence from conservative exegetes and high church theologians was also weakened when they argued not only against the ordination of women but also for apostolic succession and character *indelebilis*.[11]

---

6 Born 1910, Professor of Systematic Theology at the University of Lund 1951–77, died 2001.

7 Born 1923, Professor of New Testament Studies at Princeton Theological Seminary until 1968, in 1970 elected Bishop of Gothenburg and still the leader of the resistance in the Church of Sweden.

8 Born 1913, Professor in NT in Uppsala 1953–79, converted to the Roman Catholic Church.

9 Sandahl, *Kyrklig splittring*, 65.

10 I have myself heard Professor Riesenfeld say, "When I hear the word hermeneutics I cock my revolver." He actually used to be lieutenant colonel in the Swedish army.

11 Sandahl, *Kyrklig splittring*, 70.

How then did a confessional theologian such as Professor Linderoth argue? In a major article,[12] Linderoth gives account for Luther's strong connection between the priesthood of all believers and the ministry of Word and Sacrament, ideas that have been strongly stressed by those arguing for a functional view of ministry. But Linderoth also highlights the other side of Luther's teaching on the ministry, namely his argument against the Enthusiasts. He quotes Luther: "You are not lords [*Herren*] over the incumbents of the ministry and over the ministry of preaching and you have not instituted it, but so has the Son of God alone done."[13] "Yes, I hope you will have so much of Christian reason, that you can grasp that the ministry of the church, the ministry of preaching and the Gospel, does not belong to us or to any human being, yes, not even to an angel, but it belongs to God, our Lord, alone, who with His own blood purchased it and handed it over to us and instituted it to us for eternal blessedness [*Seligkeit*]."[14] Linderoth points out that Luther is in total correspondence with Melanchthon, who, in the Apology to the Augustana writes that the incumbent of the ministry "represents the person of Christ" (*repraesentant Christi personam*) (Ap. VII/VIII.28). And in the same article (§47) Melanchthon writes that the incumbent of the ministry acts on behalf of Christ (*funguntur vice Christi*). Further, Linderoth quotes Luther in *Von der Wiedertaufe an zwei Pfarrherrn* (1528), where he maintains that the ministry Christ has instituted has been inherited from the apostles (*von den Aposteln geerbet*).[15] In the same writing Luther admits without any reservation that we have received from the papacy the right ministry (*recht predig ampt*) as well as all other good Christian things: the right Scripture, the right Baptism, the right Sacrament of the Altar, the right power of the keys, the right catechism with the Our Father, the Ten Commandments, and the articles of the Creed. Here he differs from the Enthusiasts who do not want to admit this. But Luther himself attacks the pope and charges that he has not kept pure all these good Christian things that he had received from the apostles.[16]

In this article Linderoth also deals with the distinction between preaching and the testimonies of the faithful laymen. He attacks the strategy of the neo-Protestants who question the Scripture principle (formal principle) with the principle of faith (material principle). He writes, "Faithfulness towards the Word of God according to the reformers' view of the Bible means to take

---

12  "Kvinnan, Kyrkan och ämbetet—principiella synpunkter" (Woman, Church and Ministry—Fundamental Point of View) in the book *Kvinnan och ämbetet enligt Skriften och bekännelsen* (Woman and Ministry according to the Scriptures and the Confession) (Stockholm: Svenska Kyrkans Diakonistyrelses förlag [SKDB], 1958), 135–82.

13  Enders, ed., *Dr Martin Luthers Briefwechsel* (1914), 15:101.

14  Ibid., 99.

15  WA 26:148.

16  WA 26:147.

seriously already the outer biblical word, yes, the biblical letter." He concludes his article:

> The content of the previous is the following: You can of course be in favor of "female pastors" because of the liberation of women, in regard to the current thinking in society and the development of the culture, of political reasons or because of a pressure at the moment from the state. But from a systematical-theological point of view—and from, in this meaning, a fundamental point of view—it is not possible to bring such an enterprise into accordance with the Evangelical-Lutheran standpoint.[17]

Though at this time still a young man, Tom G. A. Hardt[18] delivered some of the strongest confessional arguments. In the crucial General Synod of 1958 one of the hardest pseudo-confessional arguments that Bo Giertz and others had to deal with was the argument that the order of ministry is an adiaphoron and that the Swedish reformer Laurentius Petri and Mattias Flacius had denied ordination of women only on the basis of human right, not on the basis of any divine commandment.[19] Hardt supplied the leading confessional warrior in the General Synod, the dean of Växjö, G. A. Danell,[20] with arguments from his investigations in the theology of Erasmus Sarcerius.[21] In Sarcerius' writings,[22] Hardt found distinctions between different classes of adiaphora.[23] There are traditions from the apostles that are necessary to keep and among them is "das die weiber unter der gemein sollen still schweigen." About this and other apostolic traditions, Sacerius writes: "Und ist von diesen kein streit zwischen uns Euangelischen und den Papisten. Denn sie billich hoch zu achten / umb jrer einsetzer willen / die da sonderliche unnd höhe werkzeuge des Helligen Geistes gewesen sein."[24] It is also worth noting that confessional theologians such as Hardt avoided the mistake from the Catholics to "liturgize" the issue. For him the prohibition in the Scripture against women preaching was rooted in the order of creation and Fall. It had consequences not only in a liturgical context but also for exercising authority in the Church. Mrs. Karin Hardt (nee Hassler), M.A., B.D., wrote an interesting article in the same book as

---

17  Linderoth, in *Kvinnan och ämbetet* (see n. 12), 168, 182.

18  Born 1934, died 1998; pastor at St. Martin, the only congregation of the Evangelical Lutheran Church of Sweden, founded by himself and a circle of friends who ordained him in 1960. Teol.dr. in Uppsala, Dissertation: "Adorabiblis et venerabilis eucharistia" (1970).

19  Sandahl, *Kyrklig splittring*, 48.

20  1908–90, Toel.dr., eight times elected bishop but never appointed.

21  Erasmus Sarcerius, Gnesio-Lutheran theologian, 1501–59 (see *Theologisch Realencyklopädi* 17:482–86).

22  *Ein Warnung büchlein/ wie man sich für alten Papisten . . . hüten sol Leipzig* (1551).

23  Nya Väktaren 1980, 27–30, 39–43.

24  Hardt, "Adorabilis," 40.

Professor Linderoth. Here she takes her starting point in the order of creation and she does not avoid the delicate question of subordination.[25]

To conclude this review of the arguments preparing the way for the decision, it can truly be said that those who opposed the new order won the discussion but lost the votes. But it is worthwhile to note that the theological arguments often were very subtle, and many conservatives had problems resisting them. The result of the theological debate in the matter of the ordination of women increased the polarization in Swedish theology and ruined the confessional center, so to say, of the Church. Those who with confessional arguments argued in favor of the new order came to follow a line of development towards a total collapse of theology. They separated faith (*fiducia*) from all elements of truth. This is now so obvious when the church deals with issues of homosexuality and other things. Those who argued against the new order on the basis of exegetical results followed a line of development towards ecumenical theology, and deserted the confession in areas other than ministry, for example, by accepting the Joint Declaration on the Doctrine of Justification. The confessional groups in the Church of Sweden lost influence when some formed their own small confessional church bodies and when there were tragic fights in those sometimes rather divisive groups. Today there are around five different confessional church bodies with around 600 members all together (which does not mean that it is wrong).

To be able to gain political influence and fight for survival within the Church of Sweden, Bishop Giertz gathered thousands of pastors and laymen in an umbrella organization called *Kyrklig Samling omkring Bibeln och bekännelsen* (Church Formation around Bible and Confession). After the decision to ordain the first women, seventeen points of advice to the faithful people was published by Kyrklig Samling.[26] Here, those against the new order were advised not to partake in worship led by female pastors, and so on. The seventeen points were understood in the mass media as doctrines. Bo Giertz became for many years the most hated person in Sweden and was under extreme psychological pressure. In Kyrklig Samling, traditional orthodox Lutherans were standing together with high-church and low-church groups. This situation is in many ways fruitful, but it has also created the problem that the question of ordination of women and nowadays the ordination of those who are against this ordination tend to be the only issues that can unite these groups with any assurance. Therefore, other confessional issues rarely have been addressed. The understanding in the Church of Sweden that a confessional pastor means simply one who is against the ordination of women has not been fruitful. With these remarks the next question already has found some answers.

---

25  *Kvinnan och ämbetet*, 206–10.

26  *Svensk Pastoral Tidskrift* 4 (1960): 56–58.

# WHAT IMPACT ON THE CHURCH OF SWEDEN HAS FORTY YEARS WITH FEMALE PASTORS HAD?

Of course it is hard to know what would have happened with the national church in a country where the emancipation of women has gone further than in any other country in the world. Without this new order the political attacks on the Church of Sweden would have continued and the Church's position as a *Volks* church would have been impossible. But the political influence on the Church did continue and increased after the decision of 1958. The Church's adjustment to the culture and the agenda of political correctness was secured by the appointing of handy liberal bishops and the activities of the secular political parties within the Church. But the Church of Sweden has not, as many prophesied, been marginalized in society. Over 80% of the people belong to the Church of Sweden, and 80% of the children born in Sweden are baptized. Most important, 90% are buried in the order of the Church. But Christianity as a religion has more and more lost its position within the Church. This situation also troubles many faithful female pastors. Some of them are openly opposing the liberal leadership of the Church, some have left their offices, some have converted to the Roman Catholic Church. But intentional or not, the female pastors are instruments for weakening the position of ministry in the Church and of the Church's Christian content. In 1960, one high-church pastor[27] prophesied that the ministry was going to become an underpaid woman's job. Nowadays a majority of those who are ordained are women, often in their second career, and there is now a lack of pastors in the Church of Sweden. Ministry in many ways has lost its status. When two women became bishops it happened only after the secular politicians had broken the positions of bishops within the organization of the Church. In the Church of Sweden a senior pastor, the church pastor (*Kyrkoherde*), traditionally has a strong position in his parishes. He can have several assisting pastors and many other employees to supervise. He also has an independent position in relationship to the parish board in pastoral and doctrinal issues. Not infrequently the parish boards boast that they are modern in choosing a woman as senior pastor. But after a while it is easy to see that their aims were only to find someone they could boss around. In the liberal diocese of Stockholm, which has the highest percentage of female pastors, the number of female senior pastors has been decreasing. The experience is that female senior pastors often get into conflicts with assisting female pastors.

With these remarks it is time to go to a more neutral source, namely a dissertation by a female pastor, teol.dr. Ulla Carin Holm, *Hennes verk skall*

---

27 Teol.dr. Alf Corell (1909–2001).

*prisa henne*.[28] Her dissertation deals with personalities and attitudes among female pastors in the Church of Sweden. Holm uses a theory by the social anthropologist Mary Douglas, presented in her book *Natural Symbols*.[29] In the English summary of the dissertation, Holm presents Douglas's theory thus:

> In a social group every individual is controlled in two ways: either through a symbolic system of shared classifications, or through group pressure, namely the feeling that you have no other choice than to follow other peoples' demands. Douglas has named these two dimensions of control GRID and GROUP. . . . Most interesting for my study is a society with strong group and grid—like the traditional villages of Palestine in the days of Jesus, and a society with weak group and grid—like the pygmies and the modern big city. In the first case we find strong classifications (high-low, sin-punishment, man-women), we find elaborated rituals deeply meaningful to the participant, the God symbol is anthropomorphic. In the second case we see no rituals, the religion consists of inner feelings (joy, good will), there are no stronger rules or punishing universe, the god-symbol is intimate and spiritual, not created after the image of Man.[30]

After investigating the profile of different psychological types of female pastors, Holm concludes about female pastors as a group compared with the Church of Sweden as a whole: Their god-symbol is more personal and intimate—less holy and almighty. Women ministers have great difficulty distinguishing between pastor and layman, meaning they are lower in grid. They also have little emphasis on sin-forgiveness. These differences could very well explain the great division in the Church of Sweden on the issues of women ministry. The debate has concentrated on the ministerial office, but rather it is two different symbolic systems trying to accommodate within the same church.[31] That these differences have opened the Church of Sweden for all the feminist theology originating from this continent and from old gnosticism does not have to be further exemplified.

## What Has Happened with the Opposition within the Church of Sweden?

I have already addressed this question in part but there is more to be said. Formally, in the legislation of the Church there are some facts to be mentioned. When the decision was reached in 1958, the government guaranteed

---

28  (Lund, 1982). Holm was born in 1948 and has been senior pastor in Malmoe since 1991.

29  (Hammondsworth, 1973).

30  Holm, *Hennes verk*, 171. The title is from Prv 31:31.

31  Ibid., 176.

the position of the opposition by a clause of conscience. According to this clause, no pastor or bishop should be forced against his conscience to interact with female pastors, and the position held in this issue should not be regarded when considering appointments to offices. But already by 1960 it was clear that the government did not want to appoint any new bishop with the old faith. When Bishop Gärtner was appointed in 1970, he was the third of the elected candidates, and was believed to be the softest. Since then, no one opposing the ordination of women has been appointed though several have been elected bishops. In 1978 the bishop of Stockholm, in a New Year's sermon broadcast on the radio, started a crusade against people of the old faith. In 1982 the law from 1958 was replaced with the common law of equality, which meant that the clause of conscience was dropped. In 1993 there came a decision of demanding acceptance of female pastors from anyone who asked for ordination in the Church of Sweden. In 2000 the Church of Sweden was disestablished from the state. In the new church order from 1999 it was decided that no one can be appointed as senior pastor who does not accept the ordination of women. The order of electing bishops is that the five who receive the most votes in the first election have to be questioned by a special committee. Anyone who does not accept the ordination of women is declared incompetent to take part in the second decisive election.

With this background, it should be clear to anyone that the legal pressure is massive on the third of the male pastors who do not accept ordination of women. The stories from the pastoral institutes of the Church, where the candidates are trained after university, is horrifying: stories of informers and psychological torture. There are sad experiences of highly talented pastors who have been stopped in their career, attacked by bishops, parish boards, and the mass media. There actually is a form of gray martyrdom going on, where people's family life, their economic life, their mental and physical health have suffered badly. But by God's grace, here and there it is still possible to find places where you can serve with loyal people around you.

## What Are Our Hopes for the Future after Forty Years of Female Pastors?

Since the acceptance of the ordination of women has opened the church for almost anything, people in general have been shocked by some events in the Church of Sweden. Some years ago the extremely liberal archbishop of Uppsala permitted a photography show to take place in the cathedral. The theme was *Ecce homo*. In different scenes, Jesus and His disciples were presented as homosexuals. This created a strong reaction in the whole society. The pope reacted by postponing the archbishop's visit to the Vatican. In January the sister of the archbishop, an influential pastor and theologian of liberation at the board of foreign affairs, was blessed with her lesbian partner during a mass in the Cathedral of Uppsala, led by the first female bishop of the Church. This and other events have caused the big middle group of the Church of Sweden to react, and other issues besides the matter of ministry have been receiving attention. This has meant that the opposition, during the past several years, has been listened to with much more respect than earlier.

Alongside the official scene there are other hopeful signs. The confessional influence within the opposition of the Church of Sweden is increasing. For example, during his later years, Tom G. A. Hardt inspired some young pastors and theologians within the Church of Sweden. Among other things, this has contributed to the forming of the North European Luther Academy (NELA), which in its turn has brought confessional theologians in Northern Europe closer together and intensified the contacts with confessional Lutherans in the USA—contacts which are of great importance. There is now a new movement in which faithful churchgoers who always have been so loyal to the structures of the Church of Sweden are now starting to form their own worshipping communities, led by young pastors ordained abroad, in Latvia and Ingria, for example. Plans are now developing to form what we call a Missionary Province in Sweden with its own structure of bishops, pastors, and *koinonias* (worshipping communities). The more the Church loses churchgoers and confessing Christian, the more the unpleasant truth is becoming clear for officials that, among those who still carry the life of our Church, not so few keep to the biblical order. The four bishops that have been appointed the last years have all been more conservative than the dominating bishops. We see many signs of a coming spring. Perhaps there will even come a day when the culture as a whole will find itself in chaos after having experimented with the roles of gender and deconstructing family, and there will be a desperate need for a change. Perhaps then someone will recall those strange people who rejected the ordination of women because of some order of creation and think: perhaps those people may have some answers to give. So, by God's providence, those who were looked on as the enemies of mankind can become healers of mankind (and womankind). Our hopes are best summarized by saying that, in spite of all our weaknesses and shortcomings, we in faith apply the words of St. Paul to ourselves:

> But in all things approving ourselves as the ministers of God, in much patience, in afflictions, in necessities, in distress. By the word of truth, by the power of God, by the armor of righteousness on the right hand and on the left. By honor and dishonor, by evil report and good report: as deceivers, and yet true; as unknown, and yet well known; as dying, and behold, we live; as chastened, and not killed; as sorrowful, yet always rejoicing [2 Cor. 6:4–8].

# The Ordination of Women and Ecclesial Endorsement of Homosexuality: Are They Related?[1]

## John T. Pless

The August 2009 issue of *The Lutheran*, the official magazine of the Evangelical Lutheran Church in America (ELCA), carried two news items side by side. First was a column under the heading "Rite Sought for Gays," reporting on requests from Episcopal bishops in six American states where same-sex marriages are now legal for permission to adapt their church's prayer book for use at these weddings. Next was a report that the Evangelical Lutheran Church in Cameroon, at its General Synod meeting last June, voted by a wide margin to ordain women.[2] Are the two matters related—the ordination of practicing homosexuals and the ordination of women?

Over a decade ago, in 1996, Wolfhart Pannenberg shocked mainline churches in Europe and North America when he declared,

> If a church were to let itself be pushed to the point where it ceased to treat homosexual activity as a departure from the biblical norm, and recognized homosexual unions as a personal partnership of love equivalent to marriage, such a church would stand no longer on biblical ground but against the unequivocal witness of Scripture. A church that took this step would cease to be the one, holy, catholic, and apostolic church.[3]

1   The following article is a slight revision of a paper originally presented at the Lutheran Theological Conference of South Africa in August 2009.

2   *The Lutheran* 22 (August 2009): 16.

3   Wolfhart Pannenberg, "Revelation and Homosexual Experience," *Christianity Today* 40 (November 1996): 37.

In the years after Pannenberg's pronouncement, Lutheran churches in North America and Europe have steadily moved toward providing liturgical formularies for the blessing of same-sex unions and the ordination of men and women who identify themselves as gay or lesbian.

In North America, the ELCA, at their national assembly meeting in 2009, endorsed proposals that allow for both the ordination of homosexuals living in committed, monogamous relationships and churchly blessings of such unions. The Church of Sweden has already had a woman, Eva Brunne, who has identified herself as a lesbian, elected as bishop of Stockholm on May 26, 2009. Furthermore, on October 22, 2009, the Church of Sweden voted to allow its priests to perform weddings for homosexual couples, who now enjoy marriage equal to heterosexual couples.[4]

Opponents see these moves as a clear and certain denial of biblical authority and an overturning of foundational moral truth, while champions of these changes see them as necessary steps for the sake of the church's mission. What is recognized by all is that change threatens the unity of the church. Those promoting change often argue that changes in church order to allow for the inclusion of homosexual men and women in the church's ministry are on the same level as previous decisions to ordain women. For example, Herbert Chilstrom, the immediate past presiding bishop of the ELCA, circulated "An Open Letter Response to the CORE Open Letter" in the summer of 2009, chiding several prominent theologians and church leaders for their inconsistency in affirming women's ordination but not the full inclusion of homosexuals in the ministry of the church. Significant voices, however, raised in support of the historic Christian teaching on sexuality insist that making provision for homosexual clergy and acceptance of same-sex unions is quite distinct from the question of women's ordination. For example, the American Lutheran New Testament scholar Craig Koester argues that to draw an analogy between endorsement of homosexual practice and women's ordination is flawed since the Scriptures are said to be inconsistent in their testimony to leadership by women but consistent in the rejection of homosexual behavior.[5] A similar case is made by R. T. France[6] and Robert Gagnon.[7] This issue will be examined

---

4    "Sweden's Lutheran church to celebrate gay weddings," *Agence France-Presse* (AFP), October 22, 2009.

5    Craig R. Koester, "The Bible and Sexual Boundaries," *Lutheran Quarterly* 7 (Winter 1993): 388.

6    R. T. France, "From Romans to the Real World: Biblical Principles and Cultural Change in Relation to Homosexuality and the Ministry of Women," in *Romans and the People of God*, ed. S. K. Soderlund and N. T. Wright (Grand Rapids: Eerdmans, 1999), 234–253.

7    Robert Gagnon, *The Bible and Homosexual Practice: Texts and Hermeneutics* (Nashville: Abingdon, 2001), 441–443.

here demonstrating nine parallels in theological method and argumentation used to defend both practices.

## I. Parallels in Theological Argumentation

1. The advocacy for women's ordination and for the ordination of homosexuals and the blessing of same-sex unions is put forth in the churches as a matter of social justice.

Church office and sexual fulfillment are seen as matters of entitlement. Just as barriers to women and homosexuals have been removed in other areas of civic life and the workplace, the same demand is made on the church. This is especially true in church bodies where social justice is seen not as a work of God in the government of the left hand but as a part, perhaps even the most important part, of the church's mission to the world. Here it is argued that the church must enact social justice in its own midst by removing barriers to equality. In fact, Krister Stendahl argues, "It seems to me almost impossible to assent—be it reluctantly or gladly—to the political emancipation of women while arguing on biblical grounds against the ordination of women."[8]

This was in large part the argument of Gustaf Wingren over against Anders Nygren in the Church of Sweden. Nygren argued against the move to ordain women in Sweden in 1958. After the decision was made to allow for the ordination of women, Nygren and others still protested. In 1974, Wingren resigned the pastoral office in protest of what he saw as a social justice issue in the resistance to female clergy.[9]

2. Churchly acceptance of women's ordination, the ordination of homosexuals, and the blessing of same-sex unions has been fueled by powerful liberationist movements within the culture rather than by biblical understanding.

Feminism had its roots in nineteenth-century equalitarian impulses that promoted social change. Many of the first women who would be seen as matriarchs of what might be more specifically identified as "feminist theology" were shaped by nineteenth-century American revivalism.[10] While feminist

---

8  *The Bible and the Role of Women: A Case Study in Hermeneutics*, trans. Emilie T. Sander (Philadelphia: Fortress Press, 1966), 39.

9  See Carl Axel Aurelius, "Wingren, Gustaf (1910–2000)," in *Theologische Realenzyklopädie*, Band 36 (Berlin/New York: Walter de Gruyter, 2004), 110. See also Mary Elizabeth Anderson, "Gustaf Wingren (1910–2000)," *Lutheran Quarterly* 23 (Summer 2009): 198–217.

10  See Melanie May, "Feminist Theology," in *The Encyclopedia of Christianity*, vol. 2 (Grand Rapids: Eerdmans, 2001), 305.

theologies exist in great variety,[11] they share a common, strong theme that women are oppressed by patriarchal structures and need to be emancipated from these restrictive, ideological paradigms and freed for access to all aspects of church life, including the pastoral office. While various gay liberationist movements are historically much more recent than feminism, they tend to have similar goals. For example, "Lutherans Concerned," a North American group, works for full inclusion of gay, lesbian, bisexual, and transgendered persons in the life of the church, that is, ordination and the blessing of those who live in committed same-sex relationships. Movements of both feminist and gay liberation insist on a revisionist understanding of biblical texts that were previously held to be prohibitive and see the gospel primarily as a means of empowerment and change.

3. In the case of both the ordination of women and the ordination of homosexuals, Galatians 3:28 is used in such a way as to sever redemption from creation.

A short monograph that would become foundational in making a biblical case for the ordination of women, first published in 1958 and then in the USA after being translated into English by Emilie Sander in 1966, was Krister Stendahl's *The Bible and the Role of Women: A Case Study in Hermeneutics*. Stendahl maintained that Paul achieved an "evangelical breakthrough" in Galatians as the distinction between male and female is rendered obsolete. Stendahl writes, "But in Christ the dichotomy is overcome; through baptism a new unity is created, and that is not only a matter discerned by the eyes of faith but one that manifests itself in the social dimensions of the church."[12] The new reality of redemption transcends and replaces the old order of creation. Paul's defense of the old order in 1 Corinthians is seen as a necessary and eschatologically limited corrective for a chaotic situation in which the gospel was not yet fully apprehended. It is a penultimate and provisional concession.

Edward Schroeder[13] extends Stendahl's basic hermeneutic to the question of the church's response to homosexuality. For Schroeder, the questions of blessings for same-sex unions and the ordination of homosexuals are answered

---

11  For a helpful survey, see Hans Schwarz, *Theology in a Global Context: The Last Two Hundred Years* (Grand Rapids: Eerdmans, 2005), 487–500, and Roland F. Ziegler, "Liberation Theology in the Leading Ladies of Feminist Theology," in *Women Pastors? The Ordination of Women in Biblical Lutheran Perspective*, [2nd ed.,] ed. Matthew C. Harrison and John T. Pless (St. Louis: Concordia, 2009), 137–152.

12  Krister Stendahl, *The Bible and the Role of Women: A Case Study in Hermeneutics*, trans. Emilie T. Sander (Philadelphia: Fortress Press, 1986), 33.

13  For a more detailed treatment of Schroeder's position, see John T. Pless, "Using and Misusing Luther in Contemporary Debates on Homosexuality: A Look at Two Theologians," *Lutheran Forum* 39 (Summer 2005): 50–57.

in the affirmative on the basis of his application of a law/promise hermeneutic that he claims comes from Luther. According to Schroeder's construal of this hermeneutic, Luther's approach to the Scriptures is to see Christ at the heart and center of the Bible. Scripture itself consists of two words from God, one of law and another of promise. As Schroeder puts it,

> Scripture's law serves as God's diagnostic agent—diagnosis of our malady, not prescription for our healing. God's Law is X-ray, not ethics. The healing for patients diagnosed by the Law is God's promise, the Christ-quotient of both OT and NT. The law's purpose (Paul said it first—after he received his "new" hermeneutics beginning at Damascus) is to "push sinners to Christ."[14]

Once sinners are in Christ, according to Schroeder, they are no longer under the law but under grace.

> Once Christ-connected they come into the force-field of his "new commandment," and it really is new, not a refurbished "old" commandment, not "Moses rehabilitated." Christ supersedes Moses—not only for salvation, but also for ethics. In Paul's language the touchstone for this new commandment is the "mind of Christ" and "being led by, walking by, his Holy Spirit." More than once Paul makes it "perfectly clear" that this is a new "law-free" way of life.[15]

Schroeder then goes on to ask and answer the question of what we are to do with all the commands and imperatives in the Bible in light of this new way of life, free of the law. He concludes, "First of all, this new hermeneutic relativizes them."[16] Here Schroeder sees himself in company with Luther, especially Luther's treatise of 1525, "How Christians Should Regard Moses,"[17] to which we shall return later. Arguing that the law applies only to the old creation while the promise constitutes life in the new creation, Schroeder asserts that human sexuality is clearly a component of the old creation, and hence is under the governance of the law.

There are things in Luther and the Lutheran confessional writings that seem to give credence to Schroeder's argument. In 1522, Luther wrote in his "The Estate of Marriage" that marriage is a bodily and outward thing: "Know therefore that marriage is an outward, bodily thing, like any other worldly

---

14  Edward Schroeder, "Thursday Theology 159" (January 28, 2001), available at http://www.crossings.org/thursday/2001/thur0628.shtml.

15  Schroeder, "Thursday Theology 159."

16  Schroeder, "Thursday Theology 159."

17  Martin Luther, *Luther's Works*, American Edition, 55 vols., ed. Jaroslav Jan Pelikan, Hilton C. Oswald, and Helmut T. Lehmann (Philadelphia: Fortress Press; St. Louis: Concordia, 1955–1986), 35:155–174 [henceforth *LW*].

undertaking."[18] Thus Luther recognizes the place of civil authority in regulating matters of sexuality and marriage.[19]

Does Luther's assessment of marriage as an outward thing, an artifact of the old creation, make questions of sexual ethics a matter of relativity, as Schroeder contends, and therefore lead to a definition of marriage elastic enough to include same-sex unions? Certainly not. There are several difficulties with Schroeder's approach. The first has to do with his understanding of the place of creation in Luther's thinking.

In contrasting the old creation with the new creation, Schroeder is concerned to show that the law is operative in creation both to deliver justice (recompense, as he puts it) and to preserve the fallen world from plunging into total chaos. Of course, these are themes that are readily found in Luther. Schroeder, however, makes an interpretative move that Luther does not make. While Luther surely sees that neither the laws of Moses nor civil laws, which vary from place to place and from one historical epoch to another, work salvifically, he does not view the law as being merely set aside by the gospel. To use the language of the *Formula of Concord*, "The distinction between law and gospel is a particularly glorious light,"[20] but it is not a light that blinds us to the normative character of Holy Scripture. To reduce the distinction to an ideology abstracted from the actual content of the biblical texts blurs both

---

18  *LW* 45:25.

19  Luther sees marriage as grounded in creation. It is not a sacrament that bestows forgiveness, but there is no higher social calling where faith is exercised than that of the family. Marriage is the arena for faith and love. In 1519, Luther still regarded marriage as a sacrament. The change is evident in "The Babylonian Captivity" of 1520. In divesting marriage of its sacramental status, Luther actually elevates marriage as he makes it equal or superior to celibacy. See Scott Hendrix, "Luther on Marriage," *Lutheran Quarterly* 14 (Autumn 2000): 355; James Nestingen, "Luther on Marriage, Vocation, and the Cross," *Word & World* 23 (Winter 2003): 31–39; William Lazareth, *Luther on the Christian Home* (Philadelphia: Muhlenberg Press, 1960); and Carter Lindberg, "The Future of a Tradition: Luther and the Family," in *All Theology is Christology: Essays in Honor of David P. Scaer*, ed. Dean Wenthe et al. (Fort Wayne: Concordia Theological Seminary Press, 2000), 133–151. For a picture of Luther's contribution to the place of marriage in Western culture, see John Witte Jr., *From Sacrament to Contract: Marriage, Religion, and Law in the Western Tradition* (Louisville: Westminster/John Knox Press, 1997), 42–73. Lindberg aptly summarizes Luther's impact on marriage: "Luther's application of evangelical theology to marriage and family desacramentalized marriage; desacralized the clergy and resacralized the life of the laity; opposed the maze of canonical impediments to marriage; strove to unravel the skein of canon law, imperial law, and German customs; and joyfully affirmed God's good creation, including sexual relations" (133). Also see the insightful treatments by Oswald Bayer in "The Protestant Understanding of Marriage," "Luther's View of Marriage," and "Law and Freedom in Marriage," in *Freedom in Response—Lutheran Ethics: Sources and Controversies*, trans. Jeffrey Crayzer (Oxford: Oxford University Press, 2007), 156–205.

20  FC SD V, 1; Robert Kolb and Timothy J. Wengert, eds., *The Book of Concord: The Confessions of the Evangelical Lutheran Church*, trans. Charles Arand, et al. (Minneapolis: Fortress Press, 2000), 581 [Henceforth Kolb and Wengert].

God's judgment and his grace. Schroeder's law/promise hermeneutic ends up with a divorce between creation and redemption, a schism between faith and life that is foreign to Luther.[21]

Luther understands creation as the arena for God's work. When Schroeder makes the claim that homosexuals are simply "wired differently"[22] than heterosexuals, he introduces into creation a relativism and subjectivism that is not in Luther. Luther, in fact, sees human identity as male and female as a creational reality. To use the words of William Lazareth, God's ordering of creation is heterosexual.[23] This can be seen in Luther's exposition of the Sixth Commandment in the Large Catechism: "He has established it (marriage) before all others as the first of all institutions, and he created man and woman differently (as is evident) not for indecency but to be true to each other, to be fruitful, to beget children, and to nurture and bring them up to the glory of God."[24] This is also expressed in a letter Luther wrote to Wolfgang Reissenbusch in March, 1527. After counseling Reissenbusch that he is free to renounce his vow of celibacy without committing sin, Luther observes, "Our bodies are in great part the flesh of women, for by them we were conceived, developed, borne, suckled, and nourished. And it is quite impossible to keep entirely apart from them. This is in accord with the Word of God. He has caused it to be so and wishes it so."[25]

In his "The Estate of Marriage" (1522), after noting God's design and purpose in creating humanity as male and female, Luther speaks of this ordinance or institution as "inflexible,"[26] beyond alteration. What Luther sees as a

---

21   Contra this divorce, see Bernd Wannenwetsch, "Luther's Moral Theology," in *The Cambridge Companion to Martin Luther*, ed. D. McKim (Cambridge: Cambridge University Press, 2003), 120–135; William Lazareth, *Christians in Society: Luther, the Bible and Social Ethics* (Minneapolis: Fortress Press, 2001); Reinhard Huetter, "The Twofold Center of Lutheran Ethics," in *The Promise of Lutheran Ethics*, ed. K. Bloomquist and John Stumme (Minneapolis: Fortress Press, 1998), 31–54. Schroeder asserts that "Huetter's conclusion really is 'the end' of the promise of Lutheran ethics"; "Thursday Theology 26" (November 12, 1998), http://www.crossings.org/thursday/1998/thur1112.shtml.

22   Schroeder, "Thursday Theology 34" (January 28, 1999), http://www.crossings.org/thursday/1999/thur0128.shtml.

23   William Lazareth, "ELCA Lutherans and Luther on Heterosexual Marriage," *Lutheran Quarterly* 8 (Autumn 1994): 235–268. Lazareth writes, "Clearly, same-sex 'unions' do not qualify as marriages to be blessed for Christians who have been baptized as saints into the body of Christ. The Lutheran church should not condone the sinful acts (conduct) of an intrinsic disorder (orientation) in God's heterosexual ordering of creation" (236).

24   LC I, 207; Kolb and Wengert, 414.

25   Theodore Tappert, ed., *Luther: Letters of Spiritual Counsel* (Vancouver, British Columbia: Regent College Press, 1995), 273.

26   *LW* 45:18.

given, biological reality, Schroeder now moves into the realm of the subjective with an appeal to the explanation of the First Article in the Small Catechism. Luther's doxological confession that "God has created me together with all that exists" and that "God has given and still preserves my body and soul, eyes, ears, and all limbs and senses" is now used by Schroeder to make God the author of homosexuality. As Schroeder writes,

> Luther doesn't mention sexuality in that gift-list, but today God puts it on the lists we have. If "hetero-" is one of the creator's ordainings, then wouldn't "homo-" also be on the gift-list for those so ordained? Isn't it "most certainly true" for both that they "thank, praise, serve and obey God" as the sexual persons they have been ordained to be? Both homosexuals and heterosexuals have a common calling to care for creation, carrying out the double agenda in God's secular world—the law of preservation and the law of recompense. If the gifts are different, the pattern of care will be different. What examples are already available within the ELCA of Christians—gay and straight—doing just that—preservation and recompense—with the sexual gift that God has ordained? Despite the current conflict, is it true about sexuality too that "what God ordains is always good?"[27]

Luther's rejection of required clerical celibacy is seen by Schroeder as a precedent for relaxing requirements for individuals who understand themselves to be homosexual. Schroeder writes:

> For outsiders to "require" celibacy of them as a prerequisite for the validity of their Christ-confession is parallel to the Roman church's "requirement" of celibacy for the clergy. Concerning that requirement the Lutheran Reformers said: God created the sexual "pressure" that surfaces at puberty. To "require" celibacy of the clergy—or anybody—is blatantly contradicting God. For those whom God "wired differently" as a student once described himself—regardless of how that different wiring came to pass—requiring celibacy for him sounds like the same thing to me. It is God, not the gay guy, who is being contradicted.[28]

Here Schroeder reveals a basic premise that is not shared by Luther, namely, that homosexuality is ordained by God. Luther does not speak of

---

27  Schroeder, "Thursday Theology 51" (May 27, 1999), http://www.crossings.org/thursday/1999/thur0527.shtml.

28  Schroeder, "Thursday Theology 159." Similar arguments are advanced by Christian Batalden Scharen, *Married in the Sight of God* (Landham, MD: University of America Press, 2000), although Scharen finally must admit that "an ethic for same-sex relationships goes nowhere with the 'letter' of Luther's views" (128). Likewise, Martha Ellen Stortz, "Rethinking Christian Sexuality: Baptized into the Body of Christ," in *Faithful Conversations: Christian Perspectives on Homosexuality*, ed. James M. Childs Jr. (Minneapolis: Fortress Press, 2003), 64–66.

a generic sexual drive or instinct but of the desire of man for woman, and woman for man: "This is the Word of God, through whose power procreative seed is planted in man's body and a natural, ardent desire for woman is kindled and kept alive. This cannot be restrained either by vows or laws."[29] Luther seldom mentions homosexual behavior, but when he does, his evaluation is always negative. For example, Luther identifies the sin of Sodom with homosexuality. Commenting on Genesis 19:4–5, Luther writes,

> I for my part do not enjoy dealing with this passage, because so far the ears of the Germans are innocent of and uncontaminated by this monstrous depravity; for even though disgrace, like other sins, has crept in through an ungodly soldier and a lewd merchant, still the rest of the people are unaware of what is being done in secret. The Carthusian monks deserve to be hated because they were the first to bring this terrible pollution into Germany from the monasteries of Italy.[30]

In the same section of the Genesis lecturers, Luther refers to "the heinous conduct of the people of Sodom" as

> extraordinary, inasmuch as they departed from the natural passion and longing of the male for the female, which is implanted into nature by God, and desired what is altogether contrary to nature. Whence comes this perversity? Undoubtedly from Satan, who after people have once turned away from the fear of God, so powerfully suppresses nature that he blots out the natural desire and stirs up a desire that is contrary to nature.[31]

Luther's rejection of homosexual activity is not merely a matter of aesthetic preference but rather a theological judgment rooted in the reality of the way the wrath of God is revealed against all ungodliness that will not acknowledge God to be the Creator and Lord that he is. For Luther, homosexuality is a form of idolatry, of false worship as we see in his lectures on

---

29  Tappert, *Letters of Spiritual Counsel*, 273. For similar statements in Luther see *Luther on Women: A Sourcebook*, ed. Susan C. Karant-Nunn and Merry E. Wiesner-Hanks (Cambridge: University of Cambridge Press, 2003), 137–170.

30  *LW* 3:251–252.

31  *LW* 3:255; also note Luther's comment in "On War Against the Turk" (1529): "Both the pope and the Turk are so blind and senseless that they commit the dumb sins shamelessly, as an honorable and praiseworthy thing. Since they think so lightly of marriage, it serves them right that there are dog-marriages (and would to God that they were dog-marriages), indeed, also 'Italian marriages' and 'Florentine brides' among them; and they think these things good. I hear one horrible thing after another about what an open and glorious Sodom Turkey is, and everybody who has looked around a little in Rome or Italy knows very well how God revenges and punishes the forbidden marriage, so that Sodom and Gommorah, which God overwhelmed in days of old with fire and brimstone (Gen. 19:24), must seem a mere jest and prelude compared with these abominations," *LW* 46:198.

Romans.[32] In attributing homosexuality to the creative will of God for certain human beings, Schroeder strangely overlooks the teaching of his mentor, Werner Elert, who maintains that creation places humanity in an ordered world of nomological existence.[33]

4. Opponents of women's ordination and those who resist the acceptance of homosexuality as a moral equivalent to heterosexuality are both labeled as fundamentalists and legalists.

Taking "the interpretation closest to hand" as that one "which allows the text to say what it says most simply," to use the language of Hermann Sasse,[34] is equated with fundamentalism. The labeling then becomes a weapon of defense from listening to what is said in the text. A simple reading of the text that yields an undesired result is dismissed (i.e., that women cannot be pastors or that homosexual acts lie outside of the realm of God's design).

Lutherans are rightly allergic to the charge of legalism. Arguments were made for the ordination of women on the basis of the freedom of the gospel, as we have noted in Krister Stendahl. In a clever statement issued by revision-ist clergy and laity in the Evangelical Lutheran Church in Canada and aimed polemically at supporters of the church catholic's traditional position on sex-uality[35] under the title, "We Believe in the Gospel," advocates of a revised sexual ethic accuse those holding to scriptural teaching as those who have revised and abandoned the gospel by "turning it into law."[36]

---

32  Luther, in his exposition of Romans 1, links homosexual behavior with idolatry: "For this reason, namely: idolatry, God gave, not only to the above-mentioned disgrace, them, some of them, up to dishonorable passions, to shameful feelings and desires, before God, although even they, like Sodom, called this sin. . . . And the men likewise, with an overpowering drive of lust, gave up natural relations with women and were consumed with passion, which overpowered the judgment of their reason, for another, men with men, and thus they deal with each other in mutual disgrace, committing shameless acts and consequently, receiving the penalty, punishment, due for their error, fitting and just for so great a sin, the sin of idolatry, in their own persons, according to the teaching and arrangement of God," *LW* 25:12–13.

33  See Werner Elert, *The Christian Ethos*, trans. Carl J. Schneider (Philadelphia: Fortress Press, 1957). Elert writes, "Creation places man into the world, *nomos* binds him to the world. In the first place, nomological under law means only that we, like all other creatures, are subject to the orderly rule of God and that we do not live in a world of chaos and arbitrariness" (51).

34  Hermann Sasse, "Did God Really Say . . . ? A Reply to Dr. Helmut Thielicke's Article 'Thoughtless, Doctrinaire, Loveless,'" in *The Lonely Way*, vol. 2, ed. Matthew C. Harrison (St. Louis: Concordia, 2002), 318.

35  For the defense of the traditional position by Canadian Lutherans, see "The Banff Commission Declaration on the Malaise That Affects the Church of our Days," in *The Banff Commission*, ed. K. Glen Johnson (New Delhi, NY: American Lutheran Publicity Bureau, 2008), 9–26.

36  "We Believe in the Gospel of Jesus Christ," accessed on July 26, 2009 from http://www.webelieveinthe gospel.org/2652.html.

5. In making the case for women's ordination and for the ordination of homosexuals and the blessing of same-sex unions, biblical texts once taken as clear are argued to be unclear or dismissed as culturally conditioned and time bound.

Some assert that the contested texts relative to women in the pastoral office (1 Cor 14:33–38 and 1 Tim 2:11–14) and on homosexuality (Lev 18:22, 24; 20:13; Rom 1:24–27; 1 Cor 6:9–10; 1 Tim 1:9–10) clearly reflect the theological worldview of the biblical writers, but that these teachings are culturally conditioned and hence open to reassessment. Typical are the arguments that the Bible represents a patriarchal and/or heterosexualist structure that may be abandoned without doing violence to the essential message of the Holy Scriptures.[37] Others argue that the disputed texts are unclear and therefore incapable of providing a sure foundation for church practice.[38] In his 2006 book *Evangelical Feminism: A New Path to Liberalism*, Wayne Grudem has demonstrated how both approaches have been adopted by some neo-Evangelical theologians.[39]

6. Ordination of women and ordination of homosexuals is seen as a matter of necessity for the sake of the gospel and mission.

The case is made that a church that excludes women from the pastoral office (which is often equated with "positions of leadership") or renders a negative moral judgment on homosexual practice will not be attractive to a world that does not discriminate on the basis of gender or sexual orientation.[40] Furthermore, it is also asserted that all Christians need to be actively involved in missionary outreach.[41] Teachings that would exclude some Christians on the basis of gender or sexual identity from full participation in the mission of the

---

37 This presupposition in regard to women's ordination is critiqued by numerous essays in *Women Pastors? The Ordination of Women in Biblical Lutheran Perspective*, [2nd ed.,] ed. Matthew C. Harrison and John T. Pless (St. Louis: Concordia, 2009), and in regard to homosexuality by Armin Wenz, *The Contemporary Debate on Homosexual Clergy*, trans. Holger Sonntag (St. Louis: LCMS World Relief and Human Care, 2006), 3–24; also Gagnon, *The Bible and Homosexual Practice*.

38 See, for example, an early attempt by Ruth Bretscher Ressmeyer, *Neither Male or Female* (East Northport, NY: Commission on Women of the Atlantic District LCMS, 1997). Ressmeyer draws heavily on Stendahl.

39 Wayne Grudem, *Evangelical Feminism: A New Path to Liberalism* (Wheaton: Crossway Books, 2006).

40 See, e.g., Karl Wyneken, "Let's Include Women," in *A Daystar Reader*, ed. Matthew L. Becker (np: Daystar.net, 2010), 152.

41 See, e.g., Craig Nessan, *Many Members Yet One Body: Committed Same-Gender Relationships and the Mission of the Church* (Minneapolis: Augsburg Fortress, 2004), 53. According to Nessan, ethical issues such as homosexual marriage have only "penultimate" significance, while the justification-centered mission of the church possesses "ultimate" significance and must not be compromised by issues of only penultimate concern.

church are seen as detrimental to effective missionary outreach and as stumbling blocks to the proclamation of the gospel, which is meant for all people.

7. Arguments for both the ordination of women and the ordination of homosexuals along with churchly blessing of same-sex unions are often made on the basis of what Alasdair MacIntyre has identified as an "ethic of emotivism."[42]

The case is made for women's ordination and an ethic affirming of homosexuality on the basis of emotional appeal.[43] The pain of exclusion, for example, is used by advocates to urge the church to respond with sympathy rather than restriction. With an "ethic of emotivism," claims to biblical authority or creedal teaching are trumped by an appeal to the emotional well-being of those who are denied access either to the pastoral office or to marriage.

8. Women's ordination and the ordination of homosexuals are urged on the church for the sake of unity and inclusiveness yet both practices fracture genuine ecumenicity.

Martha Ellen Stortz contributed an article, "Rethinking Christian Sexuality: Baptized into the Body of Christ," to the volume *Faithful Conversation: Christian Perspectives on Homosexuality*. She proposes a discussion of sexuality that begins with Baptism, thus avoiding the reality of humanity created as male and female. Her conclusions are predictable. Baptismal identity overrides sexual identity.[44] Thus sexual differentiation, distinctions between male and female, straight or gay are overcome by unity in the body of Christ. Christians may indeed entertain a variety of opinions regarding men and women in the life of the church, sexual preference, and ethics, but these differences are said not to be church divisive. Working with something akin to a paradigm of "reconciled diversity,"[45] these differences are to be lived with and even celebrated. In actuality, however, such an approach will finally exclude from unity those who hold a traditional position on these matters. When truth is sacrificed for unity, unity will finally demand the exclusion of those who insist on truth.

---

42 Alasdair C. MacIntyre, *After Virtue: A Study in Moral Theory* (University of Notre Dame Press, 1984).

43 See Scharen, *Married in the Sight of God*, 149–152; also note the emotionally charged letter of the former presiding bishop of the ELCA, Herbert W. Childstrom, entitled "My View: Questions for Those Leaving the ELCA," *Mankato Free Press*, August 26, 2010.

44 Stortz, "Rethinking Christian Sexuality: Baptized into the Body of Christ," in *Faithful Conversation*, 59–79.

45 Here see Reinhard Slenczka, "Magnus Consensus: The Unity of the Church in the Truth and Society's Pluralism," *Logia* 13 (Holy Trinity 2004): 21–39. Slenczka observes that "magnus consensus" is reduced to "reconciled diversity as an external mark of the church at the expense of truth; the question of truth is circumvented by pointing to the diversity in scriptural interpretations" (25).

In reality both women's ordination and an accommodation of a permissive ethic in regard to homosexuality have fractured churches. First of all, churches that have compromised on these issues have separated themselves from continuity with the catholic past. In that sense such communions may be said to have deserted "vertical ecumenism." They have become chronologically sectarian, introducing novelties unknown to apostolic and most of post-apostolic Christianity. Such a church can no longer confess the words of the prophets and the apostles to be the words of the living God. Second, these communions put themselves in a position that makes "horizontal ecumenism," conversation with Eastern Orthodoxy and Roman Catholicism, even more difficult. Simply put, communions which determine theology and practice by majority vote and embrace religious pluralism lack credibility in ecumenical dialogue with Rome or the East.

9. Ordination of women, ordination of homosexuals, and ecclesiastical recognition of same-sex unions are at first proposed as a matter of compromise or as a local option, but they will finally demand universal acceptance.

When ordination of women was introduced in Sweden, a "conscience clause" was included.[46] Incrementally the provisions of this protective measure were lessened and finally removed. Candidates for ordination must demonstrate their acceptance of the legitimacy of female clergy prior to ordination.[47] The Recommendations of the Sexuality Taskforce in the ELCA propose something of a local option: individual synods and congregations may opt not to have homosexual clergy or to provide rituals for blessing same-sex couples. Such a compromise, however, will hardly satisfy either activists for change or those who believe that the scriptural ethic precludes the placing in office of those who practice homosexuality. To paraphrase Richard John Neuhaus, where orthodoxy is made optional, orthodoxy will finally be proscribed.[48]

10. It is argued that by refusing to ordain women and homosexuals to the pastoral office the church is deprived of the particular spiritual gifts they possess and that these individuals are unjustly denied the opportunity for spiritual self-expression.[49]

---

46  Dag Sandahl, interview by William J. Tighe, "Swedish Dissent: Life as an Orthodox Churchman in the Church of Sweden," *Touchstone: A Journal of Mere Christianity* 13 (July/August 2000): 36–37.

47  Dag Sandahl, "Swedish Dissent," 36.

48  Richard John Neuhuas, "The Unhappy Fate of Optional Orthodoxy," *First Things* 69 (January 1997): 57.

49  See Scharen, 127–147; also note Patricia Jung and Ralph Smith, *Heterosexism: An Ethical Challenge* (Albany: The State University of New York Press, 1993), 170.

This argument relies on an understanding of the ministry that sees the ministry as an avenue for the expression of personal charismata rather than an office established by Christ and filled according to His mandates. Spiritual giftedness is confused with personal expression. Creativity and freedom to express oneself without boundary or restraint are celebrated in the name of autonomy. Given the spiritual climate of the postmodern context this becomes attractive as "gifts of the Spirit" are placed in contrast to a biblical/confessional understanding of office. Expressive individualism takes precedence over an understanding of an office instituted by Christ to serve his church with word and sacrament.

## II. CONCLUSION

Reviewing arguments made for the ordination of women in Lutheran churches in the middle years of the twentieth century, it is hard not to conclude that variants of these arguments are currently being used to advocate the ordination of homosexuals and to provide for an ecclesiastical recognition of same-sex unions through an elastic definition of marriage that ignores both "nature and institution."[50] Creation is left behind in pursuit of purely spiritual categories and relational qualities. One Lutheran ethicist, Paul Jersild, is worried that some Christians have adopted an "excessively physicalist approach to homosexuality."[51] Creation is seen as secondary, if not irrelevant. But without creation, there is no incarnation. Without creation, the new creation is reduced to a spiritualistic construct of one's own imagination.

After women's ordination was permitted in the Church of Sweden, Bishop Anders Nygren perhaps spoke prophetically when he said, "This current decision not only means a determination of the specific issue concerning female pastors, but I am convinced that our church has now shifted onto a previously unknown track heading in the direction of Gnosticism and the Schwaermerei."[52] In a tentative and somewhat ambivalent way, Helmut Thielicke would take cautious but nevertheless perceptible steps down this path when he affirmed that the writers of Holy Scripture were opposed to

---

50 Here see Oswald Bayer, "Nature and Institution: Luther's Doctrine of the Three Estates," in *Freedom in Response*, 90–118. Also note Knut Alfsvåg, "Christians in Society: Luther's Teaching on the Two Kingdoms and the Three Estates Today," *Logia* 14 (Reformation 2005): 15–20.

51 Paul Jersild, *Spirit Ethics* (Minneapolis: Fortress Press, 2000), 139. Also see Bernd Wannenwetsch's critique of the "docetic" turn taken by advocates of homosexual unions in his "Old Docetism—New Moralism? Questioning a New Direction in the Homosexuality Debate," *Modern Theology* 16 (July 2000): 353–364.

52 Quoted from *Kyrkometets protokoll*, nr. 4, 158, p. 154, in *Women Pastors? The Ordination of Women in Biblical Lutheran Perspective*, [2nd ed.,] ed. Matthew C. Harrison and John T. Pless (St. Louis: Concordia, 2009), 9.

women's ordination and homosexual practice but that these biblical prohibitions are not absolutely binding on us as the church acquires a new and deeper knowledge.[53]

In the current move to sanction same-sex unions and provide access to the pastoral office, the Gnosticism and enthusiasm that were magnetic for a departure from the New Testament mandates regarding man and woman in the church have seductively drawn Lutheran churches further away from their apostolic foundations. Those who celebrate these changes rightly see that they have created something new. Else Marie Pedersen, from the University of Denmark, argues that the ordination of women has humanized the church, yielding a new understanding of the church "so that ministry will be about the pastor's authenticity, rather than about who, on the surface, is a normal male. Authenticity and honesty as well as a solid education ought to be more important than whatever sex or sexuality a pastor has, given that the gospel is proclaimed in Word and Sacrament."[54] This vision of the church with a ministry grounded in the "authenticity" of the pastor presents quite a different picture from the one given in the New Testament. Nygren's fears are confirmed, and we are left to ponder the weight of Hermann Sasse's observation that "there are some questions raised by the devil to destroy the Church of Christ. To achieve this he may use as his mouth piece not only ambitious professors of theology, his favorite tools, but also simple pious souls. Why women cannot be ordained is one of these questions."[55]

The situation of world Lutheranism does not invite an arrogant and carnal security on the part of confessional churches that have not yet succumbed to the temptation to worldly compromise. Rather it is given to us to heed the apostolic admonitions to "keep a close watch on yourself and your teaching" (1 Tim 4:16) and "let anyone who thinks that he stands take heed lest he fall" (1 Cor 10:12).

---

53  See Helmut Thielicke, *The Evangelical Faith*, vol. 3, trans. Geoffrey Bromiley (Grand Rapids: Eerdmans, 1982), 221–22; *The Ethics of Sex*, trans. John Doberstein (New York: Harper & Row, 1964), 269–292. Also note Sasse's sharp rebuke in "Did God Really Say . . . ?," 317–322.

54  Else Marie Wiberg Pedersen, "Women's Ordination in Denmark: The Humanization of the Ordained Ministry," *Dialog* 48 (Spring 2009): 5–6.

55  Hermann Sasse, "Ordination of Women," in *Women Pastors? The Ordination of Women in Biblical Lutheran Perspective*, [2nd ed.,] ed. Matthew C. Harrison and John T. Pless (St. Louis: Concordia, 2009), 263–264. One may read Reinhard Slenczka's "When the Church Ceases to be the Church" as something of an extension of Sasse's point but now in relationship to ecclesiastical acceptance of homosexuality. His essay is published in *The Banff Commission* (New Delhi, NY: American Lutheran Publicity Bureau, 2008), 37–50.

# SECTION III

# SYSTEMATIC THEOLOGY

Is the Gospel of Jesus Christ at stake with the ordination of women? All the essays in this section offer an affirmative answer to this question. Theology, like nature itself, is characterized by a particular ecology. All articles of faith are intimately related one to another and finally converge in the Gospel itself. The Gospel is not left intact when false teaching corrupts or distorts any aspect of Christian doctrine. The Gospel itself is put at jeopardy when the apostolic mandates that govern the pastoral office are rejected.

It is the task of systematic theology to make manifest how each article of Christian doctrine is given its normative character by the Holy Scriptures and necessitated by the Gospel itself. In this section, we have examples of Lutheran theologians plying their craft to do exactly this, especially with the doctrine of Scripture, the office of the ministry, and the doctrine of the Trinity. Several of these essays (Giertz, Brunner, and Sasse) are by theologians of a previous generation. They have become classic responses to the false teaching of women's ordination. The remainder of the contributions are from living authors, and they seek to diagnose the cancerous effect of this practice on the totality of Christian doctrine.

Bo Giertz, a courageous bishop best known for his authorship of *The Hammer of God*, was a leading figure in the resistance to liberalism in the Church of Sweden. His "Twenty-Three Theses on the Holy Scriptures, the Woman, and the Office of the Ministry" were first presented in 1958. Giertz shows how the ordination of women violates sound hermeneutics, the biblical taxonomy of both creation and church, and Christian unity.

A second essay that must be described as classic is that of Peter Brunner. Brunner was professor of systematic theology at the University of Heidelberg and author of the magisterial work on liturgics, *Worship in the Name of Jesus*. First published in German in 1959 and then in English by Concordia in 1971, his monograph "The Ministry and the Ministry of Women" is included here as an example of a continental Lutheran

247

theologian who affirms the orders of creation as foundational. Brunner shows that the inclusion of women in the ministerial office runs contrary to God's design for headship within the Church.

John W. Kleinig perceptively takes up William Oddie's claim that "to ordain women as priests will be to change at its foundations our idea of God."[1] As the apostolic mission is the mission of the triune God, Kleinig focuses on the representational character of the pastoral office. Women's ordination undermines trinitarian doctrine.

Two essays in this section are by David Scaer, long-time professor of systematic theology and New Testament at Concordia Theological Seminary, Fort Wayne, Indiana. Scaer demonstrates the doctrinal inconsistencies involved for those who claim to confess a biblical view of the office and at the same time allow women pastors.

Few in the twentieth century can compare with Hermann Sasse when it comes to comprehensive knowledge of Lutheran theology coupled with ecumenical awareness. In his 1971 essay, Sasse reacts to American Lutheran decisions to ordain women and warns of the dire consequences.

Gregory Lockwood offers a comprehensive "open response" to his fellows in the Lutheran Church of Australia who advocate women's ordination, a change that would move this small church body beyond the pale of orthodox Lutheranism.

The German theologian Reinhard Slenczka has taught theology at Erlangen and Riga. His essay was originally delivered in October 1991 as a plea to the German territorial church of Schaumberg-Lippe not to allow God's Word to be overridden by a majority vote.

Dr. Armin Wenz, pastor of St. John Lutheran Church in Oberursel, Germany, points out that the ordination of women is not merely a change in practice but actually embodies a dogmatic decision that signals a change in confession. In his essay "The Argument over Women's Ordination in Lutheranism as a Paradigmatic Conflict of Dogma," Wenz documents the sobering consequences of this conflict in global Lutheranism.

Adriane Dorr, editor of the *Lutheran Witness*, examines God's design for man and woman in "Giver to Receiver," noting that the differences between male and female are reflected in God's ordering of the life of both family and church for our blessing.

---

1   William Oddie, *What Will Happen to God? Feminism and the Reconstruction of Christian Belief* (San Francisco: Ignatius Press, 1988), 26.

# TWENTY-THREE THESES ON THE HOLY SCRIPTURES, THE WOMAN, AND THE OFFICE OF THE MINISTRY

## BO GIERTZ

The following theses were worked out in Winter 1958 at the request of the Synod of Bishops of the Church of Sweden as part of their internal deliberations. Through duplication they were made accessible to a wider circle. Since the author has repeatedly been asked to do so, they are now published, albeit in shortened form.

1. *The Bible is God's Word.* This means it pleased God to reveal Himself through these Scriptures, which came to be what they are by God's design. God chose this method that He might speak to all peoples and at all times. The Bible does not only describe the history of salvation; the Bible itself is a tool for the continued history of salvation that takes place from the ascension of Christ to His Second Coming. The special status of the Bible does not rest alone in the fact that it describes unique events and personalities. In the word of the Bible itself (*Bibelwort*) there is something that makes it different from any other word. It has been sent into the world by God to accomplish His work. In its nature it is Spirit and Life.

2. *For this reason, God's Church at all times must turn to the Scriptures to receive light and guidance.* God builds His Church through Word and Sacraments. At all times and in every new situation the watchword is: *retro ad Bibliam.*

3. *Only he who submits himself to the Word can properly understand the Word.* The Scriptures are to be used as Means of Grace. Certainly they can also be read as historical documents. But if the Bible is read only as a historical work one never gets to that which is the essential thing in the Scriptures. The proper view of the Bible is from the view of salvation history. In the Scriptures we meet the living and acting God. In the Bible God addresses us. God addresses us from the first verse of the Bible to the last.

4. *The centre of the Scriptures is Jesus Christ.* It is their purpose to bring about faith in Him. If Christ receives His proper place as Redeemer, everything else in the Bible will also receive its proper place. Some things appear as preparation or fore-shadowing, some things appear as ordinances that are valid only until the beginning of the New Order (Heb. 9:10). But everything forms one great unity. That is why the Scriptures are to be interpreted with Scriptures, whereby we must remember that the truth of justification through faith in Him is the key that grants us access to the innermost meaning of the Scriptures. But that does *not* mean that the whole content of the Scriptures can be concentrated in a few "main thoughts" from which we can then logically deduce the answers to the questions that face us today.

5. *To be loyal to the Scriptures includes that we really seek out the message and the meaning of the Scriptures with the honest desire to have the Word as a light for our path.* It is a misuse of the Scriptures when we tear individual statements out of their context or when we appeal to individual passages that are in agreement with our own point of view without taking into consideration the tremendous richness of the Biblical material. On the other hand, having objectively and extensively examined the Biblical witness and having found that the Bible really has a definite opinion on a matter, then in all humility we ought to recognize this as an expression of the good and gracious will of God. And this is what the Church is to proclaim, even if it is not in agreement with presently acceptable opinions and value judgments.

6. *The corrective against a legalistic misuse of the Scriptures lies in the Scriptures themselves.* When we go into the Scriptures and conscientiously attempt to find out what God really means in His Word, then the Scriptures themselves point out what is binding and obligatory and what is not. We cannot find the lines of division outside the Scriptures, e.g. in generally accepted notions, nor can we establish theoretical rules by which we then decide on a purely logical basis what is binding for all times. This must always be the decisive question: What does God mean in His Word? In this only the Word itself can lead us.

7. *There are things in the Scriptures that, according to the witness of the Scriptures, are not designed to be obligatory for all times and peoples.* What God stipulated for Israel was to have validity until the time was fulfilled and Christ had come. Other things are valid for certain situations and for those alone. Here we can point to the prohibition to eat blood (Acts 15:29). This is the apostolic solution to the great problem that arose when Jewish Christianity came into contact with Gentile Christianity; but this solution did not have validity in the purely Gentile Christian churches, as we can see for instance from I Cor. 8:8, 10:25f., I Tim. 4:3f. We have here a classic application of the rule not to give offense, an obligation of every Christian out of love for the brethren and in deference to their qualms of conscience (Rom. 14:15, 20f., I Cor. 8:9–13, 10:23f.). There

is a long series of apostolic admonitions and advice which in the same way were always given in a certain situation but which were never designed to be applied universally. When Paul and Peter, in a series of letter endings, call upon the recipients to greet one another with a holy kiss, then we are obviously dealing with a method of passing on the apostolic greeting of the letter. It is in the nature of the matter that in other situations such a custom cannot be made the norm. (However, during debate in the Imperial Diet, the Swedish Parliament, and in certain academic quarters it was asserted that this, too, was binding if any of the other instructions of the New Testament were valid). Jesus' demands in the Sermon on the Mount, to be pure in heart, to love one's enemies, to be good and meek, yes, even to be perfect, are real demands. God's command demands that much. But this cannot be changed into civil law nor into church or canon law. In fact, all this cannot be fulfilled by those who stand under the law. Only he who lives in the Kingdom of Forgiveness by the grace of reconciliation can take up these demands of Christ and fulfill them in such moments as God grants him for this. Every Christian knows that over and over again he must confess how badly he has failed to fulfill all these demands. But he also knows that this failure in no wise entitles him to do away with any of the commands of the Lord.

8. *The fact that there is much in God's Word that is valid only in a certain situation, and much that puts us on the short end of things, does not give us the right to change God's command.* On every point we must humbly and obediently listen to God's Word, try to understand it correctly and ask ourselves, "What does God mean here?" We must stand on guard against having people isolate a number of examples from God's Word that cannot be made into church or canon law, and then have them arrive at deductions that the Church is at liberty so to arrange her life and order as contradicts the Word of God.

9. *It will not do to draw lines of distinctions in the Bible between "matters dealing with salvation" and "matters having to do with order in the Church"* and then to say that only for matters dealing with salvation does the Bible give an answer that is obligatory for all times. Admittedly this distinction has some merit. Christ did not give His Church a new law that can be compared to the Levitical Law, and the New Testament is not designed for use as church or canon law. But it will not do to divide the content of the Scriptures into matters of order and matters of salvation. The Bible itself does not make this distinction. Even the Mosaic ceremonial laws have meaning as revelations of salvation. They are "symbolic for the present age" (Heb. 9:9) and are "a shadow of the good things to come" (Heb. 10:1). In certain cases a definite outward order is necessary (as in the matter of the sacraments) because it is indissolubly connected with God's desire to save. Frequently the apostolic admonitions are of such nature that they have obvious validity for all of Christian life at all times.

10. *If the concern is to determine the content of a Biblical statement and to find out what it means today, then in every single instance the matter must be examined from the Bible itself.* The concern must be to understand what God intends with His Word. On the basis of such a conclusion it can and may be said that, for instance, I Tim. 5:9f. (regarding the widows of the congregation) is not for all times an obligatory law in the Church. This becomes clear primarily in the New Testament doctrine of Evangelical Liberty (Gal. 4:9f., 5:1f., Col. 2:16–23, *et al.*). From this it becomes also clear that such instruction (e.g., that a widow of the church ought to be at least 60 years old) do not necessarily have an inner connection with the Christian faith.

On the other hand it is equally clear that, for instance, marriage under all circumstances is to be indissoluble, and this principle (with due regard to cases of emergencies and exceptions, as the Scriptures themselves indicate) in one way or another should find expression in the dealings and arrangements of Church life. The Church does not have the liberty to dissolve what God has bound together. Polygamy or a universally assumed right to have a divorce would stand in absolute contradiction to the conception of marriage as it is set forth, for example, in Eph. 5. Here we are dealing with a "matter pertaining to order" that is indissolubly connected with faith in Christ and life in Christ. It is not difficult to find further examples of the fact that the Christian faith has necessary consequences for how the Church is ordered. The Christian Church cannot, for example, make membership dependent upon sex or race. The Church must establish certain rules for the reception of Baptism or the admission to the Lord's Supper. There must be a ministry in the Church, and its incumbents have the right to receive a salary, etc. Such arrangements are based in God's will which is revealed to us in the Word.

One cannot deny *a priori* that the problem of women pastors belongs to this category. We must at least submit this matter to an investigation.

11. *We can only answer the question, whether the Pastoral Office may be entrusted to women, after a conscientious examination of the Biblical material in its entirety.* Only after such an examination can we decide whether this question stands in organic relationship to essential elements of the Christian faith. We cannot answer the question by taking as our starting point some postulated thesis, *e.g.*, the thesis claiming that Christianity has the tendency to overstep certain limits. Such a thesis cannot but be incorrect, or in this case has been applied incorrectly once it is shown that it contradicts what the Scriptures have to say on this particular point.

The material to be considered here is rather comprehensive, beginning with the view about the relationship of man and woman represented in the Creation Accounts, Jesus' attitude about women and about the Office of the Ministry, to the interpretation and application of the Gospel by the apostles where the Gospel's concern is: Man and Woman, the Office of the Ministry and Spiritual Gifts, Equality and Diversity, and other things. I can only give a few indications of what the Biblical material, in my conviction, has to say to us. Our first task must be the attempt to determine accurately what the frequently cited passage of Paul really means when we consider it from the background of the rest of the Biblical material.

12. *Appealing to a command of the Lord and to his apostolic authority Paul teaches that the woman is not intended to hold a Teaching Office in the church (Gemeinde).* As is known, his appeal to the command of the Lord is in I Cor. 14. The authority which belongs to Paul by virtue of the fact that he is an apostle is the basis for the formulation in I Tim. 2:12.

Both passages have to do with the worship service. When in I Tim. 2:12 the word *didaskein* is used, it is a rather pregnant expression (the word means: to be a teacher in the church and to be charged by God with the proclamation of His Word). Compare the Missionary Command to the apostles in Matt. 28:20 and a number of other passages that shed light on this, among other things the combination which makes this very clear: "Teaching and proclaiming the Word of the Lord", or "to command and teach in apostolic commission and with commensurate authority" (I Tim. 4:11) or "teaching and admonishing" (I Tim. 6:2). Accordingly, the meaning of the word "teacher" in the New Testament is: Teacher of God's Word. This was already applied to Jesus as translation of the Hebrew word "rabbi". As an appellation for servants of the Word in the church we find it, among other places, in Acts 13:1, I Cor. 12:28, Eph. 4:11. In the last mentioned passage "shepherd and teacher" is used as an appellation for one and the same commission. When the Bible of the Swedish Church renders the word *didaskein* in I Tim. 2:12 as "acting as teacher", then this is quite justified. Contrariwise it would be a misinterpretation or a misuse of this passage to conclude from it that a woman should not be teacher in the Sunday School, secretary in youth groups or in any other position which obviously does not coincide with that commission to which the New Testament refers when using the words *didaskalos* or *didaskein*. The classic example, that women in the early church taught God's Word (in a connection *other* than the community worship service, is Priscilla (Acts 18:26). She had heard Apollos preach and saw that he only knew the baptism of John; together with Aquila she took him in and "expounded (*exethento*) the way of God more accurately".

I Cor. 14:34f., too, is designed to prohibit the woman from proclaiming God's Word in the worship service of the church. Any other interpretation appears to be extremely artificial and improbable. The whole chapter deals with participation in the worship service. All the decisive words used in this connection ("be silent", "speak", "church") Paul used immediately preceding in the same chapter (vs. 27–30), and it is quite clear that we are dealing here with the right publicly to participate in the worship service and there to speak of God's ways. For this reason alone the claim that the word in v. 34 (*lalein*) has a different meaning and refers only to disturbing chatter, is extremely improbable. In addition we know of Paul's preference of this term for religious speech and preaching (comp. 2 Cor. 2:17, Phil. 1:14, Titus 2:15, Eph. 5:19). Where this word has a different meaning—I have seen that Else Kähler in a specific investigation notes three such passages—this is emphasized by an object or an adverb: to speak like a fool, to speak like a child, to speak unseemly. Incidentally, I should like to point out that v. 35 would most appropriately be translated: But in case they would like to be enlightened on a certain topic they can ask their husbands at home. The Greek text uses here the little word *de*. This indicates that Paul takes up a new thought, probably a response to the objection that the prohibition to speak was all too categorical.

13. *All this the New Testament does not treat as a matter of order, but rather as a necessary consequence of a command of the law and will of Christ, based in that order which God already laid down in creation and which is now realized in Christ.* It is striking to note Paul's concern to give reasons for his standpoint. It is equally striking that Paul here does not merely point to contemporary customs and outward decency, as he does in several passages. Rather, he really attempts to give theological proof from God's Word which would be for the church undisputed authority. Having appealed to the Old Testament (to the Law in I Cor. 14:34; the Creation Accounts and the Fall into Sin in I Tim. 2:13f.), Paul points to the highest authority the early church knew, the command of the Lord Himself. Added to this is then the witness of the Spirit. Paul dares to say that anyone claiming to be filled with the Spirit would have to admit that this really is a command of the Lord. Thus, he marshalls the highest authorities of ancient Christianity: The Scriptures, Jesus' Word, and the Witness of the Spirit. Under these circumstances it is not very well possible to regard this question as "merely a matter pertaining to order" that does not have some inner relationship with the Christian revelation. And even if we say, with Wendland, that "the command of the Lord" has validity only as a principle that makes for order in the worship service, nevertheless the fact remains that according to the conviction of Paul it is part and parcel of this order that a woman is not to preach in the church.

14. *This order has an inner, organic connection with the New Testament's characteristic view of the church. On the one hand its members have become one in Christ; on the other hand they are different from one another, equipped with different gifts and entrusted with different responsibilities.* The Church is Christ's Body in which we have become members by Baptism. Thus considered, there exists among us

an indissoluble unity (I Cor. 12:20). All have equal honour and all are subject to the same gracious care (I Cor. 12:22).

One of the classic passages for this unity is Gal. 3:28. Here we are concerned no longer with Jew or Greek, no more with slave or free man, no more with man or woman. For you are all one in Christ Jesus. Frequently it is concluded at this point that between all members of the Church there must exist complete similarity. People are of the opinion that in these words we find a different, in fact, a more genuine basic New Testament stance than, for instance, in I Cor. 14:34. However, that is to tear the words from their context and to give them a meaning they do not have. For in Gal. 3:28 we are speaking of the *unity of Christ* (all are one). This unity, which finds its basis in Baptism (v. 27), is realized in fellowship with Christ, where, despite the most extreme outward differences, we form an indissoluble unity.

Therefore, the New Testament here emphasizes, as in other passages, these two: unity and diversity. In I Cor. 12 the identical thought recurs as in Gal. 3:28: "For in *one* Spirit we were all baptized into *one* body—Jews or Greeks, slaves or free men—and all were made to drink of *one and the same* Spirit." Here, too, it is shown how indissolubly this thought is connected with the actual diversities in the equipment of gifts and functions. Gifts and responsibilities differ, but they are given in such a way that in their effect they contribute to the common good. The Spirit grants to each a special gift. Yet we are one. Here Paul inserts the words cited above, but immediately he continues: "For the body does not consist of *one* member, but of many." Then he expounds on his topic: It is clear that we are different, have different functions; yet we form *one and the same body*. From this he draws at the end certain conclusions for the Office of the Ministry in the Church: "Within the church God has appointed, in the first place apostles, in the second place prophets, thirdly teachers . . . . Are all apostles? all prophets? all teachers?"

It is a misinterpretation of Gal. 3:28, therefore, to appeal to this passage as proof for the fact that the unity of man and woman must include the self-evident right of both to take up the Office of the Ministry in the Church. Here the thought of a secularized equality has pushed aside the Biblical concept.

A theology of the Body of Christ is undoubtedly one of the most central thoughts in the New Testament. Here we find ourselves quite close to the very heart of the Christian view of redemption and life with Christ. Thus the problem of women pastors has an inner and logical connection with the central thought of the Christian faith. That the ancient Christians accepted such an arrangement and carried it out is based on the fact that they had a definite view of the diversity and unity of Christians. The diversity of function was not regarded as insulting or degrading for anyone.

*15. The fact that man and woman are different is a gift of God, and it is as a result of God's will that the man and the woman have different functions both in the home and in the Church.* "Male and female He created them." The difference exists from the very beginning; it is not abolished in Christ. The New Testament directs different admonitions to the man and to the woman, according to the gifts and responsibilities entrusted to each (Eph. 5, Col. 3, I Peter 3).

Man and woman were created for one another for mutual service. Only after a joining of their abilities is the intention realized which God has with human beings. This joining finds expression in marriage and the home (see the above cited admonitions), but also in the church.

*16. This difference does not imply less esteem for the position of the woman.* That this has not been understood in some cases derives from a misunderstanding of the frequently recurring admonitions for women to submit themselves (I Cor. 14:34, Eph. 5:22, Col. 3:18, 1 Peter 3:1). If these passages are interpreted in a legal and patriarchal sense, then their meaning is different from what the Bible would have it be.

If we wish rightly to understand the command to submit oneself, then we must remember above all that we are dealing here with a Christian command that has validity for everyone (Eph. 5:21—to be subject to one another out of reverence for Christ). In the New Testament, "to be subject" (*hypotassesthai*) has a specifically Christian meaning like the word *agape*, for example, as Rengstorf, Greeven and Schlier, among others, have proven. As Else Kähler has proven in a yet unpublished doctoral dissertation (to the manuscript form of which I have access) the key to this word is to be found in I Cor. 15. There the word is used repeatedly in the well known exposition of Christ's cosmic rule (v. 25–28). There is depicted how everything has been subjected to the Son, until finally He subjects Himself to the Father who has subjected all things to Himself. Here God's grand plan is described, the order to which also the Son subjects Himself. There is not the slightest indication that this subjection was commanded. It is taken as self-evident, it is part of God's order of things. God does not establish this order for His own sake but for the benefit of His creatures. In this order Christ has been entrusted with a decisive role. Christ does not enter into this order of God by constraint, as response to a demand, but He enters into it out of love for the Father and for man.

Wherever the Bible makes mention of subjection we must keep in mind this subjection of Christ to the Father. It is a subjection not compelled through a demand or by force, rather it is a consequence of insight into God's order of things. Just as the subjection of Christ does not mean His degradation or disdain for Him, so there is no degradation in such a subjection to God's plan, God's will and God's order as the Bible demands of Christians and as is beneficial to properly arranging life in its different walks: among subjects of government, among wives, servants, children, etc. All this is based in the fact that we have gained insight into God's order of things. It means to have recognized and accepted the responsibility God entrusted to a person. People really serve God in this, not man (Eph. 6:5–8).

Again an intimate connection with the central thought of the New Testament is emphasized here. The position of the early Christians in the question of the woman and the Office of the Ministry is connected not only with the *corpus Christi* concept, but also with the concept *hypotassesthai*—fitting oneself into God's order of things, and that certainly is genuinely evangelical.

17. *The command regarding submission cannot be made a norm for society's laws.*[1] Since it is a voluntary subjection based upon insight into God's purpose and will, the admonition is always directed to the person who is to subject himself. At no time does the Bible establish it as a right for the other party, for him to whom a person is to be subject. Rather, by means of appropriate admonitions to the other party, to exercise love, kindness and concern, a sort of balance is established. The command to subject oneself is directed to everyone. Everyone, each in the position in which he finds himself, is to fit himself into God's order of things and there to serve his neighbour. The authorities are to be God's servants for the good of the subjects (Rom. 13:4). Husbands are to love their wives "as Christ also loved the Church and gave Himself up for it" (Eph. 5:25). This demand really goes beyond what is demanded of women and it is more difficult to fulfill.

This relationship between man and woman, as it is depicted, for instance, in Eph. 5, concerns marriage and can only be realized between two people who have become "one" body (comp. Eph. 5:28—as they love their own bodies). Such a mutual relationship in love and service cannot be applied to the relation of men and women in their life in society, in their life on the job, etc. This is again reason that the command to subject oneself cannot be made the norm for relationships in society. Thus, it is not an inconsistency but rather the consequence of rightly understanding the Scriptures if we maintain that this is valid only where the Scriptures say that it is valid, that is, in marriage and in the church.

For obviously there is a parallel between the church and marriage, and between the responsibilities of the woman in the home and her responsibilities in the church. This parallel is pre-eminent in the entire depiction of marriage in Eph. 5, and it is also emphasized in I Tim. 2:12.

18. *On the other hand, the chief office in the Church is to be arranged in a way that is conditioned by essential Christian considerations.* "We may not accommodate the Pastoral Office of the Church to the viewpoints prevalent in the civil community so that the factors intrinsic to being the Church are erased" (A. Nygren). The Church has a right to expect that its own members honour the order

which is based in the Gospel's own view of the purpose of man. Here subjection, which without faith in Christ makes no sense, becomes natural. The Church is not guilty of demanding too much when it asks everyone who wants to be a servant of Christ to be prepared to submit to this order. The Church, therefore, has no reason to annul this order of things. Naturally a problem arises here. Since honouring such an order of things requires faith in God's purpose and the preparedness to take up a way of life in which we relinquish any assertion of the self and follow Christ on the road of self-denial, it is easy to understand that the state holds legislation in this matter incompatible with principles the state applies at other times. But the Church must insist "that in coming to conclusions about the arrangement of the Office of the Pastors the point of departure must be the intrinsic nature of the Church as based in the Gospel" (A. Nygren).

19. *In this matter Christ's own actions and the directions given by Him were decisive for the Church.* Christ's relationship to women around Him is marked on the one hand by a superior freedom over against human ordinances and conventional rules. He makes a clean break with any degrading of the woman. All His dealings proclaim the similarity of all men. On the other hand there exists a dissimilarity of functions. Among the greatest of His disciples there are a number of women. They, too, followed Him on His journeys. But He does not entrust to them a special commission nor a place among those who are to hold office in the Church. He calls only men to be apostles and to them He entrusts the Missionary Command, the Proclamation of the Word, Baptism, the Lord's Supper and the Power of the Keys.

The office of the apostle is not as unique and as restricted to the original incumbents as some considerations in our day and age would acclaim. On the one hand it is surely the charge to be a witness of the Resurrection commissioned by Christ Himself. But on the other hand the office of the apostle gives rise to the Pastoral Office of proclamation. The great Missionary Command was given to the apostles. It applies to all peoples and extends to the end of time. Thus, the office of the apostle requires a continuation. It is overlooked all too often that on the one hand the New Testament itself bases the office responsible for leadership of the church and for proclamation on the apostles and on their authority; that on the other hand I Clement, a letter which on account of its early date (prior to 100 A.D.) is of unique historical value, expressly states that Jesus Himself gave precise instructions to His apostles how other proven men were to take over their duties once they died.

If we did not have the Letters of Paul, Jesus' choosing apostles and similar facts would hardly be conclusive. But the same would be true even of the work of reconciliation. Christ's work in our behalf is made comprehensible and is put into the proper light through the apostolic witness. Now, Christ's own actions and the manner in which the apostles continued His work form a unity without contradictions. It simply is not permissible to create a contrast here which is not present in the sources, for instance, by endowing Jesus' actions with intentions other than those which the apostles believed their Lord to have.

20. *To traditions we cannot attribute decisive significance.* Of course, there must be very cogent reasons to change a two-thousand-year-old tradition. Nevertheless, it can be done if it is merely a tradition. The Church is not bound to *traditiones humanae* (*Augsburg Confession* VII and XV).

But the matter is different when the traditions confirm that we have correctly interpreted the Scriptures. No one was in a better position to understand the New Testament linguistically and materially than the contemporaries of the apostles and their immediate successors. When we come upon a homogeneous tradition that reaches all the way back to their days, then this is *a very strong indication that a differing interpretation of the Scriptures cannot be right.*

21. *If we loyally hold to the Scriptures, then on the one hand we must say NO to the question of women pastors, on the other hand we must say YES to a utilization of women's abilities in the Church in a more intensive way than has been the practice up to now.* The New Testament presents to us a more comprehensive image than does church life in Sweden about the different gifts "in each of which the Spirit is manifested" and "which serve the common good of all" (I Cor. 12:7). A number of women are mentioned among those who with their gifts thus served the church.

Above all there is the gift of "prophecy". 1 Cor. 11:5 and Acts 21:9 consider it perfectly natural that a woman should have this gift. Prophecy is speech directly inspired by God. The prophet does not take His message from the Word but he received it through a revelation. In our churches prophecy is no longer a normal occurrence. Perhaps one reason is that now in its place we have the New Testament, and perhaps we find an indication of this development in I Cor. 13:8. But we must count on the recurrence of prophecy where and when God pleases. Something of the gift of prophecy can appear also in the Christian witness in daily life. When good, courageous women stand up and speak a clear Christian word as the individual situations may give opportunity, whether it be in the home, in the life in society, in sewing circles, on the job or wherever, then this can be on the same level as that to which the Bible refers as prophecy. The same can be true when a woman makes a presentation in a subject God has put very close to her heart, for example, Mission work. I will not undertake to draw the line in detail between such prophecy and Christian proclamation. I believe no man is in a position to do that. But the Bible does tell us that a line has been drawn and that the line cannot be redrawn at will, so that the Pastoral and Teaching Office ends up as one of those responsibilities which Christ entrusted also to His women disciples. It must further be considered that prophecy is not an office in the sense of being a commission entrusted through the church nor does a person possess prophecy as an ever on-going opportunity to serve.

But there also seem to have been occasions for such on-going service. In any case, we have indications of women "who shared the struggles in the cause of the Gospel" and who were "fellow-workers" of the apostle (Phil. 4:3) and who "toiled in the Lord's service" (Rom. 16:12). It is said of Phoebe that she was "a deaconess of the church at Cenchreae" and that "she has been of assistance to many", including the apostle himself (Rom. 16:1f.).

In any case, these indications prove that the early church made active use of the various talents of women.

22. *If it is our concern today to prepare the way for the expanded utilization of the talents of women in the Church, then we will have to take cognizance of the differences between the man and the woman and not disregard them.* An essential part of the New Testament position is the rich diversity in functions which is necessary because of the diversity of gifts. If the Office of the Pastor as office of preacher and church leader is not intended or designed for women, then it must be our concern to find such forms of service that do full justice to the differing gifts of the woman. Such forms of service must on the one hand satisfy the desire for fairness and offer the women thus working for the church an adequate salary; on the other hand they must coincide with the New Testament position in the belief that the working together of the different members works for the common good.

Among the Nordic churches the Church of Finland has probably made the most progress in this matter. In our country (Sweden) the request of the Synod of Bishops probably is the most carefully pondered and formulated request pointing in this direction.

23. *If there is serious disagreement in the Church about the proper course of action, then the Scriptures demand of us above all things to maintain two things inviolate: One is the unity of the Church, the other is loving regard for all serious qualms of conscience.*

a) *Unity.* It is probably sufficient to point to Jesus' high priestly prayer (John 17:21f.) and to the Apostle Paul's vehement intervention in the divisiveness at Corinth (I Cor. 1:10). Risking a division is always a most serious matter. This may become necessary when the concern is the purity of the Gospel, but when we are dealing with matters of order in the Church and propriety it is irresponsible.

b) *Regard for the conscience of others.* If some Christians are sincerely troubled by a certain matter so that they cannot participate without an injured conscience or are led by that into overpowering doubt and despair, then the New Testament admonishes us rather to leave the matter be than to insist on it, even though in and of itself the matter might be perfectly correct.

The early Christians had to take a position on a number of such problems. Was it permitted to consume blood, sacrificial meat or other things which for some were inextricably connected with paganism and idolatry? Was it permitted to drink wine? etc.

The answer can point in two opposite directions. When we are concerned with the basis of our salvation and if the consequence would be the reintroduction of the Law as the way of salvation, the New Testament speaks an unrelenting NO. "Not for one moment did I yield to their dictation; I was determined that the full truth of the Gospel should be maintained for you" (Gal. 2:5). But when the concern is matters of how to live, where faith in Christ and the will of commitment to Him have led people to different conclusions, there the New Testament equally openly asks us, as much as is possible, to have due regard for the conscience of the brethren. "Therefore if food be the downfall of my brother, I will never eat meat anymore, for I will not be the cause of my brother's downfall" (I Cor. 8:13; cf. all of Romans 14 as well as I Cor. 10:32–33).

These two aspects, the unity of the Church and regard for the conscience of others, ought to point the way for our Church particularly at this time. Perhaps the leaders of the Church, regardless of all differences of opinion, should arrive at complete unity and a program of action which is based on the experiences of the early Christians in their most difficult times of crises. In such a case it would be the message of mutual regard and love that would have to precede everything else. If I gauge the practical consequences correctly, the result would be that the Church with more deeply Biblical reasoning would insist that in this matter no decision be forcibly arrived at. The proposal of the Synod of Bishops, therefore, ought to be rejected. This does not mean that we all wish this rejection to be final. At the same time something ought to be done to create opportunities for the utilization of the talents of women in church positions, something the Synod of the Church has demanded previously. This must be achieved in such a way that all women can accept it, even those for whom the possibility of women pastors is unthinkable.

# The Ministry
# and the Ministry of Women

Peter Brunner

## Historic Lutheran Position

The question involved in our topic is one of those basic questions being raised with particular urgency within Christendom in this century. In the ancient church the question concerning the nature of the official service of women in the church was a very lively one, resulting from the necessary controversy with gnostic and heretical groups. The very complicated and, in its unfolding, almost tragic history of the orders for widows and deaconesses in the ancient church shows that a real question was involved here that had to be answered by an orderly ruling of the church. It must be deeply regretted that the revival of the deaconess order in the 19th century concerned itself very insufficiently with the ancient church's concern for the ministry of women and that it in no way led to a well-founded theological restatement of the office of the ministry of women in the church. Therefore we have no established living tradition that effectively deals with the ministry of women that we can cite as a guide in our present attempts to solve the problem raised by our topic. This renders a solution extraordinarily difficult.

In connection with their changing social status, an increasing number of women have undertaken the study of theology since World War I. Between the first and second world wars, their employment in the service of many of the *Landeskirchen* in Germany was regulated by church law. Although the various regulations differed greatly from one another, they were all in agreement on one point—the office of pastor was not open to women. During World War II, however, emergency situations made it necessary for women to conduct worship services and lead congregations, thus raising anew the question of "women and the pastoral office" with particular emphasis on its doctrinal and canonical aspects.

The problem acquired almost dramatic proportions during the events of the 1950s in Sweden, of which Sten Rohde reported in the journal *Lutherische Rundschau* (March 1958 and 1959). To what degree the Danish *volkskirche*, in which ordained women are already serving, is disturbed by this problem is evidenced by the controversy between three Danish pastors, Regin Prenter, and Bishop Høgsbro.[1] In the United Evangelical-Lutheran Church of Germany the question also flared up again since one of its member churches, the Church of Lübeck, in a ruling of September 1, 1958, provided a position in the *Landeskirche* for a ministry to women outside of the individual congregations, which position should be filled by a woman theologian.[2] The problematic behind this pastorate roots in the fact that she, alongside her other duties, has also been assigned to a local congregation in which she must conduct services of worship. It is well known that in churches of the Reformed tradition and in the Free Churches, women have been serving as pastors of parishes for some time now, and lately within the Anglican Church the question whether women can be ordained to the priesthood has been raised and supported with serious theological arguments.[3] Only within the Roman Catholic and the Eastern Orthodox churches is the position unquestionably maintained that women cannot be ordained to the priesthood.

If we look to the confessional standards of the Evangelical Lutheran Church, we find that they do not express themselves on the problem of the ordination of women to the pastoral ministry. They do not cite the ordinance in 1 Cor. 14:34ff. and 1 Tim. 2:11, which prohibits women from teaching in the church. Without doubt, the confessions are referring to men when they talk about pastors and bishops. The functions of these ministers are based on the commission with which Christ called His disciples and include the following: the preaching of the Gospel, the administration of the sacraments, the conferring of absolution, the rejection of false doctrine, and the excommunication of the ungodly. In this sense the office of the pastor or the bishop derives from that of the apostles, as the confessions explicitly state. On the other hand, the spiritual office under the new covenant is no longer a Levitical priesthood; it is also not bound to particular sacred places or holy persons. Instead "it is scattered throughout the world"; it is there where God has granted His spiritual gifts (according to Eph. 4:7): apostles, prophets, pastors, and teachers. Furthermore, one must remember that the church must have additional orders that do not directly derive from the above-mentioned functions of the pastoral office instituted by divine commission. These orders serve that "everything be done in good order." According to the Augsburg

---

1   *Kvinden og Kirckens Embede* (Copenhagen: Nyt Nordisk Forlag—Amold Busck, 1958).

2   *Amtsblatt der Vereinigten Evangelisch-Lutherischen Kirche*, I, 13 (July 15, 1959).

3   M. E. Thrall, *The Ordination of Women to the Priesthood* (London: 1958).

Confession, the regulation by St. Paul in 1 Cor. 11:5, that women should cover their heads with a headpiece or a veil when the congregation assembles for worship, and the instruction in 1 Cor. 14:30, that the preachers in the worship service should not all talk at the same time but in an orderly fashion one after the other, are examples of such orders.[4] Such orders are to be observed for the sake of "the love of peace," so that no one offends his brother and that everything in the church may be done in good order.[5]

When one turns to the confessional standards for an answer to the question whether or not women should be ordained to the pastoral ministry, an answer is only possible by drawing theological conclusions from them. These conclusions can be drawn, however, in various directions. If one starts from the proposition that it pleased God in Jesus Christ to trust men exclusively with the public exercise of the pastoral functions because He called only the apostles, then one can also say: the church today must take these circumstances, which do not allow for further deduction, into account and must refuse to appoint women either as pastors or as bishops.[6] On the other hand, if one starts from the proposition that the pastoral office under the new covenant is no longer considered in the "Levitic" sense but is dependent solely on the gift of the exalted Lord and in the last analysis finds its legitimization in the content of its Gospel, then one can come to the conclusion that, "from the nature of the office itself as it is described here [in the confessional books], there is no ground for the exclusion of women."[7] Starting from the concept of order and peace, one can arrive at directly opposite conclusions. There is no question but that the investiture of women with the pastoral office and the office of bishop has created a new set of circumstances serving to separate the Lutheran churches on the one side from the Roman Catholic and Orthodox churches on the other. The practice of the Lutheran Reformation of the 16th century had at this point initiated no change from that of these two church groups, as has been done by the actions in the Scandinavian countries and in Lübeck. Is this obvious widening of the gulf really necessary? Will it serve the cause of peace? On the other hand, one can ask whether the ordination of women is not necessitated by genuine needs within the Lutheran churches themselves and therefore is serving the cause of peace and the upbuilding of congregations, while the retention of the Reformation practice is a symptom

---

4   Notice that there is no reference to 1 Cor. 14:34f. in this connection!

5   Cf. Augsburg Confession and Apology XXVIII, and Treatise on the Power and Primacy of the Pope.

6   Along this line Regin Prenter has made some important observations in *Kvinden og Kirckens Embede*. Cf. there pp. 56ff. and p. 126.

7   Fritz Zerbst, Das Amt der Frau in der Kirche (Vienna: n.d. [1951?]), p. 78 (trans. Albert G. Merkens, *The Office of Woman in the Church* [St. Louis: Concordia Publishing House, 1955], p. 106).

of the kind of conservatism that must be avoided as much as possible because of the offense it gives to many in our contemporary situation. But experience has shown that just the opposite situation also exists, that the ordination of women has given offense, perhaps dogmatically ill-founded offense. But the offense the Roman Christians at the time of St. Paul took to the eating of meat was also ill-founded; in fact, their objections represented much more a rejection of the ideal of freedom found in the Gospel, and yet Paul took them into account in his instructions to the church at Rome. This train of thought also leads to no clear and obvious conclusions.

Let us turn in our question to Luther himself. He expressed himself on this subject on many occasions and in many contexts, and yet his conviction about it remained basically unchanged.[8] Already the first rather lengthy exposition on *De abroganda missa privata* (1521) contains his basic position.[9] To all Christians is given the full power to preach the Gospel, but not all Christians exercise this right in its fullness. Many can (*posse*) make no use of this full power, because they lack the necessary natural abilities, as, for example, the dumb lack the ability to speak, etc. Others do not dare exercise it (*non tamen . . . debere exequi*). Therefore women are not allowed to preach in the assemblies of the congregation even though the spiritual power has been bestowed on them. The determining factor for Luther is the aptitude of the individual, and here the difference between man and woman is important. The man is in many ways (*multis modis*) more adapted to speaking than is the woman, and it seems more fitting and proper for him to speak. The instructions the Holy Spirit gives in the Scriptures and the works He performs in the church correspond to this point of view, although, to be sure, the Holy Spirit had promised through the prophet Joel that women will also be able to prophesy, and furthermore we actually do have the account of the four virgin daughters of Philippus, who prophesied in the Acts of the Apostles. Miriam, Moses' sister, was a prophetess (Ex. 15:20); the prophetess Huldah preached the Word of God to the pious king Josiah (2 Kings 22:14ff.), and Deborah counseled the male chieftain Barak (Judg. 4:6). Yes, to this very day the Virgin Mary speaks to the church in the entire world through her *Magnificat*. Despite all this, the command of St. Paul in 1 Cor. 14:34 that women keep silent, not under all circumstances, but in the congregational assemblies, is in keeping with the work of the Holy Spirit. In the Law, the Holy Spirit had subordinated the woman to the man. If the Holy Spirit were to allow women to preach in the congregational services, He would be contradicting His own work in the Law

---

8    Cf. Heinz Brunotte, *Die Befugnisse der Vikarin, in Evangelisch-lutherische Kirchenzeitung (ELKZ)*, 10 (1956), pp. 411ff.

9    *D. Martin Luthers Werke: Kritische Gesamtausgabe* (Weimar: Hermann Böhlau, 1883–; hereafter referred to as WA), 8, 424,20–425,6; in the same place, in the German edition, 497,19–498,14.

by raising the woman above the man, but this is absolutely impossible because the Spirit does not contradict Himself (*spiritus sibi ipsi non contradicit*). This position that the Holy Spirit has assigned to the woman in her relationships with man according to the Scriptures is the reason why women are not fit to be called to the public exercise of the pastoral office. If women were to speak in the congregation where men are present, as in the church in Corinth, then both *ordo* and *honestas* would be upset, and both of these in Luther's view are definitely subject to the working of the Spirit. It is his conviction that as long as there are men in the congregation, the Spirit will much sooner come on them and inspire them to preach than He will to women. Certainly, if the situation would arise in which there are no available men, then it would be necessary for women to preach.

In later years Luther reemphasized the obligatory nature of the Pauline command to silence in his controversy with the enthusiasts (*Schwärmer*). His comments in the writing *Von Schleichern und Winkelpredigern* (1532)[10] are very interesting. Here he offers to the "Anabaptists" an argument they could have used to their own advantage as support for their conception of the charismatic calling and rights of laymen: the Scriptural proof that in both the Old and New Testaments women at times proclaimed the Word of God to men. To those figures whom he had already mentioned in 1521 he now adds the "wise woman" of the city of Abel (2 Sam. 20:16ff.) and Sarah, who ordered her "lord and master" to drive out Ishmael and his mother, a command that bore important consequences for the history of the salvation of God's people and was confirmed by God in that Abraham was commanded to obey it. He also includes the prophetess Anna in Luke 2 in the circle of women possessing charismatic gifts. With these references, the anabaptists could have "decorated" themselves and on their authority given women the right to preach in the church. Luther is not interested in investigating further "what right these women in the Old Testament had to teach and to rule," but he does emphasize that they did not do so without being called, that is, neither as a result of their own reflections nor on the basis of their own pietistic impulses.[11] The evidence for the legitimacy of the teaching and governing of these women he finds in the fact that God substantiated their ministry and work with miracles and great deeds. In this connection Luther speaks about the Pauline command to keep silent which was clearly inspired by the Holy Spirit.[12] Through St. Paul the Holy Spirit Himself determines the role that women are to play in

---

10   WA 30 III, 524,10ff.

11   According to Luther the prophetic call is something else than a *vocatio interna*; it is not a "feeling of having been called."

12   Also in the writing *Von Konziliis und Kirche*, 1539, WA 50, 633, 12ff.: The Holy Spirit has excluded women, children, and incapable people from the office of preaching.

the worship services—they are to keep silent, that is, they are not to preach. This command, declares Paul, is the command of the Lord.[13] As for the rest, women can and should "pray, sing, praise and say Amen, and read and teach one another in the household, admonishing, comforting, and also expounding the Holy Scriptures" as well as they possibly can.

Thus Luther had a very unequivocal answer to the question whether or not women should be called to the pastoral office, which can be summarized under the following points:

1. All Christians have the spiritual power to proclaim the Word of God, and that includes women.

2. In the assembled congregation, only he may preach the Word who has been called to do so by the church.

3. Only he may be called who has the ability.

4. In determining whether one possesses the ability, spiritual and natural factors must be considered.

5. The subordination of the woman to the man, as has been established in the Old Testament, has not been revoked in the New Testament; rather it has been substantiated by the Holy Spirit through the pronouncements of the apostles.[14]

6. The Holy Spirit would contradict Himself if He allowed women to preach in the services of the congregation as long as there were men present whom he has inspired thereto.

7. The *ordo*, which must be here maintained, has a spiritual character; it is the work of the Holy Spirit. The moral attitude that corresponds to this *ordo* is propriety. Neither the *ordo* nor its corresponding sense of propriety dare be violated.

---

13 It is inconceivable how the editor could surmise in the Weimar Edition 8, 524, Anm. 3, that Luther is here referring to 1 Cor. 7:10 where Paul supports his instructions with a clear directive of the Lord concerning women. There is no question that Luther had 1 Cor. 14:37 in mind, which he translated in all editions of his German Bible in the following manner: "So sich jemand lässet dünken, er sei ein Prophet oder Geistlich, der erkenne, was ich euch schreibe, Denn es sind des Herrn Gebot" (If any man think himself to be a prophet or spiritual, let him acknowledge that what I write are the commandments of the Lord). See *WA Deutsche Bibel* 7, 128 and 129. Luther read the text of the Koine version, which the Vulgate also renders: . . . *quia Domini sunt mandata*. In WA 30 III, 524, 29, Luther relates this turn of expression to the preceding command to silence and in this manner arrives at the singular, which is in fact offered in the Egyptian version and is taken up by Nestle. See footnote 27.

14 See also WA 50, 633, 20ff., where Luther says that "even nature and God's creation" prove that women can and should have no authority. Experience and God's word—Gen. 3:16—go hand in hand here. "The Gospel does not contradict natural law but confirms it as God's order and creation."

8. As long as the presupposition holds true that there are men present whom the Holy Spirit has inspired to preach, it is not proper for the woman to be called to exercise publicly the pastoral office.

9. One can safely assume that the Holy Spirit, in keeping with his directives in the Holy Scriptures, will see to it that capable men are not lacking. Should this unusual circumstance nevertheless prevail,[15] then—but only then—must women also preach in the services of the congregation.[16]

The loftiness of Luther's point of view was not shared by the fathers of Lutheran orthodoxy. The question why men and not women should preach in the church was discussed by them as part of the adiaphora problem, on which the interim had placed such emphasis. In 1549 the ministerium of Hamburg requested the faculty of the University of Wittenberg to clarify certain questions concerning secondary matters (*Mitteldinge*), whereby it was clear just what the clergymen of Hamburg considered as adiaphora, such as the custom that men can pray with uncovered heads while women must cover theirs, that men and not women are allowed to preach, and that the organ can be used in worship, among others.[17] Flacius, in his treatise *De veris et falsis adiaphoris*, publicly supports the opinions of the Hamburg clergy. The fact that men are allowed to speak in church and women are not is a ruling that cannot be supported by a divine command (*jus divinum*). As an order of human law (*juris humanum*) it is subject to the judgment of the church, though certainly not to arbitrary choice. Even the adiaphora of the Hamburg clergy were subject to an ethical norm, namely the principle of what is best for the building up of the congregation. Therefore the particular forms of church order that exist dare not contradict "what is generally considered to be proper and decent."[18]

---

15 Besides WA 8, 424, 37, see also WA 10, III, 171, 10: "Were it to come to this (which I do not intend) that no man were present, but only vain women, then a woman must step up and preach to the others, otherwise not."

16 Heinz Brunotte (see footnote 8) does not do justice to the importance of this basic principle of Luther's in his interpretation of the text in question. The fact that Luther considered the Pauline command to silence a work of the Holy Spirit, and, to be sure, a work of the Spirit who does not contradict Himself, is not considered by Brunotte. Therefore he does not sufficiently bring out the spiritual character of the "order" as one God has established. He overemphasizes Luther's dependence on the times and underestimates his dependence on the Biblical text. He overlooks the fact that one can neither dogmatically nor according to canon law achieve the situation here presented through the *schema* "*de jure divino—de jure humano.*"

17 See Paul Fleisch, *Ein Wort aus der Reformationzeit zu den Befugnissen der Vikarin*, in *ELKZ* 9 (1955), pp. 396ff. I have also taken the statements concerning Flacius from this article. One must take note how, in contrast to Augsburg Confession XXVIII, 54, the apostle's command to silence is without hesitation placed on the same level as the command concerning headcoverings and is seen as a simple question of church order.

18 Formulation according to Paul Fleisch, ibid.

Respectability and propriety are the standards that give men precedence over women in calling them to fill the offices of the church. Flacius sees this decision of the church on much the same level as the fact that mornings were chosen over evenings as the proper time of day for worship services, and that the services were begun with a worthy and modest hymn. The standard that determines respectability is obviously the general cultural attitude rather than the relationship between man and woman as it is ordered by the Holy Spirit.

The arguments Johann Gerhard presents in his *Locus XXIII* under No. 186 also fail to match the insights of Luther.[19] He understands the instructions of St. Paul that explicitly (*disertis verbis*) deny women the right to hold the preaching office in the church as a necessary reaction to the matriarchal tendencies of various heretical sects of the time, which are described in the writings of the church fathers. To be sure, there were a few women in the Old Testament who, in a very extraordinary manner, were equipped with prophetic gifts. Furthermore, Christ Himself told the women to bring the disciples the news of His resurrection, and one of the apostles even calls a woman, Priscilla, "his fellow-worker in the Lord." But no one dare conclude from this that women are to occupy the regular preaching office in the church except in cases of emergency (*extra necessitatis casum*). What constitutes such an emergency is, however, not explained. When Paul calls Phoebe a "minister" of the church at Cenchreae, he is not referring here to the public office of preaching but to the charitable ministries such as the care of the sick, the poor, and the strangers. At any rate, pious women can instruct their families and their households in the faith; in fact, it is their duty to do so. The reasons Gerhard gives for the apostolic command to silence are very heavily influenced by the anything-but-flattering judgments of the church fathers.[20] Of theological value is only the thought that Gerhard derives from Paul himself, that the woman is subordinated to the man. The moral attitude that derives from this principle is characterized by Gerhard in the concepts of "reserve" (*verecundia*) and "humility" (*humilitas*), which he uses to elucidate the Biblical concept of "hypotage." The practice of women preaching in church runs counter to the order of nature and to the Law (Gen. 3:16), which demand reserve and humility of the woman; therefore it was forbidden by Paul.

This short survey shows us that any attempt to clarify the relationship of women to the office of the ministry on theological grounds places a new

---

19  See the edition of the *Loci* by Ed. Preuss, Part VI (Berlin, 1868), pp. 125ff.

20  With Chrysostom he would like to restrict the *loquacitas, quae in hoc sexu fere nimia est*. With Epiphanius he does not trust the discriminatory faculties of women; in fact, he does not think much of their intellectual abilities at all and certainly not of their ability to carry on a logical discussion. With Anselm he agrees that it is quite in order for Paul to forbid women the right to speak, because where she did speak (in Paradise) she persuaded her husband to sin.

task before us. The declarations of the confessional standards do not give us a ready answer; rather we must, through our own theological reflection, arrive at a solution along the lines they have staked out. The assertion that the Holy Spirit has solved our problem for all time through the admonitions of the apostle can be neither the beginning nor the end of our deliberations. According to evangelical doctrine, there is no final form of church order that can be Biblically or legalistically maintained for all time. This is made unequivocally clear by the fact that in this connection contemporary Christendom has passed over St. Paul's admonition to the Corinthian women that they must keep their heads covered in church. The matter with which Paul concerns himself in 1 Cor. 11:2–11 is undoubtedly of great importance. With an extraordinary display of theological acumen, Paul is trying to make clear to the women in Corinth: You are and remain women in the worship services, and you dare not conduct yourselves as if you could take the place that God has accorded to men. The church in all ages must seek to preserve and to interpret this insight, but the situation in which it must be observed and interpreted today differs from that of Paul and the Corinthian women. No one today would think of correcting a Christian woman because she participates in the worship services or partakes of the Lord's Supper with her head uncovered. Could it possibly be that Paul's command to silence in 1 Cor. 14:34 is essentially the same as his admonitions concerning the covering of one's head in 1 Cor. 11:10 and therefore just as open to reinterpretation?

This attempt to solve the problem of the ordination of women to the ministry through our theological deliberations will involve great difficulties, because the question with which we are concerned involves many other problems about which there is no general consensus of opinion in the Lutheran churches today. Take, for instance, the question, What is the doctrine of the ministry that the church must teach today? Despite the intensive and heated controversy within the Lutheran churches of the 19th century, theological opinion differs greatly on this point.[21] Furthermore, there is the "hermeneutic" problem, which today includes the question of the authority of the Scriptures. What is the significance of the creation narratives in Genesis 1–3 for the proclamation of the Gospel? Can we make dogmatic use of this creation account in the manner in which Paul did in 1 Cor. 11:3–12 and obviously also in 1 Cor. 14:34? Can we relate the account of the fall to prohibition against women teaching in the church as is done in 1 Tim. 2:14? Is there in this passage a judaistic conception of the woman that we must reject in the light of the Gospel?

---

21  For my own treatment of the ministry see my essay *Vom Amt des Bischofs, in Schriften des theologischen Konventes Augsburgischen Bekenntnisses*, Book 9 (Berlin, 1955), pp. 5–77, and *Das Heil und das Amt in Lutherische Nachrichten*, Vol. 7, No. 40/41 (1959), pp. 4–26.

Above all else, we must take into account the theological doctrine of the sexual difference between man and woman. It is extremely necessary for the church to interpret this natural state doctrinally if she wants to present the message of the New Testament in a relevant fashion. She cannot be satisfied to borrow the insights of biology, psychology, philosophy, sociology, or medicine. Texts such as Eph. 5:22–33, Col. 3:18ff., and 1 Peter 3:1–7 show that the church must say something about what it means to be man or woman before God; it must say something that can be said by no one else in the world, because what it says is said in the light of its understanding of the Gospel. How is this to be said? What must be its content? It is my opinion that the question whether or not women should be ordained to the ministry depends on the theological doctrine of the nature and relationship between the God-given sexes.

Finally there is the question, to say nothing of many others, of the relationship between doctrine and church order. Certainly, one very important standard of measurement is already given in the distinction between that which must occur in the church *de jure divino* and that which is only *juris humani*. Certainly the principle that in the building up of the congregation orderliness and propriety are essential is valid in those things for which no direct divine imperative is evident. But are these standards and perspectives sufficient? The *Kirchenkampf* in Germany has shown us that the questions concerning church order are much more interrelated with the message of the church than was generally conceded to be the case in Protestantism. The Barmen Declaration of 1934 declared that the Christian church "with her faith as well as with her obedience, with her message as well as with her order" must witness that she belongs to Christ.[22] To be sure, this formulation, and in particular the little word *as*, needs some explanation to clarify specifically the relationship between faith and obedience, message and order, and protect it from misunderstanding. But the principle that the order of the church cannot stand in contradiction to her Gospel is one of the fundamental insights of the Lutheran Reformation. The Barmen Declaration was right when it labeled the opinion "that the church could leave the form of her message and her order up to her pleasure or to the changes in the then prevailing philosophical and political perspectives" as a heresy. It is obvious that this statement is of considerable importance to our discussion. Could it not be possible that the laws that provide for the ordination of women to the ministry in Denmark and Sweden rest on a general philosophy of life that has its roots in the Enlightenment and in the Idealism of the 19th century? Through which order does the church truly give witness that she is bound to Christ and to

---

22  See the text by Kurt Dietrich Schmidt, *Die Bekenntnisse und grundsätzliche Äusserungen zur Kirchenfrage*, Vol. 2, *Das Jahr 1934* (Göttingen, 1935), p. 94.

His Gospel, through the ordination of women to the ministry or through the prohibition thereof?[23]

Because of the many complex theological problems involved in our theme and in the light of their great difficulty, it cannot be expected that the following considerations will present an exhaustive treatment of the problem or that they will lead to a unanimously acceptable solution. It also cannot be expected that a general consensus of opinion concerning the problem under discussion will suddenly make its appearance in the Lutheran churches of the world. It cannot be denied, however, that it is a vital question for the Lutheran fellowship whether or not such a consensus will be granted her. Even though the question of the ordination of women to the ministry has been decided by church law in individual churches, yet the theological importance of this decision has not been settled. It is still open to discussion whether an order that makes this allowance may not stand in direct contradiction to the content of the apostolic proclamation of the Gospel and therefore must be rejected as an heretical order. We must not draw any hasty conclusions; instead we must exercise great patience. But above all, we must not close our eyes to the importance of this problem. With this word of introduction we are ready to begin our investigation, wherein we must first of all explain what we understand by the ministry.

## BIBLICAL ANALYSIS OF MINISTRY

The church in all ages stands under the commission of her Lord to preach the Gospel to all peoples and to administer the sacraments that He has instituted. This command takes two forms. In the first place, this commission of the Lord is addressed to each member of the church, who thereby has a share in the proclamation of the Word and the administration of the sacraments and is thus under obligation to make use of them. This he can do to the degree in which he is gifted and within the limits of the opportunities and possibilities that are opened up to him. The second way in which the church fulfills her divine commission is by calling individual members who are capable, and

---

23  Fr. Zerbst well recognized the close connection between the content of the proclamation and the order of the church as they are involved in our question when he wrote, for example: "The church cannot allow its ministers to contradict the content of their message by their personal lives. Therefore she demands from each member of the body of Christ conduct in keeping with His Word. In regard to the calling of women to the ministry, it must be carefully considered whether entrusting the woman with the proclamation of the Gospel and the administration of the sacraments does not cancel out the proclamation of the church concerning her position according to the creation. First of all, it is decisive for our problem to discover what the church as such teaches about the position of the woman and then whether this doctrine must not also find expression in the ordering of the church's ministries." (*Das Amt der Frau*, p. 80 [Merkens, *Office of Woman*, p. 109])

entrusting to them the task of proclaiming the Gospel and administering the sacraments through ordination by prayer and the laying on of hands.

The opportunities for the proclamation of the Gospel and administration of the sacraments that are open to every member of the church are the following: (1) personal missionary witness in the individual's social context; (2) personal confession of faith whether it be in the sphere of one's private life or before the civic authorities as in times of persecution; (3) the instruction in the household by mother and father; (4) daily devotions in the home; (5) the encouragement of the penitent that they are forgiven in the *mutua consolatio fratrum*; (6) the congregational proclamation of the Gospel in the services of worship through songs, psalms, hymns, and praise; (7) the administration of the sacrament of Baptism in emergencies; (8) the participation in the sacrament of the Lord's Supper and in the proclamation of Christ's death that it involves; (9) when a Christian finds himself in a place where there are no other Christians, he is challenged in a particularly new and urgent way to bear missionary witness to his faith. He must then pray that this witness will find as wide a reception as possible, and he must conduct himself as if he were sent to this place as a missionary by a congregation.

The church would disobey the command of her Lord if she only sought to propagate the faith by the first means. Therefore she must do more; she must formally commission individual members with the task of proclaiming the Gospel and administering the sacraments through a historical act, ordaining them and sending them out as messengers of Jesus Christ. This "must" is a divine imperative and dare not be based on the mere fact that it is expedient for the church. This calling, commissioning, and sending out was instituted by the risen Lord with the same words with which He called His apostles.

The office into which the individual is installed by such a call, commissioning, and sending takes two forms, which are interrelated and cannot be sharply distinguished from each other. The first form is that of the missionary who is sent to work among the heathen, the second is that of the pastor who is called to a congregation confined to one specific place. Without missionaries there could be no pastors. In this respect the missionary form of the office of the ministry is the basic one. In the exercise of his office, the missionary always has as his goal that the acceptance of the Gospel in faith and the administration of the sacrament of Baptism will result in the establishment of a local congregation. In this respect, the pastoral form of the office of the ministry is the ultimate one.

But even the pastor, within the confines of the place where he exercises his office, remains a missionary among those in his locality who do not yet believe. In like manner, the missionary as soon as he has baptized and remains among those baptized becomes a pastor, just as the pastor dare not forget that for a given locale he is also a missionary. Therefore we can speak about the missionary ministry.

This ministry will change its historical character from time to time and from place to place. Think, for instance, of the great change that the historical form of the ministry underwent in the time of the Reformation, to say nothing at all about the changes that occurred between the time of the Pastoral Epistles and the Reformation! But despite all these changes, the missionary ministry must by its very nature, that is, by virtue of its divine commission, *de jure divino*, include the following tasks, rights, and powers, which characterize the *ministerium ecclesiasticum* in its fullness: (1) the public proclamation of the Gospel throughout the world; (2) the instruction of those desiring to be baptized; (3) the granting or withholding of Baptism, the admitting to or excluding from the congregation and the Lord's Supper; (4) the preaching of the Gospel and administration of the sacraments in the assembled congregation; (5) the preservation of the apostolic teaching, which is the norm for all preaching and teaching, and the rejection of heresy, which seeks to attack or destroy this norm; (6) the excommunication of heretics or those who persist in wrongdoing; (7) the bestowal of absolution on those who in penitence have confessed their sins and who in faith desire to be forgiven and, if necessary, the renewed granting of Christian fellowship following the revocation of the excommunication; (8) the direction of the local church through the Word of God in all areas, especially conducting the church's services of worship, exercising the care of souls in its variety of forms, and the careful, responsible direction of the charitable activities of the church, everything that is included in the New Testament concept *episkopein*; (9) the responsibility for the transmission of the apostolic teaching and the pastoral office to the future generations; (10) the preservation and promotion of fellowship with the other apostolic churches, particularly with those who are "neighbors."

None of these functions can really be fulfilled by the pastor without the assistance of the members of the congregation, whether to a greater or lesser degree. The pastoral office is embedded in the many-sided charismatic ministries within the church, and it can only be fulfilled in conjunction with them. In order to strengthen one or the other of these functions, it is possible to divide responsibilities and create regular church offices besides that of the pastor, such as that of the catechist or that of the deacon, who in a very special way takes over the care of the poor and those in need; or perhaps the responsibility for the discipline within the congregation can be shared with a group of the elders. Many other forms of assistance are possible. It is also conceivable that one function of the pastoral office deliberately be given up, in case it is to be exercised by another pastor whom human law places in a superior position. Such functions are the calling and ordaining of candidates to the ministry, the imposing and revoking of the ban of excommunication, or the control over special services within the congregations. This in no way alters the fact that the tasks, rights, and powers summed up in these 10 points are included in the pastoral office by virtue of the original commission of Christ; they are not derived from the general priesthood of all believers, nor are they assumed by the pastor in the place of the faithful; instead they derive directly from the commission of the risen Lord, and only in the pastoral office do they find their fullest expression.

The Lord has reserved for Himself still a third method by which He can give His Word to mankind: the awakening of prophets. The prophet is exclusively and directly called to his prophetic ministry by God and not by men. It is impossible for the church to "ordain" one of its members to be a prophet. One either has the gift of prophecy or one does not have it—somewhat like the gift of healing. Aside from praying that it might appear, the church can do nothing to promote this gift. Over against this, in the specific sense of the word *charismatic*, the church has the duty to test these spirits wherever they may appear, and then either to acknowledge the charismatic gifts and those who possess them as genuine through her amen or to expose the pseudo-prophets and warn against them. The question as it now stands is this: Can the theologically trained women be installed in the missionary ministry as we have here described it by being called, commissioned, and sent through prayer and the laying on of hands?

## PLACE OF WOMAN IN THE CHURCH

It is beyond dispute in the Christian church that the woman, as a Christian, can lay claim to the selfsame opportunities for the preaching of the Gospel and the administration of the sacraments that are open and available to every other member of the church, as we have described them above. The woman is not a member of the congregation with lesser rank. In regard to the reception of the Holy Ghost and His gifts the woman, as woman, is in no way prejudiced against, since she is just as much a member of the body of Christ as is the man. According to Gal. 3:27–28: "For as many of you as have been baptized into Christ have put on Christ. There is neither Jew nor Greek, there is neither bond nor free, there is neither male nor female; for ye are all one in Christ Jesus." The human and historical differences that exist between people are no longer walls of division in Christ Jesus. In regard to the implanting in Christ, in regard to the sonship that is given through Christ, in regard to the promised inheritance and the reception of the Holy Spirit and His gifts, there is no difference between the baptized man and the baptized woman who live by faith in the Gospel. But this, however, does not eliminate the fact that there are various ministries in the church, even such differences in ministries, for which the very fact of being man or being woman, which state is certainly not eradicated by Baptism, can under certain circumstances be of great importance.[24]

In what has just been said it is recognized that the gift of prophecy may also be given to women. The prophecy in Joel 3, which was fulfilled on Pentecost, gives Scriptural evidence thereof. It cannot be disputed that there were women in the apostolic age who preached as prophetesses in the churches, but yet one can notice that the prophetic activity of women is more or less restricted in the New Testament writings for reasons we shall not go into at the moment. Concentrating our attention on the prophetesses of the primitive church will serve of no practical value in seeking a solution to our problem, since the ministry of the prophetess, just as that of the prophet, has its origin exclusively and directly in the inspiration of God the Holy Spirit, without any call, commission, or installation at the hands of man. Our question, however, concerns itself with just this point: whether women should thus be called, commissioned, and installed by the church into the office of the missionary ministry. In order to answer this question we will have to consider the two New Testament passages that have a bearing on the subject.

The meaning of 1 Tim. 2:11–15 is obvious: "Let the woman learn in silence with all subjection. But I suffer not a woman to teach nor to usurp authority over the man, but to be in silence. For Adam was first formed, then Eve. And Adam was not deceived, but the woman being deceived was in the transgression. Notwithstanding she shall be saved in childbearing, if they continue in faith and charity and holiness with sobriety."

---

24 Therewith we touch on the basic question around which, in the last analysis, Paul's controversy with the Corinthian women turned and which is also the central question on which the ordination of women hinges today. We agree here with Fr. Zerbst. For him also the deciding factor rests in the theological determination of the relationship between man and woman in the orders of creation and redemption. In the present-day discussion of our problem he takes seriously those theological observations "which set the order of creation over against the order of redemption in such a manner that the former is obviated and superseded by the latter. When the sacramental and pneumatic aspects are stressed as decisive, then the order of creation appears legalistic, pre-Christian, and irrelevant. The eschatological breakthrough of the kingdom of God cancels out the Law and all ties on this earth and makes it possible for the kingdom to be realized here and now. Grounded in this kind of view are both the Corinthian theology and Liberalism; Montanism as well as the enthusiastic sects throughout the history of the church which maintain a strong eschatological orientation, the theological kingdom of God optimism as well as more recent New Testament-type conceptions, which so overestimate the enthusiastic, eschatological side of the New Testament, that all earthly ties just disappear in contrast to it. After what has been said in our above discussion it is not necessary for a detailed presentation, but it must be stressed that such attempts at a theological solution are neither justified on the basis of the New Testament nor are they systematically tenable." (*Das Amt der Frau*, p. 88 [Merkens, *Office of Woman*, pp. 118–119])

The following observations are significant: Under teaching the apostle here understands, as one can already infer from the connection with the previous instructions concerning the correct conduct of the woman in worship, the public teaching in the congregation assembled for worship, that is, what we would nowadays call "preaching." This activity is forbidden the woman, just because she is a woman, in a very solemn manner since it is written in the style used for formal decrees. The reason given for this prohibition points to the order that God Himself had established at the creation: first the man and then the woman. Furthermore it refers to the different roles that man and woman played in the story of the fall. Both of these events of the protohistory, the creation and the fall, determine the status of contemporary woman, even the woman who is a Christian. The attitude that can be summed up in the concept "subject to" (*hypotage*) is seemly for her. The subjection demanded of her runs counter to the act of preaching in public. When a woman preaches in the worship services, she steps out of the role of subordination that is demanded of her and assumes by that act official authority over the man. Thus such preaching is a presumptuous abandonment of the *ordo* (*taxis*) in which even the Christian woman is placed by creation and the fall. Therefore the woman should not preach in the worship services.

One cannot doubt the general meaning of this text, even though individual points may lend themselves to variations of interpretation.[25] Much more difficult are the exegetical problems involved in 1 Cor. 14:33b–36: "As in all churches of the saints: Let your women keep silence in the churches; for it is not permitted unto them to speak; but they are commanded to be under obedience, as also saith the Law. And if they will learn anything, let them ask their husbands at home; for it is a shame for women to speak in the church. What! Came the Word of God out from you, or came it unto you only?" The following verses, 37 and 38, must be seen in the context of the entire chapter, and yet they have a bearing on the above passage.[26] Therefore we must consider them here. "If any man think himself to be a prophet, or spiritual, let him acknowledge that the things that I write unto you are the commandments of the Lord.[27] But if any man be ignorant, let him be ignorant."

---

25 These variations center mainly around the meaning of the word *authentein*, but they do not alter the general sense of the passage.

26 Concerning the question of the original position of verses 34 and 35, see footnote 29.

27 The written manuscript preferred by the exegetes reads: ". . . that that, which I write, is from the Lord." This says nothing more than our translation of the text. The variation between command in the singular and commandments in the plural is also unimportant for the meaning of the text. The plural "commandments" makes it easier to understand this text in relationship to the entire chapter. Should this not also be the case with the phrase "from the Lord"? If so, it would be in this, that an explicit command of Jesus preserved in the tradition (such as 1 Cor. 7:10) is certainly not at hand for the apostle's instructions in this chapter.

When we consider this passage only in the context of chapter 14 of 1 Corinthians, it raises no exegetical difficulties worth mentioning; Paul bids the women to keep completely still in the assemblies of the congregation. He forbids them the right to talk, even if it be merely to ask questions arising from this or that sermon or prophecy or revelation that is being presented to the congregation. When he commands them to be silent and forbids their talking in general, he is at the same time denying them the right to prophesy, the regulation of which plays an important part in this chapter. The exegetical problem in this text is this: In 1 Cor. 11:2–16, Paul presupposes that the woman can pray and prophesy in the services of worship of the congregation. There he only demands that she keep her head covered, and he seems to have nothing against her praying and prophesying[28] if she obeys this regulation. How can he then demand that women keep silent in general and completely forbid their preaching and teaching as he does in 1 Corinthians 14?

As far as I know there is no solution to this exegetical problem that is completely convincing. There are several proposals that are not convincing. One such is the proposal that verses 33b–36 are to be stricken as a later interpolation that originated in connection with 1 Tim. 2:11–15. This thesis was first proposed by Semmler (d. 1791). It was initially well received at the beginning of the century but is now held less often.[29] The conjecture that the prophesying and praying of women reported in 1 Corinthians 11 was meant in the context of the home rather than the church is even less convincing. Others are of the opinion that the speaking that Paul forbids in 1 Corinthians 14 is exclusively bound up with v. 35: women are not to interrupt the sermons, prophecies, and revelations of men. The most common interpretation, however, is that Paul forbids women the right to preach but not the right to prophesy under the direct influence of the Holy Spirit, because this is something over which he has no jurisdiction. Nevertheless, he does try to order the direct activity of the Spirit: those who speak in tongues are commanded to keep silence when no interpreter is present (v. 28). Not more than two, or at the most three, who speak in tongues should be heard at any one congregational assembly (v. 27); therefore others present must keep silent. One possessed of charismatic gifts is requested to interrupt his preaching if anyone else suddenly receives a revelation (v. 30). "The spirits of the prophets are subject to the prophets" is the basic principle to be followed. A prophet can therefore

---

28  It is no accident that v. 13 only speaks about prayer.

29  Recently the thesis that our verse is a later interpolation out of the year 110 has been advanced again by Joh. Leipoldt (*Die Frau in der antiken Welt und im Urchristentum* [Leipzig: 1954], pp. 190ff.) but without convincing reasons. The placing of vv. 34 and 35 after v. 40, as is done in various manuscripts, could have been prompted by the fact that v. 36 seems to fit directly after v. 33, while vv. 34 and 35 seem to disrupt the logical progression.

prohibit his spirit from expressing itself if it be necessary for the sake of the peace and harmony of the congregation. Thus, one can with good reason conclude that the apostle also sought to bid the spirits of the prophetesses to keep silence in the congregation.[30]

For our purposes, the question whether Paul in 1 Corinthians 14 forbade women to prophesy as well can, in view of the not-wholly-clear connection of our passage to 1 Cor. 11:2–16, remain open. Certainly Paul is forbidding women the right to that kind of preaching and teaching that depends on deliberate preparation, such as is characteristic of a sermon, in contrast to the spontaneous and inspired utterances of those who speak in tongues, of prophets, and of other charismatic personalities who depend on the immediate inspiration of the Holy Spirit.

## PLACE OF WOMAN IN CREATION

The really significant basis for the apostolic command to silence is the reference to the "subordination" (*Unterordnung*) that is demanded of the woman. Here our text and 1 Tim. 2:11 are in agreement. This subordination, with which we shall have to concern ourselves more thoroughly, is demanded by the Law and is also based expressly on the will of God. When Paul talks about the Law, he is thinking here about such passages as Gen. 3:16, where God says to the woman after the fall: "The man shall rule over you." But this concept of subordination is seen by Paul in a much larger context. If the command to be subject is based on the Law, then the story of the creation in Genesis 2 also belongs to the Law. A comparison with 1 Cor. 11:2–12 makes this clear.

It is not quite clear what standard St. Paul uses in judging the shamefulness of the conduct of the Corinthian women who spoke in the congregation. Quite often his instructions seem directly opposed to that which was the custom in the synagogue or in the Hellenistic world.[31] When seen in relationship to their day, the New Testament injunctions against women taking an active role in the congregation represent exactly a rejection of those practices that were current in the social surroundings. Thus it is not at all certain that Paul in this passage has taken as his standard one of the then prevailing value judgments as to what is decent and proper for a woman. It seems much more likely to me that the reason behind Paul's considering this kind of conduct as shameful is because it violates the express will of God, who demands such subordination. This will of God, which finds expression in the Law, is also

---

30  Ernst Käsemann made reference to these observations at a committee meeting of the Confessing Church during the Second World War.

31  In this way Paul decides against the Jewish custom in the question of covering the head. With the command to silence he separates the practice of the Christian congregation from the cultic practices found in Hellenistic religions and in Gnosticism.

in a sense written on the hearts of the heathen, so that a "natural" feeling of propriety plays a role in determining what is or is not shameful; but it by no means provides the real basis from which the apostolic injunction judges that which is respectable or nonrespectable.

The reference to the order that prevails in other congregations is of special significance in this passage. One could call it Paul's "ecumenical" argument. Already in chap. 11:16 he had stressed it with a very positive firmness, and here it seems to enclose the command to silence as in bonds of brass. In v. 36, Paul, with an almost ironical sharpness, refers as proof for his views to the order that exists without exception in the other churches, as cited already in v. 33b. It is almost as if he is shouting to the Corinthians: "Who do you think you are? Do you think that you deserve special regulations? Must I really remind you that you are only one part of the larger church?" The Word of God did not originate in Corinth, and it did not come only to the Corinthians. The church at Corinth, because of her dependence on the apostolic message, is also dependent on the church as a whole. She is not autonomous, nor does she have her own head! And she can give evidence of her dependence by acknowledging the general rule that prevails in the Christian church regarding the place of women.

Finally, however, Paid emphasizes that his instructions concerning the speaking of women in the church are not made solely on the basis of his apostolic authority but on the authority of the Lord Jesus Christ. Behind the authority of the apostle stands the authority of the Lord. It is not by accident that Paul, in his controversy with the charismatic spirits in Corinth, rests his arguments for church and liturgical order not merely on his own apostolic authority but brings Christ into the debate. He sees this question of a woman's conduct in the church not as something peripheral but as involving the whole of Christian faith. Paul judges whether true prophecy and truly charismatic spirits exist in the Corinthian church by their agreement with his instructions. It is also not a matter about which there can be valid differences of opinion. Here, as in 1 Cor. 11:16, the apostolic character of the Corinthian church is at stake, and its reaction to this problem will ultimately determine whether it remains within the folds of the apostolic church or becomes a syncretistic sect.

When one glances over these arguments of Paul, one sees that each increases in weight, in order to stress the importance of this command to silence. This shows that we have to do here with something that is central to the faith. This very important matter, on which both being "Christian" and being "church" depend, confronts us in the concept of subordination that St. Paul demands in the case of the Corinthian women and which is his strongest argument. What actually is meant when the New Testament speaks of subordination?

First of all, it is clear that we are dealing with a theological and not a sociological relationship. Whatever this subordination might mean in its various aspects, one thing is sure: it is based on the will of God, that is, it comes from God and is a divine and not a human arrangement; it is not the product of a particular social structure but is a pre-ordained order given by God to which all historical development is bound. Such a theological factor obviously has sociological consequences in its realization: where it is accepted and translated into actual practice, the results are helpful and blessed; and where men try to oppose it because of their own self-pride, the result is destruction and judgment.

The nature of this "ordering under" is actually an "ordering into" (*Einordnung*). A divinely instituted order is presupposed (*taxis*), which must be acknowledged and accepted by a concrete practical conduct of life. This being subject is first of all part of the divinely given order whereby it is mediated to the individual in question.[32]

Here we have to do with a structure that goes far beyond the relationship between man and woman. Even the relationship of Christ to God, the relationship of the Holy Spirit to Christ, the relationship of the church to Christ are determined by this fundamental principle of being set within and subject to an order that was instituted by God from the beginning. 1 Cor. 11:2–16 and Eph. 5:22–33 show the wider context in which this ordering and subordering of the woman is placed. Only in 1 Corinthians 11 the key word *subordination* is missing. But there the structure is revealed into which the practical conduct of being subordinated fits. This basic structure is a "*kephale*-structure." The man is the head of the woman; Christ is the head of the man; God is the head of Christ. The "head" is that which is prior, that which determines, that which leads. The head is the power that begins, it is *principium*, *arche*. This being the head differs depending on the structure in which it finds itself. In any case, it involves the kind of relationship for which one can never substitute a polar *schema*.

Let us look a little more closely at the relationship between man and woman as it stands within this chain. The most significant passage in this connection is 1 Cor. 11:8–9: "For the man is not of the woman; but the woman of the man. Neither was the man created for the woman; but the woman for the man." The order that prevails between man and woman is not one that has

---

32  See Karl Barth, *Kirchliche Dogmatik*, III/4, p. 192. The whole section, pp. 192–196, is of significance to our discussion of order and subordination. A critical discussion concerning the thesis of Barth is not possible within the confines of this essay. The critical reader will not have failed to observe that we have attempted to incorporate many of the observations of Barth, even though we cannot follow him at many important points and therefore come to a different conclusion in the question of the ordination of women than he does.

developed in the course of history; it was established by God from the beginning of all things and was given in the creation. What it means for man to be
man and the woman to be woman is defined by the *kephale*-structure, which
governs their relationships, a structure given once for all and not derived.
Paul is thinking here of the account of the creation in Genesis 2. There is no
reason to assume that the relationship between man and woman described
there does not correspond to the full intention of God at the creation but
represents merely the temporary beginning of a course of development that
must strive to attain the high estate anticipated in the first creation narrative, Genesis 1.[33] We will see that the relation creation set between man and
woman also participates in the history God carries through with man for his
salvation, and that it is carried along by this history even into the transformation at the resurrection. But it is just this relationship, which was established
from the origin of all things, that runs through various modalities; it, however,
retains its God-given ontological structure until the final transformation in
the resurrection from the dead.

With this we have already intimated how we are to understand Genesis 2
in relationship to the apostle's own explanation thereof. The story of the
creation of woman in Genesis 2 is certainly not meant to be the account of
an anthropological event that can be empirically investigated. It expresses,
instead, a hidden but yet very actual fundamental relationship between the
sexes. One can attempt to understand the preexistence of this order by analogy
to the, in principle, axiological givenness of a Platonic idea. Such an attempt is
certainly more faithful to the Biblical claim than the attempt to discredit the
actual import of this Biblical insight by passing it off as the result of naïveté
and an unscientific attitude. A minimum of theological understanding for the
text, in any case, presupposes the recognition that the relationship between
man and woman is determined through and through by a fundamental divine
law, which is axiologically foreordained and which transcends all experience
while at the same time influencing it. But the Biblical text goes further. It

---

33  This sentence is directed at M. E. Thrall. According to him the position of the woman
    in relationship to the man and to the image of God as God wills it can only be ascer-
    tained from Genesis 1, because the insight of Genesis 2 represents an incomplete
    intermediate stage of thought. According to Thrall, what Genesis 1 says about man
    and woman and the image of God corresponds to the new being in Christ in which
    the Christian is decisively set through Baptism. What Genesis 2 says about the posi-
    tion of the woman in God's creation corresponds to the apostolic instructions, which
    have a "growing-into" this new being in mind and which presuppose a "not-yet," a
    "becoming," and a "not yet fulfilled." The "Adam and Eve myth" can therefore never
    be accepted as "a true picture of the perfect state of human personality and human
    relations." The subordination of the woman based on Genesis 2 is therefore "only a
    stage in human development," but no permanent command for Christians. (See Thrall,
    *Ordination of Women*, pp. 32–36.) I cannot see how this concept can be harmonized with
    the basic thought of Paul and I also cannot find grounds for it in Genesis 1 and 2.

leads to the conviction that this order of God, just as surely as in every instant it acts from out of its "axiological transcendence" as a basic law, is essentially something other than such a law. It is a saving act of God done at the origin of all things. Its protohistorical reality is not testified to by a doctrine of ideas nor by a mythological description of the mystery of the ideas; proclamation must be made of a history that took place on earth once at the beginning, in which God once and for all time acted on and with mankind.

What then is the actual relationship between man and woman according to this fundamental order? The structure of the relationship can be defined by the two prepositional phrases "from" and "for the sake of." This relationship cannot be understood as a polar relationship in which the roles are interchangeable. Because the relationship between man and woman has the nature of a *kephale*-structure, the position of each in its created existence differs from that of the other for all time. Their positions cannot be interchanged. The original creaturely "from" and "for the sake of" relates to the woman; the reverse is not possible! To be sure, in the sequence of birth the man does come from woman (1 Cor. 11:11). This fact of life constitutes an important counterpart to the order established in the creation, where the woman derives from man. But this counterpart is not able to cancel out the order that was given in the creation and is in every respect prior to the succession of the generations, whereby the woman comes from the man and is there for his sake. According to her created basis the woman comes from the man, and according to his created basis he is the "head" of the woman. Both man and woman according to their foundation in the creation, under which all other characteristics are subsumed, are subject to this order with its *kephale*-structure. As a result of this order the woman is related to the man through the original creaturely associations of "from" and "for his sake," and therefore she in a unique way is subject to him as her "head." Only where the woman in her concrete practical relationships lives what she is by virtue of the creaturely existence given her in the creation is she a woman as God meant her to be and still wants her to be.

The unique *kephale*-structure of the relationship between man and woman is also evident in the event of the fall, although an important modification occurs here. According to Genesis 3 and 1 Tim. 2:14 (see also 2 Cor. 11:3) the share that man and woman had in the event of the original fall differed. Even the relationship of the man to the command of God around which the transgression centered, Gen. 2:16–18, differs from that of the woman. The man originally received these words; therefore he is the first witness to them. He is entrusted with the preservation and transmission of these words. Luther could very pictorially describe how Adam preached in Paradise, while Eve listened. According to Genesis 2 Eve can only know these words of God that were spoken at the creation of man because Adam has borne witness to them.

Already in the Garden of Eden Adam is ordered to be the preacher and the responsible custodian of God's words by virtue of his place in the creation.

It is no accident that the first transgression in the human world occurred through the woman. She is less capable of preserving these original words of God since she did not hear the word of God directly from His mouth but received it via the word of man. On the other hand, the responsibility of man and his consequent guilt are essentially greater than hers. Certainly one cannot take the sentence found in 1 Tim. 2:14 and attempt to press it into a polar scheme by saying: "Adam fell through Eve, Eve fell through Adam." One can and must say, however, that the fall into sin was finally fulfilled by the act of the man. Not until the deed of the man did the fall into sin become ripe for judgment. The first Adam proved himself also to be the "head," in that sin and death entered into the world through him. The statement in 1 Tim. 2:14 must be amplified by Rom. 5:12, and this must be said: To be sure, Adam was led astray through Eve, but through Adam the fall was "fulfilled."

One of the consequences of the judgment on this original fall was the modification of the *kephale*-structure, which determines the relationship between man and woman. A uniquely painful hardness now enters into this relationship under which the woman especially must suffer. Instead of the man being the "head" of the woman, he now, according to Gen. 3:16, becomes a ruler who possesses her. The original association of the woman to the man is now transformed into a subjugation to his desire that has an almost oppressive power.

Christ, however, redeems this *kephale*-structure that governs man and woman. In Christ the aforementioned balance is fully worked out, in that the man proceeds from the woman in the sequence of birth (1 Cor. 11:11–12). In Christ the *kephale*-structure can be described by the paradoxical formula "Be subject one to another" (Eph. 5:21). But this in no way means that in Christ the *kephale*-structure given in the creation is now cancelled out. On the contrary! In Christ this structure is seen again in its original sense; it is released from the hardness that entered in at the fall, and it receives a content that first came into the world through Christ's reconciling act on the cross and can be summarized in one word—*agape*, love. A text such as Eph. 5:22–33 shows how the relationship between man and woman that is realized in marriage has received an eschatological quality through Christ, while retaining the original *kephale*-structure. Therefore the relationship between man and woman is compared to the relationship between Christ and His church! When considering the relationship of Christ to His church, one cannot speak of a polar relationship. Here, with absolute finality, the body is body and the head is head, unchangeable and unexchangeable. The relationship between Christ and His church also includes the difference between the One who as true God from all eternity is born of God and those who to all eternity are creatures by virtue of their creation. But how deeply here the Head inclined itself! Christ offered Himself up for His church. How close is the relationship between the Head and His church even though the differences are still maintained—so close that one can say that the two are one body! In this analogical relation, the man is purposely accorded the place of Christ and the woman the place of the church. What the subordination of the woman to the man really means within the *kephale*-structure is made clear by the subordination of the church to Christ. The woman is subject to the man as the church is subject to Christ, and precisely for this reason. The man is the head of the woman, just as Christ is head of His church; therefore the man should love the woman just as Christ has loved His church.

Three events join in a mysterious way to determine the relationship of man and woman to each other: the creation in the beginning, the original fall into sin with the resulting judgment on it, and the saving act of Christ with its fruits. The closest event to us is the deed of Christ. In its light we not only see the origin of the relationship between man and woman but also that which is not as yet. The eschatological transformation in the resurrection from the dead has not yet taken place. The relationship between man and woman must still bear the fundamental elements of the *kephale*-structure that were given in the creation. According to the testimony of the New Testament, the reception of the pledge of the transformation, the reception of the Holy Spirit and His gifts, does not obviate these basic creaturely elements, even though it begins to transform them. The struggle between the spirit and the flesh shows that the consequences of the judgment on sin are not eliminated from the experience of the Christian, who is a new being in Christ, even though all is forgiven. It is to the credit of Luther's Reformation theology for having brought this actual state of affairs to the light with persistent clarity. Therefore there is no relapse into "pre-Christian" thought when the apostolic admonitions to the woman are based not only on the creation but also on Gen. 3:6 and 16. Decisive, however, is the acknowledgement that the *kephale*-structure of the relationship between man and woman that was given at the creation has not been obviated by the event of Christ, but has finally come into the light and has been brought into its own with new power and in a new way.

From 1 Cor. 11:3 and 7 we see that the *kephale*-structure of the relationship between man and woman is incorporated into a whole chain of such structural relationships. Wherever the original "from" and "for the sake of" governs the relationship between persons or spiritual forces, the *kephale*-structure is in effect. On all levels this structure demands that both partners in the relationship be incorporated into its order, which for the one partner implies a personal subordination to the other partner, the one to whom the "from" and "for the sake of" applies. This subordination, this New Testament "hypotage," is on all levels something inclusive, something total, a unified mode of behavior that determines all actions but in particular instances manifests itself as a subordination. In its totality as well as in individual actions it is related to the head, which determines this relationship and from whom its particular characteristics come. The subordination of Christ to the Father is a unique relationship that does not occur anywhere else. The same holds true for the subordination of the church to Christ and for that of the woman to the man. In all these cases we have to do with subordination, but yet each one is something unique. This shows that we are dealing here with something that is at the same time both similar and yet different, different and yet similar. Neither the difference nor the similarity dare be neglected. Therefore a certain conformity runs through all the various ways of subordination. The subordination demanded of the woman reveals a structure that is projected into the Christological depths of the saving history of God. Therefore the preservation of the *kephale*-structure for the relationship between the man and the Christian woman is nothing strange, as though it contradicted her being a Christian, her being in Christ! Instead, the maintaining of this structure on the level of relationships between man and woman actually corresponds to that which exists between the church and Christ, yes, even to that between Christ and the Father. Despite the individual differences of the various forms of subordination, the subordination of the woman to the man is mysteriously bound up with the subordination of the church to Christ and Christ to the Father. What is "subordination" for the Lord Jesus Christ is reflected in the subordination demanded of the woman, and she may see it in the light of the relationship between the church and Christ and between the Father and the Son. The Christian woman could not mistake or belie the dignity that is hers in a more basic manner than by attempting to step out of the *kephale*-structure that governs her relationship with the man and by trying to usurp and assume the place accorded to him either in the church or in marriage.

## APPLICATION TO CHURCH AND MINISTRY

With these considerations we have laid the ground for the first dogmatic theological decision that our theme demands. It is this: The *kephale*-structure governing the relationship between man and woman, which was given in the creation, and the command to subordination (*hypotage*), which is demanded of the woman in a unique way by this order, are in effect in the Christian church until the Last Judgment. Were anyone to contest in teaching and preaching the factual and effective existence of this order and the factual validity of the corresponding command, he would be proclaiming a false teaching in regard to this central point with which the whole Christian message hangs together; he would be a heretic.

One dares to hope that the Lutheran churches are still united on this point. But what does this decision mean for our question regarding the ordination of women to the pastoral office? Now arises the special ethical question: How are we to apply this theological principle today, and how are we to proclaim and make concrete the command that corresponds to it?

Do the marriage laws of the German Federal Republic by any chance contradict this theological principle? Does the practice in our society whereby women appear in the secular courts as lawyers and even as judges, passing sentences over others, contradict it? Is the subordination demanded of the woman contradicted by the practice whereby women are elected as representatives to legislative assemblies and thus not only speak out concerning but also make decisions on civil laws, and perhaps even hold posts in the ruling cabinet? Can a woman so exercise the above mentioned activities in a manner that maintains the subordination demanded of her?

It ought to be obvious that the application of our theological principle and the actualization of its corresponding demand will in many respects have to take an entirely different form today than in the 2d or perhaps the 16th century. The church will therefore have to carefully see to it, of course always with Christian freedom, that this principle and its demands are observed by her members in the realm of civic and political life. It is quite obvious that a danger threatens, which is here coupled with a great deal of insecurity and confusion; for here an area worthy of notice exists in which a variety of concrete decisions are possible by individuals and groups with the same ties. But no preacher of the Gospel and no theology professor would in our present European situation find himself in the position to flatly refuse a Christian woman the right to participate in the governmental activity of both city and state on the basis of the Word of God. The exercise of such activity does not contradict the "subordination" demanded of the woman.[34]

One might be tempted to go on from here and draw similar conclusions in regard to the ministry of the woman in the church. Does not the subordination demanded of the woman also need to be reformulated in terms of church life? Granted that for Paul very much, perhaps even the very existence of the Gospel itself, hung in the balance because of the behavior of the Corinthian

---

34  One must notice that even for Johann Gerhard women are not necessarily excluded from the exercise of public offices. He acknowledges all kinds of legitimate reasons why women should exercise the *majestas imperii* in the realm of worldly affairs. He even allows for *exempla quaedam heroicarum feminarum extraordinaria*. Such women can also in an *electio libera* be installed in the secular government provided that eligibility is not restricted to a particular family. (See *Locus XX*, no. 42, *Locus XXIV*, no. 110. Ed. Preuss, IV, 278, VI, 314ff.)

women in the congregation, so that he had to take a firm stand on women wearing a head covering and keeping silent in worship, does that necessarily mean that his instructions are still valid for our situation? In regard to the head covering, the decision has long been made. Could not the woman also preach the Gospel and administer the sacraments today without damaging the subordination required of her? Here we have a very pointed formulation of the controversy that is so deeply moving the Lutheran churches today.

There exists, indeed, unanimity of opinion that the subordination required of the woman must find such a concrete expression in the life of the church as corresponds to the social and religious situation. In the Lutheran churches there is general agreement on the necessity to distinguish between that which transpires in the secular realm and that which transpires in the spiritual realm. An argument that believes it can derive a case for the ordination of women from the changed position of the woman in modern society has no validity in the church; it cannot be advanced as proof that the ordination of the woman to the pastoral office is in harmony with the subordination required of her. On the other hand, the opposite also does not follow from this recognition. In my opinion, the deciding factor in this controversy is a dogmatic question that is directly connected with the fundamental dogmatic principle asserted above. This question must be raised in the light of the spiritual authority involved in the exercise of the pastoral ministry. The question then is: Can this spiritual authority be exercised by a woman in the assembled *ecclesia* without repudiating the *kephale*-structure of the order in which the woman stands, *eo ipso*, that is by the very act of exercising such authority, and thereby also damaging a concrete ethical consummation of the subordination implied in this order and its corresponding command?

Before I give my answer, two misunderstandings or errors must be dealt with. It would be a misunderstanding were one to say: it may be the case that a married woman would violate the *kephale*-structure that is present in marriage were the church to consecrate her as pastor, but in the case of an unmarried woman this obstruction no longer holds true because she does not have a man who *in concreto* would be her head. The misunderstanding that underlies this conception has its origin in the failure to recognize that although the *kephale*-structure does receive its most concrete and fulfilled realization in marriage, every man or woman by virtue of being man or woman is determined by and is responsible to this order even in case of actual and permanent celibacy. The state of being man or woman, even when unmarried, is subject to the working power of this creaturely existence given directly by God and to the basic order that precedes all personal existence. The difference between married and single has absolutely no dogmatic relevance for the decision involved in our controversy.

The second misunderstanding goes somewhat deeper; it already contains an important theological error. Here the command to subordination is understood as a moral demand that everyone can accept for himself through his own personal decision and inner attitude, without reference to any universal existential order. The moral decision is here completely independent of any preexistent order and falls completely within the realm of inner self-determination. The conviction that obviously underlies this conception is that what we have called the *kephale*-structure in the relationship between man and woman is in the last analysis determined by my own inner moral decision; that is, a divine order that precedes my own decision and is a part of my very being as a creature does not exist at all. The preexistence of such an order is not at all an existence that lays a claim on me without my prior moral decision, for it only involves my existence through my moral decision. This conception can lead to the opinion that an ordained woman is fulfilling the demand of subordination placed on her when she exercises her office in true Christian humility and in the proper relationship to the total congregation, free from all desires for emancipation and free from all presumptions about the office.

The error behind this conception lies in the fact that it fails to acknowledge the creative power of the Word of God spoken at the creation. It fails to realize the fact that God by virtue of His act of salvation has set certain conditions in our existence that are incessantly effectual by virtue of the divine arrangement. What is overlooked here is the fact that the *kephale*-structure of the relationship between man and woman is no less objective, no less factual, and no less a part of existence than the fact that there is a male and female sex given in an order that spans us all.

The decisive question with which we are concerned must be formulated with respect to the authority that is exercised in the pastoral ministry. This unique authority of the pastoral office is evidenced particularly at three points: (1) in those specific actions involving church order such as the basic admitting to the Lord's table, also in the occasional admitting by giving the Lord's Supper, and in the excluding from the Lord's Supper and the fellowship of the church; (2) in the public declaration of true doctrine and in the public rejection of false doctrine; (3) in the public proclamation of the Gospel in the assembled congregation.

The authority that is exercised in these acts and that culminates in the public proclamation of the Gospel is a spiritual eschatological (*endzeitliche!*) authority of the highest kind. There, where the pastor exercises the functions instituted with his office by divine mandate, as we have shown above, he stands in the place of Christ, serving as the official messenger of Christ. When the pastors perform their office by virtue of the divine institution, the Word of the Lord holds true for them just as it did for the apostles: "He who hears you hears Me" (Luke 10:16). This is clearly the teaching of the Lutheran confessional standards.[35] In the exercise of the duties involved in his ministry the pastor—even though he be a hypocrite or an evil person—represents the Lord Jesus Christ Himself. Only concerning heretics must it be said: *hic iam non funguntur persona Christi*—they no longer represent Christ (Apol. VII, 48). The pastor does not represent the church, he actually represents Christ, even though the church has installed him into this office in which he represents Christ.

The decisive question for our discussion must now be formulated in this manner: Can a woman, who as such is determined by the *kephale*-structure and analogically but really holds in it the place of the church, stand at the same time in the place of Christ as a pastor of the church and as His fully credited ambassador, while in that very same *kephale*-structure, the man, by virtue of his creation in the image and glory of God and Christ (1 Cor. 11:3 and 7) as well as by virtue of the redemption (Eph. 5:25), stands as head in the place corresponding to that of Christ? Can a woman in a regular manner— extraordinary acts of God in extraordinary situations and the awakening of prophetesses are not under consideration here—as pastor exercise over the church the highest form of spiritual authority within the realm of canonical law, which implies exercising it over a section of mankind and thereby over the man, without running into a basic existential conflict with her created (and thereby transparent for the history of salvation) being as woman? Do not being "pastor" and being "woman" contradict each other?

We are talking here about a conflict in being, which is not necessarily equivalent to a psychological, empirically verifiable conflict. The conflict with which we are concerned is carried on in the very depths and basis of created being. These depths are so hidden that only God's Word and the eye of the witness of Christ's resurrection can tell us of them. In this respect the depths and basis of being with which we are here concerned share in the hidden- ness and mystery of original sin. This conflict between being "pastor" and being "woman" is so hidden that empirical symptoms thereof are perhaps not apparent for a long time, perhaps not for an entire generation. It is quite pos- sible that the combination of woman and the office of pastor might for a long time, as far as one can empirically ascertain, be accompanied by the best of results. But finally the day will come when this conflict that is building up in the hidden depths of created being will manifest its great force even through empirical symptoms. In the long run it will eventually take its toll in the total cultural structure of an era.

---

35  Cf. Augsburg Confession XXVIII, 21f.; Apology VII, 28 and 47; XII, 40; Treatise on the Power and Primacy of the Pope, 18 sq.

This formulation of our decisive question already contains its own answer. If we see this question in the light of the observations we have already made, we must come to the following conclusion: The Biblical message about woman, as it is available to us in the applicable interpretation of the apostolic statements, and the Biblical word concerning the pastoral office, as it is defined in the teachings of our confessional standards, show that the combination of being "woman" and being "pastor" contradict each other in a manner that involves the woman in the hidden depths of her created being in a conflict that attacks her very being. This conflict roots in the fact that the combination of pastoral office and being woman objectively and fundamentally destroys the *kephale*-structure of the relationship between man and woman and therefore also rejects the "ordering into" and "subordination to" (*hypotage*) which is demanded by God's will. That which contradicts the spiritual and creaturely order with which God has invested being cannot be the good that God wills! God does not contradict Himself in creation and redemption. The apostolic command to silence, as we find it in 1 Corinthians 14 and 1 Timothy 2, cannot be explained away as the result of the peculiar theological speculation of its author, who was bound by the cultural history and the special circumstances of his day. These instructions are based much more on certain hidden, but yet extraordinarily incisive, fundamental laws and commands that God Himself established in the creation and substantiated in the carrying out of His saving counsel. These fundamental laws and commands stand directly behind the apostolic command to silence. Our dogmatic analysis has shown that the ordination of women to the ministry according to a ruling of canonical law attacks these fundamental laws and commands of God. Only God can, in an unusual manner and by extraordinary means, go beyond these basic orders and commands that all Christians in all places and at all times are bound to respect. The church must exercise extreme caution in maintaining that in a particular concrete situation such an extraordinary intervention of God has taken place. In churches that at this time are not suffering under persecution or are not blessed with the awakening of prophets in their midst, such an intervention is highly unlikely. In such churches women should not be ordained to the pastoral office.

On the other hand, one must remember that the pastor cannot exercise his office without assistance. To a certain extent he can be relieved of some of the functions included in his office, and the responsibility for them can be taken over by capable members of the congregation. These forms of assistance can be organized and carried out as offices within the church. The warrant therefore is already contained in the New Testament. And women can also assume such an official service in the church. In the ancient church the orders for widows and deaconesses, which go back to apostolic times (see 1 Tim. 5:9–16;

and probably also 3:11), were such offices for women in the church. With no dogmatic difficulties, the following functions can be separated from the pastoral office and can be organized into such an official assisting ministry into which a woman with theological training can be installed through prayer and the laying on of hands:

1. the Christian instruction of the catechumens, also confirmation instruction, above all the training of groups of members, also the introduction to the interpretation of the Scriptures that takes the form of a Bible study;

2. baptizing those who have been approved by the pastor of the congregation, and the dispensing of the cup at the Lord's Supper;[36]

3. home visitations and visits to the sick with the care and counseling that is involved, in fact, individual counseling, particularly with women, and also in hospitals and prisons;

4. devotions in houses such as retreat centers, hospitals, prisons, and charitable institutions;

5. assisting in the training of other official orders such as catechists, congregational helpers, deacons, and deaconesses;

6. cooperating in the maintenance of correct doctrine through theological research.

Those functions of the pastoral office that for dogmatic reasons cannot be transferred to women by a canonical ruling but must be exercised solely by the pastor are the following:

1. preaching in the worship services of the congregation;

2. leading the services of worship;

3. the administration of the sacraments in the worship services;

4. the decision as to who is to be admitted to the Lord's Supper; the imposing of the degree of excommunication and its revocation;

5. the granting of absolution in the confessional;

---

36  With this last proposal we pick up an important liturgical function of the ancient deacon. This function in the service should not be prohibited to women. The separation of the distribution of the cup from the *administration* of the sacrament, which is reserved for the pastor, has nothing whatever to do with a devaluation of the "second form." Christ's blood is not less precious than His body. The basis of this rule is that a decisive act of church government is connected with the distribution of the bread— admission to the celebration. In an extreme case a refusal may be necessary at the very altar. A woman should not be permitted to exercise this authority of admission. This governmental factor is not present with the distribution of the cup. Anyone who has received the bread from the pastor has been unequivocally admitted. Therefore the cup can be brought also by a woman.

6. the acts of confirmation and ordination;

7. jurisdiction over the supporting ministries and the assistants in the local church, the *episkope*;

8. the exercise of the office of diocesan bishop.

These two lists of functions, by which we have attempted to distinguish between the office of a theologically trained woman and that of the pastor, while at the same time showing their relationship to each other, is in no way intended to be conclusive. These lists and the limitations they involve will be only partially understandable on the basis of the previous dogmatic discussion. They could only be based on a dogmatic discussion of the respective individual functions, but this is not possible here, and anyway it is not necessary to our discussion. The purpose of these lists is merely to make concrete the fundamental insights that have resulted from our discussion. When the basic theological question involved in the controversy concerning the ordination of women to the pastoral ministry is acknowledged and correctly decided, the form that the office of a theologically trained woman in the church will take, its distinction from that of the pastoral office, and its relationships thereto will no longer present any great difficulties.

# THE ORDINATION OF WOMEN AND THE DOCTRINE OF THE HOLY TRINITY

## JOHN W. KLEINIG

Do we realise what we would be letting ourselves in for if we ordained women? In his book *What will happen to God?*, W. Oddie makes this provocative claim (26):

> Women's ordination . . . is thought of by many of those most commit-ted to achieving it as a means of installing immovably, in the permanent structures of the church itself, a permanent shift in the Christian tradi-tion: to ordain women as priests will be to change at its foundations our idea of God. And this is no intemperate and unfounded accusation but . . . an ambition coolly announced by the most substantial feminist writers. It may be that this ambition should be achieved; but it is right that Christian people should at least know what many of those who are seeking to bring about the change really intend.

He holds that the main change would be to the teaching on the fatherhood of God. This would, of course, result in the radical reconstruction of many other areas of doctrine.

As far as I am concerned, the assertion of St Paul in 1 Corinthians 14:34 that Christ has commanded that women should not be speakers in the liturgi-cal assembly of the congregation settles the matter for me. My conscience is bound by that word whether I understand the reason for it or not. But at the same time I will try to figure out the reason for that prohibition no matter how tentative my conclusions may be. This paper is my attempt to do so in the light of Oddie's claim, because I agree with him in his assertion that Christ's prohibition in 1 Corinthians 14:33b–38 has something to do with the doc-trine of the Trinity and our participation in the life of the Triune God through the preaching of the word and the celebration of the sacrament.

# 1. THE APOSTOLIC MINISTRY AND THE MISSION OF THE TRIUNE GOD

The three foundational texts for our teaching on the institution of the public ministry by our Lord are either trinitarian or binitarian in content and structure. First, in John 20:21–23 Jesus 'commissioned' the eleven disciples, as the Father had 'commissioned' him (cf 13:20; 17:18), and gave them the Holy Spirit, so that they could pronounce the pardon and judgment of his heavenly Father to human beings. When they forgave or retained sin, they stood in the shoes of the Father and acted by the power of the Holy Spirit.

Secondly, in Matthew 28:18–20 Jesus who had received all authority in heaven and on earth from his Father, and who promised to remain with the eleven apostles after his ascension, commissioned them to make disciples of all nations, by baptising them in the name of the Father and of the Son and of the Holy Spirit, and by teaching them all that they had received through him from his heavenly Father.

Thirdly, in Luke 10:16 Jesus gave the following promise and warning to the seventy two preachers who are regarded in our confessions as the prototypes for the public ministry of the word:

'Whoever hears you hears me, and whoever rejects you rejects me, and whoever rejects me rejects him who sent me'.

He thereby 'commissioned' them as his representatives (10:1,3), as he had been 'commissioned' by his heavenly Father (10:16).

If we take these three foundational texts together, we must conclude that the apostles and those who received the Office of the Keys from them were involved in the mission of the Triune God to all people here on earth. They exercised the keys by teaching divine doctrine and correcting false doctrine, by proclaiming divine salvation and divine judgment, by absolving and retaining sin, by baptising and withholding baptism, by admitting people to the Lord's table and excluding people from it. As they did this, they worked together with the Son who did the work of his heavenly Father by the power of the Holy Spirit.

# 2. THE PASTOR AS THE REPRESENTATIVE OF THE SON AND THE FATHER

The teaching of Jesus in Luke 10:16 shows that, when pastors preach God's word, they do not just speak for Christ but actually represent him. So those who hear their words do not merely hear Christ's words but hear Christ speaking to them. This means that Christ identifies himself so closely with preachers in their preaching that those who receive them receive him in and through them (Matt 10:40; John 13:20; cf Gal 4:14; Did 11:2,4). On the other hand, those who reject the preachers do not just reject their message and Christ's message; they reject Christ himself. The preachers of the gospel do not then function on behalf of an inactive Christ, like a person with the power of attorney for a disabled relative, nor do they represent their absent Lord, like the deputy of our Prime Minister when he is absent from office. Rather they represent the risen Lord Jesus who is actually present with his people in the liturgical assembly. So when pastors preach and administer the sacraments, we do not just hear Christ speaking; we 'see' him at work.

In his Apology to the Augsburg Confession (VII & VIII 28, 47–48), Melanchthon concludes from Luke 10:16 that those who hold the office of the ministry 'represent the person of Christ'. Like St Paul who in 2 Corinthians 2:10 forgives the sinners in Corinth 'in the person of Christ', they act 'in the person of Christ'. In their office they quite properly impersonate him. Thus, when they present the word and the sacraments to the saints, they offer them 'as Christ' (Latin: *Christi vice*) and 'in his place' (Latin: *Christi loco*), for Christ's word and his holy body and blood cannot be divorced from him as a person or received apart from him.

Pastors, however, do not merely represent the risen Lord Jesus; Jesus himself maintains in Luke 10:16 that they represent God the Father even as they represent him. They bring the kingdom of God and its peace with them personally to the people who receive them and accept their proclamation (Luke 10:5–9). Those who reject the preachers of the gospel do not just reject Christ; they reject the Father who sent him. Hence God's judgment quite properly falls on those people for their rejection of Christ's heralds. On the other hand, the people who receive those whom Christ sends receive the Father who sent him (Matt 10:40; John 13:20).

This understanding of the pastor as the representative of God the Father was elaborated by Ignatius of Antioch towards the end of the first century. He claimed that the bishop who led a congregation in its worship was 'a type of the Father' (Trall 3:1); he presided 'in the place of God' the Father (Magn 3:1). Melanchthon also alludes to this teaching in the Apology to the Augsburg Confession (XIII 12). In his discussion on whether ordination is a sacrament or not, he asserts that God is present in the ministry. This means that when a pastor publicly exercises the office of the keys, he represents God the Father. He speaks the Father's word of law or grace, accusation or absolution, disapproval or approval, judgment or blessing. Luther sums up all this rather well in a sermon on John 14:10 where he says:

> Furthermore, when Christ commands His apostles to proclaim His Word and to carry on His work, we hear and see Him Himself, and thus also God the Father; for they publish and proclaim no other Word than that

which they heard from His lips, and they point solely to Him. Thus the process goes on; the Word is handed down to us through the agency of true bishops, pastors, and preachers, who received it from the apostles.... Thus the apostles and pastors are nothing but channels through which Christ leads and transmits His Gospel from the Father to us. Therefore wherever you hear the Gospel properly taught or see a person baptized, wherever you see someone administer or receive the Sacrament, or wherever you witness someone absolving another, there you may say without hesitation: 'Today I beheld God's Word and work. Yes, I saw and heard God Himself preaching and baptizing'. To be sure, the tongue, the voice, the hands, etc, are those of a human being, but the Word and the ministry are really those of the Divine Majesty Himself. Hence it must be viewed and believed as though God's own voice were resounding from heaven and as though we were seeing Him administering Baptism or the Sacrament with His own hands. (LW 24, 66, 67)

## 3. CHRIST'S CHOICE OF MEN AS APOSTLES AND PASTORS

The incarnation of God's Son as a male person was not just a tactical concession to avoid offense in the patriarchal societies of the ancient world. It was, I maintain, an integral part of his mission to reveal God the Father to humankind in the Old and New Testaments (see John 1:18; 17:6). His incarnation as a male person led in turn to his choice of men as apostles and teachers of the word.

The case for this presupposes the scriptural teaching on the relationship between the creation of the first Adam and the redemption of humanity by the second Adam, as well as the scriptural teaching on the typological relationship between them (see Rom 5:14). To put it quite simply, Adam, the first human father and husband, is a type of God the Father and of Jesus the heavenly bridegroom, as well as a type of the pastor who represents both of them.

When God created human beings as 'male and female' (Gen 1:27), he did not just design men merely for the business of sexual procreation but also to personify his asexual fatherhood in the order of creation. God's fatherhood is therefore not the result of the projection, by analogy, of human fatherhood on to the deity, so that God is held to be something like our human fathers. Rather, as St Paul asserts in Ephesians 3:15, all human fatherhood is derived from God's fatherhood. Human fathers are meant to be like God the Father of our Lord Jesus Christ. This means that the role of human fathers is not just determined by their masculinity but is shaped by God the Father's activity in naming and providing for, assessing and approving, accepting and blessing his human children.

Neither Adam nor any human father after him has ever in reality ever remotely embodied and mirrored the fatherhood of God. In fact, we fathers seem to reflect his fatherhood to our children more by our failure than by success. As a result of our inadequacy they are often filled with a deep longing and spiritual need for some father figure to compensate for what we have failed to be to them and give to them.

Jesus became a male person to fill that vacuum and to fulfil that spiritual paternal role. He revealed the fatherhood of God the Father by perfectly embodying the divinely intended spiritual character of human fatherhood and by fully discharging the spiritual vocation of human fathers. He therefore claims: 'Anyone who has seen me has seen the Father' (John 14:9). Jesus in turn appoints mature men to be pastors and teachers in the family of God. They are, as Luther teaches us in the Large Catechism (I, 158–163), to be spiritual fathers to their charges. They are to disclose God's fatherhood by their own management of the church as God's household (see 1 Tim 3:5). Like the apostles, they not only beget 'children' through the gospel but also model and teach how to live as children of God in Christ Jesus (1 Cor 4:14–17; 2 Cor 6:13; 1 Thess 2:11,12; 3 John 4).

In his teaching on marriage in Ephesians 5:22–33, Paul maintains that, when God created Adam as the husband of Eve, he created him and every human husband as a type of Christ, the heavenly bridegroom. The role of a man as a husband was therefore spiritual as well as physical. As the heads of their wives, husbands, by their love, were meant to model and mirror the demonstrative, self-sacrificial love of Christ, the heavenly bridegroom, for his bride, the church. Now it is, of course, true that we who are husbands reflect Christ more by our failure than by our success, for who of us could ever claim that we have loved our wives 'as Christ loved the church and gave himself up for her' (Eph 5:25).

God's Son therefore became incarnate as a male person to fulfill the role which had originally been given to Adam. As the Messiah he not only revealed the typological character of human husbandhood but also redeemed both men and women by his self-sacrificial love. He husbands the church and presents the church to his heavenly Father as his lovely holy bride (Eph 5:27; Col 1:22; Rev 19:7; 21:2). Christ's maleness does not therefore disclose the maleness of God the Father, who is of course a-sexual, but qualifies him to fulfill his role as the loving redemptive head of the church.

Jesus in turn calls men who are either celibate, or who have proved to be faithful husbands of one wife (see 1 Tim 3:2; Tit 1:6), to be pastors. As pastors they are appointed to represent Christ. They are to betroth people spiritually to Christ in holy baptism (2 Cor 11:2); they are to love, cherish and nourish the church. C.S. Lewis therefore claims (239):

It is an old saying in the army that you salute the uniform not the wearer. Only one wearing the masculine uniform can (provisionally, and till the Parousia) represent the Lord to the Church: for we are all, corporately and individually, feminine to Him. We men may often make very bad priests. That is because we are insufficiently masculine.

Christ, then, did not become incarnate as a male person, nor did he confer the holy ministry on certain chosen members of the male sex, in order to indicate that God the Father was a male person, but to fulfill the role of Adam as a type of Christ and of God the Father. If we grant that this is so, then it follows that the ordination of women contradicts the spiritual vocation of men as husbands and fathers and empties marriage and family life of much of their spiritual significance. It also obscures the mystery of Christ and his work in the order of redemption. It obscures the role of Christ as the head of the church as well as the nature of the church as his holy bride. Most of all, it obscures the fatherhood of God and the role of pastors as spiritual fathers. The ordination of women creates symbolic confusion in both the order of creation and the order of redemption.

## 4. Conclusion

William Oddie claimed that the ordination of women would involve a radical change in the teaching of the church about the fatherhood of God. His claims cannot be lightly dismissed as alarmist propaganda, because many of those who have promoted the ordination of women also reject the understanding and use of the term Father as the proper name for the first person of the Holy Trinity. This is commonly justified by the claim that the term Father is nothing but a title, a metaphorical designation for the mystery of the transcendent deity. While some invoke God as Mother, most insist on the use of inclusive language for the deity in worship. They therefore avoid the use of Father as a proper name and replace it with other general designations and titles.

It is, of course, impossible to demonstrate conclusively that the ordination of women must logically lead to the rejection of God's fatherhood; or vice versa, that the rejection of God's fatherhood leads to the ordination of women. We aren't, after all, dealing with a system of ideas, a religious philosophy or ideology, but with catholic spiritual realities which are all interdependent and interconnected in a kind of ecological order. My claim is that, since the acceptance of the ordination of women may have implications for the way we view, name, and confess the Triune God, we can not ignore this issue but must deal with it fully before proceeding much further. Those who dismiss the traditional understanding of 1 Corinthians 14:33b–38 and 1 Timothy 2:11–15 and advocate the ordination of women must demonstrate that the ordination of women does not imply and will not promote the rejection of God's fatherhood.

I close with some unsettling remarks from C. S. Lewis which have kept nagging at my mind and in my conscience ever since I first read and dismissed them years ago when I was a seminary student. He says:

> Suppose the reformer stops saying that a good women may be like God and begins saying that God is like a good woman. Suppose he says that we might as well pray to 'Our Mother which art in heaven' as to 'Our Father". Suppose he suggests that the Incarnation might just as well have taken a female as a male form, and the Second Person of the Trinity be as well called the Daughter as the Son. Suppose, finally, that the mystical marriage were reversed, that the church were the Bridegroom and Christ the Bride. All this, as it seems to me, is involved in the claim that a woman can represent God as a priest does.

## BIBLIOGRAPHY

Brunner, P.

1971    *The ministry and the ministry of women*, Concordia, St Louis.

Foster, R.

1980    'Submission', *Celebration of Discipline*, Hodder & Stoughton, London, 6–109.

Harper, M.

1994    *Equal and Different. Male and Female in Church and Society*, Hodder & Stoughton, London.

Hopko, T. ed.

1983    *Women and the Priesthood*, St Vladimir Seminary Press, New York.

Jenson, R.W.

1982    *The Triune Identity. God according to the Gospel*, Fortress, Philadelphia.

Kimel, A. F.

1991    'The God Who Likes His Name. Holy Trinity, Feminism, and the Language of Faith,' *Interpretation* 45, 147–158.

Lewis, C. S.

1970    'Priestesses in the Church?', in *God in the Dock. Essays on Theology and Ethics*; ed W. Hooper; Eerdmans, Grand Rapids, 234–239.

Little, J. A.

1995    *The Church and the Culture War. Secular Anarchy or Sacred Order*, Ignatius Press, San Francisco.

Luther, M.

1961    *Sermons on the Gospel of St John*; Luther's Works 24; tr M.H. Bertram; ed J. Pelikan; Concordia, St Louis.

Mascall, E. L.

1972    *Women Priests*, The Church Literature Association, London.

Novak, M.

1993    'Women, Ordination, and Angels', *First Things* 32, 25–32.

Oddie, W.

1984    *What Will Happen to God? Feminism and the Reconstruction of Christian Belief*, SPCK.

Weinrich, W.

1991    *It is not given to women to teach. A lex in search of a ratio*, Logia, Mankato.

Yoder, J. H.

1972    'Revolutionary Subordination', *The Politics of Jesus*, Eerdmans, Grand Rapids, 163–192.

# May Women Be Ordained as Pastors?

## David P. Scaer

### Part I: Introduction

#### A. "Why Face the Question?"

The entire issue of the ordination of women as pastors has hit the Lutheran Church in our country rather recently and without much warning or preparation. I have failed to discover any significant comment in Lutheran theological literature in America on the issue in the 1950's or in the first half of the last decade.

Three books have come across my desk written by women dealing with their role as pastors.[1] The one thing they have in common is that they feel it a plot of male domination that the office of pastor never be given to women. There is also no honest attempt to discuss the exegetical issues. Each writer assumes a type of democratic principle that men and women are equal, and without ever defining what is meant by "equality," states that women should be ordained as pastors without actually defending it from a Biblical stance. *Adam's Fractured Rib*, published by Fortress Press, even predicates of the Old Testament Jews and St. Paul a type of anti-feminism.

Whatever "anti-feminism" means, it does immediately suggest the women's liberation movement of the late sixties and seventies. One suspects that as long as our nation and perhaps the western world is taken up with the movement, the concern for the New Testament teaching in this question will be secondary. It is argued this way: Since men and women are equal and

---

1   Margaret Sittler Ermath, *Adam's Fractured Rib* (Philadephia: Fortress Press, 1970); *Women's Liberation and the Church*. Edited by Sarah Bentley Doely (New York: Association Press, 1970); Elsie Gibson, *When the Minister is a Woman* (New York: Holt, Rinehart and Winston, 1970). Cf. my reviews in *The Springfielder*, Vols. 34, (3) and (4); 35, (1).

since men serve as pastors, women should have the same privileges. Many concerns of the women are legitimate. Where they have been offended by lack of promotion and inadequate salary simply because they are women, this should be corrected. Still the church recognizes that its worship procedures are based on principles determined by God who has revealed His will in the Scriptures. Certainly the political and social climate influences the church and always will, but as history has shown, these have hardly been beneficial at all times. The situation in the United States may be further complicated by the proposed constitutional amendment guaranteeing equality regardless of sex.

## B. ITS ORIGINS

### 1. Europe

The contemporary movement in Lutheranism to ordain women as pastors originated not with any theological studies but because of the connection of the church and state in certain countries of Europe.[2] The history of the ancient Catholic Church does not know of women holding the pastoral office.[3] The Montanists knew of women preachers, but the witness of a sect judged to be heretical hardly can set in itself an example to be emulated.[4] The ordination of women in Lutheran churches occurred in those countries where the church is at least in some way supported and hence regulated by the government. The roots of this problem go back to Constantine. Since then, with only a few interruptions, church and state, throne and altar, have existed in alliance. Unfortunately the Lutheran Reformation did not abrogate but endorsed this

---

2    A summary of the situation in Europe was gathered by Dr. Fred Meuser, now president of Capital Lutheran Seminary in Columbus, Ohio of the American Lutheran Church in *The Ordination of Women* (Minneapolis: Augsburg, 1970), pp. 34f.

3    The question of the canonicity of the pseudipigraphal *Acts of Paul and Thecla* was decided negatively by Tertullian because the Asiatic clergyman who confessed to being the author "made Paul guilty of allowing a woman to preach and baptize." Bruce M. Metzger, "Literary Forgeries and Canonical Pseudepigrapha," *Journal of Biblical Literature*, Vol. 91 (March 1972), p. 14. Thus the early church understood the apostolic testimony as against women preachers.

4    The Montanists had many things in common with today's Pentecostals, including special manifestations of the Holy Spirit. There is very good reason to believe that the situation of the Montanists might have been parallel with that of the Corinthian congregation where so-called Spirit manifestations and the participation of women as leaders in the church service are treated by Paul as abuses. That 1 Corinthians 14 handles both problems is hardly coincidental. It could very well be that the Spirit movement is basically incompatible with the proper institution and correct exercise of the public office of the ministry. Pentecostals tend to treasure more highly their selective worship among themselves and to neglect the regular services of the congregation. Those possessed with the Spirit in Corinth, so they thought, had the right to speak at will, regardless of qualifications. Some had tried to set their authority up against Paul's (v. 34). It is hardly coincidental that the movement to ordain women as pastors is contemporary to Neo-Pentecostalism, at least in The Lutheran Church—Missouri Synod. The precedent for this is the Corinthian congregation and the Montanists.

arrangement on an emergency basis. The emergency situation of the state controlling Lutheran church affairs to some extent has lasted nearly one half of a millenium. At first kings in certain Lutheran countries appointed bishops and pastors and provided for the church's financial support. Since the time of the Enlightenment, the power of kings has steadily declined and the real power has been placed in the hands of the parliaments representing the people on a democratic basis. The authority of the monarch to support and regulate the church has been gradually transferred to the parliaments and prime ministers. To a certain extent the church has become a political implement in the hands of the government, reflecting in its organization the desires of the government in power. Thus it is not surprising that the first decisions to ordain women in Lutheran churches were political, not ecclesiastical. Norway permitted the first women pastors in the year 1938, but the decision was made by parliament not by a church convention representing the congregations. Until 1956 a woman appointed pastor of a congregation by the government could be rejected by a congregation. At that time even this right was taken away from the congregation. It was not until 1961 or twenty-three years after the law was passed that a woman was ordained in Norway. Denmark and Sweden would follow suit. East Germany and Czechoslovakia took similar action. In each of these cases the action was taken by governments with socialist or communist leanings.[5]

A word should be said about the case in Sweden as it indicates the tension between the church and state. The ordination of women as pastors was rejected by the church convention; however, it was made law by the parliament, which in Sweden has been socialist controlled for many years. Faced with this dilemma, the church convention subsequently approved it. A number of bishops opposed it. Bishop Bo Giertz and others have fought it tooth and nail on the bases of Holy Scripture and the Lutheran Confessions.[6] Women pastors are now the rule in European Lutheran territorial churches with the exception of Bavaria. There Bishop Dietzfelbinger has made a valiant stand against his own church convention.[7] Statistically it might be said, as *Ordination of Women* claims, that "Over half of the Lutherans in the world are in churches which now have women clergy on their rolls."[8] Now that

---

5    All of the cases taken from Fred Meuser, *op. cit.*, pp. 33–39.

6    Dean Gustav Danell, acting as bishop during the illness of the regular bishop, went so far as to lock the church doors when women came for ordination. *The Springfielder*, Vol. 34, 1, (June 1970), p. 68.

7    In the summer of 1970 members of the Bavarian Church had expected that church to implement the ordination of women pastors against the desires of their bishop, who had been in ill health. Surprisingly this church has not carried through with these plans.

8    *Op. cit.*, p. 35.

two large Lutheran bodies in America have taken the step, nearly 60 or 70% of world Lutheranism endorses the practice of women in the pastoral role.[9] However, arguments for the ordination of women as pastors based on the practices of Lutheran churches throughout the world are tenuous at best, as the action was initiated by the state and not the church and was politically motivated with theological considerations secondary or non-existent. In some cases the state forced women pastors on the churches against their expressed will.

## 2. The United States

The situation in the United States can be surveyed briefly. Of course, in our country, the government does not control the church. After what some confessionally minded Lutherans have endured for the sake of conscience in Europe at the hands of the state,[10] I believe that we have something for which to be thankful. The first step to the ordination of women came when the seminaries of the American Lutheran Church and the Lutheran Church in America admitted women into their regular 'B.D.' programs of their seminaries.[11] The next step could have been predicted. The question then had to be asked of what to do with women 'B.D.' students. In 1967, the ALC's Church Council found nothing biblically or theologically opposing the ordination of women. They did indicate that there might be practical and ecumenical difficulties.[12] Here the door was opened. The only opposition was one of expediency in which some might be offended. The LCA followed suit in 1968 when its Commission on the Comprehensive Study of the Doctrine of the

9 Church statistics can be deceptive, especially in giving the membership of Lutheran churches throughout the world. In Scandinavia and many parts of Germany, the Lutheran population is basically coterminous with the resident population. They are Lutherans by law even without baptism. In the United States they are Lutherans by choice. The Lutheran churches in Europe face the prospect of de-establishment. In compiling membership figures for world Lutheranism we are adding numbers which do not in any way represent the same things. In some European Lutheran churches the attendance of the people at church does not even represent 1% of the membership. American churches have their problems, but if we dare to compare, the results will be quite obvious. Forty-one per cent attend on a weekly average in America.

10 The union between Lutheran and Reformed, as the ordination of women pastors, was instigated and enforced by the state. Most infamous is the Prussian Union of 1817 and 1830. The majority of the remaining Lutheran and Reformed churches in Europe have now willingly expressed their desire for fellowship on the basis of the Leuenberg Concord of 1971. Cf. *The Springfielder*, Vol. 35, 4, (March 1972), pp. 241–249.

11 *The Ordination of Women*, pp. 36f. More recent reports assert that 22 women are enrolled in Luther Seminary, St. Paul (ALC) with the Gettysburg Lutheran Seminary (LCA) having an equal amount. Until now the several ordained women in the ALC and LCA have been isolated incidences. In ten years this will hardly be the case.

12 This is the same attitude held now by some in the Lutheran Church—Missouri Synod. Cf. "The Orders of Creation," *Concordia Theological Monthly*, Vol. 43, 4, (March 1972), p. 177.

Ministry approved the practice. The ALC and the LCA do not have their own theological commissions as does the Missouri Synod. They rely instead on the Division of Theological Studies of the Lutheran Council in the U.S.A. Sometime in late spring or early summer 1970, the division of theological studies published the booklet *The Ordination of Women* which came to the conclusion that there was nothing commanding and nothing forbidding the ordination of women as pastors of congregations. It was declared to be what our Confessions called an adiaphoron, neither commanded nor forbidden and not a matter of revelation and doctrine.[13] The results contained in this booklet were received as the theological opinion of both the LCA and ALC at their plenary conventions in the summer of 1970 when both groups endorsed the ordination of women pastors. The press reported that there was little or no theological discussion on the issue. The vote in the LCA was nearly overwhelming, while in the ALC the vote was closer than anticipated. To date, at least one woman in each of these synods has received ordination. At its conventions in 1969 and 1971, the Missouri Synod continued to oppose the practice as doctrinally contrary to Scripture.[14]

## PART II: IS THE ORDINATION OF WOMEN AS PASTORS PERMISSIBLE ACCORDING TO THE NEW TESTAMENT?

### A. WHAT DO WE MEAN BY ORDINATION?

In answering any question about the ordination of women as pastors, the meaning of ordination must be defined. Ordination as a ceremony for entering the office of the ministry is an adiaphoron, as it is not commanded or forbidden by the Scriptures. The term can mean exactly what the church wants it to. This is true of other theological terms, the most outstanding of which may be "sacrament."[15] The public office of the ministry is not an adiaphoron but is commanded by God. Generally in the Missouri Synod the term ordination by common consent is used to designate the service in which an individual is recognized as being capable of performing all the functions of the pastoral ministry, whether or not he actually performs all of them. Thus ordination

---

13  The same position was asserted by the president of the ALC. (Cf. *Lutheran Witness Reporter* VII, (November 14, 1971), p. 3. As the matter is not specifically handled in the Lutheran Confessions, it cannot be made a matter of fellowship. This is similar to the debate between the Missouri and the Iowa synods in the 19th century. Missouri held that whatever was revealed by God was binding and Iowa held only that which the Lutheran Confessions specifically discuss is binding. Cf. Fred W. Meuser, *The Formation of the American Lutheran Church* (Columbus: Wartburg Press, 1958), pp. 56–62.

14  "A Statement of Scriptural and Confessional Principles" issued by Dr. J. A. O. Preus, president of the Missouri Synod, in March 1972 seems to support this position. Cf. p. 2.

15  Cf. Augsburg Confession XIV and especially Apology XIII.

may be the first installation service or it is closely connected with the first installation service.[16]

However ordination may be given a broader definition, depending on the needs of the church.[17] It may designate as "ordination" any service in which an individual is publicly recognized as having been assigned or called to any office in the church. Here can be included parochial school teachers, church officers who are generally inducted into service sometime after the first of the year, Sunday School teachers, and Vacation Bible School teachers. The list can be as long as there are services officially connected with the church. Evangelism and stewardship callers can also be ordained into their offices. Persons who undergo these types of ordination services are not pastors as they are not ordained or recognized as pastors. They are ordained only into the function which the congregation assigns to them and for the length of time which the congregation assigns them. A parochial school teacher may be given his task for several years or a lifetime. Perhaps a VBS teacher works two weeks, and an evangelism caller is assigned for several hours on a given Sunday afternoon. Let it be said clearly that such people publicly recognized by the congregation for specific functions possess a public office but not the office of the pastor. Strictly speaking, there can be no opposition of the ordination of women so long as that ordination is not to the office of pastor. They are by no means excluded from every office or function in the church.[18] The issue before us is the ordination of women as pastors of churches—not the question of whether they can be given certain public offices in the church in a public way.[19] The life of sanctification whereby every Christian witnesses

---

16  Until the 1960's many seminary graduates who had served as missionaries or instructors at synodical schools were not ordained because they were not called as pastors directly by individual congregations. They were commissioned. This provided an awkward situation when they accepted calls as pastors. The common procedure was to install or commission them but not ordain them. Thus there are some pastors in the Missouri Synod who have not been ordained, in the sense of having undergone a rite specifically called 'ordination.'

17  Here we are reminded that form follows function in the organization of the church. Unlike Roman Catholics, Anglicans, Presbyterians, Congregationalists, Baptists and others, Lutherans have never insisted on any one form of church government and have refrained from regarding the organization of the New Testament churches as legally binding. If such were the case, we would be faced with embarrassingly different forms of church government, e.g., 1 Corinthians with its apostles, teachers, prophets, tongue speakers, etc. and 1 Timothy with its pastors and deacons. Cf. Herman Sasse, "Walther and Loehe: On the Church," *The Springfielder*, Vol. 35, 3, (December 1971), 176–182.

18  "The Orders of Creation," *op. cit.*, seems to suggest this possibility with which I would agree. A clear definition of "professional ministerial roles" would be beneficial.

19  This position is also held by Dr. Berthold von Schenk. "There is no Scriptural reason why she should not be ordained, but she can't celebrate or preach in the Liturgy of the Eucharist, for she symbolizes the Bride of Christ." *The Springfielder*, Vol. 36, 1, (June 1972), p. 11.

to Christ continually falls not under the category of ordination, but under baptism as no specific functions are designated.

## B. CAN WOMEN BE PASTORS?

The real question is whether women can serve on a permanent basis as pastors of congregations. This is the action endorsed by the majority of the European Lutheran churches and the LCA and the ALC in America. It also has widespread and growing support in the Missouri Synod. Therefore we must pose the question to the New Testament, "Does the New Testament permit women pastors?"[20] and not the question "Does the New Testament know of the ordination of women pastors?"

### I. 1 Corinthians 14: 33b–38

*a. Context*

Of the several passages in the New Testament that might possibly speak to the issues, I Corinthians 14:33b–38 must be singled out first. Let us first attempt to reconstruct the context. Paul's great concern from chapters 11 through 16:4 is liturgical. In other words, he is interested in setting the worship life of the Corinthian congregation in order procedurally and doctrinally. In Chapter 11 he deals with the problem of women having uncovered heads and drunkenness and gluttony in the church in connection with the Lord's Supper. Chapter 12 discusses how various gifts in the congregation are to be used. Some of these gifts are connected with the worship service, for example, the utterance of knowledge and wisdom and the gift of tongues. The famous chapter on love, 13, is really a parenthetical element, following Chapter 12. Love or consideration is to be used in manifesting various gifts in the worship service of the church. This admonition applies quite specifically to the tongue speakers. Chapter 14:1–33b discusses the necessity of clarity of preaching in the church. Chapter 14:37–40 sums up Paul's authority as an apostle to interfere in the worship affairs of the congregation. Chapter 15, the great section in the New Testament on the resurrection of Jesus, deals with the content of the Christian preaching in the Corinthian congregation. Chapter 16:1–4 deals with the problem of taking up monetary collections in the congregation with the suggestion that it be done every Sunday. The remaining verses of the chapter and book are Paul's farewell greetings. We may also assume that these greetings were read right in the middle of the regular worship service. This

---

20 The question, thus worded "Does the New Testament know of women pastors" is fraught with difficulties, It is an historical question and akin to the Aland-Jeremias debate on infant baptism. The theological principle is at issue here, not the political administration of the church at Corinth. Regardless of the type of church administration adopted, the basic principle involved is whether women may lead the worship services.

might be the beginning of special intercessions for individuals read from the diptych in connection with the celebration of the sacrament.

*b. Exegesis of I Corinthians 14:33b–38*

The section dealing with the silence of women appears among other sections that deal specifically with the worship services. Whatever is meant by silence or not being permitted to speak has to do with the regular worship services. It does not mean that whenever Christians get together, that women are not allowed to speak. Let us divide our discussion of this section into three parts: I. What does Paul mean by requiring the silence of women in the church? II. By what authority does Paul enforce this regulation on the church? III. Can Paul's prohibition be interpreted sociologically as being the custom of the day and hence not applicable in another time or culture?

I. What does Paul mean by requiring the silence of women in the church?

The prohibition applies specifically to the regular worship services. It has already been shown that chapters 11 through 16 have to do with the regulations of the worship service. This pericope does not demand that women must be silent at all times. It does not forbid women from witnessing to Jesus Christ. Lydia, as we know, was instrumental in gathering Christians for the congregation in Philippi. Neither does it mean that women cannot give instruction outside of the regular worship services. Priscilla and her husband Aquilla (Acts 18:26) expounded Christianity to Apollos. This was a private instruction and had nothing to do with the public proclamation of the Word in the regular worship services. The Greek word *didasko* deals with the public proclamation and it is not used to describe Priscilla's private instruction.[21] The passage also says nothing of women as teachers in our schools, as these are not involved with the leading of public worship of the congregation. Therefore those arguments that suggest that if we take this passage "literally"[22] (whatever that might or might not mean) we could not have women parochial or Sunday

---

21  The LCUSA's *The Ordination of Women* very wisely does not use the case of Priscilla as a major part of its argument. Still it is a little more than slightly confusing in stating that she, Lydia, and Thelica had "leadership roles." The phrase "leadership roles" has all the marks of the 20th century culture and in any case seems totally inadequate in describing the functions of these women. The phrase leadership roles" may mean positions of responsibility. To assert that certain individuals, male or female, are permitted to take various responsibilities in the church hardly per se means that they are capable of assuming the pastoral office in the church, no more than a Sunday School or parochial school teacher, male or female, can be a pastor. *Op. cit.*, p. 24.

22  This view is set forth in *The Ordination of Women, op. cit.*, p. 14. "By pointing out that if it is taken literally, women may not teach in church school or parochial school, direct choirs, or even pray or sing aloud." If the question of the ordination of women becoming pastors were not so serious, one would like to suggest that the writer of this phrase has slipped from the sublime into the ridiculous. Literally Paul is forbidding not the use of female vocal chords, but the women's participation in the sermon. The prohibition to 'teach' refers to public instruction of the congregation. Cf. Bo Giertz,

School teachers, have not taken into consideration the situation to which the Apostle is speaking.

As we have defined the location to which the prohibition refers, namely the church services, we must define what it means "not to speak". Twice in this pericope Paul forbids women from speaking. A third time, he mentions that they should keep silent. Thus, within four verses there are three prohibitions. We can hardly say that this prohibition was merely a slip of the apostolic pen. The term speak used here is *lalao* and not *lego*. *Lego* means any kind of speaking or use of the vocal chords in some type of intelligible words. *Lalao*, unless otherwise modified by adverbs, when used in connection with worship services, refers to religious speaking or speaking religiously in the public way.[23] Thus Paul does not mean that women may not participate in the public singing of the congregations and the spoken prayers, i.e., the Lord's Prayer. The command to keep silent is a command not to take charge of the public worship service. The NEB catches it best when it translates the section in question in this way: "Women should not address the meeting. They have no license to speak . . . It is a shocking thing that a woman should address the congregation."[24] I Timothy 2:12 has the same intent. The situation in the Corinthian congregation can be partially reconstructed. Women in Corinth were accustomed from the association with the Temple of Aphrodite in that city to lead worship services. As there had been priestesses in the adulterous and idolatrous worship of the sex goddesses it was quite natural for them to assume the leadership roles in the Christian congregation.[25] Paul specifically forbids this.

---

"Twenty-Three Theses on The Holy Scriptures, The Women, and the Office of the Ministry" *The Springfielder*, Vol 33, 4, (March 1970), p. 14f.

23  *Ibid.*

24  Whether the Corinthian congregation had a sermon in the sense that we do is open to question. *The Living Bible* paraphrases that idea with "They are not to participate in the discussion." At Corinth there might have been something of a dialog sermon with various persons or officers of the congregation commenting on the sermon. Paul's prohibition is against their participation in this kind of activity. The question of whether ths congregation knew of 'ordained pastors' cannot be discussed here, as it cannot be determined whether the ceremony of ordination was exercised here. But if Paul is forbidding women from the minor role of theological discussion in the church service as seems the case from these words "If there is anything they desire to know, let them ask their husbands at home," it can hardly be argued or permitted to state that they should assume the task of discussion leaders.

25  *The Ordination of Women, op. cit.*, pp. 14f. suggests that the subordination of the women "is typical of the code morality which shows up in several New Testament references. It is a catechetical form perhaps taken over from the culture of the day." *If anything, Paul is going against the prevailing culture in not letting women participate in the church services as leaders.* Also it will not do to state that he is imposing his "Jewish" culture upon the Gentiles. He fought tooth and nail against imposing the Jewish circumcision regulations on the Galatians and holiday regulations on the Colossians. In the matter of hats,

II. We must now speak to the second question: "By what authority does Paul enforce this regulation upon the church?"

Paul is not slack in offering more than a few authorities in refusing women permission to exercise the leadership role in the congregation. (1) First it is not permitted by what he calls the "Law." The reference here is not necessarily to the Ten Commandments, though this is not excluded. He is referring to the Torah, the written revelation of God, the Scriptures.[26] Regardless of who wrote I Timothy 2 (and I for one still accept the Pauline authorship), I Timothy 2:14 is a further application of what Paul calls the Law. Here in I Timothy he points to the account contained in the written revelation of the creation of Adam and Eve and the subsequent fall into sin. I Corinthians 11 also refers back to Genesis 2. (2) He refers to his own apostolic office. "What! Did the word of God originate with you, . . . ?" Obviously this is not a question asked for information, but a rhetorical question. Both Paul and the Corinthians knew where the authoritative word of God originated—God has spoken through His apostle Paul. In 11:23 and 15:3, he speaks about passing things along to the Corinthians that he had learned at the hand of God. (3) He appeals to the Holy Spirit. "If anyone thinks that he is a prophet or spiritual, he should acknowledge that what I am writing is a command of the Lord." Paul appeals to those people in the congregation who have been claiming for themselves some type of unique inspiration of the Spirit. If they really do have the Spirit, and this is questionable, then with their gifts of the Spirit they should also recognize that Paul is "inspired" by the Holy Spirit so that he knows the mind of God. The background for this is 2:11–16 where those who truly have the Spirit will recognize the Spirit speaking through Paul. (4) Fourthly, Paul calls upon Jesus as an authority. Forbidding women to lead the public worship is "a command" of the Lord.[27] The Greek word *entole* has the force of a divine decree that threatens punishment to all those who break it. In the Sermon on the Mount Jesus uses the word *entole* in the plural to describe the entire Old Testament revelation as unbreakable. "Think not that I have come to abolish the law and the prophets; I have come not to abolish them but to fulfill them. . . . Whoever then relaxes one of the least of these *com-*

---

he suggests that men go bare headed and the women wear head coverings which is also against the known common Jewish usage.

26 Bo Giertz, *op. cit.*, p. 15.

27 Some have tried to mitigate the force of the word "Lord" by stating that "Lord" in the New Testament simply can refer to an honorific title for important men. The case cited was Matthew 25:37 and 44 where at the judgment Jesus is addressed as "Lord." Obviously this pericope of the final judgment uses the term in a divine sense and not merely honorific. Secondly, and here we can use the opinions of even the most radical and liberal New Testament scholars, that if the New Testament is merely a book written by the church to glorify Jesus, then "Lord" is an example of calling Jesus the Son of God. The lack of an article would only suggest that there is only one LORD.

*mandments* and teaches men so, shall be called least in the kingdom of heaven" (Matt. 5:17, 19). He places the prohibition against women pastors on the same level as the Lord's Supper and Resurrection. All three have Jesus' own authority behind them.

III. The third question is: "Can Paul's prohibition be interpreted sociologically as being the custom of the day?"[28]

Those who do not see anything in our passage dealing with women pastors generally take two approaches in interpretation. One, Paul is just reflecting current mores which did not let women speak. Two, Paul is reflecting his own "hang-ups" about women. John Reumann suggests the first in the LCUSA booklet, while Peggy Ann Way in her article in *Women's Liberation and the Church*[29] finds the latter to be the case. Let's tackle the first question. I Corinthians is written to a thoroughly Gentile congregation. It was the Jews and not the Gentiles that forbad women to participate in the worship services. The pagan cults in Canaan from the time of the Jewish invasion had female gods and priestesses. Aphrodite, a Hellenistic form of the Phoenician sex deity Astarte, was found in Corinth. Paul could hardly just be expressing custom in not letting women participate as pastors, since custom not only allowed Gentile women to participate, but encouraged them to lead in the worship. It is safe to assume that the desire of women to be pastors in the Corinthian congregation is directly traceable to the pagan influence of the priestesses at the temple of Aphrodite. This is not mere speculation, as Paul in the same epistle speaks of the Christians' relationship to idols.[30] Apparently some Christians were attending the Lord's Supper and pagan worship.[31] If the Corinthians could not totally detach themselves from their idols, no wonder that they could not detach themselves from their priestesses. The second objection in regard to our passage is that Paul is reflecting his own "hang-ups" about women. It seems unlikely that Paul was anti-feminist. He depended upon Lydia in the establishment of the congregation in Philippi and he calls

---

28 *The Ordination of Women, op. cit.*, p. 13. "Should this instruction (concerning silence of women in the churches) be brushed aside as no more binding than Paul's tastes in clothes and hairstyles? He might just have been irked with wives who had interrupted." This is hardly a serious exegetical option and is no credit to St. Paul or the writer's interpretation of this apostle.

29 Peggy Ann Way, "An Authority of Possibility For Women in the Church," *Women's Liberation and the Church, op. cit.*, p. 81. "Shall we women spend our tune developing nice little papers on what Paul really meant or how he would speak in a different cultural setting, or, on another level discovering that he was once in love with a temple prostitute who rejected him and from which came his feelings about women?"

30 I Corinthians 8.

31 I Corinthians 10, especially v. 21, "You cannot drink the cup of the Lord and the cup of demons."

Priscilla and Phoebe[32] fellow workers. In addition there are a number of things in our pericope that speak eloquently that the prohibition of women into the pastoral office is a universal prohibition, not limited in time and in space and in culture. (1) First he says, "As in *all* the churches of the saints." The prohibition is not limited to the Corinthian congregation, but Paul is putting down a principle that is applicable to every congregation. In the word "all" there is no room for exceptions.[33] (2) Secondly, he labels women's leading of the public services as "shameful". In Ephesians 5:12 he uses the same word to designate not the secret things done by the children of darkness, but the mere description of them. (3) Thirdly, Paul threatens excommunication to those who favor giving women the leadership role in the congregation. "If anyone does not recognize this, he is not recognized." There are two interpretations here possible. Paul is cutting him off from the congregation or God is no longer recognizing such an individual as a Christian. The end result in both cases is the same, exclusion from the church.[34]

*c. Other considerations in connection with I Corinthians 14:33b–38*

I. Some claim that Paul's concern was with order in the church and verse 33a is quoted in this regard. "For God is not a God of confusion but of peace." This is hardly an adequate explanation. First, according to the published Greek texts this passage belongs to the previous section. Secondly, from the context it belongs to the previous section where Paul deals with the problem of several people speaking at the same time. Thirdly, if Paul is concerned with mere orderliness or everyone speaking in turn, why does he only forbid the women from speaking? This would cure only half the problem. Does this mean that Paul allows disorderly men, but not disorderly women? If Paul was

---

32 Romans 16:1–4.

33 Some have contended that these were regulations just for the Corinthian congregation. This does not seem to be the case, but was regulation for all the churches. The prohibition against women pastors has the same type of force that the commands to baptize and celebrate Holy Communion have. They only lose their force when the final eschaton breaks through. The distinctions between male and female and hence the restriction of men to the pastoral office, pass away in the new age (Matt. 22:30). The pastoral office itself passes away at Christ's coming. Forbidding women in the pastoral office in no way speaks to the faith or glorification level of sexes. There are levels of glory in heaven, but no continuation of church offices.

34 *The Ordination of Women, op. cit.*, p. 13 suggests that perhaps Paul is not responsible for (vv. 34 and 35) these words or that perhaps Paul was not really being Pauline. "It could be that these verses were added later. Some manuscripts have verses 34 and 35 following 40; the verses do seem out of context as they are here; and it is odd to hear Paul saying, 'as even the law says.'" The one responsible for this section must, as a New Testament scholar, be aware that Paul uses the term "law" in different senses. Here the term has nothing to do with the Law-Gospel antithesis as used in classical Lutheran theology.

concerned with orderliness, then he should have suggested that the women wait their turn to speak. He doesn't. He simply tells them to be silent.

II. Some claim that I Corinthians 14:33b–38, the section on women speaking, is no more binding today than I Corinthians 11:2–16, the section on head coverings for women. The argument goes that just as we allow women to go without hats in church, so we should also allow them to be pastors. True, our churches do not demand that women attend church with covered heads, though some continue the custom as a legitimate expression of piety, but this should hardly permit us to dismiss the theological principles contained in this pericope.

The theological principles of the relationship of the man to the woman are more carefully spelled out here than in I Corinthians 14. I Corinthains 11 very much resembles I Timothy 2, as will be shown below. First, Paul identifies the eternal principle or truth with the word "traditions," *paradoseis,* the same root word which is used in connection with the Lord's Supper and the Resurrection in the same book.[35] This is something established by God and before God as true and binding. No deviation is permitted. The theological principle is this: "But I want you to understand that the head of every man is Christ, the head of a woman is her husband, and the head of Christ is God." The imagery here cannot be dismissed.[36] Paul sees in the relationship between a man and woman a reflection of the relationship between Christ and man and the relationship between God and Christ. The first one deals with the concept of the image of God, the second with the relationship between God and His Christ. Paul says in verse 7 that man is made in God's image and woman in man's image. In I Timothy 2:13 Paul says the same thing by stating that Adam was created first and then Eve. God has established in the creation a certain order or relationship. To man and woman individual functions are assigned and it is not proper, in fact, it is unlawful to step outside of this order.[37] The functions are not interchangeable. Even Christ has a position

---

35  1 Corinthians 11:23, 15:3. Cf. also 2 Corinthians 2:15, "So then, brethren, stand firm and hold to the traditions which you were taught by us, either by word of mouth or by letter."

36  This concept was both adequately and beautifully portrayed by C. S. Lewis, "Priestesses in the Church" in God in the Dock (Grand Rapids: Eerdmans, 1970), pp. 234–239, especially p. 238. "We have no authority to take the living and semitive figures which God has painted on the canvas of our nature and shift them about as if they were mere geometrical figures." Ephesians 5:21–33 applies the Christ-Church imagery to the husband-wife relationship within the family. This principle is also applicable to the congregation's worship.

37  This is substantiated by Martin Scharlemann in "Apostolic Form," a devotion delivered to a St. Louis pastoral conference on May 8, 1972. His argument is based on 1 Peter 2:13. The Greek word used is *hypotassesthai*. In the next chapter Peter discusses how the male-female principle applies to the family. Though worship services are not discussed, the same principle applies to the regulations of both family and worship services.

in regard to God that must be kept. God assigns the Messianic tasks to Christ. The reverse is not true.[38]

The question which now must be asked is: "Are women permitted to go without hats to churches?" We have already established that we are dealing with divinely established principles by which the man is the head of the woman and that the woman bears the image of the man. The practice of covering or uncovering the head belongs not to doctrine or the practice of doctrine, but to custom reflecting doctrine or principle. Paul closes the section with the words, "But if anyone wants argue about it, all I have to say is that neither we nor the churches of God have any other *habit* in worship." (NEB 11:16). The Greek word, *synetheia* means something which is expected of people, but which is not legally established. Pilate says that the Jews have a *custom* of releasing a prisoner at the feast.[39] He is hardly legally bound to take such action. There are many things in our culture that we are expected to do, but not bound by law to do so. Standing when a woman comes into the room and offering her a seat is a type of custom in our culture. We show deference and respect for the "weaker sex." Giving presents and sending cards at Christmas is another custom. Customs make up the very fiber of our culture. These we do by common consent, not because of legal compulsion. Paul is not establishing a once and for all culture. His whole strife with the Judaizers, characteristic of his ministry from the beginning, militates against this. He is saying that culture through its own forms should express divine principles when applied in a worship service. We can surmise that women without hair coverings in Corinth were expressing a type of contempt of men. Expressions of such contempt are always wrong. However in another culture women might show respect to men by having their heads uncovered. Regardless of the culture, the customs and practices derived from the culture and used in the worshipping congregation should reflect and never go against divinely established principle. The principle is that the man is the head of the woman, as Christ is the head of man. But note in this section that Paul is not setting down an eternal binding custom. Unlike Chapter 14 he does not appeal to the Scriptures, Jesus, the apostolic office, or the Holy Spirit in establishing the custom. He is, however, quite adamant about upholding the principle.

III. Some claim that I Corinthians 11:15 presupposes that women were allowed to lead in the services and that Paul changed his mind in Chapter 14.[40] Here is the passage in question, "any woman who prays or prophesies with

---

38  1 Corinthians 15:28.

39  John 18:39.

40  *The Ordination of Women* (p. 13) suggests that Paul might have changed his mind. "If it is taken seriously, a contradiction must be resolved. How can it be that Paul allowed the Corinthian women both to pray and prophesy in the previous passage (1 Corinthians 11), while in this one he forbids them to speak in the church?" The

her head unveiled dishonors her head—it is the same as if her head were shaven." What this 'prophesying' was is difficult to determine with exactness. There were many gifts present in the Corinthian congregation which the Spirit has not given to the church in the post-apostolic period and which also do not appear in other churches at that time. Chapter 12 lists these gifts as working miracles, speaking in tongues, distinguishing tongues and interpreting tongues and prophesying. There is no suggestion that prophesying and leading the worship as pastor are the same gifts or offices,[41] any more than speaking in tongues and the offices of the pastor are the same gifts. I do not wish to go into detail to explain why these gifts are not always given to the church today. The ultimate answer is that the Holy Spirit and not the enthusiasm of men decides. I will rely on the words of St. Paul, ". . . the same Spirit who apportions to each one individually as he *wills*" (12:11). Perhaps praying and prophesying meant going around in a circle and asking each to say a prayer or word of testimony, but this is only a guess and no more. Such activity must be distinguished from the actual leading of the worship.

Still the words "any woman who prays or prophesies with her head uncovered" can hardly be interpreted to mean conclusively that he approves of women who do this with their heads covered. Consider in the same chapter Paul's rebuke of gluttony and drunkenness in connection with the Lord's Supper. "For in eating, each one goes ahead with his own meal, and one is hungry and another is drunk. What! Do you not have houses to eat and drink! (12:21f.)" Does this passage mean that Paul disapproves of drunkenness in the church, but not at home? Hardly, because Paul in Galatians 5:21 stated that drunkards shall not inherit the kingdom of God. Being drunk is bad enough; but Paul pleads with the congregation not to do it in the church, bringing added offense to the congregation and damnation to themselves. Therefore Paul's words about women covering their heads when they pray and prophesy cannot by themselves be used as an apostolic endorsement of their praying and prophesying. They could very well mean, at least hypothetically, that it is a disgraceful habit for women to participate as leaders of the worship, but what is worse is that they do it with uncovered heads. Still there is no conclusive evidence that "prophesying" is identical with actually leading the worship services. Regardless of its exact meaning it probably is witnessing in which all Christians engage.

---

answer is quite obvious in that prophesying and praying were different from leading the worship service and participating in the discussion centering around the sermon.

41  However, this is just the suggestion made in *The Ordination of Women*, p. 24. "They serve as prophetesses (1 Corinthians 11; Acts 21:9), perhaps 'ordained' at Corinth, certainly speaking in the Lord's name under the Spirit." Walter A. Maier in "Some Thoughts on the Role of Women in the Church," *The Springfielder* Vol. 33, (4) 34, interprets prophesying as any type of witnessing in the Gospel.

## 2. I Timothy 2:12–14

The other passage that should be considered is I Timothy 2:12–14. There are some who consider that the author was not St. Paul and that he had no connection with St. Paul. This I am not willing to grant. But regardless of who wrote it, it must be regarded as the first commentary available to us on I Corinthians. In other words, in this passage Paul repeats his prohibition of women as pastors or someone from the first century has accurately repeated Pauline thought. Here also Paul or the unknown author is also dealing with liturgical regulations. He speaks about having intercession for civil authorities in the worship service (2:1–7). Then he goes on to say that the leadership roles in the worship service should be given to men (2:8–15). The leadership roles of bishop and deacon can only be given to men, but not to every man, so he sets the regulations for pastors and deacons (3:1–13). The second chapter ends with a type of concluding summary of these instructions. Here there are two bases for his argument. (1) He asserts his apostolic authority. "I permit no woman to teach or to have authority over men." This we have already discussed in connection with I Corinthians 14. (2) He argues from the creation of Eve from Adam and that therefore Eve was dependent on Adam. He mentions the fall into sin. The fall has not destroyed the relationship between male and female or their distinctive creative roles, but it has added tensions. The woman still bears children, but with pain. The man works, but with sweat. Men and woman still live together, but with enmity. To this Paul is referring when he says, "For Adam was formed first, then Eve; and Adam was not deceived, but the woman was deceived and became the transgressor" (v. 13f.). Paul in I Corinthians has previously established the dependency of the woman on the man at the creation (I Corinthians 11:8f.)

This is not so much an argument to Scripture as it is to creation. The argument to creation is stronger than to Scripture, simply because creation is the first act of God.[42] Jesus used the same argument to the creation when the Pharisees tried to justify divorce on the basis of the Mosaic Law. He refers to the creation, "Have you not read that he who made them from the beginning made them male and female . . ." (Matt. 19:5). What God has made may not arbitrarily be changed. In fact the written Law of God is only a reflection of the plan already established in the creation.[43] Paul's reference to the fall of

---

42 The issue comes down basically to the matter of natural law, which according to the Lutheran Confessions, precedes the written law. Cf. Holsten Fagerberg, *A New Look at the Lutheran Confessions*. Translated by Gene J. Lund. (St. Louis: Concordia Publishing House, 1972), pp. 64–75. Paul in 1 Corinthians 11 and 1 Timothy argues not from God said but what God *did*.

43 Since this article was first prepared an opposing view was set forth in "The Orders of Creation—Some Reflections on the History and Place of the Term in Systematic Theology," *Concordia Theological Monthly*, Vol. 43, 3, (March 1972) 165–178, which maintains basically the same thesis set forth in much more abbreviated form in "The

Role of Women." The latter article, appearing in *Advance* (Cf. note 45), has been widely used and quoted by those in The Lutheran Church—Missouri Synod who have supported the women pastors. The more recently published article contains further argumentation and will also receive much attention. The article cannot receive the full attention here that it requires and deserves. Still the basic argument is that even though God might have established a relationship between the male and female in the beginning, these relationships are not necessarily binding today. Basic to the argument is that God is ordering the world continually and that the church can read history so to speak to determine what God is doing. The pertinent paragraph is included here:

"Because the orders as trans-individual patterns and configurations of a whole society are historical entities, they are subject to the 'law' (that is, the Creator's law) of historical change. Cannot the same also be said about the pattern of relationship between the sexes from one age to another? In St. Paul's day it appears that womanly subordination was the Creator's order (societal placement). Today it is obvious that there has been some change since St. Paul's time and place in this cultural phenomenon. If the Creator has continued to be the Creator during the intervening years, why cannot we admit that the present growing 'equality' station of women is a work of the Creator? Into what placement is God putting women now? He is not placing them into a societal web of subordination—at least not in the Western world—nor is He placing the males into a superordinate ranking. It is in this situation of equalization of ranks that men and women are called to be God's kind of men and women. How did such a change arise? Historians and sociologists can chronicle some of the factors in the metamorphosis. Should Christians not expect that one of the abetting factors in the West may well have been Christians living their 'life under the Gospel' in the two millennia of the Gospel's history in the Western world? The CTCR report is chary about acknowledging that the 'order of redemption' can bring about concrete changes in the 'orders of creation,' but is that perhaps not a sign of weak faith, rather than of theological precision? A sweeping generalization about all orders of creation will be of little help to anyone. Yet in the particular placement of women in Western society the new order of God's Gospel has surely helped to shape some of the changes."

The concepts involved resemble process theology or philosophy whereby God continues to create the *novum*. Man in every age is capable of interpreting these actions of God. The doctrine of creation, as taught in the Lutheran Church, is that creation is an accomplished act of God. God preserves and multiples what He has already created (Genesis 1 and 2). It is also argued that if St. Paul based his opposition to the ordination of women on the signs of his times, so we in our age where women are receiving more rights should and must be able to read the signs of our times. This kind of an argument blurs the distinction between special and natural revelation. In the sense that history or culture or the like is a bearer of revelation, this concept greatly resembles the theories of revelation held by Pannenberg and other theologians connected with the 'theology of hope.' Using history by itself as a vehicle of revelation is a very dangerous thing. One could conclude that in the early 1940's that God was telling us that killing Jews was proper in that God was speaking to us through Hitler's history. But this is the very argument offered in claiming that God in history is saying that women can be pastors. The proposed amendment to the American Constitution giving equal rights to women will surely be used. According to the Apology of the Augsburg Confession what God has established in creation is not open to change as long as we are in the present aeon. *Porro ius naturale vere est ius divinum, quia est ordinatio divinitus impressa naturae* (XXXIII, 12). The Gospel can have an effect in the changes in society which is of

Eve before Adam suggests that she unlawfully assumed the religious responsibility for that first community and in so doing violated God's established order between the man and woman. Adam bore the image of God and served as God's spokesman and intermediary between God and man. By the "theological" conversation with the serpent, Eve assumed a function which God had not given her. Adam was given the command and promise and he was responsible for all "theological negotiations." Thus the woman's assuming the man's role and his assenting to this incursion are part of the first sin. Women preaching and celebrating Mass could very well be a graphic representation of the first sin.

In regard to the Timothy passage some have concluded that if we would follow this literally then women could not be allowed to teach in any capacity in the church. The word for teach is *didaskein*[44] and it refers to the official and

---

course contaminated with sin as the article indicates. We can agree with the statement: "Yet in the particular placement of women in Western society the new order of God's Gospel has surely helped to shape some of the changes." (*op. cit.*, p. 174) But the Gospel comes after the creation. Instead of violating the creation the Gospel endorses it. Only a Manichean concept of creation would regard creation *qua* creation as redeemable in any sense at all. It was the thought of Flaccius that somehow the human nature itself was sinful (Formula of Concord, I). The Formula of Concord, II, distinguishes four states of man: "1. before the Fall; 2. since the Fall; 3. after regeneration; 4. after the resurrection of the body . . ." Marriage or the relationship between male and female was created in the first time period. Sins connected with marriage or the male and female relationship are redeemable, but the relationship, since it is created by God, is not redeemable. The relationship between the sexes will only pass away after God has attained His purposes through them. According to Jesus, this happens at the resurrection on the last day. The same article claims that the phrases "order of creation" and the like are more Calvinistic in origin than Lutheran (though this case is hardly conclusive from the evidence presented) in discussing the male-female relationship. With such a suggestion it might be better to use the language of the Apology and call it a "natural right." "*Jus naturale sit immutabile*"—the natural right is immutable (XXIII, 12). Just as it is impossible to change the laws about marriage which is ordained by God, so it is illegitimate (against the immutable law or will of God) to ordain women as pastors. Stephen A. Schmidt presents both sides of the argument from creation in *Powerless Pedagogues*, 29th Lutheran Education Association Yearbook (River Forest, 1971), pp. 107f. without committing himself to either.

44 The word *didaskein* is inappropriately used of the functions of Sunday, parochial, and public school teachers. This word refers to the publicly sanctioned proclamation of the Gospel before the assembled worshipping congregation. It in no way forbids women from being teachers in various agencies of the church, as it is suggested in *The Ordination of Women*, *op. cit.*, p. 14.

Without theological or Biblical evidence, arguments used for a male clergy and hence against female clergy have been introduced into the discussion of the office of the parochial school teacher. While this entire issue must be treated at length at another time, much confusion has resulted by defining the pastor's office as "minister" and then asserting that parochial school teachers have a ministry. The implication which has become quite explicit in recent years is that pastor and parochial school teacher are equal office holders of the same ministry. Now all Christians have a ministry, but only a logical error, which St. Paul speaks against would come to the unwarranted conclusion

public proclamation of the Gospel. A teacher is one who is charged with the public proclamation of Christianity. Not even Priscilla did this type of public teaching at the Eucharist.[45] For example I Timothy 4 refers to Timothy's official tasks as pastor. Nothing here is said about prohibiting women from instructing children in the church, school or home. This does not disrupt the family "rights". In fact the Old Testament obligates father and mother to instruct their children, Proverbs 1:8. It would seem that instruction in church and school are an extention of such parental authority and obligation.

### 3. Galatians 3:28 Has redemption's orders superceded those of creation?[46]

Galatians 3:28 with the words that in Christ Jesus there is neither male or female has been used to demonstrate that God has abolished the old law

---

that all possess the same office (1 Cor. 12:28ff.). The other error involved is concluding that the admonitions concerning "teachers" in the New Testament apply to "parochial school teachers." *They do not!* Teaching in the New Testament applies to the public proclamation of the Gospel, not to knowledge conveyed about secular subjects, even when done under the auspices of the church. Stephen A. Schmidt (*op. cit.*) mentions, and rightfully so, the condescending attitude shown to women parochial school teachers. They are not included in conventions for pastors and *male* teachers. They tend to receive less pay than their male counterparts and have tenure less frequently. There is no theological or Biblical reason to discriminate between male and female parochial school teachers. Conferences for pastors and teachers should include both men and women. The arguments for putting men teachers on a higher plain than women seems to be anti-feminist. True, men teachers unlike women teachers may apply for the office of pastor; however, both men and women teachers have not been certified to have the competency to pastors. Simply because men as men have one criterion, their *maleness*, that might indicate a certain potential for the office of the pastor, lacking in women, does not give them a higher position. There are other requirements for the office of the pastor than merely being a man. In the reverse, pastors judged to be competent in proclamation of the Word of God do not per se have the competence to teach other than the religious subjects in the parochial school, unless because of the religious implications of certain secular subjects. The New Testament distinguishes between different offices, so should we.

45 The vocabulary used in Acts 18:26 in no way suggests that Priscilla engaged in public teaching. *Didaskein* or any other nearly related word is not used.

46 Galatians 3:27–28 is used by both the LCUSA's *The Ordination of Women*, p. 22 and "The Role of Women in the Church of Jesus Christ" in *Advance* (October 1970), pp. 10–12, for suggesting that women can be ordained. The latter offers the view that God is now changing the orders of creation now that the Gospel has replaced the law. Perhaps Horace Hummel's comments can best rectify this. "Nor am I able to see that more sophisticated argument from 'changing orders of creation' is not ultimately vulnerable to the same charge; it seems to me to be exegetically beside the point because Paul clearly does not argue from something he considers as result of sin, and hence subject to 'redemption,' but rather from a given already preceding the Fall." "Bible and Confession," *The Springfielder*, Vol. 35, 4, 270f.

Dr. Victor Pfitzner, professor of New Testament at Luther Seminary of the Lutheran Church of Australia also makes the point that the equality of Christians suggested in Galatians 3:27f. applies only to how these Christians appear before God and has

and therefore restrictions or roles assigned the sexes have been abolished.[47] A careful study of Galatians 3:23–29 will quite quickly show that Paul is discussing justification of the sinner before God, *coram deo*. He states that by faith we have become justified and thus all of us are sons of God and Abraham's offspring. There are no offices, no special gifts, no economic differences, no differences based on sex, as sinners stand justified by God through faith in Christ. There is only one "advantage" that qualifies before God and that is faith. In this there are no degrees of worthiness or dignity. The three year old girl in Sunday School stands before God in the same position as the Mother of our Lord, and the Apostle Paul stands in the same relationship as the ten year old who lights the candles on Sunday morning and almost burns down the church in doing so. Paul hardly suggested that the roles are exchangeable. Paul never suggests that the role of man or female could ever be exchanged, or that Greeks would become Jews or vice versa. The things ordained by God in

nothing to do with the ordering of the congregation. He also shows that as the demands for women pastors grow, there will be greater reliance on the concept that the pastor receives his office as an extension of the office which all members of the congregation hold jointly. C. F. W. Walther's doctrine of the ministry, which gives every baptized Christian the office of the ministry, carried to its logical conclusion does regretfully allow for the ordination of women pastors. To counter this Dr. Pfitzner's appraisal is given: "The equality that Luther speaks about is the equality of the redeemed *coram Deo*, Gal. 3:27f. But this does not immediately imply equal, in the sense of identical, functions in the church. Every member of the church has the right, not the duty, to participate in the calling of a servant of the Word, as he also has the duty to test and maintain the authenticity of the Word which is proclaimed on Christ's behalf. But there can be no confusion of offices and functions. . . . While the old *Uebertragungslehre* of the last century will hardly be repeated in the same terms, we can expect a repetition of the claim that the public office is merely a delegated authority. And as the plea for the ordination of women intensifies we can expect repeated references to this idea." "'General Priesthood' and Ministry," *Lutheran Journal of Theology* Vol. 5 (November 1971), pp. 107f.

47 A related argument for the ordination of women is based on the universal priesthood of all believers in *The Ordination of Women*, p. 23. It is an extremely poor one, but should be presented. "But by and large, there is agreement that the ministry of the Church of Jesus Christ is not particularly a continuation of the Old Testament priesthood. The New Testament deliberately changes it. There is a 'royal priesthood' of all baptized believers (1 Peter 2:9). Christian baptism ordains all believers. Women, then are 'priests' by baptism." John Hall Elliott in his doctoral dissertation proves that this passage has nothing to do with the cultic practices of the worshipping congregation. J. H. Elliott, *The Elect and Holy. An Exegetical Examination of 1 Peter 2:4–10 and the Phrase 'baxileinon hierateuma'* (Leiden: E. J. Brill, 1966). Cf. by the same author "Death of a Slogan: from Royal Priests to Celebrating Community," *Una Sancta* Vol. 25, pp. 18ff.

To say that all baptized people are "ordained," in whatever sense *Ordination of Women* means, would spell the end for the public ministry and would reduce Lutheranism to the most barbaric form of congregationalism. This would certainly lend credence to the thesis that the ordination of women pastors as a movement is related to all forms of egalitarian fanaticism.

creation and the divisions of society which reflect to some extent the creation of God are not annulled. The church also has orders or ranks which cannot be changed. Consider what Paul says in I Corinthians 13:29: "Are all apostles? Are all prophets? Are all teachers? Do all work miracles?" The answer is no. Justification before God through faith in Christ does not abolish the relationships that men have with each other. All are equal before God, but equality hardly suggests interchangeability.[48]

# PART III: CONCLUSION

## How Binding Is the 'Law' That Women Cannot Serve as Pastors?

As soon as the word 'law' is used we are using a freighted term, as some will say that Christ has redeemed us from the curse of the law and that the law has been replaced by the Gospel. Of course the Gospel does not destroy the law, but only means that God in Christ has fulfilled the law and all its just requirements. The law is not abolished, but its punishments are. The Scriptures use the concept of law in a variety of ways.[49]

It can refer to the ceremonial and civic law of Israel. Jesus, as is evident from his preaching was not the first to break this law. He mentions how David ate the shewbread to save his men from starvation, even though this bread was intended for priestly consumption. The Old Testament did not demand that this law be observed by non-Jews. Gentiles, who professed faith in Israel's God, did not necessarily have to obey the ceremonial or civic laws of Israel. God in His written revelation indicated when this law would apply and when it would not apply.

There is also the moral law as given by Moses and repeated by Jesus and the Apostles. This law reflects the very essence of God and was established in the world from its very creation. Man according to Romans 1 and 2 perverted this law because of his own warped nature and God had to republish it. Whenever God acts, He acts morally. He never acts amorally. In fact, He is not capable of an amoral act. All of what God does is *per se* good and just. God does not first create and then pronounce that it is good. It is good from the

---

48 Horace Hummel (*op. cit.*) suggests that the "egalitarian assumptions of our culture" might really be behind the movement to ordain women as pastors.

49 The phrase *lex semper accusat* taken out of context can cause confusion. The law always accuses in the area of justification, but the law functions in other areas. Before the Fall, the law did not accuse. In the state of glorification, the law will not accuse. For the redeemed child of God, the law does not accuse but presents to him the way on which a loving Father guides His children. The article "Orders of Creation" seems to overlook the Formula of Concord VI when it states: "According to Reformation theology, there is a twofold use of the Law, duplex usus legis" (*Op. cit.*, p. 173). FC VI deals with three uses of the law.

very beginning of the act and because God does it. Sex and the relationships between the sexes belong to God's creative acts.

Today there is a lot of "honest-to-sex" talk with the very valid comment that sex is not dirty but good. Unfortunately this talk does not go beyond telling teenagers and married people with hang-ups that they should not fear sex. But there is another step. Sex has been created by God and the relationship between male and female has been established by God in the creation. It is not an afterthought. Sex belongs to God's creative law and is reflected in the Mosaic Decalogue. The divine plan for the family is an outgrowth of this sexual relationship. Jesus in Matt. 19:2 and Paul in 1 Corinthians 11 and I Timothy 2 make specific reference to this. The relationship is endorsed by Jesus and His apostles and is in no way abrogated. In fact it is sanctified and presented to God as holy by His Word. In this set-up the children are to obey the parents and the wife is to be subordinate to the husband. The word "subordinate" unfortunately suggests the master-slave relationship with the crack of the whip in the background. Men greedy for power have either turned the relationship around or intensified it to the point of hatred. Subordination in nature has been placed there by God not to indicate that someone is more worthy than another or that one should be despised. Subordination is for the sake of function and welfare. The child is subordinate to the parents for the child's welfare, not to punish the child or to benefit the parents. Christ is subordinate to God in carrying out the task of salvation. This does not degrade Christ. The church is subordinate to Christ. The one in the superior or upper position exercises love to those in the lower positions. That's why Paul says that husbands should love their wives as Christ loved the church. Of course many do not model their family lives after the divine pattern and grief must necessarily ensue. Still the abuse of the divine pattern does not allow abrogation of the pattern because it is defiled by sin. Women pastors abrogate the divine pattern.

The church is God's new family on earth. Adam's race did not qualify as God's sons and thus in Jesus a new family, the church, has been established. The New Testament uses the term "household of the church" suggesting that it is a family. In this family God's original designs are not considered invalid or outmoded or useless. Rather, in the church, God's original intentions are again revived. God has not placed the label of "NO GOOD" over His original work, but has revived it. The church is therefore bound to the proper relationship between the man and woman established by God and that it be reflected in everything the church does. The ordaining of women as pastors, leaders, guardians, bishops, yes, "fathers" of congregations is not only a deliberate breaking of not only the Scriptures of the Old and New Testaments, but a direct contradiction of God's plans in creation. It is going directly against

God. As C. S. Lewis says, male and female may be equal but their roles are not exchangeable. It is God who loved the church and wooed her. It is men who woo their wives and love them. The late Anglican lay theologian compares the church to a ball or dance. "Sometimes the men are bad dancers, but the solution is not that we should treat all those as neuter as if they had no sex. The solution is rather that the men should be taught to be better dancers."[50]

# APPENDIX I

The proponents of women as pastors are more agreed in their objective of women as pastors than they are in the basis for establishing it. The most radical proponents are simply caught up in "women's lib." *Women's Liberation and the Church* (*op. cit.*) is a good example of raw application of unproved principles. *The Ordination of Women* (*op. cit.*) intimates that there might have been women pastors in the apostolic time. Cf. p. 24. The arguments offered for this position are obviously inferior. E.g., "They minister to Jesus during his lifetime and at his death" (Luke 8:3, Mark 15:41). With such reasoning all janitors should be allowed to conduct the Eucharist. The exegesis given here is hardly worthy of the support of serious Greek scholars! The third option is that though Paul did not let women serve as pastors at Corinth, he was reflecting a cultural opinion and thus it is not binding on us. This position is offered in the "Orders of Creation," (*op. cit.*). It reduces the question of ordination of women from a doctrinal question to a practical one. The question is no longer whether ordination of women is right or wrong, but when will the Missouri Synod be ready for it. If all arguments are to stand, and the latter two have been offered in the Missouri Synod, it would be as if a man were convicted of crime for two different and opposing reasons. Such conflicting evidence would make the old procedure spurious from the start. This is the situation in which the ordination of women stands today. The two arguments that (1) there might have been ordained women pastors in the apostolic time and that (2) Paul's strictures against women pastors were valid for his time but not for ours contain elements which are basically contradictory. Both are contained in *The Ordination of Women*.

# APPENDIX II

The Lutheran Deaconess Association with headquarters at Valparaiso University has become the center of much discussion of the woman's place in the church. This is quite natural as the office of the deaconess and her duties must relate in some way to the office of the pastor. An article in *The Lutheran*

---

50 "Priestesses in the Church?" *God in the Dock* (Grand Rapids, Eerdmans, 1970), pp. 237–239.

*Deaconess* (Vol. 48, 4) pp. 3–6 uses many of the arguments that have been discussed in this essay. The title "Woman . . . God's Creation" already indicates the position. The title can be slightly misleading and suggests conclusions that do not do full justice to the Scriptures. Yes, woman is God's creation but in a different sense than the man is (1 Corinthians 11:8f.) Man is made from God and woman is made from man by God. Regrettably, as the writer points out, women have been treated too frequently as second-class citizens in the kingdom. For example male teachers have permanent calls and woman teachers all too frequently get contracts. However, abuses against women— and they must be protested—should not be allowed as an excuse for allowing women to preach and celebrate communion publicly. The presentation rests heavily on ideas of Wartburg Seminary Professor, Dr. Julius Bodensiek, delivered at the Lutheran Social Ethics Seminar at Valparaiso University in December 1955. According to these ideas a woman's place in the church may not be determined by any principles that do not give them equal responsibility, that absolutize one historical order of society, that are based on a number of isolated texts, that have been antiquated by contemporary society. But the arguments against the ordaining of women pastors are just these. God has created male and female with different responsibilities. The order established by God is absolute, unless God's creation is capable of improvement by change instituted by men. The texts that speak to the issue are not isolated. Genesis 1–3 is hardly isolated. The procedures of any society, ancient or modern, do not determine God's principles. Working from the standard of contemporary society, the church might have to endorse and even recommend premarital sex. Of course this is being advocated by some clergymen. This is not a far fetched analogy as the relationship between the sexes is determined by God. Any view that cites present or anticipated customs or mores operates with a source of theology other than the prophetic and apostolic Scriptures.

The article offers one argument quite similar to the LCUSA's *The Ordination of Women* by asserting that, "Furthermore, the first Easter sermon of Christ's glorious Resurrection was preached by women to men." A faulty conclusion suggesting that women could then become pastors comes from using the term "preached" in a confusing way. Preaching in the church means the proclamation of the Gospel in a public way to an assembly. Sometimes the word "preach" can refer to any bringing of good news or bad. The women on Easter morning brought news about the Resurrection. They did not conduct or lead a service. Much confusion in the issue of women pastors comes through the imprecise and less than careful use of language. Too frequently using a word which can have several connotations can lead to confusion in the church.

# APPENDIX III

*Lutheran Quarterly*, Vol. 24, 2, (May 1972) 222–223, contains a review of *The Ministry and the Ministry of Women* by Peter Brunner (St. Louis: Concordia Publishing House, 1971) written by Frederick J. Gaiser. Brunner's strictures against the ordination of women as pastors is based on Genesis 2 and 3. Pastor Gaiser offers two objections to this argument based on the orders of creation. The first is essentially the same as used in "The Orders of Creation . . ." (Cf. note 42.) "Is it not possible to say that, if the course of history is determined by the Word of God, the socalled orders of creation might also function differently at different times?" Such an argument, as mentioned above, fails to distinguish between natural and special revelation or it ascribes to man the ability to discern religious information from history or nature above the fact that God exists. According to Romans and the Lutheran Confessions man is incapable of attaining true knowledge about God and His plans from nature. The whole matter of original sin is at stake here. Pastor Gaiser also failed to distinguished the creative word of God (Genesis 1 and 2; Peter 3:5, 7) and the word which is able to bring salvation (1 Peter 1:23).

The second argument, new to this writer, is that Pastor Gaiser raises the question of whether Genesis 2 and 3 is so clear on this point as to be applied to the relationship between the sexes. "Even by using all the tools of biblical research it would be difficult to read out of Genesis 2 and 3 such an absolutely certain view of God's once-for-all desired relationship between man and woman that it could be called 'a central point with which the whole Christian message hangs together." (p. 31) Gaiser has criticized Peter Brunner for the very arguments that Paul has offered in 1 Corinthians 11:7–10 and 1 Timothy 2:13f. Paul in both cases argues from the creation and fall accounts. Regardless of what position the reader takes in this debate, it has become obvious that Genesis 2–3 and its interpretations are important. If there is no agreement on the creation and fall accounts, there can be no agreement on a theology of the sexes. Further application to the ordination of women pastors become impossible.

# The Office of the Pastor and the Problem of the Ordination of Women Pastors

David P. Scaer

## I. Introduction

As I have previously pointed out, the problem of the ordination of women pastors is of rather recent vintage in world Lutheranism. It sprang up for the most part in Europe after the war and the causes for its introduction were more political than theological. What is amazing is that in the course of a generation or two, the practice is seemingly recognized as acceptable in most of world Lutheranism today.

Within the last few months, *Time* magazine took time out from reporting the Missouri Synod squabbles to tell the stories of two Lutheran pastors of the Bavarian Lutheran State Church, one associated with Neuendettelsau, a small town in southern Germany where the Missouri Synod can trace some of its roots. These two pastors felt for reasons of conscience compelled to resign their pastorates because certain women theologians were given pastoral responsibilities. Such actions were considered by the pastors to be illegal, immoral, and unbiblical. One of the pastors is seeking refuge in the Roman Catholic Church. To which *Time* editorially, and maybe even accurately, remarked that even that final haven of male ecclesiasticism might fall before the onslaught of the movement to ordain women pastors. The recent 1973 autumn convention of the Protestant Episcopal Church in Kentucky also indicated that this issue was still a live one. The majority of the delegates did favor ordaining women priests, but because of a system of block voting that resembles our electoral college at the time of American presidential elections, the matter was rejected. In this presentation I do not wish merely to repeat what has already been said, but to go after the issue from the concept of the pastoral office.

I can see two definite reasons why perhaps we should not even attempt to present this topic at this time. These two reasons are the unresolved, restless and unstable situation in our synod and the women's liberation movement in our country. First, it would seem to me that any resolution of current difficulties in the Missouri Synod should be done along theological lines. Secondly, the equal rights amendment (ERA) which is nearing final ratification, and the political and social movements behind it, only further emotionally clouds theological discussion. I see no necessary connection on how one stands on this constitutional issue of ERA and one's position on the ordination of women. One is a political issue, the other theological. But the history of a past generation has shown how a political posture can be theologically determinative. I cannot agree with the concept of God's speaking to us in our culture. We will simply have to wrestle with the problem and call "foul ball" if cultural mores become theological determinative for the church and her practices.

I would like to venture in on the problem from a direction which I have not previously undertaken. We can set the problem down in two questions:

(1) Does the New Testament, recognize the office of the pastoral ministry as a separate and distinct office instituted by Christ and the apostles?

(2) If we answer this question in the affirmative, is there any exegetical evidence which is so compelling that we can in no way permit women to enter this office and to exercise its functions?

# II. Does the New Testament Recognize the Office of the Pastoral Ministry as a Separate and Distinct Office Instituted by Christ and the Apostles?

## A. What Is Meant by Ministry?

### 1. Contemporary use of the term

One of the major arguments for the proponents of the ordination of women pastors is their concept of 'ministry.' In general terms, this concept of the 'ministry' signifies a service which each Christian performs to others within the Christian community. There is even a 'ministry to the world.' 'Ministry' becomes an equivalent term to the phrase 'the priesthood of all believers' and baptism assures and requires of the recipient 'a ministry.'

This way of speaking has become widespread in our circles in recent years. Some of its slogans are well known. 'The pastor is a minister to other ministers.' In this phrase, the functional use of the word 'minister' is stressed to the elimination of the concept of 'ministry' as a special office. The pastor is simply one 'minister' among many other 'ministers.' Another phrase expressing the platform of a more generalized form of 'ministry' is that, "The pastors job is to work himself out of a job." This means that the pastor's 'ministry' is to raise the members of the congregation to his level. But does this mean in regard to intellect or faith? I do not know. The second option would be crass Phariseeism. The goal of the pastor for the congregation is that members should operate or function at the same level at which he is functioning. He is the 'chief minister' 'ministering' to other 'ministers.' This generalized concept of 'ministry' has not been dogmatically finalized, but it now has wide ramifications even on the congregational level and is treated as a faith statement. With this type of philosophy the pastor sees himself as a type of 'enabler' within the congregational scene. Or to use the terminology of the business world, he becomes the executive officer of the church council which in turn is the 'board of directors' for the 'corporate stockholders' assembled as a voters' assembly. With this attitude, the pastor becomes expendable or at least replaceable by others in the body corporate. There are other officers who have a 'ministry' which can compensate individually or corporately and replace the pastoral office for a longer or shorter period of time.

## 2. Many ministers or ministries in the church

In The Lutheran Church—Missouri Synod, the problem has become more acute because of the recent discussions of the role of parochial school teacher, both male and female. In addition to this there are the roles of the deaconess, the director of Christian education, the youth worker, and the lay preacher. There is even some discussion of the revival of the office of the deacon. To this list can be added the entire list of congregational offices from congregational president all the way to teenage helpers in the Vacation Bible School and the sexton. One point of view regards all of these as parts of a more generalized and far embracing concept of ministry, with the pastoral office relegated to the position of *e pluribus unum*. The ministry is understood as something like the body of Christ where the relationship of each of the parts to the other is determined by function. Recently a teacher at one of our terminal schools expressed this concept quite succinctly:

> The concept of ministry must be clarified in the church at large. There is one ministry of Word and sacrament, and many forms of that ministry. Every servant of the Word—pastor, teacher, lay worker, deaconess, youth worker—is part of the public ministry. We need to expand the office to include all functions of the ministry as equal co-partners in God's service of Word and sacrament in the church.[1]

---

1    "The Future of Christian Education in the Missouri Synod: A Matter of Self-Understanding," *CTM* XLIV, 4, (September 1973), 281.

### 3. Pastor as one minister among other ministers

According to this concept, there is one 'ministry' with many forms. The pastor alone is not entitled to the title 'servant of the word' but he is to share this designation with others as equal co-partners. We can see how this type of definition could allow and even demand that women be allowed into the office of the pastoral ministry. Instead of looking for or determining suitability for a special office of pastor, we determine suitability for a more broadened concept of "ministry" which already allows for equal participation by the sexes. Since various aspects of the 'ministry' have become functions, these functions can even be exchanged. Our same source says, "men and women could specialize in one form of ministry but have access to the other functions."[2] Thus the pastoral office is *ipso facto* opened to women.

Perhaps, I could provide the following as a helpful analogy. The newer concept of ministry could be compared to a medical clinic where all the physicians are recognized as qualified medical doctors with each specializing in a field of interest or need. In their basic training they have all been adjudged capable in the general field of medicine and to maintain their competency, work in individual fields of medicine other than their particular specialty from time to time. They exchange tasks; the pediatrician becomes a surgeon, etc. In this newer understanding of ministry, the different 'ministers' could and do exchange functions.

Such an illustration might be a very attractive model to describe the church or the church's offices, but is it adequate in handling the Biblical data, especially on the pastoral office? Does the New Testament really know of a generalized office of ministry with many parts? An examination of the Biblical data might suggest an attitude or posture of ministry of service of all those in the kingdom or the church, but it in no way allows us to come to the conclusion that there is one general office of ministry which in some way is shared by all.

### 4. *Diakonia, diakonein, diakonos* in the N.T.

Basic to our understanding of the 'ministry' is a look at the New Testament word *diakonia*, 'service' or 'ministry' and its cognates, the verb *diakonein* and noun *diakonos*. To say that this word as used in the New Testament must have the same meaning or sense in every usage simply cannot be supported by the evidence. Each instance of the word cannot be applied without further ado to a generalized concept of ministry.

*a) The Gospels*

In the Gospels, the concept of *diakonia* as administering physical aid to those in distress seems to predominate. For example, the angels "minister"

---

2    *Ibid.*, p. 283.

to Jesus, who has been exhausted by His encounter with Satan (Mt. 4:11) . After she is healed, Peter's mother-in-law "ministers" to Jesus. (Mt. 8:15). One group of women are spoken of as having "ministered" to Jesus during his life of humiliation (Lk. 8:3; Mk 15:41). The use of *diakonia* as helping those in physical distress is no better demonstrated than in the final judgment scene of Mt. 25:44.

### b) Acts and the Epistles

This idea of *diakonia* as providing aid for those who are in such physical distress that helping themselves becomes impossible is carried out in various parts of the New Testament to describe the situation of the early church. A group of seven men are chosen "to minister on tables" (Acts 6:2). Here reference is to elevating the physical distress of the Greek speaking Jews who have returned to Jerusalem from the diaspora and who have not been totally integrated with the Palestinian population. This idea of physical aid is used to describe the monetary contribution of the Antiochians for the destitute situation in Jerusalem. A similar thought is expressed in Romans 15:25 where Paul travels to Jerusalem to help out in a bad situation. In Philippians 1:1 and 1 Tm 3:8–13 a special office of *diakonos* or 'minister' seems to have been established for handling the problems of physical distress. It is not a divinely established or commended office in the sense that each church must have it, but seems to have been created for a situation of necessity. There are certain qualifications, however, for the office wherever it happens to be established.

### c) Jesus' atonement as diakonia

There are uses of the word *diakonos* and its cognates which have deeper and more profound implications than providing physical aid. Jesus describes his work of atonement as *diakonein* and requires that his disciples follow His example by becoming *diakonos* "minister" and "*doulos*," "slave" (Mt 20:26ff). Here we see that 'minister' is used as a reference to the attitude of one who holds an office in the church and not to any specific office. Jesus has a particular office to carry out which He describes as "to give life as a ransom for many." In no way are the disciples given the task of surrendering their lives for anyone as a ransom. In the act itself of atonement, no one can follow Jesus. But they can follow the humble, servant-like attitude of Jesus in performing the functions and offices which God has given uniquely to them. Paul in Philippians 2:7ff. urges Christians to assume the same posture of humility as was evident in the God-Man during the days in which He was abused.

### d) Diakonia as Attitude

*Diakonia* can be used not only of giving physical aid in a type of specialized way, but it can refer to the attitude in which one carries out the office which God has given him. The common attitude of *diakonia* does not mean or even allow that offices or obligations are exchangeable. The offices are not even sub-categories under a more general type of office called *diakonia*, *'ministry.'* The prophets have their specialized *diakonia* of predicting the suffering and glory of Christ (I Peter 1:12). Christ has His specialized *diakonia* of offering His life as the ransom payment. The apostles are self-conscious that their office of being apostles is their unique *diakonia*. Peter says that Judas had a share in the *diakonia* of the apostleship (Acts 1:17) and prays that God would restore this gap in the *diakonia* of the apostleship. Paul calls his entire apostolic task a *diakonia* in his address to the Ephesian pastors (Acts 20:24), (cf. I Tim 1:12).

*e) Is it in the best N.T. usage to use* diakonia *exclusively of the pastoral office?*

*Diakonia* or *diakonos* can refer to a service or office holder without in any way suggesting that the services or office holders are interchangeable or even for that matter necessarily interdependent. Christ is not a servant for sin (Gal 2:17) and the emperor is God's servant in carrying out justice in the civil sphere (Rm 13:1).

I am not here to defend the use of the word 'minister' as the exclusive prerogative of the pastors, though our confessions consistently use the word for pastors. Not limiting it to the pastoral office might be in the sense of the best Biblical usage. Where it has been used, it has been used as a convenient synonym for those who hold the pastoral office. But to work with a general concept of 'ministry' and then to fit the office of pastor as sub-category under it is simply not allowable by the Biblical data. It is not even suggested by the Lutheran Confessions. Those arguments for women pastors derived from such a generalized concept of 'ministry' must also prove to be totally false, because the basic presupposition cannot be supported.

## B. DOES THE N. T. KNOW OF A SPECIALIZED OFFICE OF PASTOR?

Since the office of the pastorate cannot be derived from the general concept of *diakonein*, we must ask the question if the New Testament recognizes a special office of pastor. If we can provide supportive evidence here, then recognizing particular features or characteristic qualities of the pastoral office becomes easier.

### 1. The preaching of Jesus

In His earthly ministry, Jesus approaches people in two different ways. There is the invitation to faith which is offered individually and collectively. In addition, there is the invitation into a professional type of discipleship or apostleship, as it was later known. The requirements to each group and the response of Jesus to each are different.

*a) Jesus and believers*

The first group is recognized as believers in Jesus. The centurion has a faith unequaled in Israel (Mt 8:5–13). The woman with the issue of blood evokes a favorable response from Jesus (Mt 9:20ff.) as does the Caananite woman (15:21–28). The cases of the paralytic (9:1–8), Jairus and his daughter (9:18–26), and blind men (20:29–34) could all be listed. They believe, are forgiven, and whatever malady is the center of the pericope is corrected. What is lacking in these pericopes is perhaps just as important as what is included. Those who believe or who are acted upon do not join the company of Jesus on a permanent or "professional" basis, and they are not asked to. In some cases, they go home and stay there. There is no interruption in their usual pattern of living. In the case of the Roman centurion, it is possible that he never met Jesus face to face. There is no call to 'ministry' in the sense of their having been given offices or functions in the church.

*b) Jesus and the Twelve*

There is on the other hand a group of men who Jesus does pick out deliberately and for a specialized task they receive the training and instruction. This group was recognized, and recognized themselves as something special both during the ministry of Jesus and after His resurrection and ascension. This is not to say that their self-estimation and self-esteem were at all times properly self-comprehended, but it is to say they held a special office of which they were rightly self-conscious. To the Jews in general, the command was to "Repent, for the kingdom of heaven is at hand" (Mt. 4:17, 23), but only to certain men He gave the command to "follow" Him (Mt 4:18–22; 9:9). Jesus' recruitment for the special office was recognized as different from the general call to faith and some would-be applicants approach Jesus concerning the matter and are rejected (Mt 8:18–22). Unlike believers in general, they are required to give up the ordinary pursuits of life, as Peter forsook fishing and Matthew tax collecting, and to devote their lives full time to the cause of Jesus. Theirs is a profession or life-time vocation. Luke in Acts seems to concur in this observation as Peter says that the replacement for Judas must have accompanied Jesus from the time of His baptism to the ascension. There are several reasons for this. The apostles are the official guarantors of Jesus' teaching and thus had to be instructed personally by Him over a longer period of time. This is the message of Matthew. They also had to be witnesses of His resurrection as described in Acts, but which is even more basic to the arguments of John's Gospel (20:30f.). The point here is that Jesus did Himself establish a distinction between believers in general and church leaders. This difference was one of instruction and training and not necessarily faith. On the contrary, if the selection to the apostleship had been on the basis of faith alone, all of the apostles would have to have been replaced by the women,

Gentile centurions, and others. But the fact is they were not replaced, except in the case of Judas who used his office to destroy the kingdom with which he had been entrusted. The question of "great faith" does not play a role of Matthias.

## 2. The Early Church

If there is a distinction between the apostles and believers in general during the ministry of Jesus, may it not safely be assumed that this type of distinction was maintained in the early church?

### a) Apostolic self-awareness

The dominance of the apostolic office is evident. They are the church's leaders. They are the instructors. They conduct missions. They are aware that their apostolic office has two parts: witnessing to the life, death and resurrection of Jesus and pastoral care of congregations. Being aware of their own mortality, they preserve the life and message of Jesus in the Gospels. They apply that message in the epistles. Being aware of their own mortality, they also make certain that their pastoral duties, which also belonged to the office of the apostle are preserved in the church after their death by appointing pastors. The Pastoral Letters are directed to this problem. The New Testament writings do recognize one special office, established by Christ and the Apostles, with general supervision of the congregation in regard to the preservation of the truth and the proclamation of the Gospel. This office which is called by Paul in Ephesians (4:11) the office of "pastors and teachers" and was exercised by Jesus Himself in His messianic office and by the Twelve in their apostolic office. There is to be no homogenization between the office of Christ, apostle, and pastor today, because the first of these two offices is distinct and absolutely non-repeatable. Jesus was the atoner. This was not the apostolic task. The apostles were the eye witnesses of the resurrection. This 'once and for all' historical observation cannot be passed along or even be repeated by faith. There can be no apostolic succession in this sense. But there is a succession from Jesus, through the apostles to pastors today and this succession is one of shepherding and teaching.

### b) The office of congregational care as held by Christ, the Apostles, and Pastors.

To sketch this line of pastors and teaching from Jesus to pastors is hardly difficult. In fact, if needed, it can be traced to the Old Testament where Ezekiel inveighs against the false shepherds. For our purposes it is sufficient to confine ourselves to the New Testament. John attributes pastoral qualities to both Jesus and the apostles. Chapter 10 presents Jesus as the shepherd who vicariously gives His life for the sheep (v. 11). Three times Peter is given the specific responsibility of feeding the sheep of the Good Shepherd (21:15ff.). Maybe it is not necessary to note that "shepherd" in John and "pastor" in

Ephesians both translate the same Greek word, *poimen*. Any claim that the thought of Jesus as shepherd and pastor as only a later theological contribution of the church found in John does not measure up to the evidence available in the Synoptics. John's treatment of the pastoral office of Jesus is more lengthy but not necessarily more profound than Matthew's. Jesus quotes Zechariah 13:7 in application to Himself, "I will strike the shepherd and the sheep of the flock will be scattered (26:31)."

Even in Matthew, Jesus sees the pastoral office as something which is carried by others. In 9:35–38, the crowds are described as "sheep without a shepherd." This statement is immediately followed by the lament that the laborers in the harvest are few. Here we have analogies of shepherding and harvesting in such close proximity that it suggests that the task of the pastor or shepherd is also that of working in the harvest. Paul would later use the term 'worker,' *ergatas*, for a pastor (I Timothy 5:18). As previously mentioned, Peter is specifically given the pastoral functions exercised by Jesus. In his first epistle (5:1ff.), Peter addresses the pastors, *presbuteroi*, in special regard to their own pastoral functions. These functions they are to exercise in the light of the eschatological appearance of the 'Chief Shepherd,' *archipoimenos*. I can find no better place to succinctly trace the pastoral succession. He greets the pastors as a special group of people. With the words 'fellow pastor," *sumpresbuteros*, he reminds them that together they share the same responsibility of pastoral care and congregational supervision. Peter reserves for himself the title of *martus*, because he as one of the Twelve, was specifically appointed to be legal witnesses of the Lord's suffering. This is a unique function of the apostolic and not the pastoral office. As Jesus had once told Peter to feed His flock, so Peter entrusts this responsibility to the pastors, reminding them that the flock is not Peter's but God's. They are responsible to Jesus, the Chief Shepherd. Paul in his farewell to the Ephesian pastors admonishes them about caring for the sheep and feeding the church over which the Holy Spirit has appointed them overseers, *episcopoi*.

### 3. The pastor as "teacher" in N.T.

The pastoral office involves the two functions of pastoring and teaching. By teacher and pastor *only one* office is intended. With little difficulty a succession of teaching from Jesus, to the apostles, to pastors can be established. Jesus' preaching is really teaching. The conclusion to the sermon on the mount settles the issues "For he taught them as one who had authority." (Matthew 8:29). It was God's own authority (21:23–27; 28:18). Jesus regarded Himself as a Teacher, as did His contemporaries.

A brief digression here would be helpful. The term "teach," *didaskein*, in the New Testament does not suggest teaching in the sense that we use it today i.e., what a person does in a classroom. It is not a matter of primary, secondary or higher education. 'Teacher' in the New Testament rather designates a person who has been entrusted with the divine doctrine, *didache* or *didaskalia*, and is committed not only to teach others, but to commit it to designated individuals so that it will be preserved intact. The word 'teach' as used by Jesus and Paul does not really involve the duties and functions usually associated with parochial school teachers or others engaged in the tasks of Christian education, as we think of them today.

Jesus is the teacher without peer, not so much in regard to His superb educational methods, but rather in regard to His embrasive comprehensive knowledge of what God wants. But He does not regard Himself as the only teacher, as there are others, including false ones. There will be false prophets (7:15). More to the point is 5:19 in Jesus' warning that, "Whoever breaks one of the least of these commandments and *teaches* men thus shall be called least in the kingdom of heaven." Jesus' warning is not against an erring faith, but specifically and only against erring teachers. The words are specifically addressed to the disciples, but the general use *hos an* makes it applicable to anyone assuming a teaching office, Messiah, Apostle, or Pastor. Jesus here is speaking of a special office and not of believers in general. James, which I consider quite early, also singles out the office of teacher with the same type of eschatological warning (3:1). There are several places that could be selected where Jesus passes the teaching office to the apostles, but the one which is situated in a position of climax is Matthew 28:20. Jesus begins by asserting that teaching authority has been given to Him by God. He now commissions the eleven (28:16) to go to the nations and make them disciples by teaching them to observe all things whatsoever I have commanded you. All Christians have the command to believe but only a few are entrusted with the teaching task. This passage is reminiscent of 5:19 where Jesus gives the warning about breaking the least commandment. Now Jesus takes it from the top down and says all commandments and each individual one must be kept. We can speak of an apostolic obsession of preserving what Jesus had taught. For this reason the apostles gave us the New Testament and appointed pastors. John's ending to His Gospel is just as forceful as Matthew's (John 20:30f.; 21:24f.)

It was a sense of their mortality that motivated the apostles to assure, in some way, that the teaching of Jesus would be preserved. The Gospels stand as living testimony today of this devotion. In addition, they appointed 'teachers' to stand in their place. James (3:1) speaks of a situation where there were many applicants for the office. Paul in Ephesians (4:10) speaks of their being "pastors and teachers" as one office in his time. At the meeting of the Jerusalem Council (Acts 15:6), the pastors are present as a separate office along side of the apostles. As Paul and Barnabas left the churches in Asia Minor to return to Jerusalem, they appointed pastors, *presbuterous* (Acts 14:23).

As long as the apostles were alive, the pastors were subject to the apostles. The apostolic supervision was exercised through personal visits or through letters. Paul visits the Ephesian pastors (Acts 20:17). Peter, as mentioned, has special instructions for pastors in his first epistle. Most convincing is the existence of pastoral epistles which are specifically addressed to pastors in their office. I am still of the opinion that they are to be attributed to Paul and that these letters are preparing for that time when Paul knows that absence and death will make it impossible for him to exercise direct apostolic episcopal supervision. He is not permitted to pass on his apostolic office in its entirety, a thought he shares with Peter. His teaching obligations, the preservation of the teaching and the assurance that there be a succession of teachers or pastors, must remain in the church. As Peter called himself a fellow pastor among other pastors, so Paul calls himself a 'teacher,' I Timothy 2:7, 2 Timothy 1:11. Both Timothy and Titus are to 'teach' (1 Timothy 4:11; Titus 2:1). What they are to teach is the 'teaching' or the 'doctrine' *didaskalia* (1 Timothy 4:13; Titus 2:1). Timothy is given the task of preserving the pastoral office in the church (1 Timothy 5:22). Paul's instructions to Timothy in the third chapter of the first epistle certainly indicate that Timothy is now to be entrusted with the task of screening men for the pastoral office. After all isn't that a purpose of the pastoral letters?

## III. DOES THE NEW TESTAMENT EVIDENCE PERMIT US TO APPOINT WOMEN PASTORS?

I have gone to great length to show that the office of teaching and pastoring is established by Jesus and the apostles and was indeed exercised by them. This office is given to specifically designated, trained men. It is an office that is no way to be equated with the general category of the priesthood of all believers or some generalized concept of 'ministry.' Having established this, then it will perhaps be easier to accept the qualifications and limitations connected with this office. Not every male may assume the office. Jesus did not give the office to every office seeker. James wants to turn some away. Paul is quite lengthy in laying out the qualifications.

Paul in 1 Timothy 2:12 clearly denies the pastoral office to women. "I do not permit women to teach." Throughout the pastoral epistles the term 'teach' is used in the sense of receiving, preserving, and passing along the doctrine. Paul's prohibition specifically forbids women from assuming this office. Yes, the New Testament knows of Priscilla giving instruction to Apollos (Acts 18:26) and women prophetesses, but never does the NT ascribe to them the activity of teaching, *didaskein*. In fact, it forbids them to do it.

The Timothy passage is recognized as a commentary on the prohibition in I Corinthians 14:34–36. Here the word *lalain* to talk, and not *didaskein* is used. The type of talking that is prohibited the women is not the mere use of the vocal cords. The Greek word for that is *lego* and not *lalain*. In the crucial passage in Matthew 28:18, Jesus officially speaks to them as the 'teacher' so Matthew uses the word *lalain*.

If we say negatively that women are prohibited from this office, then we say positively that the office can only be given to men. This is essential for the "pastoral teaching" succession. Peter says that the successor for Judas must be male, *aner*, (Acts 1:21). So also in 1 Timothy 3:2 and Titus 1:6, the bishop must be an *aner*, a male.

There are many problems within the church which have focused on the issue of the ordination of women pastors. There is the issue of whether or not the Scriptures are culturally limited and should we use the "eye" of the Gospel to pierce through these limitations. There is the issue of whether or not the Holy Spirit is speaking through the church today with the same force as He did through the apostles. There is the issue of whether the Scriptures are binding only in regard to what is called the Gospel and not the Law and other matters. There is also Paul's deliberate connection between his prohibition against women pastors and the accounts of creation and the fall. In the Missouri Synod I see the matter of women pastors as intimately connected with our understanding of the office of the pastor. If we accept the Biblical evidence that the office has been divinely created with special requirements for entrance and special obligations, we must follow the tradition of our church, the church throughout the ages, the early church, and the apostolic church and continue to resist ordaining women into the pastoral office.

# ORDINATION OF WOMEN?

## HERMANN SASSE

During the First Session of the Second Vatican Council a lady turned up in Rome and asked for an audience with the Pope to discuss with him the question of the ordination of women to the Catholic priesthood. She was Dr. Gertrud Heinzelmann, a lawyer at Lucerne, the famous centre of the Roman Church in Switzerland. Pope John, who was otherwise kindness and patience personified, lost his patience. "Tell that suffragette that I shall never receive her. She should go back to her homeland."

## THE ROMAN CATHOLIC CHURCH

Why did the good pope, who was otherwise prepared for a dialog even with the worst enemies of the Church, give such a harsh answer? Could he not have replied something like this: "Tell my daughter that ordination of women is against the Word of God"? This was his argument when the Archbishop of Canterbury declared such ordination to be against the tradition of the Church. Could he not have referred her for further information to one of his theologians? John was not an intellectual like his predecessor. He was not a great theologian either. But he was, as his "Journals" show, a great pastor. Every pastor knows, or should know, that there are cases, when a discussion is impossible and the only answer to a question can be that "Begone, Satan!" which Jesus spoke not only to the devil (Matthew 4:10), but also to his faithful confessor, Simon Peter (Matthew 16:23).

## SUPERSTITIOUS BELIEF IN DIALOGUE

Not every question can be settled by means of a friendly discussion. It is necessary to remember this in an age which has a superstitious belief in dialog as the infallible means of settling everything. There are questions raised by the devil to destroy the Church of Christ. To achieve this he may use as his mouth piece not only ambitious professors of theology, his favorite tools, but also simple, pious souls. Why women cannot be ordained is one of these questions.

## Crusading for the Rights of Women

"That suffragette" Pope John called the woman to whom in other circumstances he would have referred as "Our beloved daughter". The term "suffragette" indicates clearly the root of the issue. Its origin is to be found not in the church, but in the world outside the church, in that great movement, in which women in modern society demanded and attained those political and social rights to which they were entitled as citizens of the modern state. As in every movement of such nature, good and bad features, rights and wrongs, just demands and unjust claims, are intermingled.

## The "Liberation of Women"

Apart from the latest development into a revolutionary "Movement of the Liberation of Women", with its exaggerated claims of full equality between the sexes, the movement on the whole has proved a blessing for modern society. That it has exercised a strong influence on the churches was unavoidable. Also these influences have been in many respects a blessing to the churches. One has only to think of the women in the teaching and medical professions. The one and only great problem is that there is one office which is not accessible to a woman. This is the office of the pastor. It is understandable that all efforts were concentrated on the conquest of this last stronghold of "male superiority". Even men and women who had no interest at all in the church and could not care less who held the service in the church, which they did not attend anyway, were waging a passionate crusade for the right of women to the full ministry in the church.

## Groups with Female Ministers

There have been Christian groups and sects, especially in America, with female ministers: the Quakers, the Salvation Army, the Pentecostals, some Methodist and Congregational churches. In Germany during the war *"Vikarinnen"* women with full theological training, who were ministering either to women in institutions, or as assistants in parishes, crept slowly into the full ministry during the war, when many pastors were drafted to the army. It is astonishing how little resistance the movement for the ordination of women met. Many of the young ladies themselves had misgivings. But their doubts soon subsided.

## COMPROMISE IN PROTESTANT GERMANY

There were several reasons for the full victory of the movement in Protestant Germany: the ignorance of the Christian people, the decay of biblical authority with the theologians, the decay of the ministry of the church which had become one of the academic professions rather than the divinely instituted office of the church, the clever and resolute policy of the "*Theologinnenverband*", an organization which was more interested in the status of the profession now open to women, than in the spiritual and ecclesiastical side of the matter. Above all, the overwhelming authority of Karl Barth, who exercised a secret dictatorship over German Protestants, must not be forgotten. The result is that hundreds of "*Pastorinnen*" are now officiating in the churches of West and East Germany. There are still pockets of resistance, especially among confessional Lutherans. But these are minorities. For German Protestantism as a whole, the question has been settled by way of compromise, as everything is settled by compromise. There may be minor splits and secessions to the Free Churches. But German Protestantism, as Protestantism everywhere in national and territorial churches, has been living for centuries on compromise. What the final results of the revolutionary movements on the churches will be, remains to be seen.

## THE DEVELOPMENT IN SWEDEN

Much more conspicuous and exciting was the development in Sweden, the most "progressive" country of Europe. The matter was under discussion for years, fostered by very active women's organizations. The church in Sweden is a state church in the strictest sense. Its bishops and ministers are public servants appointed by the king. Everyone knew that the socialist government was preparing the necessary legislation. The Swedish episcopate, once famous for its scholarship, was divided. These defenders of the faith did not know exactly whether the faith was at stake. They sought advice from outside. They asked the World Council of Churches and the Lutheran World Federation and received noncommittal answers. They asked the Swedish Labor Unions and women's organizations which were, of course, in favor. They asked the youth organizations and received the answer: No, the ordination of women is against God's Word.

## "THE GOSPEL NOT AT STAKE"

As soon as the diet had altered the law, the church assembly followed suit and altered the ordination liturgy accordingly. One of the bishops is reported to have had a crying fit and said: This is the end of the church in Sweden! He was soon soothed by his colleagues with the distinction between the Law and Gospel, that great tranquillizer for disturbed consciences in modern churches. The Gospel is not at stake! It is only an outward law which has been altered. When some of the leading churchmen later stated they had acted under compulsion, the politicians answered: Nobody has compelled you. What caused them to act as they did was the desire to avoid a clash between church and state, and to preserve to the Swedish people its national church with all its possibilities to proclaim the Gospel, whatever that may mean. It is the tragic conflict that exists within all national churches of Europe.

## Confessional Lutheranism Awakens

But in this case something happened which had not happened in other countries. A strong movement in the congregations and in the clergy arose under the leadership of the Bishop of Göteborg, Bo Giertz, and others. It was the first sign of an awakening of confessional Lutheranism, especially among the younger generation. This movement is still suffering from a lack of clarity concerning its aims and possibilities. But its influence is growing, not only in the Scandinavian countries, but also in Germany. A new "gathering around Bible and Confession" is arising everywhere as a reaction of the Christian people to that modernism in theology and church which is threatening the substance of the Christian faith. We find an interesting parallel in the rise of "Evangelicalism" in the English speaking world, especially in England and in the U.S.A., but also in Australia and in the younger churches of Asia. It seems significant that the "Student Christian Movement" (S. C. M.) is losing the academic world in favor of the InterVarsity Fellowship movement and their Evangelical Unions. One could also mention the great success of *Christianity Today*.

## The Turn of the Tide

It is significant that it was just the ordination of women which in the Scandinavian countries caused the turn of the tide. It is not always easy for the simple layman to discover a dogmatic deviation in the sermon, especially when the most dangerous modernism uses the old words of the orthodox faith, though in a totally different meaning. But if a girl appears at the altar, as the representative of Christ, everyone notices that a change has taken place. Maybe the strong liturgical tradition of the church of Sweden—Swedish is one of the finest liturgical languages in the world—stands behind the resistance of the Swedish people.

## What Is the Objection?

But what is the objection against the ordination of women? A lot of human arguments have been put forward, but they are not decisive. The Word of God is decisive and it clearly excludes women from the ministry of preaching and administering the sacraments in the church. The passages are well known and need not be explained in detail here. They are written by Paul in 1 Corinthians 14 and 1 Timothy 2. If we had only the second passage, the question could arise, whether Paul here gives an order for his mission field which might not be binding on the church of all ages and all times. However, 1 Corinthians 14 proves that the rule is indeed meant to be universal.

## The Church in Corinth

The First Epistle to the Corinthians is a truly remarkable document, a consolation for any pastor of a congregation in a modern big city. In Corinth there was a comparatively young church, the fruit of the work of a great missionary done in the space of two years, and yet a decaying church, humanly speaking dying. Corinth was one of the big harbor cities of the Empire, full of vice and superstitious cults. The moral problems of such an environment reflect themselves in the life of this church. For example, fornication in its worst form, lawsuits between members of the church, parties and strife, unbelief, such as the rejection of the article on the resurrection of the dead, an incredible ignorance going hand in hand with the pride of "knowledge", gossiping about the apostles whose merits and demerits they are discussing. The sacraments are in full decay. Paul makes it clear to them that their Sacrament of the Altar is no longer the sacrament of Christ. It has decayed into a fellowship tea without real fellowship, while Baptism has become an object of superstition. But these people have the "Spirit". It is the first case of enthusiastic "Pentecostalism" in the church. The Sunday services have degenerated into noisy, disorderly meetings in which glossolalists and people who regard themselves as prophets turn the church upside down.

## St. Paul's Amazing Patience

With an amazing amount of patience, with Christ's love for the lost sheep, with pastoral wisdom and with the energy of an experienced missionary, the great apostle does his utmost to save this church which seems to be in full decay. He believes that also this church is still church of Christ, that they in all their sins are still saints, God's holy people. For the Word of God is still present among them. Christ, the good Shepherd, is still their righteousness, sanctification and redemption.

In this context chapter 14 must be read. Paul calls the church with its noisy and sometimes almost riotous pentecostal meetings to order. He has no objection against what was regarded as work of the Spirit, such as speaking in tongues and prophecy, though already in the preceding chapter he has made it clear that these extraordinary gifts are of a definitely lower degree than the gifts which any Christian can and should possess: faith, hope and charity.

## St. Paul's Famous Passage

In this context Paul writes his famous *"Mulier taceat in ecclesia"*. "As in all the churches of the saints, the women should keep silence in the churches. For they are not permitted to speak, but should be subordinate, as even the law says. If there is any thing they desire to know, let them ask their husbands at home. For it is shameful for a woman to speak in church. What! Did the Word of God originate with you, or are you the only ones it has reached? If any one thinks that he is a prophet, or spiritual, he should acknowledge that what I am writing to you is a command of the Lord." "In church" means "in the solemn worship assembly" v. 34.

## Women Speaking in the Services

We have followed as far as possible, the RSV. The NEB, here as in other places, seems to be more interested in modern English than in the text of the Bible. It speaks of "meeting" and lets Paul forbid women "to address the meeting of the congregation". It overlooks that the public speaking includes also prayers. It had obviously happened that women who claimed to be prophets or to speak by inspiration of the spirit were speaking in the services. Maybe this claim of women and their refusal to "quench the spirit" caused the riotous "pentecostal" scenes at Corinth.

## Three Offices Conferred by God

In order to understand this, one must remember that the early church knew, apart from the local officebearers who were elected by the congregation or appointed by an apostle (e.g., Acts 14:23), three offices which God alone could confer and which were valid in the entire church: apostles, prophets and doctors (1 Corinthians 12:28). The office of the prophet was open also to women. Female prophets in the Old Testament were Miriam, Deborah, Hulda; in the New Testament the four daughters of Philip the evangelist, one of the Seven, who lived in Caesarea and moved later to Hierapolis in Phrygia, and others whose names are not mentioned in the Bible. The question was whether they could exercise their gift "in church" or only privately at home. Nowhere in the New Testament is it suggested that it could be done "in church". Even if they "prophesied" privately, they had to cover their head (1 Corinthians 11:4ff.). The main function of the prophets in the earliest church was to say the "eucharistic prayer", to consecrate the sacrament (Didache 10). While the bishop (pastor) uses the fixed liturgical prayer, the prophets are allowed "to give thanks (speak the eucharistic prayer) as much as they will" (Didache 10, last sentence). In the mighty language of the liturgy, the spiritual greatness of early Christian "prophecy" still resounds. This office deteriorated as false prophecy appeared in the church. As Paul had to fight the prophecy of women, so the great Montanist crisis of the second half of the second century led to the exclusion of prophecy from the church after the false prophet Montanus with his female companions had turned the church upside down.

## "A COMMAND OF THE LORD"

It is not only his apostolic authority with which Paul attacks the "prophetic", "spiritual" women who created disorder in the church. It is not only the authority of the entire church ("all the churches of the saints") to which he appeals. It is rather the Lord Himself on whom he relies. What he writes on the silence of the women in the church is "a command of the Lord". He must have known this, as he quotes also on another occasion a word spoken by Jesus, but not contained in our gospels (Acts 20:35). We accept this command of the Lord on Paul's apostolic authority, especially as it corresponds to the way in which Jesus acted. The followers of Jesus were well organized. There was the body of the Twelve, representing the people of God with its twelve tribes (Luke 22:30). Within this group we find the narrower circle of the Three, Peter, John and James, whom He took with Him on special great occasions (the raising of the daughter of Jairus, the Transfiguration, Gethsemane). Among them Simon Peter was the spokesman (e.g. Matthew 16:16; Acts 1:15; 2:14 etc.), the first ("primus") as he is called (Matthew 10:1), but not their ruler. There is a remarkable trend towards a primacy among the disciples, but Jesus strongly expressed Himself against any sort of primacy (e.g. Luke 22:23ff.). We hear that at a certain time of His activity Jesus appointed a wider circle of the "Seventy" (Luke 10:1ff.) to preach the Gospel. Furthermore, there was a group of "the women" who followed and served Him. They play a role in the history of the Passion and of Easter and belonged with the Twelve, with Mary and the brothers of Jesus to the nucleus of the church in Jerusalem (Acts 1:14).

# THE ATTITUDE OF JESUS

The question may be asked: Why did Jesus not invite one of them to participate in the Last Supper, not even in its preparation? Was the attitude of Jesus to these faithful followers dictated by the Jewish prejudice against the religious equality of men and women? Behind this there is, incidentally, the attitude of the Old Testament to the pagan religions of its environment in which priestesses and prophetesses played such a great role that one can say that priestesses are a mark of paganism. One may observe even that Jesus keeps a strange distance from His own Mother. Did He forsee the future cult of Mary, the first traces of which, or at least its psychological roots, may be found in His earthly days (Luke 11:27)?

# A CONTRADICTION IN STATEMENTS?

It is remarkable that the same apostle who speaks out so seriously against the preaching of women has established so firmly the principle that in Christ "there is neither Jew nor Greek, there is neither bond nor free, there is neither male nor female: for you are all one in Christ Jesus" (Galatians 3:28). If there were a contradiction between the statements in Galatians 3 and 1 Corinthians 14, as our modern feminists think, St. Paul, who after all was a keen thinker, would have noticed it. It would not have escaped the attention of the Christian women in the ancient church who played such a great role in the life of the church, not only as wives and mothers, but also as "widows" and female deacons in the direct service of the church being on the payroll of the clergy.

But we hear nothing of their desire to be bishops or elders. And if the gift of prophecy was given to some of them, they would not have based any claims on this fact. For they loved their Lord and knew that they had to obey His command.

If we ask why Jesus acted in this way, we must admit that we do not know exactly His reasons. Paul suggests that there is a connection between his rule, or rather Christ's rule, and the order of creation which made the sexes different. Equal rights in the order of salvation as children of God do not extinguish the difference between man and woman. A man can not become a mother, a woman cannot become a Father. The Son of God became man, not woman. One of the deepest reasons why a woman may become a deacon, but not a bishop or an ordained elder (1 Timothy 5:17) seems to be that in the office of the pastor there are functions which the minister performs as the representative of Christ. In the Last Supper Christ instituted not only what today even in Lutheran churches is called "Holy Communion", but the Sacrament of the Altar, in which the minister speaks the words of consecration "*in persona*

*Christi*" (in the stead of Christ), repeating the words of consecration which Christ spoke and which, as the Formula of Concord teaches, together with the fathers of the church, are effective at all times, as the words in creation "be fruitful and multiply" are effective as long as the world stands. The command, "This do in remembrance of Me", implies a sort of ordination. These words do not give a magical power, but contain the command to consecrate bread and wine so that they may become Christ's true body and blood. Certainly the command is given to the entire church, but to carry it out the church has set aside, ordained certain men, the pastors. Another occasion when a pastor speaks "*in persona Christi*" is at the absolution. Certainly the office of the keys is given to the whole church including laymen and women. But to carry out Christ's great command to forgive sins, the Church ordains a minister who "in the stead and by the command of my Lord Jesus Christ" not only proclaims the comforting truth that there is a forgiveness of sins, but who actually forgives the sins in the stead and at the command of Jesus Christ. Again, it is significant that no woman was entrusted with this office when at Easter the risen Lord gave to His disciples this power. "If you forgive the sins of any, they are forgiven; if you retain the sins of any, they are retained" (John 20.23). We all know how seriously Luther throughout his life took this power of absolution. To us modern men they have become more or less "irrelevant". So we let female "pastors" perform this no longer meaningful job. If it ever should happen that one of these ordained women asks: "Do you believe that my forgiveness is God's forgiveness?" a Christian congregation could only answer: "This we most certainly do not believe". Again we have to stick to the will of Christ and not try to interpret this in a way that pleases the old Adam. Why has He never given this office to a woman? We must leave the answer to Him. Not even to His mother has He given the power to forgive sins. The church has understood this. Like every believer, His mother could pray for sinners, as also the Apology of the Augsburg Confession admits that Mary may pray for the church, for us poor sinners in this world, though we are not entitled to take that for granted and to ask the biblical "Ave Maria" (Luke 1:28).

## THE CLEAR WORDS OF SCRIPTURE

All these considerations on the basis of the clear words of Scripture make it impossible for the Lutheran Church which clings not only to human traditions, but remains faithful to Holy Scripture as the Word of God to recognize the ordination of women as valid and permissible. Hundreds of women are now officiating in Germany as "*Pastorinnen*". They are, for us, no pastors at all. One must pity these poor girls who have been misled by false teachers. We do not deny that God in His inscrutable mercy can give His blessing to ministerial acts unlawfully performed. But no believing Christian should attend their services, not even for curiosity's sake, let alone receive "Holy Communion" from their hands. Nor can we have fellowship with pastors and bishops who perform such ordinations which are contrary to God's Word. The churches which have indulged in the introduction of this ministry will soon notice the effect on their own spiritual life. In Germany they are already obvious. False prophetesses have arisen, who as spiritual daughters of Karl Barth are teaching young mothers that they should not bring their little children to the sacrament of Baptism. Others have proclaimed the death of God and replaced Christian worship with a "Political Evening Prayer" where Christ has no place and God has been replaced by man and his alleged social needs.

What can we do?

Let us pray with our fathers:

> Lord Jesus Christ, with us abide;
> For round us falls the eventide;
> Nor let Thy Word, that heavenly light,
> For us be ever veiled in night.

# The Women's Ordination Debate in the Lutheran Church of Australia

## An Open Response to the Initial Report of the Commission on Theology and Interchurch Relations

## Gregory Lockwood

### Preface

Some may query whether it is proper for me to write a response of this nature. After all, I am not *currently* a pastor of the Lutheran Church of Australia, but a guest lecturer at Luther Seminary. Let me say in defence that this response emanates from a deep concern for the church I grew up in, have served, and still love as my "mother". After studying at Immanuel and Luther Seminaries and graduating in 1970, I served the LCA for 17 years in PNC and for three years in Bridgewater, SA. Thereupon, I accepted a call as an associate professor of New Testament and Missions at Concordia Theological Seminary, Fort Wayne, Indiana. Having completed seven years in the USA I am currently enjoying a year's sabbatical as a visiting lecturer in New Testament at Luther Seminary.

During the past months in Adelaide I have had the opportunity of following the LCA debate on women's ordination at close hand. I was also able to participate in last year's symposium on the ordination question at Luther Seminary (July 24–25, 1998).

After much soul-searching, I have decided to make a contribution to the debate at this point. I would rather do so now than have cause to reproach myself later. My interest in the topic arises from my doctoral studies in New

Testament and especially from a current writing assignment, a commentary on First Corinthians to be published by Concordia Publishing House.

The CTICR has asked for "church-wide feedback" to its initial report to be in its hands by 31 August 1999. Thus the first copies of this response will be forwarded to President Steicke and the CTICR. However, because the wider church has already become deeply involved in the issue through the recent seminars led by members of the CTICR, and because the whole church has a vital interest in the issue, I have taken the liberty of printing copies for pastors and pastors *emeriti*, with some additional copies for interested laypeople.

The financing of this project has been made possible by the generosity of some LCA laypeople who were eager to offer whatever assistance they could.

Anyone who would like to make photocopies should feel free to do so.

I commend this response to the church's prayerful consideration. My prayer is that "all things be done for the strengthening of the church" (1 Cor. 14:26).

Greg Lockwood, April, 1999
(2nd edition)

## INTRODUCTION

The Commission on Theology and Interchurch Relations has agreed, very properly, that the issue of women's ordination "is to be decided by theological considerations, based on the witness of Scripture as interpreted by the Lutheran Confessions" (Initial Report, 1). In keeping with this laudable objective, I will confine myself to the scriptural and theological evidence relating to the issue. The following analysis will draw attention to what I believe to be weaknesses in the seven "scriptural and theological" arguments for the ordination of women as listed in the CTICR's Initial Report.[1] (See Appendix B.)

It may be asked how a response which exposes the weaknesses of the "pro" case squares with the word of caution in the CTICR report: "Whether or not women are to be ordained is not to be established simply by countering the opposing argument, but by a consistent, theological argument based on the witness of the Scriptures, the creeds, and our own confessional writings"? (p. 2.B.2.)

I will not make a thorough, consistent case in favor of a male-only pastorate, as this has already been made in the CTICR report and various papers, and needs no elaboration from me. I will restrict myself (a) to addressing the principles of biblical interpretation (the "hermeneutical" principles) involved

---

1    At the CTICR meeting on 22–23 October, 1998, there were ten votes in favor of the proposition that "on balance, scriptural and theological evidence allows the ordination of women," and five votes in favor of the proposition that "on balance, scriptural and theological evidence prohibits the ordination of women."

in making a decision (Part 1); (b) stressing the significance of Paul's statement in 1 Cor. 14:37, "what I am writing to you is the command of the Lord" (Part 2); (c) [as stated above], critically analyzing the seven "arguments for the ordination of women" (Part 3).

Such critical analysis is, I believe, urgently needed at this time. Important theological issues cannot be properly clarified in an atmosphere which discourages people from raising objections to arguments they believe to be false. To use an analogy: If your friends are setting out to sea in a boat full of holes and want you to join them, is it improper for you to point out that you think the boat is leaking? They may, of course, dispute your observations. But they would be wise, wouldn't they, to double-check?

## Part 1. Basic Hermeneutical Questions (Issues in Biblical Interpretation)

### (A) The Key Texts

The key texts are 1 Cor. 14:33b–40 and 1 Tim. 2:11–15. St Paul writes to the Corinthians:

> "As in all the churches of the saints, let the women be silent in the churches. For it is not permitted for them to speak; rather, let them be subordinate, as the Law also says. And if they wish to learn something, let them ask their husbands at home. For it is shameful for a woman to speak in church. Or did the Word of God go out from you, or are you the only ones it reached? If someone thinks he is a prophet or spiritual, let him recognize that what I am writing to you is *the Lord's command*. If anyone does not recognize [this], he [or she] is not recognized" (1 Cor. 14:33b–38).

Paul also writes to Timothy:

> "Let a woman learn in silence in all submission. I do not permit a woman to teach or to have authority over a man. But they are to be in silence. For Adam was formed first, then Eve. And Adam was not deceived, but the woman was deceived and became a transgressor. But she will be saved through childbirth (or "through the birth of The Child"), if they remain in faith and love and holiness with propriety" (1 Tim. 2:11–15).

Many people today react to these texts just as the disciples reacted to the Lord's words regarding his flesh and blood being "real food" and "real drink": "This is a hard saying. Who can accept it?" (John 6:55, 60). If these Pauline texts are to be taken at face value even in the circumstances of our modern culture, they find themselves taking offense. Thus there has arisen the fierce debate in modern Christendom on women's ordination, a debate which no church can avoid.

That some find these Pauline texts hard to swallow is understandable given the climate of our times which poses a particular challenge to Christian women who seek to be faithful to the Word as revealed in Scripture. Behind these passages stands the teaching on the order of creation (the man as the head of the woman—1 Cor. 11:3, etc.) which runs counter to modern thinking. It can only be happily embraced if seen as God's good will for his creation for reasons we may not fully understand. By the same token, this is not an easy saying for many men. Not all welcome the responsibilities that headship brings.

## (B) THE SCRIPTURES—THE BASIS FOR DECIDING THE ISSUE

All Australian Lutherans should agree with John Reumann, a prominent Lutheran advocate of women's ordination in the USA, when he writes: "Any decision about women functioning in the ordained ministry must rest, in the Lutheran tradition, on careful examination of the scriptural data" (*Ministries Examined*, p. 78).[2] We would also agree with Reumann when he continues: "The whole question is basically one of hermeneutics: how do you interpret and apply the Scripture" (p. 98).

## (C) ARE ALL WAYS OF INTERPRETING THE BIBLE EQUALLY VALID?

A common approach to encouraging Lutherans to discuss women's ordination "without rancor"[3] runs like this: "All of us are equally and honestly committed to the authority of the Scriptures. That good people reach different conclusions is due simply to their different hermeneutic (approach to biblical interpretation). The hermeneutical issues involved are difficult, a matter for biblical specialists. But you may safely leave them in the hands of these experts. Whatever the outcome, you may rest assured that we all share the same fundamental commitment to the Bible. So different hermeneutical approaches which lead to conclusions quite different from what the church has traditionally held should not bother us. We should tolerate one another's

---

2   Unfortunately, we need to reckon today with the influence of the school of thought known as "postmodernism" which has no time for any authority-claims, including the claims of the Bible. For the "postmodernist," the chief authority is his or her own self, his or her personal life-experience, perception, and judgment. Someone of this mindset will say: "So, that's what the Bible says, is it? But this is what I think. . . . And what do you think?" It becomes difficult—if not impossible—for Christians who see the Scriptures as authoritative to have a meaningful debate with people who see them as merely a hodge-podge of the (often contradictory) thoughts of other humans with no more authority than "what I think."

3   The phrase comes from John Reumann.

viewpoints. After all, the issue is not church-divisive,[4] and should not be taken too seriously."

This approach begs the question: Are all ways of interpreting the Bible equally true to the Bible's self-understanding and therefore equally helpful in building up the church? The answer, I would submit, is "No." Some hermeneutical approaches encourage the practitioner to adopt a critical stance towards the authority, truthfulness, and clarity of some parts of the Bible. And that—precisely that—is the major concern of those who oppose women's ordination. The ordination of women, in itself, is merely a symptom of what they believe to be a far more serious problem: a critical stance towards the Bible's authority, a stance fraught with serious consequences for the life of the church.[5] In other words, the basic issue is hermeneutics and the doctrine of Scripture.

The real question, then, is whether we adopt (a) a Lutheran understanding of the Bible as the Word of God, a hermeneutic which allows Scripture (rather than the culture) to interpret Scripture, an approach we may call "the hermeneutics of appreciation",[6] or (b) whether we follow a critical approach to the Scriptures which questions the authority and relevance of foundational texts.

The point is not, then, whether there are honest Christian men and women on both sides of the debate. Undoubtedly there are. But an honest Christian can be honestly mistaken. And a mistaken hermeneutic can have grave implications for the church.

## (D) Two Ways Contrasted: "Proof Texts" versus "the Gospel"

The prominent Lutheran advocate of women's ordination in the United States, John Reumann, certainly does not accept all hermeneutical approaches as being equally salutary. He describes two different ways of

---

4    The issue is clearly divisive, especially because of the underlying hermeneutical issues. But if an issue is declared nondivisive, then those who take a stand are held to be at fault for jeopardizing the unity of the church, even though they may be upholding the historic position of the church and may believe (more importantly) that they are upholding the Scriptures. A classic parallel appeared in *The Australian* on March 11, 1999. The religious affairs writer reported on the call by the conservative faction Evangelical Members within the Uniting Church (EMU) for like-minded congregations opposed to the practice of homosexuality to form their own association. The article carried the headline: "Anti-gay faction divides church." But charges of troubling the church can go both ways (see 1 Kings 18:16–18!). Why not "Pro-gay faction divides church"?

5    Fortunately, thanks to what has been called a "blessed inconsistency," most scholars who practice the critical method in biblical interpretation do not apply the method across the board.

6    Cf. Ps. 119:72: "The Law (i.e. the word) from your mouth is more precious to me than thousands of gold and silver pieces."

interpreting Scripture: One approach, he writes, "argues by proof texts," the other is "gospel-centred." Thus we face the question: "Does a central gospel or do individual texts . . . prevail in reaching a decision?" (p. 99).

Already the dice are loaded. One approach is described as "gospel-centred," and therefore good. The other approach is, by implication, not gospel-centred, and therefore it is "legalistic"[7] and bad. This latter approach, it is claimed, puts too much store by "proof texts" and "individual texts."

What does Reumann mean by "proof texts?" The expression has been used, without proper definition, to disparage any appeal to the key foundational texts which have served as the church's basis in determining its teaching and practice. If Reumann means by proof-texting that a person appeals to biblical texts without regard for their context, then we would agree with him that this is bad. But what he is specifically attacking is making too much of texts that speak directly to the issue. This approach, he writes, "begins with 1 Corinthians 14, or 1 Timothy 2, which leads you to exclude women from ordination" (p. 117).

Or, it is argued, we need to be aware of the cultural, linguistic, and historical gaps between the first century and the twentieth century. What the Biblical text meant then may be different from what it means today. I personally think far too much has been made of this "gap." Couldn't the Lord, who knows the human heart, speak words that are authoritative and clear and applicable to the human condition down to the end of time? Couldn't his called apostles do the same? How much of the New Testament, the words of the Holy Spirit, doesn't speak just as directly and clearly to the believer's heart today as it spoke to people then? And if we adopt the "gap" approach, who determines what God speaks today? But I will pick this issue up again later.

I ask again, then, what is wrong with appealing to the key foundational texts? What proof are we going to use in a discussion on "scriptural and theological evidence" if we cannot use those scriptural passages that speak to the issue? Jesus himself, immersed in the Scriptures as he was, constantly appealed to "individual texts" from the Old Testament as the foundation for his teaching and practice (cf. the thrice-repeated "it is written" in Matt 4:1–13). A reading of Luther's *Small Catechism* will show that Luther quotes the Bible over and over as the foundation of the teaching he expounds.

He uses texts that speak to the specific issue. In elucidating the doctrine of baptism, for example, he does not appeal to some vague "gospel" principle (the principle of love, or the "gospel spirit" of freedom, or equality, or inclusivity). Rather, he adduces "individual texts" that deal specifically with baptism (Matthew 28; Romans 6; Titus 3). In technical language these texts are called the "*sedes doctrinae*," "the seat of the doctrine."

---

7    Other pejoratives like "fundamentalistic" are sometimes applied.

To refer to such texts is really just sanctified common sense. If we want to know what our car manual says about changing a wheel, we don't look up the section on the electrical system. Similarly, if we want to know what the Bible says about who may be qualified to serve as a pastor, we don't begin with texts that spell out the Gospel, like 1 Cor. 15:3 ("Christ died for our sins"). The Gospel of forgiveness in Christ says nothing about who should be ordained.

# PART 2. THE SIGNIFICANCE OF "THE COMMAND OF THE LORD"

## (A) THE INTERPRETATION OF 1 CORINTHIANS 14:37

Despite Reumann, then, I will focus on the key texts, 1 Corinthians 14 and 1 Timothy 2. What is the significance of Paul's statements in 1 Cor. 14:34 and 37: "Let the women be silent in the churches . . . What I am writing to you is *the command of the Lord*"? The word "command" (*entole*) is not a term that Paul uses lightly. In First Corinthians he uses it only twice. One of these texts (1 Cor 14:37) is quoted above. The other is 7:19: "Circumcision is nothing and uncircumcision is nothing, but keeping God's *commands* (*entolon*) is what matters." In Chapter 7, Paul is giving advice on various marriage matters. In some cases he gives advice simply on the basis of his own pastoral judgment (v 8: "Now to the unmarried and the widows I say . . .; v 12: "To the rest I say this (I, not the Lord) . . .;" v 25: "Now about virgins: I have no command[8] from the Lord, but I give a judgment as one who by the Lord's mercy is trustworthy"; see also v 40). At one point, however, he insists that his counsel does not rest merely on his pastoral judgment; it rests on a command from the Lord: "To the married I give this command[9] (not I, but the Lord): A wife must not separate from her husband. . . . And a husband must not divorce his wife" (vv 10–11; Mark 10:11–12).[10]

Thus Paul distinguishes carefully between his personal pastoral advice which has limited significance and does not necessarily bind the Christian's conscience, and divine commands which are to bind the conscience. A careful examination of the data in First Corinthians can only lead to the conclusion that Paul's injunction for the women to be silent belongs to the divine commands.[11]

---

8  The word used here for "command" (*epitage*) is a synonym of *entole*.

9  The verb is *parangello* ("I command").

10  Even in times when our culture and legal-system have become lax regarding divorce, we may not do away with the Lord's command. Rather we work to uphold marriage and deal pastorally with those who divorce as a result of living in a fallen world.

11  See the first argument of the case "for the ordination of men only" in the Initial Report, *The Lord's command*:

# (B) A Command That May Be Disregarded Because It Is Given Only Once?

The notion has become widespread that we may ignore this command of the Lord because it is stated only once in the New Testament. And, after all (it is sometimes added), it stems only from Paul, not from our Lord himself.

### Response

a. The command to baptise is given only once (Matt 28:19), yet no one suggests that Baptism ought not be practiced since it has only one Dominical command.

b. Paul's command that the women be silent in the churches is actually given twice (1 Cor 14:34; 1 Tim 2:12), unless we rule out the latter passage because it does not add: "this is a command of the Lord."

c. The "only once" argument also overlooks the texts which speak in a more general way of the Christian woman's submission and the man's headship (1 Cor 11:3; Eph 5:22–24; Col 3:18; 1 Pet 3:1–5; Titus 2:5).

d. Paul does not write as a private individual, but as the apostle (ambassador) of Jesus Christ. That is how he introduces himself in Rom 1:1; 1 Cor 1:1; 2 Cor 1:1; Gal 1:1 (and very strongly: "not from human beings nor through a human being"); Eph 1:1, etc. His word is not his private opinion, but the word of Christ.

Even if the Lord's command were given only once, we may ask: When parents command a child to do or not to do something, and the child disobeys, how many would be impressed by the retort: "But you only told me once"?

# (C) A Divine Command of Only Temporary Significance?

But, we may ask, is it a divine command which applied only to the church of Paul's day? A comparison with the command regarding divorce in 1 Cor 7:10–11 suggests the answer is "No." Are there any hints in the Gospels that Jesus understood his command regarding divorce as merely a temporary restriction? Or that Paul interpreted his Master to that effect? Moreover,

---

"1 Corinthians 14:33b and 1 Timothy 2:11–14 are foundational texts for the case against the ordination of women because they speak about the leadership of women in public worship. These passages clearly assert that God does not allow women to preach and teach in the divine service. This holds true even if it could be shown that the meaning of particular words and phrases is uncertain. The prohibition against speaking is not a demand for absolute silence but prevents women from preaching and teaching in public worship. The church therefore has no authority to ordain women. The apostle Paul states that this prohibition is a command from the Lord which applies to all churches (1 Cor 14:33b, 37; cf. 1 Tim 3:15) and warns that those who disregard it will not be recognised by God in his church (1 Cor 14:38)."

when we look at the rest of the New Testament, the overwhelming impression is that the word "command" when used of divine commands is that they have enduring significance. Jesus criticizes the Pharisees for transgressing the command of God on account of their tradition (Matt 15:3). The person who has Jesus' commandments and keeps them is the one who loves him (John 14:21). The Lord's Great Commission places on the disciples the duty of "teaching them to observe *everything that I have commanded you*" (Matt 28:20).[12] Divine commands have to do with matters of great and eternal significance, like faith and love: "And this is his *commandment* (*entole*), that we believe in the name of his Son Jesus Christ, and love one another, just as he has given *command* (*entole* again) to us" (1 John 3:23).

## (D) A COMMAND THAT SERVES THE ORDERLY PRESENTATION OF THE GOSPEL

It may seem, at first blush, that the above discussion focuses too much on the word "command", a word which has to do with the Law rather than the Gospel. Advocates of women's ordination have, at times, portrayed themselves as "evangelical", while their opponents are labeled "legalistic". Thus John Reumann writes: "Shall these verses [1 Timothy 2] be read 'evangelically' or 'legally', shall they be appraised in relation to the gospel (with its implications of emancipation) or as on a par with every other verse and theme in the New Testament?" (p. 92).[13]

It is important to remember, however, that in the New Testament the word "command" (like the word *Torah* in the OT—e.g. Psalm 1) is often used in a broad sense to denote the whole will and word of God, including the Gospel. We have seen that that is how Jesus uses the word in Matt 28:20 ("teaching them to observe everything I have *commanded* you", that is "all my teaching").

In this connection, it may be helpful to distinguish between commands which strictly speaking are legal commands ("Thou shalt not kill"; "Love the Lord your God with all your heart, and your neighbor as yourself"), and those commands which are specifically linked to the Gospel and implement the Gospel: "Take, eat, and drink;" "Go and make disciples . . . , baptising . . . , and teaching" (Matt 28:19–20); "Do this in remembrance of me" (Luke 22:19; 1 Cor 11:24); "Receive the Holy Spirit" (John 20:22); "Feed my lambs, tend my sheep" (John 21:15–16). "Hold to the teachings we passed on to you, whether by word of mouth or by letter" (2 Thess 2:15). Those in favor of a male-only pastorate believe that the imperatives of 1 Cor 14 and 1 Tim 2 are

---

12  The verb "commanded" (*eneteilamen*) comes from the same "word family" as *entole* ("commandment").

13  To say that opponents of women's ordination treat Scripture in such a flat manner, as if they put every verse and theme on a par, is false.

likewise designed for the proper and orderly implementation of the gospel. One could note that the order set forth in Scripture has the goal of keeping matters simple and straightfoward—as if to say, "Here is what men shall do; here is what women shall do"—without getting into endless complications and options. The simplicity keeps the focus properly on the services of the Gospel. Regin Prenter points out that the commands of 1 Cor 14 and 1 Tim 2 are not "commands of the law" (*Gebote des Gesetzes*) but "commands for the sake of good order" (*Ordnungsgebote*), "that is, commands that seek to preserve the right and proper transmission of the gospel."[14]

## PART 3. RESPONSES TO THE SEVEN ARGUMENTS FOR THE ORDINATION OF WOMEN

Of the seven arguments for the ordination of women listed in the Initial Report (see Appendix B), the first has to do with the relevance and clarity of 1 Cor 14:33b–40 and 1 Tim 2:11–15:

### ARGUMENT 1—THE RELEVANCE OF THE KEY TEXTS

"The two texts . . . are ambiguous and open to various interpretations. For example, in 1 Cor 14:34 it is not clear what kind of 'silence' Paul is commanding women to observe since women are praying and prophesying (11:5, 13). Further, it is not clear to what the 'command of the Lord' (14:37) refers, eg to the silence of the women or to the necessity for good order in worship" (*Initial Report*, p. 3).

Similar questions are raised about the clarity of 1 Tim 2.[15]

**Response**

It seems extraordinary that these passages have become "ambiguous" to scholars during the last few decades, whereas to our forebears and to the church throughout the centuries their import was clear. Our forebears were clear that these texts meant that women were not to have a leading speaking

---

14  Regin Prenter, "*Die Ordination der Frauen zu dem ueberlieferten Pfarramt der lutherischen Kirche*," 8. [The concluding two sentences of this paragraph have been added to expand and further clarify Dr. Lockwood's thoughts on this matter and to bring the cogent comment of Prenter to the fore.—Ed.]

15  The paragraph ends: "in both texts it is not entirely clear whether Paul is speaking of women in general or of wives in particular. Finally there is no clear indication that these commands are binding on the church outside their original context" (Initial Report, p. 4). 1 have already responded to the last sentence in the section in my discussion of the word "command" in the NT. The question about whether Paul has women or wives in mind does not seem to me to be a substantial issue. Most of the women likely to want to stand up and teach would have been married. If Paul wanted, at this point, to distinguish between "women" and "wives," surely he would have made that clear, as he does throughout chapter 7.

role during the worship service. They were not to lead the liturgy, they were not to preach the sermon, they were not to administer the sacraments. As for the texts themselves, it is clear that *at the least* they mean that a woman is not to stand before the congregation as "the teacher" on Sundays or whenever divine service is held. What could be clearer than 1 Tim 2:12: "I do not permit a woman to teach or to have authority over a man; she must be silent"?[16] And is 1 Cor 14:34 any less clear: "As in all the congregations of the saints, women should remain silent in the churches. They are not allowed to speak, but must be in submission, as the Law says"? In the light of 1 Tim 2:12 (according to the principle "Scripture interprets Scripture") that must *at least* mean that the women are not to teach the Word of God to the assembled congregation. Thus the *essential meaning* of both texts as they relate to the issue of women's ordination is unambiguous. At least one advocate of women's ordination has admitted as much:

> The two main texts have the following in common: women/wives are to remain silent; they are to show *submission*; they are to be *learners* or *questioners* rather than leaders and teachers . . . . The general import of the texts is clear.[17]

Questions arise mainly about the *scope* of the apostolic injunction (CTICR: "What kind of 'silence'"?). Is it to be understood more broadly than teaching? For example, does Paul (as some think) also intend to ban the women from prophesying and speaking in tongues? Or is it to be understood more broadly still, as an absolute ban on any speaking by women during church? Thus advocates of women's ordination sometimes indulge in a *reductio ad absurdum* (reducing the opponent's argument in a way that makes it look absurd) by asking, e.g., "Does that mean a woman cannot teach Sunday School?" A careful reading of 1 Tim. 2:12 should provide a sufficient answer. We need to distinguish between public teaching that exercises authority and forms of teaching in groups in the congregation under the authority and oversight of the pastor.

But proponents of women's ordination raise question after question in order to inject doubt regarding the clarity of the texts.[18] Let's take up just one

---

16 It is clear throughout 1 Tim 2 that Paul is thinking of the worship service.

17 *Ordination of Women in the L.C.A.: Yes or No* (papers presented at a Symposium at Luther Seminary, North Adelaide, 24–25 July, 1998, p. 16).

18 At the 1992 Church of England synod the second last speaker was the Archdeacon of Leicester (now the Anglican Bishop of Ballarat), Venerable David Silk, an opponent of women's ordination. The archdeacon cited Sir Norman Anderson, the chairman of the House of Laity: "In the end I come face to face with the plain meaning of Scripture." Silk continued: "I hear what is said on the headship issue and I try to follow the debate, but in the end I come face to face with the plain meaning of Scripture, and I cannot believe that God would have left its intent so obscure as to need all the fine points made

more, that "it is not clear to what the 'command of the Lord' (14:37) refers, eg to the silence of the women or to the necessity for good order in worship." I would simply suggest that you take up your Bible and read 1 Cor 14:33b–40 for yourself, and see whether you think "the command of the Lord" applies only to the need for good order (v 40), or whether it applies also to the immediate antecedent in verses 33b–36.

As for the clarity of the Scriptures in general, this is a vital point in the Lutheran Church's doctrine of Scripture. Against Erasmus, Luther argued for "the perspicuity of Scripture":

> The notion that in Scripture some things are recondite (obscure) and all is not plain was spread by the godless Sophists. . . . And Satan has used these unsubstantial spectres to scare men off reading the sacred text, and to destroy all sense of its value.[19]

Luther grants that "many *passages* in the Scriptures are obscure and hard to elucidate, but that is due . . . to our own linguistic and grammatical ignorance." In other words, the fault lies in ourselves, not in the Scriptures themselves.[20] He adds: "Those who deny the perfect clarity and plainness of the Scriptures leave us nothing but darkness."[21] On the essential clarity of Scripture, Luther quotes Ps 119:105 ("Your word is a light to my feet"), Ps 19:8; Isa 8:20; Malachi 2:7; 2 Peter 1:19, etc.

If the Scriptures are not clear and authoritative, then the church needs an authoritative teaching office besides—or above—the Scriptures. In Roman Catholicism this role has been played by the papacy. In sections of modern Protestantism, when Christians begin to lose their confidence in the clarity, truthfulness, and authority of the Bible, this role has often been assumed by the scholars. If, on the other hand, the Bible is essentially clear, then "ordinary" pastors and laypeople should be able to read it with confidence, without feeling that it is too difficult for them and its interpretation must be left to the theologians. All of us theologians can make mistakes; sometimes we make grievous mistakes. And, as C.S. Lewis wrote, every sheep has the right to bleat if it thinks its shepherd is leading it astray.[22]

---

in this debate to make it clear to me" (*The Ordination of Women to the Priesthood: The Synod Debate*, p. 72).

19 *The Bondage of the Will*, trans. J.I. Packer & O.R. Johnston (London: James Clarke, 1957), p. 71.

20 If only recently these passages—1 Corinthians 14 and 1 Timothy 2 have become obscure—does the fault lie with the Scriptures or with the scholars (interpreters)?

21 P. 128.

22 *Fernseed and Elephants and Other Essays on Christianity* (Glasgow: Collins, 1975), pp. 105, 125.

## ARGUMENT 2—THE MISSION IMPERATIVE

"The apostolic prohibition against women speaking in the worship assembly (1 Cor 14:33, 34; 1 Tim 2:11, 12) is based on a concern for the church's mission to spread the gospel. Women questioning or debating matters in the church (1 Cor 14:35) or acting in a high handed manner would have caused offence especially to the predominantly Jewish converts and potential converts. Paul's concern here is not for a male order of ministry but for orderliness in contrast to disorder, so as not to bring the church into disrepute (see 1 Cor 14:33, 35, 40)" (*Initial Report*, p. 4).

**Response**

a. The cited texts say nothing about missions and the growing of churches; their concern is for good order in the churches that have already grown.

b. It is unproved, and almost certainly false, that the Corinthian congregation consisted of "predominantly Jewish converts and potential converts." Certainly Paul always reached out first of all to the Jews, beginning each mission in the synagogue (Rom 1:16). But his special mission was to the Gentiles (Gal 2:9); he was "the apostle of the Gentiles" (Rom 11:13). Claims that his mission to Gentiles was largely a failure are unsubstantiated. The "failure" that weighed most heavily on him was that so few of his fellow Jews had accepted the gospel (Romans 9–11). Certainly, a good number of former Jews belonged to the Corinthian congregation. But if they constituted a majority, why does Paul devote most of the letter to problems to which people from a Gentile background were particularly prone: the love of sophistic rhetoric (chapters 1–4), litigiousness (chapter 5), visiting prostitutes, homosexuality (chapter 6), meat offered to idols (chapters 8–10), etc?

Far from making concessions to a predominantly Jewish culture and "going with the flow" of that culture for the sake of "mission," the apostle is countering inroads from a pagan Gentile culture which threatens the gospel. The epistle is "countercultural."[23]

c. Paul's concern was always for the clear proclamation of the gospel whether threatened by inroads from paganism or from Judaizers. Elsewhere when Paul urges Christians to refrain from certain practices, or to keep them, he makes it clear that it is in order to avoid

---

23 Most likely, it is counter-cultural in another respect. There is evidence that at various times, in various parts of the Graeco-Roman world, priestesses served in some pagan temples. Indeed, there is some evidence that this may have been going on in the Corinthian temple of Demeter and Kore in Paul's day (see Peter Gooch, *Dangerous Foods*, p. 11).

giving offence (see, for example, Romans 14:1–15:13, especially 14:13, 20, 21; Acts 16:3; 1 Cor 8:9). He is concerned that Gentiles should not be shackled by Jewish ceremonial law or custom (the whole epistle to the Galatians; Col 2:16), so he is careful to make a clear distinction between what is required and what is just for the sake of avoiding offence. Yet in 1 Corinthians 14 he makes no mention of the possibility of causing offence, but speaks of a command of the Lord.

d. The "mission imperative" argument concludes by presenting the reader with a false antithesis: "Paul's concern here is *not for*[24] a male order of ministry *but for* orderliness in contrast to disorder." So we are presented with an "either . . . or": *Either* Paul was concerned for a male order, *or* he was concerned for orderliness. And since he was clearly concerned for orderliness (1 Cor 14:40), he couldn't have been concerned for a male order of ministry.

But isn't it rather the case that the apostle's concern is to be understood as a "*both . . . and*" rather than an "either . . . or"? Indeed, a careful reading of 1 Cor 14:26–40 will show that Paul's concern for peace and order includes three aspects: i) good order requires that a tongues-speaker remain silent when there is no interpreter (v 28); ii) good order requires that a prophet be silent when a revelation comes to another (v 30); and iii) good order requires that the women be silent (v 34). Thus Paul is concerned both for good order and for a "male order of ministry" as one necessary aspect of that order.

e. Finally, does anyone seriously think that the adoption of women's ordination is likely to promote the mission and growth of the LCA?

## Argument 3—Roles Played by Women in the Early Church

"Women laboured with Paul 'in the gospel' (Phil 4:3); Priscilla taught Apollos (Acts 18:26); women prayed and prophesied in public worship (1 Cor 11:5, 10; see also Acts 2:17); Phoebe is called 'deacon' and 'patron' of the church at Cenchreae (Rom 16:1, 2). That Paul allows a woman to learn (1 Tim 2:11) is already a revolutionary step away from Jewish practice since it implies that they can then teach. It is therefore questionable whether 1 Tim 2:12 (a woman is not to teach or have authority over a man) must be read as a principle without qualifications" (*Initial Report*, 4).

### Response

a. To make too much of this argument would be to ignore the basic principle that the larger passages which speak directly to the issue (*sedes doctrinae*—in this case, 1 Cor 14:33b–38 and 1 Tim 2:11–15) should be given the most weight.

---

24 Italics added.

b. Some brief responses to each item may be given:

    i. Christian women have always laboured alongside pastors in the gospel. This does not mean they served as pastors themselves;

    ii. Priscilla taught Apollos *privately*; there is no evidence that she functioned as a public proclaimer of the Word to the assembled congregation;

    iii. That women "prayed and prophesied in public worship" does not prove that they served as pastors. It is simplistic to equate prophets and prophetesses with pastors. Passages like 1 Cor 12:28 and Eph 4:11 clearly distinguish prophets from pastors/teachers.

    iv. That Phoebe served as a "deacon" and "patron" does not mean she was a pastor.

c. That Paul allows a woman to learn may have been a revolutionary step compared with the practice of some first-century Jewish rabbis, but it is not revolutionary compared with the Old Testament. The Old Testament consistently implies that all the people of Israel are to learn the word (Deut 6:1–9); nothing in the OT restricts them from learning. One gets the impression that Mary and Elisabeth knew the OT Scriptures well. But it does not follow from their being permitted to learn that they were permitted to teach. A woman's knowledge of the Bible in OT times did not imply that she could become a priest. For that matter, a man's knowledge of the Bible did not, in itself, qualify him for the priesthood; he had to belong to the tribe of Levi and, moreover, be a descendant of Aaron. By the same token, a woman's biblical knowledge today does not imply a claim to the pastoral office.

## ARGUMENT 4—EQUALITY OF MEN AND WOMEN IN CHRIST

"The baptismal formula of Galatians 3:28[25] (cf 1 Cor 12:13; Col 3:11) gives to women a position in the church not known within contemporary Judaism. The new creation in Christ (2 Cor 5:17) confirms the equal standing of women with men before God (cf Gen 1:26–28). So, within marriage, husbands and wives are to complement one another (1 Cor 7:4) and to be subject to one another out of love (Eph 5:21). Within the church's ministry, the ordination of women is an appropriate application of this principle of equality" (*Initial Report*, 4).

---

25  Gal 3:28 reads: "There is neither Jew nor Greek, there is neither slave nor free, *there is neither male nor female; for you are all one in Christ Jesus*" (italics added).

It is a little surprising to see this argument relegated to Number 4. According to John Reumann, the New Testament scholar who has been one of the leading promoters of women's ordination among American Lutherans, this argument from Gal 3:28 "is the crucial New Testament [text] cited for ordaining women." Reumann hails this text as "the breakthrough" (*Ministries Examined*, p. 86).

## Response

a.  Gal 3:28 is part of an extensive section which argues that the Christian receives justification, blessing, and the eternal inheritance on the basis of faith in the divine promise, not by works of law such as circumcision. The immediate context of 3:28 reads: (26) "For you are all sons[26] of God through faith in Christ Jesus. (27) For as many of you as were baptised into Christ have put on Christ. (28) . . . there is neither male nor female, for you are all one in Christ Jesus. (29) And if you are Christ's, then you are Abraham's seed, heirs according to promise."

    The text speaks of *all* Christians being "sons" and heirs of eternal life. Through faith and baptism every Christian enjoys all the "rights and privileges" of being God's child and heir—access to the Father at any time in prayer (Gal 4:6), the joyful confidence of one who is no longer a slave, but a son. St Peter puts the point succinctly: Both men and women are "joint heirs of the grace of life" (1 Pet 3:7).

    The subject matter in Gal 3:28 is baptism and its implications. But where is there anything here about ordination?[27] If Gal 3:28 is taken as the standard for determining who may be ordained, what prevents us from ordaining children?[28] It has been argued that one must look

---

26  Yes, according to the Greek text both women and men are "sons" (*hyioi*)!

27  See the second argument of the case "for the ordination of men only," *The relevance of Galatians 3:28*:

    "Galatians 3:28 should not be used to support the ordination of women because it does not deal with the doctrine of the public office. Rather, it asserts that both men and women have the same status before God the Father as his adopted children, and that they have the same access to his grace through baptism. Their equality before God does not change their distinctiveness and calling as men and women with sexually differentiated and yet complementary roles in marriage, family, and the church. Their sexuality is not abolished or disregarded, but sanctified for service according to their role in the family and the church" (Initial Report, p.5).

28  Or, for that matter, homosexuals? Gal 3:28 ("neither male nor female—in Christ") can be—and has been—used in some churches as an argument for the ordination of gays. Indeed, a case can be made that the ordination of women can—and often does—prepare the way for the ordination of homosexuals. Advocates of women's ordination may protest at this linking of the two issues. Their protest is *partially* justified; on the face of it, these are obviously different issues. However, their protest is only partially

elsewhere, for example to 1 Tim 3:2 which says a pastor should be "apt to teach." And that is precisely my point. We must look elsewhere than Gal 3:28 to find the qualifications for ordination. These are set out in 1 Timothy 3:2–7 and Titus 1:5–9.[29]

b. The baptismal formula of Gal 3:28 may have given women a position in the church not known within some sectors of first century Judaism. But it is not so radically new in itself; it has deep roots in the Old Testament teaching that all believers constitute a royal priesthood (Exodus 19:5–6). It is misleading to give the impression that (a) Paul had only just managed to bring Jewish Christians to the point where they could accept that a woman could learn the Scriptures and be treated as a full member of God's people; (b) he really wanted to take them all the way to the acceptance of women's ordination; but (c) that would have been asking too much of people who had only just taken step (a).

c. Are equality and subordination incompatible? If I subordinate myself to my cricket captain on a Saturday afternoon, does that mean we are not equals? If my wife willingly subordinates herself to me in response to the apostle's word (Eph 5:22–24), does that make her an inferior being?[30] In many ways she is more than my equal! The apostles certainly saw no incompatibility between the "equality" and the "subordination" themes. Indeed, St Peter puts them directly alongside each other (1 Peter 3:5–7): "The holy women of the past . . . were *submissive*

---

justified. The pattern of argumentation for the ordination of homosexuals follows the same hermeneutical lines as the argument for the ordination of women: (a) the appeal to Gal 3:28; (b) the notion that the Biblical writers were conditioned by their culture and time, so that what they said then against homosexuality had only temporary significance; "what it meant" then is not necessarily "what it means" for us today. And so churches which accepted women's ordination after a program of debating the issue "without rancor" find themselves a few years later trying to debate — again "without rancor"—the ordination of homosexuals. The Uniting Church of Australia and the Evangelical Lutheran Church of America are only two of the many examples that could be given.

29 One of the qualifications is that a pastor must be "the husband of one wife" (1 Tim 3:2; Titus 1:6). Paul simply assumes that the pastor will be a man. How, then, can it be maintained that his position on the issue is "ambiguous" and "not clear"?

30 The Christian woman's subordination is her willing gift to her husband as a result of her love for the Lord and his word. Any suggestion that for her to give this gift demeans her has no basis in the New Testament. According to the apostolic teaching, it is no more demeaning for a woman to be subject to a man as her "head" than it is for the man to be subject to Christ and for Christ to be subject to the Father (1 Cor 11:3; 15:27–28). By the same token, any suggestion that the man's headship must be oppressive has no basis in the NT. His headship is to be modelled on Christ's self-sacrificing love for the church (Eph 2:25–33). Pastors, in their "headship" (under Christ) over the congregation, are expressly forbidden from lording it over the flock (1 Pet 5:3).

to their own husbands, like Sarah, who obeyed Abraham and called him her master. . . . Husbands, in the same way be considerate as you live with your wives, and treat them with respect as the weaker partner and as *heirs with you of the gracious gift of life*" (see Galatians 3:28!).[31]

## Argument 5—The Inclusivity of the Gospel

"The inclusivity of the gospel should come to expression also in the public ministry of the church. This inclusivity which embraced Jew and Gentile, slave and free, male and female, found tangible expression in the early church (Eph 2:11–22; Philemon 16). It is fittingly modelled by a public office which includes women" (*Initial Report*, 4).

### Response

a. The gospel is certainly "inclusive": "God wants *all people* to be saved" (1 Tim 2:4). God calls *all* people to oneness in Christ Jesus (Gal 3:28). But this does not mean that all are called to the public *ministry*. See the response to "Argument 4" above.

b. Like Gal 3:28, the texts cited (Eph 2:11–22 and Philemon 16) have nothing to do with ordination. Ephesians 2 tells us that Gentiles and Jews have equal access to God the Father in one Spirit; Gentiles are no longer strangers and aliens but fellow-citizens of the saints and members of God's household (vv 18–19). In Philemon 16 Paul encourages Philemon to treat his runaway slave Onesimus not as a slave but as "a beloved brother." He doesn't suggest that Philemon treat Onesimus as "a pastor"! In fact, it is highly unlikely that a slave in Paul's day could have served as a pastor, despite Gal 3:28 ("neither slave nor free—in Christ"), and this is certainly not what Paul was advocating in the Galatians text.[32]

---

31 According to the most common interpretation of the texts, Paul does the same thing in Eph 5:21–24: Eph 5:21 speaks of the mutual submission of husbands and wives; Eph 5:22–24 of the submission of wives to husbands. One scholar (W. Grudem) has disputed that Eph 5:21 speaks of mutual submission of wives and husbands. He notes that whenever Paul speaks of the submission of one partner in a relationship to another (wife-husband, child-parent, slave-master, citizen-government), the submission is one-way, not reciprocal (e.g. Paul does not call on parents to submit to their children, governments to their subjects, etc). In Grudem's interpretation, Eph 5:21 is a heading to the long section which deals with submission of some people to others: wives to husbands, children to parents, and slaves to masters (Eph 5:21–6:9). Whether Grudem is right or wrong, it must be said that it is illegitimate to use Eph 5:21 to cancel out everything else Paul says about wives' subordination to husbands (Eph 5:22–24; Col 3:8; Titus 2:5).

32 There is a church tradition that Onesimus later became a bishop! But that was after his release from slavery.

c. The term "inclusivity" is a buzz word which is not particularly helpful in this debate. Not only does it brand those who do not accept the arguments for women's ordination as "exclusive" and narrow-minded, in contrast to those who are "inclusive," "open" etc. It is also infinitely elastic, and raises the question: "Whom would you debar from the Lutheran ministry? Why not practising homosexuals, or children, or the intellectually disabled? Where do you draw the line? And on what basis?"

## ARGUMENT 6—THE REPRESENTATION OF CHRIST

"The first Adam embraces the whole of sinful humanity, both men and women (Rom 5:12,15). In the person of the new Adam, Jesus Christ, God redeems and restores fallen humanity, both men and women (Rom 5:15–19; 1 Cor 15:45–49). The representation of Christ by women is made possible by their incorporation into him. All those redeemed by Christ are members of his body and thus able to represent Christ to that body once they have been 'rightly called' to the public office" (*Initial Report*, 4).

### Response

a. The first two sentences of this paragraph are correct. But it is a considerable stretch from what Paul says in Romans 5 and 1 Corinthians 15 (all humanity's solidarity with Adam in sin and their reigning in life through Christ) to the conclusion: "Therefore a woman may represent Christ as a pastor." Romans 5 and 1 Corinthians 15, like Gal 3:28, do not speak specifically about the issue of ordination.

b. It is true that pastors are Christ's representatives ("we are ambassadors for Christ," 2 Cor 5:20). In the secular world an ambassador may be a man or a woman. But in the church, for reasons ultimately rooted in "the order of creation,"[33] the Lord has specified through his ambassador St Paul that only men are to be pastors.

---

33  See the fifth argument of the case "for the ordination of men only" as outlined in the Initial Report, *The representation of Christ's headship*:

"The ordination of women contradicts the reality of male headship in the church and the family which was established by God in the creation of Adam and fulfilled by the incarnation of God's Son as a male person (1 Cor 11:3,8,9; Eph 5:22–24; 1 Tim 2:13). It therefore involves disobedience to Christ, the head of the church, and disrespect for his gift of order in the church (1 Cor 14:34; 1 Tim 2:11)" (Initial Report, p.6).

Note the emphasis on "the reality of male headship in the church and the family which *was established by God in the creation of Adam*." When Jesus and Paul provide guidance for the proper ordering of marriage and the relationship between the sexes, they go back to the "order of creation" set forth in the first three chapters of Genesis. Thus Jesus, in speaking against lax attitudes to divorce, says: "*In the beginning it was not so*," and quotes Genesis 1:27 and 2:24 (see Matt 19:3–9; Mark 10:2–12). And Paul, in arguing that the

(c) In the Old Testament, women were also redeemed through faith in the promised Messiah, but clearly they were not to be priests.

## ARGUMENT 7—A LEGITIMATE CONCLUSION

"The fact that many Lutheran churches have begun to ordain women in this century, against the tradition of the church, does not necessarily imply that the church has been in error and must repent of false teaching. It means that some Lutherans have come to learn from Scripture possibilities for the life of the church which would not have been culturally acceptable in earlier ages" (*Initial Report*, 5).

### Response

a. From "the fact that many Lutheran churches have begun to ordain women . . ." this paragraph sees two possible implications: i. Either the church of the past nineteen centuries "has been in error and must repent of false teaching" (an implication which the Initial Report hesitates to draw); or ii. "Some Lutherans have come to learn from Scripture possibilities for the life of the church which would not have

---

woman is not to function as head and teacher of the church family at worship, grounds his injunction ("I do not permit a woman to teach . . .") in the order of creation and fall established in Genesis 2 and 3 ("For Adam was formed first, then Eve. And Adam was not deceived, but the woman was deceived and fell into transgression"—1 Tim 2:12–14). In other words, Adam reneged on his spiritual responsibilities, failing to exercise his spiritual headship by correcting his wife after she had given a false lead. Finally, when Paul appeals to "the Law" as the basis for his ruling in 1 Cor 14:34 ("it is not permitted for [the women] to speak . . . as the Law also says"), he almost certainly has in mind the same passages of Genesis 2–3 which he quotes in the epistle to Timothy.

The women's ordination movement, on the other hand, is uncomfortable with any talk of the original order of creation. It tends, rather, to speak in a one-sided way of the "new creation" in Christ (2 Cor 5:17). John Reumann, for example, writes of the early church's "eschatological consciousness of the Spirit's presence as a token of the New Age." The church enjoys a foretaste of the new creation in Christ or a fulfillment of God's original will for male and female in Genesis chapter 1 (*Ministries Examined*, 83, 97). Nowhere in this article does Reumann give serious consideration to Genesis chapters 2 & 3.

Recently some fundamentalist Christians in Queensland formed a nudist colony. Carried away with the excitement of becoming, through baptism, a "new creation" in Christ, they concluded that original sin had been crushed in their case and thus they could live innocent and sinless lives here on earth. They had forgotten the limitations even the most "spiritual" Christian must live under as long as we live in this world. These limitations—the man as the head, the woman as his helper, the role of marriage and the family in safeguarding the relationship between the sexes, the need for clothing as a result of the fall into sin—are all spelled out in Genesis 2 and 3. Our new creation in Christ begins to fulfill and restore God's purposes in the original creation. It is, indeed, a blessed foretaste of heaven. But we still live by faith, not by sight (2 Cor 5:7). As long as we are this side of eternity, the new creation spoken of in 2 Cor 5:17, etc., does not obliterate the provisions and the effects of the original creation and fall.

been culturally acceptable in earlier ages." The argument fails to state that there is a third possible implication: Those Lutheran churches which have begun to ordain women in this century, against the tradition of the church (and, more importantly, in defiance of the Lord's express command), are in error and must repent of false teaching.[34]

b. We need to address the argument that the culture of earlier ages, and in particular the culture of Paul's day, was so vastly different from our own. As stated earlier, I believe that far too much has been made of the gap or gulf between what has been called the "two horizons"—the first-century cultural horizon and the horizon of our own day. Thus it is claimed that we must distinguish clearly between "what it meant" at the time of writing and "what it means" for us today, as if these are two vastly different things. And so, the argument goes, whereas in Paul's day to have ordained women would have been harmful to the church's mission, in our day it would be helpful to her mission.

It is true that we must deal discriminatingly with the Scriptures. Not all is on the same level, not all has the same authority for us today. For example, much of the Old Testament law has been fulfilled, and thus superseded: the ceremonial law has been fulfilled in Christ, our great high priest; the civil law applied specifically to the nation of Israel (Luther called it the Jews' "Saxon law"), and no longer applies to us. The Ten Commandments, on the other hand, do still apply; Jesus and the apostles constantly confirmed them. And the New Testament is the great and authoritative interpreter of the OT. Consequently we need to be very careful before we conclude that some NT teaching no longer applies. To be sure, we no longer wash one another's feet (John 13). But that custom is not prescribed in the NT, anyway. Jesus simply refers to it as an "example," a "pattern" (John 13:15) of how we are to serve each other in Christian love. What is commanded, *mandated*, is that we love one another, however that love may be expressed in our modern culture.[35] Similarly, in 1 Cor 11:2–16, Paul urges the women to conform in feminine modesty to the custom of their day by wearing a head covering at public

---

34  See argument 4) of the CTICR's description of the case "for the ordination of men only," *The practice of the universal church*:

"The ordination of women, which was already advocated by some sects in the second and third centuries AD, was rejected for scriptural reasons by the bishops and councils of the early church, as well as by all orthodox churches until modern times. Luther and other Reformers rejected the ordination of women. This unanimous teaching should be changed only if we have clear scriptural authorisation to ordain women" (Initial Report, p. 5).

35  See John 13:34: "A new commandment I give you, that you love one another." The word "commandment" in Greek is *entole*, the very word Paul uses in 1 Cor 14:37 in undergirding his injunction that the women be silent in the churches: "this is a command (*entole*) of the Lord."

worship. In that day, this was a mark that they were married and so attached and beholden to their husbands. *Customs* may change, but the *principle* of male headship under Christ and female subordination (1 Cor 11:3) remains in effect. We have no authority to abrogate a command, a mandate of the Lord. To do so "involves disobedience to Christ, the head of the church."[36]

Certainly the first-century world differed from ours in a host of ways (foot-washing, head-coverings are but two examples). But the significance of these differences should not be exaggerated. Cultures vary from one another in terms of their surface configurations—thus the fascination of studying other cultures and languages. But the longer one immerses oneself in another culture, whether ancient or contemporary, the more one realizes that under the surface all human beings are the same, with the same desires, needs, aspirations, etc. It is a myth that modern men and women are thoroughly different from the people of biblical times. Deep down, we all share in a common humanity which is far more important than anything that appears on the surface.

And the same Word of God is addressed to all. From one point of view, yes, there are two horizons; we need to dig into the Bible world and its history and languages if we are to grasp it accurately. But the more we enter into that world sympathetically, with "listening hearts,"[37] the more we will hear the same Word that was addressed to people of Biblical times addressing us today. For, from another point of view (and this has not been stressed nearly enough by modern scholars), from the divine perspective, there is really only one horizon. The Old Testament prophets were taken up into God's council (Jer 23:22) and enabled to see past, present and future from God's vista. Their word continues to go forth like the rain and the snow and accomplish the divine purpose of bringing people to repentance and faith. Similarly, the apostles and evangelists of the NT are given the Word of the One who sees and foresees all human history. As H. Wheeler Robinson has observed, God's people across the generations have a "corporate personality."[38] Thus Moses can speak to the Israelites some 40 years after the Exodus and Mount Sinai: "The Lord our God made a covenant with us at Horeb. *It was not with our fathers* that the Lord made this covenant, *but with us*, with all of us who are alive here today" (Deuteronomy 5:2–3). What God said to our forefathers and mothers he still says to us "today" (Ps 95:7)—unless there are clear indications

---

36  Argument 5) of the CTICR's description of the case "for the ordination of men only" (Initial Report, p. 6).

37  According to the original Hebrew text of 1 Kings 3:9, Solomon asked the Lord to give him "a listening heart" (usually translated "a discerning heart").

38  *Corporate Personality in Israel* (Facet Books). The expression "corporate personality" may not be the most felicitous. It may be better to speak of the community, the solidarity of all human beings "in Adam", and of all believers "in Christ".

to the contrary. The God in whom there is "no change or shadow of turning" James 1:17), the Lord who is "the same yesterday, today, and forever" (Heb 13:8) has given the same clear Word to all generations of his people.

## CONCLUDING REMARKS

### (A) REMARKS ON THE ROLE OF THE PASTORAL MINISTRY IN GENERAL

As we debate women's ordination, we need to take care that the priesthood of all believers and the pastoral ministry are not played off against each other. We need to continue to uphold the pastoral ministry as God's gift to the church. The Bible teaches:

i. *the royal priesthood of all believers*, who "tell out the praises of him who called [us] out of darkness into his marvellous light" (1 Peter 2:9). They offer the sacrifices of "a broken and contrite heart," praise and thanksgiving, doing good and sharing with others (Ps 51:17; 50:14, 23; Heb 13:15–16).

ii. *the pastoral ministry instituted by Christ*. Pastors succeed the apostles in carrying out Christ's command to them to feed his sheep and lambs, forgive and retain sins, make disciples by baptising and teaching, and administer the Lord's Supper (John 21:15–17; 20:21–23; Matt 28:16–20; Luke 22:19). Paul and Barnabas appointed pastors, trained men "apt to teach," in every place they evangelized (Acts 14:23). The same epistle of Peter which speaks of the priesthood of all believers also speaks to the pastors who are charged with feeding them (1 Pet 5:1–4).

### (B) CONCLUDING REMARKS ON THE ORDINATION OF WOMEN

The points I have raised in this response refer only to Biblical arguments for and against the ordination of women. I believe there is no way anyone can prove that "on balance, scriptural and theological evidence allows the ordination of women." The Scriptures clearly state the very opposite: the Lord's command prohibits the ordination of women. Accordingly we are conscience-bound to uphold this command.

I have argued that if the LCA debate were restricted to the "scriptural and theological evidence," the outcome should be clear. The seven arguments for the ordination of women do not stand up to careful scrutiny. Moreover, this is not surprising, for the desire to ordain women does not really have its starting point in the Scriptures, but in sociology and the spirit of the age. One has the impression that the endeavor has been to find scriptural proof for a position essentially derived from the culture.

Will we nevertheless be admonished, despite the lack of Biblical evidence, to "go forward in faith, not hold back in fear"?[39] The argument sounds pious. What Christian wants to be charged with fear and cowardice, when he or she should be going forward in faith? So the conclusion is drawn: "I'd better join the progressives rather than staying with the conservatives."

But how are such admonitions used in the Bible? The passage that comes to mind most readily is the Lord's word to Moses as the Egyptians pursued the Israelites and they came up against the barrier of the Red Sea: "Tell the Israelites to go forward!" (Exodus 14:15). Here indeed was a situation where the people were called on to go forward in faith, not hold back in fear. But they were to go forward *at the command of a clear Word from the Lord*. And in doing so, he blessed and helped them through the waters of the Red Sea. It is a totally different situation, however, when we are told we must go forward in defiance of the Lord's command. In such a situation, we should take notice rather of texts like Isaiah 66:2: "[This is what the Lord says:] 'This is the person for whom I will have regard, for the one who is humble and contrite in spirit, and trembles at my word."

An analogy from the law courts may be relevant here. Before a person is declared guilty, the jury must be convinced beyond any reasonable doubt and the decision must be unanimous. Similarly, if there is any doubt at all about the legitimacy of the ordination of women, the church needs to refrain from going against the testimony of the Scriptures and overturning the position of the church for 2000 years. To decide this important issue and divide the church merely on "the balance of the evidence" (assuming the balance is in that direction) would be tragic.

## APPENDIX A

On November 11, 1992, at about 4.30 pm, the Church of England approved the ordination of women to the priesthood. The vote was carried by majorities of over two-thirds in each of the synod's three houses (bishops, clergy, and laity). The earlier part of the day was devoted to speeches for and against the legislation. Of those who spoke against the legislation, one of the most eloquent was Mrs Sara Low. Her speech may be described as a cry from the heart, or in C. S. Lewis's terms, the bleating of a sheep trying to catch her

---

39  This psychological approach played a prominent role in the Church of England's debate on women's ordination in 1992. In the final two sentences of the final speech before the vote was taken, the Bishop of Guildford said: "So I ask the Synod to take a step forward into the future, God's future, confident that he will lead us into this truth. I ask the Synod to vote firmly, clearly and confidently for this legislation" (*The Ordination of Women to the Priesthood: The Synod Debate*, p. 76).

shepherds' ear. I believe she is an able spokesperson for the quiet majority of the Lutheran women of Australia.

When I was converted to Jesus Christ in my early twenties and came into the Church of England, I was told by my first parish priest, now a bishop on these benches, that the Church of England based itself on Holy Scripture, holy tradition and human reason. This legislation gives me the gravest possible concern on all three counts.

One of the things that I have learned in my time as a Christian is that where we are faithful to the revealed truth, there the promises of the New Testament are fulfilled. The Churches that believe this and do it are, in my experience, those that are blessed.

Like many of those here, I have listened for nearly twenty years to this debate. I listened very carefully to the early arguments about Jesus' cultural conditioning and the claim that Jesus did not have the freedom to appoint women. If cultural conditioning was determinative for Jesus, then all his teaching and all his actions are thus heavily influenced. We are no longer talking about the eternal Son of God. Jesus Christ is different today from what he was yesterday, and he will be different again tomorrow. I have listened to the arguments that the early Church was equally unable to make this change, yet, on the contrary, what could have made a bigger bridgehead with the pagan world than the introduction of women priests, with which they were already familiar? I have listened to arguments on St Paul where one classic quotation [Gal 3:28] has been wrenched out of context, given a meaning that no previous generation of believers has given it, and seen it used to deny the clear teaching on headship in the rest of St Paul's letters. I have listened to the doctrine of creation being divided into greater and lesser truths, so that the complementarity of male and female has been debased to a banal interchangeability. I have listened patiently to talk of prayerful, thoughtful majorities when surely our problem is that the minority is also prayerful and thoughtful.

These are not comfortable things to say, but they must be said because if the Synod overturns scriptural authority today it will be no good coming back next time and hoping to impose it on other issues. For the Church, the authority of the Scriptures and the example of Jesus has always been determinative; I do not believe that this House has the authority to overturn them.

My second concern is the legislation itself. What of those who dissent? It seems strange, does it not, to call those who faithfully believe what the Church has always believed 'dissenters'? Bishops and archbishops may give verbal assurances that there will be no persecution against such priests and laypeople, but it is with great sadness that I have to tell the bishops that I have not met one opponent of the measure who believes them.

The reasons are simple. First, no verbal assurance can undo the fact that you are legislating for two classes of Christian; any good intentions that may exist will wither before the law and practice, as in other provinces. Second, in many dioceses the spirit of this legislation has been in operation for some years. Orthodox clergy are excluded from appointments and orthodox laity are made to feel excluded from that warm glow of official approval, as if they are suffering from some embarrassing handicap; I have experienced that myself often enough in these corridors.

However, if the human injustice of this legislation, which eases old men into retirement and condemns others to serve forever under authorities whose primary qualification is compromise, is disgraceful, it is as nothing besides its theological arrogance and blasphemy. The legislation clearly instructs the Lord God Almighty whom he may raise up to lead the Church. The Holy Spirit will be told, 'You may choose anyone you want so long as it is one of us.' A Church that denies the sovereignty of God is no longer a Church. The fruits of this debate are not the fruits of the Holy Spirit.

What of tomorrow? If you wake in the morning having voted yes, you'll know that you have voted for a Church irreconcilably divided, for whom the revealed truth of God is no longer authoritative. If you vote no, you will wake to tears and a healing ministry, but above all to the possibility of a renewed New Testament Church, for all of us could then be united in encouraging, training and funding the ministry of priest, deacon, teacher, prophet, healer, administrator, spiritual director—all promised by the Holy Spirit.

I urge Synod to vote for the authority of the Word of God, for the unity of Christ's Church and against this ruinous legislation.[40]

# APPENDIX B

Arguments for and against the ordination of women, taken from "The Ordination of Women: Initial Report of the Commission on Theology and Interchurch Relations" (pp 3–6)

## A. ARGUMENTS FOR THE ORDINATION OF WOMEN INCLUDED THE FOLLOWING:

### 1. The relevance of the key texts

The two texts . . . are ambiguous and open to various interpretations. For example, in 1 Cor 14:34 it is not clear what kind of 'silence' Paul is commanding women to observe since women are praying and prophesying

---

40  *The Ordination of Women to the Priesthood: The Synod Debate* (Church House Publishing, 1993), pp. 42–43.

(11:5, 13). Further, it is not clear to what the 'command of the Lord' (14:37) refers, eg to the silence of the women or to the necessity for good order in worship.

In 1 Tim 2 Paul is calling on women to adopt a quiet attitude which learns rather than seeks to teach. But it is unclear to whom or what they are 'to be in subjection' (v 11), or what it means to 'have authority over' a man (v 12).

In both texts it is not entirely certain whether Paul is speaking of women in general or of wives in particular. Finally there is no clear indication that these commands are binding on the church outside their original context.

## 2. The mission imperative

The apostolic prohibition against women speaking in the worship assembly (1 Cor 14:33, 34; 1 Tim 2:11, 12) is based on a concern for the church's mission to spread the gospel. Women questioning or debating matters in the church (1 Cor 14:35) or acting in a high handed manner would have caused offence especially to the predominantly Jewish converts and potential converts. Paul's concern here is not for a male order of ministry but for orderliness in contrast to disorder, so as not to bring the church into disrepute (see 1 Cor 14:33, 35, 40).

## 3. Roles played by women in the early church

Women laboured with Paul 'in the gospel' (Phil 4:3); Priscilla taught Apollos (Acts 18:26); women prayed and prophesied in public worship (1 Cor 11:5, 10; see also Acts 2:17); Phoebe is called 'deacon' and 'patron' of the church at Cenchreae (Rom 16:1, 2). That Paul allows a woman to learn (1 Tim 2:11) is already a revolutionary step away from Jewish practice since it implies that they can then teach. It is therefore questionable whether 1 Tim 2:12 (a woman is not to teach or have authority over a man) must be read as a principle without qualifications.

## 4. Equality of men and women in Christ

The baptismal formula of Galatians 3:2841 (cf 1 Cor 12:13; Col 3:11) gives to women a position in the church not known within contemporary Judaism. The new creation in Christ (2 Cor 5:17) confirms the equal standing of women with men before God (cf Gen 1:26–28). So, within marriage, husbands and wives are to complement one another (1 Cor 7:4) and to be subject to one another out of love (Eph 5:21). Within the church's ministry, the ordination of women is an appropriate application of this principle of equality.

## 5. The inclusivity of the Gospel

The inclusivity of the gospel should come to expression also in the public ministry of the church. This inclusivity which embraced Jew and Gentile, slave and free, male and female, found tangible expression in the early church (Eph 2:11–22; Philemon 16). It is fittingly modeled by a public office which includes women.

## 6. The representation of Christ

The first Adam embraces the whole of sinful humanity, both men and women (Rom 5:12, 15). In the person of the new Adam, Jesus Christ, God redeems and restores fallen humanity, both men and women (Rom 5:15–19; 1 Cor 15:45–49). The representation of Christ by women is made possible by their incorporation into him. All those redeemed by Christ are members of his body and thus able to represent Christ to that body once they have been 'rightly called' to the public office.

## 7. A legitimate conclusion

The fact that many Lutheran churches have begun to ordain women in this century, against the tradition of the church, does not necessarily imply that the church has been in error and must repent of false teaching. It means that some Lutherans have come to learn from Scripture possibilities for the life of the church which would not have been culturally acceptable in earlier ages.

# B. Arguments for the Ordination of Men Only Included the following:

## 1. The Lord's command

1 Corinthians 14:33b and 1 Timothy 2:11–14 are foundational texts for the case against the ordination of women because they speak about the leadership of women in public worship. These passages clearly assert that God does not allow women to preach and teach in the divine service. This holds true even if it could be shown that the meaning of particular words and phrases is uncertain. The prohibition against speaking is not a demand for absolute silence but prevents women from preaching and teaching in public worship. The church therefore has no authority to ordain women. The apostle Paul states that this prohibition is a command from the Lord which applies to all churches (1 Cor 14:33b, 37; cf 1 Tim 3:15) and warns that those who disregard it will not be recognized by God in his church (1 Cor 14:38).

## 2. The relevance of Galatians 3:28

Galatians 3:28 should not be used to support the ordination of women because it does not deal with the doctrine of the public office. Rather, it asserts that both men and women have the same status before God the Father as his adopted children, and that they have the same access to his grace through baptism. Their equality before God does not change their distinctiveness and calling as men and women with sexually differentiated and yet complementary roles in marriage, family, and the church. Their sexuality is not abolished or disregarded, but sanctified for service according to their role in the family and the church.

### 3. The practice of Jesus and the apostles

The exclusion of women from the public office is confirmed by the precedent of Jesus appointing only male apostles (Matt 10:24; Mark 3:14–19; Luke 6:12–16) and entrusting the administration of his holy supper to them (Luke 22:14–30), as well as by the practice of the apostles in appointing a man as a replacement for Judas (Acts 1:21) and men only as pastors of the congregations which they established (2 Tim 2:12; cf 1 Tim 3:2; Titus 1:5). Although women laboured with Paul in the gospel, they were never appointed as pastors.

### 4. The practice of the universal church

The ordination of women, which was already advocated by some sects in the second and third centuries AD, was rejected for scriptural reasons by the bishops and councils of the early church, as well as by all orthodox churches until modern times. Luther and other Reformers rejected the ordination of women. This unanimous teaching should be changed only if we have clear scriptural authorisation to ordain women.

### 5. The representation of Christ's headship

The ordination of women contradicts the reality of male headship in the church and family which was established by God in the creation of Adam and fulfilled by the incarnation of God's Son as a male person (1 Cor 11:3,8,9; Eph 5:22–24; 1 Tim 2:13). It therefore involves disobedience to Christ, the head of the church, and disrespect for his gift of order in the church (1 Cor 14:34; 1 Tim 2:11).

### 6. Pastors as spiritual fathers

Jesus chose males to represent both him and his heavenly Father in the ministry of word and sacrament (John 20:21–23). Since pastors not only speak for Christ, but also speak the word of God the Father (Luke 10:16; cf Matt 10:40; John 13:20), they therefore are to be men so that they can serve as spiritual fathers to God's family (1 Cor 4:14,15).

## BIBLIOGRAPHY

P. Brunner
*The Ministry and the Ministry of Women*, Concordia, St Louis, 1971

B. Giertz
"Twenty-three Theses on the Holy Scriptures, The Woman, and The Office of the Ministry," *The Springfielder* 33/4, 10–22 (Bo Giertz, Bishop of the Lutheran Church of Sweden, is author of *The Hammer of God*)

M. Harper
*Equal and Different. Male and Female in Church and Society*, Hodder & Stoughton, London, 1994 (a popular paperback)

J. Kleinig
"Scripture and the Exclusion of Women from the Pastorate (I)," *Lutheran Theological Journal*, August 1995, 74–81

J. Kleinig
"Scripture and the Exclusion of Women from the Pastorate (II)," *Lutheran Theological Journal*, December 1995, 123–29

G. Knight III
*Commentary on the Pastoral Epistles*, Eerdmans, Grand Rapids, 1992, 138–49

E. Leske
*The Pastoral Letters*, Lutheran Publishing House, Adelaide, 1986, 53–57

C. S. Lewis
"Priestesses in the Church?", *God in the Dock. Essays on Theology and Ethics*; ed. W. Hooper; Eerdmans, Grand Rapids, 1970, 234–239

J. Reumann
*Ministries Examined*, Augsburg, Minneapolis, 1987

# THE ORDINATION OF WOMEN INTO THE OFFICE OF THE CHURCH

## REINHARD SLENCZKA

Dear Sisters and Brothers![1]

Today you are faced with the decision whether the exception clause in the bylaw governing the office of pastors (*Pfarrergesetz*) in the United Evangelical Lutheran Church in Germany (VELKD) concerning female pastors is to be rescinded. This clause reads:

> Article 1, as far as it applies to the legal status of female pastors, first becomes effective in the Evangelical Lutheran Church of Schaumburg-Lippe when so determined by that church.

In the current situation, you are not asked to make a decision concerning the ordination of women in general; it has already been adopted by all member churches and church unions within the Evangelical Church in Germany (EKD). Instead, you are asked to decide whether one of the last two exception clauses is to be rescinded. These clauses were meant to protect the consciences of those lay members and officeholders (male and female theologians) of evangelical congregations who arrive at the conclusion that the ordination of women into the church's office of congregational leadership is

---

1 This paper was delivered at the October 1991 meeting of the convention of the Evangelical Lutheran Church in Schaumburg-Lippe (Germany). To that date, this small territorial church had resisted attempts to introduce the ordination of women, mainly because of the reputation of Bishop Dr. Joachim Heubach, who had been elected bishop in the late 1970s precisely because of his stance against the ordination of women. After his resignation from office in 1991, the convention of that church once more took up the issue, this time with a moderate, Heinrich Herrmanns, in the office of bishop. Dr. Slenczka was asked to speak against the ordination of women. Dr. Horst Georg Pöhlmann of Osnabrück University was asked to speak in favor of it (see his paper, "Ordination und geistliches Amt der Frau," in ". . . *das Weib rede in der Gemeinde*": *Erste lutherische Bischöfin: Maria Jepsen; Dokumente und Stellungnahmen* [Gütersloh: Gütersloher Verlagshaus Gerd Mohn, 1992], 49–57). Those in favor of women's ordination won the ensuing vote.

irreconcilable with Holy Scripture and the Confessions of the Church. This is also my conviction. And this is why you have invited me to speak in favor of this position.

The current situation is not favorable for deliberations and decisions. We all know and experience (regardless of where we stand) what public approval and pressure can do in all this. We also know to what degree personal interests, sympathy and antipathy, and also various kinds of emotions usually play a role here.

The different points of view should be familiar to all. The arguments have been repeated so many times orally and in written form that they are worn out. Perhaps they do not even register anymore. And the bottom line then simply becomes the ratio between "Yes" and "No" when the vote is taken, victory or defeat.

In view of this situation I would like to focus my contribution fully on one aspect. I consider it to be the most important one, though it has attracted little, if any, attention in the past years of discussion. I am speaking about the conscience, as it is bound by and responsible before God's Word. By conscience, and for it, we have to decide.

My presentation will have three sections:

I. The Conscientious Decision and the Protection of Conscience
II. The Word of the Lord
III. The Equality of Rights and the Diversity of Gifts
IV. Summary Remarks

# I. The Conscientious Decision
## and the Protection of Conscience

In 1 Tim. 1:5 we read: "Now the purpose of the commandment is love from a pure heart, from a good conscience, and from sincere faith." Heart, conscience, and faith are mentioned here as synonymous. They express what determines the feeling, thinking, and acting of the Christian. This is comprehended by the instruction, commandment, or proclamation (*parangelia*) which comes from the love of God in Jesus Christ, by which we are renewed and perfected. According to the context, this introductory remark of the Letter to Timothy refers to conflicts and arguments concerning doctrine and life which have arisen in the congregation. Among many other things also an argument concerning the public teaching of women is part of these. The correct interpretation of Scripture is explicitly mentioned as one point of contention (1:6–7: ". . . desiring to be teachers of the law, understanding neither what they say nor the things which they affirm").

Our conscience as Christians is our being bound to the Word of God. Part of this is that accusing and defending of the thoughts which, according to Rom. 2:14ff., takes place in the heart of all men. As explicitly pointed out in these verses, this accusing and defending points to the day of God's final judgment, "when God will judge the secrets of men by Jesus Christ, according to my gospel" (Rom. 2:16).

Romans 14 and 1 Corinthians 8 provide us with one example for the importance of the conscience when it comes to contentions in the congregation. These two chapters deal with the quarrels between the strong and the weak concerning the eating of meat that comes from pagan worship. We all know that this example can be claimed, or even exploited, by the strong and the weak in very different ways: the strong can use it to lord it over the weak; the weak can do the same to the strong. Yet the apostle directs the matters that, seen from a human vantage point, appear as victory or defeat to the question: How can I, with my behavior, stand before the Lord Jesus Christ who has died for me and through whom I am to receive eternal life? The *conscientious decision* has to do with the fact that "each of us shall give account of himself to God," in the words of the apostle (Rom. 14:12). The *protection of* the other's *conscience* exists so that he is not forced to do something which he cannot justify before God and his Word: "Yet if your brother is grieved because of your food, you are no longer walking in love. Do not destroy with your food the one for whom Christ died" (Rom. 14:15).

This is the core of the upcoming decision. The possible outcome is that members of the congregation, not only officeholders, will be caused, or even forced, to do something they cannot justify before God's Word, Holy Scripture. Their acts will therefore be sin because they are done with a bad conscience in the uncertainty of whether they can be justified according to God's Word and before His judgment.

I would like to clarify that now by shedding some light on the situation in which this decision takes place. I had said initially that one of the two last exception clauses is now to be rescinded. The other one besides the one for Schaumburg-Lippe is the so-called "conscience clause" of the Bylaw Concerning the Placement into Pastorates (*Pfarrstellenbesetzungsordnung*) of the Bavarian Territorial Church dating from 20 April 1980. If I am not mistaken, this clause thus first took effect five years after the introduction of the ordination of women; this was in November of 1975 when a new bishop was installed. There it says:

> The Council of the Territorial Church (*Landeskirchenrat*) has to limit the call document to male pastors, vacancy pastors, or candidates for ordination, if a pastor or a vacancy pastor serving that congregation demands it, if the latter was ordained in the Evangelical Lutheran Church in Bavaria prior to 1 July 1989 (§ 4,4).

The demand to rescind this "veto clause," which had been accepted as a mere compromise, has been under discussion for quite some time, but it has not been decided yet. A quote from a recent publication may serve as an illustration for the current situation:

> Back then this veto clause seemed necessary to me as a compromise to guarantee the peaceful coexistence of advocates and opponents of the ordination of women. Some colleagues were in office who started out under different conditions and who could not come to terms with the innovation. For them, this was a burdensome matter of conscience.

> I do wonder, however, if this can be seen in the same way today. Since November 1975 every male colleague, who is ordained in the Bavarian Territorial Church, knows that there are female colleagues in this church. In my view, the Convent of Female Evangelical Theologians in Bavaria is right about demanding that this veto clause be rescinded.[2]

It is thus foreseeable that in the EKD there will be no protection of conscience anymore for those who cannot justify the ordination of women to the office of congregational leadership according to Scripture and Confessions.

Those familiar with the situation in the Lutheran churches in Scandinavia clearly see what this means and what the results of this are. In Sweden the ordination of women was introduced in 1958. This was done because of the demands, and even pressures, of the state government. The result was that, to be certified for ordination, a declaration by the candidate was demanded, stating that he was willing to cooperate with ordained women. In view of the ongoing conflicts, "rules for the cooperation between those holding different views concerning the admission of women to the spiritual office within the Church of Sweden" were set up on 1 December 1978. To this day, the discussions continue as to "how to live together spiritually and practically in one and the same church under one and the same confession with differing conscience-based judgments concerning the question of the ordination of women."[3]

This question has not been settled to this day. And this has led to a situation where a person, if he opposes women's ordination, is not eligible for the office of bishop or, depending on the case, for ordination. The recognition of the ordination of women has thus become a condition for the bestowal of the office. One result of this is that in 1983 a Free Synod was formed in Sweden.

---

2   Marianne Pflüger, "Die Theologinnenfrage in Bayern," in *100 Jahre Pfarrer- und Pfarrerinnenverin in Bayern: 1891–1991; Stationen und Aufgaben*, ed. K. Kreßel (Nürnberg, 1991), 35.

3   *Das geistliche Amt in der Kirche*, 3d ed. (Paderborn: Bonifatius; Frankfurt: Lembeck, 1982), 103.

In Norway there exists a protection of conscience for bishops who do not want to ordain women (which currently applies to two of the eleven bishops), as well as for pastors who refuse a concelebration *in sacris*.

In Finland, where the decision was made three years ago, there are, to my knowledge, no written safeguards in effect for the protection of conscience. Yet dissenters are respected in practice. It is foreseeable, however, that similar situations of coercion will arise.

*The current discussion in Germany is not at all about how to preserve such a protection of conscience; the point is to eliminate it completely.*

However, because this is so, we will have to see and reflect on the fact that this does not only have to do with the limited question of how men and women are to relate to one another in the church. All members of the congregation can be affected by it:

It affects the *congregations* where women are to officiate and where objections are raised against this.

It affects *officeholders of the congregations* who ordain women and who are to cooperate with ordained women.

When it comes to candidates for the *office of bishop*, the question of women's ordination inevitably appears as a reason for rejection.

It affects those requesting a *vicarage*, who are told that their scriptural objections to a cooperation with ordained women make a vicarage and call in a particular territorial church impossible.

Yet it affects also, and this is easily overlooked completely, *women with theological education* who, if they do not want to be ordained because of their own objections, can only find employment in the church by way of ordination.

This means that in the EKD there exists today a mandatory recognition of the ordination of women. Yet a person who cannot accept this in good conscience does not even have the option anymore to move to a different territorial church. That person (male or female) is not eligible for ecclesiastical offices; and the entire subject matter has become non-negotiable.

However, it still holds true: "it is neither safe nor right to go against conscience" (Martin Luther, AE 32:112). And to force others to do so, to give them offense, and to cause them to fall (Rom. 14:13), this affects deeply the fellowship in the faith in responsibility before the Lord, His Word, and His judgment.

Romans 14:23 summarizes this very clearly, both concerning the conscientious decision and the protection of conscience: "But he who doubts is condemned if he eats, because he does not eat from faith; for whatever is not from faith is sin."

## II. The Word of the Lord
## according to Holy Scripture

The question dealt with in Romans 14 and 1 Corinthians 8—whether to eat meat or vegetables—might seem of minor importance. At stake is not even a mandate that could be traced back to the Lord. The apostle Paul nonetheless connects it in a surprisingly emphatic way with what decides over one's salvation, because it has to do with the faith, by which the Christian stands and falls in a final sense. This is the utter seriousness that is at stake when it comes to the conscience-based decision and the protection of conscience.

In a second step, we shall therefore now, disregarding many other reasons, focus entirely on the Word of Scripture, to which faith is bound, by which faith is also borne, and according to which faith is judged.

The following needs to be kept in mind here: Obviously, one can, and probably will, push through the ordination of women by majority vote and then enforce its recognition by way of ecclesiastical legislation. Yet one cannot change or rescind the words of Holy Scripture or the effect of this Word of God. And this is also the peculiar observation in the Scandinavian churches, but also here in Germany: that consciences at rest are unexpectedly made restless again by the Word of Scripture. I quote from another Swedish report:

> The authorities, ecclesiastical as well as civil ones, are disquieted by the fact that the conviction that female pastors are irreconcilable with the New Testament does not die out by itself; in every new generation it finds again new proponents. One speaks about the "question of female pastors" and two entirely different problems are meant. First, "How do we continue to live together in one church with such contention?" Second, "How can the resistance be stopped?"[4]

Also among students of theology (among male as well as female students, as I want to emphasize here), we experience that consciences are disquieted by God's Word. We experience this also in the congregation; we likewise experience this among those who are already ordained and who in certain cases are afflicted by God's Word, by which they are actually to be borne in their ministry.

Why this is so, and why this will always remain so, I want to show by means of the *sedes doctrinae*, 1 Cor. 14:33–40, in connection with 1 Tim. 2:9–15. Here we have the unconditional *no* to the speaking and, respectively, to the teaching of women in the assembly of the congregation. This *no* is spoken into a situation where this speaking actually occurs. Three reasons of highest spiritual authority are given for this *no*:

---

4    *Svenska kyrkans fria Synod. Die Freie Synode der schwedischen Kirche* (1986), 13.

## 1. THE *FIRST REASON* READS: "AS IN ALL THE CHURCHES OF THE SAINTS . . ." (V. 33)

This points to the ecumenical consensus, which the congregation at Corinth is breaking by its accommodation to the environment. We all know that the introduction of the ordination of women, beginning in the 1950s, has become a new church-divisive factor; it has interfered with, or even annulled, all existing rapprochements to an agreement concerning the ecclesiastical office. This, first of all, affects the relationship to the Orthodox churches of the East and the Roman Catholic Church. Yet it also affects church fellowship within individual church bodies. Currently, we observe this in the Anglican Communion.

In passing, yet not without purpose, I draw your attention to another fact that interferes with an ecumenical understanding: the administration of the sacraments by those who are not yet ordained during their internship/vicarage.

## 2. THE *SECOND REASON* READS: "AS *THE LAW* ALSO SAYS . . ." (V. 34)

This invokes the Word of God of the Old Covenant, especially also the coordination of man and woman according to Genesis 1–3.[5]

Jürgen Roloff, in his commentary on First Timothy, is certainly correct when he states concerning 1 Timothy 2: "Most of the current interpretations seek to eliminate the offensiveness of this statement."[6]

However, who reads, listens, and judges spiritually, trusting in the salutary nature of God's Word, will not miss the following: The subordination, which is talked about in these verses, is comprehended and defined by the person and work of Jesus Christ. This is why Eph. 5:21 holds true as a matter of principle for the communion among Christians: "Submit to one another in the fear of Christ." The essence of this submission, which is founded on, and illustrated by Christ, clearly consists in Christ's giving Himself for the congregation (Eph. 5:25) and in the obedience of the Son of God to the Father (1 Cor. 11:3). It would be unchristian to see this relation differently, either to defend it or to criticize it, insofar as then the relation between man and woman would be seen apart from Christ. We need to decide whether we want to take Christ or the insurmountable polarization of man and woman as the starting point of our reflections.[7]

---

5    Cf. 1 Tim. 2:13–15; 1 Cor. 11:1–6; Eph. 5:21ff.

6    Jürgen Roloff, *Der erste Brief an Timotheus*, Evangelisch-Katholischer Kommentar, vol. 15 (Zurich: Benziger Verlag; Neukirchen: Neukirchener Verlag, 1988), 140.

7    The situation is similar when the specific vocation of the woman is indicated: "Nevertheless she will be saved in childbearing if she continues in faith, love, and

The interpreters remind us that these passages are meant as antidotes against a rejection and neglect of marriage and family, which, e.g., at the time were put forth by the Gnosis.

The congregation in Corinth, which breaks the consensus with the other churches and contradicts the Word of God, is asked: "Or did the word of God come originally from you? Or was it you only that it reached?" (1 Cor. 14:36). The congregation thus has to ask itself whether it does not put its own word in the place of God's Word.

## 3. THIS LEADS US TO THE *THIRD REASON*

The following statement is opposed to every spiritual claim that does not agree with the consensus of the congregations/churches and the Word of God: "The things I am writing to you are a *command of the Lord*. If anyone does not recognize this, he is not recognized" (vv. 37–38). This invocation of the commandment of the Lord includes everything that has been said previously concerning the order of the congregation—and that means also the command to women to remain silent.

There are several such appeals to the Word and command of the Lord in Paul. In every case it is found in crucial passages: 1 Cor. 7:10, 12 prohibit divorce and remarriage of divorcees. We know how nonchalantly this is passed over among us! 1 Cor. 9:14 refers to the fact that those who proclaim the Gospel should also live from the Gospel, that is, they should and may be supported by the congregation. 1 Cor. 11:23 addresses the institution of the Lord's Supper that had been transformed into the private event of certain groups. 1 Cor. 15:3 and Gal. 1:12 appeal to the Word and command of the Lord for the content and charge of the proclamation of the Gospel. In 1 Thess. 4:15 this expression finally refers to the return of Christ and the resurrection of the dead.

Whatever other arguments there are, the Word and command of the Lord mark the highest level of obligation; and for the apostle this means: "If anyone does not recognize this, he is not recognized" (1 Cor. 14:38). This can refer to the ecclesiastical communion as well as the recognition or rejection in the

---

holiness, with self-control" (1 Tim. 2:15). Do we still hear, amid all the understandable and spontaneous objections from our experience, how here, over against the punishment of the woman after the fall (Gen. 3:16), her cooperation in the bestowal of salvation is explicitly mentioned? And in the Pastoral Epistles, which show us how the congregation is rooted in house and family, one finds direct references to what could be termed the apostolate and the apostolic succession of women in the handing-down of, and the instruction in, the faith. Paul thus reminds Timothy of "the genuine faith that is in you, which dwelt first in your grandmother Lois and your mother Eunice, and I am persuaded is in you also" (2 Tim. 1:5). Most of us owe our first instruction in the faith to this motherly apostolate. And who would not know what happens if this is neglected.

final judgment by Jesus Christ Himself. Whether we want this or not, according to the wording of the text we are here dealing with something that is decisive for salvation in the ultimate sense. *The ordination of women is therefore not a simple question of ecclesiastical order or historical custom, but for the apostle here the communion of churches and their obedience to the Word of the Lord are at stake.*

This has brought us to the point in which, seen from the Word of God, the conscientious decision concerning women's ordination consists. And to this day, the Christian congregation worldwide has always seen it this way in all churches and has acted accordingly.

Whoever decides differently has to evade and avoid, not only for himself but also for the members of the congregation, the threefold substantiation: the ecumenical consensus, the law of God, and the Word and command of the Lord. This is done, and I do not have to elaborate here, with the assertion that the pertinent verses in 1 Corinthians 14 are a later insertion based on 1 Timothy 2 or are of such a nature that they are bound to, and restricted to, the historical and social circumstances of Paul's times.

Even, and probably especially, nontheologians will realize how in this way everything will begin to slide when we—first increasingly, then completely— follow the demands of the times and the current opinion to establish doctrine and order of the Church. In various other cases, which I prefer not to mention here, this has actually already taken place by way of synodical decisions. The congregation makes itself lord over the Word of the Lord.

I tie in another remark here which seems worthwhile reflecting upon: In the history of the Church, there have always been situations in which women had to assume the ministry of men because men were lacking. Thus the Fraternal Council (*Bruderrat*) of the Confessing Church of the Old Prussian Union adopted two resolutions in 1942, that is, during World War II: "The Ministry of the Female Vicar" and "The Proclamation of the Gospel by Women."[8] Both resolutions served the purposes of filling the many vacancies and of providing pastoral care in vacant congregations. For this reason a clear delineation of duties for this emergency situation was established; however, the conclusion of a general ordination of women was not drawn from this emergency.

Contrariwise, ever since women's ordination has begun to be pushed through in the 1960s the point was never the need and the serving of congregations, especially since the so-called "flood of theologians" began already back then. Instead, demands and goals originating outside the church became decisive.

---

8   Wilhelm Niesel, ed., *Um Verkündigung und Ordnung der Kirche: Die Bekenntnissynoden der Evangelischen Kirche der Altpreußischen Union 1934 bis 1943* (Bielefeld: Bechauf, 1949), 91f.

Yet for those who reject the ordination of women into the office of congregational leadership; who also will not be ready to recognize and accept this ministry; who also will not be ready to ordain women or to cooperate with ordained women; even for theologically educated women who do not want to be ordained—for all those there is a real faith-based and conscience-based decision here, which, in one way or another, must be church-divisive and will remain so.

Therefore, whoever decides for women's ordination decides against the consensus of churches, against the law of God, and against the Word of the Lord. At the same time, that person also decides against those members of the congregation who find themselves bound to this Word. They are forced to decline to get ordained; possibly, as has already happened, to convert; possibly also to accept a compromise in bad conscience. It is terrible to hear from ecclesiastical officeholders charged with ordinations that there is uncertainty concerning the scriptural basis for women's ordination, though there are good experiences with the work of ordained women. For in this way the foundation of Scripture is replaced by the principle of success; this can be used to legitimize the violation of all commandments. It is also a terrible phenomenon if one, on the one hand, approves of the ordination of women formally but then does not do the ordaining himself. For in this way happens exactly what the apostle says: "whatever does not proceed from faith is sin" (Rom. 14:23).

## III. THE EQUALITY OF RIGHTS
## AND THE DIVERSITY OF GIFTS

The office about which we are speaking is called in Latin *ministerium*, in Greek *diakonia*—and that means service. The one exercising it calls himself, like the apostle Paul, *doulos*, that is, servant, even slave (e.g., Rom. 1:1); or also a prisoner who is led around by Christ in triumphal procession; even an offering (Phil. 2:17, see 2 Cor. 2:14ff.). We should all remember this, where the "rights of the spiritual estate" are referred to, which are either to be defended or to be conquered. It is possible that among men and women an understanding of the office has crept in which has no room for this biblical fact but has replaced it by differences in rank and pay and other such things. For all of us are of spiritual or priestly estate by virtue of our Baptism (see 1 Peter 2:9); thus we all are, regardless of race, social rank, and sex "one in Christ Jesus," as it says in Gal. 3:28, even and especially in our differences. However, the office of the public proclamation and administration of the sacraments is, as Luther said repeatedly, a "service to priests."[9] In this consists the undeniable equality of rights in the priestly estate that is given through Baptism.

---

9    See, e.g., AE 31:356; 36:312–313; 40:35.

As we now turn to the diversity of gifts, there will hopefully be a promising *yes* in addition to the clear *no*. I quote the Danish theologian Regin Prenter who years ago voiced his opinion in a way similar to Peter Brunner and Hermann Dietzfelbinger and made pertinent suggestions:

> This is why it needs to be emphasized that a No concerning the ordination of women has only force today, if it is joined to the renewal of the lost service of women in the congregation.[10]

I limit myself to a few remarks, since this subject certainly cannot be a topic for the deliberations at this synodical convention. I do think, however, that this is an important matter which certainly does not only have to do with female but also male services in the congregation in their diversity and necessity, all the while there is among us by and large a monopoly of the office of congregational leadership at the expense of other services. This is undoubtedly because of a lack of recognition and lower pay. Volunteer offices are also suffering because of this.

Assuming that the ecclesiastical order of rank and pay is by no means mandated or covered by Scripture and the Confessions, I just ask some questions for further discussion and, hopefully, later decisions: Whatever has happened to the female and male diaconate in our times? Are there not also a number of male theological students who, according to their gifts, abilities, and interests, are better suited for tasks, even in the church, that are quite different from the pastoral office? Where are there tasks in the church for which theologically educated women are qualified in a special, perhaps even in a unique and irreplaceable way, even without ordination into the pastoral office? As far as I can see, there are certainly possibilities but no suitable paths of education and employment. Are there not in certain case employment opportunities that are better served in a part-time way, which absolutely militates against the pastoral office which claims a man totally?

Practical suggestions as stimulations for further reflection have been made by Peter Brunner[11] and Hermann Dietzfelbinger.[12] In 1989 the Ecumenical Patriarchate of the Orthodox Church published a document entitled *The Place of the Woman in the Orthodox Church and the Question of the Ordination of Women* which likewise, in addition to the clear scriptural *no*, has made concrete

---

10  *Die Ordination der Frauen zu dem überlieferten Pfarramt der lutherischen Kirche*, Luthertum, vol. 28 (Berlin, Hamburg: Lutherisches Verlagshaus, 1967), 17.

11  "Das Hirtenamt und die Frau" (1959), in *Pro Ecclesia: Gesammelte Aufsätze zur dogmatischen Theologie*, 3d ed. (Fürth: Flacius, 1990), I:310–338.

12  *Mündige Welt, mündige Gemeinde, mündiger Christ: Wachstumsprobleme in der evangelisch-lutherischen Kirche* (Munich: Evangelischer Presseverband für Bayern, 1966), 58ff.

suggestions for a "fuller participation of women in the life of the church" and for tasks for theologically educated women.[13]

It is regrettable that such suggestions are not even heard. Instead, the monopoly of the office of congregational leadership is increasingly bolstered at the expense of other services and by neglecting many gifts and tasks, at least as far as the course of theological education is concerned. Here is a need for reflecting and organizing, not just for demanding and agreeing.[14]

## IV. Summary Remarks

You are facing today a decision that has far-reaching consequences for the VELKD and EKD and, furthermore, for all churches. At stake is the elimination of the last opportunity for the protection of conscience concerning the ordination of women. And this affects in the same way men and women, officeholders and church members.

This is connected with the presumably last opportunity in the foreseeable future to renew not only a specifically female service in the church but also the diversity of services and gifts of men and women.

Finally, and this ties it all together, this decision is also about this: that one church, while breaking fellowship with other churches at different places and at different times, must not superimpose itself on the Word of God and the explicit command of the Lord. For such a decision turns itself against the Church itself. The Church disintegrates where it does not observe the Word of her Lord; and she drowns in the cunning (Eph. 4:14) of human opinions and societal currents. Such a decision is null and void, even if it be made unanimously. For you cannot change the Word of God in the wording of Holy Scripture; you cannot rescind it in its effect on consciences.

May God grant to you the Spirit of wisdom and understanding for your deliberations and decisions, whom He has promised to His congregation in Jesus Christ. May He save our church from putting her own word in the place of the Word of God.

---

13   This document is now available as a summarizing conference report in *The Place of the Woman in the Orthodox Church and the Question of the Ordination of Women: Interorthodox Symposium Rhodos, Greece, 30 October–7 November 1988*, ed. Gennadios Limouris (Katerini, Greece: Tertios Publications, 1992), 21–34, esp. 28–31. See also the individual papers on pp. 197–264 of this volume.

14   A comprehensive overview, with many source documents, is provided by Manfred Hauke, *Die Problematik um das Frauenpriestertum vor dem Hintergrund der Schöpfungs- und Erlösungsordnung*, 3d rev. ed., Konfessionskundliche und kontroverstheologische Studien, vol. 46 (Paderborn: Bonifatius, 1991).

# The Argument over Women's Ordination in Lutheranism as a Paradigmatic Conflict of Dogma

## Armin Wenz[1]

### I. An Ongoing Conflict

In the June 2006 issue of the *Zeitschrift für Theologie und Kirche*, American church historian Kenneth G. Appold opened his article on women in early modern Lutheranism with the following words: "The path of Lutheranism to women's ordination is long, often controversial, and in many cases unfinished."[2] In view of the "possibilities that can, in hindsight, be connected with Luther's redefinition of the preaching office and his concept of the general priesthood of all believers," Appold finds it "surprising" that Lutheran churches have "first" since World War II started to ordain women, that, in fact, "in some Lutheran churches and congregations there is still" opposition to this practice.[3] Appold, who currently works at the Ecumenical Institute in Strasbourg—probably the most important think-tank of the Lutheran World Federation (LWF)—mentions as examples "on the forefront" of such renitent behavior the Independent Evangelical-Lutheran Church (SELK) in Germany, its largest sister church, The Lutheran Church—Missouri Synod (LCMS), but "also some churches of the Lutheran World Federation," among

---

1   Armin Wenz is Pastor of St. John Lutheran Church, Oberursel, Germany.

2   Kenneth G. Appold, "Frauen im frühneuzeitlichen Luthertum: Kirchliche Ämter und die Frage der Ordination," *Zeitschrift für Theologie und Kirche* 103 (2006): 253.

3   Appold, "Frauen im frühneuzeitlichen Luthertum," 253.

them explicitly the Lutheran Church in Latvia whose example shows "that the path to women's ordination also can be reversed."[4]

By doing so, Appold gives his thoughts a church-political dimension that is worth noting. Probably not by accident, Appold's essay appears at a time when the Lutheran World Federation is struggling for its existence. It thus fits nicely into the attempts of the LWF-mainstream to discipline deviants in Latvia and elsewhere. By way of example, I only point to the repression attempts against the Latvian church documented by Reinhard Slenczka,[5] but also to the correspondence between the two bishops of the LWF-member churches in Sweden and Kenya concerning the episcopal consecration in the Swedish Mission Province.[6] By his explicit reference to the SELK and its sister churches, Appold also weighs into the debate which is going on at least in the SELK, a church, therefore, in which, according to Appold, the path to women's ordination "is still unfinished." Appold's judgment—"Any attempt to resist women's ordination based on tradition or some 'confessional heritage' is futile,"[7]—is oil into the fire of those favoring women's ordination in the SELK.

Appold's semantics are marked by a historical axiom that is typical of much of today's Protestant theology. Resistance against women's ordination "still" takes place; the path to the desired goal is "in some cases" "not yet" finished. In some cases it is even "reversed." Such a way of speaking reveals a soteriologically charged view of history as process, which, however, strangely can no longer be made plausible to those churches exposed by Appold as *having relapsed* or *remaining backwards*. This has to do with the fact that the quarrel regarding women's ordination can be perceived in a totally differ-ent matter, namely, not as progression into a future of wholeness, but as a

---

4    Appold, "Frauen im frühneuzeitlichen Luthertum," 253. Yet for such an evaluation one would have to look carefully at how and, respectively, under what pressure the intro-duction of women's ordination in Latvia once had come about.

5    Reinhard Slenczka writes: "The consistory, working with its partner churches, is to bring to bear its influence in the Lutheran World Federation and urge considering women's ordination, as it is being questioned, as *status confessionis* (question of confes-sion)." "Die Heilige Schrift, das Wort des dreieinigen Gottes," *Kerygma und Dogma* 51 (2005): 177 n. 8. Thus reads the September 1996 resolution of the convention of the Lutheran territorial Church of Schleswig-Holstein quoted by Slenczka; cf. also 174 n. 1. For an English summary of the essay, see Holger Sonntag, "Holy Scripture, the Word of God: The Recent Debate in Germany," *Logia* 15, no. 2 (2006): 29–35. Furthermore, see Reinhard Slenczka, "Die Ordination von Frauen zum Amt der Kirche," in *Neues und Altes: Ausgewählte Aufsätze, Vorträge und Gutachten* (Neuendettelsau: Freimund, 2000), 3:183.

6    Cf. the documentation of the correspondence between Archbishop Hammar and Bishop Obare in: *Lutherische Beiträge* 10 (2005): 57–61; furthermore, see Johannes Junker, "Eine Missionsprovinz in Schweden," *Lutherische Beiträge* 10 (2005): 52–56.

7    Appold, "Frauen im frühneuzeitlichen Luthertum," 279.

paradigmatic conflict of dogma that touches on central aspects of church and theology, a reality that was pointed out already years ago by Bavarian Bishop Dietzfelbinger.[8]

This perception, however, is diligently combated by the proponents of process thinking. This can be seen especially in those churches where the quarrel is still going on, where, in other words, the path to women's ordination has "not yet" been finished, which, therefore, still find themselves in a different "phase" of the "process." For, observing the debate within the SELK and the LWF, one can make an interesting discovery. Where women's ordination has not yet been introduced, it is asserted that such a step is an adiaphoron and would by no means affect the gospel; it would, therefore, also have no church-divisive effects.[9] Yet where women's ordination has been introduced and opposing voices do not want to fall silent, condemnations are issued that are unheard of in the history of the church. In this, a new "ecumenical" consensus emerges that goes beyond confessions and countries, because the anathema hurled against criticism of women's ordination is heard in Anglicanism[10] as well as in Lutheranism, in Scandinavia as well as in Germany. The most prominent example is the 1992 statement of the Theological Commission of the Evangelical Church in Germany (EKD) on "women's ordination and the office of bishop."[11] Reinhard Slenczka, who has repeatedly examined women's ordination critically, comments on this text as follows:

---

8  Hermann Dietzfelbinger, *Veränderung und Beständigkeit: Erinnerungen* (Munich: Claudius, 1984), 319: "I am convinced that the fact, that we did not, with the patience necessary, take a joint approach to this only seemingly secondary matter that in reality affects almost all basic problems of the congregation of Christ, did significantly hinder the consolidation and inner strength of the United Evangelical Lutheran Church in Germany (VELKD)."

9  This is the oft-repeated *ceterum censeo* of a lecture series of the faculty of the Lutheran Theological School at Oberursel that has been published as *Frauen im kirchlichen Amt? Aspekte zum Für und Wider der Ordination von Frauen*, ed. Volker Stolle (Oberursel: Oberurseler Hefte, 1994). See the important critique of it in Gottfried Martens, *Stellungnahme zu Volker Stolle (Hrsg.): Frauen im kirchlichen Amt?* (Berlin, Hanover, 1995), 10. Furthermore, Hermann Sasse, in view of this argumentation, talks about the phrases "the Gospel is not at stake" and "it is only an outward law [Ordnung] which has been altered" as the "great tranquilizer for disturbed consciences in modern churches." Sasse, "Ordination of Women?" in *The Lonely Way: Selected Essays and Letters*, trans. M. C. Harrison et al. (St. Louis: Concordia, 2002), 2:404.

10  Cf. Bernhard Heimrich, "Fliegende Bischöfe fürdie unwillinge Gefolgschaft die Church of England am Scheideweg," *Frankfurter Allgemeine Zeitung*, March 11, 1994: "Who resists women's ordination errs in the faith—a little ban ex cathedra from Canterbury to Rome."

11  Kammer für Theologie, *Frauenordination und Bischofsamt* (Hanover: Evangelische Kirche in Deutschland, 1992). This document was published as no. 44 in the *EKD-Texte* series. Hereafter *Frauenordination und Bischofsamt*.

When at first there seemed to be only a question concerning church order, dealing with external peace and not with eternal salvation, opposition suddenly makes it clear that apparently there are, after all, questions involved which have to do with fellowship in the right doctrine and in the true church. The result is that a new consensus is not only demanded by disciplinary action, but also pushed through by doctrinal condemnations and exclusion from the church, even though the other side appeals to the conscience bound by God's word, which according to Romans 14 has not only a legal, but also a spiritual right to be protected.[12]

After a phase of appeasement thus follows the phase of the solitary rule of the advocates of women's ordination who demand the unconditional surrender of all who think differently.[13]

The *conclusion* of the development Appold longs for thus in fact leads to *exclusion*. The condemnations uttered show that the introduction of women's ordination has a de facto divisive effect, as it leads to the existence of two churches that *contradict each other* in many ways. In prophetic farsightedness, this was formulated already by great Lutheran theologians of the post-World War II era. Peter Brunner cautiously uttered the supposition that women's ordination could be a heretical practice, a supposition he saw validated by his inquiry.[14] Anders Nygren commented on women's ordination, recommended by the Swedish government to the church in 1958, by saying that now the Church of Sweden had committed the Gnostic aberration.[15]

---

12  Reinhard Slenczka, "*Magnus Consensus*: The Unity of the Church in the Truth and Society's Pluralism," *Logia* 13, no. 3 (2004): 21.

13  Cf. *Frauenordination und Bischofsamt*, 8. The letter, written by bishop Walter Obare Omwanza, Kenya, to Archbishop K. G. Hammar on March 16, 2004, fits well here: "The consecration of women to the apostolic priestly office is a novelty. . . . This Gnostic novelty now demands apparently not only to rule alone in the church, but also exercises tyranny because it cannot not tolerate even a minimal cooperation with classic Christianity, as this is found especially in the Lutheran confessions." The German is in *Lutherische Beiträge* 10 (2005): 60.

14  Cf. Peter Brunner, "Das Hirtenamt und die Frau," in *Pro Ecclesia: Gesammelte Aufsätze zur dogmatischen Theologie*, 3rd ed. (Fürth: Flacius, 1990), 1:319. In the same article, on page 332, he also writes: "The *kephalé*-structure of the relation between male and female established in the creation of man and the command of submission (*hypotagé*) that applies to the woman based on this order in a particular way are in force in the church of Jesus Christ to the Last Day. If a person were to contest the factually effective existence of this order and the factual validity of the command corresponding to this order in teaching and proclamation, he would, at a central point where ultimately the whole of the Christian message is at stake, proclaim a false teaching; he would be a heretic."

15  *Kyrkomötets protokoll* no. 4, 1958, 154: "Since the decision now made represents not only a decision concerning the limited question of female priests but, in my mind, at the same time includes the fact that our church changes over into a heretofore foreign track toward a view held in Gnosticism and among the 'enthusiasts,' I have to bring forward my serious complaints about the decision made and make known my reservations."

Thus, the introduction of women's ordination has led both sides to make dogmatically weighty judgments that, as all doctrinal condemnations, mark ultimate boundaries and have an eschatological quality, insofar as they bind the consciences of those judging before God. The radical nature of the *change in church and theology that took place within one generation* cannot be overestimated. It is a peculiar development that, parallel to the numerous efforts to reach convergence in the *ecumene*, the question of women's ordination has led to new confessionalizations. When dissenters are denied their right to exist by dogmatic definitions, they lose the possibility to participate in the spiritual life or in the theological discourse and are forced to continue their being the church outside the heretofore common walls. Just like at the time of the reformation, however, such an eschatological situation of crisis offers above all a chance to study aspects of the gospel, which possibly heretofore have hardly been noticed and have now been condemned by one side as error, and to build the church by doing so.

That this really takes place becomes apparent when we first shed light on the material dogmatic dimension of the conflict regarding women's ordination in order then to ask how it is possible to reach such diametrically opposed positions within the Lutheran church. For the material dogmatic decisions each presuppose fundamental theological premises in hermeneutics and, respectively, the understanding of Scripture and simultaneously have ecclesiological-eschatological consequences when they lead to the exclusion of differing positions. In this sense, the following elaborations are meant to measure the whole import of the conflict that has broken out.

## II. THE MATERIAL DOGMATIC DISAGREEMENT: BETWEEN PARADIGM SHIFTS AND DEEPENING OF THE HERITAGE

In many areas of Lutheran theology, the justification of women's ordination has led to far-reaching modifications in doctrine, reaching from the understanding of the office via the theology of creation to the image of God. This is not to say that all advocates of women's ordination follow through with all paradigm shifts in all these areas. Yet one needs to point out that also on the level of material dogmatics there has been an increasing—process-like, at times slower, at times faster—"radicalization" of the positions,[16] that therefore

---

(Quotation furnished by Rev. E. Andrae, Pittsburgh; translation into German by Rev. J. Diestelmann, Brunswick, Germany.)

16  There is not enough space here to report on the events in the SELK during the last 15 years. Some hints must be enough. The controversy in the SELK circles around the question, in what sense Article 7, 2 of its Constitution, according to which only males can be ordained to the preaching office, can be grounded theologically. After laborious work in commissions, partial results have been published in the past years, e.g., on the

the "material for sharpened juxtapositions"[17] has not decreased but increased during the last years, in the SELK as well as in the LWF or in the EKD.

For example, prominent advocates of female pastors view the churchly preaching office as merely a function or emanation of the priesthood of all believers.[18] This is the point of departure and, respectively, the central theological "principle" to be kept in mind in the statement of the Theological Commission of the EKD[19] as well as in Volker Stolle, the theological champion in the battle for women's ordination within the SELK. Accordingly, the office is seen as an order that is necessary for the sake of peace in the church.

---

question of adiaphora or on that of order of creation. A promising elaboration of the Theological Commission on "Office, offices, and services" is currently being discussed at pastors' conferences. All these efforts are an important expression of the will to walk together on a path that can be supported by as many people as possible. However, one must not be blind to the fact that in parallel to these efforts some proponents of women's ordination have further fortified and sharpened their argumentative position. This applies especially to the attempt by Volker Stolle to introduce Luther and the Lutheran tradition as chief witnesses in favor of women's ordination, which will be discussed below. At the same time, one must not overlook that Stolle's argumentation goes hand in hand with an explicit paradigm shift that affects central aspects of theology, leading to a thoroughgoing destruction of Lutheran doctrinal contents. See, for instance, Stolle's book *Luther und Paulus: Die exegetischen und hermeneutischen Grundlagen der lutherischen Rechtfertigungslehre im Paulinismus Luthers* (Leipzig: Evangelische Verlagsanstalt, 2002). This destruction affects not only the office of the church, but also the question of justification, which in Stolle is "constructed" totally from scratch. In his book, Stolle has also applied the inner-canonical material criticism, which he practices in his argumentation for women's ordination, to other areas of the New Testament and other doctrinal questions. Since Stolle is the most important theological mentor of the proponents of women's ordination in the SELK, one must expect his further paradigm shifts to be received as well (cf. as the tip of the iceberg the internet portal www.frauenordination.de, there the button "Vorgänge SELK"). Noteworthy is, for example, Stolle's compilation of clarifications, disseminated not only via the internet (the aforementioned Web site), "Ausgeblendetes, was jedoch für das Thema von großer Bedeutung ist, sowie Unklarheiten, die zu falschen Schlüssen verleiten können," on the bible study produced for the SELK's consistory: "Ordination von Frauen zum Amt der Kirche? Seminareinheit für die theologische Weiterarbeit durch die Bezirkspfarrkonvente zum Jahresthema II/2006." The way in which one then reencounters these "clarifications" in the churchly discourse shows that one indeed is dealing here with the "formation of a school," in which one person sets the tone and others follow collectively. On Stolle's "destruction of the Lutheran whole of meaning" (thus Stolle himself in his book, *Paulus und Luther*, 438), see *Lutherische Beiträge* 8, no. 4 (2003) and my critique: "Wider die alten und neuen Antinomer: Über 'Paradigmenwechsel' in der lutherischen Theologie," in *Sana Doctrina: Heilige Schrift und theologische Ethik* (Frankfurt / Main: Lang, 2004), 335–356.

17  Stolle, *Frauen im kirchlichen Amt?*, 8.

18  Cf., e.g., the position of Gustaf Wingren summarized by Regin Prenter, *Die Ordination der Frauen zu dem überlieferten Pfarramt der lutherischen Kirche* (Berlin; Hamburg: Lutherisches Verlagshaus, 1967), 15.

19  Cf. also Appold, "Frauen im frühneuzeitlichen Luthertum," who repeatedly invokes Luther's connection between the general priesthood and the office without explaining how they are both related in Luther.

Any ties back to the apostolic office or even to the institution of the office by Christ himself are questioned or simply denied. Correspondingly, there can be no talk of representation of Christ by the incumbents of the office while they exercise their official duties.[20] The question regarding an exercise of the pastoral office by women, therefore, is exclusively answered based on the criterion of "equality" or "emancipation."[21] A text like Galatians 3:28, therefore, relegates "the apostle's individual restrictive demands of silence and submission of women" to the realm of "taking care of current questions of order,"[22] that either are not at all related to the preaching office or simply have to be seen as time-bound accommodation. In Stolle one can even read: "In the Christian congregation the difference between man and woman, as it is established in creation, . . . does not matter anymore."[23] According to this view, there can be no talk of apostolic instructions that are indissolubly connected with the gospel and therefore binding even today. They are neutralized as a time-bound snapshot. The concrete shape of the proclamation of the gospel is left to the decision of the church in its "evangelical" freedom. Yet the gospel is turned into a veritable manifesto for emancipation by means of materially critical deconstructions and reconstructions. It is thus not at all surprising that occasionally there are polemics against "andristic exegeses"[24] and demands to discover the femininity of God,[25] so that in this argument for women's ordination even the notion of representation reappears in a transformed fashion, even though this is hardly done in a conscious manner.

On the other hand, the rejection of women's ordination is, at least among its Lutheran representatives,[26] based on the perception of the institution of

---

20  Cf. Volker Stolle, "Im Dienst Christi und der Kirche: Zur neutestamentlichen Konzeptualisierung kirchlicher Ämter," *Lutherische Theologie und Kirche* 20 (1996): 126.

21  On almost every page of *Frauenordination und Bischofsamt*.

22  *Frauenordination und Bischofsamt*, 6. Correspondingly, Stolle speaks of time-conditioned "structures of order" in "Neutestamentliche Aspekte zur Frage der Ordination von Frauen," in Stolle, *Frauen im kirchlichen Amt?*, 69; cf. on this the critique in Martens, *Stellungnahme zu Volker Stolle*, 31.

23  Stolle, "Neutestamentliche Aspekte zur Frage der Ordination von Frauen," 73f. Cf. on this critically Martens, *Stellungnahme zu Volker Stolle*, 37: "The claim that, in the Christian congregation, 'the distinction between male and female, as it is ordered in creation, plays no role anymore,' is perhaps true for certain Gnostic congregations, certainly not for Paul and his congregations. How one can arrive at such assertions in view of 1 Cor. 11; 14; Eph. 5; and 1 Tim. 2 is a mystery."

24  Stolle, "Neutestamentliche Aspekte zur Frage der Ordination von Frauen," 78f.

25  Cf. the elaboration by A. E. Buchrucker, *Frauenpfarramt und Feministische Theologie* (Hanover, 1995), which was not without reason published in response to Stolle, "Frauen im kirchlichen Amt?" An English translation of Buchrucker appeared in *Logia* 9, no. 1 (2000): 9–20.

26  As paradigmatic for this stance, the 1994 "Hirtenbrief zur Frage der Ordination von Frauen zum Amt der Kirche" by Bishop Jobst Schöne is to be commended, in *Botschafter*

the ecclesiastical office by Christ himself, as it is witnessed in the Lutheran Confessions, and on the perception of the biblical statements on the creation of man as male and female in the equality of rights with a difference in gifts and callings. A decisive aspect here is the notion of the representation[27] that is anchored in the doctrine of the Trinity as well as in the history of salvation and that has anthropological implications. In this way, the unity of creation and redemption and, respectively, order of creation and order of redemption is emphasized as well as the correlation between the image of God (God as Father; sending of the Son) and the office of shepherd (sending of the apostles by the Son; passing on of the office to male bishops and, respectively, presbyters).[28] We cannot here present the detailed theological reflections. Yet I will point out that the conflict regarding women's ordination in the SELK has indeed led to a deepening of neglected questions in an impressive thematic breadth. This holds for the examination of the question of whether the "one office of proclaiming the word and administering the sacraments, instituted by Christ," "exists at all and whether it can be found at least in the New Testament," done by Gottfried Martens, who works out the basic approach of the New Testament, especially of the Pastoral Letters, regarding the theology of the office.[29] There are furthermore the studies by Gert Kelter on the Lutheran Confessions' theology of the office and its position between the doctrinal decisions of the United Evangelical Lutheran Church in Germany

---

*an Christi Statt: Versuche* (Groß Oesingen: Lutherische Buchhandlung Harms, 1996), 70–82.

27 Cf. William Weinrich, "'It Is not Given to Women to Teach': A *Lex* in Search of a *Ratio*," in *Church and Ministry Today: Three Confessional Lutheran Essays, Preus, Marquart, Weinrich*), ed. John A. Maxfield (St. Louis: Luther Academy, 2001), 210: "We need to reflect upon the inner and organic connections which bind the speaking of the Gospel and the administration of the sacraments to the inner life of the most Holy Trinity." Note also the context of the quotation.

28 Cf. Schöne, "Hirtenbrief zur Frage der Ordination von Frauen zum Amt der Kirche," 79: "The image of Christ as the Shepherd and Bishop of our souls (1 Peter 2:25) pales unless there are shepherds who speak and act in his name and by his commission, whom he sent as his ambassadors (2 Cor. 5:20). Experiences and wishes, needs and expectation that are deduced from humans and are related to them, especially to women, can then quickly shape a new image of God and Christ."

29 Gottfried Martens, "Gibt es das 'eine, von Christus gestiftete Amt der Wortverkündigung und Sakramentsverwaltung'? Beobachtungen zur Frage von Amt und Ämtern im Neuen Testament unter besonderer Berücksichtigung der Pastoralbriefe," *Lutherische Beiträge* 10 (2005): 3–20. On the New Testament situation, see also the essays by Hartmut Günther, "Ordination von Frauen zum Amt der Kirche? Erwägungen zu einer umstrittenen Frage," *Lutherische Theologie und Kirche* 21 (1997): 99–113, and John W. Kleinig, "Die Heilige Schrift und der Ausschluß der Frauen vom Hirtenamt," *Lutherische Beiträge* 2 (1997): 5–20.

(VELKD) and Rome regarding the theology of the office.[30] Additional contributions shed light on the "doctrine of the orders of creation" and its being anchored in the Lutheran Confessions[31] or on the doctrine of the office in the pastoral theologians of the nineteenth century.[32] Also the question of adiaphora that is constantly brought up in the debate regarding the ordination of women has been discussed on the basis of the Lutheran Confessions.[33]

Already in 1985 and taking up the approach of Peter Brunner, the Commission on Theology and Church Relations of the LCMS also addressed women's ordination.[34] In 1993 and as an explicit discussion of arguments favoring women's ordination, this was deepened in an unmatched study by William Weinrich,[35] who, based especially on 1 Corinthians 11 and Ephesians 5, went to the bottom of the question as to why the specific correlation of man and woman in creation is reflected in the relation of Christ and his church. According to Weinrich, the apostolic instructions for the office can be seen as results of the divine economy of salvation, which is why they can by no means be qualified as time-bound, but bind the church permanently.[36] All these studies are by no means the private teachings of fanatic confessionalists; they rather bear witness to a broad doctrinal consensus with Lutheran theologians who discussed the question of women's ordination already earlier in the twentieth century on an exegetical and dogmatic level. I mention in addition

---

30  Gert Kelter, "Das apostolische Hirtenamt der Kirche als institutionalisierte Zuspitzung der potestas clavium: Entwurf einer Zuordnung von Amt, Ämtern und Diensten in der Kirche vor dem Hintergrund von CA XXVIII," *Lutherische Beiträge* 10 (2005): 21–34, and "Parochiales oder diözesanes Bischofsamt? Versuch einer Auseinandersetzung mit neuen Ergebnissen ökumenischer Forschung," *Lutherische Beiträge* 11 (2006): 71–91. Cf. also Armin Wenz: "'Vom Amt der Schlüssel'—ein Katechismusstück und seine Bedeutung," in *Einträchtig Lehren: Festschrift für Bischof Dr. Jobst Schöne*, ed. Jürgen Diestelmann and Wolfgang Schillhahn (Groß Oesingen: Lutherische Buchhandlung Harms, 1997), 542–558.

31  Armin Wenz, "Die Lehre von den Schöpfungsordnungen—ein überholtes Theologumenon?" in *Sana Doctrina*, 146–181.

32  Armin Wenz, "Ministry and Pastoral Theology of Löhe and Vilmar," *Logia* 16, no. 3 (2007): 15–23.

33  Gottfried Martens offers an important summary: "FC X shows clearly that viewing churchly practices as adiaphora . . . , where this view is taken seriously, must in the long run lead to a separation from those who contradict this view; and it admonishes us to use this terminology carefully and in a theologically responsible way." Martens, "Die Adiaphora als theologisches Problem: Ansätze zu einer Hermeneutik von FC X," *Lutherische Beiträge* 5 (2000): 127.

34  A Report of the Commission on Theology and Church Relations of The Lutheran Church—Missouri Synod, *Women in the Church: Scriptural Principles and Ecclesial Practice* (St. Louis: Concordia, 1985).

35  Weinrich, "It Is not Given to Women to Teach," 173–215.

36  Weinrich, "It Is not Given to Women to Teach," 210–211. On the commandments indissolubly connected to the gospel, see pages 212–213.

to Peter Brunner the names of the German theologians Hermann Sasse, Joachim Heubach, and Hermann Dietzfelbinger, as well as the Scandinavians Regin Prenter, Bertil Gärtner,[37] and Bo Giertz. Thus, a consensus spanning generations, countries, and confessions[38] in these questions pertaining to women's ordination can not only be attested on the side of the proponents of women's ordination.

Yet since both sides arrive at opposing doctrinal results when it comes to evaluating the relationship between man and woman, between order of creation and order of salvation, between shepherding office and image of God, between gospel and apostolic instructions, while equally invoking Scripture and confessions and, respectively, the Lutheran doctrinal tradition, we have to turn to the fundamental theological opposition in dealing with Scripture and confessions that lies behind these opposing material dogmatic results.

## III. THE FUNDAMENTAL THEOLOGICAL DISAGREEMENT

The historical-theological accusation of being "retarded"—that is, behind the times and slow to change—directed by Appold and others at opponents of women's ordination is repeated on a fundamental theological level both in the struggle for the correct use of Scripture and in the question regarding the catholicity of women's ordination, that is, its conformity to tradition or confession.

### THE DISAGREEMENT IN THE EVALUATION OF THE SCRIPTURALNESS OF WOMEN'S ORDINATION

The opponents thus are accused of espousing a fundamentalist understanding of Scripture[39] and, respectively, of arguing based on the Baroque

---

37 Bertil E. Gärtner, *Das Amt, der Mann und die Frau im Neuen Testament*, ed. Ernst Seybold, trans. Georg Stoll (Bad Windsheim: H. Delp, 1963).

38 Cf. from the Anglican perspective Günther Thomann, "Die Frauenordination und ihre Folgen für die Anglikanische Gemeinschaft—Eine kurze Übersicht," *Lutherische Beiträge* 4 (1999): 106–124; from the Evangelical camp Werner Neuer, *Man and Woman in Christian Perspective*, trans. Gordon J. Wenham (London et al.: Hodder and Stoughton, 1990; Wheaton, IL: Crossway Books, 1991); Markus Liebelt, *Frauenordination: Ein Beitrag zur gegenwärtigen Diskussion im evangelikalen Kontext* (Nürnberg: VTR, [2003]); Heinzpeter Hempelmann, *Gottes Ordnungen zum Leben: Die Stellung der Frau in der Gemeinde* (Bad Liebenzell: VLM, Verlag der Liebenzeller Mission, 1997). On the Orthodox position, cf. Peter Hauptmann, "Protestantische Frauenordination in russisch-orthodoxer Sicht," *Lutherische Beiträge* 1 (1997): 21–30. A historically far-reaching and ecumenically significant standard work has been presented by the Roman Catholic theologian Manfred Hauke, *Women in the Priesthood? A Systematic Analysis in the Light of the Order of Creation and Redemption*, trans. David Kipp (San Francisco: Ignatius, 1988).

39 This is the basic tenor of the internet portal www.frauenordination.de. It is interesting how this argument affects the so-called culture of discussion or arguing. For there is no need to listen to serious material arguments made by theologians whom one already

"proof-text" method,[40] a practice that today, in the age of the historical-critical method, cannot be regarded as an adequate way of dealing with Scripture. To counter dogmatic definitions, one points to the basic diversity of biblical "traditions" "that want to be read in their differences and in their being tied to the times"; this is why, accordingly, it is to be said: "In the bible, there is neither a comprehensive doctrine of the office nor a dogma on the role of the woman that transcends time. Rather, the history of primitive Christianity points us to different regulations in different congregational situations and resists a premature systematization."[41] Accordingly, Stolle speaks programmatically of a "New-Testament conceptualization of ecclesiastical offices."[42] Yet such time-conditioned conceptualizations are, both according to Stolle and the Theological Commission of the EKD, to be measured by the "center of the gospel." Based on this center, one can and must materially criticize misleading Scripture passages which therefore also may not claim apostolic authority that would bind the church today.[43] In Stolle one can read: "Biblical-

---

knows to be fundamentalists or fanatical doctrinaires. On the peculiar experiences one can then make in the discourse within the church, cf. the striking gloss by Gert Kelter, "Theologie und Wirklichkeit: Eine sehr populärphilosophische Glosse," *Lutherische Beiträge* 11 (2006): 253–255. What is really behind the accusation of fundamentalism is an ignoring of the Spirit-wrought reality of theology and church. Postmodern, constructivist hermeneutics thus totally changes communication. For when one no longer can agree on objective realities, including biblical statements and contents, because they are viewed as only time-conditioned constructions and because every understanding is seen as relative, then communication becomes a struggle for power, in which the strongest ("most plausible," most powerful, etc.) constructor prevails.

40 *Frauenordination und Bischofsamt*, 5: "Obedience to the Scripture cannot mean that individual biblical verses are isolated as 'proof texts' (*dicta probantia*) and their narrower and wider context is ignored."

41 *Frauenordination und Bischofsamt*, 5.

42 Stolle, "Im Dienst Christi und der Kirche," passim.

43 Cf. *Frauenordination und Bischofsamt*, 5: "When later texts and traditions mention women as causing sin in the world and demand their subordination under men (so esp. 1 Tim. 2:8-15), then this is the result of a reader response that moves away from the original meaning, but that always has to be measured anew against the liberating message of the gospel of Jesus Christ and its understanding of creation"; and Stolle, "Neutestamentliche Aspekte zur Frage der Ordination von Frauen," 77: "The limiting directives, on the other hand, take up legendary elaborations which in the texts' tradition of interpretation attached themselves to the texts and represent their timely actualization and application (1 Cor. 11:7-10; 1 Tim. 2:13-15). Under different cultural and societal conditions they, with their actual presuppositions, lose their plausibility and become meaningless." Furthermore Stolle's review of Ulrike Wagener, *Die Ordnung des "Hauses Gottes": Der Ort von Frauen in der Ekklesiologie und Ethik der Pastoralbriefe* (Tübingen: J. C. B. Mohr, 1994): "In a good and insightful manner, the study at hand leads into the hermeneutical problematic that First Timothy, in the texts discussed, deviates from the theological line of Paul and seeks to shape the congregational life based on extra-Christian societal premises. If this is perceived correctly, then the church cannot avoid the decision whether it wants to follow uncritically the ancient

theological contributions, which could help in the process of arriving at a decision, can, according to Lutheran hermeneutics, not consist in remembering apostolic orders as permanently binding decisions. Rather, they will, from the center of the gospel, take into account especially also the formative powers of the word of God. . . ."[44]

If one does not allow the fundamentalism charge to turn one off from independently looking into the biblical-theological elaborations of the Lutheran theologians rejecting women's ordination, one finds that they do not contain any undifferentiated use of contextually isolated "proof texts." This is true especially for the careful elaboration of Peter Brunner, which was probably not accidentally first caricatured and then rejected by the Theological Commission of the EKD.[45] Brunner himself, just like the many theologians following up on his work or arriving at similar results on a different path, explicitly distances himself from a fundamentalist and, respectively, biblicist-legalistic understanding of Scripture.[46] The point of departure for his exegetical observations, however, is the differentiating perception that there are in Scripture solemn divine institutions or orders that are by no means time-conditioned, which also are not only manifestations of God's will but that out of themselves—that is, by virtue of divine omnipotence—establish a universal and therefore also current reality that wants to be perceived by us. Such divine orders Brunner finds, on the one hand, in the institution of the office by Christ himself and, on the other hand, in the primeval creation of man as male and female in their specific coordination to each other. All of Scripture is permeated by the witness to the interdependence and the inexchangeability of man and woman, to the equality of rights, and to the difference in vocations of man and woman in marriage and congregation. The institution of the worldwide-missionary proclamation of the gospel and the administration of the sacraments by Jesus himself in the New Testament never takes place in an abstract way, but is always tied to persons. The two classic proof texts on the question of a preaching office of women (1 Corinthians 14 and 1 Timothy 2) thus represent within this context of the entire bible by no means cultural

---

order of society or give room to the evangelical freedom given as a gift in Christ." Review in *Lutherische Theologie und Kirche* 19 (1995): 159.

44 Volker Stolle, "I Kor 14, 26–40 und die Gottesdienstreform der lutherischen Reformation: Die biblische Grundlegung des Gottesdienstes als hermeneutische Frage," *Lutherische Theologie und Kirche* 19 (1995): 135.

45 *Frauenordination und Bischofsamt*, 4f. Cf. on this Reinhard Slenczka, "Ist die Kritik an der Frauenordination eine kirchentrennende Irrlehre? Dogmatische Erwägungen zu einer Erklärung des Rates der EKD vom 20. Juli 1992," in *Neues und Altes*, 3:201. Martens calls Brunner's treatise "Hirtenamt und die Frau" "probably the most profound negative contribution on this question." *Stellungnahme zu Volker Stolle*, 4.

46 Brunner, "Hirtenamt und die Frau," 317. Cf. Prenter, *Ordination der Frauen*, 6–8; Gärtner, *Das Amt, der Mann und die Frau im Neuen Testament*, 8.

adaptations[47] but the point where the creation-theological and the office-theological lines converge.

In this way, by observing the Lutheran hermeneutical premise that the Holy Spirit does not contradict himself,[48] a number of inner-canonical tensions can be made plausible. There is, for example, the observation that Jesus, on the one hand, could gather many female disciples around him, but, on the other hand, only called men by name in order to entrust them with the sacraments as well as the great commission. In this way, one can understand why Jesus revealed himself as the risen one to the women who had come to perform the last service of love and then sent them with a limited charge to his disciples before he then meets the disciples himself to awaken their faith and to send them out into the world. One can then understand why it is a matter of course for Paul that women are present in the divine service and involved in prayer and praise, while he at the same time prohibits them to teach in the congregational assembly.

It may be that the respective exegetes cannot answer every question to the last detail. Yet the unbiased observer will notice that the interpretations of Brunner, Prenter, Weinrich, and others, which are different and yet in agreement in their basic decisions, correspond to the hermeneutical bases of the Lutheran reformation. This is especially true of the perception that God works what he says through his solemn ordinations, a truth of faith that is frequently attested to in Scripture and that is true for all the works of the Trinity, for creation, redemption, and the work of the Holy Spirit. It furthermore has to do with the principle that the Holy Scripture of the Old and New Testaments is a spiritual, God-wrought unity.

Contrariwise, if one considers how Scripture is used by proponents of women's ordination, one, to be sure, also finds here the affirmation of viewing Scripture as God's word. This, however, is understood in a way that is quite different than in the Lutheran tradition, which becomes apparent in that in the actual use of Scripture one can observe again and again a characteristic "change in subject."[49] One no longer talks about divine institutions, but about "structures of order" conditioned by each period of time. The office of shepherd is not viewed as an institution of Christ which his apostles "hand down," as it were, for the post-apostolic period to the bishops and presbyters, but one talks instead about conceptualizations of churchly offices. The vis-à-vis

---

47  Weinrich, "It Is not Given to Women to Teach," 189: Paul argues "not on the basis . . . of the culture and society," but "on the basis of the story of creation."

48  Hans Kirsten points to this premise and its application by Luther in his essay "Luther und die Frauenordination," in *Die Kirche in der Welt: Aufsätze zur praktischen Theologie aus drei Jahrzehnten* (Groß Oesingen: Lutherische Buchhandlung Harms, 1983), 192–193.

49  Martens emphatically points to this in *Stellungnahme zu Volker Stolle*, 31–33.

of Lord and church, head and body, command and obedience is thus replaced by the concept of a tradition-historical development that can view the levels of development reached in the New Testament as time-conditioned variations but by no means as sign posts that are binding for later Christianity.[50] In fact, one can obviously ask whether the polemic against the "proof-text" method does not really fall back on the advocates of women's ordination. For the way in which texts like Galatians 3:28 are torn out of their context (which is certainly not about teaching in the worship service or a public exercise of the office of shepherd) and leveled against perceived illegitimate inner-canonical misjudgments regarding the relation of man and woman in the question of the office speaks for itself.

## The Disagreement Regarding the Evaluation of Women's Ordination's Conformity to the Confessions or Tradition

It is precisely the tradition-historical concept that is behind the motif of a process-like path to women's ordination and that shapes the way in which its proponents deal with the tradition of the church. It is claimed that, on the one hand, the Lutheran Confessions are silent on the question of women's ordination; that, on the other hand, the concept of the priesthood of all believers actually suggests the ordination of women, even if it could not yet be realized at the time of the Reformation because one had to respect the societal circumstances that have since changed. Accordingly, tradition, especially the Lutheran tradition, has cleared the path to women's ordination in increasing clarity.

Here, too, one discovers time and again—especially in the use of Luther quotes—the totally naïve use of a "proof-text" method that ignores the context.[51] It is extremely strange in this context how, for example, Volker Stolle deals with Luther's statements. "Luther apparently had great difficulties to get a theologically accurate and definitive grasp of the reality of the churchly office."[52] Luther's understanding of the office is destroyed by repeated cari-

---

50 Cf. critically on this Martens, *Stellungnahme zu Volker Stolle*, 49.

51 This applies especially to the "proofs" for Luther's alleged derivation of the churchly office from the general priesthood. Cf., for example, *Frauenordination und Bischofsamt*, 3. The fact that the Lutheran Confessions do not mention the "general priesthood" even once when they discuss the foundation of the churchly office is, for its part, not worth mentioning.

52 Volker Stolle, "Luther, das 'Amt' und die Frauen," *Lutherische Theologie und Kirche* 19 (1995): 20. Also, on page 8: "In this way, one attempts to undergird one's own culture-historical limitations in a biological and biblicist way"; and page 21: "Contrary to the word from Scripture, 1 Peter 2:9, that clearly unfolds its independent power, in fact, its critically explosive power, the commandment of silence and, respectively, the prohibition to teach, does not have any effect out of itself, but serves as the supplementary biblical foundation of convictions that appear evident based on other presuppositions."

catures, before it then is said, in summary: "The exclusion of women from the office of the church, as Luther proves it, turns out to be an element in his understanding of the office that is relative to time and that is therefore also time-bound. Accordingly, the ordination of women does not represent a break with the doctrinal tradition of the Lutheran church, insofar as Luther can be taken to be normative for it."[53]

Appold, in his overview on "women in early-modern Lutheranism" mentioned above, argues in a similar way. At first, Appold rightly points out that orthodox Lutheranism highly appreciated women and also female offices such as that of a midwife.[54] It is an equally important reminder that women as midwives and teachers could work in close contact with the office of pastor. Furthermore, Appold's hints at the beginnings of reestablishing the early church's office of deaconess are interesting. Caspar Ziegler also suggested for this a specific solemn rite of consecration.[55] Although Appold cannot adduce a single proof for an ordination of women to the preaching office,[56] he draws the conclusion: "All the presuppositions for women's ordination can be found in the 16th and 17th centuries."[57] Among these presuppositions are, according to Appold, "a clear relativizing . . . of the bible passages used against women's

---

53  Stolle, "Luther, das 'Amt' und die Frauen," 22. In "I Kor 14, 26–40 und die Gottesdienstreform der lutherischen Reformation," 134, Stolle summarizes: "The exclusion of women from the churchly office was not derived from the commission of the gospel and the call by Christ, but attributed to human orders." On page 134, note 132, Stolle calls it an "exception" that Luther himself could prove the exclusion of women from the churchly office based on the commandment of Christ. The way he deals with the quotation by Theodosius Harnack on the same page shows that Stolle can arrive at his conclusions only because, for him, order of creation always implies "human order," but not, as for Harnack, "divine" order.

54  Cf. also Eckhard Struckmeier, *"Vom Glauben der Kinder im Mutter-Leibe": Eine historisch-anthropologische Untersuchung frühneuzeitlicher lutherischer Seelsorge und Frömmigkeit im Zusammenhang mit der Geburt* (Frankfurt am Main; New York: P. Lang, 2000).

55  Appold, "Frauen im frühneuzeitlichen Luthertum," 275f.

56  Cf. Appold, "Frauen im frühneuzeitlichen Luthertum," 277: "There is no proof for women being ordained in early modern Lutheranism for the preaching office." All that Appold's observations show (and that is certainly noteworthy) is that the orthodox Lutherans were so "pro-women" that indeed numerous churchly offices existing *alongside the pastoral office* were open for them. Yet this is also exactly the proposal of numerous important Lutheran theologians who rejected women's ordination for theological reasons and therefore demand to create specifically churchly offices for theologically qualified women. Cf. Prenter, *Ordination der Frauen*, 17; Brunner, "Hirtenamt und die Frau," 337f.; Slenczka, "Ordination von Frauen zum Amt der Kirche," 195; and Schöne, "Hirtenbrief zur Frage der Ordination von Frauen zum Amt der Kirche," 81. One can also point to the fact that, in the United States, it is precisely the LCMS and the Roman Catholic Church that have by far the most women employed in qualified churchly offices—with the exception of the pastoral office.

57  Appold, "Frauen im frühneuzeitlichen Luthertum," 276.

ordination" already in Luther and "in almost all exegetes of orthodoxy."[58] Appold also claims that Luther and the Lutheran theologians did not understand the "subordination" of woman as based on creation, but exclusively as a result of the fall according to Genesis 3:16, which is why they repeatedly relativized it.[59] Accordingly, only the social-historically conditioned view of the lacking aptitude of woman for the preaching ministry prevented women's ordination.[60] Appold concludes, quite in agreement with Stolle: "Returning now to the initial thought and again asking the question whether women's ordination represents a break with the confessional-Lutheran heritage, one can unequivocally answer this question in the negative." In fact, that theological line is to be identified as "Lutheran tradition," "which stretches from Luther's view of the general priesthood and office via the many women of early modernity working in the church . . . a line which increasingly destroys the obstacles for women's ordination and prepares the path all the way to the total opening of all offices for women."[61]

Rudolf Eles, Tom Hardt, and David P. Scaer have critically discussed Stolle's "proof from tradition."[62] Their critique of Stolle can, by and large, be applied to the way Appold handles tradition. First of all, one needs to ask how Appold himself understands the repeatedly invoked connection between office and general priesthood in Luther and in the Lutheran tradition. The Lutheran Confessions, at any rate, do not speak about the general priesthood in the context of their elaborations on the theological foundation of the preaching office. According to the Lutheran view, the preaching office is founded on the mandate of Christ, not on the general priesthood. Also, the claim that the statements on women by the Lutheran theologians are exclusively founded on the fall, that is, based on Genesis 3:16, and on sociological considerations is, at least as far as Luther is concerned, not correct.[63] The

---

58 Appold, "Frauen im frühneuzeitlichen Luthertum," 276.

59 Appold, "Frauen im frühneuzeitlichen Luthertum," 277.

60 Appold, "Frauen im frühneuzeitlichen Luthertum," 277.

61 Appold, "Frauen im frühneuzeitlichen Luthertum," 278f.

62 Rudolf Eles, *Martin Luther und das Frauenpfarramt. Bemerkungen zu Prof. Dr. Volker Stolles Aufsatz: "Luther, das 'Amt' und die Frauen"* (Groß Oesingen: Lutherische Buchhandlung Harms, 1995); Tom Hardt, "Die Lehre Martin Luthers von der Frauenordination: Eine kritische Auseinandersetzung," in *Ich will hintreten zum Altar Gottes: Festschrift für Propst em. Hans-Heinrich Salzmann*, ed. Hans-Heinrich Salzmann, Michael Salzmann, and Johannes Junker (Neuendettelsau: Freimund-Verlag, 2003), 213–229; and David P. Scaer, "Ordaining Women: Has the Time Come?" *Logia* 4, no. 2 (1995): 83–85, an introduction into the debate in the SELK in the English language. Martens, *Stellungnahme zu Volker Stolle*, 52, therefore rightly rejects the attempt of "making the Reformer himself into the chief witness for the legitimacy of women's ordination."

63 Cf. Hardt, "Die Lehre Martin Luthers von der Frauenordination," passim, and Eles, *Martin Luther und das Frauenpfarramt*, 13 and passim.

reference to the office of deaconess and to an ordination to the same merely proves that some theologians could apply the term ordination to different ecclesial offices. If the statements of orthodox Lutheran exegetes really are to come into view, one would have to look especially into their commentaries on 1 Corinthians and 1 Timothy. In his church-politically motivated study, Appold dispenses with this as well as with a survey of the locus *de ministerio* in the numerous dogmatic works of orthodoxy.[64]

One can confidently question already the claim that the Lutheran confessions are silent on the issue of women's ordination. Karlmann Beyschlag writes in his history of dogma, pointing to Augsburg Confession XIV: "I venture to point out that the 'rite vocatus' of AC XIV is masculine. The Protestant 'women's ordination' to the spiritual office is thus not only contrary to Scripture but also contrary to the confessions."[65] Beyschlag has been ridiculed for this statement by those who do not want to see the reference to the male gender of the office holder in the context of the history of dogma, in which it is located in Beyschlag with inner necessity.[66] In Beyschlag one finds not only the hint that the line of tradition, in which women's ordination is located, is not the one stretching from the New Testament to the reformation, but the contrary one, namely, the Gnostic-sectarian one. Beyschlag writes on Augsburg Confession V: "What is right away significant in this formulation is that it restates the occidental conviction that reaches all the way back to First Clement, according to which the institution of the churchly office . . . enjoys priority over the gift of the Holy Spirit who works the faith. Here the AC leans on the catholic pre-understanding and simultaneously destroys the basis for enthusiasm."[67] The delimitation over against Gnosis and enthusiasm involves the perception of the office as well as the creation-based coordination of male and female.[68] Yet Beyschlag's assertion, that the Lutheran confessions contra-

---

64 Appold has shown in his habilitation that he is well-acquainted with Lutheran orthodoxy; cf. my review in *Lutherische Beiträge* 10 (2005): 261–265. It gives one all the more pause that he now throws his theological weight into the discussion in such a church-political way.

65 Karlmann Beyschlag, *Grundriß der Dogmengeschichte* (Darmstadt: Wissenschaftliche Buchgesellschaft, 2000), 2.II:401 n. 181.

66 Cf. Beyschlag, *Grundriß der Dogmengeschichte*, 2nd ed. (Darmstadt: Wissenschaftliche Buchgesellschaft, 1988), 1:150f.: "Yet what is 'the Gnostic' par excellence? When one asks for the basic motif, then one time and again runs into the same, ultimately defective structure. It is, with a word, the ontological negativism of the Gnostic doctrine of God . . . , the refusal of order of creation and of theology of creation . . . in favor of a 'soteriology of self-preservation' and 'self-realization' . . . that made Gnosticism unbearable for the church."

67 Beyschlag, *Grundriß der Dogmengeschichte*, 2.II:401.

68 Cf. Brunner, "Hirtenamt und die Frau," 310: "Due to the necessary quarrel with Gnostic and heretical groups in the early church, the question of the form of the official service of women in the church was still alive." Cf. also William Weinrich, "Women

dict the ordination of women, will certainly only make sense to the person who is willing to perceive also the broad reception of divine institutions or ordinations in the Lutheran Confessions.[69] For, in the confessional writings, the preaching office as well as the specific coordination of male and female is viewed as anchored in salvation history as well as in the holy institutions of the creator and redeemer.

## The Basic Hermeneutical Conflict

The disagreement in evaluating the conformity of women's ordination to Scripture and tradition reveals two contrary approaches to Scripture and tradition. It lies, therefore, in the area of hermeneutics.

On the one hand, we have the concept of a tradition-historical process that in its normativity by no means reached its end with the formation of the canon, but, at least in this question, reaches its end—its authoritative and irreversible conclusion—first when women's ordination is introduced. Beyond the "center of the gospel," Scripture offers any number of time-conditioned formations of tradition.[70] This view leads to the observed ongoing change in subject when it comes to perceiving the biblical contents. The evolution of the office is a human conceptualization, not the command and effect of Christ or his Spirit. The "center of the gospel," for its part, gives liberty to the church today to find contemporary solutions to questions of the church's life. This is by no means about material ("dogmatic") recognizability or even identity with earlier stages of the process. Rather, it is enough to make one's own transformations plausible as *effects of the gospel*. This effect consists, above all, in adapting the external forms and signs of the church's life to today's times.

In back of the approach is a binary and, respectively, dualistic understanding of reality. The gospel comes close to an ultimately trans-historical idea that can be separated from its canonically attested historical forms. Since, however, the historicity is a constitutive factor for the gospel of Christ,

---

in the History of the Church: Learned and Holy, but not Pastors," in: *Recovering Biblical Manhood and Womanhood: A Response to Evangelical Feminism*, ed. John Piper Wayne Grudem (Wheaton, IL: Crossway, 1991), 274: "Against the Gnostic, to maintain a distinction of male and female function was to confess a creation theology that respected the concrete, fleshly differences between man and woman."

69 Cf. Armin Wenz, *Das Wort Gottes, Gericht und Rettung: Untersuchungen zur Autorität der Heiligen Schrift in Bekenntnis und Lehre der Kirche* (Göttingen: Vandenhoeck and Ruprecht, 1996), 15–85.

70 Cf. on this idea of the "center of the gospel" as "an organizing principle in the plurality of theological conceptions that can be discerned in the tradition, especially also in the New Testament," that is at work also in the ecumenical dialogue, the critique in Gottfried Martens, *Die Rechtfertigung des Sünders: Rettungshandeln Gottes oder historisches Interpretament?* (Göttingen: Vandenhoeck and Ruprecht, 1992), 195. Martens also treats throughout on this topic and on the corresponding "change in subject" when dealing with Scripture.

because divine content (or divine Person) and earthly-historical form cannot be separated anymore by virtue of the incarnation, the explicit criticism of its New Testament forms also affects the gospel itself. The latter becomes, as Regin Prenter rightly writes, "a timeless idea," that runs the risk of losing "its historical foundation."[71]

Yet this has immediate consequences for the doctrine of justification that equally have a major impact on the gospel. For if a "center of the gospel," however that is defined, is isolated from the mandates of Christ and his apostles connected to the gospel, then the work of the Lord is ultimately replaced by the work of the church. The result is the kind of constructivism that is wide-spread in the postmodern philosophy of language. About this constructivism, Hans Ulrich Gumbrecht, a scholar of Romance languages, writes that its adherents live convinced that "man can reshape everything—from 'gender' via 'culture' to 'landscape'—according to his fancy without any further ado, because everything is allegedly 'only a human construct.'"[72] As an aside, this constructivism is not only behind socio-politically dominating "gender mainstreaming,"[73] but also behind the churchly capitulation to the homosexual movement that is connected to the former, no matter how far the effects of this capitulation have developed.

Such a constructivism was combated full force by the Reformation in its struggle against enthusiasm in all its forms. Not surprisingly, the criteria of the confessions for the shaping of the churchly life can by no means be reduced to some abstract gospel or even a "center of the gospel," but explicitly takes up the solemn (holy!) ordinations of God that alone can establish divine right in the church. According to Reformation conviction, the salvation-historically anchored commandments of Jesus and his apostles attested to in New Testament create certainty regarding what is to take place in the church by

---

71  Prenter, *Ordination der Frauen*, 18. He continues on the same page: "There is probably a line from that modern disregard for the historically conditioned external sign of the continuity between the pastoral office and the apostolate to the existence-theological view of the kerygma. . . ." Cf. on this also the elaborations of the philosopher Kurt Hübner, *Glaube und Denken: Dimensionen der Wirklichkeit* (Tübingen: Mohr Siebeck, 2001), 101–102 n. 22: ". . . a recapturing of the presence of Christ at the Last Supper, the officiating priest is his representative. This is why the demand to leave this role of his to women is nonsensical though wide-spread today. As seen, the Catholic Church's retaining of male priests does not have anything to do with misogyny. Such demands are, by the way, only an indicator of once again, as already many times in the history of Christendom, desiring to sacrifice the concreteness of the Eucharist as a matter of flesh and blood to an abstract and pale symbolism."

72  Hans Ulrich Gumbrecht, *Diesseits der Hermeneutik: Die Produktion von Präsenz* (Frankfurt am Main: Surkamp, 2004), 80.

73  Cf. Volker Zastrow, "Politische Geschlechtsumwandlung," *Frankfurter Allgemeine Zeitung*, June 19, 2006, 8.

divine right for the salvation of man and for the edification of the church.[74] This certainly is not some a-historical bondage, but corresponds to perceiving the presence of the triune God who speaks and works through his commandments that are historically handed down in Scripture. "Historical account and commandment," Prenter says, "come together in the gospel as a whole."[75]

What is at stake here is not only the authority of Scripture, which, just like the authority of Luther, is invoked on all sides, but above all its efficacy and sufficiency which by no means can be reduced to its exemplary nature in the time-conforming accommodation of the message. Rather, Scripture is effective and sufficient in that the triune God, in creation as well as in the order of redemption, works what he says by means of the words of institution handed down in Scripture. The conflict is therefore an ontological one. For if God works what he says, then we are dealing with present realities when it comes to the biblical coordination of male and female in the congregation as well as in questions of the office—realities which the living God, by means of his historically attested canonical word, establishes and defines here and now, as Dietzfelbinger put it, "not only 'time-bound,' but central and all the way to the last foundations of human existence."[76] Based on the witness of Scripture and confession, Prenter writes on the office: "It is thus part of the institution of the office . . . that it is not only an institution as the establishment of an institution which then can be administered by the congregation itself, but that it is an ongoing sending so that everybody who enters the office stands under the same divine mandate as the apostle. They thus act as representatives of Christ."[77] If one closes one's eyes to these realities; if one engages in their deconstruction to construct or conceptualize what is new and timely, then one loses the salutary things God speaks and works by his word.[78]

---

74  Cf. Prenter, *Ordination der Frauen*, 8, where he speaks of "commands of order" "which want to guard the right, appropriate handing down of the gospel."

75  Prenter, *Ordination der Frauen*, 9.

76  Dietzfelbinger, *Veränderung und Beständigkeit*, 318. Cf. Brunner, "Hirtenamt und die Frau," 328: "The order that governs the relationship between man and woman has been established by God in the beginning of all things; it did not come about in history but is given with creation. . . . Paul here looks at the account of the creation in Gen. 2." Cf. Brunner, "Hirtenamt und die Frau," 335f.

77  Prenter, *Ordination der Frauen*, 12, taking up Augsburg Confession XXVIII. On focusing this representation on the power of the keys, cf. Prenter, *Ordination der Frauen*, 13.

78  Cf. the nice conclusion by Weinrich, "It Is not Given to Women to Teach," 214–215: "A 'know-nothing' hermeneutic which finds itself satisfied when explicit and particular prohibitions are wanting in Scripture will not be competent to inquire after the inner and organic relation between word and act, between what the incarnate Word did and what the Church must do to be faithful to the Gospel."

# IV. THE ECCLESIOLOGICAL
## AND ESCHATOLOGICAL CONSEQUENCES

A final confirmation for the truth of the assertion that women's ordination is indeed not about a marginal question, but about the foundations of the church, emerges when one perceives the consequences and continuation of the hermeneutical and material-dogmatic conflict on the ecclesiological and eschatological levels. This affects the determination of the doctrinal consensus that constitutes the unity of the church and the determination of the notion of heresy connected to it. This also touches on the last things, which is finally shown in the question regarding the certainty of salvation.

### THE CONFLICT REGARDING *MAGNUS CONSENSUS* AND HERESY

Both parties to the conflict appeal to the *magnus consensus* and want to express their connection to the Lutheran Reformation also in this way. The Theological Commission of the EKD points out that the introduction of women's ordination took place by *magnus consensus*,[79] which is why objections to it cannot be tolerated. In this way, this decision, according to the Commission, even shares in the authority of Scripture and confessions and demands absolute obedience.[80] The *casus confessionis* declared within the church also affects the *ecumene* between churches. "False ecumenical considerations" in this question are harshly rejected by the Theological Commission of the EKD; in fact, precisely "out of ecumenical commitment" "the evangelical church must" teach and practice "that there are no reasons based on Scripture and confessions to exclude . . . women from the ordination to the pastoral office."[81] Dietzfelbinger still held the view that with the "step to women's ordination" the Lutheran church had "left the ecumenical center" "and allowed itself" "to be marginalized."[82]

However, Reinhard Slenczka pointed out that, according to the Reformation view, there can be no majority decisions in questions of Scripture and confessions. The *magnus consensus* formulated in the Lutheran Confession came about by setting forth the teaching that agrees with Scripture and the catholic church and by publicizing it as an offer to all Christians in this church, connected with the invitation to join this consensus. *Magnus consensus* is thus

---

79 Cf. the contrary judgment by Dietzfelbinger, *Veränderung und Beständigkeit*, 319: "That the problem, on which, after all, hinged all the centuries of church history up till now and pretty sizable ecumenical problems, had been solved or led to a consensus—that could not be said by any means."

80 Cf. *Frauenordination und Bischofsamt*, 8.

81 *Frauenordination und Bischofsamt*, 8.

82 Dietzfelbinger, *Veränderung und Beständigkeit*, 319. Cf. for the debate in the SELK the warning by Martens going in the same direction, *Stellungnahme zu Volker Stolle*, 48.

first of all about the proof of the apostolicity and catholicity of one's own doctrine, about the diachronic doctrinal consensus that spans the ages which then sustains and defines the synchronic, contemporary consensus. Thus, the consensus must not refer to the present or the future only, as it is, according to Johannes Wirsching, typical for heretical phenomena.[83] Moreover, it certainly will not do, by disregarding the distinction of the two kingdoms, to place a consensus with society or politics above the consensus with earlier generations of the church.[84] Brunner, applying the two-kingdoms doctrine, writes in all clarity: "An argument, therefore, that thinks it possible to deduce the possibility of placing women into the shepherd's office from their changed position in civil society, has no place in the church. . . ."[85]

One nonetheless can observe a reception of political consensus-finding mechanisms in the church; this holds for the introduction of women's ordination as well as for the debate on the blessing of homosexual partnerships. In the dialogical process, which is charged with quite superstitious salvific expectations,[86] there is first a stepwise change of opinion and finally a majority opinion favoring a "new consensus." However, it is quite interesting that, for example, in the EKD and in the Church of Sweden there is definitely

---

83  Johannes Wirsching, *Kirche und Pseudokirche: Konturen der Häresie* (Göttingen: Vandehoeck and Ruprecht, 1990), 176f.: The heretic "is unable to believe without supplementing the seeming poverty of his faith by additional evidences. . . . This is why the heretic also does not understand his confession of Christ as a witness to the truth of Jesus Christ in communion with the fathers and brethren (horizontal ecumene), but as a program of an elite or avant-garde congregation outdoing the fathers and brethren (vertical or futurist individualization). In this perspective, the heretic does not want to testify to something, but, above all, wants to accomplish something. . . . In all this, heresy proves to be revolutionary, not reforming. The Christian revolutionary always ends up establishing a party (meant to be church), although he wants to remain in the church and preserve it as a pure community of faith, if not even restore it as such."

84  Cf. Stolle, "Neutestamentliche Aspekte zur Frage der Ordination von Frauen," 79: "The church will have to decide the question of women's ordination today because it lives in an age that is on the way to the emancipation of women. I think the church has, based on the New Testament and today's place of man and woman in society, sufficient criteria for such a decision." Cf. on this the critique by Martens, *Stellungnahme zu Volker Stolle*, 43. Furthermore, Stolle, "I Kor 14, 26–40 und die Gottesdienstreform der lutherischen Reformation," 135; Dietzfelbinger, *Veränderung und Beständigkeit*, 317f.: "Yet the stronger emancipation movements became in the whole society, the more unequivocal, because the call of female theologians for the pastoral office and ordination like the men"; see also Sasse, "Ordination of Women?" 402–404.

85  Brunner, "Hirtenamt und die Frau," 334. Martens points out that the Scripture principle is in danger when one introduces "Scripture and society as criteria": "The latter one would then, based on the Lutheran confessions, certainly have to be called a heresy." *Stellungnahme zu Volker Stolle*, 43. Cf. also Th. Junker, "Theologische Aspekte zu den Beiträgen 'Frauen im kirchlichen Amt?'" in *Oberurseler Heft* 28 (1995): passim.

86  Sasse, especially in view of women's ordination, speaks of today as "an age which has a superstitious belief in dialogue as the infallible means of settling everything." "Ordination of Women?" 402.

not a "protection of minorities" that is customary in politics. This observation alone shows that a politicization of the church does not mesh with the gospel entrusted to it. The mingling of the two kingdoms that takes place leads to totalitarian results. The church authorities' radical calls for obedience directed at the opponents of women's ordination—calls which take place in a seemingly pluralistic and tolerant age—speak for themselves. One can certainly observe how there are already harbingers of impending totalitarianism in the phase of appeasement. Where Scripture and confessions become the objects of our de- and re-constructions, a polarization of the church takes place which theologically has to be called a hereticization in the sense formulated by Peter Brunner: "The subscription to the confessions is replaced by the subscription to the opinion of this or that theological school, which now necessarily has to assert itself with the exclusive authority of dogma. Where the authority of Scripture is lost, the *hairesis* of the school replaces the *confessio* of the church."[87] Whoever does not join the formation of schools is caricatured ("hierarchically aloof"), reviled, and met with suspicions;[88] he is declared to be unfit for dialogue or even ideologically blinkered and, respectively, stuck in traditional role-models. The confessional principle *sine vi, sed verbo* (*CA* XXVIII, 21) can evidently be abrogated in both phases, in the phase of appeasement as well as in phase of the final enforcement of the "school." The media are not infrequently instrumentalized,[89] or a seeming contradiction to secular laws is pointed out. The politicization affects even the material discussion. This is seen wherever the relation between man and woman, office and congregation, which is qualified by Scripture and confession as a spiritual-theological reality, is reinterpreted as "role models."[90] Criteria that are appropriate in the societal context but foreign to theology are brought to

---

87 Quoted in Slenczka, *"Magnus Consensus,"* 36.

88 An inquisitorial semantics of "suspicion" permeates especially Stolle's argumentation against those who do not want to share his line of argumentation on the subject, whose material arguments he thus avoids in a psychologizing manner. Cf., e.g., Stolle, "Neutestamentliche Aspekte zur Frage der Ordination von Frauen," 78; on this, see Martens, *Stellungnahme zu Volker Stolle,* 42, and Junker, "Theologische Aspekte zu den Beiträgen," 87.

89 Cf. Slenczka, *"Magnus Consensus,"* 35; Martens, *Stellungnahme zu Volker Stolle,* 47 (on the role television played in the processes of deliberation leading to the introduction of women's ordination in the Lutheran territorial Church of Schaumburg-Lippe and in the Evangelical-Lutheran Church in Baden).

90 Cf., in a particularly striking manner, Stolle writes on Luther's understanding of the office: "Roles are assigned without equivocation. The office bearers are giving; the congregation is to be receptive. And this understanding of the office is now taken into the rule of man over woman as an integral component. The doctrine of the office thus is conceptualized in correspondence to social doctrine." Stolle, "Luther, das 'Amt' und die Frauen," 16.

bear on the contents of Scripture; in fact, these criteria are to define the so-called agenda of the church more and more.[91]

The decisive criterion for defining and delimiting consensus and heresy is ultimately only social damage. Damaging or disturbing the harmonious community must not be tolerated even in cases of conscience and is therefore punished by disciplinary measures. Reinhard Slenczka rightly asks: "What has happened to a church of the reformation when it declares majority decisions of churchly entities as necessary for salvation; when those who contradict based on Scripture are defamed; and when finally consciences bound to God's word are disciplined by coercive means?"[92] It should give pause that the churches acting in this way become more and more like a quasi-papist totalitarian rule—all the way to the claim of infallibility.[93]

## THE CONFLICT REGARDING THE CERTAINTY OF SALVATION

It is all the more remarkable that precisely in this situation the legitimacy of the female pastoral office appears implausible to individuals[94] or churches, so that they return to the original consensus in spite of all resistance and countermeasures. The Reformation consensus, however, knows as highest criterion, not "social damage," but "salvation damage" (Johannes Wirsching). Here one knows that the church does not create its boundaries by itself but discovers them when God's institutions are left behind. Here one at the same time lives out of the promise that it is not we who can sustain the church, who are able to secure it by being accommodating to society and its norms; this work of sustaining and securing is done only by the Lord himself by his word and sacrament. Where it is proclaimed in its truth and purity, one comes together with those who do likewise, no matter how that might look at first on an organizational level. When churches allow themselves to be led back to Scripture and confessions, as this has taken place in Latvia, then this is a reason for joy, just as when the brothers and sisters excluded from the Church of Sweden gather in the "Mission Province." Both events are con-

---

91  Cf. Slenczka, "*Magnus Consensus*," 33: "However, to the extent that these bodies follow parliamentary precedent, consensus will become the goal that determines everything for the preservation of cohesion in the ecclesiastical polity, as well as for the pushing through of certain resolutions. Given this presupposition, it is not surprising that the spectrum of public opinion and political directions is reflected in the ecclesiastical bodies as far as the selection of topics as well as the respective attitudes is concerned."

92  Slenczka, "Ist die Kritik an der Frauenordination eine kirchentrennende Irrlehre?" 202f.

93  Cf. Slenczka, "Ist die Kritik an der Frauenordination eine kirchentrennende Irrlehre?" 205.

94  Cf. Martti Vaahtoranta, "Dies Geheimnis ist groß—der Sinn von 'des Herrn Gebot' (1. Kor. 14, 37): Einige sehr persönliche Überlegungen," *Lutherische Beiträge* 10 (2005): 35–42; and Ulla Hindbeck, "Women and the Ministry," *Logia* 9, no. 1 (2000): 21–22.

crete examples of the fact that, as Slenczka writes, also after the introduction of women's ordination, "the unchanging word of Holy Scripture continues to exercise its disquieting influence on consciences; even ecclesiastical decisions can never cancel its effect."[95]

Comparing the discussions regarding the question of certainty in the two phases of the conflict described initially leads to a highly critical point and offers an ultimate proof for the deeply *eschatological* character of the conflict. While during the appeasement phase the rejection of women's ordination based on the argument of a lacking certainty of salvation in the case of the exercise of the pastoral office by women is caricatured or even psychologized and ridiculed by pointing to a dependence on role models,[96] exactly this argument reappears in the arsenal of arguments and disciplinary measures of its defenders after the introduction of women's ordination. Thus it says in a report by the former bishop of the Lutheran Church in Hanover, Horst Hirschler, quoted by Slenczka:

> When one talks about contesting the right of the ordination of women, then a different level has been reached. This is no longer on the table in our church. Whoever has been called into the ministry of proclamation in our church does not have the right to question women's ordination. Why? Because on it hinges the question of certainty of salvation for the members of the congregation. When the ordination of women is not seen before God as an appropriate action of the church, when it is controversial, then congregants can no longer be certain that the worship service they celebrate under the leadership of their female pastor is the place of the promised presence of God. They cannot be certain that God's word is spoken to them in the proclamation; that communion is truly the Lord's Supper; that the forgiveness promised to them by the female pastor is God's forgiveness. Whoever participates in the worship service must be able to be certain that here one speaks and acts commissioned by God.[97]

In this clear statement, which is consistent in itself, are fulfilled the admonishing and warning prophecies of those who already in the first phase of the conflict knew that women's ordination in the realm of the Lutheran church

---

95  Slenczka, "*Magnus Consensus,*" 35.

96  Cf. on this Stolle, *Frauen im kirchlichen Amt?* passim, and the pertinent critical remarks by Martens: (*Stellungnahme*, 28): "Here too, the question of certainty, conscience being bound to the word of God, is only dealt with by way of caricature; not the side that changes the early church's practice, but that which retains it, is suddenly under pressure to justify itself for 'elevating' something 'as a criterion.' In this way, the problem is fully turned upside-down." *Stellungnahme zu Volker Stolle*, 28; cf. also 11f., 50f.).

97  Slenczka, "Ist die Kritik an der Frauenordination eine kirchentrennende Irrlehre?" 208 n. 16.

must lead to a division of the church.[98] This insight that last things are nonetheless at stake, in fact, salvation itself, forces a decision.[99] The theological process of clarification that can be observed on both sides has led to a deepening of the difference between paradigm shifts that go further and further and a broad and renewed reassurance concerning the traditional doctrinal consensus of the church. The claims made during the phase of appeasement—that by introducing women's ordination the gospel is not affected and church fellowship is not at stake—must, in light of the most recent developments, be considered refuted. It is thus not surprising that we now are in the process of entering a third phase of the conflict that is characterized by increasingly harsh disciplining on a church-official level and by the kind of church-historical revisions we observed in Appold and Stolle which flank these measures, confirming them either in a supplementary or advance way.

Our overview has also shown, however, that it is by no means surprising that the argument over women's ordination is still ongoing. It is grounded in the acting of the triune God in creation and redemption. We therefore affirm with Rudolf Eles:

> Office and congregation cannot be disconnected from God's designs for creation and redemption. As far as their substance is concerned, they will never be emancipated under the law of different societal concretions alien to faith which change more slowly here, more rapidly there. Only males can be called into the office that represents Christ; and the congregation, that understands itself as bride and wishes to hear the voice of the Bridegroom, resists the dissolution of this earthly symbol of its relationship to Christ."[100]

---

98 Cf. Martens, *Stellungnahme zu Volker Stolle*, 12f.: "The anathema pronounced by the Commission for Theology makes clear that a coexistence of opponents and proponents of women's ordination in a church that has introduced women's ordination is, in principle, impossible."

99 Sasse, "Ordination of Women?" 410 (my translation): "All these considerations on the basis of the clear words of Scripture make it impossible for the Lutheran Church to recognize women's ordination as valid and permissible. For this church does not cling to human traditions, but conscientiously abides by Holy Scripture as the word of God. . . . We also cannot have fellowship with pastors and bishops who carry out such ordinations that are against God's word."

100 Eles, *Martin Luther und das Frauenpfarramt*, 30.

# GIVER TO RECEIVER

## GOD'S DESIGN FOR THE SEXES

## ADRIANE DORR

*I would make a better pastor than him.*

I was sitting in a church history class as a master of arts student at Concordia Theological Seminary, Fort Wayne, Indiana, and the professor was in the process of returning graded final exams. Glancing slyly sideways, I noticed that my classmate, a second-year master of divinity student, had received a big, fat, red C-. On the other hand, I was reveling arrogantly in a sparkling, hard-earned A.

The thought seemed natural. I was clearly a better student than him, more qualified, more intelligent, better able to retain theological and historical information, and obviously a more gifted writer. An objective test had proven that. So if I was all those things, and he wasn't, wouldn't it be natural that I would make the better pastor?

Although this conclusion may seem logical to the secular culture, it stands in direct opposition to Christ and to His Word, to what He created men and women to do and to be, and to the plan for which God formed the relationships between His children, both men and women.

## EXPLAINING THE PASSAGE AWAY

"We have heard of foolish people who ordained women to the ministry," wrote Martin Sommer in 1941, "but we have never heard of any church-body where this is common practice. It is generally considered something eccentric, a thing of which the celebrated Samuel Johnson said that it was just as rare to hear of a woman preaching as it was to hear of a dog walking on his hind legs."[1]

How much—and yet how very little—has changed in the past seventy years with regard to St. Paul's words in 1 Corinthians 14: "The women should keep silent in the churches. For they are not permitted to speak, but should be in submission, as the Law also says. If there is anything they desire to learn, let them ask their husbands at home. For it is shameful for a woman to speak in church."

While it may seem as though so-called progressive women are increasingly vocal concerning the issue of women's ordination, it is just as likely that a fair amount of women throughout eras and dynasties, kingdoms and empires have never been completely enamored of this verse. It makes women indignant, men nervous, and pastors uncomfortable. Perhaps that is because, in the past, Christian denominations have misused this passage to dominate and suppress women. Others have simply tried to explain it away. Even within the Lutheran Church, women have tried to rationalize it, claiming females cannot be pastors because they are too special or delicate or unique to be doing that kind of work.

Some of this confusion can be chalked up to lack of catechesis, some to an increasingly feminized culture unused to taking "no" for an answer. But the underlying premise—whether born out of pride or perplexity—is an expectation of something more, an action, a completion, an inner fulfillment, even a sense of equality.

To be sure, some women desire to be the same as men. They want the same jobs, the same pay, the same voice, the same abilities. They want to be heard, understood, and listened to. They want to be equals. Others have more virtuous inclinations. They want to fill voids in the church, compensate for her where she lacks, and give of their gifts as they are needed. They want to be useful, and they desire to serve.

Both lines of reasoning, however, are rooted in unbelief. Women who wish to take on any portion—however small—of the pastoral office, no matter their reason, are confessing that 1 Corinthians 14 does not mean what it says, that the Lord's words are not His own, that He does not actually expect people to do as He has commanded, that there will be no consequences for actions in direct violation of His Word. That same unbelief is at the heart of every sin. It is the cause of every broken commandment, Adam and Eve's fall, each person's failings. It is the cause of the brokenness of the church and the world, and its only antidote is repentance and Christ's forgiveness.

---

1    Martin S. Sommer, "The Place of Women," *The Lutheran Witness* (November 1941): 384.

All of this leaves one wondering if there is an answer, a solution, to a proper understanding of what it means to be male and female both within the Church and in the secular environment. How ought Lutheran men and women live in relationship to each other? What is the true constitution of the male in an ecclesiastical relationship? What does it mean to be female? Does it even matter?

## INCARNATION AS EXAMPLE

The relationship of man to woman flows naturally from a discussion of what actually makes men men and women women. Irving Berlin's "Anything You Can Do, I Can Do Better" sums up the culture's view of the association between the two, contending that a woman is just as good as a man . . . even better. But what of the Church? While the world and even certain denominations within the Church militant contend there are no underlying differences between the sexes, there is one fact that cannot be ignored: our Lord became incarnate as a male. The incarnation, then, is the consummate example of what it means to be a male. Looking to Jesus and His person and work reveals the implications of a God who specifically chose maleness as the way in which He would reveal Himself.

Making a list of Christ's qualities bears witness to who He is as a man. Lutherans put justification, Christ's atonement for the sins of the world, at the top of that list. As a male, then, He was humbled by taking on Himself "the iniquity of us all" (Isa. 53:6). As a male, He sacrificed His life so that others might live. As a male, He became responsible for the sins of the whole world. As a male, He advocates for sinners before the Father and reconciles them. As a male, He sits at His Father's right hand and acts on His behalf. As a male, He has overcome sin, put death to death, and unseated Satan and his angels. As a male, He instructed those around Him: teaching, preaching, and baptizing. He gave them His Word, His truth. As a male, He has made clear the profound Word of God and opened to His children a vault of heavenly words and churchly language. As a male, He gives the faithful His Sacraments. He offers up His male body, flesh and blood, to eat and drink. He gives pardon and peace, strength and preservation until the Christian is brought to rest and eternal life.

In and by each of these actions, Christ remains in a continual posture of giving. He gives of Himself, gives His forgiveness, gives His Father's gifts of mercy and grace, and finally gives His own life. As a male, He is categorized by what He gives, what He does, how He acts. And each of those acts—those gifts—are holy, pious, perfect.

Christ gives all of this for the benefit, the protection, and the strengthening of those who receive. His gifts defend Christians against the devil, help them resist temptations, and allow them to stare death unflinchingly in the eye. In these gifts Christ offers comfort and consolation, shows compassion to the suffering, and comes alongside a world broken by sin.

Those things that make Christ who He is—and who He is uniquely as a male, as a giver—are necessary for the perpetuation and vitality of the Church. They give it form and shape, provide order in the midst of a world in chaos, and protect it from attacks that would seek to harm and destroy it.

## Man as Giver, Woman as Receiver

With Christ's maleness as its model, the Church looks to other examples of the proper relationship between male and female, most obviously in the very order of creation God established in the Garden of Eden and in Adam's reflection of Christ's maleness.

Adam gives to Eve: his rib, his affection, his completeness. He gives protection, a home, love, contentment. He shares his actual, tangible paradise with her, and together they walk with the God who created it. Adam provides Eve with food, with companionship, with no need to feel or be ashamed, even with a name: "Woman, because she was taken out of Man" (Gen. 2:23).

Eve receives, and she rejoices. Her femaleness reacts in kind to Adam's maleness. She responds by collecting all that he has to offer, and all that he offers is exactly what she needs. He fulfills her desires, meets all her demands, leaves her wanting nothing. He truly does complete her. Her response is pure and chaste love, utter unselfishness, resplendent joy.

Thus the relationship of giver to receiver begins to pattern itself, flowing naturally to the relationship of husband to wife. Like Adam, the generations of men who followed him are in the business of giving. Husbands protect their wives, offer them guidance, ensure that they have sustenance and warmth, and see that they are about the things of God and in His house.

But with the entrance of sin into the world, things that Adam did not need to give to Eve must now be given by men. Now they must offer their fidelity, faithfulness, truthfulness, and their word. Even the perpetuation of their lineage and design of their bodies manifest their creation as giver.

Like Eve, wives receive, and they rejoice in what they have been given. They submit in an anxious desire to embrace that which their husbands have sacrificed to give them. But this "subjection [is] not compelled through a demand or by force." Instead, it is a reaction, a response, to their husband's maleness, an "insight into God's order of things."[2]

To submit to her husband means that a wife responds in faith, trusting that what her husband has given her is good and true, that he means what he

---

2   Bo Giertz, "Twenty-Three Theses on The Holy Scriptures, The Woman, and the Office of the Holy Ministry," *The Springfielder* (May 1970): 17.

says when he says it, and that his gifts are those which are best and right for her. Indeed, "as the husband cannot attain to the ideal of Christ's love without self-denial, so the wife cannot conform to the ideal of the Church's love to Christ without surrender of self to Christ's precious will."[3] Thus she submits, not as one who no longer has a voice or an opinion, but as one who is open to receiving all of the best of what her husband has to give. She "learn[s] quietly with all submissiveness" (1 Tim. 2:11). That is to say, her response is one of humble gratefulness, modesty, self-control.

And so it is with the relationship of Christ to His Church on earth. "In all ages, God remains the gracious Giver, while we [the church] always remain the recipients. God is always the eternal Initiator. We receive the gifts He chooses to bestow."[4] That is to say, the Lord gives: His body and blood, His Word, eternal life, access to the Father, forgiveness, peace. And the Church— the woman—receives, and she rejoices. She is the faithful, the redeemed, those who live in and by Christ's death on the cross, His ultimate and best gift. The Church is humble and not proud. She does not demand the spotlight, nor does she look for recognition. She is "willing to receive His self-deny- ing service, even to the point of death, and then in turn being appropriately responsible to the one who has graciously taken the responsibility for [her] protection and fulfillment."[5] Just as a wife does not make outrageous demands of her husband, so the Church does not attempt to bully Christ into getting what she wants. "The Church is obedient to the call of Christ's solicitous love while enjoying the liberty with which Christ made it free. . . . It does not want to rule Christ but wants to be ruled by Him, while expressing in prayer its desires and resting to be heard."[6]

Thus what began with Christ's maleness in His incarnation, was evidenced in the first man and woman ever created, has been perpetuated through the vocation of marriage, and functions as the relationship between Christ's undershepherds and His Church on earth is the very same relationship of men to women within the Divine Service. As Christ the man gave, as Adam gave, as husbands throughout time gave, so, too, the male as pastor gives. What God gives to men in the Office of the Holy Ministry—His Word and promise— those pastors in turn give to women: God's Word, God's Sacrament, God's forgiveness. And as Eve did, as wives do, as the Church does, so the believing woman in the pew responds: she receives, and she rejoices.

3    G. H. Smukal, "Love and Obedience," *The Lutheran Witness* (September 1940): 306.

4    Dean Bell, "With Angels and Archangels: Some Thoughts on Real-Time Worship," *Logia* (Epiphany 2002): 43.

5    Kevin Huss, "The Scriptural Relation of Man and Woman; Headship: An Element of the Divine Image," unpublished, 7.

6    Smukal, "Love and Obedience," 306.

The order of creation—that is, the relationship of giver to receiver—finds its basis in Scripture and in Christ Himself. It is His order, His design, given by His own Word in creation. If this, then, is how God made men to interact with women—givers to receivers—how He designed them to complement one another, how He intended them to exist in His creation, the Christian can be assured that the relationship between the two is holy, pious, perfect.

## A Rallying Call for Men

If the men are to give and the women are to receive, if 1 Corinthians 14 is nothing more than a reminder of the way in which men and women were created and the unique paradigm into which they fall, why all the fuss? One option stands out as the most viable: that it is not the women Paul is calling to account in 1 Corinthians but the men.

Consider the account of the fall in Genesis 3. The devil targets Eve to test her knowledge of the command that God gave to Adam: "You may surely eat of every tree of the garden, but of the tree of the knowledge of good and evil you shall not eat, for in the day that you eat of it you shall surely die" (Gen. 2:16–17). Eve likely learned this commandment from Adam (Gen. 3:2–3) and was able to recite it to the devil. It was Adam's job—as male, as husband, as giver—to share that command with Eve, to provide her with what she could not have known on her own, to give her what she needed to protect herself from the attacks of the devil. It was his duty to give her Christ's gifts, indeed, to be Christ for her. Eve had no one but Adam for this. She needed what he had to give. Her life depended on it, and up to this point, things had seemed to go well.

That is why the devil next tempts her with a wholly pious sounding gift. That is why Eve is caught so unaware. She is drawn in because the devil has something to give her: the promise of knowledge on par with God. And in her emerging self-made piety (cf. Col. 2:23), Eve responds in the way that agrees with how she was created: ever ready to receive.

In that moment, Adam fails his wife. He does not give her what he promised: his protection, his paradise, an unadulterated and pure relationship with God. Instead, Adam stands by silently (Gen. 3:6) and leaves Eve to experience "the height of folly . . . to crave that which the Lord has not given her."[7] That is why, when He walks in the garden in the cool of the day, "God called to the man" (Gen. 3:9). It is Adam to whom God poses the question: "Have you eaten of the tree of which I commanded you not to eat?" (Gen. 3:11). It is Adam of whom God demands an answer: "Who told you that you were naked?" (Gen. 3:11). It is Adam who has disobeyed. It is Adam who has fallen

---

7  Sommer, "Place of Women," 384.

down on the job. It is Adam who is ultimately held responsible. Adam. The man. The giver.

Although Eve sinned first, "it is Adam who is confronted by God as having ultimate responsibility for the fatal rebellion" against Him.[8] Adam refused to do what his maleness required, and Eve's femaleness suffered the consequences.

In view of this, the answer to the questions of what women can and cannot do in the Church is answered best by what men should and ought to be doing. First Corinthians 14 is not, in fact, a condemnation of women but instead a reminder for the men of the Church to return to the task for which they were created: giving the good gifts of God to women eager to receive them. First Corinthians 14 is a blunt and formidable rallying cry for pastors, a not-so-subtle reminder that *they* are the ones who are to be teaching, preaching, and baptizing, "receiving, preserving, and passing along the [church's] doctrine."[9] First Corinthians 14 does not, as the world claims, mean Christ is unfriendly to women, that He created them as inferior beings, that they are not smart enough, wise enough, pious enough to be pastors. It means simply that God created men and women for a specific order and that order is meant for the benefit and well-being of each sex. The men, following Christ's lead, are there to give only the best to women, and the women, in turn, are there to receive the gifts with grateful and humble joy.

## RELEARNING THE SUBSTANCE OF THE SEXES

Understanding what is at the core of men and women in this way creates even more questions. How do the men, specifically pastors, reclaim this? How do women relearn what it means to be women? And where does this leave them in terms of involvement in the Church?

Any desire to return to scriptural and confessional truths must begin with repentance, and the relief for a wounded, penitent heart is the Gospel. A return to an in-depth study of God's holy Word and time spent earnestly praying the prayers and creeds of the Church are the only ways that men and women can begin to relearn how God uniquely designed the sexes to work.

In a marriage, it is the responsibility of the husband, as giver, to provide his wife with the tools she needs to reclaim the femaleness for which she was created. He can do this by recommitting himself to giving her what he has promised to give in his vows of holy matrimony. He must learn again to cherish her, nourish her, love her, and give himself up in every way for her. He

---

8    Huss, "Scriptural Relation of Man and Woman," 6.

9    David P. Scaer, "The Office of the Pastor and the Problem of Ordination of Women Pastors," *The Springfielder* (April 1974): 132.

must love her—selflessly, wholly—honor her, tend to her needs, and be faithful to her, even in the midst of a world tempting him to do otherwise.

The wife is complementary to her husband. She is receptive in every way. She takes him at his word when he tells her he loves her, lets him carry her groceries into the house, and thanks him when he shovels the driveway so that she can get the kids to school. In short, she receives what her husband has to give. She is utterly selfless in her own right. She does not fuss or scoff at his attempts to be her husband, and she does not think "herself as too exalted or too unworthy to receive his Christ-like ministry to her."[10]

## Reclaiming an Understanding within the Church

Within the Church, faithful and orthodox pastors continue to do what they do best: give. They give their parishioners God's Word, a Word that causes change and brings divine understanding to fruition. They catechize, instruct, explain. They dive into that same Word over and over again, wading in the shallow end with those who struggle or have only begun to understand, and fighting to keep their heads above water in the deep end with those who have a profound and unquenchable thirst to know the God of unfathomable love and mercy.

Faithful pastors preach. They remind the faithful that the Word given them means what it says, that it does what it promises, that it is alive and tangible and real and fleshly. They look into the eyes and souls of the parishioners even as they look into their own souls and preach the heartbreaking, immovable Law. They cut down sinners with a word, leaving them defenseless, naked, and petrified before the almighty Judge. Then with the next breath, pastors proclaim God's sweet, healing forgiveness that offers reprieve from fears, relief from guilt, and comfort from anguish. They speak Christ into the ears and hearts of a sinful people, repeating God's promise of His infinite love, mercy, and grace. They make known the Gospel, covering wounds cut deeply by sin, death, and the devil. They stand in Christ's stead and speak Christ's forgiveness, and they refuse to stop. They are Christ, in that time and in that place, to every sleeping infant, bored teenager, exhausted parent, and worried grandparent. They are Christ: real, not nebulous; tangible, not indefinable.

Faithful pastors administer the Sacraments. They give Christ's ceaseless, life-altering gifts of His male body and blood. They place the flesh of the Lord on the tongues and taste buds of their congregants, and they pour the blood of the Lord over the teeth of their parishioners.

---

10  Huss, "Scriptural Relation of Man and Woman," 7.

Faithful pastors bear the burden of the office, carrying the weight of those life-giving gifts to those who must have them to survive. Again and again, they give what the faithful must have and that for which they yearn.

Faithful pastors pray. They beg constantly that the Lord would protect their flock from false doctrine, from an arrogant desire for what the Lord has not given, for a proper understanding of the places in which God has put them. They pray for the faithful by name, for their protection, that by suffering their faith would be stretched and would grow.

Faithful pastors lead. They do not fear the consequences, the assaults of the devil, what the world might say. They answer the questions, calm the fears, guide the uncertain. They are bold, heeding the words of Peter: "Shepherd the flock of God that is among you, exercising oversight, not under compulsion, but willingly, as God would have you" (1 Pet. 5:2).

Women, for their part, are not without their own struggles. Taking on a receptive posture can be a difficult transition for women unused to thinking in such a way. Receiving can only be an outgrowth of repentance, prayer, humility, selflessness, and regular reception of the Sacraments. Ultimately, it means being and raising women and girls who have ears to hear and who take men—pastors—at their word. It means encouraging the men of the Church to be strong, Gideon-esque contenders for the faith. It means living in a quiet confidence in Christ and His gifts. It means learning to receive.

## MOVING FORWARD

Understanding male to female relationships under this ecclesiastical umbrella does not mean that women cease to be effective in the Church, that they sink into the background, meek wallflowers who must be content only to watch as the men move forward. In fact, women have just as long and rich a history in the Church as men. Indeed, "it was the mothers and wives of our Saxon forefathers who played such a large part in the founding of our Lutheran Church in this country," writes a Lutheran observer. "Let women stop exhorting and influencing their children to pray, to go to Sunday-school, to confirmation, Walther League, to church, urging their husbands to subscribe for a church paper, to attend the congregational meetings—and we could close our church doors tomorrow."[11]

At first blush, none of these pious and holy works seem as enticing as being a pastor or some other important position within the Church. But just as the Church needs Lutheran pastors, so also it needs Lutheran mothers, sisters, aunts, grandmothers, daughters—Lutheran females. It needs these women to be in the Word of God and to pray: for their pastors, for their husbands and

---

11   A. P. H. K., "Letter to the Editor," *The Lutheran Witness* (July 1940): 265.

sons and fathers, for the Church itself. The Lord promises to receive sinners, and so He hears the prayer of every faithful woman who names her request or confesses her sins before Him. Prayer returns each woman to a posture of reception: receiving the mercies the Lord has to give as His answer.

The Church also needs these women, by God's grace, to model repentance and piety, to show eager and real sorrow over their sins, and to desire true forgiveness where they have erred. That, in turn, brings about a life lived in forgiveness shown to others who have sinned against them, no matter the sin or the sinner.

The Church needs women to support their husbands and fathers, which means that they pray for them, comfort them, support them, and care for them. It means that they remind the men of their rightful place when they are tempted to give up, be lazy, worry, and not fulfill their duties. It means women raise strong, Lutheran sons, teaching them from their infancy about who Christ is, what He has done, and how His death on the cross transforms lives for eternity.

The Church needs women who humbly assist their individual congregation's needs. It means they babysit for single mothers, sit next to widows in the pew on Sunday, stop by to visit the sick and the homebound, write notes of encouragement to the suffering, and provide a listening ear to young women seeking to understand matters of the faith. It means they bring treats during Vacation Bible School, thank the organist, fold bulletins, and give children rides home after confirmation class. It means women squelch gossip when they hear it, uplift others in need of encouragement, and lead robust yet chaste lives.

The Church needs women who seek out the company of other faithful women. It means they spend time with women who rejoice in the goodness and faithfulness of the Lord and are humble, faithful, maternal, joyful. It means learning from women who have struggled through life's sorrows and have still proclaimed: "The LORD gave, and the LORD has taken away; blessed be the name of the LORD" (Job 1:21).

Women can serve in specific churchly vocations, as deaconess or Sunday school teacher, organist or choir member. They can serve the church in non-ecclesiastical vocations as well, as mother or aunt, author or cowgirl.

In each of these ways—whether through repentance and prayer or service to their churches, families, and neighbors—women receive. The burden of baptizing, teaching, and preaching is not theirs to bear. It is the male's, the pastor's, the one giving through water, Word, and Sacrament on Christ's behalf. Their strength, their femaleness, is instead found "in quietness and in trust" (Isa. 30:15).

There is, ultimately, something quite freeing about understanding Paul's admonition to Christians this way. It removes a weight of frustration and fear as it returns to the natural order, to the way it was originally intended to be, to the position in which God created men and women to exist, to the understanding that the "Bible, far from doing woman injustice, is the emancipator and protector of woman."[12]

The discussion, then, should no longer focus on what women cannot do—the no's—but on how God uniquely designed each sex. In thinking this way, and in making a concerted effort to return to this scriptural, confessional understanding, the Church may find that the men are again eager to step up, to resume their rightful place as leaders, as protectors, as givers, as men being men so that women may be women. Through repentance, prayer, and mutual consolation, God will again renew the men of the Church in who they are and what they are to do, living out Paul's words: "Be watchful, stand firm in the faith, *act like men*, be strong. Let all that you do be done in love" (1 Cor. 16:13–14, *emphasis added*). And the women may find that it is, in fact, quite easy to step aside and actually let the men be men, receiving what they have to offer. In so doing, men may learn again to pay honor to women, "who, after Jesus Christ, [are] God's best gift to men."[13]

God is faithful. He does not leave His children alone to suffer through the issues and implications of the two sexes. He sends faithful pastors and strong laymen to illustrate what it means to be men. He raises up pious, humble women to serve as confident examples of what it means to be women. Yes, He remembers what He has created, and He waits with eagerness for the day when He can gather the faithful to Himself. He longs to restore male and female alike to wholeness, and in that day, He will rejoice as they know, for the first time, the perfection—the completeness—that He intended for their unique identities.

---

12  Sommer, "Place of Women," 384.

13  Sommer, "Place of Women," 384.

# SECTION IV

# THEOLOGY OF MINISTRY

Theology of ministry is dogmatic theology in action. If dogmatics describes the necessary content of the Church's confession and proclamation, then theology of ministry attends to how that confession and proclamation are done in the acts of the Church and her ministers.

Ordination is the liturgical confirmation of the call to the office. It gives sure and certain attestation to the fact that the man put in office is put there by the Lord Himself through the call of the Church. All that would rob tender consciences of the surety of the Gospel as Christ's own word and work must be avoided. When a man is ordained, he is put in office to do what the Lord gives to be done through the office. The same cannot be said of a woman who is ordained, for this is done without the command and promise of Christ. John W. Kleinig takes up the practice of ordination as it relates to the Office of the Ministry and whether women may be placed in this office. Robert Schaibley, pastor of Shepherd of the Springs Lutheran Church, Colorado Springs, Colorado, writes on gender considerations and the pastoral office as the pastor speaks liturgically in the place of Christ.

Lutheran theology of ministry hinges on the proper distinction of Law and Gospel. Is the ordination of women categorically a question of the Law or of the Gospel? William Weinrich rightly observes that there are biblical texts that prohibit women from teaching in the Church. Such prohibitions are, by nature, law (*lex*). Given the entire biblical narrative with its trinitarian framework, what is the Scripture's own logic for a male-only pastorate? Using both the New Testament and patristic writings, Weinrich expounds the difference it makes for the ecclesial and liturgical existence of Christ's holy people.

Deaconess Kimberly Schave applies the doctrine of vocation to the issue of the ordination of women in "Vocational Boundaries," lifting up how women are called by God to serve in the home, church, and world.

The final article in this collection was written by Louis A. Smith shortly before his untimely death. Smith had served as a parish pastor, missionary, and campus pastor in the ELCA. His generation celebrated the inclusion of women in the public ministry of the predecessor bodies of the ELCA. Yet Smith changed his mind, and his article indicates how this change took place. Perhaps there will be more from his church body who follow in his steps.

# Ministry and Ordination

## John W. Kleinig

### Introduction

The Lutheran Church of Australia has been engaged in discussion on whether women may be ordained into the office of the public ministry. This question presupposes that there is agreement on two even more basic theological issues. It assumes that there is such an office or ministry, and that the rite of ordination places a person into that office.

The course of the debate before and after our General Convention in 2000 has shown that we do not all agree on these matters. In fact, we seem to have wider disagreements on the doctrine of ministry than on almost any other issue under discussion. Some of this may be the result of ignorance, as many of our members are not familiar with our traditional teaching on ministry and its biblical foundations. It is also true that some people who know it well are not convinced about our teaching on ministry. This lack of agreement on the doctrine of the public ministry has led to uncertainty, misunderstanding and a sense of frustration. So, for example, the arguments against the ordination of women are largely irrelevant and inconsequential if there is no divinely instituted office of ministry. On the other hand, many of the arguments for the ordination of women lose their force if the office of ministry is disconnected from the priesthood of believers. The time has therefore come for us to stand back a little from the debate and deal with these more fundamental questions first, before we attempt to reach some agreement on how to proceed with the ordination of women.

This paper is a tentative attempt to do just that. I am, of course, presenting my own analysis of the situation from my own perspective. My aim in doing this is to clarify what we are discussing, to ascertain where we agree, and to discover where we differ from each other, and why. It is meant to facilitate clearer communication and to stimulate more productive debate,

debate which avoids false antitheses, simplistic categorisation, and unnecessary polarisation.

# 1. The Meaning of Ministry, Office and Ordination

The debate on the ordination of women has at times been confused by our lack of clear language and by the misunderstanding of certain key terms traditionally used in our church. I shall attempt to define these key terms to avoid miscommunication.

## A. Ministry

The Greek word for this is *diakonia*. These days we tend to use the word ministry rather loosely for any kind of work in the church. It has become a virtual synonym for 'service'. Hence congregations claim that all their members are ministers. But that is not how the word has been used traditionally in our circles and in the church (Scaer). A minister was an authorised assistant, an intermediary, an envoy employed to perform a task for another person, a steward who administers the property of his employer (Collins; Donfried). A minister of Christ is therefore appointed by him to work with him and under his authority; a minister of the gospel administers Christ's gospel; the ministry of word and sacrament is their administration by duly authorised people. The word is therefore used to highlight the authority and responsibility of a person to act on behalf of the person who had appointed him. Thus, when we speak of pastors as ministers of Christ, we imply that he has appointed them as his agents, to speak his word and convey his sacraments to the people of God in the divine service. Other people may, of course, be ministers of Christ with different ministries in the same context or elsewhere.

## B. Office

This rather cumbersome term, which has played such a decisive role in our tradition, is open to misunderstanding. When people hear it used, they think first of a place where business is transacted. It speaks of what we most dislike in business, in government, in education, and wherever we have to deal with officials who care little or nothing for us as people. Nevertheless, it is still a key term for us as Lutherans, for in our tradition it has not been used to depersonalise work but to empower people to serve others.

Unlike most other orthodox churches in Christendom, who tend to speak about the 'order' of ministry with all its connotations of rank and status, we Lutherans have always spoken about the 'office' of ministry (Latin *officium*; German *Amt*). In fact, in his translation of the New Testament Luther chose the word *Amt*, 'office', to translate the Greek word *diakonia*, 'ministry'.

Traditionally, we have understood an office as a position of responsibility in a particular community. Through its leaders a community appoints a person to a position of leadership in it and authorises that person to serve in that position according to certain given terms of reference. An office is therefore a recognised position of leadership. Theologically speaking, we distinguish the offices that God has authorised and established through his word from those which have been created by human beings. Thus we claim that, while the office of the public ministry has been divinely instituted, the office of the papacy has been established by the church without explicit authorisation by Christ in the New Testament.

An office is therefore a position of delegated authority with set duties and clear accountability. It empowers a person for a task and yet at the same time limits the power of the person. It gives a person freedom to act within certain fixed parameters. It situates leadership within a community, without delivering the leader to disempowerment by that community. A leader who holds an office in a community is therefore distinguished from other people who may influence a community by virtue of their status, gifts, wealth, celebrity or knowledge, for that person has been authorised to act on behalf of it.

Thus the office of the public ministry is the position of leadership in the church under Christ as the head of the church. Those who serve in that office receive their position with its responsibilities and their authority from Christ through the church to lead the church. Their power does not derive from themselves and their abilities but from Christ and his word. They are therefore always dependent on him and ultimately accountable to him.

## C. ORDINATION

People argue that the New Testament does not speak of ordination. That is true if we turn to the modern translations of the New Testament, because none of them uses the verb 'ordain' or the noun 'ordination' as a technical ritual term. Instead, they speak about 'the laying on of hands' (1 Tim 4:14; 5:22; 2 Tim 1:6). But it is not true if we turn to the King James Version, where it is used quite deliberately and technically in Acts 14:23 and Titus 1:5. The English verb 'ordain' comes from a rather nondescript Latin word which means 'to appoint' a person to do a task. This Latin word was used in the early church to translate the Greek verb *cheirotonein*, "to stretch out a hand". This word was used in the Greek city states for the election of a person communally in a public assembly by the raising of hands or by ballot. That may be the sense of the word in 2 Corinthians 8:19. But in Acts 14:23 it refers to the choice of presbyters by Paul and Barnabas, rather than by the congregations that they served. From its use in Acts 14:23 this rather general word became a technical ritual term in the early church, as is shown by the textual addition to Titus 1:9, the subscriptions to 2 Timothy and Titus, and its use in

Didache 15:1 for the choice of bishops and deacons. It seems that the early church deliberately chose this secular term because it had no pagan religious connotations.

Even though the term ordination had by the time of the Reformation acquired hierarchical connotations of order, rank and status, it was not rejected by the Reformers but was used in two ways. On the one hand, it was used rather generally for the whole process of making a person a pastor, from the initial self-presentation for service to the installation in a congregation. On the other hand, it was also used more narrowly for the liturgical act by which candidates were received, appointed and commissioned as pastors. That is how the term is used in our confessions, and that is how it is used in this paper.

## 2. The Biblical Foundations for the Office of Ministry

The Augsburg Confession claims that God himself has instituted the office of ministry (AC 5,1). This statement has foundational significance for us. It means first and foremost that the Holy Scriptures record how Christ has established this ministry by his word. That word provides the divine mandate for the ministry of the word; it gives a secure basis for it and its operation. It establishes the office and determines its function. It also bestows the office on those who serve in it and empowers them in their work. So, in his discussion on the divine institution of the pastoral ministry, Thomas Winger claims:

> Just as Lutherans speak of the 'words of institution' for baptism, absolution, and the Lord's Supper, so also it is in keeping with the way of the Confessions to speak of 'words of institution' for the pastoral office. It is in these passages that the office receives its mandate and promise. (39)

Christ's mandate gives pastors their task and the authority to perform that task in the church. Hence Melanchthon asserts in the *Treatise on the Power and Primacy of the Pope* that 'the authority of the ministry depends on the Word of God' (Tr 10) and that the ministry of the gospel is not valid because of 'any individual's authority but because of the Word given by Christ' (Tr 26). The German translation adds this explanation of Christ's mandate and its importance for the ministers of the word:

> The person adds nothing to his Word and the office commanded by Christ. No matter who it is who preaches and teaches, if there are hearts that hear and adhere to it, something will happen to them according as they hear and believe because Christ commanded such preaching and demanded that his promises be believed.

The context makes it quite clear that when Melanchthon refers to the Word here, he is speaking about the word that institutes the ministry rather than the word that is preached by the preachers.

Secondly, the words of Christ do not just found the office of preaching; since they are the powerful, Spirit-filled, effectual words of God, they empower the office and those who serve in it so that they do the work of God in and through the office (Kliefoth). For God has created that office, like all offices, to offer and convey his gifts, his blessings, to people through it. Those who serve in it not only serve under the authority of Christ as agents of Christ, but they depend on the power of Christ's word and his Holy Spirit as they serve in it. The power for ministry therefore comes from Christ's word that establish the office and are at work in it, just as the power of baptism comes from the word that institutes it and is used together with the water in it.

Thirdly, Christ's mandate for ministry makes for certainty and confidence and boldness in a pastor. It means that those who serve faithfully according to that mandate can be sure that God is pleased with their work, for 'God is pleased only with services instituted by his Word and done in faith' (AC Ap 27, 70). They can therefore work wholeheartedly and energetically with a good conscience and defy Satan when he accuses them of unworthiness and failure. But that can only be the case if God has indeed instituted the office of the ministry and if pastors operate within their mandate.

As soon as we claim that Christ has instituted the office of ministry, people ask: 'Where, when, and with whom?'. Some Lutherans claim that our teaching on ministry is not derived from any particular passages in the New Testament but is deduced from general theological principles. Others claim that the exalted Christ has instituted the ministry of the word either through the apostles or through prophets in the early church under the guidance of the Holy Spirit. But that is not what the Lutheran Church has traditionally understood by divine institution. When our confessions speak of the divine institution of the public ministry, they speak of its institution by Christ in his earthly ministry. They therefore refer to a number of foundational passages in the New Testament (Winger: 38–40).

Our Confessions appeak to the following five texts:

- John 20:21–23: AC 28, 6–7; Tr 9, 23, 31
- Luke 10:16: AC 281, 22; AC Ap 7/8, 28, 47
- Matthew 16:18,19: Tr 22, 25
- Matthew 28:19,20: Tr 31
- John 21:17: Tr 30

Of these John 20:21–23 is obviously the most significant (Scaer: 407–408). In it the risen Lord Jesus gives the mandate for ministry to the apostles and defines their ministry as the power of the keys. He establishes the office of the keys.

The early Lutheran rites for ordination and subsequent Lutheran rites appeal most commonly to Matthew 28:16–20 and John 20:20–23 as Christ's mandate for the office of ministry in the church. They assume that Jesus addresses the apostles in John 20:20–23, just as he does in Matthew 28:16–20. They also assume that Christ's promise to be with his eleven disciples until the close of the age in Matthew 28:20 implies that they are to pass on their commission to others after them. Sasse echoes them when he claims that:

> this mandate did not cease to exist with the death of the apostles. According to Matthew 28:20, it continues until the end of time and is carried out by the bearers of the ministry in the church as the successors of the apostles and the representatives of the entire church. (1943/4: 33)

Besides these two passages, our rite of ordination and the rite in the *Lutheran Book of Worship* also use 1 Corinthians 11:23–26 as the mandate for the administration of the eucharist by pastors. This passage obviously echoes Luke 22:19,20. Its use is new, for our Lutheran rites have traditionally been wary of this passage because of its abuse by the Roman Catholics as a warrant for the performance of the mass as a sacrifice for the living and the dead.

A fourth passage could also be adduced: Luke 22:24–30. It is regarded by some exegetes as Luke's account of the ordination of the apostles. Christ appoints them to 'reign' with him in his kingdom by 'presiding' with him at his table and judging the twelve tribes of Israel. Art Just has this to say about Luke 22:30:

> This refers . . . to the responsibility of shepherding and oversight in the new Israel, the church. This is the Lukan equivalent to Jesus giving Peter the keys to the kingdom in Matthew (16:9) and his bestowal of the office of the keys upon the disciples in John (20:22–23). (849)

Many modern scholars claim that in these passages Christ does not deal with the apostles as ministers of word and sacrament but only as representatives of the church. They therefore conclude that, even though Christ did institute word and sacrament, he did not institute the *ministry* of word and sacrament. Now it is true that the apostles do indeed represent the whole church. It is also true that Christ does give word and sacrament to the whole church through them. But at the same time the words of Jesus that institute word and sacrament for the apostles also institute the *ministry* of word and sacrament in the church. Melanchthon therefore concludes that

> the church has God's command to appoint preachers and deacons. This is very comforting because we know that God wills to preach and work through men and those chosen by men. Thus it is good that we highly

praise and honour this choice, especially against the devilish Anabaptists who despise and ridicule this choice, together with the preaching office and the physical word. (German AC Ap 13, 12–13)

It is most significant that Christ did not institute the office of the ministry as something that existed by itself. Rather, in instituting this office he at the same time established the church, commissioned the apostles by his Holy Spirit as the ministers of his word in the church, and gave the sacraments as his gifts to the church. This indicates that none of these was ever meant to exist separately or apart from him. We can distinguish each one from the rest, but we must never abstract them from each other. They are all part of the same package.

## 3. BIBLICAL FOUNDATIONS
## FOR THE LITURGICAL RITE OF ORDINATION

There is general agreement that, while Christ appointed and commissioned the apostles as ministers of word and sacrament, he did not appoint and commission presbyters or pastors in the church, unless the commission of the seventy-two in Luke 10:10–20 is meant to establish the office of preachers in the church (Scaer: 409). The apostles did, however, choose men to work with them and appointed them as pastors in the congregations of the early church.

The New Testament has a range of texts that show us how this occurred. These texts have been used in our orders in various ways. They can be divided into four functional categories.

a. Some orders base the rite for the ordination of pastors on Christ's command to his disciples in Matthew 9:38, before he chose the twelve, that they were to ask 'the Lord of the harvest, to send out workers in his harvest field'. Hence the accent on prayer in all Lutheran orders.

b. The second group consists of three prescriptive apostolic texts about the appointment of presbyters. The basic text is Paul's command in Titus 1:5 to Titus, a fellow pastor, to appoint 'elders' in every city as 'bishops' and 'stewards of God', according to the criteria set out in 1:6–9. Luther claims, in one of the drafts for his rite of ordination, that Paul thereby commands us to install priests in the cities (Smith: 105). Melanchthon alludes to this in his addition to AC 14 in the Variata: 'Just as Paul instructed Titus that he should appoint presbyters in the cities'. Luther also interprets Paul's command to Timothy in 2 Timothy 2:2 to entrust the apostolic tradition to those who were qualified to instruct others as an instruction to ordain them (Smith: 105). The third text is 1 Timothy 3:1–7, in which Paul instructs Timothy on the qualifications for bishops in the church. This is replaced in some orders by the parallel text in Titus 1:5–9. Both texts were especially favoured by the reformers because they show that pastors are, in fact, bishops.

c.  The third group of texts describes the act of ordination in its liturgical context. In Acts 14:23 we read that Paul and Barnabas 'ordained' elders in the churches of Lystra, Iconium, and Antioch. They did this by 'committing' them to the Lord with prayer and fasting. This custom is amplified by Paul's reference to the ordination of Timothy in 1 Timothy 3:14 and in 2 Timothy 1:6,7. Timothy was ordained by Paul together with his fellow elders. Together they laid hands on him and prayed for his empowerment by the Holy Spirit, after a prophetic word had been spoken to him. These texts show us the features of the rite of ordination in the apostolic era. But since they merely describe the rite, they were not used in Lutheran orders as readings.

d.  The last set of texts instruct the ordinand and the pastor about the nature of the office and its responsibilities. Thus Acts 20:28–31 was used to assure the ordinands that the Holy Spirit was appointing them as bishops in the church to feed the flock and guard it against false teachers. This was replaced in some orders by 2 Timothy 3:14–4:5, which charges the pastor to teach and preach God's word. Already in Luther's rite, 1 Peter 5:2–4 was used as a charge to the newly ordained pastors about their pastoral duties and their ultimate accountability to Christ as their head-pastor.

## 4. The Difference between the Office of Ministry and the General Priesthood

The *Theses on the Office of the Ministry* rightly assert that the office of the ministry exists only in the church (TA: VI, 3,4). Pastors therefore do not stand over the church or operate apart from the church but are always, in every way, members of the church. They do not therefore cease to belong to the royal priesthood of Christ when they are ordained. The Theses go on to claim that 'the office of the ministry is not identical with the spiritual priesthood of all believers in Christ' (VI, 4). But they do not explain how they differ.

Before we can answer that question, we need to establish the nature of the spiritual priesthood of believers in Christ. As holy priests, all Christians have equal access to the presence of the Triune God. As priests with the privilege of access to God's heavenly presence, they perform two functions. On the one hand, they offer true sacrifices of themselves to God in Christ with their bodies and offerings, their prayers and praises. These are offered both for themselves and other people. They therefore represent the world and the people of the world sacrificially before God in the divine service. On the other hand, they represent God to the people of the world, communally in their corporate witness and personally in their vocation. As holy priests they bring God's love and peace and blessing to those who, unlike them, do not yet have assess by faith to God's gracious presence. The spiritual priesthood therefore straddles heaven and earth. It brings the needs of other people to God, and it brings God's blessings back to them.

There are three complementary ways of distinguishing the ministry of the word from the priesthood of the faithful. The first, which is implied in our *Theses of Agreement* (VI, 4), holds that, even though the keys are given corporately to the whole church and each congregation, Christ exercises the keys publicly in the divine service through those who are ordained ministers of his word. Luther and the reformers therefore always distinguished the *office* of the keys from the keys themselves. According to the Augsburg Confession (AC 28, 5, 21), the office of the keys involves the preaching of law and gospel, absolving and retaining sin, baptising and withholding baptism, granting and withholding Christ's body and blood, judging right doctrine and condemning false doctrine, excluding people from the congregation and readmitting them into communicant fellowship in it. It is exercised most clearly by admitting people to the Lord's table and by excluding them from it. No individual member of the priesthood may perform these tasks in the church without proper authorisation. Likewise, a pastor may not perform these tasks apart from the priesthood and the church.

The second way of distinguishing the ministry of the word from the role of the priesthood is also implied in the *Theses of Agreement*, which assert: 'the spiritual functions of the Apostolate are continued only in the ministry of the Word and Sacraments' (VI, 6). This tantalising reference is all too brief and unqualified. It is, after all, quite obvious that the role of the apostles as eye-witnesses to the risen Lord Jesus is not continued in this ministry. We may, however, infer what is meant from scriptural and confessional passages which are cited in support of it. According to the *Treatise on the Power and Primacy of the Pope* (Tr 10) in its German text, the office of the ministry derives from 'the general call of the apostles'. Here Melanchthon refers to John 20:20, which he had quoted in the previous paragraph. The authority of both apostles and pastors depends on that word of God. Like the apostles, all bishops (and pastors!) are to act corporately and collegially under Christ and together with him (SA II, IV, 9). It is, furthermore, 'a divine tradition and apostolic usage' that bishops (and pastors!) are elected in the presence of neighbouring bishops and ordained by them with the laying on of hands (Tr 13–15). Like the apostles, pastors receive their ministry from the Lord (Col 4:17), even if it is conferred on them by other pastors (Acts 14:23). Like the apostles, pastors are 'leaders' (Heb 13:17) whom Christ has appointed to 'preside' and 'rule' in his church (1 Tim 5:17; FC SD, 10, 10). Together with the apostles, they are 'elders' who exercise oversight over God's flock (1 Peter 5:1). Like the apostles, they are to preach God's word (Acts 6:2,4), teach sound doctrine (1 Tim 3:2; 5:17; Tit 1:9; FC SD, 10) and shepherd God's flock (Acts 20:28). Sasse therefore maintains. 'The preaching of the gospel and the administration of the sacraments is not the activity of the general priesthood but the performance of a mandate given to the apostles and, through them, to the entire church' (1943/44: 33).

The office of ministry may also be distinguished from the priesthood in a third way by virtue of its location in the divine service, for in ministry, as in real estate, location makes all the difference. The Augsburg Confession maintains that pastors have been called to teach God's word and administer the sacraments publicly in the assembly of the saints (AC 14; Strelan: 20). They perform that role in the divine service. So, while pastors are responsible for the 'sacramental' aspects of the divine service, by which the Triune God comes to the faithful and graciously enacts the gospel for them, the priesthood is responsible for the 'sacrificial' aspects of the divine service. Sacrificially, pastors stand together with the congregation before God, even when they lead it in confession, prayer, praise and offering. Sacramentally, they offer and convey the gifts of God from God to the congregation. More correctly, God does this through them as his mouthpiece and his hands. However, outside the church as the liturgical assembly of the saints, at home and in the world, the role of pastors does not differ theologically from the role of the priesthood.

We need to determine how the role of the public ministry differs from the role of the priesthood. It would be good to reach consensus on this matter, because confusion not only clouds the debate on the ordination of women but creates problems for the life and mission of our church. If we can clearly distinguish them from each other, we will be able to promote the maximum involvement of all our members, male and female, in the mission of God and free our pastors to be real spiritual leaders.

## 5. THE FUNCTION OF THE RITE OF ORDINATION

I do not intend to develop a full theology of ordination here but to focus on our tradition of ordination and its theological significance. First we need to clear up two common misunderstandings of our tradition. The first arises from a misreading of what AC 14 means by a call when it asserts: 'Nobody should publicly teach or preach or administer the sacraments in the church without a regular call'. While many modern Lutherans understand the call legally as a letter with an offer of appointment from a congregation or the church, Luther and the reformers understood the call theologically as the whole process by which Christ, through his church, appointed and commissioned candidates as pastors in the church. Luther, in fact, equates the call with 'true consecration and ordination to the office of the ministry' (LW 38: 211). For him the rite of ordination was therefore an important part of the call to be pastor. It enacted the call. In fact, Luther defines ordination as 'calling to and entrusting with the office of the ministry' (LW 38: 197). So, when AC 14 insists that pastors must be 'rightly called' (Latin: *rite vocatus*), it does not refer to their possession of a letter of call from a congregation; it declares that they must be both 'regularly called' by the church and 'ritually called' through the rite of ordination.

The second misunderstanding comes from the assumption that when the *Treatise* maintains that ordination with the laying on of hands was nothing but the confirmation of a pastor's election (Tr 70), and when our *Theses* maintain that ordination ratifies and publicly acknowledges the call of a pastor (TA: VI, 8), ordination is understood legally as a public announcement and official notification without any ritual and theological significance. Our *Theses*, in fact, contradict that interpretation. They argue that ordination is a 'solemn ecclesiastical rite' which performs three important theological functions: the reception of the pastor as a gift from Christ to the church, the declaration of the pastor as a minister of the new covenant, and the invocation and bestowal of the Lord's blessing on the pastor with the laying on of hands.

We Lutherans have historically understood ordination as a liturgical act by which the Triune God calls, empowers and commissions the ordinand as a minister of the gospel (Heubach). John 20:21–23 is a key text in this teaching. It shows that all three persons of the Trinity are involved in this act of ordination. The Father sends the Son, who in turn sends out the eleven disciples as his apostles to forgive and retain sin. The Son breathes on the disciples and empowers them to do the work of the Father by the gift of the Holy Spirit. The disciples, and all ministers of the gospel after them, are therefore commissioned by the Triune God.

This trinitarian understanding of ordination is confirmed by other texts in the New Testament. God the Father 'appoints' pastors as teachers (1 Cor 12:28), 'gives' them the ministry of reconciliation (2 Cor 5:18), 'gives' them the Holy Spirit (1 Tim 4:14; 2 Tim 1:6, 7; cf 2 Cor 3:6), and 'sends' them out to gather in his harvest (Matt 9:38). Through the apostolic tradition the Son hands on the ministry to the pastor who 'receives' it as a gift from him, even as he 'gives' the pastor as a gift to the church (Eph 4:11). So when Paul and Barnabas ordain elders in Acts 14:23, they commit them to the Lord. A pastor is therefore 'a minister of Christ Jesus' (Col 4:12), Christ's ambassador (2 Cor 5:20). The Holy Spirit 'appoints' pastors as bishops in the church to shepherd God's flock (Acts 20:28).

The Triune God does not ordain pastors immediately by calling them, as prophets were called, through the Holy Spirit or some charismatic experience.

Rather God ordains pastors through the church (AC Ap 13, 12; SA III, X, 3; Tr 66,67,69,72; Sasse 1986: 79–81) and its leaders (Tr 62,64,65). Consequently the rite of ordination has always been performed in our church by a pastor together with other representative pastors in a representative congregation as part of the divine service. In fact, the act of ordination has normally been performed by a bishop or regional superintendent, a president or his deputy, since candidates are ordained by the whole church for ministry in the whole church, rather than a single congregation (Sasse 1943/44: 29–30). Ordination is therefore an ecumenical event.

Luther's rite of ordination for the church in Wittenberg quite deliberately involved the congregation in its enactment. The role of the church was highlighted in two ways. On the one hand, the location of the rite was shifted from its medieval location before the reading of the gospel and made part of the offertory after the sermon. There the presentation of the candidates was associated with the offerings of the people and the prayers of the church. On the other hand, at the beginning of the rite the whole congregation was called to pray to God to send out labourers into his harvest and to empower both the candidates and the ministry of all pastors with the Holy Spirit. This prayer was made by the congregation and the choir as both the candidates and pastors knelt together before the altar. Then, when the rite was over, the whole congregation sang 'O Holy Ghost' (*LHS* 118) for all the pastors of the church.

Theologically speaking, the Lutheran rite of ordination consists of three interlocking elements: the proclamation of the word, the laying on of hands with prayer, and the commissioning of the ordained. The scriptural readings, however, are foundational for the whole rite. They not only provide God's mandate for the ministry of the word and for the appointment of people as ministers of the word, but, since these readings are the Spirit-filled, inspired word of God, they actually call, empower and commission candidates for the ministry. What God has ordained in his word is enacted performatively in the rite, for in it God's word is used in ordain, empower and commission the pastor (Kliefoth). Through his word and those who are ministers of his word, Christ appoints and sends out ordained men to be ministers of the word. Through the prayer of ordination and the act of ordination God enacts his mandate for ministry. Through this rite God confers the ministry of the new covenant on the candidates and empowers them to serve in that ministry by the power of the Holy Spirit. Through the charge and the benediction, God sends out the ministers of the word to work in his name and with his word in the church and on his mission to the world. They are therefore ordained by the word of God and prayer.

Luther is quite happy to speak about ordination as an act of consecration. In his rite from 1535 he reminds the ordinands of Paul's statement in 1 Timothy 4:4,5: 'everything created by God is good, and nothing is to be rejected if it is received in thanksgiving; for then it is consecrated by the word of God and prayer'. He then addresses the candidates with these words:

> You are not only good creatures, sanctified by the Word and the sacrament of baptism, but in a second sanctification you have also been called to the holy and divine ministry, so that many others may be sanctified and reconciled to the Lord through your word and deed. (*LW* 53: 124, n. 4; Smith: 103)

Thus, even though he categorically rejected the Catholic understanding of ordination as consecration by a bishop with holy anointing oil, he nevertheless still regarded ordination as an act of consecration by God's holy word and name in proclamation and prayer. The most holy word of God consecrated the pastor for the holy ministry. In that ministry the pastor in turn used the holy things of God to consecrate the holy people of God for their priestly service.

## 6. CONCLUSION

I end with three vital points. The first is that no matter how we regard the public ministry, we run into difficulty if we forget about the real presence of the risen Lord Jesus in the church. The keys to the Father's presence belong to Jesus and Jesus only. He has not handed them over to pope or pastors or the church to be used apart from him and to represent him in his absence. Rather he himself wields the keys publicly in the divine service through the ministers of the word and sacrament, just as he works together with all the faithful in their priestly service of his heavenly Father. The second is that Christ not only commissions pastors with his powerful word at their ordination; he continues to empower them daily in their work as pastors by that same Spirit-giving word. The third is that Luther's emphasis on prayer for the Holy Spirit in the rite of ordination has as its corollary that pastors can only fulfil their ministry by the power of the Holy Spirit and the prayer of the church for their empowerment by the Holy Spirit. Apart from the Holy Spirit neither the pastorate nor the priesthood of the faithful can do the work of God. Like the apostles in Acts 6:4, all pastors are therefore called to 'devote themselves to prayer and the ministry of the word'.

BIBLIOGRAPHY

Collins, J N
1990    *Diakonia: Reinterpreting the Ancient Sources*, Oxford University Press.

Donfried, K P
1992    'Ministry: Rethinking the term *Diakonia*', *CTQ* 56, 1–15.

Heubach, J
1956    *Die Ordination zum Amt der Kirche*, Lutherisches Verlagshaus, Berlin.

Just, A A Jr
1997    *Luke 9:51–24:53*, Concordia, St. Louis.

Kliefoth, T
1854    *Liturgische Abhandlungen* I, Verlag der Stillerischen Hofbuch-handlung, 341–501.

Luther, M
1971    'The Private Mass and the Consecration of Priests' (1533), in M E Lehman ed, *Luther's Works* 38, Fortress, 139–214.

1965    'The Ordination of Ministers of the Word' (1539), in M E Lehman ed, *Luther's Works* 53, Fortress, 122–126.

Sasse, Hermann
1943/44 'Die lutherische Lehre vom geistlichen Amt', unpublished paper.

1986    'Ministry and Congregation', *We Confess the Church*; tr N Nagel, Concordia, St. Louis, 69–83.

Scaer, David P
1992    'Augustana V and the Doctrine of Ministry', *LQ* VI, 403–422.

Smith, R E
1996    *Luther, Ministry and Ordination Rites in the Early Reformation Church*, Peter Lang, Bern.

Strelan, J G
1993    'The Privatisation of the Cultus Publicus', *LTJ* 27/1, 13–22.

Theses of Agreement
1980    'V. Theses on the Office of the Ministry', in *Doctrinal Statements and Theological Opinions*, LCA, Adelaide, A13.

Winger, Thomas M
1998    'The Office of the Holy Ministry According to the New Testament Mandate of Christ', *Logia* 7/2, 37–46.

# Gender Considerations on the Pastoral Office

## In Light of 1 Corinthians 14:33–36 and 1 Timothy 2:8–14

## Robert Schaibley

Johann Konrad Wilhelm Löhe, the Bavarian Lutheran pastor who was instrumental in establishing Concordia Lutheran Theological Seminary at Fort Wayne 144 years ago, gives the following advice to one who would be a wise teacher in the congregation:

> He does not desire to interpret precisely each conjunction and preposition, each noun, each verb, but everywhere there are clear passages which he selects and uses to confirm what the congregation already knows and to present it in a new light. His proclamation is always similar to the Creed, and he always gives his people what they can understand on the basis of the light they have already received, the light from their catechism and the gospels. Not primarily explaining obscurities but confirming and maintaining what is clear—this is his aim and intention.[1]

It is in this spirit of Pastor Löhe that I take up the consideration of a pressing issue for our day, namely the question of whether a church is biblically justified in limiting the pastoral office to males, among the other limitations that it likewise imposes upon those who would be called into the pastoral office. This is, as you know, not a new question. But there is a new and driving intensity to this question, fueled without doubt by social and cultural pressures of our day. The current status of the question in confessional Lutheran churches

---

1   Wilhelm Löhe, *Three Books about the Church*, trans. James L. Schaaf (Philadelphia: Fortress Press, 1969; reprint Fort Wayne: Concordia Theological Seminary Press, 1988).

is that we do limit the pastoral office to males, and we make the claim that this limitation is by biblical mandate.

This claim is under attack today, from many quarters and in many different forms. It is my intention to touch briefly on several of the forms of attack with which we have become familiar in recent times, and then to address more particularly a new approach that has arisen among us.

By way of introduction, it is important to note some patently true but often forgotten facts about our church's current practice of limiting the pastoral office to men. Our practice is not just a matter of some convenient device (notably the two passages in question, 1 Corinthians 14:33–36 and 1 Timothy 2:8–14) that we have used for centuries to limit the ministry of women in the church.[2] Our practice is consistent with that of the historic, orthodox, catholic church throughout her millennia of existence, with the history of the Old Testament people of God, and with the explicit teachings and actions of our Lord Jesus Christ, with regard to what we now call the pastoral office. While it might be argued that the church was in error for millennia, that the Old Testament practices are of no import to our question, and that the actions of our Lord are merely coincidental or culturally conditioned, the starting point yet remains that we who continue to recognize the validity and necessity of limiting the pastoral office to men have not been guilty of perpetrating some new fraud upon the church. Nor can one correctly assert that the question of the appropriateness of the church's practice never before arose until it was examined and corrected in the light of twentieth century discoveries. On the contrary, evidence is abundant that the question of admitting females to the pastoral office has arisen from time to time throughout the life of the church, particularly among heretical groups who advocated and practiced it, such as the Marcosians, the Quintillians, and some groups of gnostic or spiritualistic enthusiasts in the early middle ages. Moreover, such a change in practice was usually urged on the basis of the same biblical evidence often adduced today, namely Galatians 3:28.[3] So the church's historic practice cannot simply be excused and removed by an assertion of premodern-day ignorance.

Nor can one simply write off this two-thousand-year history as a matter of a low view of women. Dr. William Weinrich has shown:

> Nor, it must be said, did the church's faithfulness to the Apostle's prohibition of women in the pastoral office rest upon some notion of the natural inferiority of women to men in either intellect or virtue. One can, of course, find evidence of such thinking. But as common and certainly more

---

2   Richard J. Dinda, "Word Study: 1 Cor. 14:33–35 and 1 Tim. 2:8–12" (unpublished monograph, 1990).

3   William Weinrich, "It is not given to Women to Teach: A Lex in search of a Ratio" (monograph published by *Logia* 1991), p. 3.

true to Biblical models were other much more positive evaluations of the innate gifts and abilities of women. John Chrysostom (4th cent.), often castigated as a misogynist, could write that "in virtue women are often enough the instructors of men: while the latter wander about like jackdaws in dust and smoke, the former soar like eagles into higher spheres."[4]

In our day of the wholesale castigation of everything and anything that can be labelled "western, male, patriarchal, and linear," these words may offer little compelling evidence; however, it remains true that grounds other than male chauvinism stand under the historic practice of the church. I say this because most of the arguments against our current practice at least tacitly accuse the historic church practice regarding limitations on the pastoral office of having been in error all these years, an error we are now perpetuating.

What are some of the typical challenges to the historic practice of the Christian church? First, the earliest arguments, as noted above, appealed to Galatians 3:28: "There is neither Jew nor Greek, there is neither slave nor free, there is neither male nor female; for you are all one in Christ Jesus." This verse is marshalled regularly, also in our day, to argue that no distinction on the basis of gender should exist in the affairs of the church. But then, what about the Pauline passages cited above, which have been cited by the church throughout her history?

Three methods of facing these passages have been proffered over the years. Argument A maintains that these passages are not authentically Pauline, but rather are later additions to the sacred text, and therefore they are not authoritative for us, and women preachers are home free on the basis of Galatians 3:28. Now, there is no evidence, outside of twentieth century prejudice, that the 1 Timothy passage is not Pauline. The 1 Corinthians passage (vs. 33–35) is found in a different place in some ancient manuscripts (namely, after v. 40), leading Semler as early as the eighteenth century to suggest that these verses are not original.[5] Most scholars have found this argument quite unconvincing, leaving us with the conclusion that Argument A, namely, that these verses are not authentic and authoritative for us, is a severely wounded duck.

Argument B approaches the authority issue from a different perspective. Argument B maintains that these statements from Paul are culturally conditioned; that is to say, these arguments are what Paul had to say because of the culture in which he was raised and in which his original readers lived. They applied back then, and if we were today like they were back then in thought, tradition, and upbringing, then they would apply also to us. But, since that was then and this is now, they are not authoritative for us, just as is the case with

---

4    Weinrich, p. 3.

5    Peter Brunner, *The Ministry and The Ministry of Women* (St. Louis: Concordia Publishing House, 1971), p. 22.

the prohibition in Acts against eating blood of animals, and the prohibition in this very book of 1 Corinthians against women praying without the benefit of veils, and so forth.

Well now, what is to be said about Argument B? Those very texts have something to say about Argument B. Paul clearly shows that his appeal is not to some cultural way of thinking, for in 1 Timothy 2:13 he bases his argument on the creation of Adam and Eve: "For Adam was formed first, then Eve";[6] also, in 1 Corinthians Paul refers as the basis of his argument to the "law": "as even the Law says" (14:34), which at the very least refers to Genesis 3:16 as a result of the fall into sin, and more likely refers generally to the Torah and more specifically to the story of creation.[7] Least likely is the suggestion that this is a reference to the fourth commandment.[8] In any case, Paul seems not at all to be modifying his instructions along the lines of cultural bias, so that if his word is authentic at all (and, recalling the fate of Argument A, it is authentic), then it remains applicable to us today, thus dooming Argument B about being culturally conditioned.

This brings us to Argument C. Argument C became the godchild of the ELIM movement in the Missouri Synod in the 1970s, and goes like this: Yes, these texts are authentic (Argument A is wrong); and yes, these texts are authoritative also for us (Argument B is wrong). But these texts are law, and we live now under the gospel! Thus we are free from the law, free from 1 Corinthians 14 and from 1 Timothy 2; and that, according to Argument C, is precisely what Galatians 3:28 means when it says, "there is neither male nor female; for you are all one in Christ Jesus." This position is a clarion example of what became known as "gospel reductionism," which regarded the gospel not only as the center of the Scriptures but also, in the end, as the extent of the Scriptures.[9] Gospel reductionism was rejected by our church, and this particular argument is seldom, if ever, heard any more, even in the former AELC circles of the ELCA.

So Arguments A, B, and C have failed. But the pressure remains, and is, in fact, increasing, to admit women to the pastoral office. Whence this pressure?

---

6   How this is to be understood from an evangelical Lutheran perspective is impressively set forth by George Wollenburg, "The Office of the Holy Ministry and the Ordination of Women" (Monograph published by University Lutheran Chapel, Minneapolis, MN, 1990), pp. 11–14.

7   Wollenburg, p. 22.

8   Dinda, p. 15.

9   Christ is the center and extent of the Scriptures. As Romans 10:4 asserts, "Christ is the end of the law, that everyone who has faith may be justified." Note: Christ, not the gospel, is the end of the law. The law and the gospel remain in paradoxical tension, one with the other; the law is there for the gospel; it is under the gospel; it is temporary to the permanence of the gospel; but it is not the case for Christians that the law no longer applies to us in this life.

The pressure is sociological, cultural, and even political. And in an age when concern is rising that our church be well-regarded in society, that pressure can be unbearable. All that seems to stand between our church and capitulation to this sociological pressure are these two passages, 1 Corinthians 14 and 1 Timothy 2. If there is to be a change in our handling of the pastoral office, one of two things will have to happen: (1) we will have to eliminate the distinctiveness of the pastoral office, so that more and more it is merged into a general and murky collection of churchly functions called "ministries," (and I must say that there are many signs that just such a merging of identities is occurring),[10] but this is beyond the scope of this paper; or (2) some new argument will have to arise that will remove the binding character of these two passages on our treatment of the pastoral office. It is this second option that does fall within the parameters of this paper, and it is the case that a new argument has arisen, which I have chosen to call Argument D, because D stands for what comes after A, B, and C.

Let me tell you about Argument D. Argument D is very subtle, very persuasive, and very dangerous. Argument D masquerades as an innocuous linguistic study, as an unbiased exercise in semantic field analysis, as a scientifically disinterested effort to evaluate the Scriptural passages to which the church has been pointing for nearly two thousand years, as having no axe to grind on the results of the study, and as even seeking to help both sides in the controversy. I should like to maintain that Argument D is none of these things. It is not unbiased; it is not scientifically neutral; it is not even conducted in a methodologically appropriate way in order to answer the basic question it seeks to address.

Argument D is, first and foremost, an exercise in logic. It makes a significant case because it asserts the following syllogism:

*Major premise:*
   To be binding on the church, any doctrinal position in the church must be supported by at least one clear, distinct and unambiguous Bible passage.

*Minor premise:*
   The Bible passages cited in defense of limiting the pastoral office to men (1 Cor 14 and 1 Tim 2) do not clearly, distinctly, and unambiguously support our church's doctrinal stance.

*Conclusion:*
   Therefore, our doctrinal position is not binding on the church.

---

10   The synodical treatment of lay ministries, which include full "pastoral" functions without and apart from regular pastoral calls and accompanying ordinations, may well be a convenient device to introduce the first female-conducted sacramental exercises in the LCMS.

To be fair to Argument D as currently constituted, the conclusion stated above has not been so stated; rather, the conclusion as stated in Argument D, to date, is that *if* we are to continue to maintain our doctrinal position on limiting the pastoral office to males, *then* we shall have to find some other passages that can clearly and unambiguously uphold our position.[11] On the other hand, to be fair to our current position as a matter of church doctrine for some two thousand years, the conclusion that our doctrinal position is not binding on the church is what Argument D finally amounts to, since the idea of having to chase around the Scriptures to find other passages that have somehow eluded the church for two millennia, if we are to continue our present practice, is tantamount to conceding that our position is not binding on the church, that 1 Corinthians 14 and 1 Timothy 2 have, after all these centuries, been successfully removed as impediments to progress, and that the confessional Lutheran churches can let the ordination of women begin. Argument D is very significant and very dangerous indeed.

We begin by considering the logic: if it were the case that to be binding on the church, any doctrinal position in the church must be supported by at least one clear and unambiguous Bible passage; and further, if it were the case that the Bible passages cited in defense of limiting the pastoral office to men (1 Corinthians 14 and 1 Timothy 2) do not clearly and unambiguously support our church's doctrinal stance; is it true that, therefore, our doctrinal position is not binding on the church? The answer, it seems to me, is affirmative. The logic stands; the syllogism is sound; the conclusion flows from the premises. However, it remains to examine the factuality of the premises themselves. And we must start with the major premise.

Is it true that, to be binding on the church, any doctrinal position in the church must be supported by at least one clear, distinct, and unambiguous Bible passage?[12] The answer is, clearly, "No!" It is not the case that to be binding on the church, any doctrinal position in the church must be supported by at least one clear, distinct, and unambiguous passage. Everyone in the church would love it so to be, but that is not the character of *sola scriptura*. *Sola scriptura* embraces us through its historical-grammatical sense, its context, its unity and diversity, and through the *analogia fidei*. It is in this matrix that the perspicuity of Scripture resides. But this does not guarantee at least one "clear, cogent, unambiguous" proof text for every doctrine that Scripture teaches. For example, there is no single clear, cogent, unambiguous prooftext for the *filioque* ("and the Son" in Latin), the doctrine concerning the

---

11 Dinda, p. 2.

12 Dinda, p. 1: "That is, any doctrinal position we take we support with clear and compelling passages of Scripture. Such supporting passages, I repeat, are clear, cogent, unambiguous, and leave us with the certainty that no winds of perverse teaching will shake them."

Holy Spirit that he "proceeds from the Father and the Son." We read in John 15:26 (the passage often cited in our catechisms as a proof text for the *filioque*): "But when the Counselor comes, whom I shall send to you from the Father, even the Spirit of truth, who proceeds from the Father, he will bear witness to me." Is this a proof text for the *filioque*, clear, cogent, and unambiguous? It hardly seems so, for when Jesus says, "I shall send to you from the Father," he is *not* speaking about the eternal procession of the Spirit from the Father and the Son, for if he were, the Son would also be said to be "proceeding" from the Father, since the Father "sends" the Son (John 20:21). No, this is a reference to what happens "in time," specifically to Pentecost and the new relationship of the Holy Spirit to the church which ensues from that point in time. All that we find in John 15:26 about the internal relationship among the persons of the Holy Trinity, "outside of time," is that the Spirit "proceeds from the Father." But where do we get the phrase "and the Son"? Where is the clear, cogent, unambiguous passage that teaches us "and the Son"? The closest thing we have is Galatians 4:6: "Because you are sons, God sent the Spirit of his Son into our hearts. . . ." The phrase "Spirit *of* his Son," which by itself does not clearly, cogently, and unambiguously teach the *filioque*, but when taken together with John 15:26 concerning the Spirit "who proceeds from the Father," grounds the confession of faith to which all of us, as Lutherans, are bound, that the Holy Spirit is distinguished as that person of the Trinity who "proceeds from the Father and the Son." But it cannot be said that the *filioque* or, for that matter, the entire doctrine of the Blessed Holy Trinity is supported by at least one clear and unambiguous Bible passage.

In short, either Argument D's major premise or else the church's doctrine of God has to go. This choice leaves a Christian with no option but to reject the major premise of Argument D, and thus falls to the ground the entire argument; its conclusion does not follow, it is not proved that our doctrinal position is not binding on the church, and we can all go home!

However, that the minor premise might remain true, namely, that 1 Corinthians 14 and 1 Timothy 2 do not clearly and cogently teach what the church has for two thousand years taught, is such a troubling possibility that it demands that we stay around and take a careful look at it. Does Argument D have a point? How does Argument D make the case that these two venerable passages do not provide the necessary support for our doctrinal position?

Argument D, as recently raised among us, asserts on the basis of a word-study analysis that certain terms in both 1 Corinthians 14 and 1 Timothy 2 are vague enough, ambiguous enough, to allow for an interpretation that has nothing to do with the question of women proclaiming God's word or teaching in the worship life of the church, and therefore, it is possible to understand them in a very different light than the one holy, catholic, and apostolic church has heretofore understood them. As recently expressed here in the Texas District, Argument D points to the term λαλεῖν (the infinitive form, "to speak") in 1 Corinthians 14:33–34: "As in all the churches of the saints, the women should keep silence in the churches. For they are not permitted to speak, but should be subordinate, as even the Law says." Concerning this term, Argument D suggests two things: (a) for the passage to apply to the limitation of the pastoral office to men, this word would have to mean "to preach" in its use here; and (b) most likely, the word means "to babble" in its use here. Therefore, because it has to mean "to preach" in order to sustain the old view of limiting the pastoral office to men, but it most likely means "to babble" when referencing the manner in which women were speaking, this passage does not address in a clear, cogent, and unambiguous manner, the issue of limiting the pastoral office to men.

How does Argument D defend this observation? By conducting a "word study" of all the ways in which the term λαλεῖν is used in the New Testament. Such an analysis leads to the conclusion that when a direct object is connected to the word, such as "speak wisdom from God," then and only then could the word mean "to preach," unless, of course, the speaker is Jesus; in this case, it is preaching whether a direct object is attached to the verb or not. On those occasions when someone other than Jesus is described as "speaking," but without a direct object, then "to speak" does not mean "to preach" but only "to talk." Moreover, because of the assumed situation in the text, namely, people gathered for worship in the manner of the Jewish synagogue, when the women are speaking, this must mean "chatter" or "babbling," since they would be hidden behind a screen, separate from the men, while the latter prayed and participated in the service. So on the basis of the word study that showed that λαλεῖν could be used in other ways than to refer to preaching, together with the assumed background of a synagogue setting, Argument D asserts that 1 Corinthians 14 has nothing to say about the question of women exercising the pastoral office.

What are we to make of this? First, we need to consider the question of how one might discern the meaning of λαλεῖν in this context. While word studies may shed some secondary light on the matter, they certainly are not decisive. In fact, in this instance Argument D commits what is known as the "illegitimate totality transfer," which James Barr describes as "obscuring the value of a word in a context by imposing upon it the totality of its uses."[13] It doesn't matter if 297 of the 298 uses of λαλεῖν in the New Testament all meant "to babble." That fact would not determine the meaning of λαλεῖν for

---

13  James Barr, *The Semantics of Biblical Language* (London: Oxford Press, 1961), pp. 218, 219.

the 298th passage. It is context that is determinative for the meaning of the word, because, as Barr puts it:

> The linguistic bearer of the theological statement is usually the sentence and the still larger literary complex and not the word or the morphological and syntactical mechanisms . . . but as a whole the distinctiveness of biblical thought and language has to be settled at sentence level, that is, by the things the writers say, and not by the words they say them with.[14]

What is the context of 1 Corinthians 14? It is the context of corporate worship; it is the context of a Greek, not Jewish, gathering in which males and females are not segregated by gender nor separated by privilege; it is the context of rampant confusion[15] born of the loss of the centrality of proclamation for edification. In the context of "proclamation for edification," to λαλεῖν in tongues must be curtailed or even eliminated, because it does not bring edification. To λαλεῖν in spontaneous and unordered testimony (prophecy) is disruptive of edification, and must be controlled. In this precise context, with λαλεῖν being used consistently to describe the activity that either enhances or hinders edification, Paul says, "the women should keep silence in the churches, for they are not permitted to speak, but should be subordinate, as even the Law says." It is the context that compels us to understand λαλεῖν as a public proclamatory speech.

When Argument D posits a collection of women who are jabbering among themselves, who must be corrected by St. Paul as he interrupts apostolic admonition concerning the nature of edification in order to hush up a group of people whose murmuring causes confusion, and then follows this assumption with the conclusion that the passage is not clear and unambiguous, such a move commits the logical fallacy *petitio principii* (begging the question). Nothing in the context invites such an assumption, and therefore nothing in the context robs this passage of its clear and unambiguous message. As Barr again reminds us, it is the sentence (and of course the still larger literary complex) that is the linguistic bearer of the usual theological statement, and not the word (the lexical unit) or the morphological and syntactical connection.

As a result of the context of this verse in 1 Corinthians 14, namely the clear and unambiguous intention of Paul to rein in and regulate the corporate worship life of the church at Corinth when it came to who "speaks," the

---

14  Barr, pp. 269, 270.

15  Dinda states concerning the term ἀκαταστασία that it brought him to wonder, at the outset of his entire exercise, "Isn't Paul speaking about noisy disturbances rather than the public preaching of the Word, as we have always said?" (p. 3). But a little attention to this term, together with the context of Paul's concerns in chapter 14, would have led to the realization that the reference here is not at all to "noisy disturbances," but rather to the confusion of people and their principles!

verse in question can mean nothing else than the long held belief of the historic Christian church that, in the corporate worship life of the congregation, women are not to "speak," in the sense of public proclamation for edification, the activity we today call "preaching." In this context it cannot mean anything else, not the least of which would be a reference to disturbing noises of gossiping women coming from behind some screen in a synagogue-type setting. Therefore, 1 Corinthians 14, the first focus of Argument D's minor premise, is not the victim of ambiguity that Argument D asserts it to be.

While we are considering 1 Corinthians 14, I would like to note the nature of St. Paul's argument on account of which he asserts that women should not engage in public proclamation for edification in the corporate life of the church. After all, Paul does not just command; rather, he asserts an argument, the conclusion of which is his admonition that women are not permitted "to speak" in the church. The argument is prefaced by the assertion that this is not just Pauline opinion, or just local custom, for he begins with the reminder that this practice is true "in all the churches of the saints" (v. 33). His argument embraces four facts:

1. Women "should be subordinate, as even the Law says" (v. 34)

2. Women should deal with questions through asking their husbands at home (v. 35a)

3. "It is shameful for a woman to speak in church" (v. 35b)

4. What Paul is writing is not open to debate: "what I am writing to you is a command of the Lord" (v. 37)

These four factors boil down to one overriding issue. Paul bases his admonition on the matter of *subordination*. Both the direct reference to the role of women in the services and the relationship between his instruction and the resistance he expected from his readers boil down to the matter of subordination.

Perhaps in our social and political environment this is the most grievous part to bear of the whole matter: subordination. Our women hear that word, and they do not like it. It brings to mind all that is socially unholy and culturally intolerable today: second-class citizenship, wife abuse, rape, discrimination, and the list goes on. The word fares little better with most men, who have grown tired of being labelled chauvinist-pig, misogynist, patriarchal boor, part of that breed that is responsible for all that is wrong in the world, namely, western-European males. Many men have also grown a little tired of their fellows who truly still fit some of these labels. But most of all, both men and women have been raised in the American world of self-reliant, self-focused, self-centered individualism that rebels at the thought that anyone could inform any others that they are subordinate. Subordination just cannot be tolerated in today's world, but subordination remains Paul's chief premise in this passage under examination. What is this subordination?

To subordinate (Greek: ὑποτάσσω) is predicated of many things in the sacred Scriptures. The entire fallen creation is subordinate to futility by the will of the Creator. We Christians are to be subordinate to the government. Those who are young are to be subordinate to the elders. All believers are to be "subordinate to one another out of reverence for Christ" (Eph 5:21). St. Paul speaks of his ongoing struggle against his flesh, which resists being subordinate to God.

It is in light of this background of holy subordination, indeed in light of our reverence for Christ, that Christians acknowledge and accept the "ordering" that God does within his creation. With this background, then, we are to understand the subordination of woman to man. Paul discusses this particular ordering of God in 1 Corinthians 11 (thus making it part of the context for what we find in 1 Corinthians 14):

> I commend you because you remember me in everything and maintain the traditions even as I have delivered them to you. But I want you to understand that the head of every man is Christ, the head of a woman is her husband, and the head of Christ is God. Any man who prays or prophesies with his head covered dishonors his head, but any woman who prays or prophesies with her head unveiled dishonors her head—it is the same as if her head were shaven. For if a woman will not veil herself, then she should cut off her hair; but if it is disgraceful for a woman to be shorn or shaven, let her wear a veil. For a man ought not to cover his head, since he is the image and glory of God; but woman is the glory of man. (For man was not made from woman, but woman from man. Neither was man created for woman, but woman for man.) That is why a woman ought to have a veil on her head, because of the angels. (Nevertheless, in the Lord woman is not independent of man nor man of woman; for as woman was made from man, so man is now born of woman. And all things are from God). (1 Cor 11:2–12)

First of all, Paul makes it clear in these verses of the eleventh chapter that his subsequent reference to "as even the Law says" is not referring to the judgment over sin in Genesis 3:16 ("He shall rule over you"), nor to some specific commandment, such as the Fourth Commandment, but rather he is referring to the entire Genesis account, the creation, the original ordering of all things, as taught in the Torah (Law). And that ordering always goes back to God. Nothing about this ordering is ever independent of God. Christ to God, man to Christ, woman to man. This relationship, this ordering, which is elsewhere described by the term subordination, as we have seen, is here pictured by the word "head" (κεφαλή). Headship in Scripture is not a matter of superiority or inferiority, not a matter of master and slave, not a matter of boss and worker.

Headship is a matter of the source of life. God the Father is the eternal source of the life of the Son; Christ is the eternal source of life of sinners; and within God's created order, before the fall into sin, the man is the source of the life of the woman.

What does all this matter? It only matters in relationship to God. Apart from God, everything can be seen from its own perspective, independently. But the Christian faith recognizes what the world will not acknowledge: Nothing and no one is ever "apart from God." Therefore, within the life of the church, and especially the church at worship, the faithful are called upon consciously to order themselves with regard to the ordering of God. The same holds also in the Christian household. Therefore, St. Paul urges subordination, the ordering of God, not only in the question of whether women proclaim for edification in the services, but also in the question of whether the church will accept this instruction as it is intended: "If any one thinks that he is a prophet, or spiritual, he should acknowledge that what I am writing to you is a command of the Lord." This idea of subordination as the public, corporate, and family-household expressions of life under God is what stands behind Paul's admonition in 1 Corinthians 14, and it further informs us of the necessity of holding to the proper interpretation of this passage as it has been received and delivered in the church for two millennia.

I now want to consider briefly what Argument D does with the other passage upon which our doctrine and practice is based. For Argument D also questions the clear, cogent, and unambiguous message of 1 Timothy 2:8–14:

> I desire then that in every place the men should pray, lifting holy hands without anger or quarreling; also that women should adorn themselves modestly and sensibly in seemly apparel, not with braided hair or gold or pearls or costly attire but by good deeds, as befits women who profess religion. Let a woman learn in silence with all submissiveness. I permit no woman to teach or to have authority over men; she is to keep silent. For Adam was formed first, then Eve; and Adam was not deceived, but the woman was deceived and became a transgressor.

Concerning this seemingly clear admonition that restricts women from teaching, Peter Brunner observes:

> Under *teaching* the apostle here understands, as one can already infer from the connection with the previous instructions concerning the correct conduct of the woman in worship, the public teaching in the congregation assembled for worship, that is, what we would nowadays call "preaching." This activity is forbidden the woman, just because she is a woman, in a very solemn manner since it is written in the style used for formal decrees. The reason given for the prohibition points to the order that God Himself had established at the creation: first the man and then the woman.

Furthermore it refers to the different roles that man and woman played in the story of the Fall. Both of these events of the protohistory, the creation and the fall, determine the status of contemporary woman, even the woman who is a Christian.[16]

In the face of this, what does Argument D offer to demonstrate that this passage is unclear or ambiguous? It turns again to word studies. It notes that "men" could also mean "husbands" and therefore this might well be a passage about domestic relationships. Argument D notes that "teaching" might be something other than "preaching," that it might mean "giving working orders," so that the passage is saying that the wife shouldn't boss the husband. It notes that "exercise authority" (αὐθεντεῖν) is a word found nowhere else in the New Testament, and therefore, from a word-study point of view, could mean just about anything. And on the basis of all of these "could be's," Argument D concludes that the passage is ambiguous, and therefore not binding.

Here, as is the case with 1 Corinthians 14, Argument D again commits the linguistic fallacy that Barr calls the fallacy of "illegitimate totality transfer," the practice of "obscuring the value of a word in a context by imposing on it the totality of its uses." Clearly, that is what is happening throughout the treatment of these verses by Argument D. The result is not that Argument D uncovers inherent ambiguity in the meaning of the text in its context, but rather that Argument D creates ambiguity in obscuring the value of the word in context by imposing on it the totality of its uses elsewhere. Thus, as already observed above in connection with 1 Corinthians 14, Argument D here also commits the logical fallacy *petitio principii* (begging the question). As with 1 Corinthians 14, the text of 1 Timothy 2 brings us its own interpretive matrix in its context, a context that refers to worship gatherings, not household dynamics, and that refers to the orders God has built into creation as Paul's inspired rationale for his admonition.

So in the end, what becomes of Argument D? The answer is not yet clear! To be sure, while we have discovered that the logical structure of Argument D is sound, we also have seen that both the major and the minor premises are faulty. Thus on both counts we have seen that the conclusion is lost. So why do I say that the fate of Argument D is not yet clear? Because in our church, as in the entire church world today, a growing number of people, pastors and laity alike, just have this feeling down in their gut that this limitation of the pastoral office to men just isn't right because they don't like it. Society has imposed certain perspectives and directions of thought upon us that will not tolerate the ordering of life around the all-encompassing centrality of God in Christ. This pressure upon us, from within as well as from without, is increasing daily.

16  Brunner, p. 20.

Moreover, this pressure marshals otherwise noble and spiritual concerns as allies. This pressure reaches into the mission-minded crowd and argues that we need to draw on all the resources that both genders provide as the day is short and the night is soon coming when no man can work. This pressure reaches into the youth and says, we need to change so that you will be able to "be all that you can be," and especially so that you can be "you." This pressure reaches out to the lonely and desolate congregational settings where pastoral vacancies are many and long, and it says, why not make this change so that you can have more pastors from which to choose? And this pressure reaches to the administrative and public relations concerns in our churches, and it says, let's put a more progressive face on our church for the sake of the gospel.

And all that appears to stand between us and some accommodation to ease these pressures and satisfy the demands of the irritated are two Bible passages and the scriptural logic that stands behind them. I am convinced that the weight and momentum of opinion within the Lutheran Church today would give us the ordination of women tomorrow, no, yet tonight, if only some acceptable way could be found to neutralize the import of these two passages. Who knows whether Argument D, despite its faulty assumptions and its logical and linguistic fallacies, might not yet be appealing enough to give this majority permission to knock down the barrier of gender now placed as a limit on the pastoral office? I therefore urge you to take it seriously, and to prepare to face it head on, which will require far more than mere slogans and politics. It will require serious, sober, and alert study of Holy Scripture by us all, so that we might yet deliver unto the next generation what has been delivered unto us down through the long history of the one holy, catholic, and apostolic church. But we are not alone, just as this struggle we face is not a new one for the church. In the end, we need only be faithful: faithful to our baptism covenant, faithful to our confirmation vows, faithful to our callings, faithful to the revealed Word, faithful in our stewardship of that which has been delivered unto us, and faithful in the forms of "ordering," "subordination," and "headship" under which God placed us. God bless you in this faithfulness!

# "It Is Not Given to Women to Teach"

## A *Lex* in Search of a *Ratio*

## William Weinrich

When Tertullian in the second century wrote: "It is not permitted to a woman to speak in church. Neither may she teach, baptize, offer, nor claim for herself any function proper to a man, least of all the priestly office" (*On the Veiling of Virgins* 9.1), and when seven centuries later Photius, Patriarch of Constantinople, wrote: "A woman does not become a priestess" (*Nomocanon* 1.37), they were reiterating the prohibition of the apostle Paul. At the same time they were indicating the practice characteristic of their day and indeed were indicating that unbroken practice in all sacramental and confessional churches which until the most recent times remained unquestioned.

There were, of course, occasions in the church's history when heretical or utterly peripheral groups organized themselves in ways contrary to Paul's prohibition. From Irenaeus (second century) we learn of the gnostic Marcosians in whose sacramental rites a woman consecrated the cup of Charis into which she would drop her blood (*Adv. Haer.* 1.13). From Epiphanius (fourth century) we learn of the "Quintillians" who appealed to Eve as the prototype of their female clergy. Epiphanius explicitly says that this group had women bishops and women presbyters and that, quite interestingly, in view of modern arguments, they justified all of this on the basis of Gal 3:28 (*Adv. Haer.* 49.1–3). And from time to time in the early Middle Ages there appear to have been outgrowths of gnostic or spiritualist enthusiasms which allowed women to serve at the altar. In the sixth century, to mention but one example, two priests in Brittany allowed women to assist them in the celebration and distribution of the Lord's Supper. This elicited a vigorous response by three Gallic bishops

461

who called this practice "a novelty and unheard-of superstition."[1] Yet, despite these occasional problems, the church's obedience to the apostolic standard was unyielding and universally faithful.

Nor, it must be said, did the church's faithfulness to the apostle's prohibition of women in the pastoral office rest upon some notion of a natural inferiority of women to men in either intellect or virtue. One can, of course, find evidence of such thinking. But just as common, and certainly more true to biblical models, were other much more positive evaluations of the innate gifts and abilities of women. John Chrysostom (fourth century), often castigated as misogynist, wrote that "in virtue women are often enough the instructors of men; while the latter wander about like jackdaws in dust and smoke, the former soar like eagles into higher spheres" (*Epist. to Eph.*, Hom. 13.4). Similarly, commenting on Priscilla's teaching of Apollos in view of 1 Tm 2:12, Chrysostom says that Paul "does not exclude a woman's superiority, even when it involves teaching" when the man is an unbeliever or in error (*Greet Priscilla and Aquilla* 3).

Nor, it must also be said, did the church's obedience to the apostolic command reflect an unevangelical accommodation to social and cultural circumstances. In fact, the social and cultural context of early Christianity at times very much favored the introduction of women into teaching, priestly, or sacramental offices. In first- and second-century Asia Minor, for example, the social position of women was well developed. There were female physicians, and Ephesus had its female philosophers among the Stoics, Epicureans, and Pythagoreans, who were known to teach, perhaps also publicly. Female leadership and priesthood were well known in the local religious cults of Cybele, Isis, Demeter, and Artemis. In the Greek cults of Demeter and Artemis the holiest places were open only to female priestesses. Generally in the mystery cults women shared "equal rights" with men and were initiated into all the mysteries. Often, women performed the ceremonies and delivered the instructions, even to the male participants. This is documented, for example, in the cult of Dionysius in which all distinctions between men and women, adults and children, freemen and slaves, were broken down. Furthermore, at times the Fathers themselves show a much more positive attitude than does the surrounding culture concerning women, and they demonstrate no lack of sensitivity to unequal law and practice. Speaking of chastity, Gregory of Nazianzus (fourth century) remarks that in regard to chastity,

> the majority of men are ill-disposed, and their laws are unequal and irregular. For what was the reason why they restrained the woman, but indulged

---

1    See Roger Gryson, *The Ministry of Women in the Early Church* (Collegeville, MN: The Liturgical Press, 1976, 1980), 106; Aime Georges Martimort, *Deaconesses: An Historical Study* (San Francisco: Ignatius Press, 1986), 195.

the man, and that a woman who practices evil against her husband's bed is an adulteress, and the penalties of the law for this are very severe; but if the husband commits fornication against his wife, he has no account to give? I do not accept this legislation; I do not approve of this custom. Those who made the law were men, and therefore the legislation is hard on women (*Orat.* 37.6).

Gregory need take a back seat to no feminist in his disapproval of actual male chauvinism and self-serving.

What, then, was the basis and rationale of the church for its pervasive adherence to the apostolic prohibition of women in the office of preaching and the sacraments? There was in fact a rather broad *basis* for this practice. This basis was essentially threefold: (1) the biblical history, (2) the example of Jesus, and (3) Paul's prohibitions in 1 Corinthians 11 and 14, and in 1 Timothy 2.

Using the biblical history, Origen argues against the Montanists, and Epiphanius argues against the Collyridians. "Never from the beginning of the world has a woman served God as priest," writes Epiphanius (fourth century). And then he runs through the stories of the Old and New Testaments indicating that God's priests had always been men but never a woman (*Adv. Haer.* 78–79). Similarly, in view of the Montanist appeal to the Old Testament prophetesses, Origen (third century) argues that indeed Deborah, Miriam, and Huldah were prophetesses, yet "there is no evidence that Deborah delivered speeches to the people, as did Jeremiah and Isaias. Hulda, who was a prophetess, did not speak to the people, but only to a man, who consulted her at home." The same is true of the daughters of Philip: if they prophesied, "at least they did not speak in the assemblies, for we do not find this fact in the Acts of the Apostles" (*Fragment on I Corinthians* 74).[2]

The practice of Jesus was perceived to be fully consonant with this more general biblical history. Not only did Jesus choose for himself only males to be his apostles but, more significantly, Mary herself, the Mother of the omnipotent Son of God, was not given the task of baptizing Jesus, that task being given to John the Baptist. The prohibitions of Paul, therefore, were understood to be fully in harmony with the broad narrative of the Old Testament, as well as the New Testament histories and the practice of Christ Himself. Whenever the need arose, these three biblical bases were adduced either individually or in combination. In the Middle Ages this whole perspective received canon law expression in the ban of Pope Innocent III against the preaching and hearing of confession by powerful monastic abbesses: "No matter whether the most blessed Virgin Mary stands higher, and is also more illustrious, than all the

---

2    For the full Origen quotation, see Gryson, *Ministry of Women*, 28–29.

apostles together, it was still not to her, but to them, that the Lord entrusted the keys to the Kingdom of heaven."[3]

The church, therefore, through the centuries understood herself to be not only in continuous agreement with the Old and New Testament history but also saw herself envisioned and imaged in these stories. As Paul indicated in another context, the things of the Old Testament were written for the instruction of the people of the New Covenant upon whom the end of the ages has come (1 Cor 10:11). Such an appeal to the biblical narratives was, therefore, no mere referral to tradition or a recital of historical precedents. The appeal to biblical narrative was predicated upon the belief that the creative Word of God, incarnate in the man Jesus, revealed His will not only in the hearts of people spiritually, if you will, but also in the events and orderings of His people and in the canonical testimony to those events and orderings. It was not without reason that, to repeat the words of Epiphanius, "never from the beginning of the world has a woman served God as priest." This was rooted in the way in which God has always arranged His people so that they might be a sign of His creative will and intent. The fourth-century *Apostolic Constitutions* make the point: Jesus did what He did, and He has delivered to His church no indication of women priests, because He "knows the order of creation." "What Jesus did, being the Creator of nature, He did in agreement with the creative action. Similarly, since Jesus is the incarnate Word in whom the creation is being made new, He, as head of the church, the new people of God, typified in His ministry the new life of the church not only in its 'spiritual' but also in its fleshly contours."[4] The church did not see in the Pauline prohibitions, therefore, commandments extraneous or even alien to the new life which it had through Christ. It did not see in those apostolic statements *ad hoc* accommodations to the cultural surroundings. It saw in them, rather, apostolic exhortation and regulation which bespeaks the "shape" or "configuration" of the new community whose life is constituted in the Word of God and made active through the Spirit.

Within Protestantism, the principal Reformation and post-Reformation leaders merely assumed without question the practice of reserving the office of pastor to men. Their strong "Scripture alone" position led them, however, to rely almost exclusively on the Pauline prohibitions, with the concomitant result that appeal to the biblical history and to the example of Jesus was less frequent, if not eschewed as Roman Catholic. Within Protestantism generally there was insistence on what could be regarded as clearly applicable biblical

---

3    Quoted in Manfred Hauke, *Women in the Priesthood? A Systematic Analysis in the Light of the Order of Creation and Redemption* (San Francisco: Ignatius Press, 1988), 447.

4    The Lutheran Church—Missouri Synod Commission on Theology and Church Relations [CTCR], *Women in the Church: Scriptural Principles and Ecclesial Practice* (September 1985), 14–15.

mandate before a practice was to be regarded as required or prohibited. Luther, for example, while asserting that all Christians have the full power to preach, asserted as well, and on the basis of the Pauline prohibitions alone, that not all in fact can or ought exercise this power. He regarded the Pauline injunctions as normative for the church because they were given by the Holy Spirit: in the Law, by which Luther meant the Old Testament, the Holy Spirit had subordinated woman to man, and now in the apostles the Holy Spirit does not contradict Himself.[5] Beyond the mere fact of the Spirit's speaking through the apostle, which to be sure was for him sufficient in itself, Luther is not all that strong in explaining the whys and wherefores of the Pauline injunctions. He speaks unaffectedly of ability and aptitude: man is in many ways (*multis modis*) more suited for speaking than is a woman and it is more seemly for the man to speak. And this way of doing things, says Luther, is for the sake of order (*ordo*) and respectability (*honestas*).[6] This was apparently sufficient to the day. The whole issue of the ordination of women into the pastoral ministry was still unthinkable. For him and for his time there was no such question.

It is, however, not so for us. Today, it is important to emphasize, we are faced with an entirely new and wholly frontal assault upon the common and traditional practice of the church not to ordain women to the public office of Word and Sacrament. This assault involves not merely the higher-critical exclusion of the pertinent Pauline passages as authentically from Paul; it involves a very different reading of the Scriptures themselves. Rather than the Pauline prohibitions being understood as rooted in the creative will of God and hence instances of apostolic regulation in harmony with the full biblical narrative (there never is in all of Scripture a woman priest or apostle), the Pauline injunctions are regarded as *ad hoc* accommodations to the surrounding culture, and hence of only temporary applicability. Or the Pauline injunctions are regarded as rabbinic hangovers of Paul's pre-Christian life which now are actually in conflict with the pure gospel which Paul elsewhere preaches with such clarity. Here, almost invariably, Gal 3:28 is invoked.

---

5   *D. Martin Luthers Werke: Kritische Gesamtausgabe*, 58 vols. (Weimar: Hermann Böhlau und Nachfolger, 1883–1948), 8:424.20–25.6.

6   Ibid., 424.30–33: "Ita mulieres Paulus prohibet loqui, non simpliciter, sed in Ecclesia, nempe ubi sunt viri potentes loqui, ut ne confundatur honestas et ordo, cum vir multis modis sit prae muliere idoneus ad loquendurn et magis eum deceat." See also the discussion of John Gerhard concerning the question of whether women also must be brought into the ministry (*Loci Theologici*, Locus 23). He gives five reasons for an answer of "no." Among them: "man has better judgment, greater discretion, and a faster pace than woman"; also, quoting Epiphanius, "woman is a deceitful sort, prone to error and endowed with humble intelligence." Here Gerhard gives explanations (*rationes*) for the presence of Paul's prohibitions, which explanations are indeed very likely founded upon his own historical context, and—let us say it forthrightly—reveal an androcentric viewpoint. Obviously, such argument bears no persuasive power today.

For our own understanding of the task before us, it is necessary that we realize that the simple appeal to Paul's statements in 1 Corinthians and 1 Timothy are not sufficient anymore adequately to ground our present practice. This is not to say that, properly understood and properly related to the rest of Scripture, these Pauline injunctions do not apply as we have commonly understood them to apply. I firmly believe that they do apply. However, in the contemporary context, the appeal to these three Pauline passages is countered by a host of arguments which intend to void those passages of present authority. And this is occurring not only in the more liberal church bodies wherein we might expect to find a critical posture toward the Scriptures. It is happening just as much within American Evangelical circles whose formal adherence to the Scriptures remains similar to that of the Missouri Synod. Note, for example, the self-testimony of Gretchen Hull, who in her book *Equal to Serve* asserts that "this book is written from the standpoint of what is called a high view of Scripture: the Bible is the inspired, trustworthy Word of God written and as such stands as the true revelation of God's message, regardless of any human reaction to it." Such a high view of Scripture "affirms that the Bible texts have been proven authentic and considers them completely reliable transmitters of God's message."[7]

What could we possibly find at fault with that posture toward the Scriptures? Yet within her book Ms. Hull absolutely rejects patriarchy, equating it quite simply with male domination, and regards the patriarchal stories of the Old Testament as "the true record of the false idea."[8] The biblical accounts of the patriarchs she regards as inerrantly true (the Scriptures are inspired). But the patriarchal narratives illustrate not the will of God which is given in creation and which receives renewed and sanctified obedience in the new creation. The patriarchal stories of the Old Testament illustrate rather the perversity of human sin which has set up an ordering of human existence in opposition to that desired by God and created by Him.

Now it is quite clear that the procedure of Ms. Hull is the very opposite of the procedure of the early church fathers which I summarized above. For the Fathers, the stories of the Old Testament illustrate the will of God the creator and redeemer. The Fathers were not unaware that the stories of the Old Testament also illustrate sinful behavior and sinful attitudes. But sin was the perversion of what in itself was good. Or, as pertains to our point of discussion, patriarchy could be perverted, but patriarchy in itself revealed the will of God, that is, it revealed the way God works so that His will brings His purposes to pass. For Ms. Hull, on the other hand, the Old Testament

7    Gretchen Gaebelin Hull, *Equal to Serve: Women and Men in the Church and Home* (Old Tappen, NJ: Fleming H. Revell Company, 1987), 26.

8    Ibid., 80ff.

patriarchal stories are a kind of anti-God story wherein it is not possible to see God at work at all.

It is evident, therefore, that to the extent that Ms. Hull allows the Pauline passages any participation in the good, it can be only as a temporary accommodation to Paul's immediate historical context. The Pauline passages cannot in any case be perceived as consonant with a "true record of the true idea," as an apostolic command corresponding to Old Testament and New Testament narrative wherein women were not admitted to the priestly and apostolic office, and this in obedience to the divine will. Apart from the fact that Ms. Hull wrests from the formal principle its proper material principle, that is, empties the narrative of the scriptural record of any content as the story of God's willful activity, it is clear that fundamentally Ms. Hull (and she is by no means unique in this) is operating with an analogy of faith quite different from that of the Fathers and quite different from that of the traditional understanding of confessional Lutheranism, including the Missouri Synod. That is, quite directly put, Ms. Hull in her whole method and approach to the general question of the relation between male and female and to the specific question of the ordination of women implies a creed at variance with that which has been operative from the time of the apostles. What we are dealing with in the broad issue of the relationship between male and female and with the particular question of the ordination of women is a doctrinal and credal issue. The question is *What is the Faith?* or *What is the analogy of Faith?* or, if you will, *What is the biblical story which determines, guides, and commands our understanding of the distinctive place and role of both man and woman in the world and in the church of God?*

What makes the present moment in the church's history so difficult in this regard is that this complex question has never been forthrightly put and answered in the doctrinal history of the Christian church. While the basis for the early church's understanding and practice was broad—encompassing the whole Old and New Testament narratives, the example of Christ, and the specific Pauline injunctions—the rationale of the early church is extremely sparse if not non-existent. While we have the fact that throughout the church's history there have been women saints, martyrs, prophets, missionaries, monastics, and secular rulers, and while there have even been some women who by the Eastern tradition have been designated *isapostoloi*, "equal to the apostles,"[9] we have also the fact that there have never been women who held the public office of the bishop and pastor. But why that is so has never been doctrinally or theologically delineated. There are few if any sources in the early, medieval,

---

9    Some women who have been honored by this title are Mary Magdalene; the martyr Thekla; Helen, the mother of Emperor Constantine; and Nina, missionary to the Georgians.

or modern church which deal with this question in any explicit way. What the significance of the distinction between male and female might be, in terms of a Christian understanding of human life and the life of the church, has never been adumbrated. And, in the present situation governed as it is by an egalitarian ethos, this has easily given rise to the belief that there is no significance. The church has, therefore, experienced a ready, even precipitous capitulation to the feminist claim that restricting the office of Word and Sacrament to certain chosen male members of the Christian community is a mere vestige of an antique and outmoded way of thinking. In the present age it is in fact, so it goes, inherently arbitrary and oppressive.

In the present polemical and apologetic context, a simple appeal to the Pauline passages is futile and bears no persuasive power. For the real question lies deeper than the issue of biblical inspiration and inerrancy or the question of whether a particular passage is applicable to this or that situation. The question is rather whether the relevant Pauline passages are, as it were, imbedded in the general matrix of the Christian revelation and the corresponding vision that it engenders, so that they are perceived to arise organically out of the very preachment of the prophetic and apostolic witness to the creative and salvific work of God, and are not to be regarded as mere regulatory additions attached, for some unknown reason, to the real apostolic concerns. We seek after the organic, that is, the theological, foundations which lie at the bottom of the Pauline prohibitions and which therefore give shape, form, and content to the Pauline prohibitions.

Now before we begin this task, and it can only be a beginning, we must take note of some attitudes and concerns that have been voiced against any attempt to get to the bottom of the Pauline statements. Many say that the appeal to Paul is sufficient, and that any attempt to do more is speculation and can never have any appeal, let alone authority, for the church. To this it must again be said that Scripture is not a bundle of truisms, true stories, and legislation which somehow on their own and apart from the whole can be properly understood and appropriated. Scripture, inspired Word of God as it is, is the prophetic and apostolic witness which norms our understanding of the speaking and acting of God which began in the creation, continued through the history of the Old Testament people, was fulfilled in the incarnate Word, and now in the speech and life of the church moves toward its appointed end in the resurrection of the dead and the eternal Kingdom of God. The deep reason for the details must be sought in the whole, and where such reason cannot be found, then, argument may indeed commence whether the detail is not a true adiaphoron or a temporary incidental which now may not have, or perhaps even dare not have, any abiding authority. We seek after the biblical structure, the way of God in the world, to understand the reason why Paul, when confronted by the problems of his day, had to answer the way he did.[10]

This will not be the first time that church practice searched for its theological rationale. In the Arian conflict of the fourth century, the question arose concerning the legitimacy and propriety of prayer to Christ or to the Holy Spirit. The answer came in the form of the doctrine of the Holy Trinity which affirmed the full deity of both the Son, Jesus Christ, and the Holy Spirit. In the Pelagian controversy of the fifth century, the question was concerning the theological requirement of the Baptism of infants. The answer came in the doctrine of original sin which asserted that each individual, however small or young, was subject to the death which sin brings and therefore was in need of the redemptive work of the Savior. In the fifth-century conflict with Nestorius the question arose concerning the legitimacy of the church's liturgical reference to the Virgin Mary as the "Mother of God." What deep, theological reason made that reference not only possible but necessary? The answer came in the church's assertion of the incarnation of the Word of God whereby the flesh of humanity was assumed into the person of the eternal Son so that the humanity of Jesus was in truth the humanity of God. Therefore, that One born of Mary was in truth the divine Son of God incarnate. Mary was in truth the "Mother of God."

Today the search is after the rationale for the church's practice of reserving to a Christian man the office of Word and Sacrament. That search is in itself not speculation as some are wont to assert.[11] The beginning of all speculation is the posture of autonomy in which an idea or a principle is developed according to its own inherent dynamic. Speculation is independent in its own deductions; it is in a state of emancipation from the basis of the Scripture narrative. On the other hand, biblical theology is not creative. It is the task of serious hearing, of listening to the whispers and echoes of the biblical stories in order to hear *more*, to understand *more*, to increase *more* our wonder and awe at what God has done and what God proposes in what He has done. Biblical thinking is bound therefore to what has been spoken before. Biblical

---

10 We wish to distinguish clearly this task from the search for some "general tendency" or "main thrust" of Scripture which is then used to interpret or even to critique explicit statements of Scripture. It is a common method of many feminist writers to gather biblical data which speak of spiritual equality, mutual love, and the like, and then to declare that there is a general thrust in the Bible to level out all differences and distinctions, especially those based on gender. This "general thrust" becomes a hermeneutical tool to empty specific biblical statements, like those of Paul, of abiding significance. We seek rather to ascertain the theological structure of the Bible's own witness (one might say the credal structure of the Bible) which gives theological content to Paul's exhortations.

11 For a nice discussion of the difference between biblical theology and speculation, see Walther Künneth, "Schrifttheologie und Spekulation," in *Viva Vox Evangelii: Eine Festschrift für Landesbischof D. Hans Meiser* (München: Claudius-Verlag, 1951), 185–95.

thinking is directed toward an "is." It is not engaged in what the feminist theologian Letty Russell calls "utopic envisagement" wherein faith claims a knowledge of God's future apart from and indeed often in contradistinction to the past and present of God.[12] In trying to come to terms with the actual words of Paul, we do not speculate. We try rather to lay bare the biblical contours which lie within Paul's own words.

In the midst of the fourth century, at the height of the Arian controversy concerning the divinity of Jesus Christ, the bishop of the French town of Poitiers, Hilary, wrote of the necessity of saying things which were beyond "what heaven has prescribed." He wrote:

> We are compelled by the error of heretics and blasphemers to do what is unlawful, to scale heights, to express things that are unutterable, to encroach on forbidden matters. And when we ought to fulfill the commandments through faith alone, adoring the Father, worshipping the Son together with him, rejoicing in the Holy Spirit, we are forced to stretch the feeble capacity of our language to give expression to indescribable realities. We are constrained by the error of others to err ourselves in the dangerous attempt to set forth in human speech what ought to be kept in the religious awe of our minds. . . . The infidelity of others drags us into the dubious and dangerous position of having to make a definite statement beyond what heaven has prescribed about matters so sublime and so deeply hidden (*De Trinitate* 2.2.5).

We may take comfort and warning in the sentiments of Hilary. We have been warned by people of piety and caution not to attempt to define the ineffable nature of the human being. It is incomprehensible even as is that greater incomprehensibility of the divine nature. As we cannot approach with our understanding the essence of God, so we cannot approach the essence of our own humanity. Mankind, too, is a mystery. I accept these reservations as apt warnings. Nonetheless, the incomprehensible God has not remained in His essential hiddenness. He has revealed Himself, not in his essence directly, but in the hypostatic or personal relations in which God's essence receives its distinct representations. We know God to be Father, Son, and Holy Spirit. And we know God to be the Trinity of persons in and through His revealed activities, pre-eminently perhaps in our Baptism wherein we receive the *Spirit of Son*ship whereby we cry out *"Abba, Father"* (Rom 8:16ff.). We do not and

---

12  Letty M. Russell, *Household of Freedom: Authority in Feminist Theology* (Philadelphia: Westminster Press, 1987), 18. Russell speaks of living out of "a vision of God's intention for a mended creation." In an important sense, she writes, Christian feminists "only have this future" since patriarchal structures are such that reconstruction of woman's place "requires a utopian faith that understands God's future as an impulse for change in the present." Russell borrows the phrase "utopic envisagement" from Beverly Harrison.

cannot know God in His essence, but we do know Him in the three persons of His Godhead, in which God is in relation to Himself and graciously moves out of Himself to relate to us "from the Father, through the Son, and in the Holy Spirit." In an analogous way, might I submit, we come to know also our own human nature. For God did not create an abstract human nature to which were then contingently added the qualities of maleness and femaleness. Sexual complementarity is a gift of God's creative act. Humanity is essentially binary. "Maleness" and "femaleness" are strictly speaking not qualities or attributes at all; they are modes of human being, ways of being human. If we wish to understand humanity, it must be by considering humanity as male and female.

Nor is our task here the wholly complex one of understanding humanity as male and female. It is, however, our task to grope toward an understanding of why, from the biblical perspective, Paul made the prohibitions he did. At the outset we might make the observation that if Paul claims that man is the "head" of woman and that this "headship" must be indicated in the assembly of the church and that this indication involves at least this, as Paul says in 1 Corinthians 14, that the man speaks but the woman does not, then this claim of Paul may well be founded upon the mystery of what it means to be a male human and upon the mystery of what it means to be a female human. If Paul's point is not, in fact, merely a vestige of ancient patriarchal social forms, if Paul's point is not merely the temporary accommodation to historical circumstance, then does not the cast of Paul's injunction itself imply that there is something to being a man, and there is something to being a woman, which demands an ordering in the assembly of the church so that the distinctive modes of human being, maleness and femaleness, might be properly expressed and realized? Is it really a speculation or—heaven forbid!—a flight to catholic traditions, whether Roman or Eastern, to inquire after what we have so often called the "order of creation"? Is this not, in fact, *demanded* by the biblical text itself which does speak of the sexual distinctions within humanity and which does reflect on the place and roles assigned to them both in the church and in the home? The Bible does speak of a mutuality and reciprocity between the sexes, which mutuality and reciprocity however entails no interchangeability or confusion between the distinctions but rather a mutuality and reciprocity which has its own intrinsic order. In any case, the present feminist attack on the traditional practice of the church, whether from the liberal or evangelical sides, finds it very difficult to make meaningful sense of the distinction of male and female in the human family, let alone in the church.[13] There is rather a pervasive, and I would say docetic, tendency to denigrate and to nullify that

---

13  For example, Paul Jewett admits that he is uncertain "what it means to be a man in distinction to a woman or a woman in distinction to a man." See *Man as Male and Female: A Study in Sexual Relationships from a Theological Point of View* (Grand Rapids, MI: William B. Eerdmans, 1975), 178.

distinction as significant. This does not, of course, occur only in explicit denials of the significance of being male and being female. It occurs as well in the neglect of taking the question as significant or in the refusal to believe the question appropriate in seeking the rationale for Paul's prohibitions against women in the pastoral office.

We wish now to inquire after what among us has been called the "order of creation." We wish also to give some reflection on the relation of the "order of creation" to the so-called "order of redemption," for one still finds with great frequency the argument that in the Gospel the patterns of the "order of cre-ation" are overcome, transcended, or transformed, and this is understood to mean that something structurally totally new is come in the Gospel. Against this view, the 1985 report of the Commission on Theology and Church Relations (CTCR) of the Lutheran Church—Missouri Synod, entitled *Women in the Church*, stated that the "distinctive identities for man and woman in their relation to each other were assigned by God at creation. These identi-ties are not nullified by Christ's redemption, and they should be reflected in the church."[14] This very point was rightly reiterated by Dr. Samuel Nafzger in his presentation, "The Order of Creation, or the Creator's Order," delivered in October 1989 at a conference in Minneapolis.[15] These two presentations make an essential point: the distinction between man and woman, given in the creation, is not unrelated to ordered distinctions in the church. What is left unclear in both documents, however, is why the distinctive identities for man and woman *should* be reflected in the church. What is the nature of this "should"? It is at this point that we wish to think in a manner supplemental and complementary to what our church body has said in the past.

In a recently published article the Rev. George L. Murphy of Tallmadge, Ohio, makes "an appeal to Missouri" for the ordination of women.[16] I would like to use some of his discussion as a lead into my own. Murphy's article is divided into three parts: (1) in the first part he discusses the question of the continuing relevance of the Pauline prohibitions and other passages which he believes bespeak a biblical attitude which allows the ordination of women; (2) in the second section Murphy gives a short discussion on certain aspects of the church's tradition and argues that even Lutheran tradition appears to allow the ordination of women (he discusses a quotation from the seventeenth-century Lutheran Nicholaus Hunnius), but that in any case no tradition is in itself authoritative for a Lutheran unless it has "clear and

---

14  CTCR, "Women in the Church" (1985), 27.

15  Samuel H. Nafzger, "The Order of Creation, or the Creator's Order," unpublished paper delivered in Minneapolis, MN on October 7, 1989, 9.

16  George L. Murphy, "For the Ordination of Women," *Lutheran Forum* 24 (Advent 1990), 6–8.

unambiguous support from scripture"; (3) finally, in the third section Murphy addresses general theological issues, among them the "orders of creation," the distinction between prophets and priests, the question of the pastor's representation of the person of Christ, and the relation of the pastoral office to the church as a community of priests. Not all of Murphy's arguments are of equal weight and interest. Yet, he merits a thoughtful response. Here I have time only to be selective in my response, but I do wish to dwell especially upon his remarks in the third section concerning the relationship of the person of the pastor to the person of Christ and the relation of the office of pastor to the people as a whole.

I begin with some remarks of Murphy about the continuing validity and authority of the Pauline injunctions which traditionally make up the argument for the ordination of men alone. Murphy does not demean these passages of Paul, and it is evident that he does not wish to be facile in his use of them. His argument, he says, is not "the simplistic one that the biblical authors were 'wrong,' or that these passages are irrelevant simply because they refer to a context different from ours." Rather, he argues, "there are good reasons for believing these *authoritative* statements to refer to particular situations in the first century, and therefore not automatically binding in all other situations."[17] Acts 15:29, for example, which forbids the eating of blood, is authoritative Scripture, yet today, argues Murphy, we are not for that reason forbidden from eating blood sausage. "And this is true," Murphy notes, "even though the prohibition of 'blood' is not a mere custom but has deep theological roots in the Noachic covenant!"[18] The conditional character of Paul's statements concerning the speaking of women in the church do not mean, argues Murphy, that the church may simply ignore them. "They continue to say that in some situations it may be appropriate for some groups within the church not to hold the pastoral office. . . . But it cannot be said that *in principle* any gender or race *must* be excluded."[19]

Murphy believes that the fact that these passages are dealing with particular circumstances implies that there may continue to be situations which—presumably for reasons of peace, decency, or order—require some persons not to be admitted to the pastoral office. That is the continuing relevance of Paul's statements. However, no gender or race can in principle be excluded. We shall forego any comment on the matter of race, which here for unexplained reasons appears in the discussion. Apparently Murphy is simply overcome by a modern American sensibility which finds itself required to mention the equality of the races and of the sexes in the same breath. In any case, the

---

17  Ibid., 6, emphasis Murphy's.

18  Ibid.

19  Ibid., emphasis Murphy's.

text has nothing to do with the question of whether persons of another race may preach in the assembly. It does make the explicit statement that women ought not preach in the assembly. That is, it appears to be precisely the case that one gender is in principle excluded from the function of preaching in the assembly. And as the parallel passages of 1 Corinthians 11 and especially 1 Timothy 2 make clear, this exclusion is grounded not on the basis of what in view of the culture and society would be considered proper, decent, and in good order. Nor, we should add, does Paul argue on the basis of a covenant which arises in view of humanity's previous rebellion. Paul argues on the basis of the story of creation wherein man and woman relate to one another according to an order initially willed by the Creator: "Adam was formed first, then Eve." The apostle argues his case on the basis of a more encompassing context, namely, the creation of man and woman. Incidental irregularities do not occasion his full theological response. He could certainly have demanded decent and orderly behavior of the Corinthians on the basis of common notions of orderliness and propriety. But he did not do so. The question of a man or of a woman speaking in the assembly connoted an order given by God at the creation and an order which continues in the church.

At this point, however, Murphy makes an interesting argument. It is risky, he writes, to base the traditional argument on "the simple temporal order of creation in Genesis 2." Murphy recognizes that 1 Timothy 2 does give the order of creation as an argument for the silence of women in the assembly. However, that does not mean, he argues, that conclusions drawn from such an argument hold unconditionally. Paul uses the same argument from the order of creation for the veiling of women. If, however, despite the order of creation argument, the veiling of women is no longer required, then it is inconsistent to argue that the silencing of women prescribed in 1 Timothy must always be maintained because creation-based arguments were used to support it. This is a question worth pondering. And I would like to begin a reflective response by asking a prior question: Are the wearing of the veil in the assembly and the speaking of the woman in the assembly the same kind of activity? I would like to suggest that they are not. Of course, if today the absence of the veil in our culture were regarded as the self-assertion of the woman against the man, I suggest that we would still today have to require the wearing of the veil. And this would be so precisely for the reasons Paul indicates. However, does the absence of wearing of the veil in itself and apart from a cultural context denote the self-assertion of a woman against men? Obviously it does not. In our culture the wearing of a veil or the absence of a veil has lost its voice. Neither behavior says anything except perhaps something about the personal taste of the woman or maybe of the man she wishes to please. The wearing of the veil has no organic relation to the being of woman and her posture within the community of persons. However, there is indication in the text itself that a similar reflection cannot be made of the speaking of woman in the assembly. In 1 Corinthians 14 Paul says that "it is shameful for a woman to speak in the assembly" (v. 35). The word here translated "to speak" is the Greek word *lalein*, which is virtually a technical term for preaching (see also Mt 9:18; 12:46; Mk 2:2; Lk 9:11; Jn 8:12; Acts 4:1; 8:25; 13:43; 1 Cor 2:7; 2 Cor 12:19; Eph 6:20; Phil 1:14). That the term is used to signify the activity of preaching as a teacher may be seen from the parallel text of 1 Tm 2:11ff., where the word "to teach" or "to instruct" (*didaskein*) is used. What therefore seems to be indicated by Paul in these passages is that a woman ought not to take the position of the one who preaches or teaches in an authoritative way, that is, a woman ought not to speak the message of the church for the church and unto the church. Now, the church relates to such speaking in a vastly more significant way than the church relates to the wearing of veils. The church organically relates to such preaching and teaching as that which is created by and through such speaking. In short, the church is constituted in the hearing of faith which arises out of such authoritative speaking. And this fact, I would like to argue, possesses a substantive and organic relation to the relational order of man and woman given in the creation.

When we read in Gn 1:27 that "God created the man (*adam, ho anthropos*) in His own image, in the image of God He created him [singular], male (*zakar*) and female (*neqebah*) He created them," we gain our first clear indication of how central to the biblical vision the distinction of gender actually is. In some discussions this is denied by referring to the use of "adam" in the Hebrew or to the use of "anthropos" in the Septuagint, both of which can be used to render common humanity. Only then are the distinctions male and female indicated. Hence, the argument goes, there is a common humanity created by God which exists, so to speak, independent of and autonomous to the concrete distinctions of male and female. We are, if you will, humans first and male or female in a secondary way. However, what is not often observed is that in the Hebrew text at the word *him* ("in the image of God He created *him*," singular) there is a mark called an *athnach* which creates a pause in the narrative, something like an *id est* (i.e.), a "that is." It is after this *athnach* that the words "male and female created He them" continue. An *athnach* divides two parts of a sentence into its logical parts so that what comes second makes clear the inner logic of what comes first. In the case of Gn 1:27 we might therefore render the Hebrew like this: "In the image of God He created him and by this we mean male and female did God create in His image."[20] In short, what

---

20  For the *athnach*, see J. Weingreen, *A Practical Grammar for Classical Hebrew*, 2nd ed. (Oxford: Clarendon Press, 1959), 21. There is the opinion that an *athnach* indicates simply a pause in a verse and no more. However, even if that is so, the *athnach* in Gn 1:27 indicates a pause within a narrative, so that what comes second cannot simply

this means is that in the mention of "adam" already in Gn 1:27, no idea of a generic humanity apart from the concretions male and female is possible.[21] This *athnach* has the further effect of preparing us for the creation account of Genesis 2, where, in a clear narrative way, Adam and Eve are distinguished.

From the very beginning of the Bible, therefore, it is evident that maleness and femaleness are constitutive aspects of human being. There is no humanity, no personhood, apart from male humanity, male personhood and female humanity, female personhood.[22] Masculinity and femininity are, as I noted above, constitutively connected to the person; they are modes of human being, ways of being human. Now, if this is true, the implications are important. If masculinity and femininity are not merely qualifying adjectives alongside other adjectives like brown hair, blue eyes, and dark skin, then all that a person does is done either in a masculine or in a feminine way, and that includes what we are wont to call the spiritual activities of individuals. The gift of the Holy Spirit which we receive when we are united into Christ does not, as it were, impart some sort of spiritual nature to our natural selves so that, apart from our human selves as man and woman, there is a new, undifferentiated spiritual nature, common to both man and woman, which manifests itself by producing or allowing only the self-same, undifferentiated activities for both man and woman. The common gift of the Spirit does not mean that there can be no differentiation in spiritual matters any more than the common gift of the life-giving Spirit of creation means there can be no differentiation in the activities of created nature. But this refusal to allow for differentiation is the effect of the common contemporary use of Gal 3:28, which wishes to see in this passage the assertion that in Christ there is neither male nor female, and this in such a way that being male or being female has simply ceased to

---

introduce a novum. The "male and female" after the *athnach* indicates the content of "man" before the *athnach*.

21  We note as well that the duality of male and female is already indicated in Gn 1:26. There, God determines to create "man" (*adam, anthropon*; singular) in His image and to give "them" (plural) dominion over the creatures (Hebrew: *radah*; LXX: *arxetosan*).

22  In his commentary on Gn 1:27b Claus Westermann makes this same point: "The division of the sexes belongs to the immediate creation of humanity. A consequence of this is that there can be no question of an 'essence of man' apart from existence as two sexes. Humanity exists in community, as one beside the other, and there can only be anything like humanity and human relations where the human species exists in twos. W. Zimmerli is exaggerating when he writes in his commentary: 'A human being in isolation is only half a human being.' A lone human being remains a complete human being in his lonesomeness. What is being said here is that a human being must be seen as one whose destiny it is to live in community: people have been created to live with each other. This is what human existence means and what human institutions and structures show. Every theoretical and institutional separation of man and woman, every deliberate detachment of male from female, can endanger the very existence of humanity as determined by creation" (*Genesis 1–11: A Commentary*, trans. John J. Scullion [Minneapolis: Augsburg Publishing House, 1984], 160).

be important in the arena of the church. The "order of redemption," so the argument goes, has transformed the "order of creation" so that the order of creation simply no longer functions in the church. As illustrative of this, I would like to quote from Prof. Gilbert Bilezikian of Wheaton College, who writes the following in his book *Beyond Sex Roles*:

> The transforming power of the gospel needs to be applied to individual lives *and* to the way Christians relate among themselves. Fragmentation and divisions constitute . . . weapons in Satan's arsenal against the people of God. Where God wants to create unity and cohesion, the enemy seeks to cause alienation and separation. . . . The concept of sex roles is one of those bondages from which the gospel can set us free. Nowhere does the Scripture command us to develop our sex-role awareness as males and females. It calls us . . . to acquire the mind of Christ and to be transformed in His image (Gal 3:27; Eph 4:13; Phil 2:5; and so on). Both men and women are called to develop their "inner man," which means their basic personhood in cooperation with the Holy Spirit.[23]

Quite evident here is the spiritual monism that arises when the concretions of human being, namely, the human as male and the human as female, are not taken with sufficient biblical seriousness. Paul's "inner man" is identified with "basic personhood" and this is not in any way defined by the notions of maleness and femaleness. Indeed, sex roles, which after all is the only way fundamental gender differentiation can express itself, are for Bilezikian a "bondage" from which we must be set free by the Gospel. Hence, for Bilezikian, the works of the Spirit can be differentiated only illegitimately between the male and the female. In such a view, that there might be spiritual vocations which correspond to the distinction between male and female is inconceivable.

However, it is wholly illegitimate to understand Gal 3:28 in a way that obliterates the continuing significance of the distinction between male and female within the "order of redemption." In this regard it is important to observe that immediately following Gal 3:28, that is, in Gal 3:29, Paul introduces the terminology of human sexuality and does so in order to define our being in Christ in terms of the Old Testament covenant and therefore not surprisingly in terms of the masculine role of begetting: "For you are all one [note: this is *eis*, masculine] in Christ, but if you are of Christ, then you are the seed (*sperma*) of Abraham, heirs of the promise." There is no radical disjunction here between the patriarchal story of Abraham in the Old Testament (Abraham means "father of a multitude"; his previous name, Abram, means "the father be exalted") and the new life of unity in Christ through the Holy Spirit. Indeed, a patriarchal story is used to explicate the Gospel of Christ.

---

23  Gilbert Bilezikian, *Beyond Sex Roles: A Guide for the Study of Female Roles in the Bible* (Grand Rapids, MI: Baker Book House, 1985), 208.

Because the Scriptures in fact do consider the human race as consisting in two consubstantial forms and therefore consider these two forms, male and female, as of enduring and abiding significance, it is not surprising but rather to be expected that the Bible is not unaware of distinctive spiritual roles which correspond to roles given to masculinity and which correspond to roles given to femininity. It is not to be overlooked, let alone denigrated, that when the Scriptures speak of God or of those who represent Him to the people of God, it does so predominately through masculine imagery. And similarly, it is not to be overlooked that when the Scriptures speak of the people of God and their relation to God, it does so predominately by means of feminine imagery. And here, with our specific purpose in mind, we reiterate the fact that those figures, both in the Old Testament and in the New Testament, who serve as fundamental representatives or types of the redemptive purposes of God in Christ are male figures. There is the figure of Adam, the figure of Abraham, the figure of Moses (prophet like Moses), the kings of Israel, especially the figure of David. There is also the idea of the first-born son, and there is even the figure of the sacrificial Passover lamb, which according to Exodus 12 was to be a male lamb of one year's age (also, the scapegoat and the goat of the sin offering for the yearly Feast of Expiation were males, Leviticus 16). We mention here also the fact that the Christ Himself, to whom all these masculine types point, assumed His human nature in the masculine mode of human being, and we mention finally the fact that Christ chose as His apostles only males.

We are, of course, aware that there are arguments made that these last two items were mere divine accommodations to the patriarchal social forms of the time and that had Christ come as a woman his mission would have been correspondingly less acceptable and less effective.[24] Quite apart from the fact that his mission was rejected rather considerably as it was, this argument is one self-serving of a prior feminist interest and therefore is unwilling to take seriously the actual facts of the salvation history. Similarly, the argument that if the masculinity of the apostles is significant, then the Jewishness of the apostles must likewise have similar abiding significance, fails to recognize that while Jewishness is not a constitutive feature of human being, maleness or femaleness is constitutive of human being. Again, we are dealing here not with contingencies but with elemental features of human existence.

Does the masculinity of Jesus have anything to say to us about the question of the ordination of women? Does the pastor represent the person of Jesus in a way which creates an ecclesial propriety which is transgressed

---

24  Paul Jewett asserts that there was a cultural and historical necessity for Christ to come as a male but no theological necessity (*Man as Male and Female*, 168f.). Similarly, Letha Scanzoni and Nancy Hardesty: "Given the setting of patriarchal Judaism, Jesus had to be a male" (*All We're Meant to Be* [Waco, Texas: 1975], 177).

should a woman be placed into the office of Word and Sacrament? From the Lutheran Confessions we are aware of the view that the pastor represents Christ's person. For example, in the Apology, in the article "On the Church," Melanchthon discusses the question of the validity of sacraments administered by unworthy ministers. He writes that sacraments administered by such ministers are true sacraments because "they do not represent their own persons but the person of Christ, because of the Church's call, as Christ testifies, 'He who hears you hears me' (Luke 10:16)."[25] The reference to Luke 10 makes it virtually certain that the confessor thought of the minister as the voice of Christ rather than any kind of physical image of the Savior. In the words of the minister one hears the words of Christ, and therefore the one who hears must receive in faith the very spoken words of the minister. We of course recognize and confess this same view.

But now we inquire after the meaning of the masculine form of Jesus' humanity and how this might in fact relate to the Pauline injunctions that only a man may be a pastor. Is there something about the masculine character of the pastor which is fit and apt to represent the position of the Lord in the community of his saints? There are those, of course, who think that the very question evinces an inadmissable romanizing tendency. That is certainly not the intent. I have tried to indicate why it appears *in terms of the Bible's own thought and form* that such a question, especially in view of the contemporary discussion, is demanded, even if the answer is yet to be clearly adumbrated. But to allay any residual fears, we do not suggest that there is anything given to the ordained minister which bestows upon him some ontological capacity whereby is effected "an approximation to Christ as mediator and redemptive head of the Church."[26] If the pastor in the midst of the congregation is able in some natural way to represent Christ by virtue of his masculinity, it will not be because of something added to him by ordination or consecration. Christ redeems nature, making nature itself to be the bearer of the things of the Spirit. Therefore, any such natural representation will exist by virtue of the fact that God so willed to order creation such that it presages in itself the consummation of the Holy Spirit in Christ and His church. Or, as Susannah

---

25  See Ap. VII.29; also AC XXVIII.21f.; Ap VII.47; XII.40.

26  Hauke, *Women in the Priesthood?* 336. This book is an extremely helpful book and with considerable erudition covers a wealth of material, addressing virtually all aspects of the feminist question: biblical, historical, philosophical, sociological, biological, psychological, etc. Yet, on occasion, as in the section of the priest's representation of Christ, Hauke advances a very distinctive Roman Catholic viewpoint which is unacceptable. A further example: "This imaging relationship [of the priest to Christ] has its foundation in the sacrament of ordination to the priesthood, through which, in a way that goes beyond baptism by virtue of its *character indelebilis*, an ontological approximation to Christ is realized" (338).

Herzel has said, the creation is "prophetic material," for it points to some future which is more complete.[27]

There are many voices, and by no means only radical ones, which believe that the maleness of Christ has no significance, neither in the matter of who may become a pastor nor even in the matter of the Savior's redemptive work. I would like to refer to three worthy proponents of such a view, make to each a short response, and then briefly develop my own thoughts. Professor Eric Gritsch, referring especially to Robert Jenson, writes that when Jesus called God "Father" he did not address a male God. Jesus' historical reality—as the revelation of God—transcends such and other designations into a genuine sphere of God-talk which no longer reflects the suspicions and broken relationships of sinful human creatures. The Gospel frees us from feeling guilty about the use of imperfect language and analogies which we need to express praise and thanks to the God who justifies the ungodly.[28] To this we must simply say that in the New Testament the historical reality of Jesus—as the revelation of God—does not transcend the designation of God as "Father" and move us into "a genuine sphere of God-talk." Rather, it is precisely the historical reality of Jesus' humanity which reveals not just God but God as the Father, and therefore the name "Father" becomes the Name addressed by those who, as Paul says in Romans 8, have received the Spirit of the adoption of sons (v. 15: *pneuma huiothesias*). The God-talk of the Bible remains in every case concrete, creaturely, and historical. It does not fly off into some "genuine God-talk," and I suspect that this is so because the Bible does not believe that the things of creation need to be transcended for God to be rightly and truthfully spoken.[29] Nor is this point vitiated by the fact that in the present age the things of creation bear the brokenness of sin. It is in the revelation of the

---

27  Susannah Herzel, "The Body is the Book," in *Man, Woman, and Priesthood*, ed. Peter Moore (London: SPCK, 1978), 102. When I speak of some "natural" representation, I do not have anything especial in mind other than a representation that goes beyond that of the "voice of Christ" and sees in the physicality of Christ something that connotes the office of the ministry.

28  Eric Gritsch, "Convergence and Conflict in Feminist and Lutheran Theologies," *Dialog* 24 (Winter 1985): 11–18.

29  Note how George Florovsky speaks about the relation between the human word and the divine Word in the Bible: "When divine truths are expressed in human language, the words themselves are transformed. . . . The Word of God is not diminished when it resounds in human language. On the contrary the human word is transformed, and as it were transfigured because of the fact that it pleased God to speak in a human language" (quoted in Deborah Belonick, *Feminism in Christianity: An Orthodox Christian Response* [Syosset, NY: 1983], 11f.). The doctrine of the incarnation determines the way Florovsky understands the words of Scripture: the Word became flesh, so that the flesh of Christ was itself Word. Concerning the Scriptures one might put the same thought like this: the Word of God became human word, so that the human words of Scripture are Word of God. We cannot trade this "Nicene" way of thinking about the words and narratives of the Bible for the "adoptionism" of Gritsch's way of thinking.

Christ in the flesh, in his concrete humanity, that we see, in faith and in hope, the consummation of that given in the beginning.

Pastor George Murphy, in the article mentioned above, adduces a christological consideration to argue that it is wrong to think of the pastoral representation of Christ only in masculine terms. He refers to the classical christological doctrine of the anhypostasis of Christ's human nature. According to this doctrine, the flesh of Christ has no independent or autonomous personhood apart from the incarnation of the Word of God. In the incarnation, however, that flesh which possessed no personhood of its own received personhood by its assumption into the person of the eternal Word of God, the second person of the Trinity. Therefore, concludes Pastor Murphy, that humanity assumed by Christ is that humanity common to both men and women, and therefore both can equally represent Christ.[30] Murphy is certainly correct in the view that the christological doctrine of Chalcedon, especially those aspects most beholden to Cyril of Alexandria, understood the term "flesh"—the Word become flesh—to be a generic term referring to human nature as a whole. Christ, the Word, did not unite to Himself only one individual but united to Himself the entire human race.[31] Nonetheless, one ought not overlook the fact that the Chalcedonian fathers developed their Christology in the light of the requirements of soteriology. Christ as the Savior of all must bear the humanity of all. Nevertheless, as post-Chalcedonian discussion indicates, the Fathers were alive to the dangers of conceiving the humanity of Christ in some Platonic fashion whereby Christ's humanity was some kind of abstraction and in no way a specific humanity. That would be the worst kind of Monophysitism, a virtual denial of the true humanity of Christ. The Fathers who interpreted Chalcedon were equally of the opinion that Christ was a concrete human figure. The fact that Christ had assumed "human nature in general" did not exclude the fact that he was human within the specificities of a distinct human person, and that would have included Christ's reality as male.[32] Therefore, while it was not an explicit feature of post-Chalcedonian discussion, the masculinity of Christ was implicitly asserted.

---

30  Murphy, "For the Ordination of Women," 8.

31  See, for example, the christological reflections of Theodore the Studite (died ad 826) in his *Refutations* of the Iconoclasts: "For Christ did not become a mere man (*psilos*), nor is it orthodox to say that He assumed a particular man, but rather that He assumed man in general, or the whole human nature" (*ton kath holou aetoi taen olaen phusin*; *Refutations* 1.4; also 3.17: *taen katholou phusin*).

32  The passage of Theodore the Studite, quoted in n. 31, continues with these comments: "It must be said, however, that this whole human nature was contemplated in an individual manner (*taen en atomo theopoumenaen*), so that He is seen and described, touched and circumscribed, eats and drinks, matures and grows, works and rests, sleeps and wakes, hungers and thirsts, weeps and sweats, and whatever else one does or suffers who is in all respects a man" (*Refutations* 1.4; also 3.17).

Finally, there is the recent book by Adrian Hastings, professor of theology at the University of Leeds, who likewise argues on the basis of the incarnation of Christ, specifically referring to the words of the Nicene Creed that the Christ was made "man," *homo* in the Latin and *anthropos* in the Greek, both terms meaning "generic humanity." Hastings argues that the issue is "whether God in being incarnationally particular does or does not mysteriously break through the bonds of any and every limitation thus imposed. If the male/female wall of binary division remains operative, anymore than the Jew/Gentile wall of binary division, then not all is assumed, not all is redeemed."[33] Again, we need to say that while the generic humanity of Christ was affirmed by the creeds of the church in order to assert the universal, all-encompassing salvific work of the Savior, the specific character of Christ's humanity was never denied, other than perhaps by those of an Apollinarian or Monophysite bent. But in Hastings, too, we see the antipathy of many toward the particularities and concretions of creation. Hastings notes no difference in the distinction between male and female and the distinction between Jew and Gentile. That one is a created distinction, present inherently in the organic unity of humanity, while the other is a contingent distinction which has arisen within the movement of history, is apparently of no matter to Professor Hastings. Rather, he sees in both distinctions "walls of binary division." When that language is applied to the distinction of male and female, there is to be noted an unmistakable Manichaean negativism toward the creation as such. While making much show of being conversant with patristic Christology, Hastings is oblivious to the fact that the Fathers asserted as an essential element of their Christology that Christ is the new Adam and *as such* is the head of a new humanity, a new humanity which, to be sure, encompassed all human beings, both male and female.

In our own reflections we wish to advance two arguments. (1) In discussion concerning the continuing relevance of gender, the relation between the "order of creation" and the "order of redemption" often arises. Many think that the "order of redemption," transcending and transforming the "order of creation," presents a different configuration of human existence altogether. Many others, and here I would classify most Missouri Synod Lutherans, think of the "order of creation" as the implanted will of God in the structure of things and as such it is the expression of God's immutable will. The "order of redemption," on the other hand, constitutes a new existence in a new world brought by Christ, and this existence is determined by grace. This is, in fact, the very posturing of these two "orders" in the 1985 CTCR document *Women in the Church*. Here, to be sure, the "order of creation" is said to be sanctified

---

33  Adrian Hastings, *The Theology of a Protestant Catholic* (London: SCM; Philadelphia: Trinity Press International, 1990), 97.

and hallowed by Christ's work. There is between the two "orders" a relationship of continuity (the first is not destroyed in the second, but continues as sanctified in the second). Yet, one searches in vain in the CTCR document for any organic relationship between the "order of creation" and the "order of redemption" whereby the purposes of God for the world in Christ are already envisioned, presaged, and prophesied in the "order of creation" itself. I have already referred to the striking phraseology of Susannah Herzel, that the creation is "prophetic material" pointing to some greater and more complete future. Along that same line, I would like to suggest that the creating activity of God and the redeeming activity of God are not two qualitatively distinct ways of the divine working, but that they are organically related. The way God works creatively (and this from the beginning) and the way God works redemptively are not intrinsically different but are united in intention and purpose. Perhaps one can express the point like this: the redemptive work of God brings the creative work of God, presently under the alien dominion of sin and death, to its intended purpose and goal. If this is the case, then the "order of creation" is not transformed in the "order of redemption" but is rather illuminated in the "order of redemption." We perceive the "order of creation" most clearly in the "order of redemption." That Christ, the head of the new humanity, was male was *not* due, therefore, to some requirement to maintain the "order of creation." It is not that Christ was a male human person because in the "order of creation" God had given headship and authority to the man, Adam. Rather, God who created humankind in order that He might have communion with it in and through His Word gave the headship of humanity to the man, Adam, *in view of* the eschatological goal of humanity, which is Christ and His church. Because in the final purpose and *telos* of God for the world the man Jesus Christ was to be the head of His Body, the church (which relates to Christ as bride to bridegroom), God in the beginning gave Adam to be head to Eve. As Paul says, "the head of woman is the man" (1 Cor 11:3), and "Adam was created first [or perhaps 'as the first'], then Eve" (1 Tm 2:13). This makes perfectly good sense of two passages of Paul. The first we have already clearly implied, Eph 5:23–33. As is evident in this passage, Paul is implicitly appealing to the creation story of man and woman in Genesis 2. This passage intimately combines the creation of Eve from Adam, the recognition of Adam that the woman is "bone of my bones and flesh of my flesh," and the unity they have together as "one flesh" in the marriage bond. That Adam possesses "headship" within this "one flesh" of the marriage bond is clear. However, in Ephesians 5 Paul's point is not that Christ's love for His Bride, the church, is patterned after what was to be the case between Adam and Eve in the garden. Rather, it is in view of Christ's love for His Bride, the church, that husbands are to love their wives and that wives are to be subject to their husbands as to their head. The true marriage was not that marriage in the garden. The true marriage is that between Christ and the church. All other marriages (including that first one in the garden)—and this is true the more marriages are blessed by love—are faint images and icons of that marriage of the Lamb with His Bride, the church.

The second passage is Rom 5:14, where Adam is explicitly called "the type of the One who is to come" (*hos estin typos tou mellontos*). Here we see more explicitly still that what transpired in the garden was in view of that perfect speaking of God when the Word Himself would become man and be, as the second Adam, also the perfect Adam. Adam in himself was prophetic: he pointed toward the Christ who was to come as the man Jesus. It is utterly erroneous, therefore, to think that the "order of creation" has been overcome in the "order of redemption," for it was in view of the "order of redemption" that the "order of creation" itself was ordered the way it was. The "order of creation" is not merely sanctified and hallowed in the "order of redemption." The "order of creation" comes to its own completion, to its intended goal and end in the "order of redemption."

(2) Finally, we turn again to the fact that in Paul's discussion of the relation between man and woman the story of the creation of man and woman in Genesis 2 is foundational. Adam was created first, then Eve (1 Tm 2:13). Paul's language in 1 Cor 11:8 is more vivid and more instructive: "man is not from woman, but woman from man" (*gyne ex andros*). Adam is the source of woman's being: she is bone from his bone and flesh from his flesh (*ostoun ek ton osteon mou kai sarx ek tas sarkos mou*; Gn 2:23, LXX). Adam does not, therefore, relate to Eve merely in terms of a temporal sequence: he was first and she was second. Rather, he relates to Eve as one who has a posture, a position, a vocation vis-à-vis Eve, a vocation which earlier in 1 Corinthians 11 is indicated by calling the man "the head" of woman (v. 3). What "headship" means in part can be discerned in Col 2:19, where Christ as "Head" is the One "from whom" (*ex hou*) the whole body (here, the church) is nourished and receives its growth. Being "head" includes the notion (at least in biblical usage) of the source from which another's being, life, and sustenance is derived. Not insignificantly, therefore, Paul can designate Jesus as "the last Adam" who became "a life-giving spirit" (1 Cor 15:45). Adam is the one from whom Eve's life is derived and to whom Eve relates as the source of her life. That such derivation does not involve essential inequality is clear: Eve, coming from Adam, relates to him as "bone from his bone and flesh from his flesh." Yet, this relationship of equals is not a relationship of independent and autonomous equals. It is a relationship of equals which has its own intrinsic and organic order and which

is *not* given to interchangeability and mutual reciprocity.[34] It is a relationship of equals established in and through the creating of God, and consists in the bestowal of the self upon another and the corresponding receiving by the other of the one's self-giving. Adam relates to Eve as the one who gives of himself to her. Eve relates to Adam as the one who receives Adam's self-giving.

This relationship of giving and receiving between Adam and Eve relates to fundamental differences between the biblical creation narrative and the pagan creation accounts of the ancient Near East. First of all, in creation accounts of the ancient Near East (such as in the Babylonian *Enuma Elish*) human beings are created to be servants of the gods. However, in the Genesis account, God creates mankind and gives to it the blessings of a good earth and dominion over the earth. God creates mankind in order to be Servant to it. As creator, God gives to His creatures all those good things they need for this body and life. Already in creation, therefore, God is Lord precisely in His servanthood. He is Lord in His bestowal of life, both in the giving and in the sustaining of life.

Second, ancient creation myths frequently derived the existence of the earth from female deities. These deities were usually nature/harvest deities and were the symbolic representations of the mysterious force of the life and fecundity of the earth. The natural cycle of springtime and harvest was understood to be divine, and the natural potency and fertility of the earth were ritually divinized, the gods and goddesses being portrayed as frankly sexual beings who lusted, mated, gave birth, and were the fathers and mothers of the creatures they procreated. In such a view the rhythms of the goddess and of religious life were governed by repetition, by times and seasons. Being governed by the repetition of the seasons, these goddess religions had no functioning concept of the future nor of divine purpose. The idea of a divine Mother, therefore, is associated with the idea of a divine earth. The distinction between God and the creation is compromised and the notion of God's transcendence is lost. But with the loss of the distinction between God and the world there is the corresponding loss of the ideas of divine grace (God wills to love) and of hope (in divine purpose and in the possibility of newness).[35]

In view of such pagan ideas the theological structure implicit in naming God "Father" begins to be evident. We should, however, be aware of the important fact that the question of God's "Fatherhood" and the question of His masculinity are entirely distinct. The church has always been aware of the

---

34 One should note 1 Cor 11:3, which says that God is "head" of Christ. God and Christ, too, relate to one another as equals, but within a relationship of "begetting" and "being begotten." The Father is Father of the Son. He is not nor can become Son. The order indicates the position of relation one has toward the other.

35 It is to be noted how often feminist writers explicitly reject the idea of God's transcendence as an essential element of a patriarchal point of view.

divine prohibition given in Dt 4:15–16: "Since you saw no form on the day that the Lord spoke to you at Horeb out of the midst of the fire, beware lest you act corruptly by making a graven image for yourselves, in the form of any figure, the likeness of male or female." The pagan nature religions surrounding ancient Israel found their opposite in the Old Testament worship which excluded the depiction of God as either male or female. It was, in fact, against the heresy of Arianism that the church most clearly detailed its belief that the Triune God is transcendent to all creaturely categories, including that of male and female. The Christian church does not worship a male god, nor does it worship a female goddess.[36]

This does not mean, however, that the Christian does not worship God the *Father* and God the *Son*. For, very decidedly, the church does worship God the Father and God the Son. The prophets and the apostles and the church have simply been careful to remove God from any notion of father as a *physical* progenitor. God's fatherhood realizes itself apart from any motherhood. Therefore, while God is Father, there is no reality in God's being which can properly bear the designation "Mother." This fact is especially evidenced by the language and narrative of the New Testament, but it is by no means absent in the Old Testament. Every Semitic religion in the ancient Near East, with the exception of Israel, had goddesses. One indication of this is the practice of giving personal names which consist of a god's name plus the word for "father," "mother," "brother," "sister." For example, from Babylon one finds the name *Ummi-Ishtar*, "my mother is Ishtar," or *Samas-abi*, "my father is Samas." However, among the Hebrews there are many names in which "father" occurs, but there are none in which "mother" occurs. From the Hebrew names we may mention Abijah ("Yahweh is my father"), Joab ("Yahweh is father"), Eliab ("El is father") and Abiel ("father is El").[37]

---

36  See Ken Wesche, "God: Beyond Gender, Reflections on the Patristic Doctrine of God and Feminist Theology," *St. Vladimir's Theological Quarterly* 30 (1986): 291–308. The Arians subordinated the Son to the Father by denying the Son's equal divinity with the Father. They interpreted the Son's relation to the Father in strict analogy to the sonship and fatherhood of creatures. Since a human (male) father is temporally prior to his son and wills to beget a son, so also the Father is naturally prior to the Son and relates to the Son by will. Indeed, just as a human male need not be a father but becomes a father, so also God is not Father but becomes Father by willing the Son. Orthodox trinitarian belief asserts that God is Father in the eternal generation of the Son who is the true image of the Father since He participates in the Father's essence/deity (the "of one substance with the Father" of the Nicene Creed).

37  Abijah ("Yahweh is my father") is the name of two women in the Old Testament. Other names include Ahijah ("my brother is Yahweh"), Joah ("my brother is Yahweh") and Malchijah ("my king is Yahweh"). Among Hebrew names there is no occurrence of "my sister is Yahweh" or "Yahweh is queen." Paul V. Mankowski, a member of the Department of Near Eastern Languages and Civilizations at Harvard University, writes: "Of the 55 recorded Hebrew sentence names which are composed of the name YHWH and a verb, each shows the masculine form of that verb" (unpublished paper).

How central the fatherhood of God is to biblical understanding is indicated by God's choosing of Abram to be the progenitor of the chosen people. In the midst of a culture which possessed numerous female deities, God calls Abram, which means "exalted father" or "the father is exalted." It is to Abram that God chooses to make His promises of redemption for the nations, and in so doing God changes Abram's name to Abraham, "father of many nations":

> The Lord appeared to Abram, and said to him, "I am God Almighty; walk before me, and be blameless. And I will make my covenant between me and you, and will multiply you exceedingly. . . . Behold, my covenant is with you, and you shall be the father of a multitude of nations. No longer shall your name be Abram, but your name shall be Abraham; for I have made you the father of a multitude of nations. I will make you exceedingly fruitful; and I will make nations of you, and kings shall come forth from you. And I will establish my covenant between me and you and your descendants after you throughout their generations for an everlasting covenant, to be God to you and to your descendants after you" (Gn 17:1–7).

God makes His own fatherhood known by choosing a man to be "father" of many. But what is important to note is that God's fatherhood is indicated by His free and gratuitous election of Abraham and, in him, of Israel. God related to Abraham as a distinct Other who, while free and possessing transcendent autonomy ("God Almighty"), *chooses* to focus and to direct His love to a particular people and on behalf of a particular people. By making covenant with Abraham, God in effect *adopts* Abraham and his descendents and makes them His own. And this God does without any corresponding divine motherhood. God's fatherhood is indicated independently of any cooperating participation by another. God literally *makes* Abraham and his descendents to be His sons.[38] It is this prevenient, free, and willing making of a people that we term grace (see Dt 7:6–8). Precisely as the God of grace is God "Father." Graciously, as a father, God takes Abraham out of the nations, the tribes, and the families of the earth and makes Abraham himself to be a nation in that Abraham becomes father in the stead of Him who is Father. Abraham is released from the earthly ties of blood and family relationship and is oriented toward a future not determined by earthly bonds but by the everlasting covenant of grace and

---

38 It is interesting to note that the very words spoken to Adam and Eve, "Be fruitful and multiply" (Gn 1:28), are the words used of God's "multiplying" of Abraham and making him "exceedingly fruitful" (Gn 17:2, 6). Already in Abraham a new humanity based upon God's gracious election, that is, upon God's fatherhood, begins. This new humanity will find its fulfillment and completion in the true "son of Abraham" (Mt 1:1), who is also the true Son of the Father. The order of redemption is based upon a fatherhood but without a corresponding motherhood.

mercy in which God everlastingly chooses to be the God of Abraham and his descendents.[39]

It is in the election of Israel that God the Father becomes, in Abraham, Father to the people of Israel. And this theme is central also to the message of the New Testament. For example, the Prologue of the Gospel of John makes clear that the people of God are not made by means of a natural, sexual father-hood, but by the will of God: "to all who received him, who believed in his name, he gave power to become the children of God; who were born not of blood nor of the will of the flesh nor of the will of man, but of God" (Jn 1:12–13). Similarly, Paul indicates that the Christian is the child of Abraham by faith and that therefore the gentiles, and not only the Jews, have access to the grace of the Gospel (Romans 4). That God the Father becomes our father through the free and gracious adoption of us in Christ is nicely summarized in Romans 8:15, which refers to our Baptism: "For you did not receive the Spirit of slavery to fall back into fear, but you have received the Spirit of sonship by whom we cry Abba, Father'" (alla elabete pneuma huiothesias en hoi kratzomen abbi ho pater). The Greek word translated "sonship" really means "adopted as son" or "placed into sonship." In our Baptism into Christ, there-fore, we receive the Holy Spirit whereby we are made sons of the Father (by the Father's gracious adopting of us) and for that reason we call God "Father." It is not incidental, therefore, that in the earliest commentaries on the Lord's Prayer the introductory words "Our Father" were explained by language rem-iniscent of Christian Baptism (Tertullian, Cyprian).

Now what does all of this have to do with the maleness of Jesus? As we have noted, against the subordinationism of Arianism the church fathers fre-quently asserted that true and proper fatherhood belongs to God alone.[40]

---

39  The image of "mother" is incapable of connoting this biblical idea of grace and the idea of purpose (eschatology) which accompanies it. The earth is not free in its giving forth of fruit and harvest. It is in the nature of the earth to bear harvest. A seed is planted and the earth naturally nurtures the seed and eventually bears fruit. The earth is not gracious in doing so; it must by its nature do so. So it is also with woman. When a male seed is implanted in her, she does not will to bear a child. Her nature is such that she nurtures that seed and eventually bears a child, and this sometimes quite against her will (as we know from the abortion debate). It is important to grasp this important point of biblical imagery and nomenclature, for in the present context of feminized theology the idea of nurture is frequently advanced as the equivalent of grace.

40  For example, Athanasius, Orations against the Arians 1.21: after noting that among crea-tures fatherhood and sonship are characterized by serial succession (a son of a father becomes in turn the father of a son, and so on) and division of nature he continues, "Thus it belongs to the Godhead alone, that the Father is properly father, and the Son properly son, and in them, and them only, does it hold that the Father is ever Father and the Son ever Son" (A Select Library of Nicene and Post-Nicene Fathers of the Christian Church [hereafter NPNF], ed. Philip Schaff and Henry Wace, 2nd series [Grand Rapids, MI: Eerdmans, reprint ed. 1980], 4:319). See also Gregory of Nazianzus, Theological Oration 3.6: "He is Father in the absolute sense, for He is not also Son: just as the Son is

However, fatherhood is proper to God because He eternally generates the divine Son. This generation of the Son from the Father is not a generation on the basis of will. That would be the position of the Arians and, moreover, such a generation of the Son from the Father would be like the creaturely begetting of a son by a human father. Rather, the eternal generation of the Son from the Father involves what is sometimes called a "communication of essence" whereby the Godhead of the Father is imparted to the Son so that the Son is "of one substance with the Father" (Nicene Creed). It is, therefore, in the Son that the Father moves out of Himself, so to speak, and resides in another. It is the Son who bears in Himself the Father.

As is well known, it is New Testament witness that the eternal Son of the Father became flesh in the person of Jesus Christ (Jn 1:14). The significance of this is that in the human person of Jesus Christ the heavenly Father comes to us. The divine Father declares His will to be our Father in the person of His incarnate Son. It is the man Jesus who brings the heavenly Father to the world. Or, in the striking words of Irenaeus (c. AD 180), "all saw the Father in the Son: for the Father is the invisible of the Son, but the Son the visible of the Father."[41] Such remarks are in strict agreement with the words of Jesus Himself: "He who has seen me has seen the Father. . . . Believe me that I am in the Father and the Father in me" (Jn 14:9–11). Now the Father reveals Himself in the *incarnate* Son, that is, in the specific humanity which the Son assumed into Himself. That concrete humanity was, however, a male humanity. And it is evident why that was so. Within the order of creation it is in fact the male member of the human race who may, as God wills it, become a father. The male human being alone has the natural capacity to be a father. Within the human order, therefore, it is the masculine image which is naturally apt to connote fatherhood. Indeed, a feminine image is naturally unsuited as an image and indication of fatherhood, for a woman cannot by nature be a father. Nevertheless, it was precisely the purpose of Christ's incarnate life, death, and resurrection that He bring the Father and restore us again as children of the Father. It was in view of the very purpose of Christ's redemptive coming, therefore, that He took upon Himself a male humanity. Christ's being a male was not accidental, nor was it mere accommodation to patriarchal culture. As the eternal Son of the Father, who bears in Himself the Father's divine essence, He came to a sinful and mortal humanity in order to communicate

Son in the absolute sense, because He is not also Father. These names do not belong to us in the absolute sense, because we are both and not one more than the other" (NPNF, 2nd series, 7:302). For the creature, fatherhood is a work, a function. But for God fatherhood is a principle of being, what is called a hypostatic or personal subsistence of being. God is Father; human males may become fathers or not, as they will.

41    Irenaeus, *Against the Heresies* 4.6.6 (*Ante-Nicene Fathers: Translations of the Writings of the Fathers Down to A.D. 325* [Grand Rapids, MI: Eerdmans, 1986–89], 1:469).

and to give to the world that which He Himself possesses, namely, the relation of Son to the Father. And this relation of Son to the Father, Christ gives in and through His humanity. The flesh of Christ was not merely some abstract, passive human "stuff" which Christ assumed. It was, so to speak, the active envisagement of the Father. The flesh of Christ was, and is, the means by which the divine Father becomes Father for us. Christ in His concrete humanity remains the means by which the Father moves out of Himself in order to make us sons in His Son, the new and second Adam. Christ's flesh is not merely a dumb instrument, but it is itself flesh of the Word and therefore it speaks, "Here is your Father. Whoever sees me sees the Father, for I and the Father are one." The flesh of Christ is the active source of that new life which the Father gives by begetting us anew, as Jn 1:13 speaks of it: "Whoever believed in His name, He gave power to become the children of God: who were born not of blood nor of the will of the flesh nor of the will of man, but of God." Since God so created the human race in such a way that it is the male member who can be father, to be male is by revelation the proper mode of the incarnate Son who brings and manifests the divine Father.[42]

And now, finally, we come to the relevance all of this has for the office of the public ministry, for the question of the ordination of women into it, and for the question of women performing those functions which are distinctive of the office of pastor. We begin with the assertion of the Augsburg Confession that the office of the public ministry is the office of the preaching of the Gospel and the administration of the sacraments.[43] It is important to note that this assertion of the constitutive functions of the pastoral office comes immediately after the article on justification through faith (AC IV) which is itself intimately connected with the article on the person of Jesus Christ (AC III). When, however, the Augustana begins to speak of the office of preaching and the sacraments, it says, "In order that we might obtain this [justifying] faith, the ministry of teaching the Gospel and administering the sacraments was instituted." That is, the office of preaching and administering the sacraments is instrumental in the granting of justifying faith to the believer in which we have the new life of the Holy Spirit. The preaching of the Gospel and the administration of the sacraments are the means whereby

---

42  It would be false to say that there is something autonomously inherent or ontologically present in maleness which makes it alone apt to image and indicate God's fatherhood. As the orthodox church fathers were wont to say, God does not pattern Himself after the creature, but the creature is patterned after God. Human fatherhood is a pale image of the eternal Fatherhood which is God's. What we can say and what we must say is this: according to His will as our creator, God so ordered His creation that it is the male and not the female who can be a father. And for that reason, hidden in the will of the creator, it was Christ's male humanity which was the apt and proper humanity for Him to possess in order for Him to manifest to us His eternal Father.

43  SC V; Tappert, *Book of Concord*, 31.

Christ Himself comes, and it is the pastor who preaches and the pastor who administers the sacraments who is representative of Christ and who speaks His voice. But as we have noted, Christ does not come only to bring Himself. He came in the flesh and He comes in the preaching of the Gospel and in the administration of the sacraments as the One who brings the Father. The pastoral office is that office which God has placed in His church and by which and through which He continues to engender sons of God. For those who hear the preached Gospel in faith and for those who receive in faith the body and the blood of Christ given and shed for them for the forgiveness of sins, God continues to be "Father" in the Christ who speaks and gives Himself. Just as it is the person of the incarnate Son who in His male humanity communicates to us the Father's grace, so also it is proper and right—and this in terms of the whole salvific economy of God from the beginning—that the human instrument of the Father's grace in Christ, in the concreteness of male humanity, be an image of the incarnate Image of the eternal Father.

We need to reflect upon the inner and organic connections which bind the speaking of the Gospel and the administration of the sacraments to the inner life of the most Holy Trinity. The God who is Trinity has not kept Himself hidden from us, but for us and for our salvation has made Himself known in the coming of the Son. The movement of the Father outside Himself whereby He imparts His very being to another, namely the Son, finds its analogue in the creation of Eve whereby the bone of Adam's bone and the flesh of Adam's flesh was imparted to Eve. And as the divine Son is a distinct Other, and yet an equal Other, so also was Eve a distinct other, and yet an equal other. We see the self-same economy in the movement of the Father in Christ toward the world whereby Christ, as the new Adam, became a "life-giving spirit" and brought to pass the new Eve, which is the church. And we see finally the self-same economy in the movement of the Father in Christ by means of preaching and the sacraments, whereby children of God are engendered by grace through faith. Where the pastor forgives our sins, where the pastor preaches the Gospel, and where the pastor gives to us the body and blood of Christ, there the heavenly Father, who wills that we be His children, graciously and alone makes us to be His children, or, as Paul says, children of Abraham by faith (Rom 4). In the context of the pastoral office a male pastor remains the apt representative of the Father's grace whereby all, male and female alike, hear the words of Christ and become the Bride of the Groom.

As illustrative of the above position we take a couple of contexts from our Lutheran liturgy. First of all, we adduce the confession and absolution of sins.[44] At the beginning of the worship service, the people say, "If we confess our sins, God, who is faithful and just, will forgive our sins and cleanse us from

---

44  *Lutheran Worship* (St. Louis: Concordia Publishing House, 1982), 158.

all unrighteousness." It becomes immediately clear who "God" really is when the pastor continues, "Let us then confess our sins to God the *Father*" (italics added). It is, then, to the Father that the people confess their sins, and this is further indicated by the fact that the confession of sins which follows concludes with the prayer that God will forgive, renew, and lead us "for the sake of your Son." When, therefore, the pastor, upon the confession of the people, speaks the words of forgiveness, it is clear that he speaks the Father's forgiveness which, to be sure, has been mediated through the Son and the Holy Spirit. The pastor, standing "in the stead of Christ," stands for the Father.

Second, we take a look at the prayer spoken at the conclusion of the celebration of the Lord's Supper.[45] The prayer is addressed to "God the Father, the fountain and source of all goodness, who in loving-kindness sent your only-begotten Son into the flesh" and the prayer gives thanks to God the Father that "for [Christ's] sake you have given us pardon and peace in this sacrament." From this language it is clear that the prayer regards the ultimate Giver of the sacrament, that is, of the body and blood of Christ, to be the Father. It is the Father who for us and because of our sins gave His Son up unto death. Here then also it is evident that the pastor who administers and gives the body and the blood of Christ in the sacrament ought be representative of the Father who gives His Son for us.

To conclude we take note of the thought of two theologians who, although taking a different emphasis than we have taken, yet conclude that the ordination of women is improper or at least unwise. Regin Prenter, a Danish Lutheran theologian, has argued that the prohibitions of Paul (against women teaching in the church) are not merely commandments which are culturally determined and may not have lasting relevance. They are commandments "which intend to preserve the right and pertinent tradition of the Gospel."[46] They are similar to the commandments of Jesus, such as the command to baptize, or to 'do' the Lord's Supper, or to evangelize. Such "commandments of the Gospel" ("Gebote des Evangeliums") command the ways in which the Gospel properly is carried forth or preserved within the church.

Since the Gospel, argues Prenter, is a unity of the event of salvation history and its application through means, the external form of the means is not left

---

45  Ibid., 174.

46  Regin Prenter, *Die Ordination der Frauen zu dem überlieferten Pfarramt der lutherischen Kirche*, *Luthertum* 28 (Berlin/Hamburg, 1967), 8: "Gebote, welche die rechte, die sachgemässe Überlieferung des Evangeliums hüten wollen." The German word "sachgemäss," which I have rendered with "pertinent," means "appropriate to the thing" or "suitable to the thing." In Prenter's sentence the meaning is that Paul's prohibitions are intended to preserve the Gospel through the commanding of behavior which promotes the Gospel and the communal life it creates.

to us but is given to us from the salvific history.[47] The commandments of Paul concerning the role of Christian women in the Christian worship assembly are just such "commandments of the Gospel." Paul speaks commandments which are analogous to Christ's commands to baptize and to celebrate the Lord's Supper in that they intend, like Christ's, to order the continuing life of the church in such a way that the reality of the Gospel and the new life it engenders is sustained and maintained. Concerning the institution of the means of grace, argues Prenter, one may not merely regard them as activities and therefore believe that only their form is binding upon the church. One must also consider the office which administers the means of grace and the form in which it was instituted. "If the history of salvation and the means of grace are something historically given, then they must be continued [in the church] in the same way in which they were historically given."[48] In this view, therefore, the fact that Christ gave the command to baptize and to celebrate the Lord's Supper to His apostles is not indifferent to the question of who may properly administer the sacraments in the ongoing life of the church.

The second theologian is James I. Packer, a prominent evangelical theologian with English roots. In a recent article he summons the evangelical community to rethink its somewhat precipitous rush toward the ordination of women into the presbyterate (roughly corresponding to our pastoral office). He presents four arguments. First, the Reformation principle of the authority of Scripture includes the idea of the sufficiency of Scripture. Yet, despite the clear affirmation of women by Jesus, the New Testament nowhere indicates that women functioned as presbyters. Obedience to the Scriptures seems to indicate that it is unwarranted to introduce a practice in the exercise of the presbyteral office which is not indicated in the sufficient Scriptures.

Packer's second argument is that Christ is the true minister in all Christian ministry, and that the words and acts of Christ's ministers are the "medium of his personal ministry to us." Packer's comments at this point are worthy of quotation:

> Since the Son of God was incarnate as a male, it will always be easier, other things being equal, to realize and remember that Christ is ministering in person if his human agent and representative is also male. . . . Stated structures of ministry should be designed to create and sustain with fullest force faith knowledge that Christ is the true minister. Presbyteral leadership by women, therefore, is not the best option. That one male is best represented by another male is a matter of common sense; that Jesus' maleness is basic to his role as our incarnate Savior is a matter of biblical

---

47  Here, Prenter speaks of "an institution of salvation history" ("eine heilsgeschichtliche Einsetzung," ibid., 10).

48  Ibid.: "Wenn die Heilsgeschichte und die Gnadenmittel etwas geschichtlich Gegebenes sind, müssen sie so wie sie geschichtlich gegeben wurden, weiter überliefert werden."

revelation. . . . To minimize the maleness shows a degree of failure to grasp the space-time reality and redemptive significance of the Incarnation; to argue that gender is irrelevant to ministry shows that one is forgetting the representative role of presbyteral leadership.[49]

It is of especial interest that an evangelical theologian of Packer's stature makes this kind of argument, for it is sometimes claimed that such an argument represents a Romanizing tendency or is mere speculation. Those who make such claims may wish to take Packer's exhortation to heart and to think again about the implications of the doctrines of creation and of the incarnation for the reality of the church and its life as a renewed humanity.

Packer's third argument is that one cannot rightly ignore the significance of gender. Male and female are set in a "nonreversible relation" in which leadership responsiblity is given primarily to the man. Since presbyters are set apart for authoritative leadership, it is most proper that "paternal pastoral oversight" be reserved for designated Christian men.

Finally, the example of Mary as a supreme model of devotion and of developing discipleship is final proof of the "non-necessity of ordination for a woman who wishes to serve the Father and the Son, and of the significance that can attach to unordained roles and informal ministries."[50]

A concluding word: in matters of faith it is always a question of faithfulness, not of sight. The distinction of male and female and the biblical model for their mutual and complementary but non-reciprocal relationship is a datum of revelation and must therefore be held by the perception of faith. That Christ is the incarnate Son in whom we come to know the Father and to be known by the Father is similarly a datum of revelation, and we recognize this only by the Spirit. And finally, that Paul is an apostle of the Word who was entrusted by the Word to speak of the church and to found the church upon his apostolic testimony and activity, that too is of faith. But because all of these things are of faith and not of sight, because they are of God and not of the world, they are easily forgotten and lost when the church no longer with the requisite rigor or with the requisite credal interest finds it necessary to think on these things. A "know-nothing" hermeneutic which finds itself satisfied when explicit and particular prohibitions are wanting in Scripture[51]

---

49  J. I. Packer, "Let's Stop Making Women Presbyters," *Christianity Today* (February 11, 1991), 20.

50  Ibid.

51  Absence of explicit prohibition concerning women pastors or, say, the distribution of the Lord's Supper by women is sometimes regarded as sufficient cause for declaring the Bible unclear or the practice not contrary to the Scriptures. In its 1985 report *Women in the Church*, the CTCR rightly said that "everything depends on the nature of functions assigned to various offices" (46). Any precipitous declamations that a practice is not contrary to the Scriptures without first theologically reflecting upon the nature of

will not be competent to inquire after the inner and organic relation between word and act, between what the incarnate Word did and what the church must do to be faithful to the Gospel. It remains the unavoidable task of the church to inquire after its practice and to lay bare the theological and evangelical dimensions of those things it does which are significant for preserving and making vivid the Gospel of a new creation.

---

the function is to fail the church in the necessary task of theological and confessional leadership.

# Vocational Boundaries

## The Service of Women
## within The Lutheran Church—Missouri Synod

## Kimberly Schave

### Introduction

Although women's ordination is consistently debated within the Church today, The Lutheran Church—Missouri Synod (LCMS) has maintained the biblical and historical practice of ordaining only men to the pastoral office. Reasons for maintaining this practice are rooted in Scripture and in no way diminish the contributions that women have historically made to the Church. Scripture provides us with countless examples of faithful women whose service within vocations other than pastor are recognized and greatly respected.

The ordination of women has been a relatively recent development within the Lutheran Church, just a mere forty years ago in North America, in fact. While many offer biblical examples of women's service as support for this practice, Holy Scripture offers no support that women held the office of pastor or presbyter or performed priestly duties. Certainly women were held in high esteem, even being identified as prophetesses and disciples, but Scripture does not record that women ever entered the Most Holy Place, nor did they offer intercessory prayer, make sacrifices, or perform the sprinkling of the blood. This restriction from serving in an office that involved public proclamation in no way minimized the role of women in witnessing through the course of their vocations. The same can be said for women within the LCMS today.

### Biblical Boundaries

God placed boundaries for the benefit and protection of His creation. Genesis 2:15–17 provides the first account of God providing boundaries for man when

He commanded Adam not to eat of the tree of the knowledge of good and evil. God entrusted Adam with the care of the garden while at the same time protecting him from death. We know Eve was given this same information based on her response to the serpent in Gen. 3:2–3, but she ultimately gave in to the temptation placed before her. Satan's deceptive words mattered more to Eve than the very Word of God that had been given to her. Luther states of Satan's motives:

> He does not immediately try to allure Eve by means of the loveliness of the fruit. He first attacks man's greatest strength, faith in the Word. Therefore the root and source of sin is unbelief and turning away from God, just as, on the other hand, the source and root of righteousness is faith. Satan first draws away from faith to unbelief.[1]

Eve added to her first sin when offering the forbidden fruit to Adam. After both ate of the fruit of the tree from which they were not to eat, they hid from God in fear. Adam and Eve compounded their sin as they avoided accepting responsibility for their actions and refused to confess their sins. They both rejected God's gifts. Eve despised God's gift of protection put forth in His Word by failing to heed His command, and Adam failed to heed this same command given to him after being gifted with the task of subduing the earth and having dominion over it. Adam further despised the gift of a helpmate that God provided him by attempting to distort it instead as a burden. He appeared to accuse God in Gen. 3:12 with his words: "The woman whom You gave to be with me . . . , " for causing him to sin—seemingly shifting the burden of his guilt onto God.

As a result of this denial of God's gifts and the violation of His protective boundaries, a curse is placed upon the man and woman. For the man, as a result of listening to his wife over and above the Word of God, he now will have to engage in toilsome labor and also know death (Gen. 3:17–19). For the woman, she will now suffer pain in childbearing and will continue to be under the rule of her husband (Gen. 3:16). As a result of the fall, women will now struggle with this arrangement and attempt to claim headship for themselves. Luther states:

> For the punishment, that she is now subjected to the man, was imposed on her after sin and because of sin, just as the other hardships and dangers were: travail, pain, and countless other vexations. Therefore Eve was not like the woman of today; her state was far better and more excellent, and she was in no respect inferior to Adam, whether you count the qualities of the body or those of the mind.[2]

---

1   Martin Luther, *Luther's Works*, gen. ed. Jaroslav Pelikan, Hilton C. Oswald, and Helmut T. Lehmann (St. Louis: Concordia, 1958), 1:162 [hereafter LW].

2   LW 1:115.

Both man and woman are punished and cast out from complete communion with God in Eden. But out of love, God puts in place a plan for redemption. He also puts into place yet another boundary for the benefit and protection of His creation as described in Gen. 3:23–24: " . . . therefore the LORD God sent him out from the garden of Eden to work the ground from which he was taken. He drove out the man, and at the east of the garden of Eden he placed the cherubim and a flaming sword that turned every way to guard the way to the tree of life."

The Genesis accounts warn and guard us from erring in the same way that Adam and Eve did. Today Satan continues to try to draw us away from God's Word. Knowing Christ is the Word, we know that if Scripture is attacked, then Christ is attacked too. Like Eve, when we begin to turn away from God's Word or add to it, we are in danger of being deceived as she was. As Luther states in reference to Eve:

> But it is the beginning of one's ruin to turn away from God and to turn to Satan, that is, not to remain constant in the Word and in faith. When Satan sees these beginnings, he now exerts himself with his utmost power, as though against a leaning wall, in order to overwhelm her altogether.[3]

Today we see this attack on the foundation of the Church as more denominations turn away from the authoritative teachings of Scripture. Doctrine and practices of the historic Christian Church continue to be compromised as a result of placing our own human reason above God's inspired, inerrant, and infallible Word. Luther spoke of this in relation to the fall:

> Let these events be a warning for us that we may learn what man is. For if this happened when nature was still perfect, what do we think will happen to us now? And we have examples before our eyes. For many of those who originally thanked God with us for His revealed Word have not only fallen away but have become our adversaries.[4]

In addition to the account of the fall contained in Genesis, Moses has also handed us God's most notable set of boundaries—the Ten Commandments. In his Small Catechism, Luther speaks to the meaning of the Ten Commandments in this way:

> God threatens to punish all who break these commandments. Therefore, we should fear His wrath and not do anything against them. But He promises grace and every blessing to all who keep these commandments. Therefore, we should also love and trust in Him and gladly do what He commands.[5]

---

3   LW 1:155.

4   LW 1:156.

5   *Luther's Small Catechism with Explanation* (St. Louis: Concordia, 1986), 14.

While boundaries (the Law) play a significant role in the life of the believer, the Lutheran Church places a strong emphasis on distinguishing properly between this Law and the Gospel of Jesus Christ. Somewhat simplistically, this can be described as what we do (Law) and what God does or what God promises (Gospel). Both have important standing within the everyday lives of believers.

While Lutherans recognize that the Gospel should predominate in all theological conversations, we also recognize that the Law has its proper place. David provides us with an example of how we might better embrace boundaries (Law) when he writes: "I will lift up my hands toward Your commandments, which I love, and I will meditate on Your statutes" (Ps. 119:48). We cannot grasp the forgiveness that is ours in Jesus without first knowing that we are sinners. The Law provides the diagnosis, and the Gospel provides the cure. Although we are incapable of fulfilling the Law completely, we have assurance that this gap is bridged through the atoning work of Christ on the cross. This understanding of the proper distinction between Law and Gospel is essential as we go about our daily living in both the kingdom of the left (secular) and the kingdom of the right (sacred). God indeed places boundaries on our service (Law), but it is out of His gracious love and desire to protect us that He does so (Gospel).

## VOCATIONAL BOUNDARIES

As original sin affected the dynamics of everyday life for Adam and Eve, so does it affect us today. As it was given to Adam to labor through the day, today we labor in our careers and in the civil realm. As it was given to Eve to experience pain in childbirth and to be under the headship of her husband, today women live this out within their family vocations. As it was given to the Church to function as the Body of Christ, she continues to uphold what God has both commanded of her and gifted to her.

Within the Church, we receive God's gifts through the Word and Sacraments. After being replenished through the means of grace, we go out into the world to care for our families and to love our neighbors. Holy service is rendered through the ordinary course of daily living.

### WITHIN THE HOME

Life within the family presents many challenges, but it also presents many opportunities for witness. Through the everyday tasks of serving our spouse and rearing and nurturing our children, we are serving God. The head of the family is tasked with teaching the faith to the family. The very nature of forgiveness is taught to children through the example set by Christian parents.

Through their service to each other, a husband and wife model the submission exemplified by Christ in His own selfless sacrifice.

While God has placed women under the headship of their husbands, this is not meant to be a daunting arrangement. The husband is to put his wife's welfare first, and the wife is to respond to her husband's leading. The marriage relationship models that of Christ's relationship with the Church (Eph. 5:21–33), an arrangement born out of love. Where the biblical form of submission is found, peace, joy, and freedom also are found.

Along with service to spouse, service to children occurs within the home. Procreation requires both a mother and a father, and this arrangement within marriage provides for the stability of the family unit. We have no better example than God the Father for determining how best to teach and nurture our children. By His very nature He exhibits love, compassion, and mercy toward His children. From this we respond in kind to our own children. What parent out of love for his or her child doesn't put boundaries in place and enforce punishment when the boundaries are violated? Children do not have the maturity to know limits with respect to safety. God has placed the responsibility on parents to protect them. Motherhood is a vocation to be held in high esteem. An infant in the womb is utterly defenseless, so the mother provides protection for that child. If she is confused about this responsibility or unable to provide for the child, loving Christians can counsel the mother on God-pleasing alternatives for the future care of the child. For mothers, the selfless service to those entrusted to her care brings glory upon her, her husband, and God. Scripture provides many examples of faithful mothers, but none stands out more than Mary, the mother of our Lord. As Luther states:

> She is not puffed up, does not vaunt herself or proclaim with a loud voice that she is become the Mother of God. She seeks not any glory, but goes about her usual household duties, milking the cows, cooking the meals, washing pots and kettles, sweeping out the rooms, and performing the work of maidservant or housemother in lowly and despised tasks, as though she cared nothing for such great gifts and graces.[6]

God chose just this sort of woman to bestow the honor of giving birth to the Child who would bring about the salvation of the entire world. Mary exemplified what it is to be a servant of God through her humble act of faith and obedience. The care and nurture she provided the Christ Child through her vocation as mother was a form of service not only to God but also to her neighbor.

Care for the neighbor begins with those closest to us—our family members. This model of love and care can then extend to more distant neighbors within

---

6    LW 21:329.

our community, country, or world. It can be said that mission originates from vocation.

## Within the Workplace and the Civil Realm

After the fall, Adam and Eve were both given the burden of toiling. Today we toil as a means of receiving our daily bread. We are to "be subject for the Lord's sake to every human institution" (1 Pet. 2:13). We must meet specific requirements to hold a particular position in the workplace or civil realm, and we must submit to authority within the established hierarchy of the organization. Sometimes it is difficult to see that our work can be a source of blessing to others, but that in no way diminishes one's service in the sight of the Lord. It is not always easy to work under a boss or alongside co-workers who might not share our same values, but in so doing we serve our neighbor in love.

We also serve our neighbor within the civil realm. We are called to obey laws, pay taxes, cast informed votes, and pray for those in authority, among other things. Within the public square, Christians speak for those who cannot in an effort to protect their rights. We elect politicians with appropriate qualifications who will best represent his or her constituency. These politicians enforce the laws of the land, the boundaries that have been put in place within our communities for the benefit and protection of citizens.

The government also is an instrument of God that helps maintain order and restrain evil within society. Requirements must be met for military service, and even within this service, limits exist. Presently in the United States, the Selective Service System exempts women from registering due to limitations on their role in combat. While some combat roles in the United States military have been opened up to women, those involving direct ground offensive combat have not. Our society continues to protect women from some of the risks of front-line combat, most notably the risk of being taken prisoner by the enemy and being subject to abuse. Rather than seeing these restrictions as a burden to women, we can see them instead as a way in which our society acknowledges their value.

## Within the Church

Qualifications also exist for those wishing to hold offices within the church. God pronounces a clear "no" with respect to women (and even some men) who may desire to serve in the vocation of pastor. God's command is based on Eve's actions within the garden as well as on the qualifications for overseer that He provides within the Scriptures. This model also supports the relationship of Christ and the Church, which serves as the Bride of Christ.

Paul tells us that women are to learn quietly with all submissiveness since Adam was formed before Eve, and also because it was not he, but Eve, who was deceived and became a transgressor (1 Tim. 2:11–14). An attitude of quietness and submission makes one more receptive to what is being taught. A woman can gladly receive the pastor's teaching knowing it comes from God.

Recognizing the rhythm of our worship within the Divine Service can also help us gladly take on a posture of receptivity toward God's gifts. In the introduction to *Lutheran Worship*, we read:

> The rhythm of our worship is from him to us, and then from us back to him. He gives his gifts, and together we receive and extol them. We build one another up as we speak to one another in psalms, hymns, and spiritual songs. Our Lord gives us his body to eat and his blood to drink. Finally his blessing moves us out into our calling, where his gifts have their fruition.[7]

In worship, we rest and we receive. In Luke 10:38–42, we are told Martha busied herself with distractions while Mary sat at the Lord's feet to take in His teaching. Martha was too busy and left one thing undone—receiving what Christ wished to give her. In the church today, God has appointed His undershepherd, the pastor, to stand in the stead of Christ, so it is fitting that we should rest and receive from him the gifts God wishes to bestow upon us during worship. Within the Table of Duties of the Small Catechism we find additional scriptural support for what the hearers owe to their pastors.

The Table of Duties also addresses the expectations of bishops, pastors, and preachers based on the qualifications of overseer found in Scripture. Only certain competent males who are chosen are qualified to fill this office according to 1 Tim. 3:1–7; Paul states that a bishop must be pious, able to teach, and the husband of one wife, among other things. Luther also asserts:

> Children, women, and other persons are not qualified for this office, even though they are able to hear God's word, to receive baptism, the sacrament, absolution, and are also true, holy Christians, as St. Peter says [1 Pet. 3:7].[8]

Yet another reason for a male-only pastorate relates to the Church, the Bride of Christ. Scripture presents the theme of the bride and the bridegroom. In Genesis we read of the marriage of Adam and Eve, and in the last chapter of the Bible we read of the marriage of Christ to His Church—"the wife of the Lamb" (Rev. 21:9). In Eph. 5:22–33, the union of husband and wife is compared to that of Christ and the Church. We read of this also in John 3:29 as John the Baptist exalts Christ. In each instance, Jesus is always the groom (male), and the Church is always the bride (female). This relationship would become distorted if it were not a male standing in the place of Christ, administering the Word and Sacraments.

---

7   *Lutheran Worship* (St. Louis: Concordia, 1982), 6.

8   LW 41:154.

God has clearly restricted the Office of the Holy Ministry to certain men. Where God has said "no" to this one office, He says "yes" to countless other ways in which women may serve. While it is from a male pastor that women are blessed to receive the gifts of God, women are able to use these gifts and employ what they have learned within the areas of service that have been given to them—their vocations.

## BOUNDARIES WITHIN WOMEN'S SERVICE TO THE CHURCH

Considering we are given no examples of women in either the Old or New Testament serving as priests, presbyters, pastors, or bishops, the service of women as described in the Bible cannot be used to argue in favor of women's ordination. Additionally, we are provided with a model for the pastorate by observing the choice Jesus made to appoint twelve male apostles despite having many women available for selection. While it is clear that God chose men to serve as overseers, women in the Scriptures did make vital contributions to the Church through their various vocations, both secular and sacred.

One sacred role attributed to women in Scripture is that of prophetess. Although there is no mention of women speaking publicly on behalf of God before the assembly, they did offer private counsel, judge matters, and thank and praise God, especially through song and poetry.[9] Most notable of the prophetesses described in the Old Testament are Miriam, Deborah, and Huldah.

Miriam, the sister of Moses, led the women of Israel in song in response to the triumphal passing through the Red Sea (Exod. 15:20–21). She wrongfully pitted her gifts against Moses, which provoked God to strike her with leprosy, thus resulting in her exile from the camp for seven days (Num. 12:1–16). Despite her sinful attempt at claiming authority that was not hers, Miriam was restored as a result of Moses' prayers. She would later be honored along with Moses and Aaron by the prophet Micah—a demonstration of God's grace and forgiveness (Mic. 6:4).

The prophetess Deborah served as a judge, leading Israel and deciding cases (Judg. 4:6–10). Barak insisted that Deborah accompany him to the battlefield. The honor of victory would not go to him, since he refused to take his rightful position as a man. Deborah, like Miriam, sang a song of victory to motivate those fighting the battle (Judges 5). She served God in an important way, but she never had responsibility for priestly duties.

---

9    Edward Engelbrecht, gen. ed., *The Lutheran Study Bible* (St. Louis: Concordia, 2009), 389.

When King Josiah desired to learn more about the message found in the Book of the Law, a group led by the high priest Hilkiah went to "inquire of the Lord" through the prophetess Huldah. Through Huldah, the Lord spoke words of both condemnation and mercy to King Josiah (2 Kings 22:14–20). But note that Huldah provided private counsel rather than prophesying before the assembly.

The New Testament offers much evidence of the value Jesus placed on women within His ministry. Not only did they become disciples and support His ministry, but they also were entrusted with the care of His body. Mary was chosen to carry, give birth to, nurture, and rear Jesus. A woman anointed Jesus' feet with oil (John 12:3). Women stood by Jesus as His body hung on the cross (Mark 15:40). Women brought spices to prepare His body after it was placed in the tomb; God saw fit that these women would be the first to find Jesus' body gone and the tomb empty (Mark 16:1). These same women would encounter Jesus' resurrected body, even taking hold of His feet, when He greeted them on their way to share the angels' message with the disciples (Mark 16:9). The honor was then given to a woman, Mary Magdalene, to provide the first witness of Jesus' resurrection (John 20:18).

Although women played important roles both during Old and New Testament times, biblical boundaries that transcend time have been put in place for women. They are not to teach men or rule over them in the home (Eph. 5:21–31) or in the church (1 Tim. 2:8–14). But this command (the Law) concerning the service of women is informed by the Gospel. In worship, a Christian receives the treasures found within Word, water, bread and wine. In vocation, a Christian responds to these treasures in love for the neighbor. Love for neighbor is where women have biblically and historically excelled in their service to the Church. Today, women continue to contribute to the work of the Church in a multitude of ways apart from the pastoral office, and in so doing, they respect the very boundaries God has put in place for them.

One such way women serve is through the Lutheran Women's Missionary League (LWML). The LWML bankrolls ministry today even as the women of the New Testament era provided for Jesus' ministry. Within the trademark purple boxes of the LWML, mites are collected and offered to the church with the same trust with which the widow offered her mite in Luke 21:2–4.

In addition, theologically trained women are entrusted with the education of children within our Lutheran schools in the same manner as Priscilla, who along with Aquila explained to Apollos the way of God more accurately (Acts 18:26). Similarly, Anna was at the temple day and night, likely serving there, and gave thanks to God and spoke of Him to all who were waiting for the redemption of Jerusalem (Luke 2:38). Pious women perform acts of mercy as a form of Christian outreach in the same way Dorcas performed good works and charitable deeds (Acts 9:36).

## The Diaconate in the LCMS

Phoebe, described as a servant and helper to Paul in Rom. 16:1, serves as the example for the diaconate as women seek to care for the body and the soul. A deaconess holds a consecrated office within the LCMS, providing diaconal care and extending mercy to those in need. She may hold membership within the Concordia Deaconess Conference, which is a free association of certified and LCMS-rostered deaconesses who subscribe to and live by the confessional position of the LCMS.

LCMS deaconesses may be single, married (some to pastors), or widowed. They are mothers, grandmothers, daughters, and sisters. They have experience with divorce, abuse, depression, post-abortion syndrome, the death of children and grandchildren, and caring for aging parents, among other things. These experiences have better equipped them for recognizing when others are hurting, and these experiences aid deaconesses in providing appropriate counsel to those who are suffering, referring others to the pastor when absolution is necessary. There is no lack of need, so service in this office can be overwhelming. But there is also no shortage of blessings that result from this work. As a deaconess serves with the strength that God supplies, she brings glory to God and love to His people. There are numerous ways in which her service is manifested.

### Care within the Congregation (Luke 2:37)

Linda serves a parish with responsibility for the care of women, children, and families. She serves in various choirs and leads devotions at two Lutheran preschools. She shares the same understanding as her pastor of the Office of the Holy Ministry, the ministry of Word and Sacrament, and this understanding is foundational to all of her duties and responsibilities. This makes it a privilege for her to stand behind the Office of the Holy Ministry. It is easy for Linda to point hurting people to the pastors of the church because they preach Law and Gospel in every sermon. She was able to provide counsel to a middle-aged woman who was still struggling with a particular sin she committed as a teenager. This woman was convinced that God was punishing her now with a rare form of cancer. Linda shared the love of God by assuring this woman that Jesus already had paid for all of her sins when He suffered and died on the cross. Thus "if we confess our sins, God, who is faithful and just, will forgive us our sins and cleanse us from all unrighteousness."[10]

---

10  *LSB*, p. 151.

Ultimately, Linda pointed this woman to the pastor for private Confession and Absolution.

Dorcel also serves a parish with responsibility for visiting the sick and homebound, conducting Bible studies, and supervising Vacation Bible School classes. Her background as a library administrator and teacher has helped her perform her deaconess duties. While working at a Lutheran nursing home, Dorcel was able to share the love of Christ through Scripture reading and hymn singing with residents and families. She often fields the question of when she will preach, to which she responds with an explanation of why this is not her role as a deaconess. Instead, her work involves providing diaconal care and performing acts of mercy on behalf of the members of her church.

Nicole has served as a parish deaconess with responsibility for serving on the parish education committee, assisting confirmation students with writing assignments, leading music during Vacation Bible School, starting a women's fellowship group, and leading the fellowship group's Bible studies. Her life as a mother of a young child informs her service on the parish education committee as it works to ensure that children have opportunities to learn about God and Jesus through Sunday School and other activities. Nicole also has organized and led a mission trip to Poland, where the group offered English Bible camps for children. The expressions on the faces of the children when they heard stories about Christ and were shown His love proved memorable. The children were thrilled that the group came all the way from the United States to tell them about Jesus.

## CARE OF THE DISABLED (MATTHEW 11:4–5)

Judith is a ministry consultant with a Lutheran agency that serves those with intellectual and developmental disabilities. She ensures that the spiritual lives of clients are being supported as she collaborates with churches, agencies, volunteers, and staff to provide training. Judith has had the privilege of providing comfort at the deathbed of one of her clients until the pastor was able to arrive. She also assisted a young client whose needs were being overlooked upon the death of her mother. Judith is privileged to help make sad moments a little better for her clients by pointing them to Jesus.

Pat founded an organization that works in the Sudan to reach people with disabilities. She understands the suffering of those she serves because she is the mother of a child with Down syndrome. She knows all too well the stigma and rejection that accompanies such a disability, one that society may see as a reason for ending life. Pat enjoys bringing those she serves the reminder of the sweet relief that comes from knowing Jesus bore that stigma and pain for us. One such woman she served in the Sudan had stumps instead of fully formed feet and fingers. Pat held this woman, told her how beautiful she was in her eyes and in Jesus' eyes, and reassured her that when Jesus comes to take her home she will suffer no more pain. Pat helped this woman to understand that until that time, Jesus bathes her through her family and feeds and dresses her through the hands and feet of her fellow Christians.

## CARE OF THE LEAST OF THESE (MATTHEW 25:45)

Kim has experience serving as a deaconess in a Lutheran mission congregation with responsibility also for starting and directing a pregnancy resource center. She was charged with organizing a community-based interdenominational soup kitchen as part of the mission church's offering to those in need within the community. Her background in business prior to becoming a deaconess provided a framework for how to facilitate these projects. Kim routinely delivered leftover meals to those in low-income housing areas who were without transportation. She listened attentively at soup kitchen lunches as veterans spoke of their military experiences. Kim also counseled mothers to choose life for their unborn babies. She discovered that human care is a viable option for community outreach within the start-up of a new Word and Sacrament ministry, especially in a place where Lutheranism is not widely known or accepted.

## CARE OF THE PRISONER (MATTHEW 25:36)

Sandy works within prison ministry with responsibility for conducting women's Bible studies, overseeing a prisoner re-entry program, and providing training and resources on prison ministry. There are many angry women in prison, and Sandy helped one woman turn away from her anger by praying for someone who had hurt her in the past. Sandy reminded this woman that sin is what makes people hateful, and Christ came to destroy the power of sin and death. The inmate eventually prayed for the person with whom she was angry. She admitted to feeling that a huge burden had been lifted and that she was no longer filled with hate and anger. Witnessing God do the impossible is something Sandy experiences routinely within her work.

## CARE OF THE SICK (MATTHEW 25:36)

Sharon, a registered nurse, has served within hospital chaplaincy. Her knowledge of the hospital and medical arena and the associated staffing issues gave her a great advantage in becoming part of a chaplaincy team. It helped her serve as an advocate for the patient and family and enabled her to anticipate the needs of those receiving medical care. Sharon is now developing an inner-city ministry to assist individuals as they move from poverty to independent living. The lives of mothers and children who feel hopeless and deserted by society will now be touched with Christ's love as they are reminded of the one who has not deserted them or left them hopeless.

## Care through Encouragement (1 Thessalonians 5:11)

Mary serves as a diaconal writer with an organization devoted to working out the implications of the Lutheran doctrine of vocation and engaging contemporary culture with the truths of the Lutheran Confessions. She has been working at parsing out cultural interpretations from the written Word of God, learning the blessed role of women. This role involves representing the Bride of Christ—even representing all of humanity—as women receive sacrificial love from the God who pursues them and, in turn, serve their neighbors as they are able. She especially appreciates how a deaconess can demonstrate God's presence in both kingdoms, the sacred and the secular, and that theology is for *real life on earth*. It has an impact—for clergy, church workers, and laypeople alike.

## Conclusion

While women have played an important role throughout biblical history, there is no scriptural evidence of female pastors or presbyters. But we do have numerous biblical accounts of women serving God faithfully, and today women remain an important part of the work of the Church. Women are equipped by God to lead within the Church as the Church seeks to share works of love in the name of Jesus—to show mercy as an extension of the Word and Sacrament ministry that is at the center of the life of the Lutheran congregation. However, for their benefit and protection, the LCMS continues to respect God's boundaries for women's service to the church. Those boundaries preclude women from serving as pastors.

If we should push those boundaries or ignore them altogether, we turn our attention away from clear biblical teaching and risk falling prey to the same temptation as Eve when Satan enticed her to sin using the words, "Did God really say?" If we instead keep our focus on the most powerful tool we possess to guard against the devil—the Word—we can take God's "Thus says the Lord" to be the final word without question. A posture of receptivity during worship can be accepted with joy, knowing that it puts us in a position to receive all of the benefits that God's words and promises contain—forgiveness of sins, deliverance from death and the devil, and eternal salvation.

# HOW MY MIND HAS CHANGED

## LOUIS A. SMITH

*The Christian Century* used to run a periodic series entitled "How My Mind Has Changed." It was a chance for writers to reflect publicly on the *what* and *why* of the migration of their thinking on matters of the Church's faith. I want now to undertake such an exercise. It is a useful and salutary, if dangerous, undertaking. When done in public view, it risks alienating friends and, perhaps, comforting opponents. Should such happen in this particular case, it is in no way intended. Alas, the law of the unintended consequence seems at times unavoidable.

There is, nonetheless, a matter of accountability involved. To take a public position on any matter is no small thing. In matters of the faith, the stakes are heightened since God the Holy Trinity is part of the public. All our words are uttered before him, which means that there are no insignificant words. We are accountable for what we say. When the speaker is one to whom the office of the Holy Ministry has been committed, one is doubly accountable, both in terms of one's person and one's office.

To take a public position also means that changing one's mind is a matter of public accountability. It is a matter of changing the public record. If not exactly repentance, it is closely akin to it. Most of our sins (*Deo gratias*) do not cause public scandal and (*Deo gratias*) their effects are smaller than they could be. Private confessions and Absolution will normally be sufficient to deal with it. But some of our sin is public and scandalous and so requires public penance. Similarly, most of our words are not of sufficient public notice to warrant public correction. But sometimes they are, and when we change our mind about such public words we need to change them publicly.

The matter on which my mind has changed is the ordination of women. Since I have been on public record as supporting it, I want now publicly to record my change of mind and also to account for it.

When the American Lutheran Church (1970) and Lutheran Church in American (1972) opted to ordain women, I was for it. I lent my voice to the enterprise, enlisted women into the ranks, and even looked to those women as a source of renewal for the Church. As time went on, however, some things, unforeseen by me, became apparent.

First, I began to notice that the women who came into the Ministry were, as a group, pretty much the same cut as the men. There is nothing necessarily wrong with that, but in this case, as the 80s moved into the 90s, more and more men and women came into the Ministry with minimal catechization and substantial problematic backgrounds. They came not with commitments to the Church and her truth, but with psyches—wounded by failed marriages, bad work experiences, and other traumas—in search of religious balm. In this regard, there seemed to be little difference between men and women. Women did, however, bring an extra piece of baggage with them: feminist religion. It is, or at least ought to be, no secret that this neo-pagan religion, deeply entrenched in the modern religious academy, is anti-pathetic to the Christian faith. It has nonetheless, managed to raise a false consciousness in many women, especially the religiously inclined, that portrays them as victims of a "patriarchal" religious culture that is embodied in the historic Church and promises them a new "interpretation" of the Bible and a revision of the Christian faith.

This revision, through our seminaries, which are all too beholden to the modern religious academy, has been carried into the parish life of the Church by feminist women clergy and their male supporters. This movement is manifest in the monstrosities of so-called inclusive language and of sexual relations outside of marriage. This manifestation is only the tip of the iceberg; below the surface is a rejection of the God of Scripture in favor of the chthonic deities that the Bible was written to oppose. Now human religion has come to replace divine Biblical revelation.

At the same time that I was coming to this realization I began to hear the voices of some of the best and brightest women who had been ordained. It was not, at this point, that they questioned their own ordination, but what they did question was the sufficiency of the theological rationale and exegetical proposals that had been used to support the decision to ordain them. For me, that was a lightening bolt. The exegetical proposals and thus the theological proposals which legitimated the ordination were built on the exegetical methods in which I had been schooled, that is, historical criticism. I began to review the origin of historical criticism and soon came to see that built into the method was the effort to drive a wedge between church teaching and Holy Scriptures and thus undermine the dogmatic authority of the Church.

It is true that the historical criticism in which I had been schooled was of a moderate sort. Its product was the so-called Biblical theology movement which featured the work of exegetes like G. Ernest Wright, William F.

Albright on North American soil and monumental Europeans like Gerhard von Rad, H. W. Wolff, T. W. Manson, Joachim Jeremias, C. H. Dodd. Without a doubt, some of the output of these exegetes was enormously edifying, especially at those points where the historical took precedent over the critical. But the seeds of its own destruction were already sown. It would be seen in the gap between Biblical theology and dogmatics. Since so much of the dogmatic task had been subsumed under the general category of systematic theology what should have been seen was not recognized.

This historical-critical method of Biblical interpretation, moreover, came into connection with two of the academy's force fields: the drive to novelty in research, characterized by the cliché "publish or perish," which in the seminary became "publish or parish"; and the rise of deconstructionism which virtually turned the text into the plaything of the interpreter, turning exegesis into eisegesis. The net effect was purported interpretations that were increasingly fanciful and ideological—with feminist ideology not short in representation.

This combination of factors and its negative impact on the life of the Church could not be avoided and it required that I go back to square one in my thinking. In the course of rethinking, two things finally came to stand out—an ecumenical and a Biblical element. The ecumenical element is simple and obvious. The ordination of women is a recent novelty in the Church, a novelty introduced without the largest parts of the Church being consulted—Rome Catholic, Eastern Orthodox, and Third World churches. The Lutheran bodies in North American that made the move cared nothing about the opinion of fellow North American Lutherans. This move was arrogant and sectarian, hardly worthy of bodies intending to live as part of *una sancta catholica ecclesia*. From an ecumenical perspective it was a decision that should have never been taken, let alone come up for a vote.

What then was the driving force behind this move? I can only conclude that societal forces encroached on the life of the Church and we caved in.

The Biblical element is only slightly more complex. For some reason Lutherans (especially in the ELCA) are terrified of being called "fundamentalist," although both the accuser and the accused rarely know what fundamentalism is. So, when Scripture is quoted against ordaining women, quoters (including me) have easily backed off. But it would be a mistake to think that the Biblical issue here could be resolved merely by appealing to this or that text. Rather, a broad review of Biblical reality is called for; that reality would reveal what underlies the various texts that come into play.

While space prohibits a complete review at this point, I want to mention two things. First is the Bible's nuptial language for the relationship between Christ and the Church, the Lord and Israel. If this is not mere metaphor, but rather the expression of some fundamental reality about Christ and his

Church, so that the Church is always *she* over against her husband Christ, and if the office of the Holy Ministry has a Christological foundation, so that it might well be said that in the Holy Liturgy Christ, through his minister, is in conversation with his Bride—then the Biblical logic behind Paul's injunctions with respect to women might become transparent.

Second, I received great help in grasping the Biblical grounding of the exclusion of women from the office of the Ministry through the work of William Weinrich, professor at Concordia Theological Seminary (Fort Wayne) and John Kleinig, professor at Luther Seminary in Australia. Thanks to them several things have become clear to me. First, the Bible's reservation of the pastoral office to men, rather than being a submission to the culture of late Mediterranean antiquity, is in fact something uniquely Biblical. The world that surrounded the New Testament Church was filled with women in roles of leadership in religion. Even in the New Testament women have roles that can be considered to be of a "leadership" variety. (Our current difficulty may be rooted in the modern terminology of "leadership," which glosses over the differentiation and complementarities of a variety of roles.) Had the Apostolic Church caved in to the society around it, it would have, far more likely, included women in rather than excluded them from ordained ministry.

Second, I have seen more clearly the rich contributions to the life of the Church and the expansion of the Gospel that women have made through the history of the Church apart from ordained ministry. Professor Weinrich's article, "Women in the History of the Church: Learned and Holy, but Not Pastors" is a seventeen-page course that challenges our common understandings of the history of the Church with respect to women. It effectively reorients our ways of looking at leadership in the Church in general and the pastoral office in particular. It may well be that men who have exercised the office of the Ministry in less than faithful ways bear a large portion of the blame for our distorted views of the Holy Ministry and the push to compensate for it by including women. But I would argue that one does not straighten a crooked line by further bending it.

Third, these professors have made it clear to me that the Bible bears witness to a divine reality that takes shape in the concrete life of the Church and is indeed counter-cultural with respect to all of the world's cultures, and that this ecclesial culture might well be called the culture of the Gospel. It is true that the Gospel interacts dialectically with every other culture that it encounters, such cultures being a specific embodiment of God's Law, with the result that *a* not *the* Christian culture come about. But these "Christian cultures" are neither the Gospel nor its culture. Rather, they are new versions of the Law, available for further engagement by the Gospel. What the Church rightly preserves in her internal life is not any of these "Christian cultures," but the Gospel's own culture. Within that culture the ordination of men to the Holy Ministry has a peculiar role to play, which is complementary to a host of other roles. The importation of a secular model of egalitarianism, even if "justified" by Galatians 3:28, can do nothing but distort this picture.

What then is to be done about the *fait accompli* which currently exists with the ordination of women? Several things ought to be said and the first one is quite simple: Stop! That is always the first thing to be done when one realizes that mischief is being done. That would require, as it always does, "eating crow." But it is necessary. In the current scenario, it would mean telling women who are currently enrolled in seminaries that we were wrong to have recruited them and in effect to have held out false hopes. They may, of course, continue their studies if they so desire and even seek employment in the Church but they will not be allowed to pursue ordination. (For the orthodox and qualified there are a number of non-ordained positions that can make use of theologically trained people, including the teaching of theology in college or seminary.) As hard as that may be for all involved, it would be a necessary first step.

Next we would have to seek a humane way to deal with those who are already ordained. This is a more tricky as well as sticky wicket. Some, of course, might choose to move on to other denominations. That would (I suppose) make things somewhat easier for us, but it should by no means be looked at as a solution to the difficulty. We might also take the step of looking at the current situation as an emergency situation. (The story of Deborah in Judges might be taken as a Biblical type.) Granted, this "emergency" is one that the Church itself has created. But that is probably the case with most of the emergencies that the Church has faced, namely, that the source of the emergency lies within the Church itself. Such situations always require and allow for temporary emergency measures. So we might say that those women who are presently ordained would be allowed to continue to serve in their place of call until they make other arrangements or retire. Some might well choose to be laicized and take suitable positions in diaconal or educational ministries, thus continuing both employment and the making use of their training. In all respects, however, those presently ordained should be allowed to continue their service.

I am obligated to say something on behalf of those women who have from the outset of their ministries held faithfully to "the Lutheran Confession of the Biblical faith of the Church catholic" (as I call it). There are a number of them, some of whom I have come to know personally and to cherish as colleagues and fellow strugglers against the mischief that infects the ELCA these days. (I hope that they will know of whom I speak.) First, I want to say that I have enormous respect and admiration for their work. Unlike professions and careers, the office of the Holy Ministry sets a person in a life style. Commitment to the task often results in the upsetting of family routine—arguments for a celibate clergy are not all bad—with great burdens to maintain stability falling upon mothers who, especially in the lives of young children, are irreplaceable by even the best and best-intended fathers. Thus, faithful women have often had to carry on two fulltime jobs: fulltime in this case meaning being available twenty-four hours a day as mother and pastor. That they have survived and even prospered in such circumstance can only be chalked up to an uncovenanted act of grace on God's part. Their efforts under such conditions can only elicit admiration and thanksgiving to God for sustaining them.

I also want to say that it is not demeaning of a person to say that they ought not to hold the office of the Ministry. Were that the case, the vast bulk of the Body of Christ would be demeaned. (Might it be that the application of the term "ministry" to just about every conceivable activity is an indication that we have demeaned the universal priesthood? And might that have contributed to the inability to treat ordination as limited to males in a Biblical fashion?) When I suggest that for the Church to ordain women to the Ministry is a mistake, that is meant in no way to say anything about the person or the integrity of those women who have been ordained. Nor is it meant to say anything about their talent or capacity to serve in other aspects of leadership in the Church.

Nonetheless, if for Biblical and ecumenical reasons we should not be ordaining women to the pastoral office of preaching and sacraments, we are not doing the women that we ordain any favor. When St. Paul in Romans 12 treats the Church as the Body of Christ, he deals with both unity and diversity. The diversity among members does not deny equality before God; nor does equality before God dispense with diversity. It is precisely the diversity that produces the unity of the Body since the diversity of the members exists as a network of complementarities. When the Apostle calls on us not to think too highly, but soberly, it is precisely about our place in the Body that we are to think soberly. That means not merely accepting limits for ourselves, but recognizing the limits as from God.

The freedom which the Gospel grants is not an anarchic personal freedom in which we can do as we please, but rather freedom from such anarchy so that we can be conformed to God's intention for us. This does, of course, require an exacting discernment of both gifts and limits. If among the limits is the limitation of the ordained ministry of Word and Sacrament to those males who possess the necessary gifts, then to help women discern the proper use of these gifts apart form ordination is an element of that exacting discernment. Indeed, to say to women with a genuine interest in theology and the gifts to pursue that enterprise, "Go get ordained," is just to take the easy way out. Not to mention the fact that it promotes a clericalized church when all the theologically gifted are pressed into the one mold of ordained servants of the Church.

One would have to have a greater sense of the worth of the "professional" than I have to think that non-professional service is a demeaning of that service. That theologically trained women would not have professional avenues open to them is tunnel vision of the narrowest kind. Parish administration, catechetical instruction, Christian counseling that doesn't mimic the psychology and sociology of this world, college teaching, even seminary teaching all surface as immediate possibilities, none of which require ordination, but all of which call for in depth theological training. It may well be that by opening ordination to women we have blunted rather than sharpened our capacities for discerning gifts and roles. I wonder how many men and women, who wanted "to serve people's needs," have been sidetracked from diaconal work because ordination to the pastorate appeared to be the only "office" for service within the Church?

Years ago, C. S. Lewis said that should the Church opt to ordain women, it would very quickly find that it had brought about a whole new religion. Now, barely a generation removed from the decision, when one looks at the ELCA, his words have an uncanny prescience to them. Perhaps it is time to step back, reexamine what we have done, and if honesty requires us to say that we have done wrong, begin the necessary correction of the course. Even if it means swallowing hard.

# PUBLICATION INFORMATION

THE NEW TESTAMENT AND THE ORDINATION OF WOMEN, Henry P. Hamann, originally published in *Lutheran Theological Journal* 9, no. 3 (December 1975). Reprinted with permission. Unless otherwise indicated, Scripture quotations in this essay are from the Revised Standard Version of the Bible, copyright 1952, © 1971 by the Division of Christian Education of the National Council of the Churches of Christ in the United States of America. Used by permission. All rights reserved. Scripture quotations marked NEB are from the New English Bible © Oxford University Press and Cambridge University Press 1961, 1970.

DIDASKALOS, Bertil Gärtner, originally published in 1958 as *Ämbetet, mannen och kvinnan i Nya Testamentet* by Gleerupska Universitets Bokhandels Förlag, AB Lund, Sweden. English translation first published in *Concordia Journal* 8 (March 1982). Reprinted with permission of the translator, John E. Halborg, who credits Winston Jensen with additional editorial assistance. Throughout this essay, the transliteration has been corrected to *didaskalos*. Unless otherwise indicated, Scripture quotations are from the New English Bible © Oxford University Press and Cambridge University Press 1961, 1970. The passages from *The Epistle of Clement* are taken from the translation by Bishop Lightfoot in *Excluded Books of the New Testament*, trans. Lightfoot, James, Swete et al. (New York: Harper & Brothers, 1927). The word *ämbetet*, translated as "office," in Scandinavian usage, is derived from the Augsburg Confession and indicates, in general, a reference to the ecclesiastical order, the ministry, or, in New Testament references, perhaps apostleship.

PHOEBE, Cynthia Lumley. Scripture quotations in this essay are from the ESV Bible® (The Holy Bible, English Standard Version®), copyright © 2001 by Crossway Bibles, a publishing ministry of Good News Publishers. Used by permission. All rights reserved.

DISCIPLES BUT NOT TEACHERS, John W. Kleinig, originally published in *Ordination of Women: Interdenominational Perspectives. Interface* 8, no. 2. Edited by Cathy Thompson and Vic Pfitzner. Adelaide, ATF Press. Reprinted with permission of the author.

THE ORDINATION OF WOMEN AND ECCLESIAL ENDORSEMENT OF HOMOSEXUALITY, John T. Pless, originally published in *Concordia Theological Quarterly* 74 (2010). Reprinted with permission.

TWENTY-THREE THESES ON THE HOLY SCRIPTURES, THE WOMAN, AND THE OFFICE OF THE MINISTRY, Bo Giertz, originally published in *The Springfielder* 33, no. 4 (March 1970). Reprinted with permission. This translation is made not from the Swedish original but is based on the German translation by P. Schorlemmer; translation into English by Wilhelm Torgerson. Additional translation provided by Eric R. Andrae; used by permission.

THE MINISTRY AND THE MINISTRY OF WOMEN, Peter Brunner, originally published in English translation in *Lutheran World* 6, no. 3 (1959). The German original, "Das Hirtenamt und die Frau," appeared in *Lutherische Rundschau* 11, no. 3 (1959). This translation was first published by Concordia in pamphlet form in 1971. It is reprinted here with the permission of the Lutheran World Federation. Scripture quotations in this essay are from the King James or Authorized Version of the Bible.

THE ORDINATION OF WOMEN AND THE DOCTRINE OF THE HOLY TRINITY, John W. Kleinig, originally published in *Lutheran Theological Journal* 10 (1997–98). Reprinted with permission. The quotations from Luther's Works in this essay are from the American Edition: vol. 24 copyright © 1981 by Concordia Publishing House, all rights reserved. Extracts from *God in the Dock* by C. S. Lewis © 1970 C. S. Lewis PTE Ltd. Reprinted by permission.

MAY WOMEN BE ORDAINED AS PASTORS? David P. Scaer, originally published in *The Springfielder* 36 (September 1972). Reprinted with permission. Unless otherwise indicated, Scripture quotations in this essay are from the Revised Standard Version of the Bible, copyright 1952, © 1971 by the Division of Christian Education of the National Council of the Churches of Christ in the United States of America. Used by permission. All rights reserved. Scripture quotations marked NEB are from the New English Bible © Oxford University Press and Cambridge University Press 1961, 1970. Some verses designated as The Living Bible are taken from The Living Bible, © 1971 by Tyndale House Publishers, Wheaton, IL. Used by permission. Extracts from *God in the Dock* by C. S. Lewis © 1970 C. S. Lewis PTE Ltd. Reprinted by permission.

THE OFFICE OF THE PASTOR AND THE PROBLEM OF THE ORDINATION OF WOMEN PASTORS, David P. Scaer, originally publisher in *The Springfielder* 38, no. 2 (September 1974). Reprinted with permission. Scripture quotations in this essay are from the Revised Standard Version of the Bible, copyright 1952, © 1971 by the Division of Christian Education of the National Council of the Churches of Christ in the United States of America. Used by permission. All rights reserved.

ORDINATION OF WOMEN? Hermann Sasse, originally published in *The Lutheran* (May 3, 1971). Reprinted with permission of Lutheran World Federation.

Unless otherwise indicated, Scripture quotations in this essay are from the Revised Standard Version of the Bible, copyright 1952, © 1971 by the Division of Christian Education of the National Council of the Churches of Christ in the United States of America. Used by permission. All rights reserved. Some Scripture quotations are from the New English Bible © Oxford University Press and Cambridge University Press 1961, 1970.

**The Women's Ordination Debate in the Lutheran Church of Australia**, Gregory Lockwood, originally printed and distributed by the author in 1999. All Scripture translations are the author's own work. The speech by Mrs. Sara Low that is included as Appendix A of this essay is taken from *The Ordination of Women to the Priesthood* (Church House Publishing, 1993), pp. 42–43. Reproduced by permission.

**The Ordination of Women into the Office of the Church**, Reinhard Slenczka, permission to translate and publish this essay granted by the author.

**The Argument over Women's Ordination in Lutheranism as a Paradigmatic Conflict of Dogma**, Armin Wenz. Originally published in *Lutherische Beiträge* 12 (2007). English translation by Holger Sonntag originally published in *Concordia Theological Quarterly* 71 (2007). Reprinted with permission.

**Giver to Receiver**, Adriane Dorr. Scripture quotations in this essay are from the ESV Bible® (The Holy Bible, English Standard Version®), copyright © 2001 by Crossway Bibles, a publishing ministry of Good News Publishers. Used by permission. All rights reserved.

**Ministry and Ordination**, John W. Kleinig, originally published in *Lutheran Theological Journal* 36, no. 1 (2002). Reprinted with permission.

**Gender Considerations on the Pastoral Office**, Robert Schaibley, originally published in *Logia* 2, no. 4 (October 1993). Reprinted with permission. Scripture quotations in this essay are from the Revised Standard Version of the Bible, copyright 1952, © 1971 by the Division of Christian Education of the National Council of the Churches of Christ in the United States of America. Used by permission. All rights reserved.

**"It Is Not Given to Women to Teach,"** William Weinrich, originally published in *Church and Ministry Today: Three Confessional Essays*. Reprinted with permission of Luther Academy. Scripture quotations in this essay are from the Revised Standard Version of the Bible, copyright 1952, © 1971 by the Division of Christian Education of the National Council of the Churches of Christ in the United States of America. Used by permission. All rights reserved.

**Vocational Boundaries**, Kimberly Schave. Scripture quotations in this essay are from the ESV Bible® (The Holy Bible, English Standard Version®), copyright © 2001 by Crossway Bibles, a publishing ministry of Good News Publishers. Used by permission. All rights reserved. Quotation from *Lutheran*